EDUCATION, LITERACY AND SOCIETY, 1830–70

Reproduced as a frontispiece and on the jacket
is a page from the copybook of Richard Capell,
c. 1830 (Leeds University Museum of Education)

Knowledge promotes virtue.

Knowledge promotes virtue.

Knowledge promotes virtue.

Knowledge promotes virtue.

Knowledge promotes virtue.

Knowledge promotes virtue.

Knowledge promotes virtue.

Knowledge promotes virtue.

Knowledge promotes virt

W. B. STEPHENS

EDUCATION, LITERACY AND SOCIETY, 1830–70:
the geography of diversity in provincial England

MANCHESTER
UNIVERSITY PRESS

Published by
MANCHESTER UNIVERSITY PRESS
Oxford Road, Manchester, M13 9PL

British Library cataloguing in publication data
Stephens, W.B.
  Education, literacy and society, 1830–70: the geography of diversity in provincial England.
  1. Literacy — Social aspects — England — History — 19th century
  I. Title
  302.2'0942   LC156.G7

Library of Congress cataloging-in-publication data
Stephens, W.B.
  Education, literacy, and society, 1830–70.
  Includes index.
  1. England — Social conditions — 19th century.   2. Literacy — England — History — 19th century.
  I. Title.
  HN385.S766   1986   942.081   86-18254

ISBN 0 7190 2237 1 *hardback*

Typeset in Hong Kong
by Best-set Typesetter Limited

Printed in Great Britain
by The Alden Press, Oxford

CONTENTS

LIST OF MAPS

In all the maps the counties are registration counties

LIST OF TABLES

LIST OF APPENDIXES

PREFACE

In his inaugural lecture at the University of Leicester in 1970 Alan Everitt argued that the study of local history might be enriched by more comparative work. This study is intended both as an exercise in comparative local history and as a contribution to the growing body of historical work which eschews the compartmentalism of the discipline. I have attempted to compare aspects of the cultural experience of communities in all the various parts of provincial England in the middle decades of the nineteenth century, in respect of related demographic, educational, social, economic, religious and, to some extent, political factors. It may be noted here that part of Chapter 2 draws on material I published as an article in David Reeder's (ed.), *Urban Education in the Nineteenth Century* (1977). Also that R. A. Houston's *Scottish Literacy and the Scottish Identity: Illiteracy in Scotland and Northern England, 1600–1800* (1985) was published as my final typescript was being prepared so that it was possible to make only brief references to that excellent work.

The book has occupied me intermittently since 1978, its progress being retarded by long periods given to the completion of other publications and to other professional activities. It would not even now have been completed but for the generous support of the University of Leeds. I am particularly grateful to the University for granting me study leave in 1978–9 and also for the provision of research assistance: in the initial stages I benefited considerably from the help of two part-time research assistants — successively Dr John Seed and Mr William Meyer — both of whom were assiduous in searching many sources for me. The calculations of coefficients of correlation between literacy and schooling levels, found at several places in the volume, were undertaken by Bill Meyer. To him and to John Seed I wish to record my debt.

I have gained a great deal from conversations with higher degree students at the University of Leeds and from reading their relevant research exercises and theses. I am in debt, too, to the writers of other theses duly acknowledged in the notes to the text. In particular I wish to thank Dr David Mitch of the University of Maryland for presenting me with a copy of his excellent doctoral dissertation referred to at several places in the volume.

The work could not have been completed without recourse to numerous libraries and I am especially grateful for the assistance of the staffs of the Institute of Historical Research, the British Library, the library of University College London, and above all of the Brotherton Library of the University of Leeds. For advice and assistance with the maps in the volume I have to thank Mr Harry Tolson, Printer to the University of Leeds, and Mr Alan Haigh of the University's Audio-Visual Service.

To more than anyone, however, I owe a debt to my wife for help over the years and for compiling the index and coping with the proofs during my absence in the United States.

Finally I wish, once again, to thank the Officers of Manchester University Press for their encouragement and help.

W. B. Stephens
University of Leeds

August 1986

ABBREVIATIONS

Abstract, 1833 — *Abstract of Education Returns, 1833,* PP 1835, XLI–XLIII

App., App. — Appendix, *Appendix*

A.R., A.R. — Annual Report, *Annual Report*

BFSS — *Annual Report of the British and Foreign School Society*

BJES — *British Journal of Educational Studies*

CCE — *Minutes* and *Reports of the Committee of Council on Education* (Parliamentary Papers)

Census (es) — Published *Census (es) of Population,* etc. (Parliamentary Papers)

DNB — *Dictionary of National Biography*

Ec. H.R. — *Economic History Review*

Education Census, 1851 — *Census of Great Britain, 1851, Education (England and Wales),* PP 1852–3, XC, [1692] (reproduced 1854)

EHR — *English Historical Review*

JEAH — *Journal of Educational Administration and History*

JRAS — *Journal of the Royal Agricultural Society*

JRSS — *Journal of the Royal Statistical Society*

JSSL — *Journal of the Statistical Society of London*

Jnl. — *Journal (of)*

LME — Deposited in the University of Leeds, Museum of Education

NH — *Northern History*

Nat. Soc. — *National Society*

Newcastle — *Reps. R.C. on Popular Education,* PP 1861, XXI (followed by part), [2794–I-III, V–VI]

PP — Parliamentary Paper. Those cited in these abbreviations provide session, volume, short title, and ( ) session number or [ ] Command number. All House of Commons. Those listed as Reports may refer also to Apps., Evidence, etc.

PP 1833, V — *1st Rep. S.C. into State of Agriculture* (612)

PP 1833, XX — *1st Rep. R.C. [on] Employment of Children in Factories* (450)

PP 1833, XXI — *2nd Rep. R.C. [on] Employment of Children in Factories* (519)

PP 1837, V — *Rep. S.C., House of Lords, into State of Agriculture* (464)

PP 1834, XIX — *Supplementary Rep. R.C. [on] Employment of Children in Factories* (167–I)

PP 1836, VIII (1) — *2nd Rep. S.C. into State of Agriculture,* Part I (189)

PP 1837–8, VII — *Rep. S.C. on Education of the Children of the Poorer Classes* (589)

PP 1839, XLII — *Return of Mills and Factories, 1838* (41)

PP 1839, XLII (Reps.) — *Reports of Factory Inspectors on the Effects of the Educational Provisions of the Factories Act* (42)

PP 1840, XXIII — *Rep. R.C. on Hand-loom Weavers,* Parts I, II (43–I), (43–II)

PP 1840, XXIV, pts. IV, V — *Rep. R.C. on Hand-loom Weavers,* Parts IV, V [217], [220]

PP 1840, XXIV, (Hickson) — *Rep. R.C. on Hand-loom Weavers,* Rep. by Mr Hickson (639)

PP 1841, X — *Rep. R.C. on Hand-loom Weavers,* [296]

PP 1842, XV — *1st Rep. R.C. into Employment of Children in Mines and Manufactories* [380]

PP 1842, XVII — *Appendix to 1st Rep. R.C. into Employment of Children in Mines and Manufactories,* Part I [381]

PP 1842, XVI — *Appendix to 1st Rep. R.C. into Employment of Children in Mines and Manufactories,* Part II [382]

PP 1843, XII — *Rep. Special Assistant Poor Law Commissioners on Employment of Women and Children in Agriculture* [510]

PP 1843, XIII — *2nd Rep. R.C. on Employment of Children (Trades and Manufactures)* [430]

PP 1843, XIII (Mines) — *1st Rep. Midland Mining Commission: South Staffordshire* [508]

PP 1843, XIV — *Appendix to 2nd Rep. R.C. on Employment of Children (Trades and Manufactures)*, Part I [431]

PP 1843, XV — *Appendix to 2nd Rep. R.C. on Employment of Children (Trades and Manufactures)*, Part II [432]

PP 1843, XXVII — *Rep. Inspectors of Factories for Half Year to June 1843* [523]

PP 1844, XVI — *Rep. Commissioner on Population in Mining Districts* [592]

PP 1844, XVII — *Rep. R.C. into State of Large Towns* [572]

PP 1845, XV — *Appendix to Rep. R.C. into Frame-work Knitters: Leicestershire* [618]

PP 1845, XVIII — *2nd Rep. R.C. into State of Large Towns and Populous Districts, App.*, Part I [602]

PP 1845, XXVII — *Rep. Commissioner on Population in Mining Districts* [670]

PP 1846, XXIV — *Rep. Commissioner on Population in Mining Districts* [737]

PP 1847, XVI — *Rep. Commissioner on Population in Mining Districts* [844]

PP 1847, XXVII — *Rep. R.C. into Education in Wales*, Part II [871]

PP 1847–8, XXVI — *Rep. Commissioner on Population in Mining Districts* [993]

PP 1849, XXII — *Rep. Commissioner on Population in Mining Districts* [1109]

PP 1850, XXIII — *Rep. Commissioner on Population in Mining Districts* [1248]

PP 1850, XXVII — *Rep. to Poor Law Board on Laws of Settlement* [1152]

PP 1851, XXIII — *Rep. Commissioner on Population in Mining Districts* [1406]

PP 1852, XI — *Rep. S.C. on Manchester and Salford Education* [499]

PP 1852, XXI — *Rep. Commissioner on Population in Mining Districts* [1525]

PP 1852–3, XL — *Rep. Commissioner on Population in Mining Districts* [1679]

PP 1854, XIX — *Rep. Commissioner on Population in Mining Districts* [1838]

PP 1854–5, XIV — *Rep. S.C. on Stoppage of Wages in Hosiery Manufacture* (421)

PP 1854–5, XV — *Rep. Commissioner on Population in Mining Districts* [1993]

PP 1856, XVII — *Rep. Commissioner on Population in Mining Districts* [2125]

PP 1857(2), XI — *1st and 2nd Reps. S.C. on Employment of Women and Children in Bleaching and Dyeing* (151), (211)

PP 1857(2), XVI — *Rep. Commissioner on Population in Mining Districts* [2275]

PP 1857–8, XXXII — *Rep. Commissioner on Population in Mining Districts* [2424]

PP 1859(1), XXI(2) — *An Account of All Schools for the Children of the Labouring Classes in Wiltshire* (27)

PP 1859(2), XII — *Rep. Commissioner on Population in Mining Districts* [2566]

PP 1861, XLVIII — *Rep. to R.C. on Popular Education on Dissenters' Schools* (410)

PP 1861, XLVIII (letter) — *Letter relating to the Report of the Commission into National Education* (231)

PP 1861, L — *Return of the Average Weekly Earnings of Agricultural Labourers* (14)

PP 1863, XVIII — *1st Rep. R.C. on Employment of Children in Trades and Manufactures* [3170]

PP 1864, XXII — *2nd and 3rd Reps. on Employment of Children in Trades and Manufactures* [3414], [3414–I]

PP 1864, XXIV — *Epitome of Evidence before the Commission into the Conditions of all Mines in Great Britain* [3389]

PP 1865, XX — *4th Rep. R.C. on Employnent of Children in Trades and Manufactures* [3548]

PP 1866, XXIV — *5th Rep. R.C. on Employment of Children in Trades and Manufactures* [3678]

PP 1867, XVI — *6th Rep. R.C. on Employment of Children in Trades and Manufactures* [3796]

PP 1867–8, XVII, (a) — *1st Rep. R.C. on Employment of Children, Young Persons and Women in Agriculture, with Appendix*, Part I [4068]

PP 1867–8, XVII, (b) — *1st Rep. R.C. on Employment of Children, Young Persons and Women in*

Agriculture, with Appendix, Part II [4068–I]

PP 1867–8, XXVIII — *Reps. Schools Inquiry Commission* [3966–3966-XX]

PP 1867–8, LIII — *Return of the Number of Children in Inspected Schools in the Year ending 31 August 1867* (58)

PP 1868–9, XIII, (a) — *2nd Rep. R.C. on Employment of Children, Young Persons and Women in Agriculture, with Appendix*, Part I [4202]

PP 1868–9, XIII, (b) — *2nd Rep. R.C. on Employment of Children, Young Persons and Women in Agriculture, with Appendix*, Part II [4202–I]

PP 1868–9, L — *Return of Average Weekly Earnings of Agricultural Labourers* (371)

PP 1870, XIII — *3rd Rep. R.C. on Employment of Children, Young Persons and Women in Agriculture* [C.70]

PP 1870, LIV — *Return of Schools for the Poorer Classes in Birmingham, Leeds, Liverpool and Manchester* (91)

PP 1871, LXII — *Return of Manufacturing Establishments* (440)

PP 1874, XIII — *Rep. Inspectors of Factories for the Six Months ending 30 April 1874* [C.1086]

PP 1876, XXIX — *Rep. R.C. into the Factory and Workshops Acts*, [C.1443]

PP 1876, XXX — *Minutes of Evidence to the Rep. R.C. into the Factory and Workshops Acts* [C.1443–I]

PP 1887, XXX — *3rd Rep. R.C. into the Elementary Education Acts* [C.5158]

PP 1889, XIII — *3rd Rep. S.C., House of Lords, on the Sweating System* (165)

PRO — Public Record Office

R.C. — Royal Commission

Religious Census, 1851 — *Census of Great Britain, 1851, Religious Worship (England and Wales)*; PP 1852–3, LXXXIX [1690]

Rep., *Rep.* — Report, *Report*

Reps. Mining Districts — See references to *Reports on the Population of Mining Districts*, listed above under PP

Rev. — *Review*

S.C. — Select Committee

Stephens (1973) — W. B. Stephens, *Regional Variations in Education During the Industrial Revolution, 1780–1870*, Leeds, 1973.

Stephens (1977) — W. B. Stephens, 'Illiteracy and schooling in the provincial towns, 1640–1870' in D. Reeder (ed.), *Urban Education in the Nineteenth Century*, London, 1977.

Stephens (1983) — W. B. Stephens (ed.), *Studies in the History of Literacy: England and North America*, Leeds, 1983.

TNAPSS — *Transaction of the National Association for Promotion of Social Science*

Trans. — *Transactions*

VCH — *Victoria County Histories*

Welton (1860) — T. A. Welton, *Statistical Papers on the Census of England and Wales, 1851*, London, 1860

PART I

A GENERAL SURVEY

CHAPTER 1

The inheritance of diversity

The emphasis by educational historians on the emergence and growth of a national system of schools has tended to obscure the fact that before 1870, at least, the nature and experience of elementary education varied so much from place to place that to talk of a national condition is to distort reality. Where regional differences were great in any aspect of life the assessment of hypothetical averages and national trends, and the study of official plans and policies, may be of only limited value in recreating the past. Moreover, regional diversity in schooling is not fully explicable without some investigation of the social and economic structures in which formal education existed. This study examines the relationship of such structures to basic aspects of child life, particularly work and school, and to varying attitudes towards the formal education of the working classes throughout the English provinces. It tries, too, to relate such matters to regional levels of basic literacy, with a view to providing an added insight into the diversity of provincial working-class culture in the mid-nineteenth century, roughly from 1830 to 1870.

Only a minute examination of large numbers of individual communities throughout the country in a systematic way can, of course, provide a comprehensive picture of the state of English education in its social and economic setting. Such a task is too ambitious for the individual researcher. What is attempted here is a limited initial survey of a comparative nature at the level largely of counties and census registration districts, and, where possible, towns — based to some extent on a framework of quantitative data. This data, compiled from contemporary sources of varying degrees of reliability, falls short of the exactness that modern statisticians would find acceptable, and it has not been thought suitable for subjection to sophisticated statistical techniques. Regrettably it has not been possible to cover Wales (though Monmouthshire is included) nor to consider London, which requires a study to itself. This volume is not, therefore, likely to be definitive, and makes no such exaggerated claim. It may, however, provide a basis for more detailed local investigations and eventually a more adequate overall view.

Before proceeding to the examination of the period with which this study is concerned, the historical background of basic education inherited from the past may be considered, for communities on the eve of Victoria's accession already possessed very varied cultural attributes.

Our knowledge of English social life in the pre-industrial period and the years of the industrial revolution has been enhanced in recent years by a number of investigations of standards of basic literacy. We have now some perception of levels of literacy and their variations, over time and geographically, in the sixteenth and seventeenth centuries, and a much fuller picture of the state of affairs in the period of early industrialisation. The basis of much of this work is the quantitative evidence derived from sources showing the ability or otherwise of adults to sign their names. Many such sources are biased towards certain social classes and occupations and to men rather than women, and the extent of their survival, moreover, varies topographically and chronologically. The requirement from 1754 that all spouses should on marriage sign the parish register, or make a mark if unable to sign, however, provides a common measure for a roughly comparable age group, of men and women in equal numbers, covering all classes and occupations. From 1754 to 1839 this evidence exists, it is true, only where marriage registers have survived, but a great number of these, spread over the country and often covering long runs, is available. Moreover, from 1839 these statistics were collected by the Registrar General of Births, Deaths and Marriages and published in his annual reports — for counties from 1839 to 1914, and for census registration districts for the years 1842 to 1885, so that for these years we are not dependent on figures derived from a scatter of haphazardly surviving records, but have evidence for every marriage that took place.

It has been objected that a signature may not indicate an ability to write anything else; that reading ability, also an indication of literacy, is not measured; that some spouses may have been able to write but for various reasons made a mark. Contrariwise, illiterates might have learned the trick of signing for their marriage day merely to forget it as quickly. This has been debated elsewhere and the arguments need not be further rehearsed here. Suffice it to say that both contemporary opinion and recent research appear to indicate that signature literacy was a good indication of ability to write, if indifferently, that those who could write could certainly read. The proportions of those who marked though able to sign and vice versa are likely to have been too small to have had more than a marginal effect on figures based on marriage signatures and unlikely to have varied geographically. And indeed the gradual improvement year by year of national signature rates from 1840 without erratic fluctuations also suggests that they do reflect genuine trends. Although signature evidence is admittedly a crude and imperfect yardstick,[1] everything points to its providing a valuable measure of the maximum numbers able to write.[2] Since writing was not taught in all schools or was taught at a later stage than reading,[3] certainly more people could read to some extent than could sign their names.[4] Moreover, since the working classes generally attended school more briefly than higher social groups and had less need to practise literacy skills, the proportions of working people who could read while unable to sign their names was likely to be greater than for the better-off. And since, especially in working-class private schools, girls spent much time on learning to sew, a basis of greater female illiteracy was laid.

For the early modern period the extent of quantifiable evidence and the difficulties it presents of comparability over time and place make conclusions necessarily tentative.[5] It appears, however, that despite times of decline and stagnation between 1500 and the early eighteenth century, literacy levels for men (measured by signature evidence) rose generally from about 10 per cent at the end of the fifteenth century, to some 20 per cent in the sixteenth, to 30 per cent in the mid-seventeenth century, and to 45 per cent by 1714. Women were almost universally unable to sign their names at the beginning of the sixteenth century, but by 1641–2 about 10 per cent could do so and by 1714 about 25 per cent.

In the mid-seventeenth century, when data exists which lends itself to topographical comparison, there seems generally to have been a greater incidence of illiteracy in the north and south-west than in the midlands and south-east, though even in the south-east some counties were apparently as illiterate as northern ones. But considerable variations in literacy levels between parishes within individual counties, combined with very patchy survival rates for the data from county to county, make too definite a verdict unwise. Moreover the preponderance of the evidence is for men. There is, nevertheless, little doubt that London was more literate than the provinces, and likely, though not certain, that while literacy levels for small towns differed little from those of their rural hinterlands, larger towns, particularly in the north, may well have enjoyed superior levels.[6] The reasons for these geographical differences are difficult to ascertain. There is insufficient evidence to demonstrate a firm connection between literacy levels and puritan influences or the availability of schooling, and little more to suggest a relationship with the type of agriculture pursued.[7] As has been remarked, 'the local geography of literacy is still bewildering' for this period. Yet what is certain is that levels of literacy within a community varied according to wealth, social status, and occupation, with gentry and professional men most literate, followed by tradesmen, yeomen and servants, who were in turn superior to husbandmen and labourers. This hierarchical pattern appears to have been more or less the same over the country, though the actual level of each group may have varied regionally. Thus although other influences were also at work the socio-economic structure of local communities is likely to have affected their general levels of literacy.

Our knowledge of developments between 1714 and 1754 is particularly limited, but there is some evidence that the north of England, particularly the north-east, saw a disproportionate improvement in literacy levels over other areas, with advancement found more in the commercial classes than among industrial workers.[8] From 1754, when all brides and grooms were required to sign or make a mark in the Anglican marriage registers, a great deal of evidence becomes available. For those parishes for which registers have survived we have potential data on literacy for a roughly similar age group (the mid-twenties) for the whole period of the classical industrial revolution. The sheer bulk of the material and its physical dispersal, however, make it likely that a complete data base compiled from it will not materialise for many years to come. Moreover, the patchy survival of the registers limits the comprehensiveness of such an exercise. Nor is the parish an ideal statistical unit. Parishes varied greatly in area and population, so that literacy percentages based on such units relate to very different numbers of marriages. Where the annual numbers were small, considerable fluctuations in levels often resulted. Moreover, the smaller the area of the parish the greater the number of grooms likely to be extra-parochial, thus affecting the calculations.

Despite these drawbacks, however, tentative conclusions may be drawn on the level of literacy in this period, its changes over time, and geographical, gender and occupational variations. A statistically random sample of 274 parishes designed to show the national levels of male and female illiteracy in each year from 1754 to 1840 produced a clear indication that improvement had occurred since 1714. Bridal illiteracy, at just about 60 per cent in 1754, decreased, however, only slowly to just below 50 per cent by 1840, though the rate of improvement increased from 1800. The illiteracy rate of grooms, at about 40 per cent in 1754, on the other hand remained more or less static to about 1795, falling in the next five years, actually rising above 40 per cent by about 1805, and then falling at a rate similar to that of the brides to about 33 per cent in 1840. On average, therefore, taking brides and grooms together, about half the marrying cohort could sign their names in 1754 and about 58 per cent in 1840.[9]

National figures, however conceal considerable geographical variations and differences between types of community. Isaac Watts in 1728 observed that the 'poor who are bred in Towns and Cities should enjoy some small advantage in their Education beyond those who are born in far distant Fields and Villages'.[10] But no simple distinction between urban and rural areas is discernible. As far as towns are concerned such evidence as we have (Table 1·1) suggests that those which were predominantly smallish market centres for agricultural areas, and the larger towns that were commercial and administrative centres, tended to be superior to industrial towns and to show steady improvement over the period. The industrialising towns, particularly those with expanding populations in Lancashire, Cheshire and the West Riding, and probably the Black Country,[11] were already in the 1750s somewhat less literate than most towns in other areas and than non-industrial towns in the north (such as, for example, Wetherby and York). Not only that, but most of them experienced either no improvement or a deterioration in literacy by the turn of the century and between then and the 1830s.[12]

For the few apparent deviations from these general tendencies plausible explanations often present themselves. Thus Ottery St. Mary (Devon) was a market town with rather high illiteracy rates: but it was the seat of a highly localised domestic lace industry and, unusually for Devon, a large textile mill was established in the town in the 1790s.[13] Leamington was but a poor rural village before developing into a sizable spa.[14] And, while Worcester, Nottingham and Northampton, the first two of which saw an increase of illiteracy in 1799–1804 over the 1750s and the last little improvement, were market and administrative centres and county towns, they were also places where population was growing fast and centres of domestic industry.[15] Even so the continued decline in literacy seen in the textile towns of the north and at Dudley in the midlands is not evident in these towns.

There is further evidence, too, of the high and often increasing level of illiteracy in industrial communities at this time. In the Erewash Valley coalfield in the midlands, for example, there was a continuous rise in the proportion of

TABLE 1·1

Percentages of brides and grooms making marks in various towns, 1754–1837

Towns[1]	Approx. dates[2]	1754–62	1799–1804	1831–7
South West				
Bristol[3]		49	41	34
Exeter[4]		44	35	32
Ottery St. Mary[4]		38	51	52
Plymstock[4]		52	48	33
Penzance[5]		46	43	37
East				
Deeping[6]		62	55	48
Gainsborough[6]		44	41	32
Grantham[6]		44	34	26
Lincoln[6]		64	42	32
Louth[6]		52	44	37
Sleaford[6]		60	44	36
Market Rasen[7]		50	33	29
Barton upon Humber[7]		49	43	33
Caistor[7]		?	41	34
King's Lynn[3]		49	43	39
Oakham[8]		?	34	33
Uppingham[8]		?	40	28
Midlands				
Ludlow[9]		48	37	28
Worcester[10]		51	54	37
Nottingham[3]		46	51	35
Northampton[11]		43	41	35
Dudley[10]		57	67	73
Oxford[3]		33	29	25
Leamington Spa[12]		65	62	21

TABLE 1·1 (cont)

Towns[1]	Approx. dates[2]	1754–62	1799–1804	1831–7
North				
Doncaster[13]		?	42	31
Halifax[3]		58	53	76
Leeds[14]		68	52	?
Malton[15]		48	46	32
Richmond (Yorks)[16]		37	28	?
Wetherby[17]		50	47	31
York[18]		7	4	?
Ashton-under-Lyne[19]		58	68	90
Mottram[19]		58	50	53
Stockport[20]		50	60	52
Blackburn[21]		67	69	68
Bolton[20]		58	70	67
Burnley[21]		71	72	?
Bury[21]		57	62	72
Clitheroe[21]		50	62	?
Chorley[22]		60	64	56
Deane[21]		69	69	72
Eccleston (St. Helens)[21]		54	49	60
Kirkham[21]		47	60	58
Manchester[20]		52	62	58
Preston[21]		44	58	53

Notes
 1. Registers analysed are not necessarily for the whole of the town concerned.
 2. Dates vary but roughly fall within or very near these periods.
 3. Deduced from W. L. Sargant, 'On the progress of elementary education', *JSSL*, XXX, 1867, 128.
 4. W. B. Stephens, 'Illiteracy in Devon during the Industrial Revolution, 1754–1854', *JEAH*, VIII, 1976, 2.
 5. R. Edmonds, 'A Statistical Account of the Parish of Madron containing the Borough of Penzance in Cornwall', *JSSL*, II, 1839, 227.
 6. W. Couth, 'The development of the town of Gainsborough, 1754 to 1850', M.A. thesis, University of Wales, 1975, xxi.
 7. Rex C. Russell, *A History of Schools and Education in Lindsey, Lincolnshire, 1800–1902, Pt. I*, (Lincoln), 1965, 55.
 8. G. Young, 'Educational development in a rural society: A study of the control and provision of schooling in Rutland in the nineteenth century', M.Ed. thesis, University of Leicester, 1980, 95–8, 237.
 9. D. J. Lloyd, 'Popular education and society in Ludlow, 1711–1861', M.Ed. thesis, University of Hull, 1974, 132–3.
10. J. Grayson, 'Literacy, schooling and industrialisation: Worcestershire, 1760–1850' in Stephens (1983), 55.
11. V. A. Hatley, 'Literacy at Northampton, 1761–1900', *Northamptonshire Past and Present*, IV, 1972, 379. These figures are preferred to those given by Sargant based on two of the four parishes which Hatley analysed.
12. Deduced from F. O'Shaughnessy, *A Spa and its Children*, Warwick, 1979, 19, 59. Before 1821 the town's population was very small and might appropriately have been included in Table 1·2 below.
13. Deduced from H. C. Cottam, 'Literacy in the Doncaster poor law union, 1801 to 1860', M.Ed. research exercise, University of Leeds, 1984 (LME).
14. W. B. Stephens, 'Elementary education and literacy, 1770–1870', in D. Fraser (ed.), *A History of Modern Leeds*, Manchester, 1980, 225.
15. D. J. Salmon (ed.), *Malton in the Early Nineteenth Century*, [Northallerton], 1981, 74.
16. R. Fieldhouse and B. Jennings, *A History of Richmond and Swaledale*, London, 1978, 402.
17. R. W. Unwin, 'Literacy patterns in rural communities in the Vale of York, 1660–1840', in Stephens (1983), 73.
18. N. Yasumoto, 'Urbanisation and population in an English town: Leeds during the Industrial Revolution', *Keio Economic Studies*, X, 1973, 84. The figures selected here disguise a rise in illiteracy to about 60 per cent in the 1760s and 1770s. The figures for York are so unusual that further investigation of the sources may be wanted.
19. S. A. Harrop, 'Literacy and educational attitudes as factors in the industrialisation of north-east Cheshire, 1760–1830', in Stephens (1983), 39–40, 49, and marriage marks supplied by Mrs Harrop; Stephens (1977), 31.
20. T. W. Laqueur, 'Literacy and social mobility in the industrial revolution in England', *Past and Present*, LXIV, 1974, 99. For Manchester, M. Sanderson gives 64 per cent for the 1830s (see next note).
21. M. Sanderson, 'Literacy and social mobility in the industrial revolution in England', *Past and Present*, LVI, 1972, 82–5; K. P. C. Thorne, 'The development of education in Chorley and district from 1800 to 1900', M.Lit. thesis, University of Lancaster, 1970, 17, 134, gives for Chorley 61 per cent 1755–60, 62 per cent, 1796–1800 and 75 per cent, 1831–5.

illiterate spouses from the 1760s to the 1830s.[16] Conflated figures for a number of Lancashire and Cheshire parishes in the urbanised cotton belt also show a greater level of illiteracy in the 1830s than in the 1750s.[17] For towns in industrial south-east Lancashire and north Cheshire, additional to those listed in Table 1·1, very high illiteracy rates are recorded for the 1830s: as, for example, Eccles and Radcliffe 65 per cent, Warrington 66, Winwick and Standish 68, Oldham 69, Leigh 71, and Wigan and Rochdale as high as 81 per cent.[18] The catastrophic increase in illiteracy evidenced at Ashton-under-Lyne (Table 1·1) was commented on in the early 1840s before the Royal Commission on the State of Large Towns when J. R. Coulthard reported that 'if writing ... is to be considered a criterion of the education of a people, verily the inhabitants of this town are in a pitiable condition: and what makes the matter worse and improvement almost hopeless, is the remarkable fact that we are in a state of rapid retrogression'.[19]

On the other hand, figures for all the Bedfordshire market towns over the period support the likelihood of superior levels of literacy in such communities.[20] We have little evidence on residential suburbs of large towns in this period, but one study shows that at Childwall, a suburban parish on the outskirts of Liverpool, and St. Thomas, a fairly comfortable Liverpool parish, housing mainly the lower middle class and skilled artisans, illiteracy was much less common than in the Lancashire industrial towns. Childwall's rate fell from 44 per cent in 1801–10 to 30 per cent in 1831–40, and St. Thomas's from 23 to 17 per cent. Both places were superior to the nearby rural parish of Huyton (52 to 56 per cent in these years).[21]

Indeed, the fragmentary evidence available for rural parishes (Table 1·2) is not easy to interpret but does suggest that in the West Country, the eastern counties and the midlands rural illiteracy in the mid-eighteenth century was at a higher level than in the towns of those areas. Rural parishes in the East and West Ridings, however, were more literate than in other parts of the country, and considerably more literate than Leeds and the West Riding and Lancashire textile towns.

The data for rural parishes at the turn of the century presents a less distinct picture, but if greater emphasis is placed on those examples in Table 1·2 which embrace groups of parishes rather than single (and perhaps unrepresentative) ones, it seems likely that in most of the country the decrease in rural illiteracy proceeded more slowly than was the case in non-industrial towns. In rural Yorkshire little progress appears to have occurred, though literacy levels certainly remained superior to those of the industrial towns,[22] and over the period as a whole a lower proportion of immigrants marrying in Leeds was illiterate than was the case with native city spouses.[23]

By the 1830s a general, though not universal, improvement is apparent in rural areas, but the towns remained superior, aside from those in the north and the industrial midlands (if Dudley is at all typical). Yet it is still difficult to

TABLE 1·2

Percentages of brides and grooms making marks in various rural parishes, 1754–1837

Distribution of parishes, and number ( )	Approximate dates		
	1754–62	1799–1804	1831–7
South West			
Somerset (2)[1]	72	52	31
Gloucestershire (1)[1]	69	48	49
Gloucestershire (c.260)[2]	58	53	55
Devon (1)[3]	50	32	40
Devon (2)[3]	37	40	33
Devon (1)[3]	67	30	47
Dorset (1)[1]	?	31	39
East			
Lincolnshire (20/28)[4]	?	47	41
Lincolnshire (11)[5]	64	50	42
Rutland (13)[6]	?	36	26
Rutland (21)[6]	?	48	35
Rutland (9)[6]	?	41	44
Huntingdonshire/Cambridgeshire (2)[1]	55	61	54
Midlands			
Leicestershire (1)[1]	46	62	23
Leicestershire (1)[7]	c.64	c.55	c.57
Warwickshire (2)[1]	62	55	36
Northamptonshire (4)[1]	50	54	43
Staffordshire (1)[8]	59	38	?
Staffordshire (3)[1]	61	47	43
Worcestershire (2)[1]	61	47	34
Worcestershire (5)[9]	56	56	49
Oxfordshire (1)[1]	54	24	49
Bedfordshire (many parishes)[10]	63	c.59	61
South			
Sussex (1)[1]	50	42	22
North			
Yorkshire E.R. (1)[1]	38	50	52
Yorkshire E.R. (1)[11]	42	45	?
Yorkshire E.R. (17)[12]	49	47	38
Yorkshire W.R. (4)[13]	49	41	?
Yorkshire W.R. (29)[14]	?	47	38
Yorkshire W.R. (5)[11]	45	55	?
Yorkshire N.R. (2)[11]	33	38	27
Yorkshire N.R. (1)[15]	55	50	40

Notes   For exact references when not provided, see *Notes* to Table 1·1.
  1. Sargant, 'Elementary education', 127.
  2. J. Campbell, 'Occupation and literacy: Bristol and Gloucestershire, 1755–1870', in Stephens (1983), 23, 100.
  3. Stephens, 'Illiteracy in Devon', 2.
  4. Rex. C. Russell, *A History of Schools and Education in Lindsey*, 50–4: twenty parishes for 1800–9; twenty-eight for 1830–9. Includes towns of Market Rasen, Barton upon Humber and Caistor (See Table 1·1).
  5. W. Couth, 'Gainsborough', xx.
  6. G. Young, 'Rutland', 227–34: thirteen with populations less than 200; twenty-one with 200–500; nine with 500+.
  7. D. Levine, 'Education and family life in early industrial England', *Jnl. Family History*, IV, 1979, 372, deduced from graph.
  8. Deduced from G. Gomez, 'The endowed schools of Staffordshire in the eighteenth century', M.Phil. thesis, University of Leeds, 1977, 390 (Barlaston).
  9. Grayson, 'Literacy', 55.
 10. Schofield, 'Dimensions', 447–8: including towns. Based on an analysis of all the extant registers in the county.
 11. Yasumoto, 'Urbanisation', 83–5.
 12. W. P. Baker, *Parish registers in East Yorkshire*, York, 1961, 12.
 13. Unwin, 'Literacy patterns', 73, 75.
 14. The twenty-eight parishes comprising the Doncaster poor law union (excluding Doncaster parish and town): deduced from Cottam, 'Literacy in the Doncaster poor law union'.
 15. Salmon, *Malton*, 74 (for Old Malton).

generalise about rural parishes, for some were remote and purely agricultural, others abutted on towns, some contained mining districts, and in some cottage industry was practised. An extensive survey of some 260 Gloucestershire parishes, mainly agricultural but some mining and urban in nature, showed an overall level of illiteracy in 1835 hardly different from that in 1755 (Table 1·2). In Bedforshire, a rural county with widespread domestic industry, the illiteracy rate in 1833–44 was again only a little lower than in 1754–64 (Table 1·2). At Bushbury (Staffs.) near Wolverhampton, a mining district, very high illiteracy levels in the 1760s had fallen only a little by the end of the century.[24] At Shepshed (Leics.), a place of rural industry, average levels of illiteracy 1825–51 were no lower than in 1754–1824.[25]

There is some evidence that Lancashire rural parishes close to industrial towns experienced increases in illiteracy similar to the towns. Great Harwood, Whalley, and Newchurch in Pendle, all near Blackburn, provide examples of this. More purely agricultural parishes in Lancashire away from the industrial districts, particularly in the north of the county, however, show much lower levels of illiteracy[26] and were often superior to rural parishes in the south and midlands.

Factors bearing on rural literacy may well have varied over the country. In the Bedfordshire sample cited above, parishes which experienced a considerable increase in illiteracy over the period 1754–1840 tended to be predominantly agricultural, dominated by a single landlord, with little or no schooling available, and a high level of poor rates in the 1830s. Those where illiteracy decreased most were characterised by a tendency to have day schools, a wider dispersal of land ownership, lower poor rates, and a greater diversity of non-agricultural occupations.[27] Analysis of forty rural parishes in Rutland shows, however, that those with one or two large landowners tended to have lower levels of illiteracy than those where there were many freeholders.[28]

Complex, too, is the relationship between literacy levels and the growth of industry and population. The declining or stagnating levels of literacy in the Lancashire–Cheshire manufacturing area have been the subject of debate.[29] The social and economic changes collectively labelled the industrial revolution by historians are, however, too intricate to be explicable solely in terms of the application of factory machinery to textile production. Increased industrial output (evident from the 1740s) and galloping population growth were not confined to Lancashire nor universally attributable to the factory production of textiles. There was, for example, a great increase in the output of the domestic textile and metal trades of the midlands in this period. All the evidence suggests that, not only in the north-west but also in parts of the north-east and certainly in the midlands, falling or stagnant literacy levels accompanied burgeoning industrial output, whether based on factories or not. Existing school facilities were swamped and an extension of opportunities for child labour also militated against formal schooling, such developments probably being under way before 1760.[30]

Given the extent of migration into manufacturing areas, particularly by the young unmarried, during this period the relation of the extent of local day schooling to later literacy levels in the same place, is likely to be much less close than in more stable areas. Moreover, attempts to relate the chronology of industrial development in particular places to changes in literacy levels by application of a formula assuming that literacy largely reflected day schooling levels twelve to fifteen years before must be open to some doubt as applied to the later eighteenth and early nineteenth centuries. Local literacy levels must have been affected not only by the standards of those immigrant spouses reared elsewhere, but by the acquisition in late youth or adulthood of literacy skills by the unschooled.[31] Moreover, it was in this period that Sunday schools were introduced, attracting large numbers of otherwise unschooled children and some adults, many of whom were taught reading and some writing.[32] As day schooling became more common, of course, a stronger relationship might be expected between full-time education and later literacy levels, and this is discussed below.

Marriage mark evidence also shows the strong gender differences in literacy levels. The general superiority of grooms over brides throughout the period, alluded to above, appears to have been common to all parts of the country and to differing types of community. In most market towns, as well as in other towns outside the north of England, there was a reduction in the gap between male and female levels of illiteracy over the period 1754–1837, though rarely was the reduction very great. In the industrial towns of the north there was already a tendency in the 1750s for the gap to be greater (sometimes much greater) than in urban areas elsewhere; and this was often followed by increases in the levels of female illiteracy while male levels stagnated or sometimes also rose.[33] At Leeds in the late eighteenth century, for example, bridal illiteracy was roughly double that of grooms and a narrowing of the gap by the early years of the following century resulted more from increases in male illiteracy than from female improvement.[34]

In most rural areas, on the other hand, such evidence as we have[35] suggests a tendency for a narrowing of the gap to occur over the period 1754–1837 as female illiteracy decreased while male levels either did so more slowly, stagnated, or even increased. In the smaller parishes of Rutland, male and female levels more or less converged by 1811–20. This was so, too, in some North Riding parishes by the 1830s, though it does not seem to have been the case a generation later (Appendix D).

Dissimilar levels of literacy between different types of community were largely a manifestation of varying occupational structures, for literacy acquisition in an age when schooling was not compulsory had a strong functional ingredient. The pattern of literacy relative to social position and occupation, evident in earlier times, was still apparent in the late eighteenth and early nineteenth centuries. Those who earned their living by manual labour remained, not surprisingly, less literate than craftsmen and farmers, who in turn were bettered by professional men and the gentry.[36] In market towns and places that were more particularly commercial rather than industrial centres the stimulus of occupations connected with the expansion of trade probably encouraged the acquisition of a degree of education. Market towns contained a larger proportion of tradesmen of one kind and another for whom the three Rs were a business necessity. Moreover, such places were often ancient boroughs, traditionally centres where schools existed and educational stand-ards were superior[37] and where population growth was now not so rapid as to cause dislocation of educational facilities. It is noticeable, too, that many of these towns had benefited from improvements in road transport (for example, Wetherby) and canal construction (for example, some Lincolnshire towns) which stimulated trades in which the keeping of accounts and records and the ability to communicate by letter were useful. Oxford, a market centre, might anyway for other obvious reasons have been expected to have a disproportio-nate share of educated people.[38] On the other hand there seems every likelihood that high and increasing illiteracy rates in the industrial towns and textile areas of the north to some extent reflected growing job opportunities for women and children in factories, declining living standards among handloom weavers, a swamping by population increase of available school places, and an actual decline in rates of school attendance.[39]

The spread of the public voluntary schools following the foundation of the British and Foreign School Society and the National Society in the first two decades of the nineteenth century, and the growth of schooling generally, added to the likelihood that the incidence of schooling became an increasingly significant factor in varying cultural levels. For 1818 we have statistics on a county and parish basis for day-school pupils which, although certainly to some extent defective, provide an overall picture lacking for earlier periods. Expressed as percentages of total populations these show wide variations between counties from just over 4 per cent to more than 13 per cent (Appendix J). The counties of the far north (Cumberland, Westmorland, Northumberland, Durham and the East and North Ridings of Yorkshire), with proportions at school of between 9·1 and 13·2 per cent, form, with Lincolnshire (8·6) and Rutland (10·6), a composite area with school attendance at a much higher level than for most of the rest of the country. Only Sussex and Cambridgeshire of all other counties had 9 per cent or more at school. A group of midland counties (Derbyshire, Nottinghamshire, Northamptonshire, Berkshire and Hunting-donshire) and the south-coast counties of Kent, Hampshire, Dorset and Devon, had the next largest proportion at school (7·8–8·7 per cent). Though some of these counties were important for domestic industry, they were, on the whole, like the northern counties, predominantly agricultural. Counties with fewer than 7 per cent of the population at school included many where mining, heavy industries and the factory based textile industries were concentrated (Lancashire, Cheshire, the West Riding, Gloucestershire, Staffordshire, Warwickshire, Worcestershire, Monmouthshire, Cornwall and Somerset), together with counties where domestic industry still thrived (Bedfordshire, Buckinghamshire, Leicestershire), as well as Middlesex and Surrey.[40]

Although many doubtless still acquired the ability to write after normal school age, it might be expected that by this time schooling levels would find at least a degree of reflection in later levels of literacy — that is, in marriage signatures some fifteen years later, in the early 1830s. The number of places for which such data is available for the period about 1831–7 (Tables 1·1, 1·2), nevertheless falls short of what is required to test this hypothesis very rigorously. Yet it is observable that the extremely low proportion of 4·7 per cent at school in Lancashire in 1818 fits well with the high levels of illiteracy in the industrial towns of that county in the 1830s, while the low levels of illiteracy found in substantial samples of Rutland and East Riding parishes seem to accord with the high proportions at school in those counties in 1818 (10·6 and 9·1 per cent). There seems also no great discrepancy between the low illiteracy levels for market towns in Lincolnshire in the 1830s and the somewhat higher levels for groups of rural parishes in that county and the reasonably high level of schooling there in 1818 (8·6 per cent). More significantly, Bedfordshire and Gloucestershire, where the evidence of high illiteracy rates in the 1830s is derived from large numbers of parish registers, had only 6·2 and 5·2 per cent respectively at school in 1818.

The high levels of schooling in the northern counties support the thesis that those counties saw a disproportionate improvement in educational standards in the first half of the eighteenth century.[41] Comparison of the day-school figures of 1818 with the complete figures for illiteracy we have for 1839–45 (Appendixes D, J) also suggests that in one group of counties (across the far north of England and down the east coast, taking in Rutland) the effects of a high incidence of schooling were still bearing fruit. It is true that for English counties as a whole there was no strong statistical correlation between schooling levels in 1818 and illiteracy in 1839–45.[42] Nevertheless, of the seventeen counties with 8 per cent or more at school in 1818, twelve had fewer than 40 per cent marks in the later period and only one over 45 per cent, while of the eighteen with 6 per cent or fewer at school in 1818 all but three had 40 per cent marks or more in 1839–45 and ten had over 45 per cent.[43]

It is easier to demonstrate the levels of signature literacy and their variations between types of place and types of individual, than to explain what those figures really signify. It is unlikely that, as was once thought, the ability to write marked an immense cultural and social divide within the working classes.[44] There may have been a tendency for literate brides to marry literate grooms, and marriages where both parties made marks were commonest among labourers, but a large number of marriages were of a 'mixed' kind with one partner literate and the other not. At Shepshed (Leics.) the offspring of literate parents might be both literate and illiterate with siblings differing without any apparent explanatory pattern of age or sex,[45] and this is unlikely to be unique. Moreover, it is possible to overstress economic functionality. Many people must have had access to literacy through spouses, offspring, other relations, friends, colleagues or neighbours; members of the same trades within a locality at a particular time could be both literate and illiterate without obvious differences in prosperity. Allowing for the fact that many more people could read than sign their names, and that ability to read and write varied qualitatively very considerably, a clear line between the literate and the illiterate must in practice have been difficult to draw. It may be that a social divide in this period was there, but that the line was drawn at a higher level than possession of the bare rudiments of the two Rs considered here.[46] It is likely, therefore, that a picture of educational standards in a locality is best attained by a consideration of both basic literacy and school attendance levels, and also of the actual quality of schooling and the general nature of working-class attitudes and child life.

CHAPTER 2

Schooling and literacy: regional characteristics and influences

In the 1830s and 1840s England entered a period of expanding provision of public schooling and increasing pressure on working-class parents to take advantage of it. Growing numbers did so as opportunities for literates in the job market increased and legislation restricted the employment of young children. Nevertheless educational advance was slow and varied in extent geographically. Areas of domestic industry and of small farms dependent on family labour lingered on for many years, as did industries which employed women and children outside the home. The rate of change was affected, too, by local attitudes particularly to popular schooling and child employment. In some areas continuing opportunities for child labour, parental poverty and indifference or opposition to protracted schooling, and support by employers and others for juvenile employment, remained sufficiently strong for universal schooling of an effective kind to be unattainable without coercion. Change thus occurred at different rates and to varying degrees in different parts of the country over the period 1830–70. The remainder of this study investigates regional differences in schooling and literacy levels and seeks to explain their relation to particular economic structures and attitudes on the part of working-class parents and of the local middle classes.

The geographical, social and economic context

During the period 1840 to 1900 Britain became an increasingly literate society. The amount of reading material available to the public at large rose dramatically. Newspapers fell in price as the 'taxes on knowledge' disappeared, books and periodicals became cheaper consequent on technological and commercial changes and of the activities of the Society for the Diffusion of Useful Knowledge, religious bodies, political organisations and commercial publishers. Book clubs, commercial libraries, and adult education establishments made reading material more widely available, while letter writing was encouraged by the advent of the penny post in 1840. Over the second half of the century both working and middle-class incomes rose, and leisure time, some of which was undoubtedly spent in reading, increased.

Over the period 1850–1900 the proportion of literate persons in England was at a relatively high level in comparison with most European countries. It was lower than in Scotland, Scandinavia, Germany, the Netherlands and Switzerland, but higher than in France, Belgium, Wales, Ireland, and considerably higher than in Austria, Hungary, Spain, Italy, Russia, the Balkan states and Poland.[1] Between 1841 and 1885 the illiteracy rate at marriage for England and Wales fell from 41 to 12 per cent (Appendix D). More than half the younger generation in the early years of Victoria's reign could thus sign their names and probably more than that could read to some extent. Yet regional variations, evident in earlier periods, still persisted. At the beginning of the period London had the lowest rate, with only 18 per cent of spouses making marks over the years 1839–45.[2] Excluding the London area, the most literate parts of the country (averaged over 1839–45: Appendix D) were the far north (Cumberland, Northumberland, Westmorland, the East and North Ridings of Yorkshire) with Rutland, all with less than 34 per cent making marks. Counties with between 35 and 39 per cent marks included Durham and Lincolnshire (completing the northern and north-eastern area of high literacy), extra-metropolitan Middlesex, Kent and Surrey, and the counties of the southern seaboard (Sussex, Hampshire, Dorset and Devon), and Gloucestershire. Straddling the national average of 41 per cent marks were the midland counties of Derbyshire, Nottinghamshire, Leicestershire and Warwickshire, with contiguous Northamptonshire, Oxfordshire and Berkshire, Somerset and Herefordshire in the west, and Cambridgeshire (all between 40 and 45 per cent marks). The least literate counties (over 45 per cent) included Cornwall, Shropshire, Wiltshire and Monmouthshire in the west, Norfolk, Suffolk and Essex in the east, connecting with Hertfordshire, Bedfordshire, Huntingdonshire and Buckinghamshire, north of London, to form a block of low literacy, and Cheshire, Lancashire and the West Riding in the north linking with Staffordshire and Worcestershire in the midlands. Bedfordshire and Monmouthshire shared the distinction of being the least literate English counties, with 58 per cent of spouses making marks, more than double the proportions in the far north, and the equivalent of what prevailed in Wales.

Although the national level for marks had fallen by 1870 to 24 per cent, the geographical pattern was much the same (Appendix D). All but one of the sixteen most literate counties in 1839–45 had fewer than 22 per cent marks in 1870, while of the sixteen least literate counties in 1839–45 fourteen had 25 per cent or more marks in 1870. There were, however, some changes. Most striking is the comparatively high level of marks found in 1870 in Warwickshire (26 per cent), Nottinghamshire (27 per cent), Cambridgeshire (27 per cent) and Durham (31 per cent). The last had a generation earlier formed part of the northern area of high literacy but by 1870 was more illiterate than any other English county, except Staffordshire, Monmouthshire and Bedfordshire, which remained areas of very high illiteracy. On the other hand Oxfordshire and Berkshire improved their relative position somewhat and a very considerable improvement is observable with Essex, Wiltshire and Northamptonshire. These last three were all formerly well below average in literacy levels, but by 1870 were better than the national level and on a par with Dorset and the North Riding.

As in the period of early industrialisation some connection between levels of literacy and economic characteristics is obvious. High literacy is particularly associated throughout the period 1840–70 with certain rural areas (the sparsely populated counties of the far north and north-east, the agricultural and seaboard counties of the south coast) and with the counties close to and embracing London (Middlesex, Kent, Surrey). Reasons for the excellence of the northern counties are discussed below. As for extra-metropolitan Kent, Middlesex and Surrey, it is not surprising that counties so close to the world's greatest commercial centre, the administrative and social capital of empire, should possess concentrations of the well-to-do and educated, and attract intelligent and literate immigrants.[3] In 1870 the illiteracy rate in London itself was 12 per cent, the same as for extra-metropolitan Surrey, the most literate county.

At the other end of the spectrum some connection between low literacy levels and highly populated industrial areas is apparant. The backward state of the north-west manufacturing counties, evident in the period 1750–1830, persists through the mid-Victorian period, particularly in Lancashire and the West Riding. So too does the high illiteracy of the mining and industrial counties of Monmouthshire and Staffordshire, joined, as noted above, by Durham, which had experienced huge increases in population from at least the 1830s as mining developed. There levels of literacy remained more or less static through the 1850s. Other counties with substantial concentrations of mining or manufacturing (as Cornwall, Nottinghamshire, Shropshire, Worcestershire) remained at levels of illiteracy higher than the national, or like Warwickshire (containing Birmingham) moved into that category.

Also continuing as a region of high illiteracy were Buckinghamshire, Hertfordshire and Bedfordshire, where agricultural labour was poorly rewarded, where cottage industries were concentrated and whence London probably syphoned off the more enterprising and intelligent youths and enticed the gentry to absent themselves from their estates.[4] Other more predominantly rural areas, particularly Norfolk, Suffolk and Huntingdonshire, remained specially backward relative to national levels, while Cambridgeshire and Herefordshire had also moved into that category by 1870.

In almost all counties decreases in proportions of illiterate spouses were accompanied by a fall in the actual numbers involved (Appendix E). But in Cumberland and Durham there was an increase in the number of illiterates marrying over the period 1856–71, as was the case in the West Riding between 1856 and 1866 and in Warwickshire, Staffordshire and Nottinghamshire between 1866 and 1871. Since all these except Cumberland were industrialised areas, a further link between industrial concentration and extensive illiteracy is suggested.

Another aspect of the geographical distribution of illiteracy lies in gender differences. The inferiority of women found in earlier times continued into the Victorian period. It is not unreasonable to think that this had something to do with the fact that in mid-century, although more boys than girls were officially at work (Appendix B), fewer girls than boys went to school, and that the school curriculum for girls was less directed to writing than that for boys. In 1851 in every English county a higher proportion of girls than boys aged five to fourteen was not at school (Appendix I).[5] And in a survey of pupils in 1857 62 per cent of boys but only 56 per cent of girls were learning to write, although the proportions learning reading were about the same (88–9 per cent).[6] It is not surprising then that over the period 1839–45 more brides than grooms made marks in every single English county.

This situation, however, changed after mid-century. By 1855 the percentage of brides making marks was less than or equal to that of grooms in ten counties; by 1860 that had become fifteen, by 1865 nineteen, by 1870 twenty-one, by 1880 twenty-four, and by 1885 twenty-six counties (Appendix D). A decided pattern of change is discernible: counties where fewer brides were illiterate than grooms in any year remained so consistently in subsequent years.[7] Areas where female literacy levels were superior to male, moreover, spread outwards like liquid spilt on a floor. In 1855 female superiority existed in East Anglia, some counties in the south-east and the south midlands, and Herefordshire. In the 1860s were added other southern counties, together with some in the West Country and Rutland and Lincolnshire. More western counties were included by 1880, and Bedfordshire and Northamptonshire in the 1880s. By 1885 male superiority remained in the counties of the far north and the East and North Ridings of Yorkshire, in the northern and midland industrial counties, and in Monmouthshire. Devon alone of the counties of the south and west remained an area of male superiority, and then but marginally. Only in Lancashire and the West Riding was male superiority greater by more than 5 percentage points. The tardiness of progress towards equality in the north and midlands was doubtless to some extent the consequence of the greater differential between male and female illiteracy rates already existing at the beginning of our period. In 1839–45 that differential in the counties of East Anglia, the south, and the south midlands varied between 1 and 10 percentage points, apart from in Buckinghamshire, Bedfordshire and Northamptonshire, where it was 12 to 14 points. In the northern and north eastern counties and those of the south-west (apart from Rutland and Gloucestershire) the range was between 10 and 19 points, in the industrial midlands between 15 and 19, and in

Cheshire, the West Riding and Lancashire 25, 26 and 28 points respectively (Appendix D).

A remarkable overall improvement in the relative literacy of women from the 1850s is thus apparant. Areas of inferior female literacy remained those where women's industrial labour was most concentrated, or, as in the east, those where sparsely distributed population made school development slow and where there were few resident gentry to employ domestic servants, a class associated with good levels of literacy.[8]

Also evident, however, is that in some counties male illiteracy remained in the 1880s relatively high. Those where in 1885 a higher proportion of grooms made marks than in the country as a whole included a large number of predominantly rural southern counties where farm labourers suffered particularly from low wages[9] and the agricultural depression (Essex, Norfolk, Suffolk, Cambridgeshire, Huntingdonshire, Bedfordshire, Buckinghamshire, Hertfordshire, Dorset, Wiltshire and Herefordshire), and others where mining and manufacturing existed in otherwise largely agricultural areas (Durham, Staffordshire, Monmouthshire, Shropshire, Somerset, Cornwall, Warwickshire and Worcestershire).[10]

Contemporary social observers noted these differences between the literacy levels of various counties and between men and women and their apparent link with regional differences of an economic kind. They noted, too, the variations between urban and rural literacy and the possible influence of other social characteristics.[11] In 1847 Joseph Fletcher, a noted statistician and social investigator, went further than most in an attempt to show statistically relationships between social and economic characteristics of English counties and levels of literacy,[12] and some of his calculations form the basis for Appendix H. The evident relationship of high density of population and high illiteracy bears out the already observed connection between industrialised areas and low educational levels. More interesting are other conclusions apparent in Fletcher's calculations. His figures, for example, indicate a general connection between high levels of illiteracy and above average levels of early marriage and bastardy. Of the twenty-three counties with average or above illiteracy rates in 1839–45 all but two had above average levels of early marriage or illegitimacy, and often of both. The two exceptions, Cornwall and Monmouthshire, were perhaps explicable by the influence of nonconformist propriety in those Celtic communities. Nevertheless, of the sixteen remaining counties[13] (those with lower than average illiteracy) only five were below average for both early marriage and illegitimacy, so that, although four others were almost in that category, there seems no absolute connection between these phenomena and literacy. Other observers, however, noted that the number of marriages of minors was always greatest where industrial employment was available.[14]

The Registrar General in 1882 observed that the illiterate tended also to be improvident, and to continue to marry in times of economic depression when the more educated held back.[15] Fletcher's analysis also throws light on thrift related to literacy. Of the fifteen counties with above average savings rates nine had below average illiteracy, and it is likely that his figures showing low levels of savings in some of the highly literate counties of the far north had been affected by a recent colliers' strike.[16]

Horace Mann in 1851 rejected poverty as an important reason for failure of parents to send children to school[17] and Fletcher's figures of paupers relieved in 1844 are difficult to relate to contemporary literacy levels. Mann, however, considered only the burden of school pence and not the opportunity cost of education, while it is doubtful whether the proportion of paupers relieved in a particular year is a very useful measure. Pauper children, after all, might be schooled at the expense of the union or given instruction in the workhouse. It was those who lived on the brink of poverty and struggled to keep themselves and their children from the workhouse who were most likely to ignore school and seek employment for their children. Certainly many parents pleaded poverty as the reason for not schooling their children, and there is plenty of evidence indicating that poverty in some areas did affect the extent to which children were sent to school. The Lancashire handloom weavers were used in prosperity to school their offspring, but declining fortunes led them to set them to work, and the same situation occurred elsewhere, as in Norwich and Gloucestershire.[18] In Derbyshire, too, the domestic framework knitters lost their enthusiasm for education as their wages fell, but were more willing to school their children when incomes rose.[19] In Birmingham school attendance was low when trade was depressed[20] and such examples could be multiplied. There is also evidence, however, that in some places children were removed from school when work became readily available, and that some workpeople, as for example the prosperous Coventry ribbon weavers and the well paid metal workers of the midlands, preferred to send their children to work rather than to a school they could well afford.[21] It is not surprising, therefore, that it is difficult to relate levels of poverty or prosperity at a county level positively with literacy rates.[12]

Fletcher's figures also show a discernible but not absolute connection between good literacy levels and higher proportions of persons of independent means. But most significant is the relationship he shows between high proportions of domestic servants and superior literacy levels. Of the sixteen counties with over sixty-five domestics per thousand of the population all but three had illiteracy rates below, most well below, the national level, while all the eight counties with fewer than fifty-four domestics per thousand had above average illiteracy rates. Fletcher suggests that to this latter group could be added others, such as Cornwall and Monmouthshire, where farm servants appear to have been recorded as domestic servants in the census. This tendency must indicate to some extent the geographical incidence of middle-class employers of such labour[23] but is likely to reflect more the superior educational levels of domestics, particularly females. If county illiteracy rates of brides for 1839–45 (Appendix D) are compared with the county proportions for domestics connection between the two appears clear. Of the counties with female illiteracy rates above the national level only one, Shropshire, had proportions of domestic servants greater than sixty-five per thousand, compared with twelve of the eighteen counties[24] with better than average bridal literacy.

Of course, many domestics were illiterate. But some employers required higher servants able to read and keep simple accounts, others were less interested in educational attainment than with the training in morality, religion and obedience associated with attendance at school, or the sewing skills achieved there, and used the school as an employment agency. Parents who wanted their daughters to obtain decent household situations would, therefore, tend to send them to school. Work in the fields or the factory was coarsening and children would find it difficult to move from there to domestic service. Once in a middle-class home some domestics would have the opportunity of practising and improving literacy skills, and availing themselves of newspapers and other reading matter. Some employers were given to household prayers and bible instruction and to encouraging church attendance, which again is likely to have promoted literacy.[25] Since the extension of female domestic service over the decades following Fletcher's survey is a well known phenomenon, with a greater incidence in southern and rural counties than in northern industrial districts, it seems likely that this was a factor in the closing differential between levels of male and female literacy and the chronology of geographical changes.

The growth of domestic service for girls was accompanied by a fall-off in the numbers employed in other ways[26] and perhaps an encouragement to prior schooling. Most child labour, however, was to some extent a substitute for schooling and its varying incidence was one ingredient in dissimilar local levels of literacy. It is, however, not easy to quantify the extent to which children in the mid-nineteenth century were engaged in work. It has been suggested that by then child labour, especially for those under ten, was negligible, and that there may have been over-registration of children as workers in the census.[27] In the country as a whole only 2·0 per cent of boys and 1·4 per cent of girls between five and nine years were returned in the 1851 census as 'occupied', and by 1871 this had dropped to about 1 per cent for both sexes (Appendix B). But there was considerable variation between counties, with employment commonest in areas of domestic industry. In 1851 nearly 17 per cent of this age group (and 21 per cent of girls) were 'occupied' in Bedfordshire, and about 7–8 per cent in Buckinghamshire and Hertfordshire,[28] while in the West Riding, Leicestershire, Nottinghamshire and Northamptonshire some 4–6 per cent were officially at work. At the other end of the spectrum, in the counties of the far north, almost no children in this age group were employed. By 1871 the extent of employment of children under ten recorded in the census was negligible in most counties, though still 8 per cent in Bedfordshire and over 2 per cent in the West Riding, Buckinghamshire and Hertfordshire.

Since the numbers of five and six-year-olds formally at work must have been very small and job opportunities greatest for older children in the age group five to nine, labour must have been concentrated more in those of seven or eight upwards, when schooling might have been most effective.[29] Proportions of child workers aged seven or eight to nine may well have approached double the percentages indicated for the five to nine group, so that for some places, especially up to mid-century, the labour of young children may still have been significant.

Labour was, however, much commoner for children of ten to fourteen years, an age group where work was more likely to make literacy harder to acquire and retain. In the country as a whole 28 per cent of these children were officially at work in 1851, more of them boys (37 per cent) than girls (20 per cent). Appendix B illustrates that the incidence of these young workers was again unevenly spread. The greatest proportions were in the West Riding, Cheshire and Lancashire, with high levels, too, in the industrial midlands and in those south midland counties associated with cottage industry. The employment of boys was also at a high level in the western counties, chiefly on the land. Over the period 1851 to 1871 the proportions of boys in this age group employed in agriculture actually increased, and this was so, too, of girls in textiles.[30] In 1871 about a quarter of this age group was officially at work (including about a third of boys), and more or less the same geographical variations as in 1851 are observable.

All these figures, however, need to be viewed in the light of the contemporary context. The modern concept of 'work' and 'school' as either mutually exclusive, or likely together to embrace all children is inappropriate.[31] In most counties in 1851 over 40 per cent of boys aged five to fourteen were not at school, and in half the counties over 50 per cent. As for girls, in only three counties were more than half at school on census day, an overall figure embracing very high proportions in the textile counties, the industrial midlands, Monmouthshire and the western agricultural counties (Appendix I). Some of the children neither at work nor school, particularly in the larger towns, may have lived a life of aimless drifting,[32] but most no doubt mixed casual work about the home and elsewhere with play and many of the girls were probably engaged in looking after younger siblings and doing housework, and of the boys in casual farm work, gardening, and running errands, Nor is it unlikely that in some areas where cottage industry was prevalent some were engaged in this without being so returned in the censuses. In the south midlands attenders at plait and lace 'schools' (really workshops but regarded by parents as schools) are quite likely to have been returned as 'scholars'[33] and it is not impossible that some Sunday school pupils were wrongly returned in this way. It is likely, too, that numbers of children (large in some places) were on the school books but attended only when work was lacking, while irregular and short attendance reflected a mix of work and school by many in unknown proportions.

The data on child labour at county level appears to accord with the general geographical pattern of literacy, and the effect of child labour, officially recorded or not, was thus likely to have been of some significance in geographically differing educational standards. Considerable variations in proportions of children at school within the registration districts of individual counties[34] makes it likely that similar variations existed within county areas in levels of child labour, thus rendering its influence greater in some places in a county than others.

Such information as we have for towns also supports a spatially differential incidence of work among the young. No specific figures for those aged five to fourteen exists for towns, but statistics of young workers under twenty years old in 1851 (Appendix C) for thirty-one 'principal towns' reveal a consistent proportion of about a quarter of males at work in the towns of the north-east, the south-east and the west, but a much higher proportion in the industrial towns of the north-west and the midlands. For females proportions of about one-third or more are registered for the textile towns of the midlands and Lancashire, and in Stockport and Bradford, but smaller proportions in towns elsewhere. This probably reflected the high rate of child employment in these towns.

Fletcher like others regarded the extension of elementary education as a necessity if illiteracy was to be reduced, but he did not attempt to relate illiteracy levels in the early 1840s with levels of schooling, being aware of the difficulties of interpreting the data on schooling then available.[35] With the increase of school places and the growth of attendance clearly evident from the 1830s onwards, common sense suggests that the incidence of schooling is likely to have had an effect, if not a directly proportionate one, on later literacy levels.[36] Thus at a national level female inferiority in literacy accords with the lower proportion of girls than boys attending school remarked on above, and the likely tendency for county levels of day school attendance in 1818 to be reflected in the later overall literacy levels in the 1830s and early 1840s has also been noted.[37]

Comparison of similar school figures for 1833 (Appendix J) with the literacy levels of 1845 and 1850 (Appendix D) shows a rough consistency between higher levels of schooling and lower illiteracy levels in the northern counties and the southern seaboard shires, and between low schooling levels and some of the very least literate counties (Monmouthshire, Lancashire and Bedfordshire particularly), but once more in many cases the connection is not particularly obvious.[38] A similar exercise for day schooling levels in 1851 and illiteracy percentages in 1866, (Table 2·1), also shows a fair match, as does application of the product moment correlation coefficient formula.[39] Clearly, there was by then a tendency for the most illiterate counties to rank low for schooling levels fifteen years earlier, and for the most literate counties to have had higher levels of schooling, but there are many apparent discrepancies, and it seems that both literacy and schooling figures are in many areas too crude measures for sophisticated deduction, particularly considered at the level of county averages.

Although charity and workhouse schools and endowed grammar schools in most counties catered for too few children to affect materially the levels of literacy, the characteristics of other schools in an area may well have.

TABLE 2·1

Percentages of brides and grooms making marks, 1866[a]

	%			%	
Westmorland	16	(1)	Somerset	26	(29)
Middlesex[b]	16	(39)	Warwickshire	27	(37)
Hampshire	16	(3)	Essex	27	(19)
Surrey[b]	17	(21)	Nottinghamshire	28	(31)
Sussex	17	(8)	Worcestershire	28	(34)
Rutland	18	(2)	Cambridgeshire	28	(13)
Kent[b]	19	(6)	Herefordshire	28	(41)
Devon	20	(32)	Norfolk	30	(28)
Northumberland	21	(23)	Suffolk	30	(24)
Yorkshire, E.R.	21	(14)	Hertfordshire	30	(4)
Yorkshire, N.R.	21	(10)	Cheshire	31	(27)
Oxfordshire	21	(7)	Lancashire	31	(38)
Gloucestershire	21	(26)	Yorkshire W.R.	31	(25)
Lincolnshire	22	(16)	Huntingdonshire	31	(5)
Berkshire	22	(12)	Cornwall	31	(36)
Dorset	22	(11)	Durham	32	(17)
Cumberland	24	(15)	Shropshire	32	(33)
Northamptonshire	24	(20)	Buckinghamshire	33	(30)
Wiltshire	24	(9)	Bedfordshire	37	(40)
Derbyshire	26	(18)	Staffordshire	40	(35)
Leicestershire	26	(22)	Monmouthshire	41	(42)

a Marks percentages from Appendix D. Bracketed figures represent ranking for children on books of day schools, 1851: (1) = highest proportion (Appendix J).
b extra metropolitan area.

Elementary day schools varied greatly in size and in quality. Some were public voluntary schools, provided by churches, chapels and others, and some were private establishments run for profit. The voluntary schools were both denominational and non-denominational British; some were from the 1830s inspected and aided by government funds, others were not; some catered solely for infants, others took older children. Private schools included those for the middle classes, though most were for working-class children. Traditionally dame schools took the youngest children, private venture schools the older ones, but there were many variations and overlaps.

The age range of pupils, too, differed from one area to another, as did the length of time children stayed at school and their regularity of attendance, factors which must have influenced educational attainment. There is some evidence that the length of schooling was shorter in industrial districts than in agricultural ones and that this resulted in the school population being generally younger in, for example, Lancashire than in Lincolnshire.[40] Thus in communities in the Widnes area the same school proportions for different occupational groups later produced widely differing literacy levels, because the children of skilled workers were concentrated at school in a higher age range than those of the unskilled.[41]

Moreover the quality of education certainly varied consequent on many other factors from one area to another, and indeed from school to school. The significance of the varying incidence of public as opposed to private schooling is not simple to evaluate. The standard of the education purveyed in working-class private schools is a matter of controversy.[42] What is certain is that 'private' and 'public' are too gross classifications for firm conclusions on their relative influence on general educational standards.

Before the 1830s it is doubtful whether better elementary instruction was provided in many of the religiously orientated voluntary schools using the dubiously effective monitorial system[43] than in those private common day schools for older children which emphasised secular learning in smaller groups. And there was probably little difference in quality between the instruction given to infants in dame schools and in many Church schools. With the advent of government funding and inspection, followed by the introduction into public schools of pupil teachers, increasing numbers of trained teachers, better buildings and equipment, more generous provision of books and so on, the benefit of a sound curriculum and teaching methods, and the pressure for regular attendance, standards in inspected public schools, particularly from the 1850s, must certainly have outstripped those of schools reliant on local funding and school pence and under less external pressure.[44]

By 1851 about 89 per cent of boys and girls in the voluntary schools were learning reading as opposed to 84 per cent of boys and 87 per cent of girls in private schools. Writing was less commonly taught in the private schools (50 per cent of boys, 46 per cent of girls) than public schools (63 and 56 per cent).[45] This reflects the greater concentration of the very young in the dame schools, many of which did not teach writing — indeed some of the teachers who claimed to teach reading could not themselves write.[46] Nevertheless even in the 1850s and 1860s many unaided Church schools were little if any better than dame schools. Indeed, some 'dame schools' were smiled on by the vicar and regarded as Church schools, and may appear in statistics of public schools,[47] so that the distinction in educational terms between the unaided public and the private schools remains blurred. Not surprisingly, therefore, local variations in the raw percentages of children at 'private' and 'public' schools in 1851 are not obviously reflected in later signature rates,[48] though everything suggests that the proliferation of government inspected schools did raise standards. This is particularly likely after the Revised Code in 1862 instituted 'a crash course in literacy'[49] in the inspected schools and encouraged regular attendance.[50]

The high level of Sunday-school attendance in the nineteenth century might be expected, too, to form an additional ingredient in literacy levels. It is difficult, however, to quantify the educational effects of Sunday schooling. Some children attended Sunday schools only, others both Sunday and day schools, and yet others went only to day schools, though these variations are not often distinguished in contemporary returns of pupils. Moreover, some of those shown as attending only Sunday school had at some time been day scholars (for varying periods) or would be so later, while others never had and never would go to day school. Again, Sunday schools often had a greater incidence of older children than did day schools.[51] It is probable, too, that these factors varied from place to place and over time.

The pattern of Sunday-school attendance across counties as it related to day school figures was virtually the same in 1833 and 1851 (Appendix J) In Cheshire, Lancashire and the West Riding, in the counties of the industrial midlands, in Bedfordshire, Buckinghamshire and Northamptonshire, and in Cornwall and Monmouthshire, there was a higher attendance at Sunday than day schools. The reverse was so in the more purely agricultural counties and in Kent, Surrey and Middlesex. Much the same situation had already been apparent in 1818, with the notable exceptions of Cornwall and Monmouthshire. The connection between higher levels of Sunday over day schooling and areas where industrial employment attracted child labour is clear. Moreover in Lancashire and the West Riding, particularly in the industrialised villages and probably other densely populated industrial areas, day school facilities were swamped by multiplying populations, adding to the attraction of Sunday schooling.[52]

Religious attitudes were, however, also an ingredient in the situation. The nonconformists paid more attention to Sunday than day schooling and in the industrial counties of the north and midlands and in Cornwall and Monmouth-shire, where Dissent was strong, more children attended nonconformist than Anglican Sunday schools (Appendix L). Indeed, the data in Appendix N shows an apparent connection in 1851 between the incidence of nonconformity and Sunday-school attendance in about half the English counties, most obvious in the industrial counties. Where church attendance generally (nonconformist and Anglican together) was high there was also a tendency for Sunday schools to be well attended. In some urban areas, particularly in the north, however, the reverse was so, with Sunday schools inversely related to religious attendance, suggesting perhaps a substitution by the working classes of Sunday schools for traditional religious institutions. The low Sunday-school figures for Surrey, Kent and Middlesex may reflect the notoriously irreligious attitude of many of the working classes in the metropolitan area.[53] But because secular subjects were taught in Sunday schools, and usually free of charge, these institutions were attractive to many working-class parents aside from any religious and social pull they also had. Sunday schooling thus provided education com-plementary to day schools and in some cases a substitute for them.

It has been argued, however, that the data available (total numbers at day and Sunday schools) is insufficient to assess the significance of the substitution one for the other.[54] On the other hand it has been noted that correlation between county proportions of 'occupied' children aged ten to fourteen is consistently positive with Sunday school proportions throughout the century, whereas with day schooling the correlation is consistently negative.[55] Certainly in 1851 there is little overlap in a list of counties where day school enrolment was below the national level and a list of those where Sunday school attendance was below it.[56]

Because many children, in varying proportions, attended both Sunday and day school, and others used Sunday schools to continue education after day schooling, and because most Sunday schools emphasised reading more than writing and probably a diminishing minority taught writing at all, the educational benefits of Sunday attendance are unlikely to be reflected very strongly in levels of signatures. Certainly across counties the correlation between Sunday-school attendance and literacy levels has been found to be negative.[57] Nevertheless it is highly likely that educational benefits were conveyed. In York, where in 1826 nearly 88 per cent of some 300 children aged twelve to fourteen were allegedly able to read, Sunday schools catered for 40 per cent of the children (aged six to fourteen) not attending day schools.[58]

It has been estimated that in the 1830s and 1840s at least 25 per cent and in places up to 75 per cent of English Sunday-school pupils received no other formal education. By mid-century the proportion of such children doubtless fell as day schooling increased. At the same time the average age of Sunday scholars rose,[59] so that the contribution of these schools to training in basic literacy skills probably diminished. Some youngsters learned to read and write at evening, ragged or factory schools, but these institutions are unlikely to have affected literacy levels materially. Factory schools were concentrated in Lancashire, Cheshire, the West Riding and Monmouthshire, where literacy levels were low anyway: in 1851 80 per cent of factory-school pupils were in those counties.[60] Many factory schools, moreover, confined themselves to teaching reading; indeed, of the 'best' thirty factory schools in the Lancashire–Cheshire cotton area in 1839, six did not teach writing.[61] The impact of evening schools, too, must have been statistically slight considering the small numbers of pupils involved. The Newcastle Commission reported only 78,000 evening pupils over the whole country in 1858, with more than 1 per cent of the population found only in Bedfordshire, and actual numbers of children significant mainly in Lancashire (about 15,000), Yorkshire (6,000), and Middlesex (6,600) (Appendix Q). In evening schools for adults in 1851 the highest attendances were in Lancashire and the West Riding (9,700 and 7,800 respectively), Cheshire, Midddlesex, Norfolk and Surrey (all fewer than 2,000).[62] By 1866–7, of some 40,200 attenders at Church of England night schools spread over fourteen English counties, 93 per cent had at some time been at a day school. The concentration was again largest in Lancashire and the West Riding, and also in Middlesex, but the pupils were largely adolescents and sometimes adults.[63]

Again, ragged schools were often more philanthropic than educational institutions, and in 1858 there were but 192 daily ragged schools in England with only 21,000 pupils,[64] and for that reason, ragged schools, like charity, workhouse and grammar schools, have not been considered in this study. In seeking to relate the impact of day schooling on general levels of basic education, it is fairly safe to ignore the influence of these schools and evening schools, and in most places of factory schools.

A factor which did complicate the relationship between schooling and literacy levels in some localities, however, was the extent of in and out migration. Not all children were schooled in the county they later married in. The rate of population growth in the metropolitan counties and in some midland and northern counties, indicates considerable immigration. The poor schooling levels in Middlesex, combined with relatively good literacy rates, suggest that there was an influx of the better educated after school age. Where Irish immigrants were present a contrary situation was created, usually in urban areas.

Urban and rural dimensions

By the nineteenth century the individual English counties had each acquired distinct characteristics formed by geography, tradition and administrative structures. Nevertheless for social and economic purposes they can only be rough and ready units for comparison. They embraced both urban and country districts in different proportions, different types of towns and rural communities, unevenly spread densities of population, and locally varying kinds of economic enterprise. Most industrialised counties contained rural areas while many agricultural counties had some mining or industry within their bounds. Moreover, rural districts in one county were not always homogeneous, while some abutted on or were affected by nearby urban areas in other counties. It is thus not surprising that there were great variations in standards of basic literacy within individual county boundaries. For example, in Devon, while the average illiteracy rate for the six years 1865–70 was 21 per cent, the proportions for the twenty census districts ranged from 12 to 29 per cent.[65]

Such differences derived to some extent from the varying occupational structures of communities. All local investigations reveal, as for earlier periods, a greater tendency for some occupational groups to be literate than others.[66] Generally speaking, coal miners and their families formed the least literate group in any community, with labourers next least literate, though 'labourers' covered a wide group and in some urban areas might contain more literate men than, for example, among farm labourers. Factory hands, particularly females, were often illiterate. Craftsmen and other skilled artisans were generally more often literate than labourers, with a tendency for a relative decline in the levels of some domestic textile workers as their economic status worsened. Employers and those engaged in trading activities formed the most commonly literate group, though in the 1830s and 1840s many small farmers might be illiterate. Some in Yorkshire, in the 1840s for example, allegedly could not spell the names of their own farms.[67] As might be expected the more literate occupational groups had a greater tendency to have literate offspring than did the less literate ones, though this might be affected by falling incomes and the disruption of traditional ways of life, as for example when the hand-loom weavers' were adversely affected by factory competition which nevertheless provided jobs for their children.[68]

Other social characteristics doubtless varied, too, within county boundaries. The incidence of schooling certainly did. Thus in 1851 in Lancashire double the proportion of girls were at school in the Fylde district as in Chorlton, Salford, Ashton and Oldham; and the proportion of pupils varied over the Lancashire districts from 7 to 12 per cent of the total population. Similarly, very different levels of Sunday-school attendance within the districts of individual counties is recorded: in Cheshire in 1851 they ranged from 6 per cent in the Wirral to 17 per cent in Stockport (Appendix F).

The differing educational characteristics of town and rural areas, on which Victorian observers so often dwelt, deserves some general comment. The variety of types of English provincial town was by the mid-nineteenth century extensive. Towns included the three great industrial giants, Manchester, Birmingham and Leeds, all of which witnessed rapid expansion of population and economic growth in our period, but which differed each from the other in many ways. There were the smaller but booming textile towns of Lancashire, Cheshire and the West Riding, and also other important concentrations of population — like Nottingham, Leicester and Coventry — which were centres of industry less based on the factory than Manchester and the Lancashire cotton towns. Yet other places, like Swindon, Middlesbrough and Crewe, were virtually creations of the industrial revolution, as was St. Helens, a Lancashire town whose mixed economy, like that of neighbouring Warrington, was not tied to cotton manufacture. Then there were the ancient market towns, some of which still depended on the fortunes of local agriculture, surviving or decaying according to the region and the time; while others, the 'Banburys of England', which had developed mixed economies of trades, crafts and manufactures in the eighteenth and nineteenth centuries, continued to grow in size. Some of these towns, like Banbury itself, acted as regional centres and were clearly different in character from the predominantly industrial towns.[69] Different again were the older centres of industry which decayed or found new functions as market, social or administrative centres, like Exeter, formerly the hub of the great West Country woollen trade. It would be possible to illustrate a multitude of further diversities in towns of this period — spa towns, cathedral cities, ports — all sub-groups of the genus 'town', but with each varying within the sub-group.

The extent of school provision and attendance in these towns varied greatly and educational characteristics were manifestly related to economic function and social structure. Table 2·2 lists those forty-four English towns individually reported on in the Education Census of 1851 where the proportions of children on day school books were greater than one in every six (16·7 per cent) of the population. Certain observations may be made about the characteristics of these towns. Geographically, nearly all of them were in the south. Nearly half (twenty) were in the western counties of Devon, Cornwall, Dorset, Hampshire, Oxfordshire, Berkshire and Wiltshire; another sixteen were in counties close to London — Essex, Hertfordshire, Huntingdonshire, Buchinghamshire, Surrey, Kent and Sussex. Only nine were situated in the north or the midlands. Moreover, of the twelve with the very best proportions (those where every five persons or fewer included a child at school), all were in the south of England except Retford, East.

There also appears to have been some connection between the size of population and school attendance. Only two of these forty-four towns had more than 10,000 inhabitants (Kendal and Lincoln — the largest of the towns); only five others had populations over 8,000 (Chichester, Poole, Stamford, Weymouth, Windsor) and another eight over 6,000 (Chesterfield, Dorchester,

TABLE 2·2

Towns with more day-school pupils than 1 in 6 of the population, 1851

Population	Town	County	Day-school pupils: one in
5,187	Andover	Hampshire	4·97
2,748	Arundel	Sussex	5·10
4,026	Banbury	Oxfordshire	5·89
5,775	Bideford	Devon	4·91
2,504	Blandford	Dorset	4·60
2,544	Calne	Wiltshire	5·39
7,101	Chesterfield	Derbyshire	5·24
8,662	Chichester	Sussex	5·66
2,932	Chipping Norton	Oxfordshire	5·79
6,394	Dorchester	Dorset	5·98
4,953	Falmouth	Cornwall	5·93
4,595	Faversham	Kent	4·78
6,726	Folkstone	Kent	5·83
6,740	Guildford	Surrey	5·22
3,395	Helston	Cornwall	5·34
6,605	Hertford	Hertfordshire	4·98
3,882	Huntingdon	Huntingdonshire	4·89
2,857	Hythe	Kent	5·53
11,829	Kendal	Westmorland	5·52
3,397	Launceston	Cornwall	5·44
17,536	Lincoln	Lincolnshire	5·75
2,651	Lymington	Hampshire	4·86
4,558	Maldon	Essex	4·51
3,908	Marlborough	Wiltshire	3·39
4,096	Morpeth	Northumberland	5·41
3,959	Penryn	Cornwall	5·71
9,255	Poole	Dorset	5·59
2,943	Retford, East	Nottinghamshire	3·92
4,106	Richmond	Yorkshire	5·37
6,080	Ripon	Yorkshire	5·97
2,080	Romsey	Hampshire	5·30
5,911	Saffron Walden	Essex	5·78
6,525	St. Ives	Cornwall	5·03
2,503	Shaftesbury	Dorset	3·80
2,109	Southwold	Suffolk	5·29
8,933	Stamford	Lincolnshire	5·57
1,867	Stockton	Durham	5·82
6,043	Sudbury	Suffolk	4·99
3,901	Tenterden	Kent	5·63
4,075	Thetford	Norfolk	5·95
4,419	Totnes	Devon	5·39
9,458	Weymouth	Dorset	5·49
9,596	Windsor	Berkshire	5·96
3,588	Wycombe	Buckinghamshire	4·86

Source: Deduced from *Education Census, 1851*, Table T. Pupils here are those 'on the books'.

Folkestone, Guildford, Hertford, Ripon, Sudbury, and St. Ives). Two-thirds of the towns had fewer than 6,000 inhabitants, twelve of them less than 3,000 — so that by modern standards they were very small places. It would seem that educational provision was better in smaller than in larger towns, where incidentally the rate of population growth was also usually faster.[70]

The size and geographical position of this group of towns clearly had some relationship, too, to their economic complexion. None was a Lancashire cotton town; none was a West Riding woollen town — that is to say, school attendance in the many 'industrial revolution' textile centres was at a lower level than in the towns represented in Table 2·2. The towns listed there include both a large number of ancient boroughs and market towns, which were usually centres of agricultural regions, and also a fair number of sea and river ports, some of which were also market towns. Chesterfield, it is true, had metal industries and coal mines in its vicinity, but it was also significant for its markets and cattle fairs. More typically, Andover was an agricultural centre with important markets and fairs, as were, to name a few others, Ripon, Romsey, Stamford and Totnes. Arundel was not only a market town but also a port, exporting corn and timber and connected by canal to the Thames. Other market towns that were ports included Bideford, Falmouth, Lymington, Penryn and Southwold, and river ports like Faversham, Maldon, Stockton and Sudbury. Many of these had ancillary industries and crafts often connected with the agriculture of their hinterland, such as the making of gloves and woollens at Chipping Norton, the breweries of Guildford, the woollen manufacture of Kendal, the flour mills of Lincoln, and furniture making at High Wycombe. Dorchester, Guildford, Hertford, Huntingdon, and Lincoln were ancient county towns. In fact the towns in Table 2·2 represent to a considerable extent the traditionally important centres of trade and agriculture of pre-industrial England. This suggests that while economic growth is usually associated with the boom towns of the new industrial areas, culturally the towns of the old England, sometimes prospering as a result of expanding trade and agriculture, were superior. Indeed, in 1864 an educational observer noted that it was easier to obtain support for schools in small towns with one parish than in large towns, where a number of parishes were independent each having to seek help for itself.[71] And the Revd. H. Rigg in the 1880s attributed the superior literacy levels of Kent to, among other things, the fact that it contained 'a large number of small towns with superior educational advantages'.[72]

Appendix K, which provides attendance figures for fifty towns of over 20,000 population and 124 smaller ones, reveals that, generally speaking, the incidence of day schooling was lower, often much lower, in larger towns. To a less extent this was also the case for Sunday schooling. Analysis of day schooling in those places which the 1851 census lists as 'principal boroughs and large towns', a category embracing the main new industrial centres of the north and midlands, is provided in Table 2·3 and sheds further light on schooling levels in large places. Forty-two towns are distinguished, each with a population of over 28,000 and half of them with more than 50,000 inhabitants. In none was the proportion of registered day pupils to total population better than one in six. Moreover, only nine of these towns were in the south of England, while sixteen

TABLE 2·3
'Principal boroughs and large towns', 1851: proportions at day school

Town	Population	Day-school pupils: one in
Ashton-under-Lyne	30,676	11·88
Bath	54,240	7·20
Birmingham	232,841	11·02
Blackburn	46,536	10·93
Bolton	61,171	10·22
Bradford	103,778	10·83
Brighton	69,673	7·38
Bristol	137,328	7·67
Bury	31,262	7·93
Cheltenham	35,051	7·44
Coventry	36,208	12·90
Derby	40,609	7·81
Devonport	38,180	7·44
Dudley	37,962	10·80
Exeter	32,818	6·77
Halifax	33,582	7·68
Huddersfield	30,880	7·66
Hull	84,690	8·37
Ipswich	32,914	7·74
Leeds	172,270	7·88
Leicester	60,584	10·81
Liverpool	375,955	8·56
Macclesfield	39,048	9·72
Manchester	303,382	11·60
Newcastle upon Tyne	87,784	9·65
Norwich	68,195	8·78
Nottingham	57,407	9·68
Oldham	52,820	13·08
Plymouth	52,221	10·82
Portsmouth	72,096	7·57
Preston	69,542	9·05
Salford	63,850	12·17
Sheffield	135,310	8·66
Southampton	35,305	6·40
South Shields	28,974	6·66
Stockport	53,835	12·34
Sunderland	63,897	8·57
Tynemouth	29,170	9·64
Wigan	31,941	8·47
Wolverhampton	49,985	11·96
Yarmouth	30,879	8·69
York	36,303	6·27

Source: Deduced from Education Census, 1851, Table P. Pupils here are those 'on the books'.

were industrial towns within the Lancashire–Cheshire–Yorkshire industrial conurbation. In addition, there were the ports serving these areas (Liverpool and Hull) and also York, then developing as a railway and route centre.[73] A further seven were manufacturing towns in the industrial midlands, and other industrial towns were Sunderland and Norwich, a city with a declining hand-loom weaving industry. Fourteen of the towns were major seaports — including such significant places as Bristol, Devonport and Plymouth, Hull,

Liverpool, Newcastle, Portsmouth and Southampton. The only towns in Table 2·3 which did not bear heavily the stamp of industry or trade were Bath, Brighton, Cheltenham and Exeter, where the ancient woollen manufacture had virtually ceased in 1831 and trade as a port had dwindled.[74] Exeter, Southampton, York and South Shields, a port and market town, were the only towns represented with better proportions than one in seven.

Within this group of large towns, however, the proportions of populations on school books do not relate very strongly to the size of populations. Of the three great provincial centres with over 200,000 inhabitants each, both Birmingham and Manchester had proportions worse than one in eleven, but Liverpool, where, unusually, the corporation ran two large elementary schools,[75] had as many as one child on the books for every 8·6 of its population. The school inspectorate in the 1840s remarked of Church school provision in Lancashire and West Riding industrial towns: 'we find Liverpool the only one … approaching the right standard',[76] while the Newcastle Commission, somewhat sanguinely, found in Liverpool 'schools … within reasonable reach of almost every child'.[77] Again some smaller towns had worse proportions than the great cities (Coventry with 1 in 12·9 and a population of about 36,000; Oldham with 1 in 13·1 and 53,000; Stockport with 1 in 12·3 and 54,000), while others with over 100,000 inhabitants like Bristol (1 in 7·7, population 137,000) and Leeds (1 in 7·9, population 172,000) had relatively good proportions.

Of course the actual proportions of children in the population may have varied from town to town, a higher proportion being likely in quickly expanding industrial centres attracting young immigrants. The best that can be done to avoid the crudeness of expressing schoolchildren as proportions of total populations is to give them as proportions of those aged five to fourteen.[78] Analysis of the sixty-seven 'principal towns' of the 1851 census in this way, however, merely confirms the pattern of urban schooling outlined above.[79] Of the dozen towns with 40 per cent or fewer children aged five to fourteen at school on census day 1851, all but one, Bury St. Edmunds, was an industrial centre. The dozen included Birmingham, Wolverhampton, Coventry and Leicester in the midlands, and in the Lancashire–Cheshire–West Riding textile areas, Blackburn, Bolton, Bradford, Manchester and Salford, Oldham and Stockport. Of the eight towns with between 41 and 45 per cent of such children at school only Dover and King's Lynn were not industrial towns, the others being Macclesfield, Preston, Sheffield, Gateshead, Newcastle upon Tyne and Nottingham.

Those eleven towns with between 46 and 50 per cent at school were more of a mixture and included, outside the chief industrial areas, Bridgwater, Carlisle, Colchester, Lancaster, Plymouth with Devonport, and Great Yarmouth, as well as Derby, Stafford, Leeds, Hull and Liverpool. In the remaining thirty-six towns, where school attendance was over 50 per cent of the age group, there were only four industrial towns: Sunderland, Halifax, Wakefield and North-ampton. The large towns of Bristol, Bath, Portsmouth, Exeter and York were also in this category, but the rest had fewer than 25,000 inhabitants each and included fourteen ancient cathedral cities but a high proportion in the south and outside the industrial areas. Of the twenty towns with 61 per cent or more at school the only ones in the north were Halifax, Wakefield, Kendal and York.

Since marriage mark statistics were recorded by the Registrar General only by counties and registration districts a direct comparison of urban illiteracy rates and the incidence of urban day schooling is possible only where towns made up all or virtually all the population of the registration districts in which they were set. The twenty-four towns in this category are listed in Table 2·4 with schooling figures for 1851 and illiteracy rates for 1866. As was the case with industrial counties, Table 2·4 shows no universal relationship between the

TABLE 2·4

Marriage marks and percentages of children at school in certain towns

Town	Percentage of marks in marriages in 1866	Percentage of children 5–14 at day school on census day 1851	Percentage of marks in marriages in adjacent or nearby counties in 1866		
Birmingham	32 } 28	35·5	Warws.	27	} 32
Aston	24		Staffs.	40	
			Worcs.	28	
Bristol	22	59·1	Som.	} 24	
			Glos.		
Bury St. Edmunds	16	38·2	Suffolk	30	
Cambridge	13	54·8	Cambs.	28	
Chester	28	52·4	Ches.	31	
Colchester	21	45·6	Essex	27	
Coventry	28	29·8	Warws.	27	
Derby	18	46·1	Derbys.	26	
Exeter	14 } 15	64·4	Devon	20	
St. Thomas	16				
Ipswich	15	56·8	Suffolk	30	
King's Lynn	24	44·9	Norfolk	30	
Leeds } Hunslet	37	48·0	West R.	31	
Leicester	25	35·8	Leics.	26	
Newcastle upon Tyne	23	41·7	Durham	32	
Norwich	24	52·0	Norfolk	30	
Nottingham	26	43·0	Notts.	28	
Plymouth and Devonport	21	47·7	Devon	20	
Portsmouth	17	62·0	Hants.	16	
Reading	15	62·0	Berks.	22	
Shrewsbury	18	57·1	Shropshire	32	
Southampton	12	59·8	Hants.	16	
Sunderland	32	52·3	Durham	32	
Worcester	24	51·1	Worcs.	28	
Yarmouth, Gt.	25	48·5	Norfolk	30	

Source: Derived from Education Census, 1851; 29th A.R. Registrar of Births, Deaths and Marriages, 1867, PP 1867–8, XIX.

proportion of brides and grooms unable to sign their names in any particular town in 1866 and the proportion of children at day school there fifteen years before. All that can be said is that there was a tendency overall for towns with high illiteracy rates to be places where earlier there had been a low percentage of children at day school. Thus, in towns where 25 per cent or more made marks on marriage in 1866, an average of 44 per cent of children aged five to fourteen had been at day school in 1851; in towns where marks occurred in 19–24 per cent of cases, averages at day school had been 49 per cent; and where there were 18 per cent or less marks, 56 per cent on average had been at day school. Again, of the twelve towns with the highest percentage of marks in 1866, eight were among the worst for proportions of children at day school in 1851; and of the twelve with the lowest percentages of marks, eight were among the best twelve for children at day school.

Moreover some of the economic and geographical features noted for schooling and for earlier urban illiteracy are also evident for the urban illiteracy levels of the 1860s. Of the towns in Table 2·4 with 18 per cent or fewer marks, only Derby and Shrewsbury were not in the south, and only Derby was a manufacturing town. Those towns with 25 per cent marks and more, however, were all (except Great Yarmouth) in the midlands or the north, and all but Great Yarmouth and Chester were industrial towns. Those towns falling between (19–24 per cent marks) were mixed geographically, though none was really an industrial centre, except perhaps Newcastle upon Tyne, where shipbuilding and the manufacture of ships' goods were important. As for the relationship of population size and proportions of marks, there was again a tendency for larger towns to have worse records. Of the twelve largest towns in Table 2·4, eight were among the worst twelve for illiterate brides and grooms; of the remaining twelve towns only four were among the worst dozen for marks.

All the evidence, then, points to larger towns, northern towns and industrial towns having a lower percentage of children at day school in 1851 than smaller, southern, market and smaller port towns; and there was a two-to-one chance that the proportions of illiterate brides and grooms fifteen years later were greater in large towns, northern towns and industrial towns. However, while there was thus a general relationship between lack of schooling in a community and later illiteracy it was by no means an automatic relationship.

At local level, then, school attendance emerges as a significant but by no means the only factor in the determination of the levels of urban educational achievement in young adults of marriageable age. Apart from the imponderable impact of other educational factors, however, migration is probably an important variable here. It has been suggested, for example, that one reason for the high level of literacy in the metropolitan area and the low level for some rural counties around London is that better educated young people tended to migrate to the urban areas where they later married.[80] It may be, too, that the marriage signature figures for Lancashire towns were distorted by the influx of better educated young persons from Scotland and the extreme northern counties of England where male literacy was at a high level.[81] On the other hand it is likely that such persons were outnumbered by ill educated migrants, 'too indifferent', as Bishop Summer put it in 1838, 'to education'. Large numbers of Irish of the roughest sort tended to be concentrated in the industrial towns of Lancashire, Cheshire, the West Riding, Staffordshire and Derbyshire, many of them drifting from place to place in these areas.[82]

Even in Lancashire, however, apart from the Irish, such migration was short distance,[83] and in this context it is interesting that nearly every town in Table 2·4 had better marrriage-signature statistics than the average for those surrounding or contiguous counties, from which it might be expected to draw a large proportion of immigrants. This reinforces the likelihood that better educated young people were creamed off into the towns, at a time when there was a decline in agricultural employment,[84] thus in some places augmenting in the statistics the results of good educational facilities enjoyed by native brides and grooms, or in others offsetting the effects of poor educational standards available to the town's natives. Thus in Devon in the 1860s it was remarked of rural areas that 'the best young men, i.e. those who are the best educated, go away to the police, railways, etc.'[85]

Table 2·4 suggests, too, that the differences between illiteracy levels in towns and neighbouring counties were greatest where the town was a smaller traditional market centre set in a predominantly agricultural area.[86] In some of these districts the local market town might be a haven of culture and civilised behaviour. Thus the difference between Bury St. Edmunds and Suffolk as a whole was 14 per cent, and for Ipswich about the same; for Shrewsbury vis-à-vis Shropshire 14 percentage points; for Cambridge (and Cambridgeshire) 15. For Colchester (and Essex), Derby (and Derbyshire), Exeter (and Devon), King's Lynn, Norwich (and Norfolk)[87] and Reading (and Berkshire), differences ranged from 4 to 8 points. The figures for the port town of Newcastle upon Tyne were much better than those for nearby County Durham, reflecting the known low level of literacy in the coal mining areas, though the same pattern is not observable with Sunderland, another coal port.

On the other hand, for the large towns generally, there was a tendency for marriage signature levels to be nearer those for the neighbouring county averages. Plymouth with Devonport was somewhat worse than Devon as a whole, the urban average brought down considerably by the inclusion here of East Stonehouse, the dockland area, one of the least literate registration districts in the whole county.[88] Industrial and populous Birmingham was no better and perhaps worse than Warwickshire and Worcestershire as a whole; Nottingham little better than Nottinghamshire; Leicester and Coventry slightly worse than Leicestershire and Warwickshire respectively; Leeds (with slum Hunslet) than the West Riding (which was by no means all industrial).

An analysis of the seventy-five coastal registration districts with at least 3 per cent of adult males in occupations connected with the sea in 1851 demonstrates a strong tendency (stronger where over 10 per cent were in these occupations) for such districts to have higher marriage signature rates in 1856 and 1871 than either the national level or the level of the county in which they were set.[89] Since such evidence as exists indicates that sailors collectively were less literate than the average working man,[90] it seems likely that these signature rates reflect the more general economic structures of these districts, many of which included port towns. Such places were in a sense like market towns: they contained merchants, merchants' clerks, internal carriers, lawyers and banking staff, as well as ships' chandlers, customs officers, dockmasters, and so on, for all of whom literacy was an occupational necessity.

Another barometer of Victorian respectability, religiosity, reflects varying urban cultural characteristics. A discernible tendency has been shown to exist between the level of attendance at religious worship in 1851 in the various towns and school attendance levels and later levels of literacy. Again large towns, northern towns and industrial towns were worst.[91] Nevertheless, such towns often showed a high level of Sunday-school attendance, and it is possible that educational standards were also affected by Sunday schooling, particularly in the larger and the industrial towns, though, for reasons already mentioned, their impact is likely to have been more on reading than on the writing skills which would have affected signature statistics. It is anyway, as has been seen, difficult to tease out those children who were schooled only on Sundays. Moreover, calculations aimed at estimating the percentages of children aged five to fourteen at Sunday school are not as useful as day-school figures. The age range of children at urban Sunday schools was much greater than for those at day school. At Coventry in 1838 many Sunday-school teachers claimed that their pupils entered aged five or seven and remained until sixteen.[92] Indeed, in some towns young adults clearly attended.[93] T. W. Laqueur suggests that 'increasingly the Sunday school became the province of adolescent boys and girls'.[94] Thus the formula for day school figures used above can sometimes given an equivalent of over 100 per cent of the age group five to fourteen apparently at Sunday school. Nevertheless it may be noted that, of the twenty-one towns where the proportions of children by this formula were greater in Sunday than in day schools, sixteen had comparatively low day-school attendances (Table 2·5).

The preponderance of northern and midland towns is obvious, and it seems likely that here Sunday schools were being used as substitutes for day schools, though this was not the case in all towns. The situation also perhaps reflected the popularity of Sunday schools among nonconformists, who tended to be

TABLE 2·5

Towns where the percentage of children aged 5–14 at Sunday school on Census Sunday 1851 was greater than that of those at day school

Blackburn	Leeds	Oldham
Bolton	Leicester	Portsmouth
Bradford	Macclesfield	Preston
Bridgwater	Manchester and Salford	Stafford
Coventry	Newark	Stockport
Derby	Northampton	Truro
Lancaster	Nottingham	Wolverhampton

strongest in urban areas. In many towns dissenting Sunday schools were better attended than Anglican ones, and this was specially so in the populous centres of the north and midlands. In Sheffield, Manchester, Leeds and Birmingham Anglican Sunday schools attracted a much smaller proportion of the towns' Sunday scholars than did the dissenting establishments.[95]

Just as the situation in towns varied greatly so did that in rural districts. In 1867 W. L. Sargant took issue with the view expounded by, among others, Professor Henry Fawcett that rural areas were more generally backward educationally than the towns. He pointed out that literacy levels in the 'best' agricultural counties (Westmorland, Rutland, Lincoln, Sussex, Hampshire) compared favourably with the 'best' counties containing large towns (Middlesex, Surrey, Kent, Gloucestershire, Derbyshire, Warwickshire) while the 'worst' agricultural counties (Herefordshire and the Welsh counties) were no worse than the 'worst' counties with large town populations (Lancashire, Cheshire, Staffordshire, the West Riding).[96]

The truth is that generalisations about rural districts are as dangerous as for towns.[97] The variety of types of rural communities and settlements in nineteenth-century England was immense. Areas where agriculture dominated, population was sparse, and small villages and hamlets and isolated farmsteads were the norm, were certainly rural, though even then they were not necessarily socially and economically homogeneous. Not so easy to categorise are the mining communities and the larger villages, still less the heavily populated tracts of countryside where domestic industry flourished outside the confines of towns. Social structure, population density, outlook on life, and many other characteristics of these multifarious communities defy simple classification. Even in areas where agricultural pursuits clearly dominated, there were different types of farming and different social structures. In some country areas the land was owned in great estates by the aristocracy, in others the gentry class with smaller estates was more common; in some parts small owner-occupiers farmed the land, in yet others absentee landlords left local affairs in the hands of tenant farmers. The varying attitudes of these groups towards the provision of rural schooling was important. Again, over the century, economic, demographic and other social changes affected many communities, but not necessarily in a uniform way. Some rural areas prospered, others did not. In some population increased; in many it declined.

Certainly many rural areas had superior literacy levels to many of the industrial towns of the north and midlands, while others conformed to the picture of 'debasing ignorance' attributed to agricultural districts generally in 1831 by the British and Foreign School Society,[98] and were far inferior educationally to many towns, particularly market towns and towns in the south. Great variations between rural areas reflected differing socio-economic conditions. Significant factors included the level of wages, whether the gentry were resident or absentee, whether there were large numbers of small landowners and family farms and how prosperous these were, and whether rural industry existed or not.

Thus in areas where there was a great deal of manufacture in industrial villages and in mining communities the distinction between town and country was blurred and the educational situation may well have been worse outside the towns than in them. A witness before the Select Committee on the Education of the Poorer Classes in 1838 attested that there was 'very little education of any sort' in West Bromwich. This was three or four miles from Birmingham, with 20,000 inhabitants, though it is 'hardly a town; but over the whole surface of the parish there are nailers and other small manufacturers', and 'there is coal under ... West Bromwich; it is close to the great mining district of Staffordshire', where 'the same lamentable want of almost any education prevails'. Again, W. F. Hook, vicar of Leeds, in 1846 wrote of the populous industrial villages around that city, 'go to our poorer districts, not to our towns, but to our manufacturing villages and there you will perceive how great our educational destitution really is'.[99] The same was so in Lancashire, where children in such areas tended to attend Sunday rather than day schools.[100] Similarly in Radford, an overspill area adjoining Nottingham, the population of which had increased from 4,000 to 27,000 in the first half of the nineteenth century, schooling was much less common in 1851, and illiteracy in 1855–64 greater than either in Nottingham itself or in a nearby farming district.[101] Indeed, the commissioners investigating child and female labour in agriculture reported in 1867 that the demand for education among the labouring classes in country districts in Nottinghamshire and Leicestershire 'is exceedingly active ... but as we approach the neighbourhood of Nottingham and Leicester seaming and framework knitting absorb almost the whole population while the large overgrown villages in the suburbs of the towns ... are most ill supplied with schools ... The instances of ignorance in these districts ... far surpass anything I met with even in ganging villages.'[102] The same tendency is seen clearly, too, in Staffordshire, a county containing a great deal of rural industrial slumland where the population was unusually ignorant and degraded to a much lower level than, for example, in the Lancashire cotton areas. Thus Staffordshire as a whole had an illiteracy level much higher than Birmingham (Table 2·4). 'I suppose,' the Revd. J. P. Norris wrote of the Potteries in the 1850s, 'there is no district in Europe than can show so large a proportion of children six to seven, and eight years of age engaged in manufacture,' children, moreover, outside the scope even of the educational clauses of the Factory Acts. Here there was a lack of interest in, and a general neglect of, education among a comparatively well paid workforce.[103] In Bedfordshire and Buckinghamshire, too, cottage industry, combined with small farms, absentee landlords and low agricultural wages, created an area of educational deprivation.[104]

Areas where large numbers of smallholders and small farmers were associated with poverty and poor educational provision and standards included north Devon, south Durham, Lincolnshire and Somerset, where small owner-occupiers had to struggle to earn a living, the wages of adult labourers could not be afforded and the smallholders made do with the unpaid labour of their own children as much as possible. Such children might well be more educationally deprived than those of labourers elsewhere.[105] Similarly, in agricultural districts where wages were low — usually those remote from centres of industry which offered an alternative of better paid employment — the levels of ignorance tended to be greater than where agricultural wages were high and parents could afford some schooling. In some of the southern agricultural counties a variety of factors combined to keep educational standards low and school attendance poor.

In rural Kent, where the proportion of land occupied by smaller landowners was well above the national average,[106] one observer in the 1830s reported 'a state of semi-barbarism ... within twenty-five miles of London', in Stansted 'not above one labourer in fifteen can read and write'.[107] Yet Kentish farmers were prosperous and men comparatively well paid, the gentry resident, and the county was sprinkled with small towns,[108] and the comparatively good literacy rates are no doubt accounted for by varying educational standards within a relatively small county. In Essex, Suffolk and Norfolk silk and woollen manufacture was decaying or stagnating and the predominantly agricultural population suffered from comparatively low wages and seasonal unemployment evidenced by high poor rates and recurrent overt unrest.[109] Norfolk and Suffolk had consistently high rates of illiteracy throughout the period, as did Essex until about 1870, by which time it was embracing metropolitan overspill.

Aside from differences imposed by the existence or otherwise of domestic industry and the structure of landownership, most rural areas experienced certain common difficulties in the provision of satisfactory schooling. These included the physical hardship of travel in winter, the financing and organisation of schools in areas where population was sparse and dispersed and the demand for child labour on the land.[110] Nevertheless, considerable differences from one agricultural area to another resulted from the contrasting extent of the impact of these and other variables.

In north Devon the remoteness of the small farmers was associated with poverty and the area was one of educational backwardness,[111] and the same was so in the thinly populated valleys of rural Monmouthshire described in 1844 as 'colonies in the desert',[112] where schooling facilities were far inferior to those of the market towns.[113] On the other hand the small farms of Northumberland, Cumberland and Westmorland were remote, too, and in the last two counties small landowners were unusually common.[114] There, however, many small farmers were more prosperous than such men elsewhere, rural unrest and unemployment were rare, and there was traditionally a more amenable attitude to schooling.[115]

In poorer agricultural areas the atmosphere was different. In the eastern counties parents thought or were obliged by circumstances to act, differently, and irregular school attendance resulted from the integral part played by comparatively young children in the working of the rural economy.[116] And in Herefordshire there were 'no fewer than seven annual harvests in each of which children are largely employed'.[117]

The practice of annual hirings of whole families as well as of male labourers, still found, for example, in Dorset, Shropshire, Warwickshire, Worcestershire and Herefordshire in the 1860s, resulted in local migration which interfered with clerical influence on parents and steady school attendance.[118] Labouring parents in the northern agricultural counties, however, did not feel great pressure to put their children to work.[119] Where labourers' wages were low, as in parts of some southern, eastern and western counties, parents were bound to regard family survival through child labour as preferable to the intangible fruits of schooling. As John Woolley, a Lincolnshire labourer, who felt children should be at work by seven years of age, put it, 'And how are we to live if they don't go? I pay 6s. 8d. a week for flour for ourselves and five little children; and if a wet day comes, or two or three, how are we to go on?'[120] And in the southern and western counties when such parents fell on relief very few poor law guardians availed themselves of the right under an Act of 1855 to pay for the schooling of the children. In Northumberland, however, there was greater willingness to do so.[121] Moreover, whereas in most parts of the country farmers were antagonistic or apathetic towards the schooling of their labourers' children, in the counties of the far north many farmers were quite favourable to schools.[122] As one explained, 'I infinitely prefer an educated to an uneducated labourer; he is more easily managed, and is more amenable to reason.'[123]

The impact of the Established Church

The educational efforts of the Church of England greatly influenced the incidence of local educational provision. In much of the country the organisation, extension and maintenance of rural schooling fell largely on the shoulders of its clergy and on the larger landowners, who were themselves mostly Anglican. In the bigger towns it was easier for private schools to flourish and the concentration of dissenters enabled British and nonconformist schools to play a larger part, though in towns, too, the role of the Anglican clergy was often significant.

The local impact of Church activity in elementary education was variously affected by the extent of interest and energy displayed by parish clergy and bishops, by the amount of support they received from their better-off parishioners, by how much money was available from livings and from Church or governmental sources, and by the opinions of individual clergy on the type of education that should be supplied to the lower classes. By 1851 Horace Mann could claim that the lack of school places was not a significant determinant of why so many children were not at school.[124] The validity of this view is arguable if applied to every part of the country, but it is certainly true that the supply of public schools was greatly increased during the first half of the century, and particularly from 1820 onwards. In this expansion the Established Church played a central role. It is remarkable, however, that a comprehensive history of the contribution of the Established Church and its offspring, the National Society for Promoting the Education of the Poor in the Principles of the Established Church, remains to be written.[125] That deficiency cannot be made good here, but some attention, however brief, must be given to the impact of Church endeavour in elementary education, since that impact certainly varied from one part of England to another.

The motives of the Church, its leaders and its clergy, and the attitudes held towards the education of the poor were diverse. Certainly education became seen as a weapon against spiritual ignorance, infidelity, dissent, socialism, Chartism, profligacy, crime and immorality, as well as a philanthropic activity. Throughout the period the Church as a whole regarded its schools primarily as instruments of religious and moral instruction. Despite this, Church schools increasingly provided secular instruction and became the chief public institutions for elementary education. Though the National Society was founded in 1811 by the High Church party, it was soon supported by Churchmen generally and, with church building, was in its early decades part of a movement to restore the Church to an influential place in the new industrial society.[126] Its foundation was followed by the establishment of local societies to promote National schools such as, in 1811–12, the Durham Diocesan Society, the Norfolk and Norwich Society, the Northampton Society and the York Central Diocesan Society, and in 1816 the Rutland Society. Other local bodies founded in these early years included a Huntingdon District Committee and a National Schools Society for the Archdeaconry of Coventry.[127] The efforts of the bishops and other churchmen were, however, varied and patchy. Samuel Butler of Lichfield, for example, though a former head of Shrewsbury School, was representative of many Church leaders who were lukewarm towards the further extension of elementary schools for the poor.[128] Others, of whom William Otter of Chichester was one, were more perceptive of the dangers of taking 'refuge in ignorance'.[129]

Pressures of the 1830s including the passing of the Reform Act, the activities of the Benthamite radicals, the foundation of the Central Society of Education in 1836, and the introduction of governmental financial assistance and later the establishment of the Committee of Council on Education and of inspection of aided schools, led to an awareness that if the Church did not do more the state would assume greater responsibility for elementary education. The National Society and the more liberal bishops of the 1830s and 1840s increasingly accepted the need for a reorganisation of Church education, including a broadening of the curriculum.[130] The reports of H.M.I.s, and the letters and other contributions to the National Society's *Monthly Paper* (from 1847) are enough to indicate how far the Church schools involved themselves in secular instruction.

In the years 1837–41 diocesan education boards were established for Bath and Wells, Canterbury, Chester and Manchester, Chichester, Exeter, Gloucester, Lichfield, Lincoln, London, Monmouth, Oxford, Ripon, Salisbury and Winchester. Most of these had subordinate archidiaconal, district or local boards, some of which antedated the diocesan organisations. In 1838–40, for example, the York Central Diocesan Society formed nineteen district boards. No diocesan board existed for Hereford until 1849, but a Salop Archidiaconal Board dated from 1839. Similarly, though Ely, Peterborough and Rochester lacked diocesan boards, they had some local boards as early as 1840.[131] Not all these bodies acted with equal vigour, but an administrative framework was created which the Dissenters and the British Society could not match.[132] Moreover, by 1840 six Anglican teacher-training colleges had been established and by 1861 there were twenty diocesan colleges as well as three run directly by the Society. Diocesan inspection of schools was established by 1840, though twenty years later it was fully operational in only eighteen of the twenty-eight English and Welsh dioceses.[133]

The failure of a Bill of 1843 which might have established rate-aided half-time day schools under Church control pointed to the growing strength of nonconformity, confirmed in the 1851 religious census, and increased episcopal determination to make the Church the main educator of the people. From then on the bishops campaigned as never before for the National Society.[134] J. Garbett, Archdeacon of Chichester, called in 1844 for 'the evangelisation of the manufacturing districts' and Bishop Sumner of Chester at this time pointed to the enormous dearth of Church schooling in his huge industrial diocese.[135]

Averaged over the country the contribution of the Established Church to the provision of elementary schooling in the first half of the nineteenth century was prodigious, and in many places but for the parish priest there would have been no school.[136] By mid-century 81 per cent of public elementary schools were Anglican and these were educating 76 per cent of pupils at such schools.[137] In 1858 the proportions were similar. This compared with 10 per cent at British schools, 5·5 per cent at Roman Catholic, 4 per cent at Wesleyan and 2 per cent at Congregational schools.[138] In 1866–7 again 76 per cent of pupils in inspected schools were in Anglican ones.[139]

The proportion of the total population registered as pupils at Church day and evening schools rose, the National Society claimed, from 2·7 per cent in 1831, to 3·1 in 1837 (day schools only), 5·7 in 1847, 6·4 in 1857 and 7·7 in 1867 (Appendix M). Even so, before the 1850s were out there were some, like W. F. Hook, vicar of Leeds, Connop Thirlwall, Bishop of St. Davids, and C. T. Longley, Bishop of Ripon, able to see that the voluntary system would be unable alone to cope with the nation's future needs in elementary schooling. Schools were particularly difficult to provide in poor urban districts and remote rural areas, the result partly of the inability to meet the government's requirements for state aid.

Appendix M shows that, in the years 1837 to 1867, the proportion of children educated by the Church (expressed as percentages of total population) varied greatly from one county to another. The figures for 1837 are not directly comparable with the figures for later decades, since they do not include evening pupils,[140] but it seems likely that there was a considerable expansion in most counties between 1837 and 1847. The 1847, 1857 and 1867 figures, perhaps more reliable, reflect a number of regional characteristics. Counties which were heavily populated, containing large towns, generally had the lowest proportions at Church schools. These were often industrial counties, where dissent was strongest and British and nonconformist schools contributed more to the sum of public elementary education (Appendixes L,N).[141]

In 1847 proportions of county populations at Church schools varied from 4·1 to 10·1 per cent. Those counties where the impact of Church schooling was least effective (less than 6 per cent) at that time included Durham, Cheshire, Lancashire, Yorkshire, Monmouthshire, Middlesex and Surrey, Bedfordshire, Buckinghamshire and Leicestershire, Cornwall and Northumberland. Clearly some of these counties were characterised by high density of population and all by industrial activity or mining. Aside from Middlesex, Surrey, and perhaps Warwickshire, they all ranked high for proportions of attenders at nonconformist places of worship. At the other end of the scale (8 per cent or more at Church schools in 1847) were Westmorland, Rutland, Oxfordshire, Berkshire, Sussex, Hampshire, Dorset, Northamptonshire and Huntingdonshire, all predominantly rural and with all but the last two ranking low for dissenting worshippers in 1851 (Appendix N).

The comparatively low levels of Church schooling in the industrial counties in 1847 was despite considerable efforts by Churchmen. In the north-west, for example, J. B. Sumner, Bishop of Chester, and leading clergy in the manufacturing towns were extremely active. Moreover the National Society from the 1830s at least, followed a policy of spreading its funds unevenly to give preference to certain industrial areas. Lancashire was given particular attention and by 1839 had received 13 per cent of the Society's total grants to schools for England and Wales. Moreover in the 1830s 22 per cent of all treasury grants for elementary education were channelled to Lancashire through the Society. In the 1840s special funds to assist Church schools in the mining and manufacturing districts were raised and in 1846–7 Lancashire, Yorkshire, Cheshire, Staffordshire and Derbyshire received *per capita* grants from the Society higher than for any other county.[142] That Lancashire should still in 1847 lag behind in the provision of Anglican schooling has been regarded as a failure by the Church. On the other hand the task was a colossal one, and advance, particularly in Derbyshire and Staffordshire, respectable (Appendix M). The situation would certainly have been infinitely worse without this external funding. All these counties in the 1840s themselves raised less money for Church schools *per capita* than most other counties in response to the appeal for industrial areas.[143]

It is difficult to be very definite about school incomes in the 1850s for the available data is confusing. Nevertheless it appears that a disproportionate share of public funds continued to go to some of the industrial counties. Between 1833 and 1859 treasury grants to voluntary schools, most of which were Anglican, were above average, proportionate to population, in Cheshire, Lancashire, Staffordshire and Yorkshire. But public elementary schools in these and other industrial counties in 1858 had levels of income, apart from government aid, at or below the national average. Some rural counties, like Wiltshire, Hampshire, Hertfordshire and Dorset, where Anglicanism was strong, received both above average amounts of treasury grants and also had other income above the general level. On the other hand some other industrial and mining counties, particularly Monmouthshire and Cornwall, where dissent was strong, received well below average from the state while yet having very low incomes from other sources (Appendixes O, P).

For these and other reasons, although the Church's share of pupils rose in all counties between 1847 and 1867 (Appendix M), the rate of advance was not uniform. Despite the extraordinary financial support given to the industrial counties listed above, the counties which experienced the greatest increases in proportions of Church pupils (4 percentage points or more) were rural ones, though in some cases having domestic industries. They were Oxfordshire, Dorset, Rutland and Berkshire (in all of which levels had already been comparatively high in 1847) but also Wiltshire, Buckinghamshire, Somerset and Bedfordshire. The National Society's annual reports indicate that most of these counties were within the areas of the most active diocesan education boards — those of the sees of Bath and Wells, Oxford, and Salisbury.[144] Respectable advance was made, too, in Leicestershire, Nottinghamshire, Huntingdonshire, and Shropshire, and in the counties of East Anglia, again agricultural counties with some industry, largely of a domestic kind.

The least improvement took place mainly where Church schooling had been weakest in 1847. Of the eighteen counties where the advance by 1867 was less than 3 percentage points, only three had had over 7 per cent at Church schools in 1847. After all its external funding, Lancashire, certainly, improved by 3·4 points, but Staffordshire, Cheshire and Yorkshire only by 2·2 or less. Indeed, the counties with the lowest proportions at Church schools in 1867 (fewer than 8 per cent of the population) included Lancashire, Yorkshire, Staffordshire, Warwickshire, Durham, Cornwall and Monmouthshire (all mining or industrial), together with heavily populated Surrey and Middlesex, Northumberland, where dissent was widespread, and Devon, where nonconformists were relatively numerous in the west of the county. Nonconformists sometimes preferred private schools to Anglican ones, so that low Anglican numbers did not necessarily mean high British or dissenting ones.

So, although there was a rough correlation between the incidence of Anglican church attendance in 1851 and registration at Church schools, there was by no means a strict match.[145] Varying degrees of clerical effort, unequal distribution of public and Church funds, the concentration of nonconformist activity in urbanised areas, the patchy distribution of private schools, and the differing levels of school attendance generally, were all factors affecting Church influence in education at the local level. Nevertheless, compared with the dissenters, who probably approached Anglicans in numbers by mid-century, the achievement of the Church in education was remarkable. To some extent it is attributable to the ready-made administrative structure for school promotion possessed by the Church in its diocesan and parochial organisation. The possession of an educated clergy, the adherence especially in rural areas of the better-off laity especially among the landed classes, and the unifying effect of the National Society and other affiliated societies, and of the large number of Church training colleges, must also have helped.

The dissenters on the other hand were split into numerous denominations, many of them numerically weak outside urban areas, their adherents containing fewer of the better-off and well educated. Moreover, even where, as in some industrial towns, wealthy dissenters and large congregations existed, they often preferred to support Sunday schools, adult education and mission work at home and abroad rather than day schools. Some were fundamentally opposed to the acceptance of governmental aid for schooling. The British and Foreign School Society, which, though nominally non-denominational, was regarded as nonconformist, was less well organised than the National Society, lacked the managerial and financial resources of the Church, and failed to attract anything like the amount of state aid.[146]

Some counties illustrate the influence of nonconformity in reducing the proportions of Church scholars (Appendixes L, M, N).The Church, however, took the lead in schooling even where dissent was strong. Lincolnshire, for example, had more Methodist than Anglican places of worship in 1851, but Methodism had but a small share of schooling.[147] Indeed, by the 1850s, and probably before, Church scholars outnumbered British, dissenting and Roman Catholic pupils in every county by a very considerable proportion (Appendix L). British schools were found most in the towns,[148] particularly in London and the industrial cities, where attendance at private schools was also higher than in rural areas. Nevertheless, even in the conurbations the Church still did remarkably well. In the nonconformist strongholds of Birmingham, Sheffield and Leeds Anglican schools in mid-century accounted for more pupils than dissenting and British schools. In Manchester, the home of wealthy and influential Dissent, Protestant nonconformist and British schools had fewer pupils than Anglican ones.[149]

Not all Church schools, however, were in receipt of government assistance, for the government would give only to schools meeting certain requirements. Particularly in poor rural areas, where absentee or indifferent gentry combined with clergy unwilling or unable to provide what was needed from their own pocket, Church schools were absent, or, if there, unaided.[150] Indeed on the eve of the 1870 Education Act Forster claimed that only half the parishes of England and Wales had government-aided schools.[151] Of course, some of these were small places served by schools near by. Nevertheless the Church itself reported that in 1866–7, excluding those dame schools considered to be 'Church schools', 58 per cent of Anglican day schools were not in receipt of annual treasury grants, accounting for 57 per cent of pupils in Church schools.[152] And surveys of Liverpool, Leeds, Manchester and Birmingham in 1869 show that many urban children, particularly those of the poorest classes, were not being attracted to voluntary schools.[153]

Demand from below

Much has been made in recent years of the motive of 'social control' inherent in the provision of schooling for the masses in the nineteenth century.[154] It is not intended here to examine that topic from a national viewpoint, though regional attitudes of employers, clergy and other middle-class people in various parts of the country are considered in subsequent chapters. The expansion of school attendance cannot, however, be explained solely in terms of increased supply by the better-off classes. Since schooling generally was not free and did not begin to become compulsory until the 1870s, the rising school attendance figures over the two generations before that must reflect a growing demand from working-class parents for formal schooling, however minimal.[155] The popularity of the largely free Sunday schools, too, cannot be said to have stemmed solely from working-class religious enthusiasm,[156] and the increasing secular curriculum and better organisation of the voluntary schools was certainly in part the price promoters had to pay for working-class attendance.

Moreover, the continued existence of proletarian private schools, accounting for at least 50–60 per cent of school children in most counties in 1833, indicates that middle-class supply was only part of the schooling equation. In 1851 the proportion of day-school pupils attending private schools still amounted to one-third or more in twenty of the forty-two English counties, and in only three counties (Hertfordshire, Herefordshire and Wiltshire) did the proportion fall short of a quarter. Reliance on private schools was generally strongest in many northern counties, the midlands and some southern and eastern counties.[157] Methodist Cornwall, however, stood out as the only county with more children at private than voluntary schools at mid century. (Appendix J). In the towns, too, there were wide differences. At Hull and Portsmouth, for example, more children attended private than public day schools in 1851, at Ashton-under-Lyne the proportions were roughly equal, at Blackburn the ratio was five to one in favour of public schools. The proportions are not, moreover, the only consideration, for the numbers attending private schools in a town could be very large even when they catered for a minority.

The growth of parental demand for education is simpler to demonstrate than to explain. No doubt many parents were influenced by religious motives, by aspirations to the respectability of which schooling may have been a hallmark, and by the proselytising of local clergy and others. Some individuals, particularly older children, doubtless saw attractions in reading for pleasure and the ability to communicate with relations living at a distance. Some saw political advantages in the possession of some education. Thus miners' leaders in various parts of the country spearheaded the demand from below for compulsory schooling.[158] The economic advantages of literacy, both real and hoped-for, must, however, have furnished a very strong motive. Evidence taken by official commissions and committees abounds in instances of members of the working class attesting to the belief that they would have succeeded better in life had they been schooled or expressing the view that education would provide better job opportunities for their offspring. But evidence of the economic advantages of literacy is difficult to interpret. Certainly the least literate were concentrated more in jobs at the lower end of the social scale, particularly in labouring, whereas in some employments the functional advantages of literacy were obvious, as for tradesmen, shopkeepers, over-seers, storekeepers, and the like. In the growing ranks of clerks literacy was a necessity. On the other hand literate labourers earned no more than illiterate ones, and like craftsmen of various kinds their employment required the use of physical skills rather than literacy.[159] Literacy even in the mid-nineteenth century was not a functional essential for a high proportion of working people.[160]

But literacy was increasingly a product of schooling, and schooling, particularly 'public schooling', imparted other qualities than the purely academic, so that it is not always possible to distinguish the economic advantages of literacy from the wider contextual advantages of schooling. Although, particularly in some agricultural areas, education for labourers' children was disliked by some farmers as likely to lead to migration and a dearth of labour, a growing number of employers, including those of manual labourers, valued schooling for its ability to inculate self control, acceptance of discipline, understanding of rational explanations, cleanliness and moral qualities, and as an antidote to political disaffection and moral turpitude.[161] Thus even when literacy was not a requisite of a particular job, employment was increasingly more easily obtained and retained by literates, or rather the schooled, and this must have affected the outlook of parents.[162]

These developments occurred at the same time as the changing structure of industry and legislative restrictions reduced employment opportunities for the very young, and among parts of the working classes a general rise in prosperity made it less essential for wives and children to work. As schooling became the norm the completely unschooled became increasingly untypical, a situation which must have brought its own pressure to conform. On the other hand there are plenty of middle-class complaints that some working-class parents failed to accept that schooling would be of benefit to their children. In 1851 the 'Grand Cause' of failure to send children to school was allegedly parental indifference.[163] Indifference certainly existed, particularly in the slum areas of large towns and in some industrial and mining counties,[164] but it was sometimes assumed where the real cause in some social groups and certain communities was inability to pay for schooling,[165] or a conscious decision that early employment was more sensible. Some working parents in certain localities realised that education beyond a mere smattering of the elements was unlikely to affect their children's future prosperity if they merely followed their parents' occupations. In some rural areas escape from farm labour was difficult, in certain manufacturing and mining districts high wages could be earned by the illiterate.[166] Taught for generations not to look beyond their station, it was hardly surprising, as Horace Mann acknowledged, that some parents should deem a 'thorough' elementary education not worth the time and money, and also to be mindful of the value of practical training in employment.[167]

In this context geographical variations in literacy levels and in school attendance were to some extent a reflection of different attitudes on the part of working-class parents in different types of community, and these attitudes were themselves influenced by the socio-economic structure of those communities. Where manual labour was the only outlet, as in remote agricultural districts and districts of cottage industry, or where manual labour or work requiring acquired skills rather than formal education were easy to come by, as in the textile factories, and often well paid, as in some of the midland industries, there was less incentive to educate children than, for example, in or near ports, market towns, and commercial centres where well paid jobs in railway stations, the police, and as clerks, shopworkers, warehousemen, errand boys and the like required or favoured some basic education. In these latter places, too, bodies of self-employed shopkeepers and traders existed to whom literacy was an advantage if not a necessity and these people might be thought to favour education for their young.[168] It is the growth of commercial and service employment that marked the difference between the years 1780–1840 and those from 1840 onwards. In the earlier period falling literacy levels, especially in industrial areas, indicated a situation where a general lack of education was no drawback to an expanding economy.[169] From 1840 schooling appears increasingly desirable socially and also functionally advantageous in an increasing number of jobs.[170]

Moreover, the vast expansion from the 1830s of didactic evangelical and utilitarian publications, of political and commercial literature, and of newspapers, radical and otherwise,[171] attests to a working-class society in which the ability to read must have added to the economic advantages political and social ones.[172] These influences, and attitudes to schooling, not only differed between occupational groups but varied geographically and were subject to change over time. They must be seen as contributing to the statistical manifestations of schooling and literacy levels discussed in detail elsewhere, though themselves not amenable to quantification. Indeed, to the framework provided by figures it is necessary to add the details obtainable from more subjective contemporary sources in order to provide an understanding of the patchwork quilt of inter- and intra-county differences in schooling and literacy levels. Such evidence is abundant, though not always easy to interpret.

Geographical differences in literacy levels reflected many things: demographic changes, occupational structures, attitudes of parents, employers and others, and levels of schooling. Similarly statistics of school attendance provide a general impression of the educational state of an area but they must be interpreted warily. The proportions of children said to be at school in any particular year, for example, represent but part of the existing body of local children who at some time had attended school. By mid-century a large proportion of children must have experienced some day schooling, even if brief, and others some sort of formal education even if only in Sunday or evening schools. On the other hand, the accuracy of the Newcastle Commission's conclusion that the average school life of English children in about 1860 was five to seven years, has been a matter of debate, and is probably too high.[173] At all events this time probably included years spent as toddlers from three years of age upwards, and anyway, being an average, varied greatly from place to place,[174] and was in practice reduced by irregular attendance.

Moreover, despite what has been said of the growth of working-class demand, all the evidence suggests that only some form of compulsion combined with state assistance could bring what was generally considered as adequate schooling to the poorest and 'submerged' classes in the large towns, to children who continued to form part of family work units in areas of increasingly poorly remunerated domestic industries, to some child workers in other industrial areas where small business units made application of the half-time system hard to enforce, and perhaps to the offspring of smallholders and the owners of poor family farms. Certainly not all families were able to view the loss of children's earnings with equanimity.[175] A proper assessment of the effect of parental attitudes on the extent and nature of schooling in different parts of the country must, therefore, take into account, too, their views on the suitable length of school life, the types of schooling favoured, and the importance of regularity of attendence, and also the opportunities they perceived to derive from schooling measured against the opportunities of the workplace and the needs of the family budget.

In this initial survey of cultural change as represented by the spread of schooling and the extension of literacy, the significance of geographical diversity has been a recurrent theme. The next chapter looks at these local variations in the northern and eastern counties, and the subsequent three chapters examine them in greater depth for a contiguous block of twenty-three of the forty-two English counties — those comprising west and central England.

A common statistical framework of social and economic data (set out in the appendixes) is used to set local levels of signature literacy and school attendance, against the background of the local social and economic structure and of the contextual attitudes to schooling of the local middle classes and of working-class parents. The basic territorial units chosen for examination are census registration counties and districts[176] and, where possible, towns.

Admittedly, the individual registration district, comprising a number of parishes, is not an ideal unit. Some districts were economically and demographically homogeneous; many, however, contained within their boundaries differing types of communities — sometimes one or more towns of various sizes and types, as well as rural areas. On the other hand, the existence of detailed and like statistical information on population, occupation, schooling and literacy for every district is an enormous advantage. The districts for which information is provided for schooling in the 1851 Education Census, for religious worship in the 1851 Religious Census, and for signatures annually for much of our period by the Registrar General, are the same territorial units for which the decennial census provides demographic, and occupational data.[177] Sufficient evidence exists to treat some towns, especially large ones, separately. In some respects the registration district is, moreover, preferable to the parish as a comparative unit. Covering a much larger area, it avoids the statistical difficulties arising from small numbers and short-distance migration. Marriage signature figures in sparsely populated parishes, with a handful of marriages a year, for example, tend to fluctuate considerably, and in parishes of small area disproportionate numbers of grooms come from elsewhere.

Since so much evidence exists at the level of counties, any attempt at regional comparison must be based on groups of contiguous counties, rather than on topographical divisions reflecting solely physical or economic characteristics. No such grouping meets all requirements. A division by regions based on the districts supervised by different school inspectors has, considering the subject matter involved, attractions. But such districts were subject to alteration over the period under consideration, differed for Anglican, Roman Catholic, and dissenting and British schools, and at times cut across county boundaries. The arrangement adopted takes some account of economic characteristics and topographical contiguity, as well, to some extent, of the inspectorial areas for Anglican schools, and the need to avoid a multiplication of regions.[178] Counties have, therefore, been grouped as follows: (1) the far north and north-east, (2) East Anglia and the south-east, (3) the industrial north-west — all covered in Chapter 3, and (4) the midlands, (5) the south midlands, and (6) the western counties — covered in Chapters 4, 5 and 6. The information provided in most of the appendixes is arranged in these groupings.

Finally it may be noted that much of the statistical evidence provided in the tables in this chapter, and in the appendixes, is based on data culled from the official censuses, the annual reports of the Registrar General of Births, Deaths and Marriages, and on official educational surveys of 1818 and 1833, the Newcastle Commission's report of 1861, and various surveys of the National Society. Of these, the evidence from the census and the Registrar General's reports may be considered reasonably accurate, the rest much less so, though not sufficently erroneous to be disregarded and still in most cases valuable for comparative purposes.

CHAPTER 3

A survey of northern and eastern England

The counties of the far north and the north-east

In the early 1840s the counties of the far north and the north-east (Cumberland, Durham, Lincolnshire, Northumberland, Rutland,[1] Westmorland, and the East and North Ridings of Yorkshire) still retained their former superior levels of literacy (Appendix D). For the northernmost counties this has traditionally been attributed variously to a social affinity with nearby lowland Scotland, where schooling was more common than in England generally and education was respected, to an unusually large number of dispersed charity schools, and to a high proportion of independent freeholders, combined with a type of farming which left time, especially in winter, for self-improvement and permitted boys to stay at school longer than usual. At least to 1800 the prevalence of living-in farm servants as opposed to day labourers created a class open to the informal education provided in farmhouses.[2] Certainly the 1851 census schedules show in these parts a goodly number of Scots born.

In all the eight counties, except Durham, the dominant occupation in 1851 was still farming, and much of the region remained purely rural. Durham, however, had by then twice as many men engaged in mining and manufacture as in agriculture, and parts of the north-east were being transformed into industrial conurbations of economically related colliery districts, manufacturing towns and ports. In the coalfields, and on Tyneside and Teesside generally, population was expanding greatly, much of it consequent on immigration from other parts of England, and from Ireland, Scotland and Wales. Watering places like Cleethorpes, Whitby and Scarborough developed, and by mid-century there were seven towns in the region with over 26,000 inhabitants and another nine with over 12,000.[3] Conversely, in the rural parts of the region, labourers left the land for manufacturing towns and independent small landowners and farmers suffered somewhat from agricultural recession, though retaining a modest prosperity. It was a period, too, of railway and dock construction which brought temporary influxes of navvies to various places, spawned new centres, and subsequently reduced the remoteness of many towns and rural areas.

All this affected the overall social composition of the region and the state of education. As schooling became commoner elsewhere, and particularly as public grant-aided schools pioneered improved elementary instruction the northern region ceased to stand out as so significantly better schooled. Increasingly, sparsely populated areas were faced with the difficulties of providing the sort of schooling that attracted government assistance, while the burgeoning mining and industrial developments of Tyneside, Teesside and elsewhere created societies akin to those of the industrial midlands, Lancashire and the West Riding, and with similar educational problems.

The proportions of the population returned as day scholars in 1818 and 1833 were substantially above the national average in all eight counties, and in 1833 higher than in almost all other counties. By 1851 all the eight remained above the national level, but no longer as strikingly so — except for Rutland and Westmorland, which still bettered all other counties but Middlesex for proportions of day-school pupils on the books (Appendix J). Figures for attendance at Anglican public schools in 1837 (Appendix M), however, show levels well below the national average in Cumberland, Westmorland, Lincolnshire, and probably in the North and East Ridings, suggesting (considering the high overall levels for 1818 and 1833) a reliance on other types of school.[4] Nevertheless, although dissent was strong in all the counties except Westmorland and Rutland (Appendix N), by 1851 Church efforts had resulted in a clear lead in the provision of public education in the region. Surveys of Church school pupils in 1847, 1857 and 1867 show proportions above the national average except in Northumberland (Appendix M) and general surveys of 1851 and 1858 show a clear lead over dissenting schools (Appendix L).

Despite this, by the 1850s the proportions of day-school pupils attending *all* public schools was, apart from in Westmorland and Rutland, not exceptionally high compared with other regions (Appendix J). To some extent this may reflect trends in financial support. In 1858 day schools in the strongly Anglican counties of Westmorland and Rutland, and to some degree in Lincolnshire, had incomes (mainly for Church schools) from other than government sources well above the national level, whereas the more populous Durham, Northumberland and Yorkshire (as a whole) fell below that level (Appendix P). Government grants to schools over the period 1833–59 were substantial only for Durham (Appendix O). The region as a whole appears to have had to rely to a large extent on local and Church money for school provision.

County statistics, however, disguise considerable variations in the educational scene which emerged as the region became increasingly differentiated with sparsely populated agricultural areas, and industrial and mining communities. Throughout the period the general educational level was notoriously low in the mining districts which had a way of life as unwholesome and degraded as that of the coal and iron districts of Staffordshire.[5]

In the early 1840s many children in the pit villages of Northumberland and

Durham were receiving either no education at all or very little. The miners, themselves extremely ignorant, were remarkably indifferent towards educating their offspring. They earned comparatively high wages, but their work was dangerous and continuous employment uncertain: boys could find work in the pits and add to the family budget at an early age, while girls were useful at home and as domestics. The value of schooling was not perceived. Moreover some parents exercised little control over their children amongst whom there was strong antipathy to attending school. The more respectable miners were usually dissenters and did not readily accept Church schools, and Primitive Methodists and other dissenting sects popular in the villages generally lacked funds to establish schools. There is some evidence, too, that Roman Catholic parents were influenced by their priests against sending their children to Church schools.[6] Many parents thus preferred the many small private schools to which they might send, irregularly, those of their children too young to work. Such institutions often lacked their own buildings, were ill equipped, poorly organised, and run by incompetent and ignorant teachers. The Anglican clergy found themselves charged with areas excessively overpopulated, ill endowed, and lacking any well-off lay residents. In the circumstances the establishment of adequate schools was difficult.[7]

Some help came from employers. The lead mine owners, mainly in Cumberland, had a long tradition of providing libraries and schools for the offspring of their employees and for adult workers.[8] The coalowners, who had shown little inclination to assist in the early decades of the century, were provoked in the 1840s into a new zeal for education. Following Chartist disturbances in 1839, and strikes in the Northumberland and Durham field in 1826, 1831, 1832 and more particularly in 1844 and 1849–50, some employers established libraries and began to support schools.[9] At first, assistance was extended to existing private schools, as in a few cases had been the custom before, but from the mid-1840s and in the 1850s many company schools, day and Sunday, appeared and substantial assistance was given to some Church schools.[10]

This policy, intended to produce civilised workmen who would apreciate the mutual benefits of co-operation, was supported by the school inspectorate, and by the commissioners appointed to report annually on conditions in the mining districts in the 1840s and 1850s, and who regarded the pit villages not only as sinks of depravity, sloth and savagery, but nests of incipient political subversion.[11] And to the wish to inculcate habits of industry, obedience and morality through schooling were added other motives. Deeper pits, more complicated machinery, and so on, accentuated the advantages of a literate workforce which could understand regulations and written instructions.[12] There was also the hope that provision of good schools would reduce the habit of workmen to move frequently from one colliery to another.[13] The colliery schools were not simply engines of social control. Humanitarianism and paternalism played a part in their establishment[14] and the education provided was certainly not inferior to that of Church schools.[15] By 1853 most coalowners supported half-time education for boys of ten to fifteen.[16]

Advance was, however, slow. The considerable ill will felt by the miners to their employers limited their reponse. Libraries were often ignored, private schools preferred,[17] but gradually attendance at Church and colliery schools increased. Standards even at inspected voluntary schools, however, remained low. Attendance was very irregular and confined to the very young, children often changed schools, and attainments were low; they 'soon forgot all or nearly all they had been taught'.[18]

A very different situation existed in agricultural areas, though they were by no means homogeneous in levels of education. Attitudes to schooling, particularly in Westmorland and Cumberland, were still more amenable than in rural districts elsewhere. To a large extent this was the result of traditionally better educated parents, comparatively high farm wages, a smaller need for child labour, especially in winter, and maybe proximity to Scotland.[19] In Cumberland and Westmorland freeholders, farmers and labourers favoured an extended school life to thirteen or fourteen.[20] Farm labourers in Northumberland and Durham supported schooling much more than the better paid miners. A Northumberland vicar in the 1830s claimed that 'I scarcely know an instance in which the children of an agricultural labourer have not been sent to school, for the most part at his own expense',[21] and an H.M.I. reported in 1869 of that county that 'education is not found to be inconsistent with agriculture. The labourers ... are the best educated and most intelligent of their class that I have met with, and they are generally very anxious that their children should attend school as regularly as possible'.[22] Indeed, of one Northumberland village it was said in the 1860s that 'public opinion would send any man earning wages ... to the position of a brute who did not send his child to school'.[23] Some parents, moreover, looked further than the fields for their children's future. The Newcastle Commissioners noted that the London counting houses 'are much supplied with the country lads from Cumberland and Westmorland'.[24] Moreover, farmers in the area were unusual in favouring schooling for their labourers' children, sometimes meeting the cost, and were not opposed to legal restrictions on child labour, and the Newcastle Commissioners reported that it was 'quite usual in Cumberland and Westmorland to go to school in the winter till fourteen or fifteen'.[25]

Although illiteracy rates remained low, especially for men (Appendix D), this state of affairs represented to some extent the traditional culture of a past age, by the 1850s recognised as 'the remains of an old civilisation wearing out', as the independent yeomen diminished in numbers and prosperity. Fears were expressed that the north was failing to keep up with generally improving educational standards.[26] A decade or so later the still numerous endowed grammar schools and charity schools, the basis of earlier cultural superiority,[27] no longer fitted the needs of the time. The grammar schools, which often served as elementary schools, were considered ripe for reform,[28] the charity schools were allegedly inefficient, poorly staffed and badly managed. Some of the remaining 'statesmen' (yeomen), like the smaller tenant farmers, had a need of their children's labour at an earlier age than before. Parents were criticised for withdrawing children for casual farm work.[29]

Outside observers pressed the need for inspected elementary schools of the kind becoming common elsewhere.[30] In the 1850s there was still a considerable dearth of certified teachers and of inspected schools in the rural areas of Westmorland and Cumberland,[31] where even by 1863 there were still only thirty-eight inspected schools in towns and fifty-six in country districts. Rural schooling was hampered by difficulties in meeting the requirements of the Revised Code and raising money from the small yeomen.[32]

The similar difficulties faced in rural Northumberland are illustrated by the comparatively low proportions at Church and other public schools.[33] By the 1860s the numbers of schools were adequate but quality lagged behind. On the eve of the 1870 Act shepherds in remoter parts still provided education for their children by hiring teachers whom they lodged and boarded.[34] Little Rutland, on the other hand, maintained a superior standard of education throughout the period. Anglican allegiance was strong and by 1838 there was said to be a parish for every 400 inhabitants and as many charity schools as parishes. Private schools were efficient and in the growing numbers of Church schools attendance was unusually regular.[35] By the 1850s some rural parts of the county lacked efficient schools,[36] but Rutland experienced little population growth in mid-century and lost population, 1851–71, so that on the whole its schools were able to meet demand and improve in quality.[37]

In the rural parts of the other counties in the region parental attitudes though not antagonistic were somewhat less favourable. There was more scope for child labour, greater insecurity for labouring families,[38] and the problem of irregular attendance was greater.[39] Large parts of Lincolnshire suffered from the lack of a resident gentry, and in that county and the North and East Ridings the farmers, while educating their own children, were generally less enthusiastic for schooling for labourers' offspring.[40] 'If I were a scholar,' said a Lincolnshire labourer in the 1860s, 'I shouldn't be here, and that's the reason why the farmers hold against this 'ere scholarship.'[41] School attendance in the county was relatively high in the 1850s but there were few trained teachers and many of the Church schools were uninspected.[42] By the 1860s there were more aided Church schools and few parishes without a school,[43] but school life remained short, with most children in the age group five to nine. There was a tendency for even earlier leaving than before and a large residuum of uneducated children. Schooling was particularly backward in the Marsh area, where there was an absence of resident clergy and middle-class laymen, and in the sparsely populated Fens, where the children of small freeholders had less schooling than those of labourers.[44]

Generally speaking, the East Riding was well provided with schools by mid-century, and in some parts the presence of interested resident gentry had a good effect on school attendance. Nevertheless, not all resident landowners in the county showed an interest, and in both the East and the North Ridings there were parts where schooling was backward — especially in the moorland areas and the wolds. Many parishes even in the 1860s had no grant-aided schools and some no National schools at all. Moreover, conditions in the fishing villages were said to be at a lower level than in manufacturing towns, with schooling confined to infants.[45]

As for towns in the region, the national pattern of large towns and industrial towns having a worse record for day schooling than small towns, particularly market and cathedral and administrative centres, is borne out by an examination of the twenty-three towns in the region for which separate schooling figures were provided in the 1851 census (Appendix K).[46] Moreover, five of the eight towns with more than 20,000 inhabitants had lower proportions at school than the average for their own county, while the opposite tendency is clear for the smaller towns (Appendixes J, K). Market centres like Beverley, Boston, Kendal, Richmond, Stamford and the two cathedral cities of York and Lincoln stand out as having the highest proportions of children at day school.[47] Stockton in this category, too, was in an industrial area, but was also an ancient market centre. Apart from Tynemouth and Durham, however, the older towns of the region tended to have better school figures than the industrial towns of Lancashire, the West Riding and the midlands. And many of these smaller towns had greater proportions on the books of public schools than in their county generally. York, with 76 per cent on public school books, was exceptional in this respect — as was Grimsby[48] at the other end of the scale with only 28 per cent (Appendix K).

The continued superiority of market towns is suggested by other evidence,[49] but the larger non-industrial towns had problems before 1870 of attracting all children to school. Surprisingly, the Anglican share of day-school pupils in York and Lincoln in the 1860s was only about one-third of the total, and in Lincoln about half the children 'of school age' were not at school in 1868.[50] In Hull and Sculcoates the proportion of such children was less than half in 1858, the average school life two and a half years, and the average leaving age ten and a half.[51]

Problems in the industrial towns of the region were greater, though not as overwhelming as in the mining districts. In Newcastle upon Tyne in 1838 many children were not at school and the schools themselves offered but little instruction mainly to the very young who attended irregularly, and the teachers were 'about as ignorant as the scholars'.[52] By the 1850s population growth in the town and in others like Hartlepool, Sunderland, Gateshead and South Shields resulted in a remarkable lack of school places despite limited demand.[53] In fast expanding Middlesbrough, with a population 'as heterogeneous as in the frontier towns of the American West',[54] circumstances even in the 1860s were 'very unfavourable to education', the Church organisation was inadequate, neighbouring industrial places ill supplied with schools, and such pupils as attended were of the 'most unruly description'.[55]

In many of these towns Church influence was weak, though the diocesan education society channelled funds to populous areas.[56] Similarly, some of the employing classes who gave little support to education began by the 1860s to be more sympathetic.[57] Thus William Peel in the 1860s favoured increased provision of schooling for the class of child ('the poorest and most ignorant') he employed in his Newcastle match factories.[58] In these towns and the ports, like Hull, the main difficulty in reaching the residuum was the indifference of unskilled, though sometimes well paid, parents faced with opportunities for child employment. To them, schooling was an irrelevance or meant merely a smattering of letters taught to infants.[59]

Child labour was certainly an important factor affecting school attendance in the region, even though the censuses suggest that its incidence was comparatively low. Both in 1851 and 1871 the recorded employment rate for boys and for girls aged ten to fourteen was below the national average, and in most of the eight counties well below. In some counties, particularly Durham, however, there was an increase in actual numbers in 1851–71. Few children aged five to nine are returned as employed and again both in 1851 and 1871 the levels were well below the national average (Appendix B). Again, proportions of employed persons under twenty, male and female, were lower in the main towns in 1851 than in those of the industrial north-west and midlands, and on a par with southern towns (Appendix C).

In 1851 the largest proportions of employed boys in the age group ten to fourteen were in farm work (11–14 per cent in Rutland, Lincolnshire and the North and East Ridings, and 3–4 per cent in Westmorland and Northumberland), in coal mining (4 per cent in Cumberland, 7 per cent in Northumberland, 15 per cent in Durham), cotton manufacture (3 per cent in Cumberland), and as messengers, porters, and the like (5 per cent in the East Riding). By 1871 farm work accounted for 16–17 per cent in Rutland and Lincolnshire, 7–9 per cent in the East and North Ridings, but only 2–5 per cent in Northumberland, Cumberland and Westmorland. Coal mining accounted for 10 per cent in Durham, 6 per cent in Northumberland and 3 per cent in Cumberland. For girls in this age group cotton manufacture accounted for 4 per cent in Cumberland in 1851 but domestic service was the only significant employment, varying between 3 and 8 per cent across the counties. By 1871 that proportion had increased in all the counties, substantially so in all but Northumberland and Durham, with a range of 6–12 per cent.

These employment statistics do not, however, give the full picture. Far larger proportions of children aged five to fourteen were not at school on census day 1851 than are recorded as employed (Appendixes B, I). For girls this varied from three to seven times as many over the counties, and for boys half as many again. Aside from children ill or temporarily absent,[60] some of these, particularly girls, were kept at home to mind younger children and do household chores,[61] others, both boys and girls, in the larger towns, were probably in a state of semi-employment, doing odd jobs and intermittently idling and playing. In 1853 it was alleged that many such children at Newcastle upon Tyne were 'abandoned to a life of precocious crime'.[62]

In agriculture there was less incentive for extensive full-time child labour than in many rural areas, for labourers' wages in all eight counties were well above the national average, the lowest (Lincolnshire) being 2s. a week above it in 1867–8.[63] Nevertheless, life for labourers was not easy, children were employed fully at a relatively early age and part-time work was common, while seasonal absence from school could last weeks or even months. The position was probably worst in Lincolnshire where children from eight or younger were employed for potato picking, weeding, tending sheep and so on. Particularly in the Fens there was constant work for young boys, and in the Fens and the Marsh areas of the county children were also found as members of gangs sometimes travelling long distances.[64] Children in the East and North Ridings even in the 1850s and 1860s were often employed from the age of eight, particularly in the summer.[65] Some agricultural gangs existed in West Cumberland and Westmorland but they rarely contained children younger than ten. 'Generally speaking, there was much less demand for young children to work on the land in those counties and in Northumberland and Durham, for the type of farming gave little scope for it, except perhaps in summer.[66] On small family farms in south Durham and the Lincolnshire fens in particular, children worked extensively for their parents,[67] though possibly not appearing as workers in the census returns. In the coastal villages fishermen generally took their offspring away from school in summer, and the growing holiday resorts claimed many children in the season.[68]

In the mining districts child labour was regular and full-time, so that the census figures represent a truer picture — but, of course, the county averages disguise much higher proportions in the colliery villages. In the coal mines of Durham and Northumberland, and to a lesser extent Cumberland, very young boys worked underground regularly, and in the lead mines children of nine to ten are recorded in the 1840s. Even after the Act of 1842 ten-year-olds were still illegally employed in some coal pits, and as late as 1870 boys of twelve upwards worked below ground for longer hours than adults.[69] In the industrial conurbations young children, through the period, worked in iron works, earthenware, and cotton manufacture, tobacco processing, glassworks, metal production[70] and the like in concentrations not evident in the census county averages.

The age structure of the school population, and the length of school life reflected opportunities for child labour and parental attitudes. Older children were found most in rural schools, particularly in the northernmost counties, least in the colliery and industrial districts, with town children somewhat in between.[71] In Durham and Cumberland in the late 1850s, for example, the ages of pupils in mining villages ranged from five to ten, and in agricultural districts from seven to thirteen.[72] But almost universally school children were bunched in the younger age groups. In the inspected schools of Cumberland, Durham, Northumberland and Yorkshire in the 1850s, 70–80 per cent were under the age of ten, and only 10 per cent over eleven to twelve.[73] At Middlesbrough in 1864, 84 per cent of pupils were under ten and only 4–5 per cent over twelve.[74] Such examples could be multiplied.[75] Moreover schools were always in a state of flux consequent on a combination of early leaving and migratory parents. At a school in Houghton-le-Spring about 1850, ninety of the children out of 105 came and went in the year.[76]

Sunday and evening schools do not appear to have contributed greatly to secular instruction in the region. The dispersed nature of the rural population rendered evening classes impracticable and in all counties attendance at such schools was negligible (Appendix Q).[77] As for Sunday schools, except for Rutland from 1818, and for Lincolnshire in the 1850s, attendance in the region fell below the national average (Appendix J), and was lowest in those counties with most dissenters (Appendix N). All eight counties in 1851 had proportions attending day school higher than or equal to those at Sunday school (Appendix J) and this was also generally so in the towns of the region (Appendix K). Neither at county nor at registration district level is there any obvious relationship between Sunday schooling in 1851 and later literacy levels (Appendixes D, F, J). Such facts provide little evidence that Sunday schools were being used as substitutes for day schools on any large scale. A limited exception may have been the lead districts of Alston and Reeth, where Sunday-school exceeded day-school attendances by 4–5 percentage points in 1851 (Appendix D). Other evidence suggests that in coal villages and some of the industrial and port towns poorer children may have attended only Sunday schools, but, generally speaking, instruction seems to have been at a very low level, with children who had attended for years still illiterate or nearly so.[78]

The social, economic and educational pattern is both reflected in the marriage mark statistics and further illuminated by them. In 1839–45 all eight counties returned a lower proportion of marriage marks than the national average, and Cumberland, Northumberland, Rutland, Westmorland and the East and North Ridings had better proportions than all other English counties (Appendix D).[79] By 1870 equally good or better levels were being achieved by some southern and western counties, though all but Durham of the eight counties retained a relatively high position. Durham, however, had above the national average proportion of marks by 1855, and from then on the county's figures rose progressively above the national level. In 1875 Durham still had a higher proportion of illiterate brides and grooms than Cumberland had in 1865. Moreover it was the only English county where, though proportions of illiterate spouses fell, actual numbers were greater in 1866 than 1856 and greater again in 1871. This reflected a huge increase of population (of approximately 80 per cent) between 1851 and 1871 as coal production expanded. Population changes in the other seven counties ranged from a 4 per cent decrease in Rutland to a 27 per cent rise in Northumberland.

Throughout the period 1839–85 there were more illiterate brides than grooms in all the counties except Rutland and Lincolnshire. In those two the same was generally the case until the mid-1860s, after which a position of comparability pertained in Lincolnshire. In Rutland, however, where the initial gap between men and women had been relatively small in 1839–45, male illiteracy levels rose above female. Indeed, Rutland's proportion of illiterate brides was 20 percentage points lower than the national average in 1845 and did not drop to less than twelve points below until the 1880s. The excess of female illiteracy rates over male, though generally diminishing, remained considerable in Westmorland until 1865, in Durham until 1880, and in the other five counties at least till the 1870s. And though in 1839–45 female illiteracy levels were lower in Cumberland, Northumberland, Rutland, Westmorland and the East and North Ridings than in most other English counties, this was a situation that was not maintained. By 1880, though Rutland's proportion of illiterate brides was lower than any other county, twenty counties had lower female rates than the East Riding, which itself was superior in this respect to the North Riding, Cumberland and Westmorland. By then the female illiteracy rates were higher in Durham than in any other county except Staffordshire and Monmouthshire. As for male illiteracy, levels better than most counties prevailed in 1870, except for Durham and to a lesser extent Lincolnshire. By 1880 Durham had a higher proportion of illiterate grooms than in all but eleven other English counties.

Analysis of illiteracy rates in registration districts underlines their relationship to economic and demographic features. In 1856 (Maps 1, 2, 3 and Appendix E) there was only one area of high illiteracy — that comprising a number of contiguous districts in north Durham (Gateshead, Chester-le-Street, Houghton, Durham, Auckland, Easington). Every district in Westmorland, Northumberland, the North Riding and Rutland had rates below the

MAP 1

Percentages of marriage marks, 1856: Northumberland, Cumberland, Westmorland, Durham. Bold figures indicate percentages above the national level of 35 per cent.

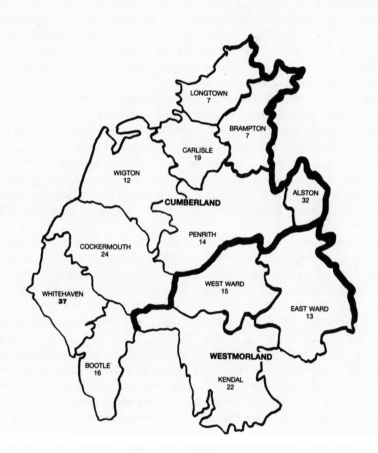

MAP 2

Percentages of marriage marks, 1856: North and East Ridings of Yorkshire. Bold figures indicate percentages above the national level of 35 per cent.

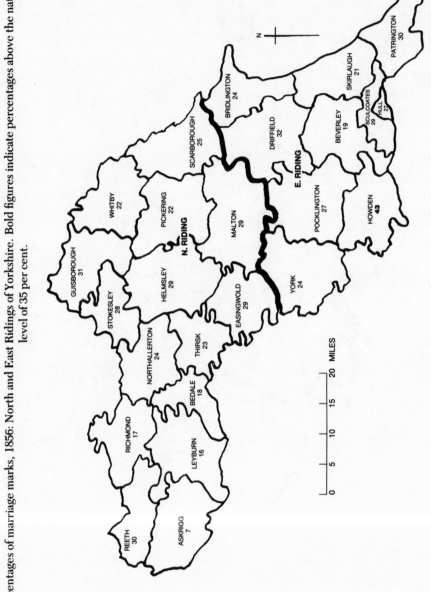

MAP 3
Percentages of marriage marks, 1856: Lincolnshire, Rutland. Bold figures indicate
percentages above the national level of 35 per cent.

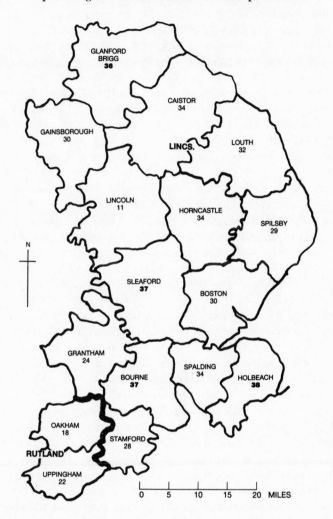

national level (35 per cent), and the same was so in all but one district each in
Cumberland and the East Riding (Whitehaven, Howden). Lincolnshire had
four districts somewhat above the national level: Glanford Brigg, Sleaford,
Bourne and Holbeach, the last three of which included fenland and the first the
Isle of Axholme. A separate study of Lincolnshire based partly on marriage
marks at parish level shows that illiteracy was worst in areas of the Isle of

Axholme, the Fens and the Marshes, where there were large numbers of small freeholders.[80] Generally speaking, levels improved moving from south to north, with the least illiterate districts close to the Scottish border.[81] Belford was the only English district where no illiterates were married in 1856, but several others registered levels between 3 and 8 per cent.

The placing of the registration districts of the counties covered in this section in a league table of illiteracy as measured by marriage marks is perhaps a rather contrived exercise, for it deals with these eight counties as a closed block. Nevertheless, without accepting any strict mathematical validity in the rank order, it does shed some light on the relative educational levels of the different types of community over the period. Thus Appendix G ranks the seventy-seven districts in 1866 with the least illiterate first, and compares that with the order in 1856 and 1871. Fourteen were consistently among the twenty-three most illiterate districts in 1856, 1866 and 1871. They included Guisborough (N.R.), close to Middlesbrough, which experienced a huge influx of population between 1851 and 1871, Holbeach in fenland Lincolnshire, Howden (E.R.), and all nine of the Durham colliery districts. These Durham districts all had enormous population increases over the twenty years from 1851. Auckland, the most illiterate district in the eight counties bar one experienced a growth of 68 per cent 1851–61 and 37 per cent 1861–71. Stockton, which included the new boom town of Middlesbrough, grew by 75 per cent in 1861–71. The five most illiterate of the colliery districts, moreover, had exceptionally high concentrations of miners: 35–49 per cent of adult males in 1851.[82]

Also among the twenty-three least literate districts in 1856 were Whitehaven (Cumberland), where 12 per cent of men were miners in 1851 and there were many Irish immigrants (two likely ingredients of illiteracy),[83] and Alston (Cumberland), where 59 per cent of men were lead miners, a higher proportion than anywhere else. Lead miners, however, were well known to be generally more literate than coal miners,[84] and Alston's illiteracy level in 1856, though high by Cumberland standards, was still 3 percentage points better than the national average. Hartlepool, where the town of that name mushroomed in population, attracting many casual Irish and other labourers to its new ironworks, shipyards and shipping,[85] was not a separate district in 1856 but had very poor literacy rates in 1866 and 1871.

As a contrast, the twenty-seven most literate districts in 1856 were largely those studded with market towns. All but six of the twenty-seven were also in the most literate category in 1866 and 1871. They included (in 1856) practically all the districts of Northumberland and Cumberland, all the districts in Rutland and Westmorland, the districts of Teesdale (Durham) and Askrigg (N.R.), both bordering Westmorland, with Askrigg's neighbours, Leyburn, Richmond, and Bedale (N.R.), as well as a group made up of Pickering and Whitby (N.R.), and Beverley and Skirlaugh (E.R.).

Several other districts are worthy of comment. Cockermouth (Cumberland) fell from the thirty-fourth most literate district in 1856 to sixty-third and sixty-ninth in 1866 and 1871, whilst its proportion of marks actually rose as new coal mines and blast furnaces were established at Workington, Seaton, Flimby and Great and Little Clifton. At Weardale (Durham) the proportion of illiterates remained constant at 23 per cent in 1856, 1866 and 1871, with an influx of Welsh and Cornish lead miners and the establishment of a coal community.[86]

The districts including Scarborough and Whitby had good literacy rates, but as these old fishing ports developed as resorts both districts suffered a rise in illiteracy rates: Scarborough between 1866 and 1871 and Whitby district between 1856 and 1866, though both were still comparatively good (Appendix F). Children in these resorts were taken from school to help with the holiday trades from May to November.[87] On the other hand Kendal, containing a flourishing market town with some industry, improved its literacy rating in 1866–71 as better rail communications attracted an influx of well-off residents.[88] Kendal had a full range of social and cultural institutions, as indeed did Newcastle upon Tyne and Hull. It is perhaps because of this that literacy levels in the districts containing these towns were thoughout better than the national average, despite the growth of population and industry and the deficiencies in schooling described above. These were clearly differenced from more purely industrial towns by the range of occupations connected with trade and the fact that they were traditional centres of culture. The same was so for York, despite its high influx or Irish.[89]

A general relationship between proportions of boys aged five to fourteen not at school in 1851 and male illiteracy rates in 1866 is discernible at county level, though this is not as obvious for females (Appendix I). Application of the product moment correlation coefficient to the relationship of actual school attendance in 1851 and the illiteracy rates in 1866 in the various districts of each county shows the strongest connection in Northumberland (-0.79) (indicating that schooling may have accounted for some 60 per cent of later literate spouses), the North Riding (-0.57) and Durham (-0.52) but little or no relationship in the other counties.[90] For the districts of the region as a whole, the coefficient is low (-0.34), lower than that for any of the other regions investigated in this volume — perhaps an indication of the loss of educated youngsters to other parts before marriage. The observable relationship is presented simply in Table 3·1.

At registration district level the generally lower illiteracy rates for males in 1866 may reflect the fact that more boys than girls were at school in almost every district in 1851 (Appendix F). And it may be observed that of the seventy-seven districts in the region only five had proportions at day school in 1851 below the national level, and in view of the clear deficiencies of education in parts of the region even in the 1860s, noted above, the importance of

TABLE 3·1

Illiteracy rates and schooling

% population in attendance at day school, 1851	Illiteracy rates 1866: number of districts		
	6–17% marks (26 districts)	18–22% marks (26 districts)	23–45% marks (25 districts)
15		1 ⎫	
14	4 ⎫	1 ⎪	⎫
13	1 ⎪	3 ⎬ 19	1 ⎪
12	11 ⎬ 21	9 ⎪	5 ⎬ 14
11	5 ⎭	5 ⎭	8 ⎭
10	4 ⎫	5 ⎫	8 ⎫
9	⎪	2 ⎬ 7	⎪
8	⎬ 5	⎭	3 ⎬ 11
7	1 ⎭		⎭

Source: Based on Appendix F. Hartlepool (Durham) existed as a district in 1866 but not in 1851, and is therefore omitted from these calculations.

regarding not only numbers of schoolchildren but quality of schooling and regularity of attendance is underlined. Certainly it was the official opinion even in the 1860s that only compulsion could effect regularity of attendance, and an extension of the length of a child's school life, in the Northumberland and Durham coalfields,[91] and it seems doubtful if that conclusion should be confined only to the colliery districts.

East Anglia and the south-eastern counties

Although agricultural employment dominated[92] in the eight counties considered in this section — Norfolk, Suffolk, Essex, Sussex, Hampshire, and extra-metropolitan Kent, Middlesex and Surrey — they were not socially or economically homogeneous. Broadly speaking, East Anglia and Essex were backward rural counties with few towns. Much of Kent, Sussex, Hampshire, and south Surrey, too, was farming country, but rurality was interspersed with much more urban development, while Middlesex and north Surrey were fast becoming adjuncts of the metropolis.

In East Anglia, with central and north Essex, conditions for farm workers were unenviable. Villages were often remote and culturally backward. Smallholdings, especially in Norfolk, were increasingly absorbed into bigger estates. Large expanses of countryside were inhabited by a surplus of labourers, low paid when in employment and often seasonally reliant on the poor rate.[93] Poverty was widespread and the poor law was manipulated to the advantage of employers but to the detriment of the men, and the prevalence of closed parishes in some areas raised housing rents in nearby open parishes. The widespread use of gang labour further divorced farmers from personal responsibility towards their workers and not surprisingly relations between labourers and employers were hostile and at times, as in the 1840s, incendiarism and other violence flared up.[94]

The misery of farm workers in this eastern area was compounded by lack of alternative employment, for the traditional woollen and hempen-linen manufacture had all but disappeared by 1850, adding further to the overstocked labour market. Attempts to establish a factory based silk industry in its place largely failed. In a restricted area of south-west Suffolk and north Essex, domestic and a little factory silk production persisted, as did straw plaiting, lace manufacture, and, around Ipswich, stay making.[95] Populations therefore grew slowly, and actually declined in Norfolk and Suffolk 1851–61, and there was a high level of migration overseas, to the industrial north, and to London, perhaps creaming off the better educated and more intelligent.

Conditions in East Anglian towns were better than in the countryside. Despite the plight of rural labourers profitable farming went on and the produce of the many large estates and farms induced a modest prosperity in market centres, like Bury St. Edmunds and Stowmarket, which also became centres of industries connected with agriculture.[96] Norwich, certainly, had large numbers of bitter indigent handloom weavers struggling on in a changing industry. Otherwise, however, its cloth manufacture continued and it enjoyed relative prosperity as a market and cathedral town and a centre of mixed industries. King's Lynn, Ipswich, Yarmouth and Lowestoft numbered among other towns which developed some industry and were trading and fishing ports, while the last two also developed as resorts.[97]

In south Essex, proximity to London gave opportunities for market gardening, while the West Ham area began from 1850 to develop as a residential district with employment opportunities in the expanding docks, railway works and other manufacturing and service industries. Wages were thus higher than in other parts of East Anglia.[98]

South of the Thames different conditions prevailed. Much of Kent and the southern parts of Sussex and Hampshire were dotted with well populated thriving market towns, opulent watering places and ports. These areas, and parts of Surrey and Middlesex, had a goodly proportion of wealthy residents and generally contrasted with the paucity of such people in Norfolk and Suffolk, where above average early marriages and illegitimacy prevailed, and there were fewer domestic servants (Appendix H). Middlesex was 'a sort of demesne to the metropolis, being covered with its villas, intersected with innumerable roads leading to it',[99] and north Surrey acquired a heavily suburban character. By mid-century Deptford, Chatham and Sheerness were both dockyard and industrial towns,[100] Portsmouth and Southampton substantial centres of shipping, trade and industry, and Brighton a considerable concentration of population and opulence. All this provided centres of consumption for local agricultural produce.[101] In parts of Middlesex, Kent and Surrey, close to London, hay, fruit and hop production and market gardening were stimulated and smallholders often prospered.[102] In Kent the yeomanry in the 1840s were said to be 'a superior class'[103] and in that county, and in parts of Surrey and south Hampshire, farm wages were relatively high.[104]

In the northern parts of Hampshire and Sussex and south Surrey farming was more backward, rural population thinner, and the towns, their former cloth trade defunct, virtually bereft of industry — 'quiet and half forsaken except on market and fair days'.[105] Farm labourers were less well paid, and in the Weald and its environs there were many poor smallholders. Caird noted the ignorance and stupidity of Surrey farmers, many 'being scarcely able to sign their own names'.[106]

The incidence of child labour as recorded in the census was comparatively low in the region (Appendix B). For youngsters aged five to nine it was heaviest in Norfolk, Essex and Suffolk, but even in those counties the numbers involved in 1851 were relatively small, and by 1871 they had declined considerably. By then only for boys in Norfolk and Suffolk did proportions exceed the national average. Many more older children (ten to fourteen) were officially occupied, though in 1851 none of the eight counties had proportions either of boys or girls above the national average. Such proportions were generally lower than in the industrial counties and the rural west, though above those of the northern rural counties. By 1871 there had been an increase in the number of occupied children in this age group in all eight counties, though a fall in percentages, but in Norfolk and Suffolk the proportions of employed boys had risen above the national average.

Proportions of employees under twenty in the four 'principal towns' of the area for which the 1851 census provides data are generally on a par with those of the counties of the north and north-east, though with somewhat smaller percentages for males and somewhat higher ones for females. Norwich had by far the heaviest incidence, with much the same proportion as Birmingham (Appendix C).

In 1851 the largest proportions of boys in the age group ten to fourteen were employed in agricultural labour (18–23 per cent in Essex, Norfolk, Suffolk, Sussex; 13–15 per cent in Surrey, Kent and Hampshire; only 6 per cent in Middlesex), the only other significant proportions being of messengers, porters and the like in Kent and Norfolk (3–5 per cent). In 1871 agriculture was still the main occupation for boys of the age group, but by then only 7–10 per cent were employed in this way in Surrey, Kent and Sussex and Hampshire, and 2 per cent in Middlesex. In Essex, Norfolk and Suffolk, however, 18–20 per cent were still so occupied and actual numbers had increased in each of these counties.

For girls aged ten to fourteen general domestic work was the chief employment in 1851: 5–6 per cent in Surrey, Kent, Hampshire, Middlesex and Sussex; 3–4 per cent in Essex, Norfolk and Suffolk. Plait and silk manufacture accounted for 5 per cent in Essex, 3 per cent in Suffolk. By 1871 domestic service survived as the only significant occupation, accounting for 9 per cent in Sussex and 6–7 per cent in each of the other counties, and actual numbers so involved had roughly doubled in every county since 1851.

Very much higher proportions of ten to fourteen-year-olds, however, were not at school on census day 1851 than were returned on that day as at work (Appendix B, I).[107] In Hampshire the proportion of boys not at school was 10 percentage points above the proportion officially occupied; in the other counties the difference ranged from 16 to 23 points. For girls the difference was greater, ranging from 35 to 38 points more in Hampshire, Kent and Middlesex, and from 43 to 46 in the other counties. In Surrey, for instance, 8 per cent were returned as occupied in the Census, but 51 per cent were not at school. We may assume that many of these children were in at least intermittent employment.[108]

The diverse economic and social pattern of the region is reflected in its educational structure. The proportions of day scholars in 1818 were above the national level in all eight counties, apart from Middlesex (including its metropolitan districts).[109] This was so, too, in 1851 except that extra-metropolitan Middlesex had a higher proportion of day pupils than any other English county (Appendix J).

Though British and nonconformist schools functioned in the area,[110] by 1851 the Established Church had a clear lead in the provision of public schooling in all the counties (Appendix L). Surveys of Church school pupils 1837–67 (Appendix M), moreover, show that Essex, Hampshire, Kent and Sussex had proportions generally above the national average, as did Norfolk and Suffolk from 1847. In Middlesex and Surrey (including their London districts) below-average proportions persisted, and these counties were the only ones of the eight where the proportions at *all* public schools were below the national average in 1858 (Appendix J).[111] Though neither ranked high for dissenting worshippers (Appendix N) both had higher proportions at dissenting schools in 1851 and 1858 (Appendix L) than the other counties in the group, except Essex. The London population of Middlesex and Surrey, however, greatly outweighed that of their extra-metropolitan districts and these figures largely represent the situation in London, not covered in this study.[112]

Other evidence demonstrates the variations of quantity and quality of schooling embraced in the county figures, and in particular the differing experience of rural, suburban and urban areas. The schools in extra-metropolitan Surrey and Middlesex included those in small towns and suburban villages, those in well-off middle-class suburbs, and purely rural establishments. In all, the presence of a sufficient proportion of the better-off ensured, except perhaps in the remoter parts of south Surrey, that there was little difficulty in raising funds for elementary schools. This contrasts strongly with the situation in the metropolitan parishes of the two counties, where heavy concentration of the labouring classes created communities where school provision was difficult.[113]

Nevertheless general progress occurred in public school provision and its quality in Middlesex and Surrey over the 1850s and 1860s.[114] In the late 1840s one small rural parish in Surrey at least had two-thirds of those between ages five to fifteen at school and only twelve children in regular work. Boys began farm work full-time at the age of twelve, considerably older than in, for example, East Anglia, and girls as in other southern counties tended to stay at school longer than boys.[115]

In rural Norfolk and Suffolk the poverty and ignorance of the labouring classes led them to acquiesce in the early employment of their offspring and large numbers of farm labourers and even many farmers and tradesmen were in the late 1830s completely illiterate. Many parishes contained only Sunday or inadequate day schools, poorly staffed and equipped. Of 207 children in five Norfolk villages, for example, only sixty-eight attended day and forty-eight Sunday school.[116] Many inland Essex villages lacked day schools in the 1840s,[117] and throughout the period the inspectorate reported large tracts of East Anglia to be deficient of adequate schooling. In the late 1850s 630 square miles of Norfolk, 280 of Suffolk, and 420 of Essex had no inspected schools,[118] and a decade later fifty populous Norfolk villages had no Church schools,[119] though in some of these places private schools of unknown quality existed.[120] In the 1850s a period of economic depression resulted in a fall-off in school attendance,[121] and the general quality of education in Church schools in Norfolk and Suffolk was criticised by the inspector, who found a decline in the average age from twelve to eleven.[122] There was a lack of a resident gentry in many villages, arising from the existence of large estates, and also less frequent willingness on the part of the landed classes to support schools than was the case in some parts of the country.[123]

Throughout the period diocesan education societies in the area complained of lack of local financial assistance, and indeed subscriptions were often very low. In five Suffolk parishes in the mid-1840s they averaged £6 p.a. and in another nine, £16.[124] In the 1850s subscriptions in Suffolk actually declined, and there was a continual fear that the burden would prove too much for individual priests or the Church itself.[125] Tenant farmers, in many places the best-off inhabitants, were often dissenters opposed to Church influence and antagonistic to the schooling of children on whom they relied for labour. Indeed, they put pressure on already apathetic and poor parents, even in the 1860s and 1870s, to send their children into the fields.[126]

The onus of school provision in rural East Anglia thus fell largely on the parish clergy,[127] a situation that brought its own difficulties. Non-residence was common in parts of Suffolk and Norfolk into the 1840s, and day schools in such parishes had to await resident parsons.[128] Even then many parishes were tiny and the incumbent's income small, so that rural schools were often poorly equipped, and staffed by uncertified and inadequate teachers and found it difficult to qualify for government grants. Clerical independence and conservatism, moreover, militated against applications for such aid and also against the formation of central schools, large enough to serve a number of parishes. Such difficulties were made harder by the natural obstacles of widely dispersed cottages and hamlets and poor communications impeding school attendance over long distances. Those schools that did have government aid faced repeated criticism from the H.M.I.s for their poor quality.[129] Indeed, government grants over the period 1833–59 were exceptionally low for Norfolk, and well below average for Essex and Suffolk (Appendix O). Though progress occurred — annual grant-aided schools in Essex, for instance, increased by 50 per cent, 1865–70[130] — advance was slower than in the southern counties. Even by 1870 there was little support from the county clergy or the landowners of Hampshire and Surrey for universal compulsory schooling, though there was some approval for prohibiting farm labour for the very young.[131]

Seasonal work on the land followed by regular employment at an early age kept school attendance in East Anglia irregular and confined largely to the very young. Children of eight to ten years old were often absent for one-third of the year, and by nine or ten left altogether; some boys never attended at all.[132] In the late 1850s two-thirds of pupils still left school by ten and only some 5 per cent were over twelve. Even after the 1870 Education Act some boys in Norfolk and Suffolk were at full-time work at age seven or eight.[133] The gang system, prevalent in parts throughout the period, had a particularly pernicious effect in sucking the very young, particularly girls, into a life of endless toil, and though those under eight were barred by an Act of 1867 from public gangs they continued to be used in private gangs.[134]

In parts of north Essex and west Suffolk straw plaiting took girls from school early and spawned plaiting schools, like those in the south midlands, which were preferred to public schools by some parents. This led to plaiting being introduced into some Church schools, further diluting their quality. Domestic and factory silk production and corset making also interfered with schooling in the area.[135]

The inspectorate was less critical, but also less informative, of conditions in rural Kent, Sussex and Hampshire. Proportions of children at school in 1851 in the various registration districts of those counties were, in general, noticeably higher than in those of Essex, Norfolk and Suffolk (Appendix G). Nevertheless the rural parts of the southern counties, in some of which distress resulted in violent disturbances in the 1830s,[136] shared some of the same educational deficiencies and difficulties. Lack of financial support, early leaving and irregular attendance were the perennial complaints of the inspectorate and others.

Many parishes in Kent and Hampshire were without Church schools in the 1830s and 1840s.[137] A survey of some Kentish villages about 1840 revealed communities with only a small minority of children being schooled and those irregularly. Moreover, most went to schools, some Church-supported, which taught only reading and sewing.[138] In 1855, 65 per cent of pupils in inspected Church schools in the county were under ten and only 6 per cent over twelve.[139] Few children were employed regularly on the land till the age of twelve for girls and eleven for boys, but market gardening and hop and fruit culture created in Kent and parts of Hampshire and Sussex a heavy seasonal demand for child labour, making school attendance light for long periods.[140] At Fordingbridge (Hants.) British School, for example, pupils in the 1840s generally attended only a half to a third of the time,[141] and in Hampshire through the 1850s and 1860s the majority of pupils at dissenting and Church schools were under nine or ten.[142]

The H.M.I.s, however, reported continuous progress in the southern counties over the period. The numbers of inspected schools, certified teachers and pupil teachers increased steadily and the quality of teaching improved.[143] By the mid-1850s inspected schooling in Kent, Sussex and Surrey was reckoned as good as anywhere in England, with some 80 per cent of schools inspected in 1858 graded as 'good' or 'fair',[144] and in the early 1860s many excellent rural schools were reported in Hampshire.[145] Energetic diocesan activity increased Kentish provision, so that few places in the 1860s were out of reach of an inspected school.[146]

Nevertheless, though improvement was more obvious than in rural East Anglia, voluntary effort found it increasingly difficult to provide adequate schooling. In the late 1860s a hundred Hampshire parishes, including twenty populous places, had no inspected school, some no school at all and without prospect of improvement.[147] By the early 1870s three-quarters of Hampshire school-age children were said to be under efficient instruction, but in the open downs thinly populated villages and hamlets were unable to support effective schools. Central schools for larger areas, however, were still resisted by clergy and landowners.[148]

Indeed, few large landowners in Kent established or supported estate schools[149] and in some rural parishes in the southern counties, as in East Anglia, advance was delayed into the 1840s by the non-residence of clergy.[150] Though nearly all the more populous parishes of rural west Sussex had access to schools by the 1830s, the quality of schooling continued to lag behind that of the east of the county into the 1870s, and the smallness of parishes created the same difficulties as in East Anglia of obtaining government assistance.[151]

Even the greatest clerical enthusiasm could not overcome the financial difficulties. Hampshire and Surrey, for example, certainly benefited from the drive for school provision promoted by Charles Sumner, Bishop of Winchester.[152] Yet the Hampshire Society for the Education of the Infant Poor suffered through the 1830s from small and diminishing local subscriptions.[153] Its successor from 1835, the Winchester Diocesan Board of Education, supported by a network of diaconal boards and a training college at Winchester, helped to expand Church schooling but suffered similar difficulties and from 1852 was unable to continue financial assistance to schools.[154] By the early 1870s the voluntary system in Hampshire and Surrey was said to have reached its 'extreme limit of elasticity and progress', and compulsory attendance would have shown school provision still inadequate.[155] All this was despite the fact that by 1858 public schools in all the counties considered in this section (except Middlesex as a whole) had income from other than government sources at or above the national average (Appendix P). These figures, of course, covered urban as well as rural areas.

The state of urban education differed from rural. The region's towns in general had better attendance levels than towns in any other area except perhaps the western counties, and only four (Dover, Bury St. Edmunds, Harwich, King's Lynn) fell below the national average (Appendixes J, K). Fourteen towns in the region were among the forty-four in the country with the best enrolment figures.[156] The larger towns (over 20,000 population) had higher enrolments than the industrial towns of the north and midlands.[157] Attendance rates in the towns of the region were generally comparable with or somewhat higher than those of their own counties, while those in the smaller towns tended to be distinctly higher.

The best attendance rates (15–18 per cent) were found in fourteen towns: Southwold, Sudbury (Suffolk); Maldon, Saffron Walden (Essex); Thetford (Norfolk); Guildford (Surrey); Faversham, Hythe, Tenterden (Kent); Arundel, Chichester (Sussex); Andover, Lymington, Romsey (Hampshire), of which all but Guildford and Chichester had populations of 2–6,000.[158] A distinction between some of the more important towns of East Anglia and those of the southern counties is, however, discernible. Aside from Dover and Rochester, the proportion of children at school in 1851 in Norwich, Yarmouth, Bury St. Edmunds, Colchester, Harwich and King's Lynn was lower than in any of the thirty-nine towns in this group of counties for which the census provides such information (Appendix K).

As to private schools, in 1876 half Winchester's day-school pupils attended them,[159] and in 1851 the towns of Essex, Norfolk, Hampshire and Kent[160] tended to have lower proportions at public school than the counties in which they were set, suggesting a greater reliance on private schools than in rural areas. Standing out were Deal and Sandwich with only 23 and 29 per cent of schoolchildren at public schools, while the large towns of Portsmouth and Yarmouth had somewhat more children at private than public schools, and Southampton 58 per cent at public schools. Notable exceptions in these counties were Norwich (67 per cent at public schools), Hastings (80) and Romsey (91). No tendency for large numbers at private schools is obvious in the towns of Suffolk, Surrey and Sussex.

The presence of numerous thriving towns with a good proportion of the better-off was an ingredient in the generally higher level of education prevailing in the southern counties. Though some towns, like Southampton, grew as rapidly in the century as those of the industrial north, they were never as bereft of schooling. Portsmouth, Portsea, Gosport, Southampton and other southern towns were generally well provided by the 1850s.[161] In the early 1860s, in these and other Hampshire towns, Church schools were reckoned to be as large and efficient as in any towns elsewhere.[162] The problem was increasingly less one of mere provision than of encouraging regular attendance over a reasonable number of years. Brighton, for instance, had the remarkable number of 189 private schools (many middle-class boarding establishments) in 1851 and twenty-nine public schools, yet still some 6,500 children aged five to fourteen in the town were not at school.[163] At Gravesend a decade later many children did not attend school,[164] and no doubt such examples could be multiplied.

There were, of course, in some southern towns opportunities for regular and casual child labour that were absent in the countryside: for boys in the dockyards and arsenals of the Thames and Medway, Southampton and Portsmouth; for children generally as domestic servants, shop hands, errand runners and cart drivers; for girls as outworkers and factory hands in corset and shirt making and the like;[165] and in a whole gamut of seasonal work in the resorts. The ports spawned on- and off-shore work connected with fishing and other maritime activities, while in some places hopfields and fruit farms called whole families to the countryside in summer.[166] All this interfered with schooling, particularly for the poorer classes.

East Anglian towns presented a more diverse picture than did the rural parts of that area. Many from an early date possessed large and efficient Church and charity schools: but they also had many other public and private institutions, while the larger towns contained numerous poor labouring families indifferent to schooling or unable to afford it, with some children getting no education or only that of the Sunday school. Other towns, like King's Lynn, were in the early 1840s poorly provided with public schools.[167] Norwich, the largest town in the area, had many public schools by the early 1840s, but few well equipped or staffed. Within its bounds large numbers of depressed hand-loom weavers, hostile to authority, married young and put their children to work at the earliest age, some bargaining for factory work for them in the Monday 'children's market'. One-third of Norwich weavers' children about 1840 received no day schooling, the remainder a very limited one.[168] The 'poorest of the poor' put their children in lucifer match manufactories in conditions as unwholesome as in the Potteries.[169]

In the 1840s the income of town schools in Essex, Norfolk and Suffolk was said to be lower than that of rural schools.[170] In the 1850s middle-class financial support for popular education was allegedly still ungenerous in Ipswich, Yarmouth and Norwich, subscriptions actually declining in Norwich. The zeal of the clergy mitigated the situation in some towns, like Ipswich and Yarmouth, but was less effectual in Norwich.[171] Public schooling in Colchester, King's Lynn, Yarmouth, Ipswich, Bury St. Edmunds and many smaller towns expanded, if sometimes slowly, through the 1840s, 1850s and 1860s and in Yarmouth and Ipswich, at least, many children attended private schools. In those two towns, and probably others in the area, educational advance by 1860 was such that the superiority of the younger generation was clearly discernible. Yet ignorance persisted particularly among the poorer labouring classes who were unwilling to school their children regularly to a reasonable age: for many indeed schooling was a luxury they could still ill afford. John Glyde concluded of Ipswich in 1850 that only a local rate could provide sufficient schools for the community.[172] In Norwich, in particular, 'stagnation' prevailed into the mid-1860s with a system of district Church schools failing to meet needs and public support for education limited.[173] Not until the late 1860s was improved public school provision, quality and attendance reported: even then many city children were not at school.[174]

The marriage mark statistics both reflect and illuminate the social and economic patterns already outlined. They reveal Kent, Middlesex, Hampshire and Sussex as among the most literate English counties for both brides and grooms throughout the period, with Surrey well placed for brides and improving its ranking for grooms. By the 1880s 90 per cent or so of spouses in those five counties were literate.[175] Norfolk, Suffolk and Essex, however, had overall proportions of marks well above the national average in 1839–45, and though they moved close to the average over the period they remained inferior to the southern counties (Appendix D).

The overall mark proportions, however, disguise important and changing differentials between men and women. Male illiteracy was considerably above the national average in Essex until the early 1870s and in East Anglia through the period 1841–85, whereas the other five counties returned male levels below the national average throughout. As for female illiteracy, proportions below the national average pertained in all but Suffolk and Essex in the 1840s and in those counties from the 1850s. In the five southernmost counties female illiteracy was remarkably low — by 1885 less than half the national average. Indeed, compared with the prevailing ignorance of agricultural labourers, improvements in female literacy levels *vis-à-vis* those for men, perhaps consequent upon the growth of schooling for girls and of female domestic service, are striking. At the beginning of the period more brides than grooms were illiterate in all eight counties. From 1845, however, Surrey had more illiterate grooms than brides, and from the mid-1850s this was so, too, in all but Kent and Hampshire, where nevertheless a position of approximate parity had been reached.

Analysis of illiteracy rates at registration district level refines the geographical pattern. In 1856 while all but five Norfolk and Suffolk districts had overall proportions of marks above the national average (Map 4, Appendix F), King's Lynn, Norwich, Bury St. Edmunds and Ipswich districts (containing the towns of those names), and Mutford, which included the port of Lowestoft, were below that level. Apparantly the towns contained sufficient proportions of the better-off and middle-class to offset their many unschooled and under-schooled inhabitants.[176] In contrast, an area of particularly high illiteracy comprised a group of contiguous districts in south-west Suffolk and north Essex,[177] some of which were centres of silk production. Indeed north and west Essex generally had levels worse than the national average. South Essex was better, West Ham having a very low illiteracy rate, and Romford and Billericay around the national average. Colchester, containing the town of that name, too, stood out with a level about as good as that of Ipswich and King's Lynn.'[178]

In Middlesex, Kent, Surrey and Sussex there were comparatively few districts in 1856 with illiteracy rates above the national average and the same was so of south Hampshire (Map 5, Appendix F). Exceptions included a connected group of districts in east Surrey and north-east Sussex, another in west Surrey and west Sussex,[179] and those comprising north-east Hampshire. As in Devon and Dorset the districts nearer the coast tended to be more literate than those inland.

Appendix G ranks the 145 districts of the eight counties with the least illiterate in 1866 first, and compares that with the ranking in 1856 and 1871.[180] The fifty-seven most illiterate districts in 1856 (40–61 per cent marks) included thirty-eight in Essex, Norfolk and Suffolk, mostly agricultural (including Halstead and Braintree, Essex, where there were concentrations of silk and plait workers),[181] and some districts in Hampshire, Surrey, Sussex and Kent, almost all in rather remote rural areas. Hoo (Kent), for example, where illiteracy was at a very high level, was an isolated rural backwater, with no rail links until the 1850s, which registered in 1851 a low attendance at Anglican worship despite a dearth of dissenting chapels.[182] Midhurst, Uckfield, Petworth and East Grinstead were all in the thinly populated rural north of Sussex, and Godstone, in Surrey, bordered East Grinstead. Alton, Whitchurch, Droxford and Kingsclere comprised an area in north Hampshire of woodlands and small unimproved farms where wages were lower than in the

MAP 4

Percentages of marriage marks, 1856: Norfolk, Suffolk, Essex. Bold figures indicate percentages above the national level of 35 per cent.

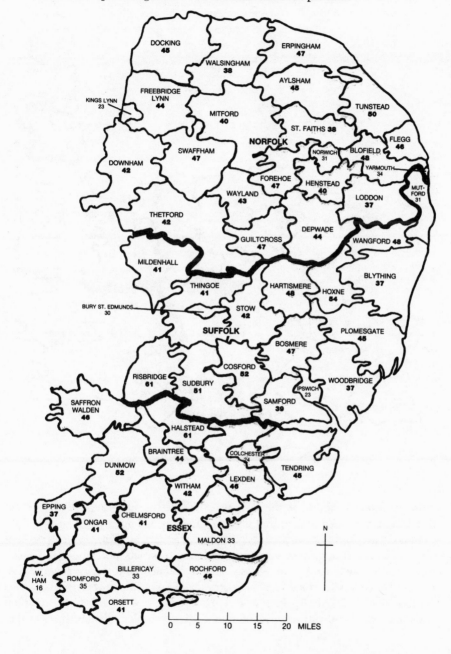

MAP 5
Percentages of marriage marks, 1856: Hampshire, Sussex, Surrey, Middlesex, Kent.
Bold figures indicate percentages above the national level of 35 per cent.

more prosperous south of the county. Most of the fifty-seven least literate districts in 1871 were still in that group in 1871 or had not moved far out of it.

In contrast, the forty-eight least illiterate districts in 1856 (14–28 per cent marks) consisted largely of growing residential districts near the metropolis, those containing coastal towns, those centred on fairly large inland towns (often market centres with some local industry), and some of the more prosperous rural districts of Kent, Sussex and Hampshire. Most of these retained comparatively good ratings in 1866 and 1871. Examples of such districts that

were affected by the spread of population from London included fashionable residential areas of Surrey which experienced an influx of the better-off and an exodus of labourers to inner London,[183] four of the six extra-metropolitan Middlesex districts,[184] where much increase was of the educated classes, and West Ham (Essex). West Ham saw the expansion of the London docks and the establishment of railway works and other industries with a concurrent large population growth, yet maintained a high level of literacy presumably because immigrants included many skilled, semi-skilled and clerical workers. Also in

this group were Dorking, Reigate and Guildford (Surrey) (districts centred on
substantial market towns with local industries and good rail links to London),
together with Colchester,[185] Winchester,[186] Canterbury and Maidstone (all
containing important towns), as well as many districts embracing ports, resorts
and watering places along the south coast: Hastings, Eastbourne, Worthing,
Christchurch (containing Bournemouth), Brighton, and Dover, Gravesend,
Eastry (containing Deal), Portsea Island (containing Portsmouth) and Southampton.[187]

Districts falling between the least and the most illiterate in 1856 (29–39 per
cent marks) included some in the otherwise heavily illiterate counties of
Norfolk, Suffolk, and Essex; those containing the main towns — Norwich, Bury
St. Edmunds, Yarmouth and Mutford (containing Lowestoft), Romford (con-
taining Barking, an important fishing port) and Epping (containing Epping and
Waltham Abbey). In this category, too, were similar districts containing towns
in the southern counties like Rye, Andover, Medway (including Chatham and
Rochester), Alverstoke (containing Gosport), and many largely rural areas.
Most of these districts remained in the middling category in 1866 and 1871.

Comment may be made on some trends. The fact that of the twenty
Hampshire districts three showed no improvement in literacy levels 1866–71
and eleven registered an increase in the proportion of marks appears to link
with the poor schooling facilities noted into the 1860s,[188] and the almost static
population. A great improvement in the relative ranking of Cuckfield (Sussex)
must be related to the large population increase after the London and Brighton
railway made commuting to the capital and to Brighton possible. The failure of
Farnham's (Surrey) illiteracy rate to fall 1866–71 appears to be connected with
the establishment of Aldershot army camp,[189] while Milton (Kent), where the
rate remained static 1851–61, had an influx of unskilled labour when a large
brickfield was set up.

Indeed population trends appear to be an ingredient in literacy levels in
many places. Of the ninety-two most literate districts in 1866 only five suffered
population decline, while the others averaged an increase of 22 per cent. In the
fifty-three least literate districts (28 per cent marks) twenty-nine lost population
and in the best the increase averaged only 10 per cent. The bulk of the districts
where literacy increased with population growth were in the southernmost
counties, representing influxes of the better educated into urban and
residential districts. Norfolk and Suffolk stand out as counties where rural
depopulation was associated with a slow improvement in literacy.

Use of the product moment correlation coefficient formula shows that the
relationship between schooling levels in 1851 and illiteracy rates in 1866 was (at
-0.49) stronger than in all the other regions except that comprising the
counties of the industrial north west. The coefficients for individual counties,
however, vary greatly. In Middlesex (-0.59) and Suffolk (-0.56) it was

TABLE 3·2

Illiteracy rates and schooling

% population in attendance at day school, 1851	Illiteracy rates 1866: number of districts		
	8–17% marks (45 districts)	18–27% marks (47 districts)	28–52% marks (53 districts)
16	1 ⎫	0 ⎫	0 ⎫
15	7 ⎪	1 ⎪	0 ⎪
14	1 ⎬ 27	2 ⎬ 18	0 ⎬ 9
13	8 ⎪	7 ⎪	4 ⎪
12	10 ⎭	8 ⎭	5 ⎭
11	8 ⎫	12 ⎫	11 ⎫
10	6 ⎪	14 ⎪	16 ⎪
9	2 ⎬ 18	3 ⎬ 29	12 ⎬ 44
8	2 ⎪	0 ⎪	2 ⎪
7	0 ⎭	0 ⎭	3 ⎭

Source: Based on Appendix F.

strongest; in the other counties it was weak: Essex (−0·29, Norfolk −0·03, Surrey −0·24. Kent −0·20, Sussex −0·31 and Hampshire −0·41).[190] Such tendency as there was for a relationship between local day schooling and illiteracy levels is shown in a rudimentary way in Table 3·2.

It is unlikely that Sunday or evening schools affected educational standards materially. Night-school attendance was highest in Norfolk, Suffolk and Essex, but although in those counties it may have served for some as an alternative to day schooling, schools of all kinds were difficult to maintain in rural areas and evening pupil numbers in all eight counties appear small (Appendix Q).[191] Sunday instruction, as in most rural areas, was rudimentary — in Hampshire even in the late 1860s the teachers were, though earnest, allegedly incompetent,[192] and the same was probably so in the other counties. In all eight, proportions at Sunday school in 1833 and 1851 were below the national average,[193] while in 1851 there were higher proportions at day than Sunday school in most of the towns in the region and all the counties — in Middlesex, Surrey and Sussex twice as many (Appendixes J, K). Of the 145 districts in the eight counties only fifteen had higher proportions at Sunday than day schools, ten of them — all with high illiteracy rates in 1866 — in Suffolk, Norfolk and Essex (Appendix I), suggesting that the part played by Sunday schools as substitute day schools was limited,[194] though undoubtedly some children attended no others.

All in all the educational level in these counties was very mixed, but despite high literacy levels in some, for working-class children in the remoter and poorer rural areas, and in those towns where child labour was concentrated, the situation left much to be desired. There is little evidence to suggest that by 1870 adequate schooling for all children could have been made a possibility without compulsion and increased public assistance.

The counties of the industrial north-west

Although the counties covered in this section — Lancashire, the West Riding and Cheshire — all had much agricultural land they were dominated economically by industry and mining (Appendix A). Factory production of textiles was widespread, with the West Riding specialising in woollen and worsted manufacture, Lancashire and Cheshire in cotton, and the Macclesfield and Congleton area in silk. Metal trades and engineering were strong in south Lancashire, the Sheffield area and other parts of the West Riding, and coal mining was spread across the manufacturing districts of the West Riding and Lancashire. A multitude of other industries existed in the area, too, in particular chemicals and glass in the Widnes and St. Helens district, salt in parts of Cheshire, fustian cutting around Manchester, Oldham and Warrington, calico printing, bleaching and dyeing in many textile districts and paper making, especially in Lancashire. The expansion of many of these contrasted with the continuing decline of the traditional hand-loom weaving of the area.

Urban development included the great commercial and manufacturing cities of Manchester (with Salford), Liverpool and Leeds and the other large industrial centres of Bradford and Sheffield, together with a network of other industrial towns interspersed with tracts of industrial hinterland. Near some of these large towns were, by mid-century, residential areas with significant proportions of the better-off — the Wirral peninsula and the West Derby district served Liverpool in this way, as Altrincham and Chorley districts did Manchester, and Otley and Knaresborough districts Leeds. Outside the industrial concentrations the cathedral cities of Chester and Ripon, the rising resorts of Southport and Blackpool, and market towns in all three counties, also contained higher proportions of the better-off and educated and of those in trading occupations than did the industrial centres.

Throughout the area were many small farms and holdings, and around the towns market gardens. Dairy farming predominated in Cheshire, but while parts of north Lancashire (the Fylde, the Lune Valley and Furness) contained rich arable land, much of rural Lancashire and the West Riding comprised remote, backward hilly districts given over to sheep.[195] Opportunities for industrial employment in the region kept rural population sparse. Half the farms in Cheshire in 1851 employed no labour.[196]

In contrast the industrial districts were heavily peopled and the population of the three counties doubled, 1851–71, to over 5 million. Labour was sucked in from far and wide, including large numbers of poor Irish. Many of the textile towns consisted largely of the operative class, though larger towns also contained significant numbers of middle-class people. Both urban and rural wages were relatively high,[197] but distress in industrial districts accompanied periodic trade crises. Living and working conditions were often unenviable and totally working-class communities tended to eschew middle-class standards of thrift, cleanliness, religiosity and general propriety. Early marriages were more frequent than in most parts, and illegitimacy in Lancashire and the West Riding well above average (Appendix H).

Children were regarded as an economic asset and the prevalence of child labour was a characteristic of the area. Bishop J. B. Sumner of Chester, whose diocese included the cotton factory belt, felt in the 1830s that 'new schemes of education would be a waste of labour ... so long as the demands for child labour are so great', resulting in schools being largely nurseries for infants.[198] In the 1830s and 1840s legislation excluded the youngest from the cotton and woollen mills, calico printing and the mines, and for older children in these industries reduced hours and imposed part-time schooling in some textile trades. Children over twelve, however, continued to be employed in textiles on a large scale and younger children to toil long hours in the many other industries unprotected by law into the 1860s, including bleaching, dyeing, fustian cutting, card setting, metal manufactures,[199] and silk production.[200] In agricultural districts there was much seasonal child labour, though pastoral farming gave more opportunities for schooling than was often the case in manufacturing areas.[201]

The 1851 census recorded (Appendix B) that children aged five to nine in Lancashire and the West Riding were employed proportionately as much as in the industrial midlands, though below the levels of Bedfordshire, Buckingham-shire and Hertfordshire.[202] Numerically, however, many more of such children were returned as workers in Lancashire and the West Riding than in any other county. Moreover, the situation improved less quickly than elsewhere. By 1871 the proportions of this age group returned as employed in the West Riding were a high as in Buckinghamshire, and in the West Riding and Lancashire they greatly exceeded in proportion and numerically those returned for the industrial midlands despite the many unregulated domestic industries of that area.

As for older boys and girls (ten to fourteen), again far greater numbers were returned as workers in 1851 in Lancashire and the West Riding than in any other county. In Cheshire numbers were lower but still substantial. By 1871 numbers of such children had actually risen in all three counties.[203] Even the proportion in Lancashire had not fallen and it joined the West Riding in having higher proportions of this age group at work than any county except Bedfordshire.

Further evidence of the high incidence of juvenile employment is provided in the proportions in 1851 of occupied persons under twenty in certain of the area's towns. These were on a par with those of the midland textile centres and much higher than those of towns elsewhere. The four great cities (Man-chester–Salford, Leeds, Liverpool and Sheffield), with more diverse economies and greater proportions of the middle classes than the smaller industrial towns, returned much lower levels (Appendix C). The low level in commercial Liverpool reflects the lack of jobs for under 14s in the city.[204]

In 1851 the largest proportion of boys aged ten to fourteen returned as employed was in the textile trades: 17 per cent of the age group in Cheshire, 21 per cent in Lancashire, 25 per cent in the West Riding. Coal mining and the iron and steel trades accounted for 5 per cent in Lancashire and 8 per cent in the West Riding, farm work 6 per cent in Cheshire, 3 per cent in the West Riding and 2 per cent in Lancashire, and employment as messengers, porters and the like 6 per cent in Lancashire and 3 per cent in the West Riding. By 1871 textiles still accounted for 10 per cent of the age group in Cheshire, 18 in the West Riding and 17 per cent in Lancashire, and coal mining and iron and steel trades 4 and 16 per cent in Lancashire and the West Riding. The only other significant proportions were those for agricultural labour in Cheshire and messengers and porters in the other two counties (all less than 4 per cent).

The majority of occupied girls returned in this age group (ten to fourteen) was in textiles in 1851: Cheshire 20 per cent, Lancashire 24 per cent, West Riding 27 per cent. The only other significant employment was in domestic service and 'nursing' (a euphemism for baby-minding): 6 per cent in Cheshire and Lancashire, 5 per cent in the West Riding. By 1871 textiles still accounted for 15, 23, and 25 per cent of these girls in Cheshire the West Riding, and Lancashire respectively, and domestic service (and nursing) had risen to 7 per cent in Lancashire and the West Riding and 8 per cent in Cheshire.

The census figures of child employment, however, provide only a partial picture. The proportions of children aged ten to fourteen not at school in 1851 (Appendix I) were, except for West Riding boys, much higher than those returned as employed. This was especially so for girls in all three counties. Of girls aged seven to ten not at school in Castleford (W.R.), for instance, the ratio of those at home to those at work was 8:1.[205] As in other regions,[206] many were doubtless employed at home or elsewhere, but the large towns contained bands of idle children.[207]

The swamping of traditional school facilities during the great expansion of population in the area from the late eighteenth century, combined with increased opportunities for child labour, created communities where regular day schooling was not the norm.[208] All three counties returned proportions of day-school pupils in 1818 below the national average, and though Cheshire rose above that level by 1833, Lancashire and the West Riding were still below it in 1851 (Appendix J). The comparative backwardness of the industrial towns of the area and their hinterlands has been discussed in Chapter 2.

Expansion of day schooling occurred slowly,[209] in 1840 many industrial towns lacking efficient inspected schools. Over the next three decades there was a gradual growth in the numbers of inspected schools, especially in the larger towns, but in those, and especially in the mining villages and smaller industrial towns, black spots remained, and improvement in the standards of public schooling was slow and erratic. In the 1850s, for instance, the proportions of Yorkshire Church school pupils learning to write declined.[210] Education in the West Riding was said to be as backward as in Siberia,[211] and in the 1860s to contain many children untaught 'as though they belonged to Fiji rather than to England'.[212] The well known enquiry of 1869 into Leeds, Manchester and Liverpool, however flawed in detail, showed with little doubt that thousands of city children, especially of labouring parents, lacked proper or often any schooling.[213] In rural parts there were fewer completely unschooled children but grant-aided schools and qualified teachers were often lacking.[214]

The efficacy of day schooling was affected greatly by the migratory habits of workpeople, many children seldom staying at one school for as long as a year and teachers continually 'attempting to fill the sieve which cannot . . . hold the water'.[215] The length of school life is difficult to determine. It was somewhat longer, especially for girls, in the rural areas than was the case in industrial districts,[216] where most pupils in public schools appear to have spent one to two years in the 1840s, rising to three years at the most in the 1860s, with girls leaving earlier than boys. At least three-quarters of pupils in those districts were aged ten or less even in the 1860s.[217] In the 1850s the length of school life in the West Riding actually fell with more children leaving before they were ten.[218] School contact was further reduced by great irregularity of attendance, most evident in girls.[219] Thus average attendance at Church schools in Sheffield even in 1871 was less than 54 per cent of the roll.[220] Indeed in the towns there were often more places in inspected schools than pupils, though not always in the right location.[221]

Religious factors were particularly significant in the region. The spread of Church schools and of grant-aided schools generally was hampered by the strength of Dissent (Appendix N), the deficiency of Anglican church provision in densely populated areas, and an influx of uneducated immigrants, particularly poor Catholic Irish.[222] In the smaller manufacturing towns and the industrial and mining villages a substantial Anglican middle class was often lacking; in the larger towns many leading citizens were strongly nonconformist. In some places in the 1830s and 1840s dissenters were unwilling to send their children to Church schools, said at Sheffield to be 'under the spiritual police of the state clergy',[223] while the Roman Catholic clergy sought to keep their flocks from Anglican schools despite the inadequate provision of Catholic ones.[224]

Church schools became acceptable to many dissenting parents,[225] but local financial support was meagre. Despite the campaign to expand Anglican schooling by channelling into the area disproportionately large amounts of Church and treasury monies,[226] which undoubtedly led to an expansion of Church schooling, many Anglican schools, especially outside the largest towns, persistently suffered from insufficient permanent funds to provide good staff and equipment.[227] Parish clergy often had to shoulder most of the burden of management and make good financial deficiencies.[228] Without this, advance would have been much slower, and where clerical enthusiasm was lacking, as in Ashton-under-Lyne and parts of Sheffield, Anglican schooling did not flourish.[229] Consequently many Church schools were not grant-aided and even in the 1850s some Lancashire clergy diverted parliamentary grants intended for day schools to Sunday schools.[230]

Nevertheless, the dissenters were less enthusiastic for day schooling than the Anglicans, disliked accepting government grants, and found it harder to equip and staff their schools. Moreover the British and Foreign School Society found it difficult to divert funds to the industrial north-west. In rural areas resources for nonconformist funding were lacking, and while in towns the dissenting employing class did provide assistance, even in places like Leeds, Bradford and Rochdale, concentrations of well-off dissenters failed to give support commensurate with their wealth and influence. In the 1850s, for example, Bradford subscribers to the British and Foreign School Society raised nor more than £15 p.a.[231] Manchester and Liverpool were unusual in supporting a large number of dissenting and British schools.[232]

Thus, while about a quarter of public-school pupils in Lancashire and the West Riding were at dissenting or British schools in 1851 and Lancashire had a higher proportion at Roman Catholic schools than any other county,[233] the vast majority of pupils attended Church schools, and even though Lancashire ranked well below the national average for Church scholars until 1857, by 1867 it had about reached that level (Appendixes L, M).

In the poorest areas where religious adherance was weak and in some places with concentrations of Irish Catholics, it was particularly hard to meet government requirements for grant aid or to find school pence.[234] Catholic public schools came late. Money was granted 'where least needed', complained the Catholic Poor School Committee in 1849, faced with the difficulties of schooling Manchester Catholics.[235] Despite the capitation grants of the 1850s such areas continued to find funding difficult.

The absence of significant numbers of middle-class people in the smaller manufacturing towns, the mining communities, the industrial hinterlands of towns, and even in some large conurbations like Sheffield, unincorporated until 1843, was another factor in the lack of local support for public schools. The larger merchants and manufacturers were too busy to interest themselves in education and often lived outside the industrial districts or left on achieving prosperity.[236] Nevertheless, for reasons of benevolence, practicality, and social control some textile manufacturers, both before and after factory legislation, provided evening, Sunday and sometimes day schools for their young workers and others, and this is well documented.[237] But while a minority became genuinely enthusiastic in promoting education, the vast majority showed little interest.[238] Some at first connived with parents to evade the law, or pressed them to send their children to the mill at the earliest opportunity.[239] Likewise, while some coalowners in the area provided or supported schooling[240] and railway companies established schools at Crewe and Doncaster,[241] employers outside textiles were usually totally indifferent to the welfare of child workers, ceasing to employ children coming under the half-time Acts. Before young children were banned from underground work Yorkshire coalowners were allegedly uncaring 'whether they were educated or debased'.[242]

In Lancashire there was still in the 1850s some prejudice against schooling the lower orders at all.[243] In the Sheffield metal district, where children were not directly employed by works owners, works schools were uncommon and even in the late 1850s the employing classes showed great reluctance to supporting any but Sunday schools.[244] No employers of hand-loom weavers are known to have provided schooling.[245]

In agricultural areas there are many examples of the landed classes supporting schools: in Cheshire they continued to do so despite great losses in the cattle plague of the 1860s.[246] In Doncaster district school provision was better in estate than freehold parishes, and this was probably so elsewhere, too.[247] In areas of small farms and market gardens little direct support came from the farming class. At mid-century Yorkshire farmers were allegedly 'opposed in every way' to education for labourers' children,[248] and both West Riding and Lancashire farmers were themselves considered less well educated than those elsewhere.[249] The smaller Cheshire farmers were not socially distinct from labourers and often illiterate.[250] In the 1860s some Yorkshire farmers were active as school managers,[251] but the attendance of offspring of smallholders and some farmers in the area was less regular than those of of such children in counties to the north.[252]

Parental indifference to schooling in the area was attributed by official observers sometimes to poverty but more often to greed and ignorance,[253] and while there is some evidence for this, a logical view of education differing from that of the middle classes is also discernible. A smattering of reading with perhaps a little writing at most was desired, but for all but infants earnings were often preferable. When legislation barred young children from textile mills parents sought to evade it, or placed their offspring in the mines at ages earlier than previously.[254] When legislation was applied to the mines Yorkshire parents for years collaborated with colliery officials to flout the law.[255] In the textile industry no pecuniary return appeared to attach to education.[256] Parents at Pendleton in 1838 saw no advantage in schooling and to many in Oldham in the 1840s no day schooling was acceptable even in prosperous times,[257] while labouring parents in Sheffield saw no need for anything more than Sunday schooling.[258]

When some mine managers were completely illiterate and owners of small mines barely schooled, it is not surprising that many colliers, though well paid, had a 'prevailing disinclination' to provide their children with day schooling.[259] In some Lancashire districts attempts to start Church schools in the 1840s failed through lack of demand, the only call being for dame schools for infants.[260] In some Yorkshire pit villages day schools were completely lacking and Sunday schools satisfied even parents who aspired for clerical jobs for their children. Even in the town of Barnsley fewer than one-third of children went to day school in 1841.[261]

Similarly in the fustian trades, where many masters in the 1860s were still largely illiterate, children were put to work as soon as possible, few ever attended day schools even though Mondays and Tuesdays were taken as holidays, and many were 'too tired' for night or Sunday schools. Thus at Warrington in the 1860s, 40 per cent of fustian cutters under thirteen and 60 per cent aged thirteen to eighteen could not read and the rest only indifferently.[262]

The excuse of poverty was frequent. In the bleaching and dyeing trades in the mid-1850s some parents claimed poverty or employers' pressure for early child employment, but times of prosperity often led to a fall in school attendance[263] while in unemployment free schooling was rejected.[264] A Bolton surgeon alleged that those with large families lived on their children's wages: 'they are quite aristocratical among workpeople'.[265] Many attended no church and did not send their children even to Sunday school so that at eight or nine they began work completely illiterate.[266]

There were, of course, those who could genuinely not afford schooling, among whom were depressed hand-loom weavers of the three counties, in 1840 still favouring education but requiring their children's labour or wages to make ends meet. Thus few of their children over age eight attended day school and Sunday attendance was limited by lack of decent clothes.[267] A survey of Manchester and Salford about 1850 showed lower school attendance in the poorest districts, with far more children idle than at school or work, half of whom (aged three to fourteen) had never been to day school.[268] Further surveys in the 1860s revealed much the same situation in Manchester and Liverpool with numbers of such children on the increase, and also with many slum dwellers hostile to civilised behaviour and having no control over their offspring.[269] There were indeed sizeable numbers of the 'submerged' classes in the industrial towns, living in conditions of destitution and near savagery, who certainly had no interest in education.[270] In Bradford in the 1850s they included 13,000–20,000 migratory Irish,[271] and Liverpool, Leeds and other Yorkshire and Lancashire textile towns had similar concentrations.[272] Mary Carpenter in 1861 described 'a large class' of degraded children in Warrington, 'who swarm the streets utterly untaught and uncultivated'.[273]

Nevertheless, growing school rolls illustrate that increasingly some working-

class parents were appreciative of education.[274] In Manchester and Salford
about 1850, for instance, 37 per cent of children from the poorest districts were
attending school, three-quarters public school,[275] and though the poverty
resulting from the cotton famine of the 1860s affected school attendance,[276] the
eager take-up of special free schooling by unemployed younsters and adults
shows some desire for learning, though the accompanying free food and
avoidance of stone breaking under the poor law no doubt was also influential.[277]

The half-time system, at first disliked, became accepted in the textile
industries by parents and others as a practical fusion of the needs of schooling
and work, and for some time the educational standards of half-timers
compared favourably with those of other children.[278] Poor schooling in factory
and other schools, however, persisted[279] and as school attendance generally
improved the factory children fell behind.[280] In the late 1850s none of a group
of Bradford mill girls could read.[281]

Again the use of Sunday schools, night schools and adult institutions attest to
the existence of some appreciation of education. The industrial north-west was
remarkable for its concentration of mechanics' and other institutes and other
organisations, demonstrating political and cultural interests among a section of
the working classes. The strength of dissent and radical politics suggests, too,
the existence of a literate, if proletarian, culture to set against the evidence of
widespread cultural degredation.[282]

In many parts of the area the Sunday school often met working-class needs
better than the day school and was seen by parents and the dissenting middle-
classes as equally important.[283] For many children it was the main, often the
sole, means of formal education. Consequently Sunday attendance was high
(Appendix N) with pupils at dissenting establishments greatly outnumbering
those at Anglican ones. In the 1830s through the 1850s Sunday attendance
exceeded day-school attendance at county level, in almost all towns for which
data is readily available, and in the majority of registration districts (Appendixes
F, J, K).[284] The excess was greatest in industrial and some remote rural areas,
and least in residential and many country areas, underlining working-class use
of the Sunday school, which was free and did not interfere with child labour, as
an alternative to day schooling.[285] In Oldham, for example, they were in the
1840s 'the schools' for most parents.[286] In Liverpool, however, lack of
opportunity for child labour, resulted in the 1830s in lower Sunday-school
attendance than in Manchester and Salford, but higher day-school attendance.[287]

The Sunday schools were undoubtedly part of the working-class culture of
the area, but their educational impact is difficult to assess. They catered for an
age range older,[288] and perhaps more receptive of instruction, than the infant
day schools, and attendance was extended over long periods, sometimes into
adulthood. Many undoubtedly learned to read there and a much smaller

number to write.[289] Yet although they probably provided a civilising influence[290] and contributed to a reading culture, sabattarian objections to writing instruction led to it being dropped especially after mid-century, or transferred to night schools.[291] Moreover, in exclusively working-class areas, Sunday-school teachers were drawn from manual labourers, some mere children themselves, whose own standard of education was minimal.[292] Thus many attended for years without acquiring any useful literacy skills.[293] 'I go to Sunday school: I cannot read or write' (boy aged sixteen, 1841) was a common statement to investigators.[294] Night schools, which throughout the period also catered for those deficient in other schooling, had in comparison with other regions a relatively high proportion of pupils (Appendix Q),[295] but not sufficient in numbers to have greatly affected local educational levels.[296]

In the areas particularly reliant on Sunday schooling, like many pit villages,[297] educational standards were strikingly low. In 1842 only a quarter of boys aged thirteen to eighteen in a Lancashire sample could write their names and less than 1 per cent of girls, while in two groups of West Riding mine boys (aged six to eighteen) only 6 and 2 per cent could write, and of 150 young worsted workers at Halifax 11 per cent could do so.[298] Of some 500 boys (ten to seventeen) at a Bradford iron company in 1845 over 80 per cent could not write, though many claimed to read.[299] Such examples could be multiplied.

Marriage mark statistics bear out the persistent educational backwardness of much of the area. From the 1840s through the 1860s all three counties returned overall proportions of marks well above the national level. The national average was approached in Cheshire only from 1870 and in Lancashire and the West Riding not until the 1880s. Even in 1870 Lancashire and the West Riding had reached only a level achieved thirty years before by some counties further north (Appendix D).

Levels of bridal illiteracy were a crucial ingredient of this poor showing. In the 1840s male illiteracy in the area was only a few percentage points above the national average, closing to that level by the mid-1850s in the West Riding, and by 1870 in Lancashire and Cheshire. Bridal illiteracy in Lancashire, 1839–45 however, exceeded that of every other county and in the other two counties was exceeded only in Monmouthshire. Not until the late 1870s did the Cheshire female rate approach the national level, while bridal illiteracy in the West Riding and Lancashire was still 6–7 percentage points above it in 1885.

It follows that high levels of bridal marks were characteristic of the most illiterate districts. In Lancashire in 1841–5 they reached 80 per cent and more in Blackburn, Rochdale, Burnley, Ashton-under-Lyne,[300] Oldham, Haslingden, Bolton, Wigan, Bury and Chorley, while grooms' marks in those districts ranged from 49 to 61 per cent, higher than men in the rural districts of the area and in Liverpool and Manchester.[301] Likewise in the most illiterate Cheshire districts in 1845 (Stockport, Macclesfield, Northwich, Nantwich) female illiteracy ranged from 61–75 per cent and male 37–50,[302] and a similar difference is discernible in the least literate West Riding districts.[303]

An analysis of marriage marks in 1856 (Maps 6, 7 and Appendix F) reveals a belt of districts with illiteracy levels above the national average, from Ormskirk and Prescot in the west, to Tadcaster and Pontefract in the east, and including Lancashire, as far north as the Clitheroe and Preston districts, and parts of the northern West Riding, and in the south most of Cheshire and parts of the southern West Riding. Districts with rates lower than the national average comprise parts of north Lancashire and north and south-east West Riding, together with West Derby, Wirral and Great Boughton abutting on the Mersey estuary, and Altrincham and Chorlton straddling the Lancashire–Cheshire border.

Appendix G provides comparisons of the rates by districts in 1856,[304] 1866 and 1871 and reveals certain patterns. The twenty-one least illiterate districts in the three counties in 1856 (20–34 per cent marks) included rural parts of north Lancashire and the north West Riding (predominantly pastoral like the highly literate districts of the North Riding, Cumberland and Westmorland on which they abutted)[305] which tended to have static or declining populations[306] and in some cases diminishing concentrations of textile workers. Also in this category were other largely rural West Riding districts[307] and the rural districts of Wirral or West Derby, which were also residential areas for Liverpool, with contiguous Great Boughton, embracing the cathedral city of Chester, and further east Chorlton and Altrincham (including Knutsford and Wilmslow), where the better-off from Manchester increasingly settled.

A middle category (35–46 per cent marks) comprised districts embracing the larger cities and their environs (Liverpool, Manchester, Salford, Leeds, Sheffield–Rotherham), the district containing Wakefield, a county town with some industry and mines, and some districts containing industrial and market towns as well as farming areas.[308] Within the different parts of these districts there were probably wide variations: in Pontefract district, for instance, the market town of that name had a much lower illiteracy rate than did Castleford, the mining and industrial part of the district.[309]

The twenty-four most illiterate districts in 1856 (48–60 per cent marks) were characterised mainly by textile production and mining and included almost the whole of industrial south Lancashire with adjoining Stockport (Ches),[310] and a connecting group of West Riding woollen districts (Todmorden, Keighley, Bradford, Dewsbury) as well as the coal district of Barnsley, the metal district of Ecclesall Bierlow (W.R.), and the salt mining district of Northwich (Ches). Of the fifteen most illiterate districts thirteen were in Lancashire.

In general the 1856 pattern persisted in 1866 and 1871, the most striking changes over the period being improvements in the relative positions of Halifax, Ormskirk, Todmorden, Keighley, Skipton, Pateley Bridge, Ashton-

MAP 6

Percentages of marriage marks, 1856: Lancashire, Cheshire. Bold figures indicate
percentages above the national level of 35 per cent.

ULVERSTON
34

LANCASTER
30

GARSTANG
31

CLITHEROE
36

N

FYLDE
35

PRESTON
56

BURNLEY
56

BLACKBURN
59

CHORLEY
55

LANCASHIRE

HASLING-
DEN
52

ROCHDALE
57

ORMSKIRK
52

WIGAN
61

BOLTON
54

BURY
45

OLDHAM
53

MANCHESTER **39**
SALFORD **43**

LIVERPOOL
37

W.
DERBY
22

PRESCOT
55

LEIGH
59

BARTON
U.I.
48

CHORLTON
29

ASHTON U.L.
53

WARRINGTON
61

STOCKPORT
53

WIRRAL
20

RUNCORN
47

ALTRINCHAM
31

MACCLESFIELD
45

NORTHWICH
50

GREAT
BOUGHTON
33

CHESHIRE

CONGLETON
46

NANTWICH
43

0   5   10   15   20   MILES

MAP 7
Percentages of marriage marks, 1856: West Riding of Yorkshire. Bold figures indicate
percentages above the national level of 35 per cent. District boundaries are from the
Census, 1851. By 1856 the new districts of Wetherby and Great Ouseburn had been
formed, largely out of Knaresborough district: the new boundaries of this area are not
shown here.

under-Lyne, Rochdale and Oldham, and a decline in those of Pontefract,
Thorne, Sheffield, Hunslet, Liverpool, Salford and Ulverston. Some of the
changes, as in Hunslet and Pontefract, certainly resulted from alterations to
district boundaries. Ormskirk benefited from the growth of Southport as a
resort, watering place, and as a residential area for Liverpool and Man-

chester,[311] while Ulverston's decline coincided with the growth of iron and cotton manufacturing and the virtual creation of Barrow-in-Furness as an industrial centre, and Sheffield's with a great expansion of metal and coal production. Pateley Bridge may have improved consequent on the migration of rural workers and the closure in the 1860s of a railway works, and Skipton from an exodus of hand-loom weavers and lead miners. Improvements in other districts, especially Halifax, Rochdale, Oldham and Ashton, are not easily explicable in demographic terms. Manchester and Liverpool districts showed slower rates of improvement, 1841–71, than other Lancashire registration districts, perhaps as the better-off moved to nearby areas.[312]

Considering the large scale immigration into the region, the greater than usual impact of Sunday and adult education,[313] the incidence of half-timers, and the high proportion of infant pupils, a close match between local schooling levels and later illiteracy levels might not be expected. Application of the product moment correlation coefficient formula to the data for the registration districts of the region provides, for the relationship between day-school levels in 1851 and illiteracy in 1866, coefficients of -0.55 and -0.54 for Lancashire and the West Riding, though only -0.20 for Cheshire,[314] and an overall -0.60 for the region. The tendency for a connection between the two variables is illustrated for the districts of the region as a whole by a simple exercise presented in Table 3·3.

In Lancashire, where twenty-two (of twenty-six) districts in 1866 had illiteracy levels above the national average, sixteen had had lower than average proportions of day-school pupils in 1851.[315] In Cheshire however, seven (of ten) districts in 1866 had above-average illiteracy, but only one (Stockport)

TABLE 3·3

Illiteracy rates and schooling

% population in attendance at day school, 1851	Illiteracy rates 1860: number of districts		
	10–28% marks 34 districts	29–34% marks 17 districts	35–59% marks 21 districts
15	1 ⎫	⎫	⎫
14	2 ⎬ 11	⎬ 2	⎬ 1
13	2 ⎪		
12	6 ⎭	2 ⎭	1 ⎭
11	5 ⎫	3 ⎫	5 ⎫
10	3 ⎪	8 ⎪	1 ⎪
9	3 ⎬ 13	3 ⎬ 15	5 ⎬ 20
8	2 ⎪	— ⎪	6 ⎪
7	— ⎭	1 ⎭	3 ⎭

Note
Some districts omitted because not in existence in 1851 or 1866. Boundary changes in others represented above make the comparison between schooling and later levels of marks less feasible than in most other parts of England. These figures can only be approximate.
Source: Based on Appendix F.

below-average at school in 1851. In the West Riding, too, while seventeen (of thirty-seven) districts were above average for marks in 1866, only six (of twenty-nine)[316] had previously had less than average proportions at school (Appendix D). The persistently high illiteracy rates of brides, however, certainly bears out what we know of girls' schooling. In fifty-seven or the sixty-four districts more boys than girls were at school in 1851 and in none were there more girls attending than boys (Appendix F).[317] In the industrial places girls attended school more irregularly and for a shorter time than boys, and when at school often spent more time on sewing than writing or arithmetic.[318]

County proportions of pupils at private schools were above average in 1851 in Cheshire and the West Riding (Appendix J). For reasons discussed elsewhere[319] a direct relationship between these and later literacy rates is unlikely, and indeed no very obvious connection at district level is discernible (Appendix F), though some districts of high illiteracy, like Stockport, did rely heavily on them, and there was a tendency for girls to attend them more than boys.[320] All the official reports commented adversely on the dame and common day schools of the area, often probably with justice, but many of the large number of unaided and uninspected public schools and some assisted schools were also held in low esteem by the inspectorate. Thus the uninspected public schools of Liverpool were said to be proportionately more numerous than Manchester's and of lower quality.[321]

The continued widespread, if diminishing, use of uninspected and private schools in the area[322] at a time when aided school standards were improving probably worked to the educational disadvantage of the area.[323] Moreover, the threefold expansion of half-timers in the textile industry, 1838–68,[324] merely added to the numbers for whom full-time schooling was impossible — and in the Cheshire silk mills full-time work could start at eleven.[325] Nor did the exclusion of the youngest from the textile factories guarantee they were sent to school.[326] Outside the textile industry extension of the half-time system tended only to result in refusal to employ children covered by the Acts and their dispersal to trades difficult to regulate or to idleness at home,[327] or, as in Manchester following the Workshops Regulation Act of 1867, widespread disregard of the law.[328]

While it is true than many more people in the area could read to some extent than could write[329] and that for many working-class people this seemed enough, the marriage mark statistics do reveal a level of literacy in the industrial districts of the north-west far below that of much of the country. This, in conjunction with other evidence, such as the revelation of widespread educational deprivation in Leeds, Liverpool and Manchester in 1869,[330] makes it difficult not to agree with some contemporary observers[331] that only compulsory full-time aided schooling was likely to meet the needs of an area where such high levels of child employment and concentrations of poverty existed. W. F. Hook, vicar of Leeds, had advocated state schooling in the 1840s,[332] and by the 1860s even erstwhile opponents like Edward Miall, the Bradford M.P., and Edward Baines, of Leeds, realised that the voluntary system could not cope alone.[333]

PART II

DETAILED STUDIES

CHAPTER 4

The midland counties

Economic and social structure

The six counties considered in this chapter — Derbyshire, Leicestershire, Nottinghamshire, Staffordshire, Warwickshire and Worcestershire — were characterised in the mid-nineteenth century by their concentrations of industry and population.[1] By 1851 the west midlands was the third most populous English conurbation, embracing Birmingham (233,000 population), Leicester, Nottingham, Wolverhampton, Derby (40,000–60,000), Coventry, Dudley, Worcester and Walsall (26,000–36,000), Kidderminster (18,000), many centres of 6,000–12,000 and a number of smaller towns. Many midland towns, were, however, not distinct urban centres set in rural hinterlands. The textile towns of Nottingham, Derby, Leicester and Coventry, for example, were surrounded by populous industrial villages, while in the Potteries and the Black Country town merged into town in a vast blanket of industrial activity. These areas experienced considerable population growth, and by 1901 the population of the six counties had more than doubled over 1851.

Coal mining was especially significant in Nottinghamshire, Derbyshire and Staffordshire, with some parts having a very high density of miners: in Dudley district about a quarter of the male population in 1851. With coal went the various metal manufactures important in Staffordshire, Warwickshire, Worcestershire and to some extent Derbyshire. Pre-eminent in this activity were Birmingham and the Black Country, the latter covering a rough quadrilateral, with Wolverhampton near its north-west corner, the Walsall area at its north-east, its south-western fringes taking in Stourbridge, and in the south-east — around Harborne and Handsworth — merging into Birmingham. In ten registration districts in the Birmingham–Black Country area in 1851 a quarter of the metal workers of the country were to be found. Twenty-nine per cent of adult males and 7 per cent of females were engaged in such work, though within the Black Country there was a high degree of local specialisation in the types of metal goods produced.

In the Potteries coal was important but earthenware dominated, centred around the parishes and townships of Stoke-on-Trent, Longton, Fenton,

Hanley, Shelton, Cobridge, Burslem, Longport and Tunstall. In the Stoke registration district in 1851 38 per cent of adult males and 20 per cent of females were engaged in the industry and at Wolstanton 32 and 17 per cent. These larger townships were interspersed with smaller industrial hamlets including Wedgwood's Etruria. Hosiery and lace making was focused on Derby, Leicester and Nottingham with their scores of satellite villages and small towns. By 1844, 90 per cent of British stocking frames were found in this area and high proportions of men and women were engaged in these trades. Silk manufacture was centred in and about Coventry, Foleshill and Nuneaton (Warwicks.), Derby and in Leek (Staffs.), linking with the Cheshire silk centres of Macclesfield and Congleton. Many females were employed in glove making in the Worcester area, and carpet weaving was significant at Kidderminster. Other important midland industries included glass making at Stourbridge, Kings Norton, Birmingham, Aston, West Bromwich and Dudley, salt production at Stafford and Weston-upon-Trent, and shoemaking at Stafford and Stone, while Burton-on-Trent, isolated from the main industrial areas, owed its population growth entirely to brewing.[2]

The six midland counties thus represented a remarkable concentration of industrial occupations. All had well above the national average (10·2 per cent) of adults employed in manufacture in 1851: Derbyshire 17 per cent; Leicestershire 21; Nottinghamshire 21; Staffordshire 17; Warwickshire 19; and Worcester 17. Only Lancashire (24) and the West Riding (26) had higher proportions than Leicestershire and Nottinghamshire, and only by Cheshire and Bedfordshire were the other four midland counties surpassed in this respect.[3] In addition child labour, discussed below, was at a high level. Nevertheless, agricultural employment in 1851 was also significant in some parts (Appendix A): in Derbyshire, Nottinghamshire and Worcestershire the proportion of adult men so employed was near the national average of 26·5 per cent; in Leicestershire above that. In Staffordshire and Warwickshire it was considerably lower (17 and 19) but because of the high total population the actual density of men employed in farming was above the national average — in industrial south Staffordshire, for example, nearly as high as in Hertfordshire, while Warwickshire had more persons in agricultural occupations than Worcestershire. In Staffordshire, markets, including cattle markets, remained important even in the larger industrial towns, while outside the manufacturing districts other towns (like Uttoxeter) were essentially market centres. Whereas proportions of industrial workers continued to rise, by 1881 percentages of farm workers had, however, fallen in all the midland counties to about half that forty years before.[4]

Forms of industrial organisation determined the social structure of local communities.[5] The midland manufacturing districts in the first half of the nineteenth century illustrate very well how misconceived is the view of the industrial revolution as an ubiquitous conversion of rural workers into townsmen, and the general replacement of the domestic system of production by power-driven factories. The various textile industries of the midlands were, indeed, in this period to a great extent found in rural as well as urban settings and based for the most part on the labour of hand workers unassisted by power, working in their own homes or small workshops. The metal trades of the Black Country were similarly structured. Even mining and iron manufacture was conducted by workers organised in small units, and though larger units of production were found in pottery manufacture, there was certainly no dominance there of power-driven machinery. The midland industries were, with some exceptions, highly labour-intensive, with the merchant capitalist, the middleman, the small master or partnership, and the individual working family the norm.

Partly as a consequence, industry was topographically less concentrated than in Lancashire, with higher proportions of semi-skilled workers, and was less diluted by any sizable class of superior artisans, tradesmen, shopkeepers and clerks, as might be found in, for example, market towns, or where manufacturing was confined to urban centres surrounded by agricultural districts. Despite these common characteristics the varying economic fortunes of the dominant industries and differences in the structure of those industries, resulted in diversity in midland communities, and this diversity was reflected in, among other things, general attitudes towards education and the place of children.

The structure of the hosiery industry (with silk wares concentrated mainly in Derbyshire, cotton mainly in Nottinghamshire and woollens mainly in Leicestershire) was chiefly domestic, with the larger towns acting as marketing and putting-out centres, and in which the more skilled processes were carried out. The run-of-the-mill production was found not only in these centres but throughout the village communities whose inhabitants tended to be less skilled and more poorly paid, being unprotected by agreed 'list' prices sometimes exacted from the merchants by better organised town workers. At the bottom of the social scale was the individual domestic framework knitter operating in his home alone with his family or with a journeyman or two. But this was not the sturdy independent home worker selling at will his own products. Both he and the small-scale employer, producing in sheds and workshops, were usually tightly tied to middlemen, variously called undertakers or bag hosiers, who acted as links with the merchant hosiers, distributing raw materials and taking back finished articles. A vicious system of frame renting, prevalent in Leicestershire and Nottinghamshire but also present in Derbyshire, was the chain binding the individual worker to the middleman or direct to the merchant. Merchant hosiers and middlemen charged a 'rent' to each knitter to whom they gave work, whether the frame was theirs or the knitter's. In slack times work was spread over the same number of frames as in busy periods, or even more, and generally encouragement given to the use of frames by as many as possible, including women and children and semi-skilled rural folk, so that rent income could be maintained. By the early nineteenth century there were very few independent knitters. In the Nottingham area a comparatively small, and reducing, number of large and medium-sized Nottingham firms controlled thousands of domestic weavers in the city and the hinterland villages. A similar situation pertained in Leicester and Leicestershire. Except in parts of Derbyshire the midland textile merchants tended to work, especially in the villages, through middlemen. Of these, bag hosiers, who combined middlemen functions with direct employment, dominated some villages, which fared worse at their hands than they would have at those of the larger firms and their agents. The middlemen and bag hosiers were often drawn from the ranks of the framework knitters, or from those who had started as small farmers or even from labourers. Admittance to the status of the merchant hosier was more difficult for the ordinary workman. In Nottingham it was very unusual for those lower in the economic hierarchy to rise into the ranks of the small group of hereditary 'gentlemen' hosiers, as they called themselves, who came generally from the educated middle class. Indeed, the gulf between these men and the framework knitters was, it has been said, 'much greater than between the Manchester cotton manufacturer and his workmen'.[6] It is true that in some villages and in the town of Derby a situation existed somewhat similar to the cotton factory system where employers including small masters, employed substantial numbers of hands directly in their own workshops. But the regularity of hours and factory discipline was lacking, and wages were no better than the earnings of the domestic knitters.

With an excess of labour where other employment was lacking the hosiery industry in this period was in long-term decline, and workpeople were caught in a conservative and inflexible structure, with real wages falling. Understandably, but against reason, they clung to a way of life for themselves and their children that involved increasing labour and deepening poverty. Chartism found support from the Nottingham weavers but the generality of knitters were too concerned with basic survival for political activity. Technical difficulties delayed the application of steam power but, more important, the stockingers had no wish to change their domestic status and feared the competition of factories, while manufacturers and middlemen were not inclined to give up frame renting and low wage costs to invest large sums in fixed capital. Steam-powered factories were established in Leicester and Loughborough in the 1840s and within the next decade such factories were on the increase in both Nottinghamshire and Leicestershire, but hand-frame production continued to be significant until frame renting was abolished by law in 1874.

Other developments in these districts towards mid-century tended to promote greater prosperity. Though they involved factory production, however, they also spawned domestic work. The introduction of boot and shoe making in Leicester after 1848 required little capital and the typical business unit was the family, and much outwork was undertaken on hired machines. More important was the progress of the machine-made lace industry which offered in Derbyshire, Nottinghamshire and Leicestershire expanding and regular employment, higher income and better working conditions to a growing number of superior artisans. From the mid-1820s only a modicum of capital was necessary to set up as an employer or small independent operator, and opportunities for social and economic advancement increased still further from the 1850s. The industry was, however, despite its name, essentially a domestic one. From 1836 some thirty steam-powered lace factories existed in Nottingham and forty large workshops with concentrations of hand-worked machines, but the typical unit of production until the late 1840s was the small workshop. Merchant capitalists, renting out machines, existed side by side with independent artisans employing a few women or relations. Steam power only gradually took over during the period 1840–60. Even then there was much domestic outwork involved in finishing processes and in 1861 two or three times as many women and children were engaged in this way as in the factories. Even by 1865, when there were 135 'larger factories' in Nottingham, small production units and individual operators still continued, sometimes combining to hire power. For much of this period, therefore, the social distance between lace employers and workmen was much less than in the hosiery trade, and the social relationship between small manufacturers, independent operators, and skilled workmen was close. The Chartists drew little support from the Nottingham lace workers. And for most of our period, a society was perpetuated in the hosiery districts in which putting-out centres like Belper, Nottingham, Leicester, Loughborough and Derby controlled the domestic outwork of whole families dispersed through a large number of towns and villages.

The domestic system was also significant in the silk ribbon industry of the Coventry and Leek areas[7] which prospered until the slump of the 1860s. In Coventry the socio-economic relationships in the industry were flexible and upward mobility possible. In Coventry by the 1830s the ribbon industry was in the hands of a numerous class of small independent capitalists ('manufacturers') employing between ten and a hundred looms and an even larger class of 'first-hand journeymen', who were, despite their name, independent manufacturers on a smaller scale. Between these men and their employees ('second-hand journeymen') there was little social division, for advancement to 'first-hand' status came with age, and 'first-hand' men with luck and application could hope to become 'manufacturers'. The application of power to ribbon production created a class of unskilled factory hands, but even by 1860 there were few factories and this class was comparatively small. Coventry's second industry, the prosperous watchmaking trade, was, moreover, both skilled and domestic.

In Foleshill and the country districts round Coventry, however, the depressed picture of the framework knitters was repeated, for there ribbon production continued on the outdated single-hand loom and the weavers, unable to compete with the multiple looms used in Coventry, earned far less and were the first to feel the pinch in recessions. Between these extremes was the situation at Leek and Derby, where power production of ribbons both created an unskilled factory class and depressed the domestic producers. Hand-loom production remained significant in the broad silk trade organised similarly to Coventry's with less prosperity but without the degradation of the framework knitters, though both undertakers and journeymen sent their children into the factories.[8]

Kidderminster by mid-century accounted for a large proportion of British carpet manufacture.[9] Most of the working population was directly or indirectly concerned with this trade which was concentrated in large shops with men and youths working unpowered machines for wages, though favouring the irregular hours typical of domestic industry. The advent of steam-driven looms in the 1850s abruptly changed the picture, causing massive unemployment and large-scale emigration, with those remaining subject to the discipline of the powered factory. The quick death of the hand-loom carpet weavers thus compared with the lingering one of the hosiery villages.

Burton-on-Trent differed from other midland centres in its concentration on brewing, which by mid-century was in the hands of a few large-scale employers. A great economic gulf existed between the workforce and the employers, who kept down costs by taking on farm labourers from the surrounding countryside in winter.[10]

In the coal, metal and earthenware districts working conditions were as unpleasant as in the textile districts, but the social structure and outlook were often very different. In the Staffordshire, Derbyshire and Nottinghamshire coalfields some landowners, like the Duke of Devonshire, worked their own mines direct or through agents and bailiffs. More often large proprietors leased to entrepreneurs who tendered the day-to-day running to self-employed contractors, called butties — unskilled small capitalists, drawn from the ranks of the ordinary miners, to whom they remained socially akin. As large coal and iron companies emerged by mid-century, mining engineers, colliery managers and other officials became more common, but the butty system survived and the mining communities remained almost exclusively working-class, culturally rough and uncivilised, but relatively well paid.[11]

In north Staffordshire the miners lived partly in distinct mining villages, partly mixed up with the potters. In the Black Country miners, metal workers and others lived more generally cheek-by-jowl.[12] Coal mining and iron production were indeed linked and firms frequently had an interest in both. Though there were large-scale operators, however, many Black Country ironmasters were in business on a very small scale, sometimes as a sideline to coal or clay mining. Important landed proprietors, like Lord Dudley, leased large blast furnaces, forges and rolling mills rather than worked them direct,[13] but on the whole landed property in south Staffordshire was much dispersed. Hence, it was said, 'there is a colliery in almost every field', and the small coal producers often combined to run furnaces, as did groups of local tradesmen. Such operations were much dependent on loan capital. Thomas Butler, who visited the area in 1815, found that 'there is hardly an ironmaster in this neighbourhood worth a groat',[14] but though relatively small scale in production terms their total workforce could number hundreds.

Of the structure of the multifarious metal manufacturing industries of the Black Country, Birmingham and elsewhere in the midlands, it is difficult to generalise.[15] In most metal trades workpeople enjoyed some prosperity. In the Birmingham area small-scale entrepreneurs and a multitude of small work-shops, not using power, were the rule, with little economic or social gap between master and man, since most owners of workshops and small factories had themselves been workmen. Even in 1870 probably fewer than twenty Birmingham firms in these trades employed over 500 people. In many of these trades a class of factors organised finance, marketing, co-ordination of processes, and so on, and provided a social and economic cement, quite different from the exploiting middlemen found in the hosiery industry. Much of the labour force in the metal crafts was skilled and well paid, and even though working conditions were sordid labour relations were good and strikes few. Moreover, owing to the great variety of occupations, members of the same family frequently worked in different trades, 'so that if one trade is in a depressed state, another may be in a thriving condition'.[16]

Two exceptions to these relatively satisfactory conditions existed — in the Birmingham pin workshops, depressing places of exploitation employing large numbers of children, and in the nail industry.[17] The nailers of Derbyshire, Worcestershire, the Black Country and Birmingham were often technically independent.[18] In fact their situation was similar to that of the framework knitters: they were in the hands of merchant capitalists and their agents (or 'foggers') who put out raw materials and collected the hand-forged nails. An excess of numbers depressed earnings and resulted in endless toil for whole families, with, as at Belper (Derbys.), nailers among the most pauperised sections of the community.[19] From 1830 a losing battle against machine-made nails was fought, the employers weapons being low wages and the truck system. Like the framework knitters, the nailers unwisely continued to put their children to the trade in the perverse hope that things would improve, so that they survived to the 1890s as an anachronistic domestic trade. There was considerable social distinction between the large nail masters and the nailers, but the smaller factors were described in 1841 as 'only one degree above' the poorest class of nailer. Chain making, as carried out in the Stourbridge area, was similarly organised.[20]

The pottery industry, concentrated mainly in the Staffordshire region to which it gave its name but also present in Derbyshire, had by 1841 many enterprises with more than 800 employees each, and large-scale 'factories' increased in numbers in mid-century. Yet the typical firm was a family business or partnership, and many were small. Most potters were weekly wage earners, but advance was possible: as late as 1860 almost all the sixty potteries in Longton, for example, were run by men who had started at the bench. Moreover, though steam power was used by some large enterprises, much of the work could be undertaken only by highly skilled hand workers, perhaps accounting for the absence of Luddism in the Potteries, and for the absence, too, of a strong trade union movement until the second half of the century — though there were strikes and unrest in the 1840s.[21]

Despite differences midland industrial areas were thus characterised by the prevalence of domestic, small-scale enterprises using family labour and not dependent on power and by the concentrated sprawl of urban communities and industrial villages. Also striking was the extent to which workmen, small (and often large) masters and middlemen were socially akin, producing an overwhelmingly working-class ethos.[22] Thus the proportions of persons of independent means in the six midland counties, it was reckoned in 1841, fell short of the national average by 20 per cent in Worcestershire and Warwickshire, 43 per cent in Staffordshire and 27–32 per cent in the other three counties (Appendix H). Whole areas given over to concentrated manufacture were environmentally unattractive and retained only those forced to inhabit them for a livelihood.[23] Of the Black Country in 1847 it was written that 'those who are not acquainted with such districts can scarcely form a conception of how [they] ... appear to be occupied by *workpeople* alone'.[24] Considering this and the sordid, overpopulated unpleasantness of most of the midland industrial towns and districts in mid-century and later,[25] it is not surprising that early marriages were well above the national average in all the midland counties (except Warwickshire), while in Nottinghamshire, Warwickshire, and Worcestershire illegitimate births also exceeded the average for the country as a whole (Appendix H).

Despite the concentration of industry in the midlands, however, the large population provided a ready market for food, and farming on the whole prospered in the area in mid-century.[26] Pasture farming predominated in Derbyshire, and Leicestershire, and was significant in Nottinghamshire and Warwickshire, while there was more arable in Staffordshire and Worcestershire. Dairy farming and market gardening was profitable near towns and in the Evesham and Pershore districts there was a concentration of fruit and vegetable growing. Patterns of land ownership and occupancy, however, varied somewhat. In Derbyshire, Nottinghamshire and Staffordshire much agricultural land was in the hands of large proprietors. Some 31 per cent of the area of Derbyshire and Staffordshire (excluding waste) was held in estates of over 10,000 acres; in Nottinghamshire 38 per cent, concentrated in the west of the county. In Warwickshire the national average of 24 per cent pertained, while in Leicestershire (14) and Worcestershire (16) large estates were much less common.[27]

A great deal of land in the midlands, however, was leased and there were also many small freeholders. In Derbyshire farms were generally small with very few of over 300 acres; in Nottinghamshire, where 31 per cent of the land was owned in estates of less than 1,000 acres, and gentry were generally resident, farm sizes averaged 300–500 acres in the north, but only 70–150 in the southeast. In Warwickshire, too, there was a large body of resident landlords and a high proportion of smaller landowners. Farms in the rich Avon valley were largish, averaging 300 acres; in the south-west, however, farms varied in size from 150 to 200 acres, but many were smaller. In the south-east a large number of small occupiers held farms of 100 to 150 acres, while in the north, particularly in the Birmingham area, farming merged into market gardening. In Worcestershire, too, there were many small landowners, in some areas specialising in market gardening and fruit growing. In Staffordshire James Caird in 1850 noted the large class of tenants with smallholdings, especially in and around the towns, who had little capital and were worse off than the agricultural labourers. Despite the large estates, 36 per cent of the land was owned in parcels of less than 1,000 acres, for small freeholders were common in Needwood Forest and Cannock Chase. Actual farms varied from twenty-five to 500 acres or more. In Leicestershire the bulk of the landowners were small owner-occupiers, many farming from fifty to 500 acres. Annual tenancies militated against improvements, as did the fact that there were few resident gentry, country houses being let in winter for fox hunting. The large numbers of small farms, together with the prevalence of small freeholders and the concentration of market gardening in some districts, gave an impetus to the family work unit which avoided the use of extra labour wherever possible.

Levels of working-class prosperity thus varied considerably within the midland counties. Metal workers and colliers on the whole earned high wages, and in the Potteries, where the mixture of light and heavy industry provided jobs for men, women and children, family wages were higher than where employment opportunities favoured men only. Farm wages in the 1860s were around the national average, rather comparable with those in the south-east and better than those in the west, improving as one moved from the south of the region to the north, and generally being higher in and around industrial areas. In contrast, wages were low in the sweated nail and chain trades, while the textile hand workers often earned much less than farm labourers.[28]

Viewed generally, the midland counties were remarkably working-class in character, though containing communities differing greatly in prosperity, independence and outlook. The social and occupational structures of these communities had implications for child labour and schooling.

Child labour

The incidence and nature of child employment was a significant element in educational standards. The censuses probably underestimate the numbers involved but are useful for comparative purposes.[29] Except in Worcestershire in 1871 the proportions of children aged ten to fourteen officially at work in 1851 and in 1871 were well above the national average (Appendix B) and the actual numbers of such children considerable. In 1851 Nottinghamshire, Derbyshire, Leicestershire, Warwickshire and Staffordshire had higher proportions of such children at work than any other county except Bedfordshire, Northamptonshire, Buckinghamshire, the West Riding and Lancashire, and Worcestershire was not far behind.

By 1871 all six midland counties had experienced reductions in child workers in this age group of 4–5 percentage points (compared with a national decline of 2 points), though their position relative to other counties had improved only marginally, except for Warwickshire, which by then had lower proportions of the age group at work than eighteen other counties.

The census totals of children aged five to nine in employment (Appendix B) are probably less reliable than those for older children, but they do reveal that in the midland counties much higher proportions were working than in most other parts of the country. Though in 1851 they fell below the levels that pertained in Bedfordshire, Buckinghamshire, Hertfordshire and Northamptonshire, where the domestic lace and plait trade claimed so many infant hands, Leicestershire equalled the West Riding's high proportion and, like Nottinghamshire, was well above the Lancashire level. Each of the other four midland counties had roughly the same proportion of their young children at work as did Lancashire. By 1871, though higher proportions of very young children were still employed than in most counties, the relative position of the midlands had somewhat improved, being better than in the north-western textile counties and the outworking counties of the south midlands.

For the older age group (ten to fourteen) the proportion of boys employed was much higher than that of girls both in 1851 and 1871, though the gap between the sexes narrowed over these decades. For younger children (five to nine) a higher proportion of girls than boys was at work in Derbyshire,

TABLE 4·1

Proportion of children (10–14) occupied, 1851, 1871

(a) BOYS	1851			1871		
	(b) % occupied	(c) Main occupation	(d) % in (c)	(e) % occupied	(f) Main occupation	(g) % in (f)
Derbyshire	42	lace & silk workers cotton workers coal miners	7 5 5	38	coal miners cotton workers	7 5
Leicestershire	44	hosiery workers agricultural labourers	15 9	38	agricultural labourers shoe makers hosiery makers	9 5 4
Nottinghamshire	42	hosiery workers agricultural labourers lace workers	7 7 4	36	coal miners agricultural labourers hosiery workers lace workers	6 5 3 2
Staffordshire	46	earthenware workers coal miners iron workers indoor farm workers	8 7 4 2	35	earthenware workers coal miners iron workers indoor farm workers messengers, porters, etc.	5 4 4 2 2
Warwickshire	45	agricultural labourers messengers, porters brassworkers	7 7 3	36	agricultural labourers messengers, errand boys, etc. gold and silver smiths, jewellers brassworkers	5 5 2 2
Worcestershire	41	agricultural labourers nailers carpet makers, etc.	8 5 4	31	agricultural labourers nailers iron workers	6 3 2

(a) GIRLS	1851			1871		
	(b) % occupied	(c) Main occupation	(d) % in (c)	(e) % occupied	(f) Main occupation	(g) % in (f)
Derbyshire	34	cotton workers silk workers general domestic	12 7 4	29	general domestic cotton workers silk, satin workers	9 7 4
Leicestershire	33	hosiery & lace workers general domestic	17 5	28	general domestic hosiery workers	8 7
Nottinghamshire	35	hosiery & lace workers general domestic cotton workers glovers	17 5 2 2	29	general domestic hosiery and lace workers	8 11
Staffordshire	23	general domestic earthenware workers silk workers nailers	8 5 2 2	21	general domestic earthenware workers	9 4
Warwickshire	25	general domestic silk and ribbon workers button makers	8 5 2	23	general domestic silk, satin workers	8 2
Worcestershire	22	general domestic nailers glovers	7 4 3	21	general domestic nailers	9 2

Leicestershire and Nottinghamshire in 1851, though except in the last named this was no longer the case by 1871 (Appendix B). This probably reflects the increasing opportunities for farm labour for boys as they grew older, and the fact that girls perhaps took more easily to domestic trades at a younger age.

Specific figures for young workers in certain important towns, provided by the 1851 census, show that in the metal towns of Wolverhampton and Birmingham the proportion of males under twenty was a half to a third greater than that of young female workers, while in the textile towns (Coventry, Leicester, Nottingham and Derby) the proportions for males and females were much more on a par (Appendix C). At a county level, however, agricultural labour was in 1851 one of the largest single employments for boys aged ten to fourteen in Warwickshire, Worcestershire, Leicestershire, and Nottingham-shire (Table 4·1). In Staffordshire coal, iron and pottery work provided employment for significant numbers of boys, as did nailing in Worcestershire. In Leicestershire, Nottinghamshire and Derbyshire a sizable proportion was employed in the various textile industries. Twenty years later proportions employed had fallen but textiles were still important for boys in Leicestershire, Nottinghamshire, Warwickshire and Worcestershire, as were coal and iron in Derbyshire and Staffordshire, pottery in Staffordshire, hosiery and lace in Leicestershire and Nottinghamshire and cotton in Derbyshire.

General domestic service was the largest single occupation for girls of ten to fourteen in 1851 in Staffordshire, Worcestershire and Warwickshire, but was less important proportionately in the other three counties, where the various textile industries continued to employ large numbers. For girls earthenware was important in Staffordshire, nailing in Staffordshire and Worcestershire, gloving in Nottinghamshire and Worcestershire, and silk and ribbons in Warwick-shire. By 1871 domestic service accounted for 8–9 per cent of girls in this age range in all the six counties, being the most significant single employment except for lace and hosiery in Nottinghamshire and cotton and silk in Derbyshire. Leicestershire still had 7 per cent in hosiery.

All these percentages omit children not returned as workers in the censuses, though the known irregularity of school attentance and the likelihood that some, particularly younger children, those who worked part-time, and those who worked under the family roof (especially in home tasks), were not listed as workers, suggests that the statistics are underestimates. It is possible, too, that some children who attended only Sunday schools were returned as 'scholars' in the census. Appendix I showing the proportions of children aged five to fourteen not on the books of day schools in 1851 includes both employed children and those neither at home nor formally at work. In each of the six midland counties there was a higher proportion of girls than boys not enrolled as pupils, and in only one of the sixty-nine midland registration districts in 1851 was there a higher proportion of girls than boys at school (Appendix F). All this reinforces the likelihood than many girls not listed in the census as employed, may well have been occupied at home, often as drudges, sometimes in domestic manufacture.

Again the proportions at work so far considered are on a county basis. Since opportunities for child employment were much greater in some districts than others the proportion of young workers in some places in the midlands must have been very high indeed, particularly in some age groups. A survey of over a thousand Birmingham families in 1856 showed 42 per cent of 1,373 children at day school and 33 per cent in employment. Twenty-five per cent were neither at school nor work but the survey was taken in winter and this reflected a seasonal reduction in employment demand. Even so the proportions at work increased from 5 per cent at ages seven to eight to 25 per cent at ages nine to ten, to 61 per cent at ages eleven to twelve and 72 per cent for those aged twelve to thirteen, with higher proportions for boys than girls. Employment ranged over seventy-seven occupations for boys and thirty-two for girls.[30]

The nature of child employment in many of the midland industries differed from that in the textile mills of Lancashire and the West Riding, where, if conditions were harsh and hours excessive, the use of steam powered machines ensured some regularity of working hours. Some children in the midlands worked in factories, but the vast majority of child workers were employed in their own homes and outhouses, workshops, warehouses, potteries, furnaces, forges and so on, where steam-powered machinery was not used or did not dominate production. Except in a few processes, like chevening (embroidery work) and pinheading, the tendency was not to group large numbers of child workers together. 'It would be rare,' it was said of Leicester's hosiery industry in 1842, 'that ten children are engaged together, usually two or three according to the size of the family or shop.'[31] A common characteristic of the midlands was indeed the prevalence of family labour, with men, women and children hard at work, variously spurred on by high wages or extreme poverty. When not working with parents, children were usually, even in the large workshops, attached to individual workers and thus subject to the extremely irregular hours adult midland workers preferred. In some cases the child worker was employed directly by the workman and not by the master. This, combined with the multiplicity of small industrial units and family domestic production, rendered legislative control to ameliorate children's conditions more difficult than in the factory districts. Consequently, much of midland industry for long remained outside the Factory Acts and the half-time system.

In the circumstances it is difficult to be specific about the hours of work and ages at which children began employment, and the evidence produced by successive Children's Employment Commissions in the 1840s and 1860s is confusing and often contradictory. A few general conclusions may, however, be made with some confidence. In the midland industries taken as a whole, an average of ten working hours a day, exclusive of meals, would be quite common for children, but the practice of irregular working frequently meant youngsters working up to twelve to fourteen hours in a day, or, on occasions, up to eighteen.[32] The age of starting work varied, but often children were very young when they began. Such generalisations, however, cover a considerable variety of experiences.

In 1858 J. P. Norris, H.M.I., wrote that 'in no part of England has the evil of premature employment presented itself in a more aggravated form than in Staffordshire'.[33] Certainly the earthenware manufacturers of Staffordshire and Derbyshire, who did not come under legislative control until 1864, used a high proportion of child labour both in the pottery making processes and in the finishing trades of painting, gilding, burnishing and scouring. Some of the work was comparatively light, but much was extremely arduous and, especially in some of the finishing processes, injurious to health.[34] Child employees were often very young, for the habit of early marriages resulted in large familes and parents could not cope without their earnings.[35] In the 1830s and 1840s children began work as early as the age five or six in the Staffordshire potteries and at seven in Derbyshire, such employment becoming common at seven or eight and general at eight to nine. Of some 124,000 workers noted in returns made by the principal Staffordshire pottery manufacturers in the early 1840s, 12 per cent were under thirteen years of age and many were between thirteen and twenty-one.[36] The Children's Employment Commission of the early 1840s found that in this arduous trade the hours were usually twelve and a half a day, in overheated workshops, and frequently an extra four hours. Those in the finishing trades, often girls, also worked twelve or more hours. Overtime was not common in Derbyshire, except in Chesterfield, but frequent in Staffordshire.[37]

When another official investigation took place in the early 1860s, conditions had hardly improved. There were still in 1862 some 6,300 boys and youths employed in the pottery side of the industry, and some 11,000 children and young persons, many of them girls, in the finishing operations. Conditions of work in certain jobs remained atrocious and dangerously unhealthy.[38] The 'normal' working day of twelve hours was frequently exceeded as a result of commercial demands and the irregular habits of the adult workpeople.[39] Nine-year old William Wood, a moulder, began work when still seven years of age, and claimed to work from 6 a.m. to 9 p.m. six days a week. A few years later a French observer commented that 'because of the greed of certain parents, you would . . . come upon children of six or seven or under'.[40] As late as 1870 there were still some 3,000 children aged under thirteen in 315 Staffordshire pottery works.[41] In the Black Country brickyards some children began work at six, many at seven or eight, labouring at arduous tasks exceedingly long hours to suit the adults they served, who usually employed them personally.[42] The visiting American, Elihu Burritt, reported that two-thirds of the largely female workforce in these yards were girls aged nine to twelve.[43]

Girls were not employed underground in the midland coal mines but until 1842 boys commonly worked there. In Derbyshire some began at five, many at six and seven, few after eight, and in south Staffordshire commonly at seven or eight, generally at nine.[44] In the Bilston area it was alleged that the majority of children in coal, ironstone and other mines began at seven or eight but were often taken down the pit as young as four to sit and get accustomed to it. In the north Staffordshire, Warwickshire and Leicestershire pits, there were generally far fewer very young children because the coal hewn was hard and in large lumps. Usually the children worked twelve-hour shifts, though in Derbyshire longer.[45] Despite the prohibition of the underground employment of boys under ten in 1842, the law was commonly disregarded in the early 1850s in Staffordshire, and in the late 1850s it was alleged that most colliers' sons were being removed from school at ten or earlier to be sent down the mines. In Derbyshire expansion in coal mining after 1850 produced an increased demand for boys.[46] Moreover, as J. P. Norris remarked in answer to his own question ('Do the children kept out of the colliery [by the Act] . . . go to school?'), 'No: they are at once absorbed by other trades in the district.'[47]

In the multifarious metal industries of Birmingham and the Black Country children were almost ubiquitously employed and unaffected by legislation until 1867 and from then slowly. In Willenhall in the 1840s, for example, no less than 900 to a thousand boys were employed in the metal trades out of a total population of 5,695.[48] In the Staffordshire and Worcestershire iron districts children worked in blast furnaces and iron mills: even in the early 1860s some 1,200 boys under thirteen and double that number aged thirteen to eighteen, as well as some young girls. The work was hard and the hours were long: 'rollers', aged fourteen upwards, worked day and night shifts of twelve hours and were said to run eleven miles in a shift. In the foundries of Wolverhampton seven-year-olds could be found. Nine and ten-year-olds worked bellows, boys of thirteen to fifteen struck with hammers, and so on; and much of this activity took place in very high temperatures, while some processes, as in brass and bell founding and casting, were specially injurious to health. In the hoop mills of Wednesbury boys began at nine years old. In the japanning, tinplate, varnishing and like trades in the Wolverhampton area in the 1840s children's work was said to be 'seldom laborious'; nevertheless twelve hours a day was common and often longer. Work in screw making, and in the production of shoe tips and washers, undertaken by women and girls in factory conditions, required long tedious labour in the same physical position, often causing disablement.[49]

The Birmingham area had as high a proportion of juvenile labour as any in the country, much of it employed domestically or in small workshops. In the 1840s many children began work in the metal trades at seven, eight or nine and in the 1860s such work was still general at age nine or ten. It was estimated that in 1862 some 2,000 children under ten were employed in Birmingham alone, a quarter of them under the age of eight. Work hours varied much but throughout the period these children worked as long as adults, commonly a ten to twelve hour day, though on the whole, especially in the light metal trades, labour was less fatiguing than in other industries, being dependent on manual skill and dexterity.[50] In the pin factories, however, where the average age was only eight or nine, and where, unlike in many trades, children were herded together to work *en masse* under the surpervision of a few adults, hours were very long and tasks were exhausting and carried out in close and crowded conditions.[51]

Of other child metal workers in the Black Country probably the most degraded were those engaged in the hand-made nails and chain trades which were generally carried on in domestic buildings, outhouses and small workshops. Parents and children worked together in most unsavoury and sordid conditions. At Stourbridge and Willenhall children began as early as age four, elsewhere often at six or seven, or at least eight or nine. The trades were nevertheless not unpopular with many adults, who preferred the freedom of irregular hours, and consequently in the 1860s nailers' children were called on to labour from 5.00 a.m. to 10.00 or 11.00 at night on some days of the week. Even in the 1870s the hours worked were so long towards the end of the week that child assistants were said to have to remain at their tasks night and day for several days at a time.[52] Moreover the mechanical repetition of the work was tedious and (as was said of Wolverhampton nailers) 'wearies and indeed wears out the soul with the body'.[53]

In the midland textile communities child and female labour was very common. Out of 28,000 persons employed in connection with the Leicestershire hosiery and glove trades in 1833, 15,000 were under the age of eighteen.[54] The lace and hosiery industries were still basically domestic, with the family or extended family the common unit, and even when production was based on hand machinery in large warehouses, childen and adults tended to work together. As wages fell and parents worked longer and longer hours, similar conditions were pressed on attendant children.[55] In the early 1840s, it was said, 'almost all the children of the labouring classes in the Nottingham, Leicester and Derby districts are engaged in ... lace manufacture and hosiery'. Children began work at six, seven, or eight or even younger in the hosiery trades in the 1830s; in lace the average age of starting was eight and a half.[56] In Leicestershire hosiers' children 'as soon as they can begin to hold a needle, or are big enough to stand at the wheel, they must either seam or wind';[57] in Nottingham they were started 'as soon as they can tie a knot or use a needle'.[58] Children often began young with their parents or small masters, progressing to larger workshops and warehouses at eleven or so. Hours of work varied but were irregular and often very long. Boys, for example, who began winding in the lace industry at five or six, worked the same hours as the men. Girls, beginning to seam at seven or eight, worked with women up to fifteen hours a day.[59] Adult workers in the hosiery trade in the early 1840s rarely worked Mondays and frequently not Tuesdays. Children, often very young, were thus overwhelmed towards the end of the week, and at times when orders had to be met. In the lace industry in the 1840s hours were so irregular that they could not be computed precisely. Some children at times worked sixteen to twenty-two hours at a stretch. In the hand worked trade they might also have to move from workshop to workshop. Even when not officially at work they might be 'on call' often in the workshop where no sleeping facilities existed, and all in unpleasant conditions.[60] In comparison with these wretched places, it was said in 1845, 'factories are elysiums'.[61] Young children engaged in the embroidering of goods like gloves and stockings had a particularly distasteful lot at the hands of the mistresses under whom they worked in groups, rather like the unfortunate pin headers of Birmingham. R. D. Grainger, the employment commissioner, in 1842 felt that 'the toil to which these poor children, infants some of them ..., are subject, is altogether disgraceful in a Christian country'.[62]

In the 1850s and 1860s conditions were much the same, both in lace and hosiery, except in large lace warehouses where the average working day was some two hours shorter and overtime restricted. In such warehouses children were by then generally over nine or ten, but children as young as three and a half were still found in small lace shops and parents' houses, and children of eight and nine were sometimes made to work all night. In the Nottingham area alone in the early 1860s it was reckoned that 8,000 — 10,000 children and young persons were employed in the machine lace industry, and another 10,000 in the finishing aspects of the trade.[63] In this period in the depressed hosiery villages outside the towns conditions remained especially bad, with the labouring population much worse off than other workers and 'very neglected and demoralised, socially, morally and intellectually'.[64] For instance, at Bulwell, a large straggling village outside Nottingham, with a population of nearly 4,000 housed along narrow dirty lanes, dependent on the production of gloves on hand frames, one middleman reported that 'a child begins works at about nine years old' and works from breakfast to nine to ten at night, though often past midnight.[65]

In the 1830s comparatively few children in the midland cotton or silk industries were employed in factories,[66] but large numbers worked in the domestic ribbon industry of Coventry and its environs. Many 'first-hand' journeymen and women working their own looms relied on their own families for labour. In 1838 of 6,796 working members of such families in Coventry itself, 2,587 were children under the age of fourteen, over half of whom were under seven. Of 1,520 'second-hand' workers employed by first-hand men, 435 were under fourteen, most of whom were under seven. Of the poorer 'single-hand' weavers three-quarters were females and of the rest about one-third were boys aged twelve to sixteen. They were assisted by younger children who began winding at about eight years of age. Those then employed in Coventry factories numbered only 965, but over a quarter of them were under seven.[67] The ribbon trade subsequently suffered severe trade depression, but by 1866, when the number of engine looms had been much reduced and wages generally fallen in the Coventry district, there were still 8,000 weavers, two-thirds of them women and children, and boys of seven upwards, for example, were engaged in the heavy task of loom turning for twelve to fourteen hours a day.[68]

In the silk industry at Leek some children worked in factories but many more as outworkers. In factories children's hours were regulated, but even in 1870 only fifty of the 286 silk workshops in the town ranked as factories. Large numbers of women and children were employed outside the aegis of the Factory Acts, some, even in the late 1860s, beginning work at or below the age of eight. Though the work was comparatively light they toiled rarely less than ten or eleven hours a day. In 1861 of the total number engaged in Staffordshire's silk manufacture (most in Leek, with some in Newcastle under Lyme) 40 per cent were under twenty-one.[69]

In the Kidderminster carpet industry boys began to work at home at age six or seven, working four, five or six hours a day and progressing at eight or nine to longer hours. In the large warehouses, where much of the production was concentrated, children from nine or ten were engaged not by the master but the operatives they attended, and consequently often worked as long as these adults and as irregular hours. Employers in 1833 admitted that children were thus considerably overworked.[70]

This survey does not, of course, comprehend all the types of child employment. There were many other industrial occupations followed by children. Young boys were still, for example, working twelve to sixteen hours a day in small workshops in the boot and shoe trade in Leicester in the early 1870s.[71] Many were employed from very young ages in a multitude of different ways, as domestic servants, errand boys, shop workers, stable boys and so on, to say nothing of acting as surrogate housewives and nurses in the absence of working mothers.[72] The Burton-on-Trent brewing industry was one that employed few children. There were, for instance, only sixty-three boys out of 956 employees in fifteen breweries in 1851.[73] Likewise the Coventry watch trade, which boys did not enter until the age of fourteen, was another exception.[74] The overall view of the midland manufacturing districts in the period 1830–70, however, is of a working community in which children from an early age were as a matter of course more than fully employed alongside their parents and neighbours. The organisation of the majority of the trades in which they worked was such that their lot was unlikely to be improved merely by industrial legislation.

In many rural districts of the midland counties children were not usually engaged on a permanent basis at the very early ages found in local industries. Less labour of all kinds was required for pasture farming, and, although ploughboys were needed on the clay lands, this occupation could not be undertaken by the very young. In Leicestershire and Staffordshire there was little demand from farmers for the occasional labour of children, but boys started work with horses in Staffordshire at about the age of ten or eleven and in Leicestershire between ten and twelve. In Derbyshire boys were not regularly employed until twelve or thirteen, in Warwickshire between eleven and fourteen[75] In Worcestershire, however, there was a considerable call for child labour in the summer in the market gardens of the Vale of Evesham and an all-year-round demand for ploughboys.[76] In Nottinghamshire the increasing cultivation of root crops and the disinclination of women to work in the fields were given in the 1860s as reasons for the increase of child labour on farms, and at an earlier age — even as young as eight. In the west of the county light work was done by 'troops of children' employed all summer and part of the winter for stone picking, and Nottinghamshire was the only one of the six counties where the miserable agricultural gang system was to be found.[77] Child labour in agriculture, however, was hardly affected by official regulation before the 1870s. Farmers in many parts of the area did employ young children occasionally for specific jobs, especially in the spring and summer months. In Derbyshire in the 1860s, for example, children of seven or eight upwards, in Warwickshire from about eight, were employed from March to September. Girls below the teens were found much less often than boys in regular or occasional agricultural employment.

The smallness of farms and the prevalence of family labour, was, however, one of the causes of a lack of farm work for hired children, and such parents regularly employed their young offspring. Moreover, where industrial employment was available, as particularly in the hosiery and lace districts and the potteries, farm labourers' young children found work there. This was so, for example, in Derbyshire. In the thinly populated rural districts of Leicestershire and Nottinghamshire, outside the 'open' industrial villages, agricultural areas were kept by the landowners deliberately 'closed' against the infiltration of framework knitters and the like, who might fall on the poor rates. To these, farm labourers from the 'open' villages travelled daily, but their children were often employed in the home village in manufacture.[78]

Attitudes to education

Evidence of working-class parental attitudes to schooling may be inferred from school attendance figures and the like, but more directly from the statements of working people made to official investigations and from the observations of government inspectors, commissioners, politicians, clergy, employers, landowners, and so on. A lack of unanimity in the views and evidence of members of the same class or social or occupational group is, however, very common and conclusions are made more difficult by the variables of place and time. Again, the diversity found in working-class views reflects not only the varying impact of different industrial influences on communities but also the fact that the 'working classes' embraced within them parents ranging from the skilled artisan to the ignorant and depraved slum dweller. The spectrum of midland working-class society was in fact so varied that only the broadest of generalisations are possible here. Certain tentative points may, however, be made.

First, very few members of the working-class communities just surveyed, with their long established acceptance of child labour as an integral part of their way of life, generated any interest in schooling for its own sake, and it is doubtful whether the possession of a smattering of letters brought any special social status.[79] Particularly up to the late 1840s and 1850s, many parents in the midland trades, which invariably required no educational qualifications whatever, could see no economic advantage in book learning for their children. The depressed hosiery workers were especially short-sighted, looking back to better times when their own lack of education had been no bar to comparative comfort, and forward to an unwarranted expectation that if their own children merely followed in their footsteps better times would come. Generally they saw no further than this, or less sanguinely were primarily concerned in keeping the wolf from the door by exploiting their children's labour, which brought in about as much as their own. Poor education then restricted the children from seeking clerical employment and their general physique resulting from poor diet precluded them from farm or other heavy labour.[80] In the more prosperous trades hedonistic tendencies were equally antagonistic to schooling.[81] George Coode, reporting to the Newcastle Commission in 1859, distinguished between a 'want' of education, only too obvious in the Black Country, and a 'demand' for it from those who needed it most.[82] Highly paid workmen owed their prosperity not at all to schooling and saw no reason why their sons should not be satisfied with following in their footsteps. To the mass of parents enjoying what seemed a reasonable, even a desirable, way of life dependent on manual labour and often the earnings of the whole family, the advantages of education were hardly apparent. The highest paid nailers at Rowley Regis in 1859, for instance, were mostly illiterate yet owned valuable breeds of pigeons, spending 4s.–5s. a week on bird food and devoting their spare time to flying them. They 'could not afford' to send their children to school and set the standards of ambition for most boys in the neighbourhood.[83] Even those who might have sought some sort of advancement in their local industry for their offspring could hardly be blamed for ignoring book learning as a necessary step towards it. Manual dexterity learned early was often a necessity,[84] and in the iron and coal districts there were many prosperous employers who had risen from the lowest occupations in the pit, the furnace or forge, and even the nailers' shop without ever acquiring the rudiments of reading or writing.[85]

The Children's Employment Commissioners of the 1860s in reporting on the Birmingham metal trades carefully distinguished between skill and schooling. Men capable of accurate and difficult work might be illiterate yet highly paid. Only boys apprenticed to a trade requiring a high degree of literacy or mathematical knowledge would be expected to be educated to any level, and these were a rarity indeed.[86] Similarly the coalowners of the Black Country, with few exceptions, did not live near the colliers or even employ them directly, so that the most successful men in mining communities were perceived as the small masters, the butties, contractors who hired and paid the men, and the mine agents (or underground bailiffs) whose job it was to direct workings. These, drawn from the same social background as the workmen, were often quite uneducated. In 1850 H. S. Tremenheere reported that in ten important coal and iron companies, each employing twenty to thirty contractors, only half such men could write and some could not read — yet they conducted their affairs apparently without difficulty, controlling hundreds of workers and often accepting important contracts. Even the mine agents, carrying extensive responsibilities, were little better schooled. In 1850, of the sixty such men in the south Staffordshire coalfield, at least a quarter could neither read nor write, and only twenty-five might be called 'educated'. Many could not understand a plan and worked without one. Their efficiency was said to be impaired by these deficiencies, yet this had not affected their success in life.[87]

A common saying in the midlands in the late 1850s was 'The father went down the pit and he made a fortune, his son went to school and lost it'. Nor did workmen admire the regularity of the work of the clerk at his desk or the shopkeeper at his counter, preferring the greater freedom to work or to 'play' when they wished.[88] The Revd. W. Lewis, of Sedgley, a diocesan inspector of schools, in 1858 reported that such men 'do not value the instruction they themselves have done without', observing that a little education did not raise the earning capacity of their children, 'valuing little that training and improvement of the mind or elevation of the character which makes man superior in his portion to what he would otherwise have been'.[89] George Coode, reporting on the Dudley district to the Newcastle Commission, summed it all up:[90]

> To the mass of parents in this ... district, the advantages of education ... cannot be very apparent, while its attendant disadvantages are manifest ...

They see some of the most prosperous men in the world who have attained
this prosperity without any other education than that of the nail shop, the
pit or the forge ... they see no greater if any equal, prosperity attending
the people who read and keep books, shopkeepers, lecturers, ministers of
religion. Learning is rather thought a drawback.

There was indeed in many parts of the midlands little demand for youths with a
smattering of letters and even employers active in promoting schooling
admitted that their most skilful and best paid workmen were not necessarily
those who were literate. Attempts in the 1850s by well-meaning employers in
the Dudley district to give preference to children who had attended school had
little effect since the demand for child labour exceeded the supply.[91] Sending a
child to school, moreover, meant doing without the money it might earn
without any compensation in enhanced wages at a later date.

Ambition for offspring was commonest in the ranks of the small tradesmen
and artisans, and in the countryside among some farmers and craftsmen. In
Worcestershire in the 1860s such persons were said to be 'really anxious to
have their children well educated' choosing schools carefully and keeping their
children at them until they had made good progress. Usually, in that county
and in Derbyshire, some farm labourers were also mindful of economic
advantages of schooling. In Staveley (Derbyshire) it was said that proportionately the schools were 'more appreciated and better attended by
agricultural labourers' children than by those of any other class of labourers'.[92]

The minority of working parents who saw advantage in schooling noted the
unsatisfied demand for clerical workers in the offices and counting houses of
businesses, factories, solicitors, railways and so on. Such outlets, particularly in
the Birmingham area in the 1850s, led to higher wages for those boys who could
read, write and sum. Jobs like these were not, however, attainable by a few
years at a dame school, but rather by attendance at a sound charity or voluntary
school until the age of twelve or so.[93] In the county town of Worcester, a
market centre with a high proportion of artisans, craft workers and small
masters, and with a relatively low proportion of labourers, education was more
appreciated and cultural levels were higher than in neighbouring industrial
districts, and no doubt this was the case, too, in other such midland towns
where schooling had an economic value.[94] In some, however, the majority of
well-off workmen in the industrial communities saw no advantage in education
though they might have afforded it, while those who were poorer looked to
their children's earnings to retain their independence and avoid the workhouse, and the profligate and idle led easier lives cushioned by family
earnings.[95]

Contemporary middle-class opinion tended to overlook the apparent absence
of economic advantage seen by workpeople, frequently asserting that parental

greed or parental need were the causes of failure to educate children. Poverty was, indeed, the main reason given by parents. In periods of unemployment or underemployment, when depressed trade or strikes affected family incomes, this excuse was certainly genuine. Such conditions applied frequently in the declining textile trades, but were also found among the poorer workmen in other trades. Thus the education of the children of the Foleshill ribbon weavers was allegedly affected by poverty in 1833.[96] In the early 1840s the Catholic priest of Longton in the Potteries believed that many poorer workmen could neither afford school pence nor do without their children's earnings, a state of affairs still pertaining there among young parents in the 1860s. Similar conditions were evident at Kidderminster when foreign competition resulted in large-scale unemployment in the carpet industry.[97]

The Revd. W. Lewis of Sedgley noted in 1858 that with poor families with large young families and the families of widows, found especially in such trades as nailing, there was indeed too little of the parental income left for schooling, besides which, older girls were needed as surrogate mothers and household drudges to release mothers for work. He remarked that at any time of the day in the industrial districts of north Worcestershire and south Staffordshire groups of children aged ten or below were always observable neither at work nor at school.[98] In the Ashby de la Zouch coalfield in the 1840s another clergyman pointed out that there poverty forced parents to send their children down the mine at an early age.[99] In the declining hosiery trade, too, it was generally accepted that children's wages were essential to family survival.[100] Contemporary complaints by hosiers of low earnings have the ring of truth. Joseph Benson, a Leicester framework knitter, for instance, declared it was 'not in a poor man's power to give his children any education; and even if a man gets his child into a charity school, he cannot afford to maintain them'. Many hosiers attested in the 1840s that they could not afford even to clothe their children decently enough for Sunday school, let alone day school.[101] In the 1840s and still in the 1860s the Leek journeymen (as opposed to the undertakers) certainly needed all their family earnings to exist.[102] The Revd. H. W. Bellairs, H.M.I., using Birmingham child labour as an example, stressed the enormous aggregate earning power of children and the consequent difficulty of a situation when 'compel them to go to school, and you drive the family into the workhouse'.[103]

Such claims of poverty were not, however, always believed by middle-class observers who were probably correct in feeling that quite a large number of midland workmen could have afforded more schooling for their children, though not always appreciating that failure to do so often reflected a different set of priorities rather than pure wickedness or avarice — though undoubtedly the latter was present. Certainly, many comparatively well paid workmen in the Black Country for long tended to put the comforts attainable by family wage earning above the advantages of schoooling. The Children's Employment

Commissions of the 1860s found few poor families who did not profess to see the advantage of education. The prevalence of private schools indicated this. 'They have known of cases where some in their own status of life have raised themselves' by education 'and this is . . . a strong inducement'. But they set their standards very low, and took their children away from school as soon as employment in or out of the home was possible.[104] A Stourbridge clergyman in 1841 felt that the real reason for working-class failure to educate their children was 'want of a moral and religious feeling . . . [they] cannot resist the temptation to profit from their children's labour'. It was alleged, too, that nailers in this area often gave up work at thirty or forty to 'idle about, living upon the labours of their family — mother, boys and girls'. The Revd. H. S. Fletcher of Bilston reported that to the mother of a child of seven who could earn half a crown a week in the mines, this money was 'of more importance than the education for which she has to pay 2d. a week'.[105] In the Birmingham area in the early 1840s it was alleged that some parents were happy to live in idleness on their children's wages.[106] H.S. Tremenheere, the commissioner for the mining districts in the 1850s, felt that few Black Country workmen would not have been able to dispense with the labour of their young children, but put them to work for mere greed.[107] The availability of well paid industrial work[108] made it hard for schools to retain boys even below the age of nine, while girls were removed to prepare food and take it to the menfolk.[109] In Stratford in the 1860s excuses for absence included 'He's gone with his father's dinner,' 'She's holding the baby.'[110]

The Revd. H. Moseley, H.M.I., in 1845 found the south Staffordshire mining districts very prosperous, with earnings relatively high, yet men degraded, profligate, and willing to spend money on bottled wine and port, but not on schooling.[111] In the 1850s, too, it was the experience of a mine agent in the south Staffordshire coalfield that periods of high wages resulted in more drinking and less attendance at work, yet the children were still taken from school 'at the earliest moment they can earn anything' 'to enable the father to idle away a part of his time'.[112] It was in this coalfield in the 1840s that employers reported themselves 'constantly beset by parents entreating them to employ their children before they are fit for labour, and often insisting upon it as a condition of engaging to work themselves'.[113] At Wednesbury, and other districts in the Wolverhampton area in the 1860s, opinion was that 'the parents who sent their children at the earliest age to work were, in most cases, well paid operatives who wasted their earnings'.[114]

Not dissimilar attitudes were found in the Potteries in the early 1840s, where it was reported that some parents often earned as much as £2 to £4 a week but still were totally indifferent to the education of their children, caring 'so little about their immediate or future welfare, as to be equally satisfied whether they continue in ignorance or not'. Among the better paid textile workers, too, schooling was not for many a high priority. R. D. Grainger, who investigated the lace districts of Leicestershire, Nottinghamshire and Derbyshire in 1841 for the Children's Employment Commission, found that, whatever was the case in the hosiery trade, the early age children were set to work in the lace industry was not due to parental want. The Houghton family, who lived in the Nottingham area, for example, put all their children to work at two or three years of age despite the husband's regular wage of 23s. a week.[115] Coventry ribbon weavers, even in their period of prosperity, showed as little desire to school their children as the less fortunate single-hand country weavers, who probably could not afford it. Coventry teachers in 1838 thought more children were kept from school 'through carelessness and indifference' than want.[116] In Derbyshire in the early 1840s the sole desire of parents seemed to be, it was said, 'to make all they could of their children at as early an age as possible without regarding their future welfare'.[117]

Among the comparatively well paid farm labourers of Staffordshire failure to send children to school in the 1860s was felt to be due to neglect and rarely connected with poverty. Indeed, in the midland agricultural areas generally children were valued as workers on their parents' own plots, and some parents were prepared to pay for private schools where regular attendance was not demanded, rather than take advantage of free schools where it was.[118]

Education pressed on workers by others was certainly not often appreciated. Freedom to put their children to work was preferred. When one owner of an ironworks in south Staffordshire offered, about 1845, to pay 2d. a week for any of the children of his 1,500 workpeople sent to school, only thirty accepted, though most workers' children did not go to day school.[119] In the 1840s, too, the vicar of Dudley sought to establish a free school for girls at his own expense, together with free clothing, without any great success.[120]

In Birmingham and district in the mid-1850s an H.M.I. reported 'no lack of good schools ... the accommodation is good, the teachers are good. The parents do not complain of religious intolerance or of heavy school payments. But some send their children to remunerative labour, and some to steal, or to idle about the streets and beg; and so they are not found at school'.[121] Many parents clearly regarded control of their own children as an important prerogative. Self-employed operatives often worked their children harder than employers. One such at Wolverhampton, 'a very steady man' and a Mormon preacher, worked his sons in the 1860s from four in the morning to twelve at night, for two or three weeks at a time.[122] In some Derby silk mills in the 1830s the only children under nine or ten were those whose ages parents had misrepresented to the employer.[123] Parents at Wolverhampton in the early 1840s with a few exceptions were opposed to any legislation preventing child employment in mines and workshops.[124] In 1864 the vicar of Walsall predicted public agitation against any attempt to bring the Factory Acts there.[125] In 1859 it was the parents of child workers in the Potteries, rather than the employers, who were opposed to the element of compulsory schooling in proposals to extend the half-time system to earthenware manufacture.[126] Even in the late 1870s many Black Country parents were hostile to the school boards.[127]

Appreciation of schooling was evident most, as we have seen, among the petty bourgeoisie rather than the workmen proper, and perhaps among some handworkers in the depressed textile trades. Some domestic textile workers in the 1840s expressed regret to official investigators that they could no longer afford some day schooling for their children, though in more prosperous times they had been able to.[128] It would be unwise to accept these protestations at their face value, and an exaggeration to suggest that such workpeople were deprived in their decline of a golden age in which schooling had been the normal lot of their happy children. Nevertheless there seems to have been in the depressed industries a hankering after such a provision not found among the better-off workers elsewhere in the midlands. Generally speaking, many who protested poverty as a reason for not sending theirs children to school were speaking in relative terms. As the Revd. J. P. Norris put it:[129]

> 'Times are bad, and we cannot afford it.' The clergyman lowers his fee, but still they 'cannot afford it'. He offers to pay for their schooling; *to oblige him* they send the children to school for a week or two, but very soon they drop off again. 'Times are bad, and they cannot afford it'. Cannot afford what? — cannot afford *to give up the value of their child's time*. This was what they meant from the first ... Their time is worth 2s. or 3s. a week and this is what the parents grudge ... the school fee is a mere trifle.

Prize schemes, inaugurated to compensate parents in the mining and industrial areas for loss of child earnings, by giving money payments for some intelligent boys to stay at school till the age of thirteen, had a very limited success in the midlands. The prizes tended to be won by lower middle-class children who would have stayed at school anyway. The vast majority of colliers' children for whom the schemes had been inaugurated were still leaving school at ten or earlier to go into the mines.[130] The verdict on the prize schemes of the rector of St. Thomas's, Birmingham, in the late 1850s, seems sensible: 'To suppose that any considerable number will be allowed for a few shillings' worth of books, to stay at school for any effective learning, is surely delusive.'[131] And in the hosiery districts, as the vicar of Shepshed pointed out in the 1840s, free schools were not the answer 'unless we could pay each child th equivalent of what he could earn at home'.[132] The generality of working parents in the midlands certainly had no wish for their children to go to school after the age of eleven and had a very limited view of what schooling was needed before that age.

All this is not to suggest that every working-class parent in the midlands area in the 1840s, 1850s and 1860s sought to deny his children any education. In the 1850s G. Loveday of Wigston (Leics.), an undertaker in the hosiery trade, felt that there was a growing desire among the labouring classes for education for their children: 'I think there is scarcely an instance to be found in the village, unless it is among the very lowest who have no education, in which the parents would not make every effort to send their children to school'.[133] In the Erewash Valley coalfield miners began to appreciate, as better jobs in the pits became more technical, that their sons might benefit materially from a little education.[134] Occasionally, too, an outstanding teacher would stimulate labourers to send their children to a school, where good buildings and equipment had failed to attract them. Thus a school at Hanley in the 1850s retained a minority of its boys longer than normal and these later obtained clerical and similar jobs with higher wages than other child workers. And at Tipton a certificated teacher built up a school from three to 180 pupils in fifteen months, retaining most even during a colliery strike.[135] Similarly in the 1860s a female nailer told Elihu Burritt that 'she was determined that her children should have a little schooling, for she had seen the want of it herself'.[136] In Birmingham in the 1860s Quaker Sunday schools were favoured by parents because they taught writing.[137] And by 1869 it was felt that even in the midlands the labouring classes would send their children to schools if they felt they were good schools.[138]

Statistics, discussed in detail below, of growing attendance at day and Sunday schools in all the midland counties over the period of this study attest to the fact that some children were sent to school, and were usually paid for. The conflict of these facts with the evidence of widespread child labour and the ubiquity of ignorance noted in official reports is partly explicable by the difference between working and middle-class views on what constituted satisfactory schooling. To the hosiery workers, in the 1840s, 'a knowledge of reading and writing is deemed education, rather than ... the instruments through which it must be acquired'.[139] Similarly, government inspectors found in Worcestershire and Staffordshire in the early 1850s that most workmen felt enough had been achieved when children could read a few simple words, 'put down figures', and 'write a little more than their names'. Many mine workers urged teachers 'to finish their boys quickly'.[140] All they wanted, it was said in 1858, was the three Rs; 'grammar and geography, the parents care little about'.[141] The increase in the proportion of children attending public as opposed to private schools in the midland counties over the period (see below) does not suggest any great political objection to middle-class or religious domination of elementary education, or any ambitions to obtain political control of education. Working-class unrest and political activity in the midlands are discussed below as a stimulus to middle-class action in the educational field. As a medium for working-class endeavour in self-education organised labour does not appear to have been very important.

It is true that at the height of their agitation in 1842 the Chartists established a school at Bilston and a People's Hall and school in Wednesbury the next year, and when Samuel Cook, the Dudley Chartist leader, stood as parliamentary candidate for Wolverhampton in 1847 he demanded secular schools for all children.[142] The *Flint Glass Makers Magazine*, a trade union organ in Stourbridge in 1851, stressed the importance of education for every man in the trade: 'get intelligence instead of alcohol ... get knowledge and getting knowledge you get power'.[143] And in the 1850s working men's institutes and mutual improvement societies were founded in Stourbridge and Dudley.[144] Such ventures were, however, fleeting and few and do not suggest any widespread political interest in education in the area. Moreover the support for socialism and Chartism, even in the Black Country, came more from the minor tradesmen than the workmen class.[145] Often the poorest workmen, such as the hand-loom weavers, were the most politically apathetic, and although trade unions in the hosiery district organised strikes, and there were periodic outbursts of popular violence, the view that the midland handwork villages were centres of dangerous political extremism is dubious.[146] The adult school at Leicester run by Thomas Cooper, the Chartist, had to be abandoned in 1842, the men being 'too despairing to care about learning to read': 'What the hell,' said some, 'do we care about reading if we can get nought to eat?'[147] At Leicester, too, the mechanics' institute, founded in 1843, rejected politics as part of its activities, and indeed attracted a largely middle-class membership.[148] Between 1852 and 1860 some fifteen mechanics' institutes were established in the Black Country, but Thomas Coates found midland artisans indifferent and the institutes did not appeal to the labouring classes. The *Dudley Weekly Times* thus considered in 1857 that the town's institute in its first decade had been enjoyed 'almost exclusively by the middle classes'.[149] An analysis of the membership of the Stourbridge Mechanics' Institute in 1847 found most members to be of the lower middle class, especially tradesmen and clerks. The proportion of 'mechanics' rose at its highest point only to 26 per cent and was generally much lower, and it is doubtful whether more than a few of these were labourers. A similar situation existed at the Wolverhampton Athenaeum.[150] We must conclude that had the limited ambitions of the midland workers and their restricted views on schooling prevailed, little educational improvement could have occurred. Middle-class views of the nature and purpose of popular elementary education were, however, different. The interaction between the different outlooks of the various social groups moulded the development of schooling in the midlands during our period and determined how effective it was.

Pressure for an extension of working-class schooling came both from official investigators and the local middle classes and was often morally based. Outside investigators, like H.M.I.s and members of royal commissions and select committees, were shocked by what they found in the area. They deplored the existence of working-class communities indifferent to religion and with many children growing up little better than pagans. They were affronted by the popular attitude to work and to play, the general profligacy, immorality and fecklessness and the widespread lack of parental responsibility in child raising. The low proportion of 'persons of independent means' in the midland counties (Appendix H) is likely to have been a factor in the lack of any widespread provision and supervision of British and nonconformist schools, except in the larger towns. Local middle-class opinion was consequently dominated by the views of the Anglican clergy and of employers. Churchmen registered distaste and horror at the incidence of immorality and licence. In 1841 it was said of Wolverhampton that 'a stream of prostitution . . . flows through the streets . . . after dark'.[151] Magistrates at Dudley in the 1850s reckoned that among the nailers 'it is held rather a shame to a young woman not to have, than to have, a bastard child', and an assistant commissioner about the same time found the sexual morals of the young in the Potteries 'repulsive', 'even the power of skilful drawing' being used to deface public places.[152] In the hosiery and lace districts of Leicestershire, Derbyshire and Nottinghamshire adolescent immorality was held to be rife throughout the period.[153] Outside observers and officials were usually less condemnatory than the local middle classes about sexual morals, often finding such verdicts exaggerated or unproven, and they recorded some evidence of a growing respectability among workers, such as the increase in the numbers of friendly societies and savings banks and the decline of cruel sports.[154] R. H. Horne, who investigated Wolverhampton for the Children's Employment Commission in 1841 was struck less by any positive working-class viciousness as by their overwhelming apathy and degredation.[155]

What was even more disliked, however, was the rejection of the middle-class virtues of thrift, temperance, respectability and religiosity. In a society where hard physical labour was common and in some areas wages were often relatively high, recreation was found in drinking, in the music, dancing and rude drama provided by the alehouses, and in cruel sports, rather than in amusements deriving from religious inclinations or intellectual curiosity. Earnings were spent while they lasted and an extra day's holiday preferred to savings. In the Black Country generally, few were willing to work on Mondays and many also 'played' on Tuesdays and half Wednesdays. Among the midland miners the higher the wages the less time was worked. Parents at Wolverhampton in the early 1840s were allegedly usually drunk once a fortnight, some of them two or three days at a time.[156] In the Potteries families bringing in up to £4 a week were 'proverbially improvident and . . . squander the proceeds of their labour in gaudy dress, or at the skittle ground and alehouse'.[157] Of the midland mining districts in the 1840s it was complained that as a rule 'those who have the greatest amount of wages are the worst ordered in their own conduct and their families worse provided for' since the money was spent on drink and debauchery.[158] Similar was the complaint about workers in the Staffordshire coal areas a few years later that 'the half savage manners of the last generation have been exchanged for a deep and almost universally pervading sensuality'. Better times did not bring thrift and piety but 'reckless extravagence'.

> Poultry, especially geese and ducks; the earliest and choicest vegetables (e.g. asparagus, green peas, and new potatoes, when they first appear on the market); occasionally even port wine, drunk out of tumblers and basins; beer and spirits in great quantities; meat in abundance, extravagently cooked; excursions in carts and cars; gambling, etc., are well known objects upon which their money is squandered ... devotion to mere animal indulgences.[159]

Middle-class opinion generally was appalled at the extent and nature of child labour in the midlands and much exercised to find ways to alleviate what was often felt to be a moral scandal. Compassion, however, was more often an attribute demonstrated by outside observers than by those who lived and worked in the area. It was the *Quarterly Review*, for example, which expressed horror that 'multitudes of these poor children can never have seen a primrose by a river's brim, or heard the song of a lark'.[160] The recipe for reformation of this hedonistic and immoral working-class culture and for the physical and moral well-being of the children in the midland industrial districts was seen to be through general social legislation such as restriction of the truck system, which encouraged drunkenness[161] and improvement of public health regulations, and also very much in the extension of sound elementary schooling.[162]

The Black Country experienced riots and periods of social unrest particularly from 1835 to 1860 and, however dubiously based, there was fear that unless better education was promoted the heavily populated midland industrial region might become the centre of a political explosion. The Children's Employment Commissions and the various investigations into the moral, economic and social condition of the working population in the midland mining districts were clearly affected by the unrest of the early 1840s. The hosiery districts periodically erupted with strikes and violence, and Hampden clubs had been formed in a number of midland towns after the Napoleonic wars. More particularly, Chartism established a national focus in Birmingham, long a centre of radical politics, and found violent expression throughout the midland industrial districts, and particularly in the Potteries and the Black Country, where mass unrest and rioting were especially severe in 1842.[163] The Midland Mining Commissioners who investigated workers' grievances after the upsets of 1842 connected those disorders and the influence of Chartism to the failure of religious and moral institutions to keep pace with the rapid increase of population. Whatever the immediate causes of unrest had been, the latent cause was felt to be a want of clergy, churches and schools to provide religious education and moral training.[164] In 1844 the Revd. H. Moseley, H.M.I., likewise left that the Potteries were notorious 'not less for the wilder forms of religious belief than for the *infidelity* prevalent' and the 'madness of its political combinations' because the elementary education available was 'probably worse than in any other district'.[165] A decade later the Revd. J. P. Norris, H.M.I., considered the ignorant working masses of north Staffordshire politically dangerous, and the situation to be alleviated only by an element of compulsory education under the Factory Acts: 'Every year's delay brings us nearer to a crisis', and he reported the 'angry looks and muttered threats' of strikers he found 'gathering in knots at every meeting of the roads'.[166] There is no evidence of any significant support for keeping the workers politically weak by withholding education, and indeed Norris, a few years later, attacked the view that it would be dangerous to give an extended education to the child of the Black Country worker:[167]

> Dangerous to give him any other than bodily pleasures! Dangerous to extend his view beyond the next reckoning night; to school him into the habits of industry and honesty and obedience; to teach him his greatest foe is not he who bears authority over him, but his own rebellious will! . . . Monopolists of education may one day find that their folly has endangered their monopoly of property. Signs are not wanting that people will endure neither monopoly much longer. It behoves us . . . to anticipate an infidel and disloyal education by giving one that is sound and Christian.

Again H. S. Tremenheere in the early 1850s stressed the peril of leaving the education of Black Country workers to the Sunday schools, the moral influence of which he felt was ephemeral. A smattering of letters enabled them to read seditious literature without having the moral or intellectual strength to discern its falseness. Such literature could 'only exist in consequence of the low degree of intelligence' of the mass of its readers. In south Staffordshire he found men who had been influenced by such writings, 'exaggerating the principle of equality before God and the law . . . to a social and moral equality', and antagonistic to their employers. At Wednesbury and Bilston he found circulating cheap, anti-religious, socialist, anarchical and Chartist publications often purveying views identical to those of the 'Republican and Socialist literature of the Continent', and fomenting bitterness and strife. He saw particular danger in the fact that these were read by the artisan and tradesman class as well as by other workmen and saw the solution in a greater effort to provide 'sound and effective education among the lower classes' along Christian lines, especially through Church day schools. 'The schoolmaster should always be regarded as a powerful assistant to the clergyman' in raising the sights of the young above such literature: 'If children were to stay at school till eleven or older, they would make better servants . . . less liable to be led astray by false

advisors'.[168] And when the 'quiet, patient bearing' of workers of south
Staffordshire in the depression of 1857 was noted, it was held by J. P. Norris,
H.M.I., to result from the great expansion of schooling over the previous
decade.[169] 'Formation of character should be the most important of
educational aims', thought another H.M.I. 'Good conduct in manhood follows
as surely upon religious training in youth, as the rich harvest of autumn follows
upon the careful weeding and tillage of spring'.[170]

The motives of local clergy, many of whom were active in promoting education in the midlands,[171] were mixed. Often they, too, rated the strengthening
of the existing social order highly: 'a deference to authority is to be inculcated',
said one clergyman in the Potteries in 1841.[172] Others, like the vicar of Walsall
in 1848, were more interested in combating moral lassitude and the con-
comitant lack of religious observance.[173] Concern was, for instance, expressed
that two-thirds of the Leicestershire workers ignored the churches.[174] Some
Anglican clergy were no doubt stimulated by the need to combat Dissent,
which in Staffordshire, for example, had made inroads where parish churches
and chapels were comparatively thin on the ground.[175] In Birmingham, the
greatest city in the region, the bulk of voluntary school provision came after
1830, when evangelicalism became stronger, and much of it was the fruit
of interdenominational rivalry.[176] And the vicar of St. Mary's, Warwick,
described British schools as 'dreadful machines', 'full frought with moral and
religious evil to Church and Country'.[177] As early as 1823 the Leicester Society
for the Education of the Infant Poor (an Anglican organisation) recommended 'a
sound religious education ... [as] the surest bulwark against fanaticism'.[178]
Dissenting congregations put more emphasis on Sunday than day schools. Thus
in the south Staffordshire mining areas Anglican clergy in the 1840s felt
strongly that Sunday schools would not themselves meet local educational
needs.[179]

Nevertheless the lack of a resident gentry to provide social leadership and
financial aid hindered the extension of Church schooling in industrial
Staffordshire and the Black Country.[180] Tremenheere felt it also resulted in an
absence of cohesion between the classes and a 'spirit of insubordination'
expressed in trade unionism and strikes damaging both to worker and
employer. This state of affairs was exacerbated by the lack of education of the
contractors, who in the mining districts, with their absentee coal owners, were
the effective employers of the men, and who continued to employ young boys
underground illegally but with impunity.[181] The paternalism of the north-
country factory masters was less evident in the midland textile trades, where
commercial capitalists employed dispersed domestic workers, often indirectly,
and where the industrial unit was small. Such employers were often
unsympathetic to schooling. The chairman of the West Bromwich poor law
union, a magistrate, in 1837–38 felt that 'a great mischief arises from the outcry

against sending young children to work'.[182] Black Country employers in the 1840s considered that they had no responsibility for the social welfare of their workforce.[183] Even as late as 1858 the Revd. W. Lewis of Sedgley found in south Staffordshire and north Worcestershire that 'employers care but little whether their workpeople are educated or not' so long as they did their work.[184] The pit agents and butties in particular saw no harm in early labour for children nor any advantage in schooling. Thomas Rawling, a Derbyshire agent and Sunday-school teacher, felt in 1842 that restrictions on children under ten working in the mines would harm the industry and saw nothing against eight-year-olds being so employed.[185] Even in the late 1850s Black Country pit masters, though reconciled to the expansion of schooling, felt it made boys less effective workers.[186] Among the coalowners in the area there was general opposition to the age limit for underground working being raised from ten to twelve, and some disquiet about limiting the labour of older boys. In this way they were in accord with the owners of south Wales and Scotland, but out of tune with those in the north-east.[187]

In the Potteries employers discouraged public discussion of the application of the Factory Acts to their trades and saw considerable economic disadvantage to those firms employing large numbers of children. By 1858, however, they were willing to submit to some legislation, unlike the parents of the young workers who totally opposed restrictions on child labour.[188] Yet in the Birmingham and Wolverhampton hardware districts, as late as the 1860s, the generality of employers, especially the smaller ones, felt that legislative inteference with the employment of the young would be 'uncalled for' and 'distasteful'.[189]

Despite these widespread attitudes, some employers in the midlands, particularly those operating on a large scale, either actively promoted schooling or saw advantages in its extension. Their motives were mixed. Cerrtainly there was in some the feeling that educated workpeople made better employees, less inclined to political mischief or trade unionism. Others, probably a minority, appear to have been activated by genuine paternalism and humanitarian feelings, and there is some indication that such interest increased in the 1850s and 1860s.[190] The Whitwick collieries on the Ashby de la Zouch coalfield provided a day school and refused to employ children under ten before the Act of 1842 forbade it.[191] Edward Webb, a horsehair manufacturer in Worcester, established a girls' factory school in 1846.[192] At Stourbridge employers with strong religious motives promoted dissenting schools, and W. O. Foster, a large employer there, provided a reading room and library for his workmen. Messrs Bagnall, who employed many workers in iron works and colleries, set up evening schools for their employees in the early 1850s at Golds Hill and Capponfields as well as libraries, a sick club and recreational facilities, and paid a clergyman to minister to the spiritual needs of the workforce, later building a church.[193] In the Black Country, too, Chance Brothers, large-scale glass makers, established at Smethwick in 1845 a reading room and a school for 500 children, and in 1851 another school at Oldbury. This firm resolved then 'to discountenance the employment of boys and girls in our works who do not possess ... a fair acquaintance with the elements of reading, writing, and arithmetic with the addition of freehand drawing for the ornamental department'. Chance's young employees were to attend school several times a week in the day or evening and to sit an annual examination. These employees were, however, socially superior and more skilled than most in the Black Country.[194]

By the late 1850s other employers in the Black Country, like the British Iron Company at Congreave, as well as some employers in the Potteries, provided or supported day or evening schools. And in the Potteries, as at Hanley and Burslem, for example, leading dissenting employers established numerous schools to provide religious education. The subscription lists to the prize schemes contained the names of many employers, especially iron and coal masters, though, it is true, many more gave no support.[195] A belief in the socialising effect of education is clearly evident. At the colliery village of Kidsgrove (Staffs.) in the 1830s the coalowner built a church, a day school and a Sunday school, claiming to have converted the 'notoriously ignorant, vicious and depraved' inhabitants 'Little removed from barbarism' and a 'terror to the surrounding country' to industrious hard-working souls, 'regular in their devotional exercises' and 'respectful and obedient to their superiors'. By 1842 a thousand of these admirably converted workmen turned out 'with cudgels to keep off Chartist rioters' attempting to foment a strike. By 1850 there were 600 children in the schools and 'not one person to be found in a public house' on a Sunday, and similar examples in the district were cited.[196]

R. D. Grainger found, in his report on conditions in the industries of Nottinghamshire, Derbyshire, Leicestershire and Birmingham in the early 1840s,[197] that far from employers of 500 to 2,000 workers fearing political danger in popular education, they agreed 'without exception' that educated workmen were more trustworthy, more respectful, more accessible to reason in disputes over wages or changes in routine, better conducted in their social duties, and more refined in their tastes and use of language. Similarly some Leicestershire and Nottinghamshire lace employers found educated workers easy to handle[198] and R. W. Winfield, one of a number of Birmingham manufacturers who supported works schools, remarked in 1857 on their influence, 'We have no strikes, no disorder,'[199] and Samuel Turner, a Birmingham button manufacturer employing over 500 hands, in 1840 declared that 'the educated workman is unquestionably of much greater value to his employer than the uneducated'. He would not knowingly take on 'even one of

the very lowest mechanics who could not read. He found the extent of education to be directly proportionate to the hand's respectfulness and good behaviour. In any disagreement the ignorant were the first to complain. The
educated sent their children to Sunday schools and eschewed drunkenness and
bad behaviour. He and others who attested similarly made it clear that they
were not talking of mere acquaintance with the three Rs but of 'such a process
of mental and moral training as will develop the intellect and promote religious
conduct'.[200] It is clear, nevertheless, that they often believed such an education
obtainable through Sunday schools alone, and were not envisaging any
advanced secular instruction.

Similar views were being expressed in the late 1850s. Some employers saw
education as a direct antidote to unionism and political radicalism. Coalowners
in north Staffordshire blamed strikes on the misguided attractiveness of trade
unions to the ignorant: 'very many would not have joined the Union at all, had
they not erroneously imagined that by doing so they would benefit their master
as well as themselves'.[201] At Golden Hill and Mow Cop collieries disturbances, the growth of trade unionism and attempts to force up wages were
connected with a superfluity of beerhouses and an absence of schools. Robert
Williamson, the owner, reported later that at Mow Cop 'we are now well
supplied with churches and schools' and he anticipated a solid improvement:
these and other social amenities had led to lack of support for a strike.
Similarly Tremenheere felt that the Chances' educational efforts, noted
above, were 'well repaid by the general good conduct of their workmen', trade
unionism being unheard of.[202] At Ironville (Derbys.) , a village owned by the
Butterley Iron Company, the clergy promoted evening lectures and activities
and libraries, while the company indicated its support for education, letting it
be known that preference in employment would be given to educated youths
and workmen who schooled their children and offering financial assistance
to large families. The failure of a trade union-sponsored strike in 1844 and of
Chartism to find support was attributed to the company's paternal policies.[203]
At Clay Cross (Derbys.) in the 1870s more blatant blackmail was evident in
Charles Binn's mining company's threat to withdraw support for schools if a
trade union were established.[204]

The purely technical advantage of a better educated workforce, especially in
the coal and iron industries, was less obvious to midland employers than to
outside observers, though some did see such a need. In the 1840s a few
employers in the metal, pottery and textile trades were urging the establishment of schools of design.[205] At least one large employer accepted in 1850 that
'the ignorance of the underground bailiffs had caused the loss of immense sums
of money to Staffordshire',[206] and support for the prize schemes was an
indication that some employers saw the writing on the wall for the British metal
trades. The prize schemes aimed not only at raising general educational

standards but also at improving the scientific knowledge of skilled workmen —
mine agents and butties included — 'on whose skill . . . the material interests of
those important mining districts so much depend'.[207] The competition the
Staffordshire iron industry was meeting from producers elsewhere, it was felt,
could be matched only by an improvement in the technical education of the
skilled men, which had to rest on sound elementary education and a general
rise in the *per capita* productivity rate, itself adversely affected by undis-
ciplined, illiterate workmen.[208]

    The employers of agricultural workers varied in their outlook. Working
farmers were, as elsewhere, generally less in favour of the extension of
elementary schooling than were resident landowners. In Nottinghamshire,
even in the late 1860s, farmers were opposed to the curtailment of child labour,
which in some parts was used extensively, and some saw nothing against boys
starting work as young as seven.[209] In Warwickshire some farmers would let
cottages to labourers only on the condition that wives and children worked for
them, 'and press the women to come out oftener and the children younger than
they otherwise would do'.[210] Derbyshire farmers were antipathetic to
educated labourers and indifferent to the schooling of their offspring but since
very young children were not employed on Derbyshire farms there was little
positive opposition.[211] Among tenant farmers in the Black Country, however,
there was still antagonism, though landowners like Lord Hatherton were
supporters of schooling.[212] In rural north Nottinghamshire the presence of
aristocratic estates whose owners were sympathetic to popular education was
beneficial to the labourers,[213] and in Derbyshire, too, some landowners gave
handsomely to support schools, and villages with resident landowners fared
best.[214] In rural Leicestershire, where there were so many absentee landlords,
farmers even in the late 1860s were hostile to elementary schools and put
pressure on parents to send young children to work.[215]

    Landowners, however, were not unanimous, and some were cautious in
supporting too extensive interference with child labour. A meeting of
Warwickshire landowners at Exhall in the late 1860s was fully in favour of
forbidding child employment under ten and of legal restrictions to thirteen,[216]
but in 1870 some did not see how boys in farming districts could be kept at
school till they were twelve.[217] About the same time a similar meeting, of the
Staffordshire Chamber of Agriculture, revealed a variety of opinions among
landowners, farmers and other local people. Some supported a restriction to
ages ten to eleven. Others, including the Earl of Lichfield, favoured eight as
the age, since older children would otherwise merely go into neighbouring
industries not covered by the Acts. The Revd. R. W. Essington of Shenstone
opposed any interference in child labour in agriculture until free education
was provided by the state, but the meeting eventually resolved on support for
prohibition until eight and half-time schooling until eleven.[218]

Schooling and literacy

The cultural characteristics of midland communities and the attitudes of workmen and middle-class people towards education and child labour are reflected in the incidence of elementary schooling and the level of literacy. Each of the six counties show over the period 1841 to 1885 a considerable reduction in the proportion of marriage marks (Appendix D). Nevertheless in Derbyshire, Nottinghamshire, Staffordshire and Worcestershire the 1845 proportions of illiterate spouses were equal to or greater than the average for 1939–45. Again, while from 1850 most counties show an unhesitating decline in illiteracy, there was little if any improvement in Staffordshire between 1865 and 1871, and by then that county had achieved only the levels reached by Derbyshire, Leicestershire and Warwickshire in 1845 and Nottinghamshire in 1850. Indeed, Staffordshire fell far below the national level for the whole period, while Worcestershire, too, was considerably worse throughout, and Nottinghamshire for most of the time. The figures for Derbyshire, Leicestershire and, until 1870, Warwickshire, were equal to or slightly better than the national level. But on the whole the midland counties combined an absolute improvement in the proportion of illiterates with a decline relative to other counties, and in all but Worcestershire improvement took place at a slower rate than in the nation as a whole. Staffordshire, moreover, dropped to a position in 1880 where its proportion of illiterate spouses was higher than those of south and north Wales and of every other English county except Monmouthshire. Moreover percentage changes disguised the extent of illiteracy in numerical terms, for the midlands experienced a great population growth. The actual numbers of illiterate grooms in Derbyshire in 1866 was greater than in 1856 and the overall decline in numbers of illiterate brides and grooms taken together was relatively small in Derbyshire, Leicestershire and Staffordshire. Moreover in 1871 there was a slight increase over 1866 in the numbers of illiterate brides and grooms in Nottinghamshire, Staffordshire, and Warwickshire and of illiterate brides in Worcestershire (Appendix E).

A survey of the illiteracy statistics for individual registration districts (Maps 8, 9 and Appendix F) demonstrates that in 1856 there were three geographical concentrations where illiteracy was worse than the national level (35 per cent). First, in Staffordshire all districts in the east of the county from Leek in the north to Wolverhampton, Dudley and West Bromwich in the south, were in this category and these abutted on a number of districts in Worcestershire (Stourbridge, Kidderminster and Bromsgrove) and the populous Birmingham district, which in turn linked with the districts of Tenbury, Martley, Alcester, Pershore and Evesham. Together these formed a deep wedge of relatively high illiteracy from north Staffordshire to south Worcestershire, connecting with similarly illiterate districts in Shropshire, Herefordshire and north

MAP 8

Percentages of marriage marks, 1856: Staffordshire, Worcestershire, Warwickshire.
Bold figures indicate percentages above the national level of 35 per cent.

LEEK
39

WOLSTANTON **55**
NEWCASTLE U.L. **42**
STOKE O.T. **48**

CHEADLE
41

STONE
46

UTTOXETER
29

BURTON
O.T.
30

STAFFORD
37

STAFFS.

N

PENKRIDGE
40

LICHFIELD
27

TAMWORTH
32

WALSALL
55

ATHERSTONE
35.

WOLVERHAM-
PTON
64

DUD-
LEY
54

W.
BROMWICH
48

ASTON
29

NUNEATON **46**

BIRMINGHAM **36**

STOUR-
BRIDGE
57

MERIDEN
32

FOLES-
HILL
58

KINGS
N.
16

SOLIHULL
22

COVENTRY **39**

KIDDER-
MINSTER
45

BROMS-
GROVE
53

WARWICK
19

RUGBY
25

TENBURY
47

MART-
LEY
43

DROITWICH
33

WARWICKS.

WORCESTER
31

ALCESTER
45

SOUTHAM
35

STRATFORD
O.A.
33

PERSHORE
42

EVESHAM
49

SHIPSTON O.S.
34

WORCS.

UPTON
O.S.
33

0   5   10   15   20   MILES

Gloucestershire.[219] Secondly, in east Warwickshire another such block
comprised the districts of Coventry, Foleshill and Nuneaton (Warwicks),
connecting topographically with five districts in Leicestershire (Market
Bosworth, Hinckley, Ashby-de-la-Zouch, Blaby and Barrow-on-Soar). A third

MAP 9

Percentages of marriage marks, 1856: Derbyshire, Nottinghamshire, Leicestershire.
Bold figures indicate percentages above the national level of 35 per cent.

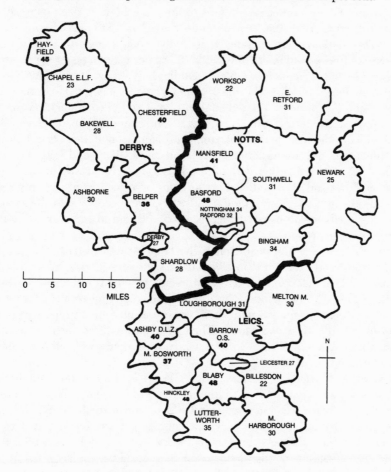

such group was made up of the districts of Chesterfield and Belper (Derbys.)
and Mansfield and Basford (Notts.). These connected with the Sheffield and
Doncaster (W.R.) districts, other areas of poor literacy. Not far off was Hayfield
(Derbys.), which was really part of the Lancashire–Cheshire industrial area of
high illiteracy.[220]

These heavily illiterate areas largely comprised the Potteries, the Black
Country, and parts of the midland mining and hosiery districts. Apart from the
towns of Derby, Nottingham and Leicester (all coinciding almost exactly with
the districts bearing their names), the remaining parts of the midland counties

were predominantly rural, though containing some market towns, some industrial centres (like Burton-on-Trent), and some mining areas, as in the Bakewell district.

Appendix G represents an attempt to compare literacy rates over all the midland districts, with the least illiterate district in 1856 ranked one, and so on.[221] This ranking demonstrates that in that year the bottom third (most illiterate) of the sixty-nine districts (with 42–64 per cent marks), twenty-two in number, included Wolverhampton, Dudley, Walsall, Stourbridge, West Bromwich, Pershore (all in the Black Country and its environs), together with Alcester and Bromsgrove, related centres of nail and needle manufacture, the carpet town of Kidderminster, and Stone, a centre for home-made gloves. Also included were the heavily concentrated hand-loom ribbon districts of Foleshill and Nuneaton, and the hosiery districts of Basford, Blaby and Hinckley, plus Hayfield (Derbys.), together with all the Potteries — Newcastle under Lyme, Stoke-on-Trent and Wolstanton. Pershore and Evesham were the only really agricultural districts represented, and they were dominated by market gardening, a labour-intensive activity using child labour to a greater extent than most farming operations.

Very different was the character of the twenty-three districts forming the top (least illiterate) one-third in 1856 (16–30 per cent marks), all well below the national level. Certainly districts embracing two industrial towns — Derby and Leicester — were included, but these were county towns and commercial centres as well as manufacturing places, where a substantial proportion of the better-off middle class was found. Then there were three districts close to Birmingham: Aston and Kings Norton, which were then partly rural and partly mixed residential suburbs, and Solihull, which was mainly agricultural. The largely rural districts of Lichfield and Warwick were dominated by the cathedral city and county town, neither a centre of industry, which gave them their names. Worcester, another county town and cathedral city, did have some glove manufacture, but was the centre of a predominantly farming district.[222] Other districts in this category were mainly agricultural in character, containing within them some mining and manufacture, but also market towns — like Uttoxeter, Bakewell, Chapel-en-le-Frith, Ashbourne, Rugby, Newark, East Retford and Worksop. Burton-on-Trent, the brewing centre, was surrounded by a farming area employing land workers in the winter months. A few lace and hosiery districts were represented, like Billesdon, Southwell and Shardlow and the districts to which the market towns of Loughborough, Melton Mowbray and Market Harborough gave their names. While industry was thus not absent from the districts of better literacy, these districts lacked heavy concentration of manufacture.

The middle-third group of districts in 1856 was, as might be expected more of a mixture. Included in it were districts dominated by large towns, particularly Birmingham itself, but also the ancient industrial towns of Coventry and Nottingham. Other districts included manufacturing centres like Leek and Chesterfield, and the county town of Stafford, which had some industry. The bulk of the lace and hosiery districts, too, were in this middle group — Radford, Bingham, Belper, Ashby de la Zouch, Lutterworth, Mansfield, Barrow-on-Soar and Market Bosworth, some of them embracing mining and other industrial activity, too. In addition, there were some largely agricultural districts containing market towns, as, for example, Shipston on Stour, Meriden, Stratford-on-Avon, Cheadle, Southam and Upton-on-Severn.

The variety apparent in this middle group indicates the danger of attempting to attach too exact a relationship between degrees of illiteracy and particular types of community, but taken all in all this analysis does show beyond doubt the relatively poor cultural state of Black Country and the Potteries, the comparatively good state of rural areas with market towns, and the fact that the hosiery and lace districts, perhaps because set in rural areas, were more literate than the more prosperous heavily industrialised areas.

A similar analysis undertaken for 1866 and 1871 (Appendix G) indicates some changes in the relative position of districts, though a substantial core of good and poor districts remains. Of the best (least illiterate) third (twenty-three) of the districts in 1856, sixteen were still in that third in 1866 and fourteen in 1871; of the worst third (twenty-three) in 1856, sixteen were in that category in 1866 and fourteen in 1871. In 1871 the continued relationship between industry and high illiteracy is clear: the most illiterate twenty-three districts then represented substantially the Black Country (now also with Birmingham), the Potteries, the silk districts of Foleshill and Nuneaton and Leek, a few textile districts like Hinckley, and several other manufacturing centres. Radford, not in the category in 1856, was substantially an overspill industrial suburb of Nottingham populated by the poorer, less skilled workers. The predominantly rural districts and those with market towns were still not to be found in among the most illiterate districts.

It is clear, too, that the extent of educational deprivation represented by illiteracy was increasing over the period in the midland industrial area. The gap between literate and less literate communities widened. The range of illiteracy in the sixty-nine districts in 1871 (from 9 to 59 per cent) was greater than in 1856 (16 to 64 per cent) and 1866 (12 to 58 per cent) (Appendix G). For males the difference between districts actually increased somewhat, from 42 percentage points in 1856 (15–57) to 43 in 1866 (11–54) and to 44 in 1871 (9–53). For females there was also an increase in the range, which remained greater than that for males: 1856, 53 percentage points (17–70); 1866, 54 points (8–62); and 1871, 62 points (2–64). The differences between districts is accentuated when percentages of illiterates are converted into actual numbers, for the industrial districts were the most heavily populated. Of the fourteen districts of over 50,000 in 1861, for example, ten were among the worst twenty districts for illiteracy in 1866. Of the other four, only Derby was relatively good.

Some recent studies support the significance of occupational structure as a factor in literacy profiles. In the Erewash Valley coalfield, miners and their daughters were less literate than the average male and female in the area until the 1870s and the rate of their improvement was related to their economic circumstances. Similarly literacy levels of frameworkers in the valley varied over time according to their levels of prosperity.[223] A comparison of occupation and literacy in Worcester and Dudley is similarly revealing. In Dudley, a town dominated by nail making, mining and unskilled labour, an average of only 31 per cent of grooms and 18 per cent of brides signed their names in the decade 1841–50. Then and later the literacy levels of nailers and miners in the town were lower even than those of labourers. In Worcester, a county and cathedral town, containing a large number of craft trades with many small masters and artisans, comparatively few labourers and an unusually large professional middle class, the comparable percentages were 72 and 59. Not surprisingly, there was also demonstrably better school provision in Worcester than Dudley.[224]

Additionally Dudley experienced a much larger increase in population over the period than did Worcester, and shifts in relative illiteracy levels within the midland registration districts (Appendix G) were manifestly related to population change. Many districts which experienced only a small population increase, or a decline, mainly predominantly rural areas and market towns, improved their relative positions. Thus, to cite only a few examples, Melton Mowbray, Meriden, Lutterworth and Southam, in all of which population declined 1851–71, rose considerably in the literacy table (Meriden from twenty-fourth to first). Indeed, fourteen districts in the top third in 1866 and 1871 had only modest increases or actual declines in their population over the period and nearly all these experienced substantial decline in percentage of illiterates from already relatively low levels. The same trend occurred in districts lower down the table.

On the other hand, where there were large population increases, and this was so particularly in districts comprising the larger towns, illiteracy rates tended to show no or little improvement, or even to get worse. The rate remained more or less static at Kings Norton (where population rose 53 per cent 1851–61 and a further 41 per cent 1861–71) and at Aston (also becoming part of greater Birmingham and experiencing a similar huge increase of numbers). Aston dropped from fourteenth place in 1856 to forty-ninth in 1871, and Birmingham itself fell from thirty-sixth to fifty-eighth. At Leicester, Chesterfield and Nottingham substantial increases in population went hand-in-hand with little improvement in literacy levels. Moreover in districts already highly illiterate in 1856 which saw high rates of population increase — as in the

Potteries and the Black Country — illiteracy levels showed little or no improvement, 1866–71, and in some cases a worsening. At Penkridge the proportions of marks actually rose 10 percentage points in that period. But even where population growth in industrial districts was moderate, illiteracy levels did not always diminish. The district containing the cathedral town of Warwick, on the other hand, retained a high ranking despite increases of population.

All this suggests not only the perpetuation of poor educational standards in the Black Country and the Potteries, but the likelihood of a halt in any considerable advance in other growing midland industrial towns. Eighteen districts showed a greater percentage of illiteracy in 1871 than in 1866. One factor in the high illiteracy of the midland counties was the consistently poor showing of brides. In each county female illiteracy was greater than male over the whole period (Appendix D). In the early years the gap between the sexes was considerable, and it closed only slowly until the mid-1860s, the difference remaining greater for longer in Nottinghamshire and Staffordshire. For Nottinghamshire and Worcestershire, and for Staffordshire in particu'ar, brides' achievements were worse than the national level throughout the period, in Warwickshire about that level till 1865, and in Derbyshire and Leicestershire slightly better. Even so, Staffordshire and Worcestershire were also below the national level for grooms throughout the period, Staffordshire considerably so, and the other counties around or slightly above, though Warwickshire lost ground from 1870. Over the period 1841 to 1880 improvement in literacy levels relative to other English counties was experienced in the midlands only in Leicestershire and Nottinghamshire for grooms and in Worcestershire for grooms and brides (Appendix D).

However, while in most places in the midlands many more brides than grooms were illiterate, this was not the case everywhere, as examination of marks at district level shows (Appendix F). In 1856 female illiteracy was greater than male in forty-nine of the sixty-nine districts, in forty-two by a margin of 5 percentage points or more. In 1871 the comparable numbers were forty-three and twenty-seven. Eighteen districts showed persistent concentration of female illiteracy of 8 percentage points or more over males in each of the years 1856, 1866 and 1871. These were the Potteries districts of Wolstanton, Stoke-on-Trent and Newcastle under Lyme, the four silk ribbon districts (Leek, Nuneaton, Coventry, Foleshill), the cotton district of Hayfield, the hosiery and lace districts of Hinckley, Leicester, Radford, Basford and Nottingham, and the central Black Country districts: Wolverhampton, Dudley, Walsall and Birmingham. All were places of high female employment where girls as well as boys found jobs early, and in most there were higher proportions of boys at school than girls in 1851. In Warwickshire in the 1850s, moreover, standards in boys' schools appear to have been higher than in girls'.[225]

The districts in which male illiteracy predominated over female were fewer in number, and largely but not entirely agricultural. In such areas there was less female employment and more men were labourers. There were seventeen such districts in 1856, nineteen in 1866 and twenty-three in 1871. Less of a permanent core is evident than is the case with districts of higher female illiteracy: only seven districts had greater male illiteracy in all three survey years: Market Harborough, Lichfield, Stratford-on-Avon, Shipston-on-Stour, Southam, Martley and Upton-on-Severn. The degree of difference between male and female proportions was less extensive than with the districts of greater female illiteracy. In 1856 in only six of the districts was male illiteracy greater than female by more than 5 percentage points, though by 1871 there were fourteen such districts — an indication perhaps of the decline in female knitters in country districts, and the growth of domestic service.[226]

There was then, an undeniable connection in the midlands between industrial concentration and poor literacy. Agricultural districts were better, particularly where market towns were included. The absence of resident gentry and the large numbers of smallholders in Staffordshire may have contributed to that county's low literacy levels and the same may be said of market gardening districts in Worcestershire. Generally, however, there appears to be no very obvious connection between literacy levels and types of farming or estate and farm size,[227] perhaps because the demand for the labour of young children was generally less than in some parts of the country.[228]

Schooling was certainly an important ingredient of literacy. Although the proportion on day-school books seems to have increased greatly between 1818 and 1833 and again between 1833 and 1851 in all the midland counties, both in 1833 and in 1851 the figures for Staffordshire, Warwickshire and Worcestershire fell below the national average. By 1851 Nottinghamshire had also fallen below it, while Warwickshire was superior only to Monmouthshire, Herefordshire Bedfordshire, Middlesex and Lancashire. Staffordshire and Worcestershire were better only than these counties and Cornwall. In 1858 in Derbyshire alone of the six counties did the proportion at public schools rise above the national average (Appendix J).

In the smaller towns of the midlands the situation was generally better than in the counties as a whole, but in the larger towns worse. Of the eight towns with over 20,000 inhabitants separately treated in the 1851 census, all but two had lower proportions of their populations at school on census day than the average of the county in which they were set, and those two (Nottingham and Walsall) only equalled the county average. Of the twelve smaller towns for which figures are supplied, only one, Lichfield, did not have better ratios of children at school on census day than the county average, and in most cases their superiority was substantial (Appendixes J, K).[229]

For the nine midland towns in a list of sixty-seven 'principal' English towns for which it is possible to express school attendance as a percentage of children

aged five to fourteen, seven fell below the average of 52 per cent:
Wolverhampton, Coventry, 30 per cent; Leicester, 36 per cent; Nottingham 43
per cent; Stafford 50 per cent; and Worcester 51 per cent.[230] And other
evidence, too, illustrates the educational backwardness of the industrial towns
of the area. In the towns of Warwickshire in 1866 there was reported 'a class of
children which does not exist in rural parishes, children who do not profess to
go to any school and who pass the day idling about the streets'.[231] In 1857 fewer
than half the children in Birmingham under ten were at school,[232] and even
in the late 1860s a large part of the city's population was considered 'not in any
way reached by our present system of education',[233] and there were allegedly
over 50,000 child idlers on the streets.[234] As late as 1870 only 21 per cent of
children aged five to thirteen were at day school in Willenhall, 32 per cent in
Wednesfield and 45 per cent in Wolverhampton.[235] As noted in Chapter 2,
the educational situation was often worse in the heavily populated industrial
areas outside the towns than in either the towns or the more purely agricultural
areas. Instances of this are provided in West Bromwich, not a 'town' but
covered with working nailers and other industrial workers, in the textile
manufacturing areas outside the larger centres of Nottingham, Leicester, and
Coventry, where domestic industry was concentrated, and in the Potteries.[236]

In the sprawling and densely populated districts of south Staffordshire and
north Worcestershire 'a large proportion of the children are still found
unaffected' by schooling in the 1860s,[237] and Brierley Hill in the Black
Country, with 11,000 inhabitants, was said in 1866 to have had fewer children
at school than any comparably sized place in Europe outside Spain or Italy.[238]
Generally the proportions of children at school were greater in the midland
agricultural areas, though not invariably so.[239]

Factors like migration and adult education make it unlikely for there to be a
directly proportional relationship between the day schooling levels in a
particular place and later literacy levels there. Appendix I does, nevertheless,
suggest that at county level a general connection existed between proportions
of boys and girls aged five to fourteen not at day school in 1851 and illiteracy
rates in 1866. A rudimentary analysis of all the registration districts in the six
counties also demonstrates a discernible relationship betwen the incidence of
day schooling in mid-century with illiteracy rates fifteen years later (Appendixes
F, G). Despite many exceptions, there was a tendency for districts with better
school proportions later to produce lower illiteracy rates (Table 4·2).[240]

Nevertheless, application of the product moment correlation coefficient
formula to the data for the registration districts of the region yields a coefficient
of only −0·43, about the same as for the western counties and the south
midlands. Within each county the strongest correlations (−0·70 and −0·69)
were found in Warwickshire and Staffordshire; a weaker one (−0·53) in
Nottinghamshire; very low correlations in Derbyshire (−0·30); and effectively

TABLE 4·2

Illiteracy rates and schooling

% population in attendance at day school, 1851	Illiteracy rates 1866: number of districts		
	12–22% marks	23–29% marks	30–58% marks
13	3 ⎫	3 ⎫	1 ⎫
12	3 ⎬ 16	2 ⎬ 14	1 ⎬ 6
11	5 ⎮	5 ⎮	2 ⎮
10	5 ⎭	4 ⎭	2 ⎭
9	4 ⎫	1 ⎫	7 ⎫
8	2 ⎬ 6	6 ⎬ 9	5 ⎬ 18
7	0 ⎮	2 ⎮	3 ⎮
6	0 ⎭	0 ⎭	3 ⎭

Source: Based on Appendix F.

no correlation in Leicestershire (+0·03). In Worcestershire there was actually a positive correlation — a tendency for better school attendances later to produce higher levels of illiteracy. Thus while the two counties embracing the Black Country and the Potteries show the strongest correlation, even there only some 50 per cent of the literacy levels can be associated in this way with the incidence of local day schooling.

A less sophisticated examination of the illiteracy and schooling figures (Appendixes F, G) shows a tendency for the heavily industrialised districts and those dominated by large towns to have high illiteracy rates and low school rates. This is particularly evident in Birmingham, the position of which in the illiteracy rankings (Appendix G) fell from thirty-sixth to fifty-eighth between 1856 and 1871. Poor literacy rates in the Potteries and Black Country districts were reflected in day school attendances in 1851 that were below the national level; and the same is so of the silk districts of Coventry, Foleshill and Nuneaton.[241] The hosiery districts were mixed, showing much less of a connection.

The better school-roll figures for most of the smaller county and market towns, noted above, appear to provide a partial explanation of the tendency for the registration districts in which they were set to have relatively better literacy levels (Appendixes G, K). Warwick is the most striking example: the town had 15 per cent of its population on school books in 1851 and Warwick registration district ranked as the least illiterate in the midlands in 1866. Yet in quite a number of cases no obvious relationship between school attendance and illiteracy levels is observable. Some apparent discrepancies, however, appear to have demographic causes. It is, for example, not surprising that Kings Norton's low 8 per cent of population at school in 1851 bore little relationship to its very low illiteracy rate in 1866 (only 14 per cent), since between 1851 and 1861 its population increased 53 per cent and in the following decade by another 41 per cent. In this case it seems likely that the influx included comparatively educated people. With Chesterfield, population increase was of a different kind. There a modest 10 per cent at day school in 1851 was followed in 1866 by a high illiteracy rate in 1866 (37 per cent), but the population increase of 35 per cent 1851–61 and 25 per cent 1861–71 was probably of industrial workers. Billesdon was consistently good in literacy (third, first, first in 1856, 1866, 1871): yet had only a modest 9 per cent at day school in 1851. Here, however, there was only a small increase of population (4 per cent 1851–61; 3 per cent 1861–71). Not dissimilar was Meriden, where there was a small decrease in population.

From the 1830s public schooling spread. In 1833 private schools catered for at least a half[242] of day-school pupils in all but Warwickshire; by 1851 public schools accounted for 58 per cent in Nottinghamshire and somewhat over two-thirds in the other midland counties (Appendix J). By mid-century seven of the twenty midland towns treated separately in the census had 74 per cent or more pupils at public schools (Appendix K). Comparison of the 1866 illiteracy rates in the sixty-nine midland registration districts with day-school proportions at public day schools shows no relation whatever (Appendix F) — not surprisingly, since, aside from other factors like migration, many public schools were unaided and uninspected and as often condemned by the inspectorate as were poor private schools,[243] and certainly less efficient than the inspected schools. It was reckoned that in the uninspected schools of Birmingham less than a quarter of pupils would have passed the appropriate examination under the Revised Code.[244] Moreover two districts with the same proportion of public-school pupils could have very different percentages not at school at all.[245] At the level of basic literacy, improvement may have derived less from the growth of all public schools as from the spread of schooling generally, though we may suspect that the expansion of the numbers of aided schools, not distinguished from other public schools in the 1851 census, was a significant ingredient.

The bulk of the public schools provided in the midlands, as in most parts of the country, was increasingly Anglican. In the mid-century nonconformity was relatively strong in Derbyshire, Nottinghamshire, Leicestershire and Staffordshire, but less so in Worcestershire and Warwickshire (Appendix N). The approximate proportions of British and dissenting schools in 1833, however, reflect that pattern only very obviously in Derbyshire and Nottinghamshire, but even there such schools numbered only about one-third of all public schools and in the other midland counties a much lower proportion (Appendix L). Even in the towns, where more dissenters were probably concentrated, the Anglican dominance was evident. At Warwick, for example, two National schools were founded in 1815 and 1833, but no British school until 1845. In Coventry a British school founded in 1811 was followed in 1813 by a National school and by the establishment of an archidiaconal National Schools Society, so that before long the Church had established a clear lead in the city.[246]

By 1847 the proportion of Church school pupils in the population was above the national average in all the midland counties (Appendix M), and by the 1850s Anglican domination in public schooling was very clear: with some three-quarters or more of public day school pupils at Church schools in every county. Nottinghamshire stands out as an area when Church schooling was particularly strong. Roman Catholic schools were most evident in Staffordshire and Warwickshire (Appendix L). By 1867 proportions of the population at Church schools were around or above the national average in all midland counties, but lowest in Staffordshire and Warwickshire (Appendix M). The success of the Established Church in an area where dissent was strong reflects the advantages of organisation and wealth discussed above.[247]

It is likely that Anglicans represented the wealthier section of many communities and that the lack of unity of dissenting sects gave the Established Church the advantage. Where bigger dissenting congregations, with some better-off members, existed the share of the Church in schooling was less. At Birmingham, Coventry, Derby, Leicester, Nottingham and Wolverhampton in 1851, for example, it varied between 60 and 68 per cent — well below the county averages. Yet even in such dissenting strongholds the Church did surprisingly well. Expressed in actual numbers of pupils, 6,000 of the 10,000 Birmingham public day-school pupils were at Anglican schools and over a thousand at Roman Catholic ones. By 1869 the figures were 18,660 (Anglican), 2,780 (R.C.) and 3,773 (British and nonconformist),[248] a situation perhaps reflecting conflicting views over day-school provision among Birmingham nonconformists,[249] but also the energy of the Church. In Nottingham, too, where dissenting schools had twice the number of pupils as Church schools in 1833, the nonconformist interest waned and by 1851 1,800 pupils were at Church schools and only 848 at nonconformist and British schools, while by 1870 the figures were: 5,300 Church; 1,200 British and protestant nonconformist, 400 Roman Catholic.[250]

The mid-1830s had seen the formation of the Lichfield Diocesan Extension Society, which was followed by much Church building, often with National schools, to serve the expanding populations.[251] Moreover, despite Samuel Butler's personal lack of enthusiasm for popular schooling, his episcopate at Lichfield (1836–9) witnessed the establishment of a system of district boards and a diocesan college for training male teachers. Within six years 271 schools (12,000 pupils) were in union with the board.[252] By 1858 Church schools in the midland counties collectively had a much larger income from non-governmental sources than did British and dissenting schools (Appendix P). Moreover, because of the number of Church schools, they received the bulk of parliamentary grants. Much of this funding was concentrated on Staffordshire, which received from the treasury over the period 1833–59 grants at the same high level as Lancashire (Appendix O). Staffordshire and Derbyshire were also among those counties chosen by the National Society for extra assistance in the 1840s, though both ranked very low in the amount of money locally subscribed following the Queen's exhortatory letter of 1843.[253]

Despite all this the impact on the educational needs of the area must not be exaggerated. While schools were provided where otherwise there would have been none, and while Church dominance of public schooling in Staffordshire, the centre of Primitive Methodism and the Methodist New Connexion, was something of a triumph,[254] nevertheless only five other English counties had lower proportions of their populations at Church schools than Staffordshire, and Warwickshire's rate was only on a par with that of Lancashire (Appendix M).

All the midland counties except Staffordshire received a lower rate of government funding than the national average, 1833–59, though it is true that Church schools in Derbyshire, Leicestershire, and Warwickshire had above average incomes from other sources in 1858 (Appendixes O, P).

Consequently, in the 1830s and 1840s in particular, there was a considerable lack of school places in some parts of the area. In Dudley no National school was opened until 1836, and a British school only the previous year.[255] In 1833 the number of places where the only school was a Sunday school, and where it could not be presumed that children could attend any other school, was twenty-nine in Leicestershire, twenty-six in Worcestershire, twenty-three in Nottinghamshire, eighteen in Derbyshire, sixteen in Warwickshire, and seven in Staffordshire. This, however, probably gives a sanguine picture of the availability of decent schooling. Reports that the midland mining and manufacturing districts were deficient of schooling recur throughout the period,[256] particularly with reference to outlying parts of parishes away from village centres and to the new suburbs of industrial towns, as in Derby in the 1860s.[257] Assessment of such deficiences was, however, often based on an unreal conception of local demand for schooling.[258] Often the supply of public school places exceeded that demand. In 1844 the Revd. H. Moseley, H.M.I., visited ninety-four midland schools with a capacity for over 11,000 children, but found only some 6,350.[259] In the mining village of Audley (Staffs.) another H.M.I. found in the 1840s 'an excellent school-house in the centre of a large population of colliers, unoccupied'. A survey of Anglican day schools in the Potteries in 1844 revealed accommodation for over 5,000 children, but actual attendance, of 2,273, and in 1852 only 40 per cent of the places in fourteen schools in the Black Country were filled, and those mostly by very young children.[260] Similarly, in 1858 in the unions of Dudley, Stoke-on-Trent, Newcastle under Lyme, and Burslem and Wolstanton, the average daily attendance at public elementary schools was less than 9,500, though there were some 17,000 school places.[261] Similarly in the hosiery districts schools were said never to be full.[262] In Leicester itself over the period many schools were unfilled, and by 1870 there was accommodation for 75 per cent of the city's children aged three to thirteen, but only 56 per cent were in attendance.[263] By the 1860s the situation in rural areas, where dispersed and small populations made provision of schools difficult, had improved considerably. By then very few parishes in Nottinghamshire and Worcestershire did not have their own school or access to one nearby. In rural Derbyshire schools were widespread, and in Leicestershire, some sort of school was 'seldom wanting', though the absence of resident landowners meant that good schools were fewer.[264]

Even for children who attended school, however, the effectiveness of the education provided was affected by their age, the length of school, stay, their regularity of attendance, and the quality of teaching. The reports of the inspectorate indicate increasing numbers of trained teachers as the period progresses, but there is no evidence that the monitorial system prevalent in the 1840s resulted in any better instruction than that given in the smaller private schools. In 1845 one H.M.I. reported of the public schools in the midlands generally that 'with very few exceptions the children are taught by one another'.[265] In many schools the younger children, all grouped together and not organised in classes, were left entirely to monitors, who were on average younger than eleven.[266] Where there were no monitors, however, the position was not necessarily better: in 1846 at Arnold, a town of framework knitters, the school contained 131 children of all ages in sole charge of a nineteen-year-old mistress.[267]

The pupil–teacher system, an improvement over the monitorial, gained ground from the late 1840s, but in the midland manufacturing districts, especially in prosperous periods, intelligent youths were attracted to the better paid jobs in commerce, the railways and so on.[268] Moreover, in 1849 only six pupil teachers had been recruited in Leicestershire, and then and in the 1850s the inspectorate felt there were too few trained teachers in the midlands generally and the inspected schools were still very defective.[269] It was really only in the 1860s, as the numbers of trained teachers increased, that the inspectors reported many well organised and conducted schools. Even then many midland children were abysmally ignorant despite attending day school. Of rural children leaving school at nine to ten in Nottinghamshire and Leicestershire it was said in the late 1860s: 'the little knowledge they have thus gained appears to be very quickly lost . . . many of the farm servants might, to judge by what they know, have come from Central Africa'. Yet ignorance was far greater in the manufacturing districts of the area.[270] Joseph Rockley, an eleven-year-old glove worker, had attended day school for two years from the age of seven, but could read only a few short words, and read 27 as 72 and 21 as 12. Anna Rockley, aged nine, in attendance at school, could also read only a few words like 'cow' and 'sea'.[271] Thomas Cooper, a worker of eleven in

Birmingham, after two years at day school knew only individual letters, and could write only his own name. He could not multiply three by three. Caroline Falkener, aged seventeen, a worker in a pen factory could likewise tell letters but not read despite two and a half years of school. At William Aston's button factory in Birmingham 86 per cent of eighty girls between seven and sixteen were unable to read, and none could write at all.[272]

Facts like these provide a warning against placing too much reliance on the significance of school attendance figures. The age structure of the school population, for instance, affected the level of instruction experienced. Neither the 1833 survey nor that of 1851 provides statistics of the precise ages of pupils. The 1833 survey did, however, attempt to classify schools according to the ages of the children catered for and gives an overall impression for the midland of a day-school population dominated by the very young. Indeed, even in 1845 the average age in inspected public schools was eight to nine,[273] with few children over twelve, and the average in the private schools was probably much lower. To a large extent this reflected the general age at which children were put to work.

In 1841 in the parliamentary borough of Wolverhampton (comprising Wolverhampton itself and the townships of Bilston, Sedgley, Wednesbury and Willenhall), where only a quarter of children under fifteen attended any day school, the proportions of children on the books of public day schools were recorded as 23 per cent under five, 52 per cent five to nine; and 17 per cent ten to fifteen.[274] At Stourbridge in the same year the curate of Old Swinford reported of his day school, 'they come in and out so young that it is little better than an infant school'.[275] In 1852 it was said of the minority of Black Country children who attended public schools that the general practice was to enter at seven, attend three or four days a week for twelve months or so, and then leave.[276] Even in the mid-1860s a survey of south Staffordshire showed only 17 per cent of pupils over the age of ten, and 5 per cent over twelve. This compares with 55 per cent over ten in the rural East and North Ridings of Yorkshire.[277] In Birmingham in 1838, 25 per cent of children at day schools were under five,[278] and twenty years later only 21 per cent of boys and 17 per cent of girls over ten were still at school.[279] The situation in the Potteries was certainly no better. At Burslem, for instance, in the early 1840s, the curate reported that the children who did attend school were 'too young to make much progress'.[280] In 1851–2 only 10 per cent of a sample of children aged seven and upwards in inspected National schools in the Potteries were over ten.[281] About the same time in sixteen National schools in north Staffordshire 48·5 per cent of pupils were under seven and 42 per cent were aged seven to ten.[282] Even in the 1860s only the infant school prospered in Burslem, and the Revd. H. Sandford, H.M.I., reported that in all but one National school in the Potteries the mass of children were under nine; indeed, only 13 per cent were over ten and less than 4 per cent over twelve.[283] In 1864 the schools in the mining districts of north and south Staffordshire were said to 'lose their children at an earlier age than those of any other part of England'.[284] In the textile districts a similar situation pertained. At Leek, where there was a heavy demand for girls' labour, only 13·5 per cent of girls in National schools in the late 1860s were over ten, 4·5 per cent over twelve.[285] In the Nottingham textile area in 1842 teachers complained that if trade was good 'in a fortnight half the school would leave'.[286] The vast majority of children in ten schools in the area in 1857 was under ten and only 18 per cent had been at school for two years or more.[287]

Even in the 1860s a Nottinghamshire middleman admitted that 'Very few girls between the ages of seven and twelve go to school except on Sunday, as most of them are seaming'.[288] In Leicestershire the situation was much the same.[289] Moreover, one H.M.I. in 1845 alleged that the average age of children in public elementary schools in the midlands generally was actually falling: 'we may be educating *more*, but they are, I believe, younger children, and stay with us a less time'.[290] There were similar observations in the 1850s, and between 1856 and 1862 the percentage of children over ten in schools in the Potteries fell from 21 to 15.[291] Between 1862 and 1866 the proportion of children in school aged over ten in south Staffordshire also decreased.[292]

The situation was somewhat better in agricultural areas, though children's school life was short there, too. In Warwickshire and Worcestershire country children left school on average before they were ten; in Derbyshire more often they stayed till the age of twelve or so.[293] In rural Staffordshire in the 1860s only 43 per cent were said to leave school before age ten, compared with 75 per cent in the Potteries, and the percentage of older pupils was much higher than in the Potteries.[294] Educational standards in even the ganging villages, the most depressed agricultural districts, were said to be better than in hosiery districts round Nottingham and Leicester.[295] Nevertheless, in the 1860s, of 100 children in Nottinghamshire and Lincolnshire inspected schools over the age of six, only 8 per cent were older than ten and few of those were farm labourers' children. In the Worksop area children were said to be working on the land at an earlier age than formerly, many leaving school at eight. About the same time in fifteen rural Leicestershire parishes, of 1,000 to 1,200 farm labourers' children registered at day schools the proportions were higher: 26 per cent in summer and 30 per cent in winter were older than nine.[296]

In all parts of the midlands the number of years spent at school was small and attendance irregular. Two surveys of schools in the Dudley–Wolverhampton area in the late 1840s and early 1850s put the average 'school stay' of working-class schoolchildren at fifteen to thirty months.[297] A survey of south Staffordshire schools found that even in the 1860s only 29 per cent of boys had been at school longer than two years, compared with 55 per cent in rural Yorkshire.[298] In the 1860s at Leicester, too, children attended 'some only a month or a week' and most rarely more than eighteen months and then irregularly. At one city school only about a half the pupils had attended more than 100 days in the preceding year.[299] As one Birmingham teacher said in the 1840s 'the school is constantly changing and few receive benefit'.[300] In the 1850s the average attendance at one boys' school in the city was eight months and at another seventy-one days.[301] Such information is generally available only for inspected schools. It is unlikely that the situation in private and uninspected public schools was better and probable that it was worse.

Efforts at improvement by teachers and H.M.I.s were often counterproductive Generally, especially in mining communities, 'the better the school the shorter the time the children remained at it', since parents felt they reached the required standard earlier. Mining populations tended to move about in search of higher wages and this, too, militated against regular schooling.[302] Certainly, parental attitudes often did not coincide with those of the inspectorate. In rural Warwickshire even in the late 1860s parents thought satisfactory schooling possible 'if a child goes ... when he has nothing else to do',[303] and throughout the rural midlands attendance was worse in summer than winter.[304] Henry Moseley, H.M.I., commenting on the midlands generally in 1845, felt that the low average length of schooling resulted in as many or more children leaving school unable to read as children who could.[305]

Many parents made do with Sunday schools, important features of the life of many communities, at which attendance was impressive. In 1833 far more children attended Sunday school than day school, the excess being particularly evident in Nottinghamshire, Leicestershire, Derbyshire and Staffordshire, where Sunday school proportions were considerably in excess of the national average. In 119 places (mostly in Nottinghamshire, Leicestershire and Worcestershire) only Sunday schools existed, catering for over 5,000 children.[306] In 1851 and 1858 the same county pattern is discernible (Appendix J). At registration district level in 1851, twenty-one districts in Leicestershire, Derbyshire and Nottinghamshire had a Sunday-school attendance above the national level, and only seven below that; and in Staffordshire the ratio was nine to seven. The likelihood of Sunday schooling being a substitute for day schooling, either entirely or for older children, is strong in these counties. In Worcestershire and Warwickshire the position was reversed, with two-thirds of districts at or below the national level (Appendix F).

Sunday schooling was particularly popular in certain towns. In 1834 20 per cent of the population of the extensive borough of Stoke-on-Trent were Sunday-school pupils. In 1838 there were 12,500 Sunday scholars in Birmingham, in Coventry 1,350; in the 1840s 2,500 at Kidderminster, 1,600 at Leek, 10,500 in Nottingham and 8,000 in Leicester.[307] In 1868 only 16 per cent of a sample of adolescents in Birmingham had not attended Sunday school.[308] Nevertheless of the twenty towns separately treated in the 1851 census[309] all but fourteen had proportions at day school on census day equal to or greater than at Sunday school, suggesting that the Sunday establishments were less of a substitute there for full-time education than in some parts.

That cannot, however, be said of Derby, Leicester and Nottingham, nor of Coventry, Wolverhampton and Newcastle under Lyme (Appendix K). There is plenty of evidence to show that for many children in districts where work began at an early age Sunday school provided virtually all their formal education. In Burslem in the Potteries in 1833 there were 3,168 children at Sunday school but only 700 at day schools.[310] About 1840 73 and 78 per cent of children at Sunday school in Birmingham and Coventry respectively attended no other school, these proportions representing 46 and 44 per cent of children receiving some sort of education in those places.[311] In the Wolverhampton district, including Willenhall, Bilston, Wednesfield, Sedgley and Darlaston, and in Dudley, Walsall, Wednesbury and Stourbridge, in the early 1840s Sunday schools, though attracting only half the child population, were said to be 'the chief means relied on for the education of the working classes',[312] and the same was said of the mining districts of Warwickshire, Leicestershire and Derbyshire. In West Bromwich in 1839 20 per cent of children aged two to fourteen attended only Sunday school, 27 per cent some sort of day school, and 53 per cent no school at all.[313] In the Potteries two years later nearly 18,000 children attended Sunday schools, compared with 2,000 in public day schools.[314] In Leek Sunday schooling was extensive, providing in 1840 'nearly all the instruction the children obtain', the only public day school being a small charity establishment.[315]

The proportions of Sunday scholars in manufacturing villages was lower than in the towns, but in agricultural districts the reverse was so. Thus in 1851 some 80 per cent of children aged five to fourteen in Nottingham attended Sunday schools, a somewhat higher percentage in Bingham, a nearby agricultural district, but only about 46 per cent in Radford, a cluster of industrial villages just outside Nottingham.[316] In the hosiery and lace districts in the 1840s and 1850s many children attended only Sunday schools. 'Were it not for the Sunday-schools,' said William Bott, a knitter of Barwell (Leics.), 'the condition of the labouring classes, as respects education, would be appalling indeed.'[317] And another knitter, Thomas Alsopp of Hinckley, reported that 'hundreds of children . . . never knew what it is to go to any other school . . . If it was not for the Sunday schools . . . I think we should be at the lowest pitch of depravity that human mind is capable of conceiving; and even as we are, we are in a low and dreadful state'.[318] Even in the late 1850s the proportions attending only Sunday schools was reduced, but still probably high in some places. A survey of 1,373 working-class children aged seven to thirteen in Birmingham in 1857 showed 34 per cent at Sunday but not day school, 31 per cent at both day and Sunday school, and 11 per cent at day school only.[319] About the same time in the Black Country parishes of Dudley, Tipton, Sedgley and Rowley Regis there were 137 Sunday schools and over 22,000 pupils, while only 18,000 attended any sort of day school.

Analysis of the thirty-eight midland districts with Sunday-school attendance above the national level in 1851 (Appendix F) suggests that in about a quarter of them high Sunday-school attendance was an accompaniment of low day-school attendance. Nevertheless in the remaining twenty-three districts higher than average Sunday school attendance was paralleled by above average day-school attendance, suggesting communities where parents regarded both Sunday and day schooling as a desirable part of child rearing.

The popularity of Sunday schools certainly had a religious aspect. Nonconformists in the midlands were more willing or better able to provide Sunday than day schooling. In 1833 the proportion of pupils at Church and Dissenting (including Roman Catholic) Sunday schools was approximately 9 : 11 in each of the six midland counties except Nottinghamshire where the proportion was 11 : 9. By the 1850s the nonconformist lead had increased in all but Warwickshire and Worcestershire, though even there about half the Sunday scholars went to dissenting schools. In those two counties, and in Derbyshire and Nottinghamshire, a definite connection between the incidence of Sunday schooling and religious allegiance is discernible (Appendixes L, N). Such a relationship is not obvious in Staffordshire, but the likely preference of non-church-going parents in the industrial areas, particularly the Potteries and the Black Country, for nonconformist Sunday schools is suggested by the very high proportion of Sunday scholars attending nonconformist establishments: at Burslem 67 per cent in 1833; at Hanley and Shelton 79 per cent; 81 per cent at Newcastle under Lyme; 84 per cent at Wolverhampton; 100 per cent at West Bromwich; 72 per cent at Leek.[320]

Despite this, evidence of beneficial educational effects deriving from all this Sunday activity is sparse. At county level Sunday-school attendance rates in 1851 bear little obvious relationship to literacy levels in 1866 (Appendixes D, J). Nor is any strong relationship discernible at registration district level, though in the thirteen (of sixty-nine) midland districts with Sunday-school proportions more than 4 percentage points above day-school proportions, nine were among the thirty least literate districts in 1866 (Appendix F). They were mainly in Staffordshire and the areas of domestic textile production. Sunday-school attendance in the midlands was, of course, characterised by a wider age range than the day schools, a much higher proportion of older children (at Wolverhampton, for example, in 1847 only 10 per cent under five, 39 per cent over ten), and longer school stay — quite often as long as ten years.[321] At Leek the mean entrance age in 1838–40 was eleven.[322] These factors, as well as the overlap with day schooling, render a discernible relationship with literacy levels difficult to find. Yet it would be surprising if all this activity had no educational impact. Sunday schooling attracted many midland parents because it was free, gave moral training within the ambit of their own religious beliefs, and did not interfere with child earnings — but also because it offered secular instruction. No comprehensive statistics are available but all the evidence suggests that in the 1830s and early 1840s in the midlands virtually all the Sunday schools taught reading, though a minority taught writing.[323] At East Retford Wesleyan school in 1839, however, less advanced pupils were actually kept from morning chapel to receive extra coaching in writing.[324] In 1843 the Methodist New Connexion Sunday school at Hanley taught reading and writing to about 1,000 pupils.[325]

Throughout our period, however, sabbatarian objections limited the teaching of writing[326] and by the 1840s it was no longer taught in many midland Sunday schools, especially Anglican and Wesleyan establishments.[327] In Kidderminster, for example, writing was forbidden in all but Unitarian Sunday schools by 1840. Here, however, parental ambitions were recognised by the provision of writing lessons on Monday evenings. Such provision by Sunday-school teachers existed, too, in other parts of the midlands. In many schools in Nottinghamshire writing and arithmetic were not taught on the Sabbath but provided, for well behaved children, in the week.[328] At Thumaston, a hosiery village in Leicestershire, the Primitive Methodists allowed Sunday writing, but the Wesleyans provided it on Monday evenings.[329]

Various surveys of educational levels attained by midland Sunday-school pupils suggest that the main impact was on the extension of reading and to a lesser extent on the writing of individual letters and short words.[330] Analysis of a report on Friar's Lane Sunday school in Leicester about 1840, for forty-seven girls and fifty-three boys aged mainly ten to thirteen, provides the following:[331]

	Girls (%)	Boys (%)	% Boys and girls
Able to read	96	87	91⎫ 98
Able to read a little	4	9	7⎭
Unable to read	—	4	2
Able to write	51	60	56⎫ 72
Able to write a little	26	8	16⎭
Unable to write	23	32	28

A larger sample, of the New Meeting Sunday School, Birmingham, in 1841 (168 boys, 105 girls, aged mainly nine to fourteen), yields very similar evidence:[332]

	Girls (%)	Boys (%)	% Boys and girls
Able to read	64	58	60⎫ 98
Able to read a little	33	39	37⎭
Unable to read	3	2	3
Able to write well	38	43	41⎫ 79
Able to write a little	33	42	38⎭
Unable to write	29	15	21

In each case most of the children unable to write had begun work at an early age, often six or seven. In the Leicester sample 15 per cent were also at day school, and in the Birmingham set 13 per cent. The larger proportion of Birmingham boys able to write is not matched at Leicester. The very high proportion who, it was claimed, could read to some extent is, however, common, as is the lower, but not dissimilar, proportion supposedly able to write to some extent. Considering the emphasis in the schools on reading rather than writing this is to be expected, and other evidence supports the fact that many more Sunday-school children could read a little than write.[333] A smaller sample of young pinheaders aged seven to twelve at Palmer and Holt's pin factory in Birmingham about the same time, indicates a very much lower level of attainment. Of the boys 67 per cent and of the girls 58 per cent could not read at all, and 81 per cent of boys and all the girls were unable to write at all. More than half these children (and three-quarters of the girls) did not attend Sunday school. Thirty-eight per cent of the boys had been to school at some time, but of these all but one had attended only a matter of weeks or months. No girl had attended school more than three years.[334]

The educational significance of Sunday schools must, therefore, not be exaggerated. Standards were not high. Many working-class Sunday-school teachers in the midlands were barely literate, unsuited to teaching and often little more than children themselves.[335] Despite the examples cited, the time given to secular subjects was often very limited. Evidence taken by the various Children's Employment Commissions as late as the 1860s indicates that many children who claimed to be able to read and write could often barely say their ABC, while many left quite unable to read or write and in a state of abysmal ignorance:[336] 'Has been at the Methodists Sunday school at Ripley five years; only reads a b ab, cannot spell in the least; cannot tell what d o g spells — he says "gun",' is a common example.[337] In the 1860s 127 children out of 256 at one Potteries Sunday school could not write their names and 138 could not read.[338]

It is unlikely, too, that evening-school attendance in the midlands was extensive enough to affect educational standards materially.[339] In 1851 fewer than 4,000 adults were at night schools in the whole six counties.[340] By 1858, 10,000 children, mostly boys, were at evening school in the area, with proportions above the national average in Warwickshire, Nottinghamshire, Leicestershire and Derbyshire but below in Worcestershire and only half the national level in Staffordshire (Appendix Q). About then there were only 4,360 evening pupils in the Potteries and the Dudley area, and some of the classes were not for the working class.[341] Standards in many were low and children too tired to learn.[342] Of works and mines children at thirteen night schools in the Potteries in the 1860s 44 per cent could not read and 47 could not write (for mines' boys: 64 and 60 per cent).[343] All in all, the contribution of

Sunday and evening schools to basic literacy, particularly writing, must have been limited, their greatest impact being perhaps on those who had already attended some years at day schools whom they helped to retain elementary skills.

The difficulties besetting the extension of sound education in the midlands in the 1830s and 1840s were still there in the 1860s. Despite a growth of schooling and school attendance, illiteracy remained relatively high in many districts, and the educational standards of many children very low. It is likely that by 1870 there were sufficient school places for children who wished to use them, but child labour remained common, school attendance brief and irregular and, apart from the offspring of artisans and small tradesmen, mostly confined to younger children. Many parents were indifferent, or, in the case of some lower groups, antagonistic to day schooling. Many employers were uninterested and the absence of a large body of resident gentry in industrial towns and some country areas was a disadvantage.

Despite the considerable efforts of local churches, particularly the Established Church, substantial improvement was unlikely to come from within midland communities. Moreover in Birmingham, the greatest city of the area, both Church and Chapel were complacent about the state of educational provision already existing.[344] Governments of the day tended to seek a spread of education through the extension of the Factory Acts. The various investigations into child labour in the midlands, however, pointed to the difficulties of this approach. First, large scale employers, like the Lancashire factory owners, whom the state could use as accountable agents in enforcing legislation, were comparatively few. Instead, with children often only indirectly employed by commercial capitalists and effectively in the hands of middlemen and parents, and a multitude of small workshops and home employment dispersed over large areas, often neither town nor country, official regulation was unlikely to succeed. Such legislation as was introduced was not very effective. When child labour in the lace and hosiery industries was brought under regulation, it had some effect in Leicester but much less in the industrial villages, and it was laxly enforced by unenthusiastic magistrates, at first ignored by employers and also by parents and later blatantly evaded. A serious loophole was the recognition of lace 'schools'[345] as schools rather than the workshops they really were. Though more effective in the Potteries, legislation had there, too, a limited effect, and in the Black Country the Acts were in the 1860s regarded as a failure.[346]

Even where heeded, the Acts resulted less in attendance at school than in a shift to unregulated types of employment, or to mere idleness. Thus in the 1860s in Leek the factories, when brought under regulation, ceased to employ young children, but these continued to toil in unregulated workshops[347] In Nottinghamshire children excluded from work by the Acts simply did not attend school.[348] In Warwickshire in 1868 the H.M.I.s believed that there was a large and growing number of children who attended no school at all, and in the midlands generally a very large number who neither worked nor went to school.[349]

As early as 1841 the Commissioners on Unemployed Hand-loom Weavers had predicted such difficulties, and, in advance of their time, had recommended that the only solution was for communities to be forced to provide schools and parents to send their children to them.[350] By the late 1860s there is every reason to believe that only universal compulsory education could meet the needs of the midlands.

CHAPTER 5

The south midlands

Economic and social structure

The eight counties to the west and north of London covered in this chapter —
Bedfordshire, Berkshire, Buckinghamshire, Cambridgeshire, Hertfordshire,
Huntingdonshire, Northamptonshire and Oxfordshire — had a population in
1851 of about 1,300,000, less than half that of the West Riding and only about
twice that of Staffordshire. The most populous county was Northamptonshire,
while Huntingdonshire had but 60,000 inhabitants. As in other largely rural
areas, population grew comparatively slowly over the period 1841 to 1871, with
Huntingdonshire actually losing numbers from 1851. Cambridgeshire, where
reclaimed fenland increased the demand for farm labour, experienced an
increase of population between 1841 and 1851 of over 13 per cent (just above
the national average) but lost population in next decade, and Bedfordshire
had an even larger increase of 15·5 per cent, 1841–51, with Luton, centre of
the hat industry, recording a 40 per cent increase.[1] The area contained no large
conurbations and few towns of any size. Aylesbury, Cambridge, Oxford and
Northampton had populations in 1851 of 27,000–28,000 each, while the only
other substantial towns were Reading (21,000), Bedford (12,000), Luton and
Wisbech (11,600 each). Some thirty others had populations of 3,000–11,000.
The general pattern was one of small market centres and rural villages.

The occupational structure of these counties was dominated by agriculture,
with a high proportion of men of twenty and over engaged in farming in 1851.
Indeed of the fourteen English counties with at least 45 per cent of adult males
engaged in agriculture, six are found in this group (Appendix A). In actual
numbers Cambridgeshire had most (25,000), with Nottinghamshire, Oxfordshire, Hertfordshire and Berkshire, all between 20,000 and 24,000, tiny
Huntingdonshire with 8,000 and Bedfordshire and Buckinghamshire with
16,000 and 18,000 respectively. Conditions of life for most of the inhabitants of
the area were determined largely by the nature and state of agriculture, but
also in some parts by the fortunes of industry, largely domestic. Economic
activity in the small market towns of the area was related to the needs of
agriculture and the marketing of domestically produced goods.

As in most counties, the proportion of the total south midlands occupied population engaged in agriculture fell between 1841 and 1881. Nevertheless it remained relatively high and even in 1881, when only seventeen English counties had more than 23 per cent employed on the land, about a quarter of the working population in Bedfordshire, Berkshire, Buckinghamshire and Hertfordshire was so employed, while in Oxfordshire the figure was 29 per cent, in Cambridgeshire 37 per cent, and in Huntingdonshire 40 per cent. Only Northamptonshire (20 per cent) was not found in the seventeen counties mentioned. Of course, much higher proportions of men (than of all adults) were occuped in farming.[2]

Though the development of railways diminished the advantages the counties near London had in supplying food to the capital, agricultural activity in the south midlands was much influenced in our period by proximity to the metropolitan market and to a lesser extent by the demands of smaller but affluent communities like Bath, Oxford and Cambridge.[3] Corn was grown in all counties, but particularly in central Buckinghamshire, the Vale of the White Horse (Berks.), north Cambridgeshire and south and east Huntingdonshire. Other types of farming were particularly labour-intensive. Fruit orchards were evident especially in south-west Hertfordshire, market gardening was exten- sively practised, for example, in the vale of Bedford, and dairy farming in Oxfordshire, south-west Northamptonshire, the vale of Aylesbury (Bucks.), and in Berkshire in the Vale of the White Horse[4] and the vale of Kennet. Cattle were fattened for the London tables in Northamptonshire and around Aylesbury, while barley for London and local breweries was grown particularly in Oxfordshire, where the soil was often poor, Cambridgeshire, and in Hertfordshire, where hops were also cultivated.[5] Large flocks of sheep were raised on the Berkshire downs,[6] in Northamptonshire, the Huntingdonshire fenland, south and east Cambridgeshire, Bedfordshire, Hertfordshire and Buckinghamshire. Horse breeding was carried on in the valley of the Cam and in Northamptonshire for the London market, while hogs (for bacon) were reared in Berkshire and Huntingdonshire.

The underlying structure of land ownership as revealed towards the end of our period was a mixed one.[7] Cambridgeshire stands out as a county of small landowners, freeholders and owner-occupiers. A third of its land was held in estates of 300 acres or less, and over a half in estates of 1,000 acres or less. The other seven south midland counties conformed more to the national level for estates up to 1,000 acres (39 per cent). For great estates (over 10,000 acres) Northamptonshire was most prominent, with 30 per cent of its land so held. Bedfordshire, where the Duke of Bedford owned much land, and Hertford- shire were nearer in this category to the national level of 24 per cent. Cambridgeshire had only 11 per cent of its land in great estates, and the remaining four counties (Berkshire, Buckinghamshire, Huntingdonshire,

Oxfordshire) had relatively low proportions ranging between 15 and 19 per cent. For gentry estates (1,000 to 10,000 acres) Berkshire and Oxfordshire had rather high proportions (37 and 40 per cent) and Northamptonshire a rather low one (26 per cent), against a national average of 29 per cent of land in estates of this size. The other counties ranged between 30 and 34 per cent.

Despite these differences in patterns of land ownership, what is significant about the south midland socio-economic structure is that it was generally an area of small farms. In mid-century, of the eight counties, Cambridgeshire had the largest number of farms of over 1,000 acres, but even so there were many owner-occupiers and most of its farms were of between twenty and 200 acres, and the vast majority below 500. Large areas of fenland had been brought into cultivation by 1840 and the standard of farming in that part of the county was generally high. But in the south-west, especially between Cambridge and Huntingdon, farmland was poor and agriculture backward. In neighbouring Huntingdonshire the fenland in the east was drained and cultivated but most of that small county was given over to pasture, poorly drained, with farms small and not particularly prosperous. The farms of Buckinghamshire were largest in the vale of Aylesbury but averaged less than 200 acres and were generally between 100 and 400, with fewer than fifty larger than that. Caird found many rich farmers, but the small farmers in the clay country between Aylesbury, Wendover and the Chilterns scraped a poor living. In Bedfordshire, where many smallholders engaged in market gardening, farm size averaged only about 150 acres, with few over 500 acres, and farmers in the northern district were said to be very poor. In Northamptonshire, too, despite large estates, the majority of the farms were of between 100 and 250 acres, and few were above 400. Good farming, however, according to Caird, was the exception, with land-lords apathetic. There and in Hertfordshire, another area where farms tended not to be large, those with holdings of fifty to sixty acres struggled for a living, ranking economically little above labourers. The sheep farms of the Berkshire chalklands were of 400–1,000 acres but elsewhere in the county smaller farms were the rule. In south-east Oxfordshire most farms were of between 200 and 600 acres; in the west of the county they were larger, but Caird reported that 'the county exhibits a poverty stricken and neglected look', with poor relationship between tenants and landlords.

Farm wages in Bedfordshire and Northamptonshire in the 1850s and 1860s were somewhat above those in the other six counties, but on the whole the south midlands was a low wage area, certainly better than the western counties but comparing adversely with the counties of the north and the more industrialised midlands. Thus in 1851 agricultural wages in all the eight counties were below the national average, and lowest in Cambridgeshire and Berkshire, and in 1867–8, except in Northamptonshire, they were still relatively low.[8]

Lack of regular employment made matters worse for the rural labourers. Seasonality of employment was a characteristic of corn grazing land, of which, as noted, there was a high proportion in Hertfordshire, Huntingdonshire, Cambridgeshire and Bedfordshire. In the last three and in Northamptonshire farmers commonly employed large groups of casual itinerant labourers for short terms, minimising the need for permanent local workers. In Berkshire also labourers were dismissed when work was scarce. Too often in the area work was available for only eight months of the year. Not surprisingly, the proportion of paupers in the population was high, particularly in the 1840s in Buckinghamshire and Oxfordshire.[9] High cottage rents were accompanied by poor living conditions often in neglected accommodation, frequently inconveniently distant from farms in closed parishes.

Class relationships were most unhappy. Many landlords, often absentees, were uninterested in improving agriculture, disliked by their tenants, and apathetic to the alleviation of social misery. Between farmers and labourers there was much antagonism, with employers as a matter of course throwing their workmen on to relief in the workhouse whenever they could be done without.[10] Working-class resentment was particularly strong in Cambridgeshire and Huntingdonshire, where rick burning still occurred in the 1850s, and in Berkshire, Buckinghamshire, Northamptonshire and Oxfordshire.[11] Bedfordshire experienced widespread rioting and disturbances consequent on overpopulation and distress, particularly in the period 1815–34, and the farm worker continued after that to face 'an employment oligopoly of farmers who had no intention of breaking a tradition of low pay', and no alternative to erratic and seasonal employment.[12]

The surplus of male farm labourers restricted regular employment of women and girls on the land, though they were used extensively at harvest time and on small family farms. This and the low wage structure gave an impetus to large-scale female and child engagement in domestic industry. This employment was high in three of the south midland counties: in Bedfordshire 19·3 per cent of adults were employed in manufacture in 1851, far above the national level (10·2 per cent) and lower only than in Lancashire, the West Riding, Nottinghamshire and Leicestershire. Buckinghamshire and Northamptonshire had over 13 per cent, Herfordshire had 7·9 per cent and Oxfordshire 4·5 per cent, and these proportions did not take into account the considerable number of children and young people under twenty engaged in such work.[13]

The industries and trades of the south midlands rested to a large extent on the agricultural basis of the local economy. In a largely rural area the towns and larger villages had concentrations of multifarious crafts supplying the local population with their daily needs. The larger places were market centres for agricultural and other produce and for such industries as agricultural engineering which expanded in the latter half of the century. Brewing, too, was widespread in the area, with some tendency from the 1850s to become concentrated in larger units in the towns, and being most important in Northampton, Abingdon and St. Neots.[14] Paper making established itself particularly in Buckinghamshire, Hertfordshire (especially Watford and Hemel Hempstead) and to a lesser extent Oxfordshire. As it became a mechanised factory industry it employed large numbers of young persons, especially girls of thirteen to eighteen.[15] In Wycombe and Amersham (Bucks.) there was already a concentration of male chair makers. At Banbury agricultural machinery was produced, and there and in other parts of Oxfordshire (particularly around Witney and Chipping Norton) were remnants of the ancient West Country woollen industry, though of comparatively little importance. Silk mills existed in Tring, Watford and St. Albans.[16]

From the point of view of numbers employed, the main industries of the area were domestic ones, but while they offered an additional income to many rural families some of these trades suffered decline in the nineteenth century and that decline aggravated the poor social conditions of the rural districts. On the other hand improved transport facilities from the 1850s tended to prolong the continuance of the domestic industry of the area.[17] Glove making was concentrated around Woodstock (Oxon.), organised in cottages and workshops as in the West Country.[18] The lace-making area of the south midlands extended from Kettering (Northants) to Thame (Oxon.), embracing north Buckinghamshire, north Bedfordshire and parts of Northamptonshire as well as adjoining parts of Huntingdonshire and Oxfordshire. In 1851 over 33 per cent of women of twenty years and over in the registration district of Newport Pagnell were employed in lace production, and in the other districts very high proportions were similarly engaged: in all, an average of 21 per cent of adult women.[19] Very large numbers of children were employed by masters, dealers, and in so-called 'schools'.[20] Large 'manufacturers' operated very traditionally, not formally employing the home workers but selling them the raw materials and purchasing the finished product, sometimes travelling around to conduct their business direct with the makers or operating through middlemen, small dealers and shopkeepers.[21] Some, however, did operate a putting-out system keeping ownership of the materials themselves.[22] The truck system and the binding of workers by the extension of credit were evils adding to the general misery of the area,[23] which increased as work hours lengthened and earnings fell in the face of the competition of machine-made lace. Compulsory schooling and the demise of the lace schools resulted in further decline, so that by 1881 the trade was no longer significant,[24] though for the mid-Victorian period it remained important.

Two other related domestic industries[25] were straw plait production and the making of the plait into hats, bonnets and fancy articles. This activity was concentrated in thirteen registration districts in Bedfordshire, Buckinghamshire and Hertfordshire centred on the town of Luton. In these trades 10,600 adult women were employed in 1851, embracing 60 per cent of women in Luton registration district, and between 24 and 29 per cent in the districts of St. Albans, Hemel Hempstead, Berkhampstead and Leighton Buzzard. In Luton district over 10 per cent of men were also working in the trades, mainly in hatting.[26] As in lace making, many children worked in the less skilled straw trade: in 1861, for example, over 5,000 girls under the age of fifteen. Plaiting was traditionally a rural occupation, hatting more a town one. The plait workers were organised more loosely than the hatters, often buying their own materials from shopkeepers, farmers or middlemen straw dealers, and selling not only to manufacturers and their agents but also direct into local markets. Young children were often organised in 'plait schools', where, unlike the lace schools, the parents provided the raw material and sold the products. The trade was adversely affected by the Workshops Acts of the 1860s, which restricted the numbers in plait schools, the Education Acts, and around 1860 by the import of cheap foreign plait.[27]

The more capitalistically organised hatting industry survived better than plaiting. Though affected by foreign competition, the industry overcame it by simulation and innovation. On the other hand, whereas the local lace industry was adversely affected by the factory production which developed outside the region, the already urban-based hat-making trade moved towards a factory organisation established locally, particularly in St. Albans and in Luton, where in 1855 there were over thirty large manufacturers and many smaller ones. Domestic outworking, however, continued, with plait workers often turning to sewing.

The boot and shoe industry of Northamptonshire was concentrated in six registration districts: Daventry, Northampton, Hardingstone, Wellingborough, Thrapstone and Kettering. In these an average of 20 per cent of male adults were so employed in 1851 and some 13 per cent of women were shoemakers or shoemakers' wives.[28] The organisation of the industry was very mixed.[29] The process of 'closing' (stitching parts of the upper shoe) was undertaken by women and children for weekly wages in premises belonging to 'masters' who collected prepared materials from the manufacturers' warehouses and returned the worked products. Many of those in the trade, however, were outworkers operating in their own homes, dealing direct with the manufacturers and earning piecework wages. Various towns and villages acted as distributing centres, preparing materials for putting out to surrounding hamlets and other villages, and outworkers were recruited from the ranks of declining woollen, lace and silk workers. From the mid-century the trade was stimulated by better rail communication, and factory production spread, with the main manufacturers maintaining large premises but also putting out work to smaller employers owning a few machines. Outwork, particularly finishing, however, continued into the 1880s, and although the machines took over tasks undertaken by children, especially younger ones, many children continued to be employed in the factories.

However approximate Joseph Fletcher's analysis of social characteristics in the south midlands in the 1840s (Appendix H) may be, it accords remarkably well with those aspects of life just described. He found that all the eight counties (except Berkshire) had well below-average proportions of persons of independent means. Bedfordshire had the lowest proportion of any English county and Northamptonshire was not much different. Early marriage was rife; again, in all but Berkshire it was above the national average, with Bedfordshire at an amazingly high level, far above any other English county. Cambridgeshire, Hertfordshire, Huntingdonshire and Buckinghamshire also had very high rates. Illegitimacy was also above average in all the counties except Northamptonshire, though not at as high a level as in some counties elsewhere. In proportions of paupers relieved in 1844, again all the south midland counties were above average, with Buckinghamshire sharing with Essex the highest rate in the country apart from that of Wiltshire. Oxfordshire was not far behind. Deposits in savings banks in the same year were below average, too, in all the south midlands counties.

The picture of the area in mid-century is of a predominantly poor rural working-class culture, inward looking, often resentful, and, apart from Berkshire, lacking a substantial middle and upper-class leavening. And change was very slow. The prevailing dominance of farming and the lack of alternative male employment rendered the area, despite heavy emigration in the early part of the century, overstocked with labour and with continuing working-class deprivation. Poor rural housing was common, employment uncertain and pauperism widespread. As E. H. Hunt has remarked, the rural south-east was 'pre-industrial in 1760, pre-industrial in 1850, and in most respects pre-industrial in 1911'.[30]

Child labour

Child labour was extensively used in parts of the south midlands. Those counties with concentrations of domestic industry had the highest proportion of children aged ten to fourteen at work (Appendix B). In 1851 Bedfordshire had the largest percentage of such children in any English county (50 per cent), while Northamptonshire (40) came third after the West Riding. Other south midland counties, too, had levels similar to those of the industrial midlands: Buckinghamshire (35, about the same as Lancashire), Hertfordshire (34). Huntingdonshire equalled the national level (29 per cent), while Oxfordshire (26), Berkshire (25) and Cambridgeshire (22) were somewhat below it. By 1871, when the national level had dropped to 27 per cent, all the south midland counties except Oxfordshire and Berkshire were still above it, Bedfordshire and Northamptonshire considerably so (45 and 35 per cent respectively). In Cambridgeshire the proportions had actually risen over 1851 by 7 percentage points and in Huntingdonshire by 4. Moreover, quite large numbers of children in the age group were involved — more than 46,000 in the south midlands in 1851 and over 50,000 in 1871 — roughly a quarter in each census year of the numbers employed in the Lancashire–Cheshire–West Riding factory belt.

Even more striking is the fact that comparatively high proportions of younger children were also at work (Appendix B). In 1851, when the national proportion of working children aged five to nine was 1·9 per cent, 17 per cent of the age group in Bedfordshire was occupied, 8 per cent in Buckinghamshire, 7 in Hertfordshire and 6 per cent in Northamptonshire — proportions far higher than in any other English county. By 1871, when the national proportion was 0·8 per cent, the only counties outside the south midlands with over 1 per cent of such children at work were Lancashire (1·4) and the West Riding (2·7). Bedfordshire, however, still had nearly 8 per cent and Hertfordshire over 3 per cent, while Buckinghamshire equalled the West Riding, and Huntingdonshire and Northamptonshire approached 2 per cent. Only Berkshire and Oxfordshire in the south midlands returned less than 1 per cent.

In the largely agricultural counties of Berkshire, Oxfordshire, Cambridgeshire and Huntingdonshire far higher proportions of boys than girls in the age group five to nine and in the group ten to fourteen were returned as at work in 1851 and 1871. Between those two years, however, the percentage of girls aged ten to fourteen in employment rose in all those counties, apparently because of increased opportunities for domestic service. In the other four counties, where domestic industry was found alongside agricultural work, the situation was different. In Bedfordshire a higher proportion of girls aged ten to fourteen than boys was employed in both census years. In Buckinghamshire, Northamptonshire and Hertfordshire a smaller proportion of girls than boys was at work, but the proportion of employed girls was nevertheless high — roughly at the same level as in Lancashire and the West Riding and those midland counties where domestic industry was widespread. Specific figures for the towns of Cambridge and Bedford in 1851 show that the percentage of females under twenty at work approached more nearly that of males than was the case even in the midlands and the north-western textile towns (Appendix C).

Table 5·1 illustrates the main types of employment of children aged ten to fourteen in 1851 and 1871 in the area. For boys, farming was clearly the largest single source of employment. Only shoemaking in Northamptonshire and straw crafts in Buckinghamshire offered other employment on a large scale. In Cambridgeshire, Huntingdonshire and Oxfordshire the proportion (and numbers) of employed boys in the age group actually increased (in Hunting-

TABLE 5·1

Proportion % of children (10–14) occupied, 1851, 1871

(a) Boys	1851			1871		
	(b) % occupied	(c) Main occupations	(d) % in (c)	(e) % occupied	(f) Main occupations	(g) % in (f)
Bedfordshire	50	agricultural labourers straw workers	28 8	44	agricultural labourers general labourers straw workers	25 6 4
Berkshire	38	agricultural labourers	21	34	agricultural labourers	19
Buckinghamshire	44	agricultural labourers	25	39	agricultural labourers	22
Cambridgeshire	34	agricultural labourers	23	43	agricultural labourers	27
Hertfordshire	42	agricultural labourers	22	37	agricultural labourers	19
Huntingdonshire	42	agricultural labourers	27	48	agricultural labourers	36
Northamptonshire	48	agricultural labourers shoemakers	24 12	45	agricultural labourers shoemakers	23 9
Oxfordshire	38	agricultural labourers	23	38	agricultural labourers	24

(a) Girls	(b) % occupied	(c) Main occupations	(d) % in (c)	(e) % occupied	(f) Main occupations	(g) % in (f)
		1851			1871	
Bedfordshire	51	straw workers lace workers	34 12	46	straw workers lace workers	30 10
Berkshire	11	general domestics agricultural labourers	5 2	13	general domestics	9
Buckinghamshire	34	lace workers straw workers	18 9	28	lace workers straw workers general domestics	11 7 5
Cambridgeshire	10	general domestics agricultural labourers	4 3	15	general domestics agricultural labourers	8 4
Hertfordshire	26	straw workers general domestics silk workers	18 3 2	24	straw workers general domestics	14 5
Huntingdonshire	16	lace workers general domestics	8 3	18	general domestics lace workers agricultural labourers	8 3 3
Northamptonshire	32	lace workers shoemakers general domestics	18 6 3	27	lace workers shoemakers general domestics	7 7 7
Oxfordshire	14	general domestics lace workers glovers	4 3 2	15	general domestics	8

donshire very considerably) over these twenty years, and in most of the other counties of the south midlands the proportion did not diminish greatly. For older girls the significance of industrial occupations remained great but in all the south midland counties, except Bedfordshire, employment in domestic service claimed increasing proportions in line with the national trend.

For children aged five to nine, more girls than boys were returned in the census as at work in the counties of cottage industry (Bedfordshire, Buckinghamshire, Hertfordshire), but fewer in the other south midland counties. Census figures, however, do not tell the whole story. Many child workers were apparently not returned as such to the enumerators.[31] Nor for 'scholars' is full-time education necessarily to be inferred. 'When the girls learn to make lace, or are otherwise useful at home, they come to school only half days,' reported the incumbent of Willen (Bucks.) in 1857.[32]

Fewer girls than boys were at school in almost every registration district in the south midlands in 1851 (Appendix F), and of children aged five to fourteen in 1851 a higher proportion of girls than boys in every south midland county was not on the books of schools (Appendix I). This supports the likelihood that girls who worked part-time or stayed at home to do domestic chores did not appear in the census employment statistics. In addition to these children there were doubtless others who, while on school books, rarely attended.

The picture given by statistics is supported by much other more detailed evidence on the extensive use of child labour, throughout the period, in the glove, lace and straw industries.[33] Lace making was much more skilled than plaiting, and an early start was considered essential for a proper mastering of the technique. Children thus began to learn the craft at the age of four, five or six in the lace schools which were prevalent throughout the lace districts and in some places the only schools. These institutions were usually small, overcrowded, ill ventilated and thoroughly unhealthy. Moreover the methods of working were harmful to the physique, and the practice of continuing to labour by candlelight allegedly impaired eyesight. Children of five or six often worked four to eight hours a day for 2d or 3d a week and older children (who stayed till aged twelve to fifteen) toiled twelve hours or as much as sixteen in busy periods. Certainly many of these children matched in time their fathers' work day in the fields. In the 1840s wages were low, girls of ten to thirteen earning but 1s to 2s a week; in the 1860s, 1s 6d to 2s 6d. Such toil required harsh taskmistresses, and one such, Mrs. Saunders of Princes Risborough, recommended that a child be sent at six for 'you can beat it into them better then'.[34]

In the straw plait crafts[35] toddlers began under their mothers' instruction and were sent to a plait school 'usually at four years old, some at three and a half', paying the mistress 2d or so a week.[36] In summer, work might be done out of doors, but in winter atrociously dirty and unhealthy conditions prevailed, for the plait schools were often more crowded than the lace ones. The practice of the schools was less to instruct than to keep the children at work (often with sticks and canes) at tasks set by their parents on materials they brought from home: 'the mistresses who get the most work out of the children are the most patronised'.[37] Younger children attended for five to eight hours a day, those over ten for ten hours, though failure to complete the stint could result in longer incarceration.

In the 1840s, in a time of bad trade, girls of nine to eleven were earning very little at plaiting (6d to 1s a week).[38] In the 1860s when plait was still prospering a woman and her two offspring could earn as much as her farm labourer husband. Twelve-year-old Ruth Stombridge, a Bedfordshire worker, claimed in 1863 to make 5s a week, and she had a brother and two sisters also on the job.[39] Both plait and lace schools were restricted by legislation of 1867.

Gloving, largely in Oxfordshire, was organised as a cottage industry but also in workshops employing large numbers of women and girls. Girls began somewhat later than in the lace and plait trades, generally at ten or eleven, earning little till about thirteen.[40] Silk mills in Aylesbury (Bucks.) paid 1s to 1s 6d, a week to eight-year-old girls.[41]

In the boot and shoe industry small master closers and middlemen employed girls, some only seven or eight, as 'closers', while boys assisted the men who sewed the soles to the uppers. In 1851 a school inspector remarked of Northampton that 'there is no locality in which children are retained for so short a time under instruction as in this town where the shoe-making business is carried on to a great extent, and in certain departments of which very young children can be employed'.[42] These children worked for twelve to fourteen hours a day, often in small overcrowded, ill ventilated rooms in the houses of the masters for 1s to 2s 6d a week.[43] From the mid-century machines began to drive out younger children and to edge the industry towards a factory system, but much outwork was still undertaken in the mid-1860s and children of both sexes were employed in workshops, even young children being retained as knot-tiers, earning 1s 6d to 3s a week for days of eleven hours or more. In the factories older children earned higher wages and worked somewhat shorter hours.[44]

In the paper industry of the 1840s many youngesters of thirteen to eighteen were employed, though few under thirteen. Wages were relatively high (girls earning 4s–9s a week), but hours were long (nine to fourteen a day) and in some jobs stints of twenty-four hours were required on alternate days. Mechanisation resulted in an expansion of employment in the 1850s and 1860s for young people aged under twenty.[45]

Farming in the south midlands gave little regular paid employment for girls or for boys under ten. Such as there was for girls aged ten to fourteen was concentrated in 1851 in Cambridgeshire and Berkshire, where there was little cottage industry, and even in those counties more were employed in domestic service (Table 5·1). For boys, however, farming was the largest employment in all eight counties, roughly a quarter of boys aged ten to fourteen working on the land. On the whole few were regularly employed under thirteen, though in Northamptonshire and Oxfordshire boys of eight were used and those of ten quite commonly, and it was alleged that employers put pressure on their labourers to allow their young sons to work. It was in the districts where smallholders and poor farmers were to be found that child labour was at its greatest, for, unable to afford hired labour, these men used their own wives and children extensively. Thus in south Cambridgeshire there was a great deal of child employment, from as young as six years of age.[46]

Particularly noxious was the gang labour found in those parts of Huntingdon-shire, Northamptonshire, Bedfordshire, and, particularly, parts of Cambridge-shire, where larger farms existed. The so-called public gangs were peripatetic groups of ten to forty persons, half of them children, managed by a master who contracted with the farmers for seasonal work. The gang children, usually aged seven upwards, worked long and exhausting hours, often, moreover, walking long distances to and from work. In three Huntingdonshire parishes in the 1860s 69 per cent of the males in public gangs and 39 per cent of the females were aged seven to thirteen; in six Cambridgeshire parishes the proportions were 60 and 30 per cent. Notorious for their drinking, violence and depravity, the gangers earned no more than ordinary labourers. Sympathetic observers were convinced that the work demoralised the children rendering girls coarse and unfit for any more skilled work. Mixed gangs allegedly led to juvenile prostitution and immorality, and few children in the public gangs continued any schooling. Larger numbers of young children were, however, employed by farmers in their own private gangs starting at six or seven, and although the work hours were less excessive, this, too, was not conducive to schooling.[47]

Attitudes to education

In an area where domestic industry, small farms, and consequently child labour were widespread and where farm labourers were downtrodden and ill paid, it is easy to understand the verdict of one H.M.I. who reported of the outlook of working-class parents in Hertfordshire in 1848 that 'the value attached to the blessings of education would seem to be but slight'. Somewhat simplistically he blamed this partly on a generally slovenly way of life with a propensity to petty crime, especially poaching.[48] Indeed, middle-class sup-porters of schooling tended to speak of parents' apparent indifference to schooling in this area as evidence of greed and improvidence and of a resultant perpetuation of ignorance — with young parents forcing on their children the way of life that they had had imposed on themselves, where the prime object was to maximise the parents' income.[49] It is, in fact, difficult to provide explicit evidence of the motives and attitudes of working-class parents in the south midland counties in respect of formal education. Our verdict must be based largely on inference.

In 1839 both employers and men in the wool trade at Witney asserted that the hand-loom weavers were 'anxious for the education of their children' but the evidence for this appears to have been support for Sunday schools.[50] In areas where farm labour and domestic industry provided the mainstay of life the assignment of children to day schools was unlikely to have seemed sensible to many whose family economy, with every member contributing towards the common need, was coherent and rational, even if incompatible with middle-class standards of propriety and household maintenance. Book learning was not perceived as a basic necessity and young people soon acquired independence of their parents without it and, as noted above, early marriages were commoner than in most parts of the country.[51]

One H.M.I. in the 1850s pointed out that the object of education was to fit a child for his career in life and that in the south midlands the various employments open to children all required some degree of manual dexterity.[52] The three Rs were of little help in that. Working parents were thus not necessarily greedy and indifferent when they sought to introduce their children to the tasks at which they would have to earn their livings. The lace and plait schools, so disliked by contemporary educationalists and philanthropists, could be regarded less as evidence of parental exploitation than indicative of parental responsibility in securing for their children the practical education of the apprentice in crafts where skills had necessarily to be mastered at an early age. Such an argument is more acceptable for the lace than the plait schools, for plaiting was a not a difficult skill and was soon acquired. The task of the plait mistress was less to instruct than to ensure that children completed the daily work stint set by their parents.[53] The skills of lace making were, however, more advanced and required instruction over a period of years.

This does not necessarily imply outright antagonism to formal elementary schooling. In the 1860s those engaged in the lace trade claimed that lacemakers could generally read, though not write, having been taught at home and at Sunday and evening schools, or even in the lace schools.[54] Indeed, that a minority of plait and lace schools gave a smattering of formal education, usually reading,[55] suggests that not all parents were averse to part of the working day being devoted to attaining the rudiments of literacy — though in fact very little real education took place.[56] Most such establishments were probably the 'little pestiverous workshops' that Joseph Fletcher considered them.[57]

On the other hand the parental view that craft training should dominate childhood was so widespread that it was often recognised by the promoters of voluntary schools. Joseph Fletcher remarked in the 1840s that 'Every item connected with Bedfordshire seems to be influenced by the combination of remote ignorance with a profligate dependence of the man, in part, upon the earnings of the women and childen,' and the Revd. F. C. Cook, H.M.I., reported of that county in 1844: 'it appears to be difficult, indeed ... impossible, in most places ... to keep up a girls' school', because of the preference of parents for lace and plait schools. There were, for example, at this time, no girls' National schools in Luton, Dunstable or Leighton Buzzard while in villages the attempt to maintain a girls' school was rarely made. Cook suggested that the National schools in Bedfordshire should include lace and plait making in their curriculum, hoping to combine such lessons with moral instruction.[58]

Where this was done, however, it was not always very successful. The incumbent of Ickleford (Herts.) provided for plaiting, and limited formal teaching to an hour and a half a day, but even so pupils were removed as soon as they were old enough to go to a school offering more plaiting and less 'education'.[59] In some Church schools in Buckinghamshire, too, plaiting occupied most of the day: 'without offering it we should not have any scholars'.[60] In the Northampton British schools even in the 1860s youngsters in the shoe trade were allowed to bring their work with them.[61]

Attempts were made, too, to improve the general atmosphere of the plaiting schools by organising common village establishments where a literate teacher devoted some time to moral instruction and reading. All this suggests attempts of well-meaning middle-class people to nudge what was an acceptable type of education to local parents somewhat more towards literary instruction than might otherwise have been the case, though it is doubtful whether any great effect on general educational standards resulted.[62]

There were, moreover, other factors at work than the dominance of parental inclination. The prevalence of child labour, often at an exceptionally early age, reflected to some extent economic necessity. It is true that some families in the Buckinghamshire paper industry earned very high wages while their children remained educationally neglected even in the 1860s,[63] but this situation was not typical of the south midlands. In some agricultural districts child labour was not infrequently forced on parents, particularly by the employers of farm labourers. One H.M.I. reported 'many instances' where parents wanting to send children to school 'have been informed that they must give up the child or be dismissed from labour themselves'.[64] Twenty years later another inspector, reporting on an area including Northamptonshire, alleged that farmers still took advantage of their ill paid workers: they 'practically coerce parents ... to send them [their children] at seven years of age into the fields, often miles away from their homes, where they work from dawn to dusk, in wet and cold, insufficiently fed, thinly and raggedly clad, till they suffer both in health and brain'.[65] Similar pressure appears to have been used by at least some industrial employers, as for example at a silk mill at Aylesbury in the later 1850s when trade was brisk.[66]

Poorer parents were, moreover, not encouraged to send their children to school by the way the poor-law guardians interpreted the law. Even in the 1860s in Hertfordshire, it was reported that 'every child is calculated as a source of income capable of producing so much toward the general support of the family. The amount is accordingly deducted from what would otherwise be given as relief to the parents'.[67] Guardians in Northamptonshire likewise ignored their right to pay for the schooling of the children of those on outdoor relief, so that as soon as parents were thrown on the parish they withdrew their children from school.[68] At workhouses at Buckingham and Newport Pagnell children were taught plait and lace making.[69]

Moreover, in a rural area where adult employment was irregular and uncertain, the pence children could earn in the fields or in cottage industry were likely to seem more important than any advantages a smattering of schooling, which had to be paid for, could offer. In Bedfordshire in the 1840s poverty was recognised as contributing to indifference to education.[70] And of Oxfordshire labourers in the 1850s it was discerningly noted that to blame rural parents of 'cupidity and wickedness' for sending their children to work in the fields rather than to school, was to ignore the fact that 'poverty is a hard master, and where the wages of a full grown man amount to something between 6s and 8s a week, one can scarcely feel surprise'.[71]

Where labourers did not have permanent employment the family had to rely on the labour of their wives and children. In Bedfordshire as late as 1868 'a large proportion of so-called catch workmen expect the female plaiters to maintain them throughout a great proportion of the year'. When the plait trade was depressed in the late 1860s, one-third of the population of Toddington (Beds.) was on poor-relief.[72] In such circumstances formal day schooling might seem a dangerous indulgence. Again a young child might assist its mother in her own toils, either releasing her from household duties, or actually helping her in her paid work. Thus at St. Albans in 1864 eight-year-old Edward Giddings helped his mother by threading her needles for the hat sewing she was engaged in, in preference to attending school.[73]

Uncertainty of the future and the general lack of security certainly led some parents to seize any available opportunity for their children to earn a little extra. The Revd. D. J. Stewart, H.M.I., blamed labouring parents in the south midland counties in the 1850s for taking children from school 'whenever any casual employment is to be had', and when the work ends returning them 'demoralised in character and intellectually depressed',[74] On the other hand this suggests parents had some regard for schooling, though not at the expense of a chance of extra income. In 1864 Stewart was more magnanimous when, reporting on a decline in funding for schools in Cambridgeshire, Huntingdonshire and Bedfordshire, he noted that if fees were raised it would 'simply put the children of the poor out of it'.[75] That more boys than girls attended school in this area[76] was a reflection that employment was easier to obtain for girls, but also that education was at least thought to be a preferable alternative to unemployment.[77]

There is a little evidence that by the early 1860s parents in the area were becoming more sympathetic to day schooling. More children were attending ordinary schools until eight or nine and there was said to be more parental demand that they should at least be able to read,[78] and night schools were also said to be popular.[79] In Berkshire growing opportunities for schooled youngsters made some farm labourers conscious that their children should have some education.[80] Elizabeth Emerson of Newport Pagnell sent her two small daughters to night school after their day's lace making, saying, 'I never could pay for schooling for either of them before they were at the pillow.'[81] Such a trend must, however, not be overstressed.[82] In areas of cottage industry the attitudes of many parents to child labour and formal education had changed very little even by the late 1860s. 'A farm labourer,' it was reported at that time, 'treats it as a matter of course that his daughters will be sent to a lace school at four or five years of age, and that from the time of their leaving school to the time when they leave his house for good, it is his wife's business to see that they stick to their lace pillow and work as many hours as he does himself.'[83]

Indeed, in these parts formal schooling and restrictions on child labour had to be forced on unwilling parents. The Workshops Regulation Act of 1867 was successfully evaded by the plait and lace schools until a test case determined that they were covered by the legislation. From then children under eight were excluded from the craft schools and those aged eight to thirteen in formal employment had also to attend an approved elementary school for ten hours a week. Even so, children could and did work with impunity in their own homes, and parents and employers connived with the craft school keepers to evade the law. Lace and plait schools did diminish in numbers but it was an uphill fight, and the decline of those establishments was more the result of economic recession than legislation.[84] As late as 1876 it was reported that 'there appears to be a general disposition among the workpeople at this trade to evade the law. The children at the schools will not tell how they work; the existence of the plait schools is concealed; the arrival of a stranger is telegraphed about'.[85] About this time the inspector of factories for the Bedfordshire and Hertfordshire plait and lace districts wrote of the indignation of the workers there 'looking upon the law as heartlessly interfering with their earnings and their privileges, to whom the weekly earnings of their children, small though they may be, are of vastly greater importance than prolonging, or even making regular, attendance at school'.[86] Even after elementary schooling became compulsory many Oxford-shire parents co-operated as little as possible, keeping their children away from school as often as they dared, even preferring to pay fines.[87] In 1877 the log book of the board school as Shillington (Beds.) recorded that 'girls are kept at home plaiting and boys are going to work'. In Biggleswade (Beds.) in 1886 the attendance officer reported 'a quantity of children illegally employed'.[88]

The large numbers of children employed in agriculture were not affected by the Workshops Acts and although the Agricultural Gangs Act of 1867 prohibited the employment of children under eight it did not apply to 'private' gangs employed directly by individual farmers.[89] Boys were more often employed than girls and in Croxton (Cambs.) in 1851 it was said that farm labourers were more inclined to send their daughters than their sons to school.[90] Many children, moreover, worked on a casual basis in agriculture especially in the summer[91] and of both farmers and parents in the south midlands it was said as late as 1867, 'As a general rule neither the one nor the other is willing to make any sacrifice to obtain an education for the children.'[92] When an Act of 1873 prohibited the employment of children under eight on the land Oxfordshire magistrates and clergy reported that it was largely ignored,[93] and in Bedfordshire such legislation was said to be a 'dead letter'.[94]

Lack of parental demand for education was compounded by weakness in willingness or ability to promote supply.[95] The relative paucity of paternalistic resident landowners in parts of the area was a definite drawback. Moreover, as already noted, the proportion of persons of independent means, who might have been expected to help financially and otherwise, was well below the national average in Bedfordshire, Buckinghamshire, Northamptonshire and Huntingdonshire, and only Berkshire of the other counties in the area had a proportion of such people above the national level (Appendix H). The middle-class beneficence found in big urban concentrations was largely absent; so, too, for the most part was the sprinkling of paternally inclined factory and mine owners influential in some other parts of the country. As in the midland areas of domestic industry, the middlemen showed no interest in either the education of those dependent on them or other aspects of their social welfare. The relationship was entirely a cash one. Though social unrest certainly existed it was not the threat to the fabric of society that it was in the populous midland counties and did not act as a spur to school provision for socialising purposes. Consequently, as far as local support is concerned, it was the outlook of farmers, clergy and landowners that was most significant in the development of popular elementary education.

The poor relationship between agricultural employers and their labourers in this area has already been touched on. Not surprisingly the attitude of farmers to schooling for the poor was generally antagonistic or at best indifferent and where they formed the *in situ* dominant class the provision of schooling was difficult. Moreover, many farmers in the area, particularly in Cambridgeshire and Huntingdonshire, were small men with little time and less money to devote to paternalistic activity even had they been so inclined. Often they needed their own children's labour. They were hardly likely to favour provision for labourers' children of the education they denied their own. Thus only a few south midland farmers actively supported schools, and then usually by providing free transport for building materials rather than in regular money subscriptions.[96] By the late 1860s a few more discerning of the larger farmers were becoming aware that education might be needed where machinery was used. 'I have an engine,' said one Northamptonshire farmer, 'and the men are useless with that unless they can read and write ... they can't read the indicator of the engine ... I used to have machines broken ... because the men were uneducated.'[97] But the majority were unwilling to contribute financially and often viewed the whole question of the education of labourers' children with great suspicion, or actual hostility. Even in the late 1860s they were reported as not wanting the men 'to get above themselves', fearing labourers' children might become better schooled than their own[98] and having 'an ill defined fear ... that the school will in some way increase the price of labour'.[99] The propensity to insist that labourers' offspring should be available for work has been noted above.[100] To other qualms was added the spectre of having to pay education rates if schooling became compulsory. In 1870 the tenant farmers of Buckinghamshire and Oxfordshire still objected to the removal of juvenile labour from their fields to the classroom.[101]

Without the efforts of the parochial clergy the educational situation in the south midlands would certainly have been far worse than it was. Of all social groups their efforts, in organisation and financial support, were the most widespread and consistent. In Hertfordshire incumbents kept Church schools going in the face of enormous difficulties and often at great personal cost.[102] Examples could easily be provided of similar sacrifice in other parts of the area, the financing of the school often being met largely or in part by the clergyman himself.[103] Dependence on the clerical pocket, however, limited the quality of the education provided,[104] and made it difficult to get government aid. Dependence for schooling on the clergy in Northamptonshire in the 1850s was declared almost impossible unless the living were rich or the incumbent had an ample private income.[105] Thus accommodation, equipment, teachers' wages and so on, had to be tailored to the available funds, and where the clergy were poor schools might never exist or disappear when difficulties arose. Consequently, in Northamptonshire and some adjoining counties as late as 1867, such parishes had either inferior uninspected schooling or none.[106] Knowledge of financial difficulties of this kind, moreover, led, it was alleged, 'even to diocesan inspectors to advocate a lower standard than that which is proper'.[107]

Lack of resident clergy was also a drawback. In the early decades of the century the fens and some of the clay lands of Huntingdonshire and

Cambridgeshire were disadvantaged by having few resident incumbents, and although by the mid-1840s this was no longer the case, the neglect of schooling was not quickly rectified. At that time an H.M.I. complained of Huntingdonshire, Cambridgeshire and Bedfordshire that money raised by the archidiaconal boards of education went unclaimed by the clergy of the area whose efforts in education were but moderate.[108]

The impact of the Church on schooling, was moreover, limited by the restricted light in which some local clergy viewed education for the poor. To many the object of schooling was chiefly to obviate the immorality and vice supposedly prevalent among young domestic and agricultural workers, and to inculcate religious knowledge and principles. In 1856 parish schoolmasters in the Oxford diocese were told that 'when you have manufactured a steady, honest, God-fearing, Church-going population, then you have done your duty as schoolmasters'.[109] As late as 1866 an H.M.I. complained of some clergy in Berkshire and Oxfordshire that they regarded their responsibilities for education 'to extend only to religious instruction'.[110] At this time the Bishop of Oxford was opposed to compulsory education even for children younger than ten, believing compulsion would necessitate an education rate, stopping voluntary aid and putting 'an end to religious teaching in our schools'.[111]

Concentration on religious and moral instruction often brought with it the policy of inculcating attitudes to authority and society associated with 'social control'.[112] Certainly from Churchmen in the area there was no emphasis on the promotion of upward social mobility through education. Indeed, Bishop Wilberforce at the annual meeting of the Oxford Diocesan Association of Schoolmasters in 1857 stated plainly that the object of schooling was not to deprive the land of workers, and felt there was 'too much outcry against children being taken from school to work on farms'.[113] At parish level, moreover, some clergy had very possessive and exclusive attitudes to their own parish schools. Thus one in 1844 was excessively proud of a small, overcrowded and generally inadequate school in which an H.M.I. felt no real education possible.[114] The incumbent of Wigginton (Herts.) was convinced in 1847 that a plaiting school was sufficient for the needs of his parishioners.[115] Again, one rural dean, commenting on an adverse report on schooling in Bedfordshire, Cambridgeshire and Huntingdonshire at this time, pointed out that many clergy regarded Sunday schools as the mainstay of education, since only very young children attended day schools. Betraying his view of the function of education he expressed satisfaction that as a result of Sunday schools 'I rarely *now* meet with a person not well acquainted with the great principles of his faith'.[116] As general levels of schooling and the expectations of the inspectorate rose, the weaker uninspected Church schools, once better than none, were seen as a drag on progress. Thus criticism was directed in 1867 at clergy in Oxfordshire and Berkshire whose schools could afford only uncertificated teachers yet who persisted in running their own establishments and discouraged children from going to more efficient schools outside the parish, over which they had no control.[117] H. W. Bellairs, H.M.I., reported lack of proper clerical supervision and alleged that those who had in the past been the fount of education were by 1870 resentful of others who would interfere to raise standards.[118]

Compared with the Anglican clergy, however, the influence of nonconformity on the spread of schooling in the south midlands was small. More school provision by dissenters was found in Huntingdonshire and Cambridgeshire, areas of small owner-occupiers, Bedfordshire and Buckinghamshire, centres of domestic industy, than in the other south midland counties.[119] Even so, nonconformists in country districts and small towns consisted of divided and weak groups who generally found it financially difficult to establish schools. In Fenny Stratford (Bucks.) for example, they tried and failed to set up a Lancasterian school in the early part of the century and a British school was not opened until 1865.[120] In the larger towns British schools were more common and here Anglican fears of nonconformity led to rival schools.[121]

The influence of the landed classes on educational provision in the area was varied. In Oxfordshire in 1849 a meeting of landowners determined to raise £5,000 to help establish training schools,[122] and in the area generally numbers of schools owed their existence to gifts of land and subscriptions from individual landowners.[123] Where, however, there were few resident gentry, as especially in parts of, Bedfordshire, Buckinghamshire, Cambridgeshire and Huntingdonshire, there was a dearth of schools.[124] Moreover, there is plenty of evidence (particularly in H.M.I.s' reports) to suggest that as a whole members of this class were not generally as sympathetic as in other parts of the country. In 1844, for example, the Revd. John Allen, H.M.I., wrote bitterly of the attitude to elementary school provision prevalent among the better-off classes in Bedfordshire, Huntingdonshire and Cambridgeshire:[125]

> One theory that caused me considerable pain during my tour in these counties, was the avowal in conversation with persons, who themselves were blessed with every advantage of early training and the soundest education, of the opinion that schools were but of doubtful good; so that even where pains were taken towards their maintenance, I found instances of persons speaking as if they chose the establishment of a school as the least of two evils, under the impression that if a teacher were not set to work subject to their influence others subject to worse would find employment in the district. Until I went to this part of England I think I never had official intercourse with any that maintained such a position ...

Money was hard to extract from such people and clergy and school managers often complained of a lack of financial support: 'I have met with so much "cold water",' wrote one in the early 1850s in the area, 'that I have not been able to build yet. I shall have hard work to get up the subscriptions.' And another confirmed 'that our experience of the sympathy to be met with from the landed proprietors is sadly like the cases you deplore'.[126] In the mid-1860s there were still those who felt 'the poor are better without education', and in Bedfordshire, Buckinghamshire, Cambridgeshire and Huntingdonshire generally landowners' support remained tepid.[127] The lack of interest evidenced by wealthy lay proprietors in Berkshire in the education of the poor was remarked on in the 1830s and as late as 1858;[128] and by 1867 the clergy in parishes with non-resident landowners in Berkshire and Oxfordshire favoured legislation to compel landlords to contribute towards the expense of school provision.[129] Berkshire, however, did have numerous resident gentry and contemporaries attributed relatively high levels of literacy in the county in the 1880s to this.[130]

Detailed studies of Hertfordshire have shown that the members of the hereditary aristocracy, with the sole exception of Earl Cowper, were sadly deficient in providing local leadership for the spread of popular education, and at best their modest activities were confined to their own parishes. Those Hertfordshire towns that had aristocratic neighbours (Hatfield, Watford, St. Albans) fared poorly educationally. On the other hand the gentry of the county, particularly the parvenus and *nouveaux riches* were more sympathetic and generous. The Abel-Smiths, for example, built and maintained a number of village schools; the Giles Pullars were similarly enthusiastic, and both families co-operated in the establishment in 1853 of a teacher training college at Bishop's Stortford.[131]

As with the clergy, however, the concept of what kind of education should be provided was a restricted one. One dame school assisted by a 'wealthy person' in the 1840s contained 'not a single child able perfectly to tell all its letters', yet such schools were thought sufficient for local needs.[132] Many landowners and clergy, like local farmers, were less sympathetic to the imposition of age restrictions on land workers than was the case in some parts of England. In 1867 agricultural employers in Derbyshire and other counties where demand for the labour of children under twelve or thirteen was small were sympathetic to the idea of prohibiting the employment of children under thirteen. In Hertfordshire, however, there was virtually no support for restricting farm labour to those over ten. Lord Salisbury, the most vehement opponent of compulsory schooling among the county's landowners, declared in the House of Lords that as a magistrate he would refuse to convict farmers breaking any such law.[133] The Hertford Board of Guardians made a plea that nine-year-olds who had reached a certain educational level should be employable; and the Hatfield, St. Albans and Hitchin guardians opposed any age restrictions.[134] In Oxfordshire, Bedfordshire and Buckinghamshire there was a general feeling that even a half-time regime would be impracticable for ploughboys aged ten to thirteen, though Boards of Guardians differed as to restrictions, especially for the under tens.[135] In Cambridgeshire it was felt that to deprive the small owner-occupiers of their own children's labour would be insupportable: 'they are too poor to hire labour and the assistance rendered by a child of eight or nine years is of great value'. Similarly, the clergy recognised what appeared to be the facts of life. The Bishop of Oxford in 1867 felt that children under eight should be allowed to work on the land half-time and that those of nine (having passed an educational test) and all ten-year-olds should be employable without restriction.[136] The clergy of Northamptonshire were convinced of the impracticability of compulsory schooling even on a half-time basis and could think of no other remedy to general ignorance than extension of the existing voluntary system and better night schools.[137]

In the areas of domestic industry even in the mid-1870s the general view was that any compulsory full-time schooling to the age of ten would be impracticable and would destroy the trades vital to the subsistence of the working classes.[138] Indeed, by 1870 it was pretty evident that a substantial extension of schooling in the area was unlikely to be effected by local effort or influence. Even better-off parishes lacked people willing to organise a school.[139]

Schooling and literacy

The social characteristics of the south midlands revealed by the type and distribution of agriculture and industry, levels of child labour, and attitudes towards education, are further illuminated by the extent and distribution of adult literacy and the incidence of elementary schooling. Except for brides in Oxfordshire and Berkshire, each of the counties in the area had levels of illiteracy in those marrying in the early 1840s above the national level (Appendix D). Moreover in Huntingdonshire, Northamptonshire, Bedfordshire, Buckinghamshire and Hertfordshire the proportions of illiterate spouses in 1845 were either the same as in 1841 or greater; in Huntingdonshire and Buckinghamshire greater by 4 percentage points. In five of the counties (Cambridgeshire, Huntingdonshire, Northamptonshire, Buckinghamshire, Hertfordshire) the level in 1845 was either no better than the average for the years 1839–45 or actually worse. This decline may reflect to some extent the educational position of children in the 1830s but the cause is uncertain. Certainly, as elsewhere, all eight south midlands counties show a steady decline in the proportion of illiterate spouses from 1850 down to 1885. Nevertheless, aside from Oxfordshire and Berkshire, where illiteracy rates were below the national level, the south midlands was an area of high illiteracy, with some counties having especially poor records. The worst, Bedfordshire, where domestic industry was particularly concentrated, had in 1860 reached a level of literacy only as good as Berkshire's in 1841, and in 1880 it had achieved the level reached or bettered by all the other seven counties of the area ten years or more before.[140]

Declining illiteracy percentages were accompanied in all the counties (except Cambridgeshire, 1866–71) by a drop also in the actual numbers of illiterate spouses (Appendix E). In some of the counties improvement came with falling populations. In the four counties which showed a decline in the numbers of illiterates between 1856 and 1871 of over 40 percentage points, Cambridgeshire and Huntingdonshire experienced a fall in population, 1851–61, Oxfordshire's population remained almost static, and Berkshire's rose by only 2·5 per cent (Appendix F). Of the two counties which had the lowest proportional decline in numbers of illiterate spouses, Bedfordshire had a population increase of over 8 per cent. In Hertfordshire, Northamptonshire and Buckinghamshire no likely connection with population changes is observable.

The marriage mark statistics for the individual registration districts show more exactly the geographical pattern of illiteracy in the area. Those for 1856 (Map 10 and Appendix F) reveal a solid phalanx of districts with illiteracy rates above the national level (35 per cent) stretching from Cambridgeshire in the north-east to Berkshire in the south-west, fringed to the north and south by a number of districts where rates were better than the national level. In every district in Huntingdonshire and Bedfordshire, and in almost every district in Cambridgeshire, Buckinghamshire and Hertfordshire, the illiteracy rates were above the national level, exceptions being the small Cambridge district, dominated by the university town, the Hatfield district (Herts.), and six districts in south-east Berkshire: those containing the towns of Reading, Newbury and Windsor, together with Eton (Bucks.), adjoining Windsor and the seat of Eton College, as well as the districts of Buckingham and Newport Pagnell (Bucks.). In Oxfordshire, where the situation was more mixed, Banbury, Woodstock, Oxford and Headington districts formed a contiguous group of districts around and including the university town of Oxford with rates better than the national level. Northamptonshire appears as the most literate county, with every district better than the national level, except for Potterspury and a central group comprising Wellingborough, Kettering and Thrapston, all of which contained lace workers. Wellingborough also had a concentration of shoemakers.

The areas of high illiteracy linked with similarly illiterate districts in other areas: those in Berkshire with districts in east Wiltshire and Hampshire (Map 5, 12), those in Cambridgeshire and Huntingdonshire with districts in East Anglia and Essex (Map 4). The districts of above average literacy in Northamptonshire joined with superior districts in Warwickshire, Leicestershire and Ruthland (Maps 3, 8, 9).

Appendix G represents an exercise like that undertaken for other regions,[141]

MAP 10
Percentages of marriage marks, 1856: Cambridgeshire, Northamptonshire,
Huntingdonshire, Bedfordshire, Oxfordshire, Buckinghamshire, Hertfordshire,
Berkshire. Bold figures indicate percentages above the national level of 35 per cent.

and provides further illustration of the nature of the topographical variations in
literacy levels in the area. A rough division of the sixty-eight south midland
districts into three groups, shows for 1856 that the twenty-one with the lowest
illiteracy rates (fewer that 36 per cent marks) included those containing the
cathedral city of Peterborough and five of the eight county towns: Cambridge,
Oxford, Northampton, Reading, Buckingham, the first four of these comprising
four of the five largest places in the south midlands, two the seats of universi-
ties. There was also the district including fashionable royal Windsor (with a
thousand soldiers in residence) with the adjoining districts of Easthampstead,

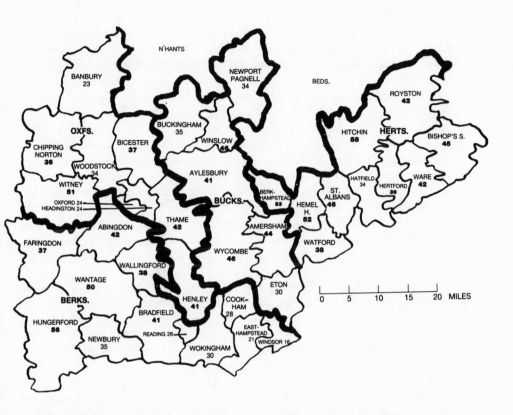

Cookham and Eton, together with Headington and Woodstock, all containing a rather high proportion of the middle ranks and of domestic servants and the like. Only four districts in this group contained significant numbers of lace and straw plait workers: Towcester, Hatfield, Newport Pagnell and Buckingham, all of which, however, contained the market towns that gave them their names. Woodstock district had glovers and contained Woodstock, Blenheim Palaces's dependent town. The superior literacy levels of Bedfordshire market towns in the period 1754–1844 has already been noted.[142]

The other districts in the best twenty-one were all situated in the Oxfordshire and Northamptonshire fringe and south Berkshire, and included those containing the ancient market town of Banbury (where the traditional woollen industry was declining but where domestic service occupied many women), Oundle, Brixworth, Daventry (where males were occupied mainly on the land and to some extent in shoemaking, and in the last two of which some women were engaged in lace making) and Wokingham and Newbury, dairy farming areas in the Vale of Kennett, with women in domestic service.

The twenty-three districts with the highest illiteracy rating in 1856 included a concentrated contiguous group in Buckinghamshire, Bedfordshire and Hertfordshire: Leighton Buzzard, Ampthill, Biggleswade, Luton, Berkhamstead, Hitchin, Hemel Hempstead, St. Albans, Wycombe, Winslow, Amersham and Woburn. These contained areas of labour-intensive agriculture, such as fruit growing in south-west Hertfordshire and market gardening in the Biggleswade and Ampthill districts, and the corn-growing districts of Buckinghamshire. All had heavy concentrations of workers in lace and straw plait, Wycombe and Amersham were also furniture making centres, and St. Albans had silk mills, too. Also in the bottom group were Hardingstone and Wellingborough, adjoining districts in Northamptonshire, both heavily concerned with lace and shoe production, Hungerford and Wantage (Berks.), and Witney (Oxon.) districts. In the last three, which embraced part of a corn-growing area, a high proportion of men were employed on the land and an unusually large number of women were agricultural labourers. In Witney women were also engaged in blanket and glove making. Other districts in the category were, in Cambridgeshire and Huntingdonshire, the contiguous Newmarket and Linton, Caxton and adjoining St. Neots, and Bishop's Stortford (Herts.). Much of this area was agriculturally backward, with small unprosperous farms; all these districts had high proportions of male agricultural workers. St. Neots, unlike other Huntingdonshire districts, was also a lace-making district and had some brickworks, and it was said that many of the more enterprising young men emigrated to North America and Australia.[143]

The twenty-four districts falling between the best and the worst were mixed in character. They included districts containing the market town of Chipping Norton, seat of a declining woollen manufacture, the county towns of Huntingdon, Hertford and Bedford (also a lace centre), and seven other districts noted for lace making and in some cases straw plait manufacture (Brackley, Kettering, Potterspury, Aylesbury, Henley, Bicester and Thame), together with Thrapston, a shoemaking district. Additionally, there were a number of districts where farm labour was the main characteristic. These included in north Cambridgeshire the districts of Whittlesey, North Witchford, Wisbech and Chesterton (distinctive also for containing few schools, ill attended, and large numbers of small farmers), Ware and Royston (Herts.), and the Berkshire districts of Faringdon, Wallingford, Bradfield and Abingdon. Brewing also took place in Abingdon but domestic industry, except for some shoe production in the Berkshire districts, was conspicuously absent from these districts.

There was a clear tendency for the best and worst districts in 1856 to remain the same in 1866 and 1871, despite overall improvements (Appendix F). Thus, of the twenty-one most literate districts in 1856, sixteen were in the best twenty-three in 1866 and fourteen in the top twenty-one in 1871; of the least literate twenty-three districts in 1856, eighteen were among the worst twenty-four in 1866 and nineteen among the worst twenty-four in 1871. Eight districts (Windsor, Cambridge, Easthampstead, Banbury, Oxford, Headington, Reading and Cookham) were in the best twelve in 1856, 1866 and 1871; five (Caxton, Hemel Hempstead, Woburn, Hitchin and Ampthill) were consistently in the worst dozen in those three years. All these last five were straw plait areas and Caxton and Ampthill also lace centres.

The gap between the best and worst districts, however, fell from a range of 16–59 per cent in 1856 to 10–48 per cent in 1866 and 6–42 per cent in 1871 — a still considerable difference. For males the difference between districts fell from 42 percentage points (18–60 per cent range) in 1856 to 39 percentage points (9–48) in 1866 and to 31 points in 1871 (8–39). For females, the difference remained greater and fell more hesitantly: 48 points in 1856 (13–61), 37 points in 1866 (10–47), and up again to 42 points in 1871. By then the 3 per cent of illiterate brides in the best district (Windsor) contrasted strongly with the 45 per cent in the plait district of Leighton Buzzard.

Despite the general tendency for more or less literate districts to remain in that relationship to each other, there were, however, notable exceptions. Some changes undoubtedly resulted from the fluctuations in percentages of marriage marks found where there were a relatively small number of marriages, as, for example, at Whittlesey (Cambs.) and Hatfield (Herts.). In some districts demographic change seems to have been a factor. Northampton district (embracing Northampton itself) experienced very large increases in population between 1851 and 1871 as the boot and shoe industry expanded and several iron foundries were erected. In Northampton town average illiteracy fell from 30 per cent in the decade 1841–50 to 25 per cent in 1851–60, but the actual numbers of illiterate spouses increased. In the decade 1861–70 the rate had dropped in the town to 18 per cent, but the fall in actual numbers of illiterates was comparatively small.[144] The literacy ranking of the Northampton registration district in the period 1856–66–71 worsened from ninth to fourteenth to twenty-eighth. This contrasts with Kettering, another shoe-making district, which improved its literacy rank from eighteenth to fourth (1866–71), but which had a much more modest increase in population. Again Watford's position in 1866 (eighteenth) fell (to thirty-second) in 1871, as it underwent a considerable growth in population with railway development and the introduction of paper mills. On the other hand a remarkable improvement in ranking occurred at Wokingham (Berks.) 1866–71 (thirty-first to fourth) as population increased quickly with improved railway communications and the establishment of 'New Town' as a suburb of Reading where most of the inhabitants were employed at the biscuit factory. In other, largely rural, districts, relative ranking improved with loss of labouring population. Thus, for example, the position of Brixworth (Northants) rose from fifteenth and eighteenth (1856, 1866) to fourth in 1871 following a 10 per cent reduction in population 1861–71 as workmen left for higher wages in the towns. At Witney (Oxon.) the position improved (ranking fifty-ninth in 1856, forty-ninth in 1866, twenty-first in 1871) as migration to manufacturing districts and the amalgamation of small farms thinned the population. At Hungerford (Berkshire), where population also fell, relative improvement was even more striking (sixty-sixth, thirty-first, thirty-seventh, with illiteracy percentages halved, 1856–66) as again smallholdings were absorbed into larger farms, demand for agricultural labour fell and young people migrated to the towns. In St. Neots (Huntingdonshire) (fifty-third, fortieth, twenty-first) demand for labour fell with the exhaustion of extensive clay pits in Great Paxton parish which caused the dispersion of brickmakers, and surplus labour generally moved to manufacturing districts. To this we may juxtapose Biggleswade (Bedfordshire), a straw plait and market gardening district where the expansion of brickyards and coprolite works caused population increases of 8 and 10 per cent, 1851–61 and 1861–71 and a fall in literacy ranking from fifty-sixth to sixty-eighth to sixty-second.

Not all changes lend themselves to such plausible explanation. In some largely rural districts falling populations were accompanied not only by a deterioration in literacy ranking but by actual increases in the proportion of those making marks. Oundle (Northants) fell from fourteenth to thirty-fifth in 1866–71, and male illiteracy rose by 10 percentage points; the position of Thame (Oxon.), a lace as well as a farming area, dropped from twenty-fifth to fiftieth in the same period, and that of St. Ives (Hunts.) from forty-second to fiftieth, in both cases with an increase in male illiteracy percentages. The ranking of Newport Pagnell (Bucks.) fell from fifteenth to sixty-fourth, 1856–66, with both male and female illiteracy rising; that of Woodstock (Oxon.) experienced slight rises in male illiteracy, 1856–66, and in female, 1866–71, as its position fell from fifteenth to twenty-fifth to thirty-seventh (1856–66–71). Common causes of falling populations in these districts were reportedly migration to manufacturing districts and emigration to Australia and North America. In the case of Newport Pagnell heavy concentration on Sunday rather than day schooling may have been a factor,[145] and indeed it may be that its early comparatively good level was more surprising — Francis Hill remarked particularly in 1836 on its 'exceedingly low' state of education with only 2 per cent of children and 1 per cent of labourers and their wives able to write.[146]

Illiteracy was not uniformly spread between the sexes. In the 1840s more brides than grooms were illiterate in each of the south midland counties, though to a varying extent (Appendix D). In Hertfordshire and Berkshire the difference in 1839–45 was only 5 and 3 percentage points respectively; but in the other counties female illiteracy ranged between 9 and 13 points higher than male, with the greatest differences in Bedfordshire and Northamptonshire. By the 1880s, however, the situation had changed radically and in every county fewer brides than grooms were illiterate. In five of the counties (Cambridge-shire, Huntingdonshire, Oxfordshire, Hertfordshire and Berkshire) the change-over occurred some time in the decade 1850–60; in Buckinghamshire by 1870. In Bedfordshire and Northamptonshire the preponderance of illiterate brides was not reversed until the 1880s, by when considerably higher proportions of brides than grooms were literate in Cambridgeshire, Hunting-donshire and Hertfordshire. By 1860 in all the south midland counties, except Bedfordshire, the proportion of illiterate brides was lower than the national level, and this appears to have remained so into the 1880s. Male illiteracy, on the other hand, was higher than the national level throughout the early part of the period. The grooms of Northamptonshire and Oxfordshire showed the best records, with the male rate in these two counties equalling the national level by 1870. Berkshire was in that position by 1875. By 1885 a lower proportion (by 1 point) of grooms in these three counties was illiterate than in the nation as a whole.

These developments were reflected in the levels of literacy relative to those of other English counties (Appendix D). Here an improvement is observable in 1880 over 1841 in Cambridgeshire, Northamptonshire, Oxfordshire, Hertford-shire and Berkshire, both for brides and grooms. In Huntingdonshire and Bedfordshire the relative position for males remained the same, but whereas Huntingdonshire brides improved their position very considerably, those of Bedfordshire remained approximately unchanged. In Buckinghamshire a slight improvement in the brides' position was offset by a slight decline in that of grooms. The most striking changes overall are the relatively improved position for males in Northamptonshire (twenty-fourth to fifteenth) and the relative improvement of brides in Cambridgeshire (thirty-fourth to twenty-first), Northamptonshire (twenty-seventh to nineteenth), Oxfordshire (eighteenth to tenth), Hertfordshire (thirty-fourth to twenty-sixth), Berkshire (fifteenth to sixth) and Huntingdonshire (twenty-fifth to sixteenth). Bedfordshire, however, stands out with consistently low female literacy and formed with Hertfordshire an area of very low male literacy.

Statistics for the individual registration districts further illuminate the relative levels of male and female illiteracy (Appendix F). In 1856 female illiteracy rates were higher than male in thirty-six of the sixty-eight districts (in twenty-six of them by 5 or more percentage points), and male illiteracy was greater than female in thirty-one districts (in eighteen of them by 5 or more points; nine of these were in Berkshire and five in Hertfordshire). By 1871 the tables had been turned and the number of districts where female illiteracy rates were greater than male was twenty-five (only in twelve by 5 percentage points or more). Males by then had higher rates than females in thirty-six districts (in twenty-five by 5 points or more).

Males were consistently less literate than females in the Berkshire districts over the period and in some instances the extent of female superiority was quite remarkable: 18 percentage points in Bradfield, 1856, and 9 or more in Hungerford, Abingdon, Wallingford, Wokingham and Easthampstead. In half the districts of Hertfordshire, too, females, in 1856, were more literate, by 9 points or more: in Ware the gap was 23 points; in Bishop's Stortford 21; in Hertford 20; and in Watford 24. In all these districts agricultural labour was by far the main male occupation, while domestic industry for women was conspicuously absent (except for a few plait workers in Hertford and Watford). Even in 1871 male illiteracy still exceeded female in Berkshire by 11 points in Wantage, 13 in Newbury, 15 in Wallingford and 9 in Cookham, and in Hertfordshire by 15 in Bishop's Stortford, 11 in Ware and Royston, 10 in Hertford and 24 in Hatfield. By then male illiteracy at substantially higher levels than female had also emerged in some other south midland districts, as, for instance Chesterton (Cambs.) (13 points), Newmarket (Cambs.) (10), and Oundle (Northants.) (19). The reversal by 1871 of the overall superiority of men over women that had existed in 1856 is thus accentuated by its concentration in certain areas and by the extent of female superiority. On the other hand female illiteracy was consistently higher than male in Bedfordshire and Buckingham-shire over the whole period. In Woburn district in 1856 there was a difference of 14 percentage points, in Leighton Buzzard and Luton 12, in Wycombe 10, and in Buckingham district 11. By 1871 the gap had narrowed but there were still differences of as much as 9 points at Ampthill, Luton and Wycombe.

Employment patterns are clearly a key to the changing relationships between male and female illiteracy in the region. In areas of domestic industry, where a high level of employment for women and girls continued, the relative position of female literacy was depressed. In predominantly agricultural areas, more boys than girls were employed, at a younger age and in some cases in increasing proportions. The relative position of male literacy was thus adversely affected in those areas particularly, since farm labourers in the area lived an existence of mindless physical toil. The growth in domestic service for girls, more pronounced in those counties where domestic industry was not concentrated (Table 5·1 above), is likely also to have been significant.

The relationship between elementary education, child employment and later literacy levels is, however, a blurred one. School provision and attendance varied over the area, with the situation on the whole less good in rural districts than in towns, but the towns of the area were neither sufficiently large nor sufficiently numerous to affect the general picture greatly.[147] In the country districts, to the difficulties of remoteness were added the factors of indifferent and absentee landlords, the predominance of small farms with an overriding interest in economic survival, and in some parts domestic industries hungry for child workers. The last was very significant and the counties where these industries were concentrated tended to fare less well for schooling than other counties in the region. Thus, in 1833, while Huntingdonshire had but nine places where the only school was a Sunday school and where it could not be presumed that children could attend any other school, Cambridgeshire had fifteen, Hertfordshire sixteen, Berkshire seventeen and Oxfordshire twenty-three, Bedfordshire had fifty-seven such places, Buckinghamshire fifty-nine and Northamptonshire sixty-seven.[148]

In all the south midland counties the proportion of the population on day-school books increased between 1818 and 1833 and again between 1833 and 1851. Even so, Bedfordshire was still below the national level in 1851, and indeed rated worse than any other English county except Monmouthshire and Herefordshire. Buckinghamshire's proportion approximated to the national level, Northamptonshire was just above it, and Cambridgeshire, Oxfordshire, Huntingdonshire, Hertfordshire and Berkshire well above (Appendix J).

In some of the towns school attendance was better than in country areas. Of the sixteen towns in the area with populations under 20,000 separately treated in the 1851 education census, all but St. Albans had higher proportions at school on census day than the average of the county in which they were set and only Abingdon and St. Albans a lower proportion 'on the books'. Some, including the county towns of Bedford, Buckingham, Hertford and Hunting-don, and the market towns of Banbury and Chipping Norton, together with Windsor and Wycombe, had much better proportions both enrolled and in attendance.[149] And although five larger towns (with over 20,000 inhabitants) for which separate figures exist, tended to have a smaller proportion on the books of day schools in 1851 than the county average, all had higher proportions in attendance on census day (Appendixes J, K). Expressed as a percentage of children aged five to fourteen, school attendance at Reading was 62 per cent in 1851, at Wisbech 60 per cent, and at Cambridge 55 per cent, compared with an average for all the 'principal towns' for which the census provides such information of 52 per cent.[150] At Bedford, where the Harpur Trust provided copious free elementary schooling and where it was said 'education ... represents what other forms of industry do in other towns',[151] the proportion was 64 per cent.

Even so, Cambridge in the mid-1840, had been considered undersupplied with schools,[152] and school provision was by no means satisfactory in many of the south midland towns, particularly those connected with domestic industry. There was, for example, no National school for girls at that time in Luton, Dunstable or Leighton Buzzard.[153] In 1836 children in the Dunstable area had been reported as 'in a deplorable degree destitute of daily instruction'.[154] The smaller towns of Hertfordshire like Hitchin and Hoddesdon benefited from interdenominational rivalry in school provision, but Watford and St. Albans were particularly poorly off. Watford had a population of over 12,000 in 1861, but only in 1856 had it acquired a school efficient enough to be permitted to train pupil teachers, and the situation at St. Albans (population over 10,000), was similar. There, in five Church schools, there was not a single certificated teacher. In both these towns school boards were required after 1870.[155] And while the Berkshire towns in the early 1870s were significantly better-off than the country districts, there was by then a considerable deficiency at Reading, which had experienced a large population rise since 1861. The Revd. C. D. Du Port, H.M.I., reporting on visits to twenty-seven rural private schools, twenty-nine in Reading and thirteen in other Berkshire towns, claimed that only one was efficient and that the 600–700 Reading children at such establishments 'are not at school at all in any proper sense of the word'. He felt that only the advent of school boards would compel closure of 'these nurseries of inaccuracy and superficiality'. Compulsory attendance brought an immediate increase of 20 per cent to the town's school rolls.[156] In the mid-1860s the town schools inspected in Bedfordshire, Buckinghamshire, Cambridgeshire, Hertfordshire and Huntingdonshire were considered less satisfactory than rural schools.[157]

Indeed, statistics of schools and pupils present for all the counties an exaggerated position of the strength of elementary education in the area. The quality of many of these schools was by all accounts very poor. The inspectorate was acknowledgedly antagonistic to private schools for the poor but its strictures on them in the south midlands have the ring of truth, and the inspectors were often as equally critical of many unaided Church schools and roundly condemnatory of the shortcomings of some grant-aided schools in the area. So one H.M.I. in the early 1840s reported that 'no schools or only schools of the humblest class' existed in sixty-five of Bedfordshire's 123 parishes, fifty-seven of Cambridgeshire's 164, and forty-nine of Huntingdonshire's 104; and 30 per cent of the inspected schools in the remaining parishes he considered almost worthless.[158] Certain districts were at this time particularly deprived. On the Huntingdonshire–Bedfordshire border, an area of high illiteracy,[159] for example, a group of fourteen or so parishes had no reasonable schools for the working classes and a similar concentration of eighteen contiguous parishes existed in north-west Huntingdonshire, while the fen area of north Cambridgeshire was 'sadly deficient' in this respect. In the Bedfordshire plait and lace districts, attempts to provide Church schools for girls were rarely made, for they preferred the lace and plait schools or no schools at all.[160]

The assertion common in the midland region that plentiful school provision was not taken up by parents, is not found to any great extent in reports on the south midlands. For many places large numbers of the public schools were not of sufficient standard to be grant aided. There were only thirty-one inspected schools in the whole of Northamptonshire in 1848, and, though numbers increased in the 1850s, in the 1860s it was reported that no aided Church schools existed in a large part of the north of the county and some small towns in south Northamptonshire had no inspected schools at all. In Cambridgeshire in the later 1850s a line drawn from Wisbech in the north to Linton in the south would pass near only four grant-aided schools, while another from Wisbech to the extreme south-west of the county would pass only three such schools. At the same time there were only two grant-aided schools in the northern half of Huntingdonshire, while in that part of Bedfordshire north of Ampthill (well over half the county) there were none.[161] All this accords with what we know of areas of high illiteracy at this time, and Oxfordshire, where literacy rates were better, was reported to be better provided at that time with schools than any other county except Wiltshire and Westmorland.[162]

Provision of school places improved over the period. By the late 1850s there were increased numbers particularly in Hertfordshire, and in the 1860s most children in that county lived within reach of a day school,[163] and the same was so of Oxfordshire and Berkshire.[164] In Northamptonshire conditions improved,[165] and by 1868 schools of some kind existed in every village and Church schools in all but thirteen parishes. Even so, the quality of these publicly-provided schools left much wanting particularly in small rural parishes.[166] The Oxfordshire and Berkshire clergy were criticised by the inspectorate for persisting in running their own uninspected schools with uncertificated teachers rather than encouraging pupils to attend more efficient schools in neighbouring parishes. Many of the unaided Northamptonshire Church schools were really dame schools smiled on by the incumbent but with low levels of attainment.[167] In one such school 'a common labourer (whose respectability was his single qualification) [had been] promoted by the clergyman to the office of schoolmaster'.[168]

The situation in Buckinghamshire, Bedfordshire, and to a lesser extent in Cambridgeshire and Huntingdonshire, remained particularly poor even on the eve and morrow of the 1870 Education Act. Indeed, in 1868 it was alleged that the efficiency of the Church schools of Cambridgeshire, Bedfordshire and Huntingdonshire had actually declined: 'good reading', it was said, was 'becoming rare'.[169] Quite populous villages in those counties were still allegedly without a decent school. In the district of Newport Pagnell, for instance, only six schools in the thirty-eight parishes and townships were in receipt of a regular government grant, and another eight were receiving aid but not annually.[170] Of 219 places in Bedfordshire and Huntingdonshire in the early 1870s, sixty-four, it was said, had no reasonable school and eighty-two were considered adequately provided for.[171] In Kneesworth, East Hatley and

Steeple Morden, to give samples from Cambridgeshire, no Church school was opened until 1867, 1874 and 1867 respectively.[172] The private schools in these counties, too, even apart from the lace and plait schools, were particularly poor: 'One ancient lady said that her children did no writing, "for you see" ... "I lost the use of my right hand, and that's what drove me to school keeping." "They only come to be kept quiet," said many others.'[173] At Bassingbourn (Cambs.) the new board school found even the ex-pupils of the closed National and British schools barely literate.[174]

The high and sometimes increasing proportions of boys of ten to fourteen, employed on the land[175] and the decline in male literacy standards in some agricultural districts[176] suggest that school attendance for boys in some parts, as for girls in industrial areas, may have been poor. Appendix I indicates that at county level a general connection existed, except perhaps in the case of Northamptonshire, between the proportion of children aged five to fourteen not at day school in 1851 and illiteracy rates in 1866. Application of the product moment correlation coefficient formula to the relationship of actual day-school attendance in 1851 and illiteracy rates in 1866 in the various districts of each county reveals correlations of -0.65 and -0.63 for Hertfordshire and Bedfordshire, lower ones for Northamptonshire and Oxfordshire (-0.56, -0.55), and very low correlations or none at all for the other four counties.[177] From these figures it may be argued that, while a relationship was most evident in the counties where domestic industry was most heavily concentrated, even in Northamptonshire and Oxfordshire only some 40 per cent of the literacy rate can be associated statistically with earlier schooling levels locally. Taking all the registration districts of the region together, the correlation coefficient is only -0.44, similar to that found in the western counties and the midlands. Nevertheless, the existence of a tendency is demonstrated in a rudimentary fashion in Table 5.2.

This relationship was close in the districts of four of the eight counties (Appendix F). In Bedfordshire all the districts with day-school attendance proportions below the national level in 1851 had illiteracy rates of 29 per cent or more in 1866, while of the two districts with day-school proportions at or above the national level one had an illiteracy rate of below 29 per cent. In Northamptonshire all the districts with day-school attendance at or above the national level in 1851 had illiteracy rates below 29 per cent in 1866, while two of the four with the worst school attendance had over 29 per cent illiteracy fifteen years later. The districts of Berkshire and Oxfordshire showed a similar relationship. In the other four counties the relationship though discernible is not quite as strong. Of the twenty districts in the eight counties with day-school levels below the national in 1851, however, only seven had illiteracy rates less than 29 per cent in 1866, and only two had rates below 26 per cent. (Potterspury, Northants, 22 per cent; Easthampstead, Berks., 10 per cent).

TABLE 5·2

Illiteracy rates and schooling

% of population in attendance at day school, 1851	Illiteracy rates, 1866: number of districts		
	10–22% marks	23–29% marks	30–48% marks
16	1	0	0
14	2	2	1
13	3 } 11	2 } 7	1 } 5
12	5	3	3
11	4	7	6
10	0	4	4
9	0 } 6	2 } 17	7 } 22
8	1	4	4
7	1	0	1

Source: Based on Appendix F.

Over the period the relative proportions of day pupils attending public, as opposed to private, schools increased. In 1833 public day schools accounted for about half or slightly more of day-school pupils in all the south midland counties except Cambridgeshire and Huntingdonshire. By 1851, in all the counties apart from Cambridgeshire, over 70 per cent of day-school pupils were at public day schools, and in Cambridgeshire that proportion was nearly approached. In 1858 all the south midland counties had proportions of their population at public school above the national level (Appendix J). As for the twenty towns in the area separately treated in the 1851 census, all showed a higher proportion of pupils on the books of public than private day schools, but the proportions varied greatly. Eight had between 67 and 72 per cent at public schools; six above that (Bedford, Daventry, Hertford, Maidenhead, St. Albans and Wycombe) and the remaining six below 67 per cent, Newbury the lowest, with 56 per cent. There is not as clear an indication as, for example, in the western counties of a heavier incidence of private schooling in the towns than in the country districts generally. In only eight of the twenty was there a higher proportion at public than at private schools (Appendix K).

Despite the limited enthusiasm for popular education shown by many in the Church in the south midlands, the expansion of public schooling was nevertheless attributable largely to Anglican activity. The Oxford Diocesan Education Board was founded in 1839 and soon set up training establishments for teachers, though a system of diocesan inspection was not instituted until 1850–1. [178] The 1851 religious census shows that nonconformity in the south midlands was strongest in Bedfordshire, Cambridgeshire and Huntingdonshire, relatively strong in Northamptonshire and Buckinghamshire, and weakest in Oxfordshire and Berkshire. [179] The number of dissenters' public schools in 1833 reflects this pattern, except for Oxfordshire, which had a surprisingly large proportion of nonconformist schools. Even so, the Anglican schools were in a considerable majority in all the counties of the area, though less so than, for example, in the western counties. British and protestant dissenting schools accounted for 46 per cent of public schools in Bedfordshire, 28–30 per cent in Buckinghamshire, Cambridgeshire, Northamptonshire and Oxfordshire, 23 per cent in Hertfordshire, 19 per cent in Huntingdonshire, and 14 per cent in Berkshire. In 1851, when we have information on the distribution of pupils in the schools, the pattern was more or less the same. The Church of England by then had a considerable lead in each county, with only Bedfordshire, Huntingdonshire and Cambridgeshire approaching as much as a quarter of scholars in dissenting schools. By 1858 the Church had increased its lead in every county in the area except Berkshire, and in none were more than 20 per cent at nonconformist schools (Appendix L).

Statistics of Anglican schools, compiled, on a different basis, for the years 1837, 1847, 1857 and 1867 (Appendix M), confirm the growing strength of the Church in the provision of public schooling. By 1847 attendance at such schools was well above the national average in all the south midland counties except Bedfordshire and Buckinghamshire, while by 1857 and in 1867 those two counties also fell into that category. Church effort is indicated also by the fact that in 1858 Anglican schools in the south midlands (except in Cambridgeshire) received income apart from treasury grants at a level about the national average, while in five of the counties British and nonconformist school income of this kind fell below the national average for such schools (Appendix P). Nevertheless, over the period 1833–59, all except Hertfordshire received in government grants less than the national average per head of population, a fact perhaps attributable to the large number of Church schools of a standard too low to apply for aid.[180]

For reasons already discussed[181] it is difficult to test any relationship between the spread of public schooling and literacy levels, and indeed the ten south midland districts with over 80 per cent of day pupils at public schools in 1851 had little in common in later literacy ratings: they ranged from 18 to 40 per cent in illiterate spouses in 1866. What examination of these districts does show, however, is once again a tentative connection between literacy rates and proportions at day schools as a whole (private and public) (Appendix F).[182] However, marriage signatures tested only a very basic literacy, and the rising standards revealed by them, and suggested by the spread of day schools, should not be exaggerated. In particular, they beg the question of the quality of education purveyed. Other evidence, particularly official reports, although often impressionistic, does something to fill in the picture and suggests that the south midlands was a region of persistent educational backwardness. The 1833 survey reveals that day-school pupils were heavily concentrated in the youngest age range. Moreover in Bedfordshire, Buckinghamshire, Hunting-donshire, Northamptonshire and Hertfordshire there were also large numbers of young children in lace and plait schools who were not included in the return. In rural Northamptonshire even in the 1850s it was admitted that most Church schools were 'little, if anything, more than Infant schools'.[183] In Banbury the proportion at school over the period 1851–71 did not rise, but the numbers attending included gradually more older and fewer younger children.[184] But more commonly high proportions of young children persisted through the period.[185]

In the districts of domestic industry the converse of starting work at an early age was the concentration in the schools of the very young, and this was particularly so of girls. Thus the incumbent of Marsh Gibbon (Bucks.) in 1857 complained that lace making 'draws the girls from school before they are six years of age and makes it impossible for me to have a girls' school'.[186] Jane Alcock, a nine-year old in Bedfordshire in the 1860s, had attended day school for six months prior to entering a lace school; she had never attended Sunday school, and could spell 'do' but had no figures. Mary Benning aged six and Sarah Cooper aged seven, at lace schools in Buckingham, had already finished with day school, and such examples could be multiplied. Some of these girls claimed to attend Sunday school and evening or Saturday schools to learn writing, but this was by no means the norm.[187]

In 1855, 79 per cent of pupils in inspected schools in Bedfordshire, Buckinghamshire, Hertfordshire and Middlesex were aged ten or less: an increase of 13 per cent since 1853.[188] Up to the age of ten more boys than girls attended school in the industrial districts of Northamptonshire, Bedfordshire and Buckinghamshire. For instance, in Woburn district (Beds.) in the late 1860s 25 per cent more sons than daughters of farm labourers in this age group were at school, and another 4 per cent in the age group ten to thirteen.[189]

In those districts where agricultural labour was the main occupation the situation differed somewhat but was still unsatisfactory. The school age structure certainly seems to have been little better. In inspected schools in Wiltshire and Berkshire in 1851–2, 56 per cent were aged eight or below and 78 per cent below ten, a proportion higher than two years before.[190] In 1868 a similar survey in Berkshire and Oxfordshire revealed 87 per cent under ten.[191] Nevertheless in the late 1860s a much higher proportion of farm labourers' children was found at school up to age thirteen in sample districts of Oxfordshire and Hertfordshire than in the plait and lace districts of Bedford-shire and Buckinghamshire. Moreover the attendance pattern of the sexes was reversed. In the agricultural districts more girls than boys were at school, particularly over the age of ten. Even below that age boys' attendance fell off much more than that of girls in the summer months.[192]

The impact of domestic industry on the schooling of girls is demonstrated by the fact that in only six registration districts in 1851 did the proportion of schoolgirls exceed that of schoolboys (Appendix F). Four of those districts were in Berkshire, and one each in Cambridgeshire and Oxfordshire. The extent of the excess of boy over girl pupils tended to be greatest in the districts of Bedfordshire and Buckinghamshire. The data in Appendix I, which assesses the proportion of children aged five to fourteen not at school in 1851, further illustrates the situation. In Bedfordshire and Buckinghamshire some two-thirds of girls in this age group were not at school; in Northamptonshire about 60 per cent. Cambridgeshire, perhaps because of the preponderance of small family farms, also had nearly 60 per cent, but in the other four south midland counties the proportion was around half. For boys the proportion of non-attenders was highest in Bedfordshire (56 per cent) and in the other counties was about half. Census day, it is true, was in March, so that attendance was probably less affected by farm work than in the summer. Thus, while a mathematical relationship between district schooling rates in 1851 and later differences between male and female literacy levels is difficult to demonstrate, the impression outlined earlier of the effect of differing employment patterns for boys and girls on male and female literacy levels is reinforced (Appendix F).

Proportions of children not at school at a particular time do not, of course, show that none of these children had ever been at school, but they do underline the shortness of school life, and this is supported by other evidence. In 1855, for example, only 17 per cent of pupils at inspected schools in Bedfordshire, Buckinghamshire, Hertfordshire and Middlesex had been there for over two years.[193] Farm work was less of a hindrance to school attendance than domestic industry. In the more purely agricultural areas school stay may have been a little longer, but the evidence is slight. In rural Oxfordshire in 1850 children were said to 'come to school under favourable circumstances at two years, and remain, with occasional interruptions, until they are eight, ten or twelve, when their school-days are over',[194] and in rural Berkshire the average length of school stay was two years nine months.[195] In the Cambridgeshire fens, however, where schools anyway were not numerous, the average stay was eighteen months in the late 1860s,[196] and everywhere the seasonal demands of agriculture gravely affected the attendance of boys and sometimes girls, particularly in the summer, and in rural schools children went less regularly than in towns. In 1846, for instance, over 20 per cent of pupils in village schools in the 'eastern district' (including Cambridgeshire and Huntingdonshire) were always absent even at 'the best seasons of the year',[197] and this persisted. In Cambridgeshire in the 1860s children absented themselves for weeks at a time when needed on the land,[198] and irregular attendance was still a problem in rural Oxfordshire and Berkshire in the 1870s, even after the introduction of compulsory schooling.[199] Eleven-year-old Mary Middleton of Pytchley

(Northants) attended a charity school in 1863 'but has never been for more than a few months at a time, and leaves in summer for out-door work and gleaning'.[200]

As to Sunday schools, it is evident that attendance was in 1833 particularly significant in three of the south midland counties. In Bedfordshire nearly two and a half times the number of children were attending Sunday as day schools and in fifty-seven places only Sunday schools existed (they catered for 3,100 children compared with 6,630 children at day schools in the whole county); in Buckinghamshire there were almost twice as many Sunday as day scholars; in Northamptonshire, one and a half times the number. In Buckinghamshire, Bedfordshire and Northamptonshire 183 places, mostly those where domestic industry dominated, had no schools but Sunday schools, which catered for thousands of pupils. This is reflected in the proportion of the population at Sunday as opposed to day schools in those counties. In the other five counties the number of places relying entirely on Sunday schools was not great and only in Oxfordshire and Huntingdonshire were there slightly more Sunday than day-school pupils.[201] Something of the same pattern is discernible in 1851. Then Bedfordshire, Buckinghamshire, Northamptonshire, Hertfordshire and Huntingdonshire had more Sunday-school pupils proportionate to their population than was the case nationally, while Oxfordshire, Berkshire and Cambridgeshire had fewer. In 1858 Bedfordshire still had double the number of children at Sunday school as at public day-school and proportions were relatively high in Buckinghamshire and Northamptonshire (Appendix J).

At registration district level in 1851 all but one district (Eton) in Bedfordshire and Buckinghamshire had a Sunday-school attendance rate above the national level. Since half these districts had below average day-school attendance, it is evident that Sunday schools were here serving as substitutes for full-time educaton (Appendix F). Similarly in Hertfordshire there was a clear tendency for districts where Sunday-school attendance was above the national level to have below the national level of day-school attendance and conversely where Sunday-school attendance was below the national level. In Oxfordshire and Berkshire, where only three of nineteen districts were below the national level for day-school attendance, eight districts were below that level for Sunday-school attendance. In Cambridgeshire and Northamptonshire no such clear relationship is discernible. In Cambridgeshire there was a tendency for districts with higher levels of Sunday-schooling also to have higher levels of day school attendance. In Northamptonshire attendance was above the national level in both Sunday and day schools in half the twelve districts.

The connection between areas of domestic industry and greater reliance on Sunday schools is thus evident. That connection is made even clearer if the actual numbers of pupils are considered. In only eleven of the forty-three registration districts in Berkshire, Oxfordshire, Cambridgeshire, Huntingdonshire and Hertfordshire did Sunday-school attendance in 1851 exceed day-school attendance, and these included the plaiting districts of St. Albans, Hemel Hemstead and Berkhamstead. In Bedfordshire every registration district showed a higher attendance at Sunday than day school, in Buckinghamshire all but one (Eton), and in Northamptonshire all but two (Oundle and Peterborough). In some districts, the excess was very considerable: more than double in Ampthill, Luton, Woking and Newport Pagnell, for instance (Appendix F). In towns, however, the situation differed. In only a handful were there more Sunday than day scholars in 1851[202] and in none, except perhaps Chipping Norton, does it seem that Sunday schools were being used extensively as day-school substitutes (Appendix K).

The incidence of Sunday-school attendance probably also had something to do with religious affiliations. The nonconformists found it easier to provide Sunday than day schools and the religious complexion of the area is better reflected in Sunday-school than in day-school attendance, even though the Established Church still catered for the bulk of Sunday as it did for public day pupils: in 1833 two-thirds or more in each of the south midland counties, except Bedfordshire, Buckinghamshire and Hertfordshire. By the 1850s there appears to be at county level a rough relationship between the incidence of nonconformity and the popularity of Sunday schools generally (Appendix N). By then, too, the nonconformist share of Sunday schools had risen in each county except Oxfordshire, substantially so in Berkshire and Cambridgeshire: in 1851, in all but Oxfordshire, over 40 per cent of Sunday scholars were in dissenting schools (Appendix L).

At county level there is no very obvious relationship between the incidence of Sunday schooling and later literacy percentages, except for Bedfordshire, Buckinghamshire and Oxfordshire, (Appendixes D, J). In the first two of these counties there is an apparent connection between poor literacy levels in 1866 and relatively high proportions of Sunday-school pupils in 1851, combined with proportions at day school below the national level. This bears out other evidence that in these areas the Sunday school was still for many children the main medium of education and one connected with low levels of attainment. Conversely Oxfordshire, the most literate of the south midland counties in 1866, had the smallest proportions at Sunday school in 1851, but a day-school attendance well above the national level. Similarly Berkshire, with proportions of Sunday-school pupils below and proportions of day-school pupils above the national level, was next best to Oxfordshire in standards of literacy.

The districts where proportions at Sunday school in 1851 were more than 4 percentage points greater than proportions at day school (sixteen out of sixty-eight) were mainly districts where domestic industry was common. And twelve of them were among the thirty districts with the worst literacy rates in 1866 (Appendixes F, G): again, Sunday schooling as a not particularly successful substitute for day schooling is suggested. Moreover three of the sixteen districts (Newport Pagnell, Buckingham, Towcester) had ten years before been among that third of the districts with the best literacy ratings, and it is tempting to see continued preference for Sunday schooling as an ingredient in their relative decline.

The availability of secular instruction on a part-time basis would seem the strongest reason for the attraction of Sunday schools. Edward Early of Witney reported in 1839 that over a thousand children were taught reading in the town's Sunday schools and taught to write on Saturday evenings.[203] In 1851 some 2,600 adults in the south midland counties attended evening schools (excluding mechanics' and literary institutes), and these probably included adolescents, the heaviest concentrations being in Bedfordshire and Buckinghamshire.[204] Certainly in 1858 Bedfordshire, Northamptonshire and Hertfordshire had a higher proportion of their population at night school than any other English county. Oxfordshire and Buckinghamshire did not lag far behind, and Cambridgeshire, Huntingdonshire and Berkshire also had well above the national level. In all of them a far higher number of boys than girls attended (Appendix Q). In the early 1860s night schools existed in two-thirds of the parishes of Oxfordshire and Berkshire and over half those of Bedfordshire and Buckinghamshire. G. Culley observed that they supplemented or substituted for day schools but did not feel they were efficient enough to have government grants.[205]

Night schools in rural Northamptonshire were reported by the clergy in the late 1860s as unsuccessful, being poorly attended, with indifferent pupils taught by inefficient teachers.[206] Given the uncertainty of their educational contribution to those who attended, and the comparatively small numbers involved, it remains doubtful whether night schools affected general cultural standards greatly in the south midlands and they must have been less significant than the Sunday schools.

The picture of the south midlands provided by the marriage signature statistics as, on the whole, an educationally backward area is thus supported by qualitative evidence. Domestic industry, poorly paid agricultural labour, small family farms, remote and dispersed rural populations, poor communications, and indifferent and absentee landlords,[207] all combined to create cultural backwardness that persisted into the 1860s and beyond. Remedies in the form of schooling were more difficult to provide than in areas of urban concentration. Thus Cambridgeshire and Huntingdonshire suffered particularly from poor roads and the paucity of towns and large villages able to furnish central schools for surrounding countrysides; attempts to establish such schools in the early part of the century failed and the parish school, too small and poor to be efficient or often to attract grant aid, became the norm.[208] The common difficulties in rural areas of applying the half-time system to young farm workers pertained in the area, too, and with particular force to the numerous family farms whose children worked for their parents. Likewise the widespread presence of domestic industry in large parts of the area represented a greater problem of control for educational purposes than did, for example, the factory children of the north. Thus it was difficult to provide good schools and often hard to get children to attend them.

Financial constraints on the extension and maintenance of sound public schooling in the area were very great. Where resident gentry and aristocracy took an interest things were better, but often this support was lacking. In Hertfordshire, for example, access to sound schooling varied greatly from one part to another according to whether there were landowners willing to promote it.[209] Farmers in the south midlands helped little and where the landed classes were also lukewarm the burden fell heavily on the clergy, whose resources were limited. The H.M.I.s' reports over the decades of the 1840s, 1850s and 1860s stress that the clergy who ran schools were forced to run them cheaply with uncertificated teachers and poor equipment; they were thus unable to obtain government grants and a bad situation was compounded. Some were forced to close their schools.[210]

F.C. Cook, H.M.I., in 1845 reported of his district, which included Bedfordshire, Cambridgeshire and Huntingdonshire, that the need for economy in public schools was impairing their educational value and in 'many places where the clergy have hitherto made great sacrifices to keep their schools open ... it will not be possible for them to struggle much longer'; the same lack of local financial support was preventing the establishment of schools in parishes where there were none.[211] Hence, said another inspector in 1851, 'we have both bad schools and no schools'.[212] In 1868 an actual decline in scholars in the Church schools in these counties was attributed to difficulties of raising funds.[213]

Likewise in Berkshire and Oxfordshire in the late 1850s and 1860s not only were the numbers of schools getting government grants limited by the widespread use of low-paid uncertificated teachers, but some schools were losing aided status as they shed certificated teachers because they could not pay them.[214] Thus many schools in the area, although deemed 'public', were in a low state of efficiency.[215] In Berkshire and Wiltshire in 1850 only 84 of 682 National schools had pupil-teachers.[216]

The uncertificated teachers were not greatly superior to those of private schools: 'some have merely passed a few months in a National school of a neighbouring town; not a few have been domestic servants'; some still devoted their leisure hours to domestic industry.[217] In some areas the teaching was so poor that children were removed to dame schools where, it was said, 'they at least learn to read, which is more than can be said for those who remain two or three years in the schools alluded to'.[218] Even in 1872 many schools in rural Berkshire had no certificated teachers.[219]

Everything points to the likelihood that in many parts of the south midlands educational improvement would come only by a combination of an infusion of public money and compulsory attendance. As early as 1850 Henry Moseley, H.M.I., reporting on Oxfordshire and Berkshire, was suggesting some form of local rates,[220] and almost twenty years later some clergy in Oxfordshire and Bedfordshire wanted legislative action 'to compel the owners of property to bear a fair share' of the expense of supporting schools.[221] The mere provision of schools, however, would not, in an area where child labour was so entrenched, be enough. In 1870 H. W. Bellairs, H.M.I., saw no hope of improved rural schooling in Berkshire and Oxfordshire while the introduction of compulsory attendance was permissive. In the towns where compulsion would be applied there would be improved education; in the villages where it would not, ignorance would reign 'in its old glory'.[222] In the areas of domestic industry it was clear that, despite legislation on child employment, only some form of compulsion would get all the children to school.[223]

CHAPTER 6

The western counties

Economic and social structure

The maritime counties of the south-western peninsula (Cornwall, Devon Dorset, Somerset) and Gloucestershire, together with inland Wiltshire and the border counties of Monmouthshire, Herefordshire and Shropshire, the subject of this chapter, covered a considerable area. Their total population in 1851, however, amounted to only some 2·75 million souls, considerably less, for example, than the combined population of Lancashire and the West Riding.[1] Devon, Gloucestershire and Somerset were the most populous (Appendix I), though over the period 1841–71 Monmouthshire had the largest increase of population. Wiltshire is remarkable for being the only English county in which population actually declined between 1841 and 1851, and the county's population fell further in 1851–61. Similarly, Cornwall experienced a 2 per cent decline, 1861–71, and by 1871 its population was about the same level as twenty years before. Herefordshire, one of the most thinly peopled of English counties, saw little population growth between 1841 and 1871. Indeed, the western counties embraced two of the four largest groups of registration districts of decreasing population (1841–51) in the country, and part of the third. One of these areas comprised five registration districts on the south Devon coast[2] together with six other Devon districts in the centre and north of the county[3] and the adjoining Cornish district of Stratton. Another was made up of neighbouring districts in south Gloucestershire, north Wiltshire, east Somerset[4] and Shaftesbury (Dorset). Both these areas were traditionally connected with the West Country woollen industry, by then in decline. Further north, the districts of Wem, Ellesmere and Oswestry formed part of a third area of falling population which spread over the Welsh border into Montgomeryshire.

If the populations of urban and industrial areas are excluded from total county populations, Cornwall, Devon, Dorset, Herefordshire and Wiltshire saw a continuous decline in population from 1861 to 1901, and Monmouthshire, Gloucestershire and Shropshire slight increases between 1861 and 1871, with decline after that.[5] There were few large towns. In 1851 Bristol stood out, while

Plymouth with Devonport formed the only other large conurbation. Towns with around 20,000 or more inhabitants included Bath, Cheltenham, Stroud, Exeter, Gloucester and Shrewsbury. Hereford, Taunton and Newport (Monmouthshire) were the next largest. A score of others, including Truro, Salisbury, Poole and Weymouth–Melcombe Regis, were in the range 7,000–12,000 and about fifty communities had populations of 3,000–7,000.

Joseph Fletcher's statistical analysis of social characteristics in the 1840s (Appendix H) demonstrates a lack of uniformity in the western counties, which, as will be shown later, is evident, too, in the occupational structures of the area. Proportions of persons of independent means fell below the national level in Cornwall, Monmouthshire and Shropshire, all partly industrial, and in rural Wiltshire, but in the other four counties was above average. Early marriages were at low levels — except in Dorset and, especially, in Wiltshire, reflecting, no doubt, the degradation of farm labourers in those two counties, as does the high level of relieved paupers there. Some match is evident in Cornwall and Monmouthshire between a lack of persons of independent means and below-average levels of savings deposits, but Fletcher's figures here are not easy to interpret.

Certainly the distribution of the chief types of industrial employment in the nine western counties was a significant element in the varying characteristics of local community structures. In particular, the coal and iron districts of Shropshire, the Mendips, the Forest of Dean and Monmouthshire, where mining was often combined with metal manufacture, presented social attributes similar to those found in parts of the north of England and the Black Country, though the organisation of the extractive industries of Cornwall and south Devon gave some communities of those areas more distinctive structures. The declining West Country woollen industry and lace and glove manufacturing provided social ingredients in some areas deriving both from factory organisation and domestic work, reminiscent on the one hand of Lancashire and the West Riding, and on the other of parts of the midlands. In Monmouthshire miners outnumbered farm workers by two to one by 1851 and parts of Shropshire shared in the industrial expansion of the Black Country. Nevertheless the most striking feature of the occupational structure of the nine western counties in the mid-nineteenth century is the dominance of agriculture in most of them, a dominance persisting for the rest of the century.[6] Herefordshire in particular was almost exclusively a farming county, while Wiltshire, Dorset, Shropshire, Devon and Somerset also had large proportions of men listed in 1851 as farmers or farm labourers (Appendix A). Proportions of those attached to the land in the other three counties were smaller but still significant. Since the size of county populations varied considerably the picture derived from actual numbers employed in agriculture is different. Devon had most (66,000 persons), while Somerset (54,000) and Wiltshire (49,000) had the next largest farming populations. Gloucestershire, Cornwall and Shropshire had about the same number in each (36,000, 35,000, 34,000), while Dorset had 26,000, Herefordshire, a sparsely populated county, 19,000, and Monmouthshire 12,000. And, although the proportions of the occupied population engaged in farming fell between 1841 and 1881 in each western county except Cornwall, the decline was much less than in many parts of the country, particularly in Gloucestershire, Herefordshire and Shropshire.[7]

The great variety of soils and terrain, however, combined with other factors to produce diverse types of farming and landowning and tenancy structures, and consequently working populations enjoying differing degrees of prosperity and life style. Most types of farming were found.[8] Sheep farming was pursued on Dartmoor and Exmoor, the Blackdown Hills, the Cotswolds, and in Herefordshire, Dorset, Cornwall, south-east Wiltshire and Monmouthshire. Grazing and dairy farming were variously found in many parts, particularly in Devon, in the Exe valley, the vale of Exeter and Honiton and the South Hams, in east and central Dorset, in Somerset, north-west Wiltshire and Cornwall, in south and west Shropshire and in Gloucestershire in the vales of Evesham, Gloucester and Berkeley. Corn was grown especially in Herefordshire, Shropshire, Monmouthshire, south-east Wiltshire and Cornwall, while orchards were significant in west Devon, Herefordshire, Somerset and Monmouthshire. Hops were produced on Herefordshire's border with Warwickshire, and potatoes extensively in Cornwall. Around Yeovil there was market gardening.

More significant for the social historian than the actual types of farming activity, however, was the nature of land ownership and tenancy. By 1870 Cornwall, Devon, Somerset, Gloucestershire and Herefordshire were conspicuous for the proportions of land held in estates of 1,000 acres or less: 42–6 per cent as against a national average of 38·5 per cent. On the other hand Wiltshire, Dorset and Shropshire had comparatively few small landowners and above average proportions owning over 1,000 acres. Indeed, in Wiltshire and Dorset 36 per cent of the land was in estates of over 10,000 acres.[9] In those two counties the existence of large estates was characterised by a greater number of large farms, whereas most of those counties where small estates were common also had a large number of small farms.

In Cornwall farming practices were generally backward, at least to the mid-century, and very labour-intensive. By the 1870s, 7–9 per cent of the total population of the county were said to be engaged in agriculture, and the proportion of farmers to the number of cultivated acres was high. Property was much divided, with an immense number of small occupiers who, with their families, managed their enterprises without outside help. Farms of between twenty and seventy acres were common and in addition much land in certain areas was held in small parcels by working miners and cottagers. With the decline of the mines and the arrival of the railway the farmers of west Cornwall turned the fields into market gardens and the pilchard fisheries were similarly expanded.[10]

Devon, with a large agricultural population, was, like Cornwall, a county of small farmers, and this was particularly the case on the poorer soils of north Devon and on the fringes of Dartmoor.[11] Though there were some farms of 600–700 acres the majority of Devon farms were between sixty and 250 acres. In addition there were many smallholders whose social and economic condition was little above that of labourers. Many landowners were resident, but in mid-century the quality of farming was generally held to be inferior to that in most other counties. In Somerset, too, most of the farms were small. In the western hill area the occupiers of some tiny holdings were little better off than labourers, though some farms ranged from 170 to over 300 acres, generally larger in the Quantocks. In the vale of Taunton farms averaged around 200–220 acres but there were many of less than 100. In east Somerset in mid-century about a thousand acres were run as field gardens divided among 5,200 families. Gloucestershire was another county of predominantly small farms. In the vales of Evesham, Gloucester and Berkeley the great majority were of less than 150 acres and few exceeded 300 acres. In the sheep areas of the Cotswolds they ranged from 200 to 1,000 acres with the smaller holdings more common in the south. Monmouthshire possessed some large estates, but property was a good deal subdivided, and the size of farms was generally small, ranging from sixty to 300 acres, though farms of 300–400 acres were common in the lowland parts of the county.

In Shropshire, where 44 per cent of the land was held in middling sized estates of 1,000 to 10,000 acres, farm sizes varied. On the Welsh border they were very small, many not exceeding twenty acres, while in the east they varied between 100 and 500 acres or more. In the south-west the district of Clun Forest was divided into small freehold properties with the owner-occupiers and their families doing most of the work themselves. In 1848 it was reckoned that 40 per cent of Shropshire farmers were poor men unable to carry out improvements. In Herefordshire, however, where the proportion of land in middle-sized estates was about the same as in small estates,[12] resident landowners were common and the size of farm was somewhat above the average elsewhere, and the bigger estates were divided into farms of 200–400 acres. Small farms were decreasing in number, but there were still many in 1851.

In Dorset estates were large, and there were more big farms, while some great landowners, like Lord Portman at Bryanston, farmed their own land. The standard of farming was high, especially in the arable–sheep economy of the uplands. In Wiltshire the south-east was chiefly in large farms of 800 to 5,000 acres, with farmers generally of a 'superior class'. These men often occupied the manor houses, since the landowners were frequently non-resident. In north Wiltshire the farm size varied from fifty to 250 acres with some of up to 500 acres. On the more numerous smaller farms family labour usually dispensed with the need for hired hands.

The ubiquity of small farms in most of the western counties was not conducive to very advanced agricultural practices, and although progressive methods were moderately represented in Dorset and Wiltshire during the period of high farming (1840–80), in the other western counties there was comparatively little advance. Indeed, small farms meant a countryside where a large proportion of the population concentrated its efforts in making ends meet. Not only were farm labourers the lowest paid of most occupational groups in the south west but their wages compared unfavourably with farm earnings elsewhere. In 1861 the nine English counties with the lowest agricultural wages included seven of the western counties (that is, all but Shropshire and Monmouthshire),[13] largely because in the west the labour market was overstocked and alternative employment at a premium. Farm labourers fared better in Monmouthshire and Shropshire, where industrial jobs were available.[14]

The overall picture of the rural west is thus one of small farms, much family labour and, except in a few areas, a lack of alternative work. The state of farm labourers, a significant occupational group throughout our period, was unenviable even in areas of large farm units, and often exceedingly miserable.[15] Yet wages in other occupations in the west tended also to be below those in most of Britain.

Occupations connected with the sea accounted for over 3 per cent of adult males in twenty-two western registration districts in 1851, but only in six were over 9 per cent so employed (Poole, Falmouth, Bideford, Bridport, Stoke Damerel, Plymouth).[16] Only Devon and Cornwall had a substantial interest in fishing, and much of the work in the pilchard fisheries, including the preparation of the catch on land, was seasonal and undertaken by labourers, miners and by women who had other callings, so that no large group of permanently employed workers existed. With improved land transport the drift fisheries became more important, employing more than the seine fisheries, and though they, too, became capitalised, the small independent fishermen survived into the latter part of the century.

Proportions of adults engaged in manufacturing in the western counties fell well below the national average (just over 10 per cent) the highest proportions being in Monmouthshire (7 per cent) and in Wiltshire, Gloucestershire and Somerset (all about 6 per cent). Nevertheless, when child labour is taken into account, there were districts where industrial employment was significant. Certainly mining of one kind or another was very important in some parts. In particular Cornwall had a higher proportion of adult men so employed in 1851 than any other English county, while Monmouthshire nearly equalled Durham, which came second to Cornwall (Appendix A). Together with the Tavistock district of Devon, the Cornish mining districts accounted for 26,000 of the 37,000 employed nationally in the mining of copper, tin and lead. In the Redruth district 54 per cent of adult men were miners, and six other Cornish districts plus Tavistock had between 20 and 31 per cent of its men engaged in mining these minerals. In Monmouthshire it was coal and iron mining that was important. There 11,000 adults were so occupied: in Abergavenny district 36 per cent of the adult men, in Pontypool 26 per cent, in Newport and Monmouth districts 12 and 14 per cent respectively. Another 9,000 men were employed in coal mining in Gloucestershire, Shropshire and Somerset, the bulk in the last two of those counties. In the Coalbrookdale area of Shropshire (Madeley and Wellington districts) 22 per cent of adult men, and in the neighbouring Newport district 11 per cent, were engaged in coal and iron mining. In the Forest of Dean area (Westbury-on-Severn district) of Gloucestershire, adjoining Monmouthshire, the proportion was 18 per cent; and in the Somerset (Mendips) coal-mining area (Clutton and Keynsham districts) 22 per cent. In the same areas metal manufacturing was important. Monmouthshire's proportion of adult men engaged in these industries (12 per cent) exceeded that of all but three other English counties (Warwickshire, Staffordshire and Worcestershire), while in the Coalbrookdale area of Shropshire (where the Coalbrookdale Company was the largest ironworks in the country) the proportion was over 16 per cent.[17]

The organisation of the Cornish mining industry, which expanded and prospered in the first half of the century,[18] produced an occupational structure strikingly different in character from the industrial areas of the north of England. Landowners sometimes worked mines themselves but more often leased them to companies of 'adventurers' who supervised operations through pursers and agents or 'bal captains'. The captains, risen from the ranks of miners, controlled operations on the spot. The miners were, however, self-employed and essentially profit-sharers rather than wage-earners, working in gangs of two to three men assisted by boys whom they employed. 'Tributer' gangs contracted to dig out a section taking a share of profits; 'tutworker' gangs contracted to dig shafts and galleys for a fee. In addition numerous women and children who prepared the ore on the surface were employed by the company or the tributers, but some skilled surface work was undertaken by independent workers.

While independent, however, the miners depended greatly on fortune, and competition kept their incomes down. In times of bad trade they experienced great hardship. The growth of overseas competition from around the middle of the century, combined with rising costs as deeper mines were needed, resulted in the end of prosperity for Cornish mining, particularly in copper production.

The Cornish population reached a peak in 1861 but the financial crisis of 1866 dealt a savage blow to an already weakening industry. Production fell, unemployment rose and the great wave of Cornish emigration began as 'Cousin Jack' took his skills to the far ends of the earth.

Some degree of relief came with the stimulus given to vegetable growing and fishing by the opening in 1859 of the railway link with the capital, and by expansion of china clay production, particularly in the area between Roche and St. Austell. The china clay industry was heavily capitalised and the size of the units of production increased as the century progressed. The large workforce was a wage earning one, although local carriage was often contracted to farmers.[19]

In Monmouthshire and Shropshire the ironworkers and coal miners were employed sometimes directly by the mine owners or companies, or more often through sub-contractors or butties who hired the workmen. The contractors rose from the ranks of the colliers, and were traditionally illiterate. The coalowners employed their own agents, ground bailiffs and clerks, but professional managers were few.[20]

The West Country was also, from medieval times, one of the chief areas of textile production, and in the nineteenth century textile manufacture continued to provide employment on a substantial scale in parts of Devon, Dorset, Gloucestershire, Somerset and Wiltshire. Woollen cloth production was found in a large number of districts, including parts of central and east Devon and contiguous parts of Somerset and Dorset, but was concentrated particularly in two groups of registration districts, one in Gloucestershire (Stroud and Dursley districts) and the other not far off on the borders of Wiltshire and Somerset (Bradford, Melksham, Westbury and Frome districts). In these two areas, taken together, an average of 19 per cent of adult men and 20 per cent of adult women were occupied in this way in 1851, and more cloth workers were also found in the districts of Warminster and Shepton Mallet, adjoining the second group, and Wheatenhurst, next to the first. Melksham and Stroud districts were remarkable in having some 30 per cent of their adult males engaged in textile manufacture.

Domestic production of cloth by master weavers attached to capitalist 'manufacturers' still persisted in the mid-century. These men employed journeymen or put work out to smaller independent weavers. There was great competition for work, and the small one-loom weavers often worked for journeymen's wages and were the first to suffer unemployment when trade was depressed. The years after 1825 were on the whole ones of decline for the West Country industry, with distress widespread, especially in the 1830s and 1840s. The number of weavers was too great for the demand, and in 1840 two-thirds of those in Somerset and Wiltshire allegedly earned only as much or less than farm labourers.[21] In Gloucestershire the Hand-loom Weavers' Commission

found that weavers were worse off than workhouse inmates. At Uley
(Glos.), for example, in the late 1830s, where wages were paid in truck (as
in many places) and distress was said to be extreme: 'their clothes are clearly
wearing out; their children are half naked; they have scarcely any bedding,
and actually sleep under tattered rags. Every article that would bring money
has been sold, and the population is destitute of money and almost destitute
of work.'[22]

Despite a considerable increase in power-driven machinery in mills and a
consequent depletion in the numbers of small masters employing home
workers, the mills, however, continued through our period to employ
outworkers, and hand-looms were also worked in the factories. In Gloucestershire, in particular, the mill owners set up hand-looms in large quantities in the
mills, employing journeymen direct. In some areas, especially in Devon,
domestic work was a part-time occupation, weaving being undertaken by
women and girls while the man of the family earned wages on the farm or as a
craftsman, or ran a shop.[23] In Wiltshire, factories spread slowly.[24]

However, almost all the clothing towns in Gloucestershire, Somerset,
Wiltshire and Devon decreased in population between 1841 and 1851 as the
wollen industry declined. The period was characterised by bankruptcies as well
as unemployment and low wages. The number of small manufacturers fell in
the face of the competition of those who could afford costly machinery. In the
Cullompton (Devon) area, for example, there was by 1840 only one
manufacturer, employing 500 hands, where thirty years before there had been
forty small capitalists.[25] Improvement in the 1860s was effected by greater
mechanisation rather than increased employment.

Other West Country industries characterised by low wages, long hours and
domestic drudgery included the manufacture of lace, gloves, and linen and
hemp products. The lace industry of the south-west was partly factory-based
and partly domestic. The manufacturers of machine-made lace in, for example,
Barnstaple, Chard and Tiverton employed adults and children directly in the
mills, but also as outworkers. At Heathcote's factory in Tiverton to 800–850
mill workers in the 1830s were added about 1,500 outworkers.[26] Many more
domestic lace workers were engaged in pillow-lace manufacture. East Devon
with adjoining parts of Dorset was one of the two main centres (the other being
the south midlands) of what has been described as a survival of outwork in its
most primitive form. The industry was controlled by a few large manufacturers
who did not directly employ the workers but (often through middlewomen or
other agents like shopkeepers) sold them the raw materials and patterns at
exorbitant prices and bought back the finished goods. Although technically
independent, the workers were tied to particular employers and eked out an ill
paid existence. Child labour was common in the family home, in warehouses,
where they were hired by other workpeople, and in so-called lace schools.[27]

Silk production was to be found in a number of registration districts in the mid-century, including Shepton Mallet (Som.) and Sherborne (Dorset). Glove making occupied some 6,000 adults (mainly women) in one area of Somerset and Dorset centred on Yeovil, and another 3,200 in north Devon, the adjoining Stratton district of Cornwall, and the Cricklade area of Wiltshire. The glove trade was organised like the domestic lace industry. In the 1860s London firms used local agents who employed men and boys in cutting shops to produce the pieces, which were put out to large numbers of women and children. The decline of the domestic woollen industry and the need to supplement low agricultural wages provided a docile and exploited workforce used to working in their homes. Glove schools, similar to the lace schools, appear to have existed.[28]

Outdoor needlework for government clothing contractors was found around the seaports, as at Devonport and Poole.[29] More important in east Dorset, particularly around Yeovil and Bridport, was the production of rope, twine and thread and linen. Linen was also produced in Mere (Wiltshire), Chard (Som.) and in Crediton (Devon) and Plymouth.[30] These manufactures (particularly sailcloth and hemp production) were partly organised in power-driven factories, but also domestically, in warehouses, 'spinning walks' and private houses. Work was given out from the warehouses to smaller places. Netting in particular was made largely in country villages. Much of the work was not controlled directly by the manufacturers, who rented the sheds to middlemen who employed outworkers. The domestic workers again employed their own and other children.[31]

The districts of Plymouth, East Stonehouse and Stoke Damerel were remarkable in housing 18, 38 and 35 per cent respectively of men employed in defence occupations, mainly the navy, army and marines. Thus, although agriculture was the most significant general provider of employment, the incidence of various other occupations was significant in certain districts. Moreover Somerset and Gloucestershire were peculiar among the nine counties in containing several large 'fashionable' places as well as commerce, agriculture, mining and manufacturing. Consequently they had a higher proportion than usual of 'attendants and distributors of wealth'.[32] Thus in Gloucestershire 33 per cent of adult males, and in Somerset 31 per cent, were shopkeepers and small traders in 1851. In Devon the holiday industry had similar results, with 30 per cent so employed.[33] In Gloucestershire and Shropshire nearly 19 per cent of adult women and in Devon and Somerset over 15 per cent were employed as domestic servants.[34] In the fashionable town of Bath 26 per cent of women were employed in 'menial' work, in Cheltenham 24 per cent, and in Bristol and Clifton 18 per cent.[35]

Declining fortunes in mining and woollen manufacture, exploitation of workers in domestic industries, heavy concentration in some places of mining, poorly paid but numerous farm labourers, and many small farmers and smallholders, with child labour concentrated particularly in certain parts in manufacturing and extractive industries, characterised the western counties at mid-century.

Child labour

The low wages generally found in the western counties meant that the income earned by children or the work done by them on family farms was important for the family budget. For the age group ten to fourteen, however, the proportions officially at work in the western counties were not, in aggregate, outstanding (Appendix B). In 1851 the heaviest incidence in the nine counties was in Cornwall. Devon, Dorset, Monmouthshire, Somerset and Wiltshire approximated to the national average of 29 per cent, while Gloucestershire, Herefordshire and Shropshire were somewhat below that.

By 1871 the national average of such children at work had dropped only 2 percentage points. In the western counties there had been a reduction of some 3–4 points in Cornwall, Devon, Dorset and Herefordshire, and 1–2 points in Monmouthshire, Gloucestershire and Shropshire. Somerset remained at 28 per cent and in Wiltshire there had been an increase of one point.

In each county, in 1851 and 1871, much larger proportions of boys than girls in this age group were recorded at work, but whereas the proportion of boys dropped in each county over the twenty years 1851–71 (except Wiltshire, where it remained constant) the proportions of girls increased or remained roughly the same in every one of the nine western counties — except Devon and Dorset, where it fell 1–2 percentage points. Much of this was probably due to increasing use of girls as domestic servants,[36] and since many girls probably also performed domestic functions at home the census figures may anyway give a somewhat distorted picture.

The data in Table 6·1 shows that the largest single employment for boys aged ten to fourteen in most of the western counties in 1851 was still agriculture (including indoor farm servants). Monmouthshire, where only some 4 per cent were employed in this way, was an exception: there a quarter of boys found work in mining and manufacturing. Of the other western counties only Cornwall, with 18 per cent in mining, employed a large proportion of boys of this age in industrial jobs. In 1871 farming still dominated as an employment for male youths in every western county except Monmouthshire (with 15 per cent engaged in the iron and coal industries) and Cornwall, where proportions employed in mining and the metal trades were about the same as on farms.

In 1851 the highest proportions of girls aged ten to fourteen in any single category were employed in general domestic service. In Dorset general domestic work was outnumbered by gloving and silk; in Cornwall double the

TABLE 6·1
Proportion % of children (10–14) occupied, 1851, 1871

(a) Boys	1851			1871		
	(b) % occupied	(c) Main occupations	(d) % in (c)	(e) % occupied	(f) Main occupations	(g) % in (f)
Cornwall	47	indoor farm servants copper miners tin miners agricultural labourers shoemakers	9 9 9 6 2	40	miners (various) & tin manufacturing indoor farm servants agricultural labourers	12 6 5
Devon	36	indoor farm servants agricultural labourers	13 6	29	indoor farm servants agricultural labourers	8 4
Dorset	43	agricultural labourers	23	36	agricultural labourers	18
Gloucestershire	32	agricultural labourers woollen workers	11 2	29	agricultural labourers messengers, porters general labourers	8 4 3
Herefordshire	32	agricultural labourers	12	36	coal miners iron workers	10 5
Monmouthshire	43	coal miners iron workers & miners indoor farm servants	13 10 4	36	agricultural labourers indoor farm servants	8 7
Shropshire	35	indoor farm servants agricultural labourers	9 6	29	indoor farm servants agricultural labourers	7 4
Somerset	36	agricultural labourers	13	35	agricultural labourers messengers, errand boys coal miners	11 2 2
Wiltshire	42	agricultural labourers	26	43	agricultural labourers	23

| | (b) | (c) | (d) | (e) | (f) | (g) |
(a) Girls	% occupied	1851 Main occupations	% in (c)	% occupied	1871 Main occupations	% in (f)
Cornwall	16	copper and tin workers indoor farm servants general domestic service	6 3 3	16	general domestic service connected with mines	6 3
Devon	20	general domestic service indoor farm servants gloving & lace workers	5 5 4	18	general domestic service lace making	11 2
Dorset	16	gloving & silk workers general domestic service	4 2	15	general domestic service gloving	6 2
Gloucestershire	15	general domestic service wool & silk workers	6 3	16	general domestic service	8
Herefordshire	13	general domestic service	8	14	general domestic service	10
Monmouthshire	11	general domestic service	5	13	general domestic service	8
Shropshire	15	general domestic service	9	18	general domestic service	12
Somerset	20	gloving general domestic service indoor farm servants	6 5 2	20	general domestic service gloving	9 3
Wiltshire	16	general domestic service woollen & silk workers agricultural labourers	4 3 3	14	general domestic service	8

number worked in tin and copper production and an equal number on farms, while in Devon domestic industries, domestic service and indoor farm work each represented 5 per cent. In Somerset gloving accounted for 6 per cent and general domestic work for 5, and there appears to have been quite an increase in the employment of young female glovers in that county since 1841. By 1871 general domestic work far outstripped all other occupations for girls in all the nine counties.

In the age group five to nine much lower proportions were returned in the census as being employed (Appendix B). Generally the figures for the western counties fell below those of the midlands, the south midlands, and the Lancashire–West Riding areas in this respect, but they were larger than those in the counties of the far north and north-east and those of the south and east — apart from Essex, where domestic industry existed. The highest incidence in the western counties was in Dorset, Somerset, Wiltshire and Cornwall in 1851 and in Cornwall in 1871 — though by 1871 very few children of this age group were officially at work.

Percentages of children aged five to fourteen not on the books of day schools in 1851 cannot be related to the proportions recorded as at work in the censuses because all children not at school were not necessarily in employment; and children employed at home or on family farms may not have been returned as such for the census. Clearly, however, the proportions of children at work or at home were high: well over half in Cornwall, Herefordshire, Monmouthshire and Shropshire for both boys and girls, and 40 per cent or more in the other counties (Appendix I).

Whereas the proportion of boys aged five to nine and ten to fourteen at work was almost always higher than that of girls at county level (Appendix B),[37] the proportion of girls aged five to fourteen not at school (Appendix I) in 1851 exceeded that of boys in every western county. In only two of the 122 registration districts in the nine counties, moreover, was the proportion of girls at school greater than that of boys (Appendix F). In the two largest conurbations (Plymouth-Devonport and Bristol) far larger proportions of males than females under twenty were returned in the 1851 census as being at work (Appendix C). All this suggests that larger numbers of girls than boys were engaged at home, and probably more of them than boys in domestic manufacturing, but not always returned in the censuses. Again, since large parts of the western counties were given over to agriculture, county averages obscure the situation in some districts, where proportions engaged in industry of one kind or another were much higher than over the county as a whole.

The high level of child employment in Cornwall is largely attributable to the opportunities for such labour in the tin and copper districts. By the early 1840s, as steam power made deeper workings possible and mining expanded, some 8,000 boys and girls (to the age of eighteen) were employed out of a total mine workforce of some 25,000. Of these, 2,335 were under the age of thirteen. The Mines Commission report of 1842 noted that, while no children under the age of eight and no girls at all were employed underground, boys usually began work down the pits between the years of nine and ten, and there is some evidence of employment at earlier ages than had previously been the case. These youngsters were first engaged on working air machines and later in the laborious activity of wheeling barrows, generally working for up to eight hours at a stretch. Wages varied greatly (1s 6d to 15s a week) according to age, hours and type of job. At times, boys worked in association with fathers and other relatives, working as long hours. One witness recalled, 'When about fifteen, I used to stay once or twice a month for three twelve-hour courses in succession, merely coming to surface for a short time between each stem of twelve hours to take some food.'[38]

Nevertheless the atrocious conditions of contemporary coal mines were absent, and the working hours were much shorter than those of workers in the local foundries and farms.[39] Surface work, which included dressing ore, employed large numbers of women and girls, and children as young as seven or eight, though mostly aged ten upwards. They toiled in the open as employees of tributers at piece work in very exposed and often unenviable conditions, and for nine or ten hours a day, earning according to their abilities from 2d a day to 10s a week. The Cornish slate quarries similarly employed children under and over thirteen for long hours but in far fewer numbers. To hours of work had to be added, often, the time walking three or four miles to and from work. Such conditions also applied to the associated mining area over the Devon border.[40] Despite legislation in the early 1860s, 4 per cent of the underground workers in the Devon and Cornish mines were aged ten to fourteen. Twenty-one per cent were between fifteen and nineteen; on the surface children of seven upwards were still being employed.[41]

The coal-mining districts of the western counties also employed young children, particularly before the Act of 1842. Though hardly any girls worked underground in the coalfields of Shropshire, north Somerset, south Gloucestershire and the Forest of Dean,[42] children of both sexes from as young as five, but more often from seven, eight or nine, were employed above ground. Boys were commonly employed from six, seven or eight in these fields, and from five in the South Wales coal area, of which Monmouthshire formed a part. Girls from eight upwards were employed in Monmouthshire as tip girls on the surface of coal mines and as pilers in the iron mines. In Shropshire many girls worked at preparing iron ore on the surface.[43] In Monmouthshire, in particular, lower wages and the high cost of food (partly resulting from the prevalent 'truck' system) made it difficult for parents to avoid sending their boys down the pit. The Revd. E. C. Jenkins, and Independent clergyman of Bedwellty parish, for example, was obliged to sent his five-year-old son to work underground as an air-door boy for 8d for a twelve or thirteen hour day. Many very young children in Monmouthshire and Glamorganshire assisted their fathers in cutting coal for similarly long workdays.[44] In south Gloucestershire, too, young boys, ill fed and unhealthy, hewed coal where the seams were thin, and in the Forest of Dean pulled coal trucks for long hours for wages varying from 2s to 18s a week.[45] In the Gloucestershire iron foundries boys found work as young as ten years of age for up to twelve hours a day, and, where employed directly by workmen as assistants, kept the same hours as their masters.[46] In the Shropshire iron mills, forges and furnaces, boys and some girls were employed from eight years old.[47] The Mines Act forbade the employment of children under ten below ground, but in the South Wales coalfield, including Monmouthshire, young children were still being so used illegally in 1850.[48]

Children worked extensively in the early nineteenth century in the West Country textile industries. The woollen districts were by the 1830s employing children in powered mills, where generally they worked the same hours as adults. In Gloucestershire, for example, children as young as six or seven, though more commonly from nine, worked from ten and a half to twelve hours a day for low wages. Though many mill owners denied the existence of corporal punishment, others admitted the use of straps and switches, and such treatment was doubtless not uncommon. In Wiltshire young boys were worked uninterruptedly without meal breaks for fourteen hours at a stretch. Here children as young as six were employed, though most started at age nine or over. In Somerset children from eight years worked with adults for the same long hours.[49]

Factory legislation resulted in a sharp decline in the number of mill children. Only 130 below thirteen years were so employed, for example, in Wiltshire in 1839. But even in the 1850s there were still many hand-loom weavers in the western counties, and children countinued to be employed in domestic industry. Similarly the Dorset rope, twine and sail industry, centred on Bridport and carried on in factories and workshops, employed in the 1840s children aged seven upwards for twelve-hour workdays at 1s 8d a week.[50] By the 1860s few so young were employed in the mills consequent on legislative restrictions, but many still found work in unregulated workshops, warehouses, so-called spinning works, and in private houses. Youngsters from age eight to twelve were commonly used to turn wheels for very low pay. Girls began to spin at about the ages of twelve to fourteen, often working for their own parents and for the same hours. A Bridport twine spinner in the 1860s reported, 'It is long hours to work but we must do it to live.'[51] As John Betts, a Bridport relieving officers, told the Children's Employment Commission of the 1860s, 'It is a kind of modern slavery.' The children were consequently often stunted in growth and generally unhealthy, and David Hounsell, a foreman directly employing several children admitted, 'Bridport is an awful place for children.'[52]

There were other places equally awful for children in the West Country. The lace factories of Devon and Somerset employed young children for a pittance for long hours, including night work. At Tiverton in the 1840s all children were employed by the 'master', but at Barnstaple by the factory hands, and at Chard children worked for the mill owners and then overtime for some of the men.[53] Many others were indirectly employed among the outworkers, who could outnumber the actual factory workforce.[54] The mill children were protected by legislation in 1861.[55]

In the Dorset, Devon and Somerset lace districts, however, a large number of working-class children were employed in the traditional pillow-lace industry either by their parents or in other domestic establishments. They began work as young as five or six, 'or as soon as they can turn the bobbins'. In the so-called 'lace schools', common in these districts, young children worked a three-year or so 'apprenticeship'. For a few pence a week they put in exceptionally long hours, at busy times from breakfast or earlier to midnight.[56] Generally pillow-lace production was a sweated industry in which in 1843 it was said, 'a young woman must work hard for fourteen or fifteen hours a day to earn 3s 6d a week'.[57] In the 1860s it was found that children under ten would be lucky if they made as much as a shilling a week. The numbers involved in this domestic trade were falling by the 1860s as a result of the competition of the machine-made lace, but large numbers of youngsters, especially girls from age five upwards, were still employed in unhealthy conditions and the lace schools still flourished. The Education Act of 1870 and the subsequent spread of compulsory education, however, changed the situation and a commission in 1888 found a diminishing and ageing labour force, with the lace schools in decline.[58]

Around Yeovil, Hereford, Ludlow and Leominster glove making employed many women and childen in their own homes and in gloving 'schools' and shops. The industry had been adversely affected by the removal in 1862 of restrictions on the import of French gloves, better in quality and cheaper, which pauperized the English glove makers until improvements in quality resulted in a slow recovery. In 1842 at least 5,000–6,000 women and children (mainly girls) in the Yeovil area were employed in domestic gloving.[59] Girls were put to sewing at age six or seven and work was generally from 6.00 a.m. to dusk, frequently continuing to 9.00 p.m. or, towards the end of the week, later. Not all workers, however, devoted all their time to gloving; for many women and children it was a part-time occupation. In the factories where gloves were prepared, cut out and later finished by skilled workmen and apprentices who did not start until aged fourteen, helped by younger boy workers, the tasks were laborious and the conditions unpleasant. But men's wages were above those of agricultural labourers, and women could earn 4s to 7s a week and younger children 6d to 1s.[60] Conditions were not very different in the 1850s and 1860s, when children were still beginning domestic work at six or seven years of age and working long hours, suffering consequent physical deformities. [61] In the overheated factories and warehouses boys of ten and upwards were still employed, though not in large numbers. [62]

Other West Country industries employing children included button making, organised like glove making, in Dorset around Blandford, Shaftesbury and Sherborne, and the Bristol potteries employing for twelve hours a day children of ten upwards, mostly girls. [63] In the Bristol area children found employment, too, in glasshouses, potteries, brick works, soap boiling, tobacco manufacture and so on. [64] At Bristol nail making organised in workshops employed mainly young boys, sons of agricultural labourers. In the 1840s children as young as nine were employed and had to keep the same times as the men who worked irregular hours, sometimes twenty-four or even thirty-six at a stretch. By the 1860s boys were mainly of thirteen or so upwards and the work hours had become more regular, though still long. [65]

In the West Country many children worked in agriculture. By the 1840s in Wiltshire, Dorset, Devon and Somerset, however, few girls were employed out of doors on a regular basis. At that time in Devon boys began regular farm work at age seven upwards, but generally between nine and twelve. In that county, however, and in neighbouring parts of Dorset and Somerset boys, particularly those on poor relief, were still compulsorily apprenticed to farmers at the age of nine or even younger, though this system was on the decline. The lot of such children varied greatly according to the individual master. [66]

By the 1860s in Devon and Cornwall few boys under ten were regularly employed on farms, and there was little casual work for those under twelve; girls did not regularly work in the fields till they were fifteen or sixteen. [67] Many youngsters in the Cornish mining areas anyway preferred the much better wages they could earn in the mines. [68] The small family-run farms of these counties, however, relied greatly on the labour of their own children. The district of small farms in south-west Shropshire bordering on Wales also depended much on family labour. Wages were low and there was little call for outside children for farm work. Girls, however, were commonly taken as drudges in the farm houses at ten or eleven. [69]

The many small tenant and freehold farmers of Monmouthshire, too, employed their own children from an early age, in arable districts boys commonly from the age of seven. Few other children below the age of ten to twelve found employment in so-called 'Welsh' farms where labourers lived in, though in the hill farms boys of eight upwards were engaged. There was little farm work for girls who generally went into service in the farm houses at thirteen or so. [70] Family labour was common also in those parts of Dorset where farms were small, while in other parts of that county the system of hiring whole families for agricultural work was a characteristic. The consequence was that in the 1840s boys of seven were set to work in the fields, and even in the 1860s this was still the case: 'some at six or even younger'. Then the proportion of child labour on Dorset farms was unusually high: boys of six, seven and eight were commonly employed with horses, being put to plough at eight or nine, much younger than thought suitable elsewhere. Low wages, it was said, 'make every labourer anxious to send his children out, although near Dorchester this is certainly surpassed by the eagerness of the farmer to get them'. Indeed, the Children's Employment Commission noted in 1867 that in Dorset the 'proportion of boy labour is excessive', and since many men were laid off in the winter 'boy labour has partly displaced that of men'. Young girls were, however, used little except at hay time and harvest, though many older females did work in the fields.[71]

In the areas of Gloucestershire where small dairy farms were common (as in the Thornbury registration district) family labour was used, though boys were not needed for regular work till they were eleven or twelve. In arable districts of the county, too, boys were not employed regularly till strong enough to do a day's ploughing, so that the youngest boy workers were generally between ten and thirteen.[72] In Somerset some boys in the 1840s were in regular farm employment at the age of nine or ten, but being a pastoral county there was less work for children than in arable areas. Exceptions were the valleys and slopes of Exmoor and its offshoots and the cold soils of Somerton where arable exceeded pastoral land. In the 1860s there is some evidence of the employment in Somerset of children through the gang system and the intermittent labour of young boys and girls, and children were also employed in the market gardens around Axbridge and Yeovil. The youngest children in employment were those of small farmers.[73]

In Herefordshire and Wiltshire, areas of larger farms, there was no excessive use of permanent child labour. Boys in Herefordshire began work regularly at ten or eleven in the 1860s, in Wiltshire at nine or ten, though younger ones were employed intermittently. Girls were not generally employed until in their teens. In the hop district in the centre of Herefordshire, however, considerable employment was given to women and children and in that county there were frequent harvests because of the variety of different crops, all of which interfered with schooling.[74]

Attitudes to education

How far lack of elementary schooling in the West Country was the result of parental need, greed, indifference or antagonism is difficult to ascertain. Certainly official and other middle-class observers throughout the period put apathy and selfishness as an important reason for working parents keeping children from school altogether or sending them irregularly and withdrawing them at an early age. Poverty, however, was also frequently given as a reason, and the inability of families to do without children's earnings or, less frequently, to pay school pence was stressed by parents themselves and by more sympathetic observers. Opinions based on some knowledge and honest enquiry are not hard to come by, yet are inevitably generalised and to varying degrees subjective.

There is little evidence that parents' religious enthusiasm, or the lack of it, had much to do with whether a child was sent to a particular day school or to school at all, though it may well have affected Sunday-school attendance. Day schools were chosen for their convenience or, by the discerning, for their supposed efficiency. Denominational issues, so great a concern to the middle classes, do not appear to have worried working parents greatly, and the preponderance of Anglican schools in areas where dissent was strong derived from the principle of supply rather than demand. Thus, while a large proportion of children of dissenting parents were to be found in the central National school, Dorchester, the teachers 'never knew an instance of parents objecting to the catechism' being taught. Similarly, in Sherborne (Dorset) nonconformist parents appear to have preferred a good National school to a British school thought less efficient, despite a newspaper campaign to persuade them to change their allegiance.[75] At Bristol and Plymouth in the late 1850s parents were indifferent as to the religious connections of their children's schools. At St. Paul's National School, Bristol, 46 per cent of parents were dissenters and over 20 per cent had no particular religion.[76] Patrick Cumin, the assistant Newcastle Commissioner for Bristol and Plymouth, reported one dissenting father who sent his boy to a Church school because there his 'learning is first-rate', claiming, 'Do you think if they put anything into the child's head during the day about religion which I did not approve, that I could not shove it out at night?'[77] Throughout the West Country in town and rural areas, the better-off, more 'respectable' workman was likely to avail himself increasingly of good schooling. Regional differences in parental attitudes and practices as they pertained to the generality of working folk, however, derived very much from the nature of the dominant occupations and the social *mores* of the communities concerned.

In the mining and iron districts of Monmouthshire, the Forest of Dean and Shropshire the position was akin to that of certain parts of the Black Country.[78] While no doubt many were poor, poverty was not the most important reason for indifference to schooling. These were rough, tough areas of high employment and mushrooming migrant populations, where physical strength and manual dexterity gave substantial returns. In the Monmouthshire mining districts, for example, wages except in periods of depression were high, attracting people from all over Wales and elsewhere. They were societies whose way of life was condemned by contemporary middle-class opinion. Thus the Forest of Dean, a long neglected area, spawned similar predominantly working-class communities, the spiritual destitution of which the Bishop of Gloucester reported in 1858 'well nigh filled him with despair'.[79]

As to the Monmouthshire mining areas it was alleged that 'Evil in every shape is rampant ... demoralisation is everywhere dominant ... the whole district with the exception of Newport teems with grime ... with scarcely a rag of mental or spiritual intelligence ... physical strength is the object of esteem and gain their chief god.'[80] This view, contained in the report on education in Wales in 1847, was echoed in the reports on the state of the population of mining districts in that decade and the next. The inhabitants of this part of Monmouthshire were 'a people immersed in habits of sensuality and improvidence, earning very high wages, wasting nearly one week in five in idleness and drunkenness; working their children in the mines and elsewhere at the earliest possible age; a very small porportion of the adults of either sex able either to read or write'.[81] In the 'lowest state of intelligence, and sensuality, ignorance and perverted views' they were guilty of 'a reckless sacrifice of their children to their own cupidity'.[82] 'The more wages they get the more they spend on drink [and] the less they spend on the education of their own children,' for 'not withstanding their own ample earnings, the moment there is the least demand for their children's labour, they take them from school at the earliest age at which they can earn anything, whereas when employment is slack they are content that they should be left at school, provided it costs them little'. At the same time men refused extra work themselves even when available.[83] It was Monmouthshire parents rather than the coalowners who, when legislation restricted child labour in the mines, conspired illegally to continue working girls and under-age boys underground.[84] And in the Forest of Dean such children, excluded from employment in the pits, were not nevertheless sent to school.[85] In that area, it was held, the miners 'with very few exceptions, ... ought to have no difficulty in giving their children ... education at day schools', but preferred the extravagance of excessive drinking.[86]

Such indictments have a ring of truth, though the disapproval is underlaid with fear, for Monmouthshire had been the seat of a Chartist rising in 1839.[87] For more docile Cornwall, a mining area of a different kind, accusations of parental debauchery, barbarity and indolence were absent.[88] The Cornish were seen as 'a shrewed intelligent race of people not unwilling to avail themselves of a good education for their children when they can do so without self sacrifice'. But they, too, took them from school as soon as they could earn in the mines.[89] Nevertheless the Cornish, including the miners, were often religiously inclined and read tracts and newspapers. Of 150 miners in 1842 who could read, sixteen had learned at evening school and twenty-seven were self-taught.[90]

The Revd. E. P. Vaughan, diocesan school inspector for Bath and Wells in the 1850s, did not feel poverty prevented working-class parents from sending their children to school. Clergy in Bristol and Devonport held the same view. Only extreme destitution, it was said, would force Bristol parents to withdraw their children from day school.[91] At Bath in 1850 the Wesleyan Education Committee reported mainly labourers' children at its school.[92]

The claims of poverty were, however, in many cases, more genuine than some middle-class observers would admit. Certainly , there were many in the mining districts who felt that poverty drove their children to work, and there is plenty of evidence of periodic poverty during depressed times in the colliery areas.[93] Cornish miners, too, because of the economic structure of the industry, suffered from considerable fluctuations in income with a need to live on credit in lean times and an unwise though understandable tendency to profligacy in good. Ill health was common and many men died early.[94] Normally high wages have to be seen against a background of lack of savings, large families, widowhood and , especially in Cornwall and Monmouthshire, early marriage. In Monmouthshire, too, children became physically and financially independent at an early age, leaving home and evidencing no interest in education.[95]

Looked at from a different point of view, apart from meeting present family needs, child labour might well have seemed to many parents a more practical preparation for earning a living than the multiplication tables. Middle-class opinion recognised this in a disapproving way in such statements as (of Monmouthshire) 'the best conceivable education will remain untouched so long as ignorance obtains ready employment'.[96] The coal and iron areas of Monmouthshire, like parts of the Black Country, were almost entirely populated by working folk, conservative, inward-looking and seeing for children, especially girls, small advantage in a little 'learning'.[97]

In Cornwall economic advancement and prosperity were clearly not connected with education;[98] the influential and prestigious mine captains, for example, had sprung from the ranks of ordinary miners with little book learning,[99] and in the western mining areas generally lack of education was no obstacle to what in the eyes of most inhabitants was satisfactory employment; 'success ... being the result of mechanical skill ... the higher qualities of the mind are called into play to a comparatively small degree. Even those appointed to situations of responsibility possess in general very slight attainments'.[100] Nevertheless Cornish miners were felt to be more aware of the value of education than miners elsewhere, though they wanted good schooling which would not prevent children also working.[101] Only in such occupations as the police and the railways was education advantageous, and these syphoned off boys with some schooling who often then left the neighbourhood.[102] The Bishop of Wells in the 1850s conducted a class in reading and arithmetic for railway navvies 'who know that some of the richest contractors have risen from being mere navvies, but that such a position it is impossible to reach without a knowledge of reading, writing and arithmetic — especially the latter'. But it is unlikely these were typical. In the late 1850s at Bedminster parents objected to geography, grammar 'and such subjects as useless in their station in life'.[103]

In the decaying hand-loom areas of the west the position of parents was different. Here wages were low, depression and unemployment a common fact of life. The reports on the conditions of the hand-loom weavers in the 1830s and 1840s were full of evidence of real poverty and its effect on schooling. The older children's wages were needed for survival, and for the younger school pence could not be found nor clothes decent enough to attend in.[104] Though some clergy blamed the poverty on beer houses and general profligacy, alleging apathy towards education, most observers agreed that the depressed state of the woollen industry rendered the weavers too poor to support day schooling.[105] 'In Chalford Vale [Gloucestershire] the weavers are unable to avail themselves of education for their children, because they require their services ... they cannot afford the weekly payment to the school, to which must be added ... the amount which they could earn ...'[106] Moreover, whereas they sometimes earned more than farm labourers their earnings were uncertain, leading to fluctuations of attendance among children who did go to school.[107]

There is also some likelihood that factory legislation, which closed the woollen mills to weavers' children, pauperised those families, leaving less money available for the schooling of younger brothers and sisters: 'the means of education are', an assistant commissioner felt, 'diminished by the very law that was intended to promote it'.[108] In Gloucestershire in 1865, daughters of weavers were in some places less literate than those of labourers.[109] Most protested a desire for their children to be schooled, and sometimes this was genuine. In fourteen Gloucestershire hand-loom weaving parishes, it was reported in 1839, the proportions attending school were greatest when wages were above average. At Uley (Glos), where employment was lacking at that time but free schooling was available, 300 children plus infants were sent to day school.[110] At Twerton (Som.) parents, though little schooled themselves, were 'sensible of the value ... of giving the best education their means will afford to their children', and there seventy-five of 103 weavers' children attended some kind of school.[111] No weavers were, however, found in any of the mechanics' institutes of Devon, Dorset, Somerset or Wiltshire in the 1840s,[112] and on the whole hand-loom weavers' children were less likely to attend school than those of other workers, and districts where they were concentrated were felt to be more ignorant than most. Thus in 1840 at Trowbridge (Wilts.) of 127 hand-loom weavers' children none attended day school and less than half Sunday school, and at nearby Hilperton and Hilperton Marsh a similar situation existed. At Rood (Som.) only nine of forty-nine such children attended day school and twenty-five Sunday school.[113] At Wellington (Som.), of 430 children at day (excluding dame) school only sixty-nine were weavers' children, while the figures for Sunday schools were 595 and 191.[114] And of 535 children of shop-loom operators in the weaving area of Gloucestershire only eighty-six attended day school and 195 Sunday school.[115]

In other domestic industries of the West Country not in decay the educational state of children was probably as bad. Gloving, lace making, button making and rope and twine manufacture created, it was said, 'a complete bar to anything like education',[116] for they were based on a workforce containing large numbers of children. Moreover these industries too long escaped any legislative restrictions on child labour, and as we have seen very young children could be usefully employed. The parents of gloving children in the Yeovil area were said in the 1840s to be generally uneducated and careless of their children in this respect,[117] and as late as 1869 the Revd. Salmon of Martock (Som.) reported of the gloving children: 'they grow up in a state of deplorable ignorance, very few of them being able to write even their own names. At an early age they become independent of their parents and submit to no control ...' Sunday schools do a little for the best of them, but the roughest will not attend'.[118] Of the Dorset button makers, it was said that 'parents refuse to allow their children to go to school although their earnings were only a few pence a week'.[119] In fact, however, earnings of children could add 3s to 6s a week to a family's earnings, and in Devon young lace maker's wages were said to be 'considerable'.[120] Generally, it was felt that of the parents of child workers in Dorset, Devon and Somerset, 'many are prejudiced and suspicious about [education] ... unwilling that their children should attain more than their own measure of information'. Their attitude was *cui bono*; they could see no reason for it. On the other hand, it might be considered that parents regarded early labour as a form of apprenticeship for a lifelong occupation — a kind of education. Certainly they supported the lace and glove schools.

In the districts of the large towns of Plymouth and Bristol there was a tendency to send small children to school merely to keep them off the streets and out of the way. For older children in such places there was plenty of work as errand boys and domestic servants, and even in the late 1850s labouring parents took their children from school as soon as they could earn wages. On the other hand, superior working people sent their children to school more regularly and evening schools were patronised with the specific intention of securing the sort of employment requiring literacy and numeracy.[121] Dockyard apprentices and boy naval entrants at Plymouth, for example, had to pass competitive examinations, and the ability to read and write was recognised by parents as needful for entry to the police, railway jobs and even for some porters and errand boys. In Bristol, Devonport and Plymouth many such parents recognised the potential benefit of education and were able to judge a good school. An increase in the number of private schools in Plymouth in the 1850s was felt to indicate an 'anxiety for education'.[122] In Bristol in 1860 the British and Foreign School Society reported parents' increased interest in schooling, exemplified by willingness to pay for lesson books.[123] In the 1860s, artisans in Bristol and Gloucestershire were aware of the advantage of education, though this was still not so of miners and labourers.[124]

The attitude to schooling of parents in areas which were largely agricultural was doubtless affected by the low wages of farm labourers in the West Country. There appears to have been little outright antagonism, and none of the debauched outlook attributed to the better off workers of, for example, the colliery districts. In 1843 a report on child labour in Wiltshire, Dorset, Devon and Somerset stressed a considerable day-school attendance in agricultural parishes and a 'universal feeling in favour of both day schools and Sunday schools amongst the labouring population'.[125] In that year at Launcells (Cornwall), farm workers freely gave their labour in the building of a school.[126] And about the same time Mary Puddicombe, a Devon labourer's wife and mother of six who could neither read nor write, felt education desirable and sent all her childen to school. A Wiltshire labourer's wife who sent all her nine children to school, however, did not 'let them go long ... for they must be earning something'.[127]

The opportunity to earn regularly at an early age was not as available on the land as in industrial occupations (except perhaps for boys in Herefordshire),[128] but schooling was affected by other factors. One evident throughout the agricultural areas was the irregularity of attendance induced by seasonal employment at the various harvests. Another not infrequent factor was early leaving because of lack of school pence. As the vicar of Witheridge (Devon) remarked, 'in general, the burthen of their maintenance is too great'.[129] Regular schooling was affected, too, by the habit, common in some parts, as for example Dorset, of farmers employing whole families.[130] The practice of apprenticing children whose parents were receiving poor relief was also detrimental. An assistant commissioner investigating female and child employment in agriculture in the 1840s remarked that 'I did not hear of a single apprentice attending a day school, and not of many attending Sunday schools,' though some employers attempted home tuition.[131] Nevertheless in the 1840s through the 1860s outside observers felt that lack of education in the West Country agricultural districts was due to the low wages. Child earnings were not high, but 'high enough ... to outbid the school, and to make the poor ignorant parent think that what was education enough for him ... must be education enough for his child'.[132] A diocesan inspector reporting on the financial plight of Somerset agricultural labourers in the 1850s felt that 'the poor man supporting his family ... on 10s a week cannot be expected to keep his child at school if that child can earn 3s a week ... I doubt whether those who value education the most would keep their children to school after ten'.[133] In 1868–9 in the Wimborne and Cranborne union of Dorset low wages were still 'a great detriment to the proper education of our agricultural poor',[134] and in the poorer parts of Monmouthshire in 1870 a good many children were kept from school 'because of the penny'.[135] Parental indifference was undoubtedly present — as was reported, for example, at Pimperne and North Wootton (Dorset) in the 1840s,[136] and of the poor in small rural parishes in the West Country more generally in the 1850s,[137] but as school became more general in rural areas those who failed to send their children stood out more than before.[138]

James Fraser in 1859, while finding that the majority tried to get the best education they could, reported that some, mainly in country towns like Ledbury, Bromyard, Ilchester and Yeovil, from 'indifference, thriftlessness, recklessness' kept their children from school even though not setting them to work. These were, however, centres of domestic industry where the outlook of the workers in those industries may have dominated.[139] This complaint was echoed a decade later in east Somerset, where it was found that schooling was least appreciated in the larger parishes near small towns.[140] At that time parental indifference rather than the need for child earnings was said to be the cause of poor school attendance in rural Shropshire,[141] and at Morebath (Devon) a survey suggested that 'caprice or indifference was a greater factor in poor school attendance than a genuine need for child labour'. A survey of the parish of Hentland (Herefords.) about this time found that, out of 108 children between the ages of six and twelve, fifty-three did not attend school: nine were absent owing to poverty, want of money, clothes or food; eight were out at work; two were absent because they lived too far from school; thirteen were kept at home to mind the house or nurse; while seventeen were absent owing to the indifference of parents.[142] In Devon and Cornwall it was by then less the employment of children on the land than the employment of the mother that militated against schools, older children being kept at home to look after the younger ones. Yet, 'in almost every parish will be found some parents who are utterly indifferent to education'. But F. H. Norman reported of agricultural areas in a number of counties including Wiltshire and Herefordshire, 'the number of these is becoming fewer every day'.[143] In those parts of western counties where there were settled gentry, active support for popular education came mostly from the landed classes and the Anglican clergy. In areas of small-holdings and small independent farms, and where there were concentrations of industry, such support fell more heavily on the clergy with less middle-class backing. To some extent this reflects the varying proportions of 'persons of independent means' in the different counties (Appendix H). In 1841 Devon had 36 per cent above the national average of such persons, Gloucestershire 32 per cent, Somerset 22 per cent, and Dorset of 14 per cent. Cornwall and Herefordshire were a little above the average; but Monmouthshire, Shropshire and Wiltshire had 30, 22 and 17 per cent below the national average.

In the industrial parts of Monmouthshire, Gloucestershire and Shropshire the situation was similar to that in the midlands. The spiritual and educational needs of the mushrooming concentrations of population drawn in by the opportunities of employment were at first ignored. West Country business-men, with a few exceptions, were not active in support of elementary education for the poor.[144] In Monmouthshire the employing classes were for long indifferent to the lack of churches and schools and the clergy too poor to fill the gap.[145] The Chartist outbreak of 1839 in south Wales and Monmouthshire was followed by reports on the inadequacy of churches and schools in the area, and the observation that some places not suffering the deficiency did not experience the unrest. Subsequent building of churches and chapels-of-ease was some-times funded by local works companies. Thus at Court-y-Bella, near Blackwood (Mon.), a seat of disaffection in 1839, Sir Thomas Phillips, mayor of Newport and a coalowner, expressed the view that political unrest was connected with ignorance and he contributed substantially to the building of a school. At Pontypool schools were established by the British Iron Company and by the Pentwyn and Golynos Company, and other such examples could be provid-ed.[146] 'Generally speaking,' a report on the area in 1846 declared significantly, 'the most intelligent workmen are found by the masters to be the best disposed, and most easily guided ... Good schools will bring to the employers who support them their own reward.'[147] At Coalbrookdale in 1848 Abraham Darby claimed to give his workmen 'the best means of education', and provided them, too, at his own expense, with a publication spelling out the unfortunate results of the Chartist movement and of the 1848 French revolution 'to prevent the growth of disorder'.[148] The Darbys established day schools as well as providing technical education for older employees.[149]

Cornwall was remarkably free of Chartism,[150] which was opposed by Methodist zealots and indeed the Cornish appeared to be largely 'indifferent to political agitation'[151] and, although there were strikes, trade unionism was weak.[152] In some Cornish mining parishes evidence of the realisation of the need of some sort of advanced elementary education of a kind teaching subjects related to mining was found at Illogan and Trevenson (supported by Baroness Bassett), St. Agnes and Gwennap, the last set up by subscriptions from mine agents.[153] In Monmouthshire, however, many landed proprietors, coalowners and farmers turned a deaf ear to requests from the clergy for money for schools,[154] and, generally speaking, employers who took an interest were in the minority.

In Swindon (Wilts.) the Great Western Railway Company opened a school in 1845 for its own employees' children, also admitting others,[155] but this was not typical of the area. There is, for example, little evidence that those who organised the work of the hand-loom weavers or the various other domestic industries had any great interest in extending education. One S. Marling of Ham Mills (Glos.) in the early 1840s, however, provided an infant school for his employees' children and some other examples could be given.[156] At Heathcote's at Tiverton, all workers under seventeen who did not attend school as half-timers were required by the firm in the 1860s to attend the works' evening school. At that time some 270 young persons were at the school.[157] The impact of works schools in the western counties generally must, however, have been very small.

In the vast areas of the rural West Country the availability of schooling was dependent largely on the existence of resident landowners and enthusiastic clergy with funds available.[158] In areas where resident gentry were few, and farms small and poor, the provision of schooling lagged behind. This situation pertained most in rural Monmouthshire, and in large parts of Cornwall and north-west Devon, in the last area the difficulties being compounded till the 1840s by absentee incumbents.[159] In Dorset, where rural riots occurred in 1830,[160] on the other hand, many of the owners of large estates, like Lord Digby, the Earl of Shaftesbury, the Duke of Bedford, Lord Rivers and the Marquess of Westminster, built and maintained schools or contributed generously towards them, and lesser gentry, too, commonly gave assistance.[161] In Wiltshire the Marquess of Lansdowne, the Marquess of Ailesbury, the Marquess of Bath, the Earl of Suffolk, Earl Nelson, Lord Arundel of Wardour, and others were similarly active.[162] The support of the landed classes was not, however, uniformly strong.[163] In the 1840s the landowners of Herefordshire were said to be as antipathetic to popular education as the tenant farmers.[164] In other cases, as in Gloucestershire, support from landowners was limited.[165] At Ebrington (Glos.), for example, a Sunday school was supported by Lord Harrowby, the chief landowner, and Lord Fortescue, the lord of the manor, but no National day school was set up until the 1860s.[166] In the late 1860s landowners in Wiltshire and Herefordshire were said to support education in theory, some resident ones contributing handsomely to schools, but the situation was less happy when the landowner was not resident.[167] 'When a proprietor does not live there,' the Revd. J. Fraser had reported to the Newcastle Commission of rural districts in Herefordshire and Dorset, 'to a very great extent he does not spend'.[168] Even in 1870 it was difficult to get help from landowners in parts of Shropshire.[169]

Throughout the period West Country farmers were generally antagonistic to the spread of popular education, the larger grudging cheap labour, the smaller burdened with mortgages and anxious that labourers' children should not better in education their own, whom they could ill afford to spare for schooling. In the 1830s it was alleged that in Devon many poor-law overseers drawn from the ranks of farmers could not write their own names,[170] so that a high regard for schooling for labourers' offspring was not to be expected from them.

Generally most farmers were fearful that extended schooling might destroy the relationship between labourers and employers and render men unfit for manual labour, over-ambitious and rebellious. They shared with some landowners and clergy the view that keeping children at school too long would make it impossible for them to gain the necessary skills for agricultural work because of late initiation.[171]

The claim by farmers in Shropshire, reported in 1868, that 'the best paid labourers are the least educated' must be viewed suspiciously when coupled with the view that therefore labourers' children ought to start work as soon as they could get it, by which means 'the children of the smaller farmers will keep ahead of their labourers in respect of education'.[172] Similarly an editorial in the *Shrewsbury Journal* in 1872 considered that increased education would result only in the poor 'studying newspapers written to show them all their hardships were the fault of the government of the upper classes'.[173] In Somerset the fear was expressed that education taught the labourers more than their employers knew. Certainly in north Devon the children of small farmers, who were forced by economic necessity to use their children's labour, were less well educated than labourers' offspring.[174] Farmers in Dorset, Wiltshire and Somerset were said, as late as 1868, to be 'especially suspicious of education, because it is found in practice that the low wages drive away almost all the young men who are sufficiently well educated to go', and could result in a pressure for higher wages on the land. Not many in Herefordshire and Wiltshire would admit to education making a man a better labourer.[175]

There were, of course, exceptions among the farmers. In the 1840s a Mr. Tarver of Blandford (Dorset) preferred his labourers to have had some schooling, a Devon farmer felt that some education in a boy indicated a respectable background, and a Devon labourer reported being taught to read by his master.[176] In 1858, in some rural parts of Dorset and Herefordshire, farmers admitted they would rather have a carter or bailiff able to read, write and keep simple accounts,[177] and one large Cotswold farmer in the 1860s felt that the advent of complicated machinery would create a need for educated labour while reducing the need for boy labourers.[178]

By the late 1860s farmers in Devon and Cornwall, who employed few children under ten, had in general no objection to legal restrictions on the employment of young children on the land, though a meeting of the Devon Chamber of Agriculture at Exeter declined to co-operate with the Royal Commission on the Employment of Women and Children in Agriculture. A minority of farmers in the county, however, supported compulsory schooling,[179] and in the West Country generally there was something of a *volte-face* after the 1870 Act, with farmers contributing to Church schools, 'anxious to avoid a vote for the furtherance of an object towards which they have as yet contributed little besides hostility'.[180]

Schools in market and other towns found it easier to obtain local financial support than rural schools, and were therefore superior in quality. In the 1840s, for example, the Revd. H. W. Bellairs, H.M.I., noted such schools in existence at Shipston on Stour, Tewkesbury, Cheltenham and Wimborne. Cheltenham, where there were efficient and plentiful schools, was held to be a place 'easy to raise a school to a state of efficiency'.[181]

Not all the clergy supported the need for more extended schooling for the working classes. The archdeacon of Stow in the 1820s felt that education for those destined to earn their living manually might be positively dangerous.[182] The Gloucester Diocesan Board of Education complained in 1841 about the managers of uninspected rural Anglican schools who were unwilling to be associated with the board or to become subject to diocesan inspection.[183] A few years later, however, Exeter Diocesan Board itself considered dame schools which inculcated mainly religious habits best suited to rural areas where children began work at nine or ten.[184] Indeed, in the late 1850s the Newcastle Commission was told that the absence of public day schools in many rural West Country parishes was due to a body of clergy 'by no means small or uninfluential', who were opposed to state interference in schools and had a limited idea of the levels of instruction required.[185]

Yet it was the clergy who were most active in promoting schooling, and indeed in rural areas of the west if the landowners were not supportive the burden largely fell on the clergy, who were often unable to provide sufficient funds for an efficient school. Frome Bishop (Herefords.) and Little Rissington (Glos.) were two of many schools in the West Country entirely supported by the parochial clergy in the early 1840s. At other places any deficiency in school income had to be made up by the clergy, and when that was not done schools would close or their efficiency suffer.[186] In Herefordshire local clergy were said in the 1880s to contribute eleven times as much as an average subscribing farmer and six times as much as an average subscribing landowner.[187] In Somerset there was said in the late 1860s to be generally 'a sort of struggle going on between the clergyman and the farmers' over keeping labourers' children at school.[188] In Dorset the clergy stepped in in those parishes where large landowners were absent — as at Charlton Marshall, Halstock, Haydon, Portland, Spettisbury, Stock Gayland and Tolpuddle, where the schools were entirely or largely supported by the incumbents.[189]

Many such schools were insufficiently provided for to be eligible for government grants, and unaided public schools also resulted from antagonism on the part of some of the large landowners who did set up schools. In Dorset, even on the eve of the 1870 Act, many landed sponsors, like Lord Ilchester, opposed seeking government aid and opening the schools to the H.M.I.s. Similarly Lord Shaftesbury, who maintained a number of schools, hated the government system: the laity should provide the funds to enable the clergy to run the schools without the danger of the state interfering in matters of religion. The result was that Dorset had 104 aided Church schools in 1868 but 179 unaided ones; for Somerset the numbers were forty-five and 111 respectively.[190]

The Revised Code, permitting small rural schools under ex-pupil teachers to be recommended for grant, facilitated the spread of government-supported schools.[191] But where lay support was limited and rural areas were sparsely populated, remote and poor, as in Herefordshire, voluntary schools found it hard to meet the requirements for government financial assistance so that difficulties were compounded. Moreover the prejudice of some managers and clergy against accepting government aid continued to impede the spread of inspected schools in the 1860s.[192]

Indeed, the system of state support for elementary education tended to perpetuate rather than cure, for as a Devon clergyman in the 1860s said, 'Under the present system of granting aid rich localities who are able to pay certificated masters get all, the poorer who are not able get none. Torquay under the present system is in receipt of state aid to the amount of several hundreds a year while the poorer parishes in the neighbourhood get nothing.'[193]

Among religious promoters purely educational motives were often not uppermost. The need to strengthen religious adherence, to raise moral standards and combat vice seemed to many the main task of schooling for the lower classes. At Bath and Bathforum British school in 1840 success was felt to be entirely due to 'Him in whose hands are the hearts of all men'; in 1840 at Devonport the parents' duty to God in having their children schooled was stressed; at Truro in 1845 regret was expressed that children were found strolling 'idly about the streets' instead of being 'instructed in the nurture and admonition of the Lord'.[194] Interdenominational and even interparochial rivalry, too, was clearly present. In Bristol in 1868, for example, Church and dissenting schools existed side by side some 'avowedly . . . built to empty those of other parishes or of rival denominations'.[195]

Religious proselytising in areas felt to be in need of moral regeneration was evident in the extension of schooling in the Forest of Dean, where the clergy were very active. An Act of 1838 divided the previously ex-parochial Forest into four ecclesiastical districts with resident clergy and schools, but here political advantages were also seen: 'No educated man has any doubt of the soundness of the social and economical principles on which our institutions rest.'[196] Indeed, fears for the fabric of society were sometimes clearly evident in Church thinking. A Salisbury diocesan report of 1840 connected the agricultural riots of the 1830s with lack of education and noted that there were still 'the materials for such an explosion . . . in some of the rural parishes of Dorset and Wiltshire. Those materials are poverty and ignorance'.[197] At Cheltenham, in 1842–3, clergy pointed to the need for Church education to avoid crime and the civic disorder that had occurred elsewhere. 'We were bound,' said one, 'to educate the lower classes ... on the ground of *national safety*.'[198] And a report of 1841 on a National school in the poorest and most densely inhabited district of Bath called for an expansion of Church education, since the teachers when visiting pupils' homes found 'much Chartism and Socialism, and they greave that their labours in the School are grievously counteracted by rebellion and neglect at home'.[199] Such sentiments were not, however, as prominent in contemporary thought towards the West Country as they were when the potentially explosive condition of the industrial midlands and north-west was considered.

The National Society was not as generous with its grants to Monmouthshire schools as it was with, for example, Lancashire and Staffordshire. Indeed, Monmouthshire presented a particularly unfortunate example of active clergy working with inadequate funds. The difficulty was especially evident in the poorer rural areas, where clerical livings were not sufficient to bear the costs of schools and the parents too poor to pay more than a few pence.[200] The Llandaff Diocesan Board for Education was set up in 1838, which encouraged the establishment of Church schools, increasing the number of pupils in such schools from 1,339 in 1838 to 2,373 in 1848. In 1847 the Welsh [Church] Education Council, together with the National Society, supported an agent to promote the establishment of schools. All three bodies provided some money, but still the main costs fell on the clergy and their parishioners.[201] By the later 1850s an expansion of public schooling was evident (Appendix J), but small rural Monmouthshire schools still found great difficulty in raising funds.[202] They were too poor to become efficient and too inefficient to attract government aid.[203] In areas like this, and there were others similarly if not so badly placed in the rural Westcountry generally, the voluntary system was evidently unable to meet the needs of the time.

Schooling and literacy

Further evidence on cultural levels is provided by marriage mark statistics. In the 1840s five of the western counties registered a decline in the levels of basic literacy in those marrying (Appendix D). The proportion of marks in 1845 in Cornwall, Devon, Dorset, Monmouthshire and Shropshire was higher than in 1841. In Dorset a substantial rise of 8 percentage points is recorded. In these five counties and in Herefordshire the proportion of illiterate spouses in 1845 was equal to or greater than the average for the years 1839–45. This suggests the possibility of a decline in educational opportunities around the period of agricultural distress and unrest in the early 1830s,[204] though the complexity of data on schooling makes it impossible to relate the trend to any fall-off in educational provision.

From the 1850s down to 1885, however, all nine counties show a steady and unbroken decline in the numbers[205] and percentages of illiterates getting married, with the proportions for Devon, Dorset and Gloucestershire better than the national average throughout, and those for Somerset and Herefordshire wavering about the national level. The proportions of illiterates for Cornwall, Shropshire and Monmouthshire, on the other hand, were consistently higher than the national level throughout the period. Monmouthshire, which experienced a population growth 1801–51 greater than Lancashire, and had over 6 per cent Irish born in 1851, was by far the least literate of all the nine counties. By 1885 it had reached only the level achieved by Devon, Dorset and Gloucestershire twenty years earlier and had double or more the proportion of illiterate spouses that those counties had in 1870. Indeed, Monmouthshire literacy levels in 1885 were worse overall, and for grooms, than the very low levels that pertained in south Wales (all spouses: 20 per cent marks; grooms: 16 per cent). Wiltshire presents a less consistent picture. Starting badly, with figures rather similar to Shropshire's in the 1840s, it improved relatively from the 1850s, when it achieved levels better than the national average, and by 1885 its percentage of illiterates was as low as Dorset's and it had become one of the most literate of the nine counties. This coincided with a population decline between 1841 and 1861: in 1871 the county's population was only marginally above the 1841 level.

An analysis of the statistics of individual registration districts refines the topographical pattern of illiteracy. In 1856 (Maps 11, 12, 13 and Appendix F), there were certain areas where illiteracy was above the national level (35 per cent marks). One such consisted of an unbroken band of districts from mid-Devon to Land's End. It included all the registration districts west of Bodmin, together with Liskeard to the south and east. Liskeard district abutted on the Devon districts of Tavistock and Okehampton,[206] embracing Dartmoor, and Crediton, the only Devon districts with levels worse than the national average (apart from urban East Stonehouse, where there was a shifting population of service personnel). In addition to this area the districts of Holsworthy (north Devon) and Camelford (north Cornwall) had literacy ratings at the national level, while Launceston (north Cornwall) and Torrington (north Devon) were only one percentage point better. These were areas of sparse population, small farms, and poor land, where wages were low and communications poor.[207]

Another extensive area of illiteracy above the national level was in Somerset and neighbouring parts of Dorset, Wiltshire and Gloucestershire. This stretched from the districts of Bridport, Beaminster and Sturminster (Dorset) in the south, to Axbridge and Keynsham (Somerset) and Thornbury and Chipping Sodbury (Glos.) in the north, and from Wellington on the Somerset–Devon border in the west to Mere and Blandford districts (Wilts.) in the east. Exceptions within that area were the districts centred on the county town of Taunton, on the cathedral city of Wells, and on the towns of

MAP 11

Percentages of marriage marks, 1856: Cornwall, Devon. Bold figures indicate
percentages above the national level of 35 per cent. The percentage shown for
Okehampton is for 1857: see Appendix F, note 12.

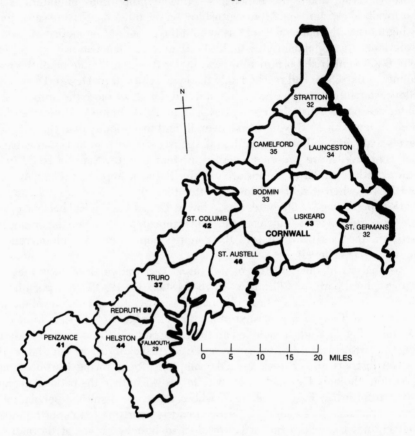

Frome and Sherborne, but all these had ratings only 1 percentage point better
than the national level, as did Williton in north-west Somerset.

A group of four topographically connected districts wth above-average
illiteracy was in east Wiltshire: Highworth, Marlborough, Pewsey and
Devizes.[208] The districts of Warminster, adjoining Devizes, was only 1
percentage point better than the national level, while its neighbour Tisbury
had a rating equal to the national average. These two districts abutted on Mere,
linking the east Wiltshire area of poor literacy with the larger one centred in
Somerset, noted above. Similarly the adjoining districts of Chippenham,
Cricklade and Calne[209] in north Wiltshire (all also only 1 percentage point

better than the national level) provided a second link (with Chippenham abutting on Bradford and Chipping Sodbury). Indeed, there was a continuous band of districts exhibiting illiteracy rates of 34 per cent and more from Axminster in east Devon, embracing almost the whole of Somerset, to the Hampshire border, broken only in Wiltshire by the districts of Melksham and Westbury.

The districts in the border counties of Herefordshire and Shropshire were almost universally above the national illiteracy level. A great block of such worse-than-average districts stretched from the north and east Gloucester-shire districts of Westbury-on-Severn, Newent, Tewksbury, Winchcomb and Northleach to the Cheshire border, with the districts containing the county towns of Hereford and Shrewsbury and the district of Ross the only districts

MAP 12
Percentages of marriage marks, 1856: Somerset, Wiltshire, Dorset. Bold figures indicate
percentages above the national level of 35 per cent. The percentage shown for
Malmesbury is for 1857: see Appendix F, note 15.

MAP 13
Percentages of marriage marks, 1856: Shropshire, Herefordshire, Monmouthshire, Gloucestershire. Bold figures indicate percentages above the national level of 35 per cent.

with rates equal to or better than the national. This area of poor literacy joined a chain of other similarly poor districts in Worcestershire and Staffordshire (Map 8), and through Westbury-on-Severn they linked with the districts of Monmouthshire, all five of which had ratings worse than the national level (Map 13). In the north they connectd with the below-average districts of Nantwich and Congleton (Ches.) (Map 6).

Areas with relatively good levels of literacy included in Cornwall only the Falmouth district. In Devon the south-coast districts, together with Exeter, were all (except East Stonehouse) better than the national level, as were the coastal districts of north Devon. Of these, Barnstaple district in the north, the Plymouth and Stoke Damerel districts, and the contiguous districts of Kingsbridge, Totnes, Newton Abbot, St. Thomas and Exeter were areas with particularly good literacy levels, and the same could be said for the coastal districts of Dorset (except Bridport), together with Dorchester and Shaftesbury. Indeed, apart from the central districts of Crediton, Okehampton and Tavistock in Devon, and the districts of Beaminster, Bridport and Stourport in Dorset, the whole of these two counties had ratings equal to or better than the national level. In south-east Wiltshire the three districts centred on the cathedral city of Salisbury (Wilton, Alderbury and Salisbury) formed another area of superior literacy.

In Somerset, Dulverton, on the Devon border, and the district centred on Bath showed, as might be expected, a very good level of literacy, while not far distant the districts comprising the city of Bristol and its environs (Bedminster, Bristol and Clifton) made another area of high literacy. The districts of central Gloucestershire, too, were better than the national level, with especially good proportions in Gloucester, Cheltenham, Tetbury and Dursley districts. In the border counties only the small district centred on the town of Shrewsbury had a good rating.

This picture of the geographical variations in literacy levels within the nine counties in 1856, can be filled out by an examination of the characteristics of the 123 registration districts involved and a comparison of their literacy ratings in 1856, 1866 and 1871. Appendix G ranks the districts in order, with the least illiterate first, for each of these three years, in similar fashion as adopted in previous chapters for other areas.[210] It reveals that the forty-five worst districts in 1856 (with 41 per cent or more spouses making marks) included most of the coal and metal mining and metal manufacturing areas: in Monmouthshire, Abergavenny and Pontypool (the least literate districts in the whole of the nine counties, and in the case of Abergavenny far worse than any other English district),[211] Newport and Monmouth districts; in Gloucestershire, Westbury on Trym, part of the Forest of Dean mining area; in Shropshire, Cleobury Mortimer, Newport, Shifnal, Atcham, and the Coalbrookdale iron complex in the Madeley and Wellington districts; the Mendip mining area (Clutton and Keynsham and Chipping Sodbury); and the Cornish copper and mining districts (Penzance, Redruth, Helston, St. Austell, St. Columb and Liskeard).[212]

Among this, the worst, third of the districts, were also many where the making of clothing, particularly gloves, was carried on, largely by females and often in domestic conditions. These included in Somerset the districts of Chard, Langport, Wincanton and Bridgwater; in Gloucestershire Newent and Winchcomb; and in Herefordshire Ledbury and Bromyard. Among the forty-five least literate districts were also Shepton Mallet (Som.) (silk making and ironworking), Whitchurch (Shropshire) (silk), Bradford and Mere (Wilts.) and Wellington (Som.) (all woollens), and the hemp making centre of Bridport, the only Dorset district represented.

Many of these poorly literate mining and manufacturing districts had large agricultural populations as well as industrial ones, and there were also among the worst districts some where agriculture predominated — as, for example, in Shropshire, Wem, Market Drayton, Clun, Church Stretton, Bridgnorth; in Devon, the large Okehampton district embracing part of Dartmoor; and the Wiltshire districts of Marlborough, Devizes and Pewsey. Figures for East Stonehouse suggest a particularly illiterate district, but it was small, with a barracks and a naval hospital. It is likely that its marriage statistics reflect to some extent a shifting population.[213]

A connection between high illiteracy rates and certain economic and occupational characteristics is thus clearly evident in many of the western districts. Indeed, a glance at the maps shows a connection between districts of poor literacy and areas of industry and of poorer farming and concentrations of small working farmers.

Certain districts with better literacy rates can be shown to have shared some of these same characteristics, but other reasons for their better showing can usually be made. In the thirty-nine districts which make up in 1856 the middle third in the ranking of illiteracy (40 to 33 per cent marks) mining was important: for example, in the districts of Oswestry (Shropshire), Tavistock (also metal manufacture), and Bodmin and Truro. Truro district, however, included the cathedral city, the largest town in Cornwall, Bodmin was the county town, Tavistock an ancient borough the population (approximately 8,000) of which made up one-third of that of the district, and Oswestry contained the relatively prosperous market town of that name. Also in this group were the gloving districts of Sturminster and Yeovil, the textile districts of Crediton and Tewkesbury, and Beaminster, where net making employed women and girls. Yeovil itself was a market town of 5,000 and all four other districts also contained the market towns which gave them their names.

Even so, all these districts still had literacy rates worse than the national level, as did others of the thirty-nine districts in the middle category — for

example, Ellesmere, Leominster, Weobly and Ludlow, agricultural areas with
market towns along the Welsh border, and the agricultural districts of
Northleach (Glos.), Thornbury, (Glos.) and Axbridge (Som.).

Other districts with a literacy rate equal to or better than the national
average, yet still in the middle third of districts in the rank table of 1856,
included only a few where literacy levels are hard to reconcile with
occupational structures. Thus Frome, Camelford and Launceston had substantial proportions of adult miners in 1851 and Frome was also a woollen-
making district. Gloves were produced in Torrington, Holsworthy, Sherborne,
Bideford and Blandford districts, lace in Axminster district, and textiles in
Wheatenhurst (also a centre for canal bargemen) and Warminster. The
populations of the towns of Bideford, Sherborne, Blandford, and Warminster,
however, accounted for a third to a fifth of those of the districts that took their
names, and Axminster included the town of Lyme Regis.

The remaining districts in this middle category (Taunton, Wells and Williton
(Som.); Ross and Hereford (Herefords.); Cirencester (Glos.); Cricklade,
Chippenham, Calne, Tisbury and Amesbury (Wilts.)) were predominantly
agricultural. Since all these contained towns and Taunton, the county town,
made up 40 per cent of the population of the district named from it, it is
surprising literacy rates here were not better.

The thirty-nine most literate districts in 1856 (14 to 32 per cent marks), all
considerably better than the national level, included the districts containing
most of the large towns. These numbered the two cathedral cities of Salisbury
and Exeter, both with very good literacy rates, the spa towns of Cheltenham
and Bath, together with the county towns of Shrewsbury and Gloucester, and
also Shaftesbury and Plymouth, the second largest town in the nine counties.
All these towns accounted for substantial proportions of the populations of the
districts which bore their names.[214] In addition there was Stoke Damerel
district (part of the Plymouth conurbation and including much of the town of
Devonport), Newton Abbot, which included not only the small market town
and railway centre of that name but also the town of Torquay (by 1850 calling
itself 'the Queen of the Watering Places' and 'the Montpellier of England'),[215]
Totnes (which included the towns of Totnes, a market centre, Paignton, an
incipient watering place, Brixham, Devon's foremost and prosperous fishing
port,[216] and Dartmouth), and Dursley (which included the market towns of
Dursley and Wotton-under-Edge).[217] Alderbury district included in it the
cathedral close of Salisbury, and Wilton district abutted on Salisbury. St.
Thomas district surrounded Exeter and included part of suburban Exeter,
while Plympton St. Mary encircled the Plymouth conurbation. The city of
Bristol was covered by the two districts of Bristol and Clifton, and the
Bedminster district was also part of the Bristol conurbation. Moreover the
populations of the towns of Weymouth, Wareham, Dorchester and Tiverton

(of which only the last could be considered industrial) made up from about a quarter to a third of those of the districts of the same name. Also among the best thirty-nine districts were Melksham (embracing Trowbridge), Westbury (Wilts.) and Stroud, all of which contained market towns still centres of a once prosperous but now declining woollen manufacture and which experienced emigration.

Towns tended to have better communications and in Devon anyway there was a correlation between districts of higher literacy and those with good rail, road and sea communications.[218] The remaining 'good' districts were largely agricultural, often embracing some small but ancient market towns, as, for example, Tetbury, Stow, Malmesbury, Stratton, St. Germans, South Molton and Wimborne. Detailed research into Gloucestershire literacy, based on parish records, shows that literacy levels in the market towns of Dursley, Tewkesbury, Wotton-under-Edge and Stroud were considerably higher than those for a sample of rural parishes over the period 1815 to 1865.[219] Similarly, while the parish of Ludlow (Shropshire) had only some 28 per cent making marks in the 1850s, the registration district of that name in 1856 had 60 per cent doing so.

An analysis for 1866 and 1871 similar to that undertaken for 1856 (Appendix G) reveals some changes in the relative position of districts but a strong tendency for the best and worst to remain substantially the same. Thus, of the best thirty-nine districts in 1856, thirty-one were among the best forty in 1866, and thirty in the best forty-two in 1871,[220] while, of the forty-five worst districts in 1856, thirty-four were among the worst forty-seven in 1866 and thirty-six among the bottom forty-nine in 1871. Moreover, of the nine districts in the best thirty-nine in 1856 but not in the top forty-two in 1871, four had not slipped far out of that category, and, of the dozen in 1871 in the top set which had not been in that category in 1856, eight had similarly not been far below it. The gap between the best and worst districts fell from a range of 14–70 per cent making marks in 1856, to 8–55 per cent in 1866 and 9–50 per cent in 1871.

Plausible explanations of changes in the relative literacy ranking of districts, 1856–71, can often be made. Atcham's rise from 112th position in 1856 to twenty-third in 1871 certainly derives from the combination of that district with that of Shrewsbury, which ranked sixteenth in 1856 and 1866. Sometimes, particularly in rural districts, considerable fluctuations in percentages derived from the small numbers of marriages, as, for example, at Weobly and Ledbury (Herefords.).[221] In other districts population changes were probably responsible. The improved position of Highworth, which rose from sixty-ninth and seventy-seventh in 1856 and 1866 to twenty-third in 1871, was consequent on the 98 per cent increase in the population of the railway centre of Swindon between 1841 and 1851 and a further 41 per cent increase in the next decade, and thus perhaps the result of the immigration of skilled workers. Newton

Abbot district, which retained its relatively high position in the literacy table, included the town of that name, which from 1846 also became a railway centre. The improved position of Axbridge from seventy-fifth in 1856 to forty-fourth in 1871 seems related to the 92 per cent rise in the population of the watering place of Weston-super-Mare between 1841 and 1851 and an actual doubling in the next decade,[222] and it may be noted that the districts of Cheltenham and Weymouth which sustained high positions throughout while experiencing considerable population increase had in them the spa town and seaside resort which gave them their names and no doubt attracted literate people. Cheltenham had particularly good school provision: 'the public opinion of the place rules ... decidedly in favour of education', it was said.[223]

The fall in the relative position in the literacy table of certain districts traditionally connected with woollen cloth production may have had some connection with the decline of that industry in the West Country and consequent static or falling popultions. Thus we have Westbury (Wilts.) (sixteenth in 1856, forty-fifth in 1871); Dursley (Glos.) (twentieth, forty-fifth) where male illiteracy remained at 23 per cent in 1856, 1866, and 1871; Wilton (Wilts.) (twenty-fourth, eighty-third),[224] where male and female illiteracy was at the same levels in 1866 as ten years before, and South Molton (Devon) (thirty-fourth, fifty-seventh). It must be admitted, however, that, with some other districts associated with the declining woollen industry and falling populations, there is no apparent connection with changing relative literacy levels. Bradford (Wilts.), for example, rose from 119th to forty-second, 1856 to 1866, only to fall back to ninety-second in 1871; Stroud (Glos.) improved from thirty-fourth to sixteenth, to ninth.

Certain agricultural districts also suffered a relative decline in their position. Stratton (Cornwall) fell from thirty-fourth and twentieth in 1856 and 1866 to 115th in 1871, a considerable increase in both male and female illiteracy occurring, 1866–71. It had experienced a population decrease of 9 per cent 1841–51, 6 per cent 1851–61, and 2 per cent 1861–71, emigration, perhaps of the more intelligent, being blamed on agricultural distress. Tetbury (Glos.) fell from fifth place in 1856 to 116th and seventy-fifth in 1866 and 1871, with illiteracy doubling from 20 per cent in 1856 to 40 per cent in 1866, and still at 24 per cent in 1871, when grooms performed worse than in 1856. Williton (Som.) fell from forty-sixth in 1856 to one hundredth and 108th in 1866 and 1871 with a decline in the literacy levels of brides between 1856 and 1866. The introduction before 1861 of some hundreds of navvies employed on railway and harbour works may have had some connection with this.

The other changes are not easy to explain. Dorchester district fell in rank from twenty-seventh in 1856 to fifty-fourth and sixty-seventh in 1866 and 1871, without apparent cause, though there was an increase in the number of soldiers at Dorchester barracks. Totnes, where male illiteracy actually increased between 1866 and 1871, fell from thirteenth in 1856 to forty-fifth in 1871: its population had declined in the 1840s and materially in the 1850s.

Some agricultural districts improved their relative position. They included Northleach (Glos.) (sixty-ninth in 1856 to eighteenth in 1871), Wem (Shropshire) (116th to thirty-eighth), Market Drayton (Salop.) (eighty-third to forty-fourth) (in all of which there were noteworthy improvements in female literacy levels) and Ledbury (Herefords.), also a gloving area (ninety-ninth to twenty-fourth).

At Church Stretton (Shropshire), which rose from 102nd place to twenty-third with a great improvement in the performance of grooms, a decrease in population was due in part to a reduction (1851–61) in the numbers employed in a colliery and the completion of a railway. At Chepstow (Mon.) (eighty-third to forty-fourth) some railway workers left the district between 1851 and 1861. Indeed, the movement of railway labourers in the West Country in this period, when much track laying went on, may well have had a significant effect on the changing levels of literacy represented in the marriage marks statistics, though such a hypothesis would require detailed local research to substantiate.

If male and female illiteracy rates are distinguished in the county figures (Appendix D), an interesting development is revealed. At the beginning of the period the proportion of illiterate brides was greater than that of illiterate grooms in all the nine counties. By the end of the period there were higher percentages of illiterate grooms than brides in five of the counties — Dorset, Herefordshire, Shropshire, Somerset and Wiltshire. A position of rough equality had been achieved by 1856–66 in Dorset, Somerset and Wiltshire, in Herefordshire somewhat earlier, and in Shropshire by the 1870s. In three of the counties (Dorset, Herefordshire and Wiltshire) about twice as many brides as grooms could sign their names by 1885. The relative position of brides improved also in the other four counties over the period. They achieved about equal levels of literacy with grooms in Gloucestershire by the mid-1860s, in Devon and Cornwall by 1880 and in Monmouthshire by 1885.[225] In the case of Cornwall the closing of the gap between male and female illiteracy levels, from 20 percentage points in 1841 to 10 in 1856 and then completely by 1880, appears to represent a very considerable change in the educational position of women.

In relation to the national level, however, bridal illiteracy remained at a higher rate in Cornwall throughout the period, and the same was so in Monmouthshire, and on the whole, until the 1880s, in Shropshire. In Devon, Dorset, Somerset, Gloucestershire and Herefordshire, however, female illiteracy was at a lower rate than the national level throughout the period. In Wiltshire the proportion of illiterate brides was greater than the national level before 1850, but from then on it fell below it. Indeed, it is the proportionate increase in bridal literacy that accounts to a large extent for the relative overall improvement in the literacy figures for that county.

The record of grooms in the nine counties, relative to the country as a whole, was less satisfactory. In Cornwall, Herefordshire, Monmouthshire, Somerset, Shropshire and Wiltshire male illiteracy was higher than the national level throughout the period — in Monmouthshire much higher. Devon and Dorset had male levels better than the national throughout the period and Gloucestershire for most of it.

Examination of the records of the individual registration districts sheds further light on the differences between male and female literacy levels (Appendix G). The gap between the best districts for male literacy and the worst closed little between 1856 and 1866 (10–65 percentage points to 8–63 points) but much more by 1871 (9–45 points). For females the gap closed more steadily but remained wider (14–74 points, 1856; 8–63 points, 1866; 9–54 points, 1871). Nevertheless the overall relative improvement of female literacy is striking. In 1856 female illiteracy rates were higher than male in seventy-eight of the 123 districts (by 5 percentage points or more in fifty-two districts), while males were more illiterate than females in only forty districts (in twenty-six by 5 percentage points or more). By 1871 the position had been reversed, with sixty-nine districts showing better proportions for brides compared with forty-three for grooms.[226] Male illiteracy rates greater by 5 percentage points or more than female were found in thirty-seven districts, compared with nineteen districts where female rates exceeded male by 5 percentage points or more.

In very few of the western districts in 1851 were there higher proportions of girls than boys at school (Appendix J), and the differing economic structure of the communities is a more likely factor than schooling in explaining sex differences in literacy levels. Districts where female literacy levels were consistently worse than male (in 1856 and 1871) included most of the Cornish districts, the three covering the Plymouth–Devonport conurbation, Bristol and Clifton, the Weymouth district, the Monmouthshire districts of Abergavenny, Pontypool and Newport, together with Wellington (Shropshire), Tavistock (Devon), and Keynsham (Som.). These districts contained the West Country's two largest towns and many mining districts. Other such districts included some where women were employed in textile manufacture of one kind or another: Yeovil, Whitchurch (Shropshire), South Molton, Torrington, Melksham, Warminster and Westbury. Holsworthy, a glove-making district where women had been more literate than men in 1856, experienced a remarkable relative deterioration in brides' standards, with 7 percentage points greater illiteracy in 1871 than in 1856, double the proportion of illiterate grooms. It seems likely that declining employment in agriculture led to an increase in women glovers between 1851 and 1871.[227]

Districts where male illiteracy was persistently greater than female did, however, include some where women were to some extent employed in domestic manufacture, as in Axminster and Blandford, and also mining or industrial districts like Monmouth, Cleobury Mortimer, Clutton and Chipping Sodbury and the woollen centre of Bradford. Many districts where male illiteracy predominated were primarily agricultural.

The districts which accounted for the great increase in those where male illiteracy was greater than female by 1871 included, for those with a difference of 5 percentage points or more between the sexes, many farming districts, and districts where both manufactures and farming were represented, like Sturminster and Wincanton, where gloves were made. Westbury-on-Severn (Glos.) was the only mining district among them. It would appear that depressed agriculture, a comparatively high demand for boys' labour, and low wages, combined sometimes with the decline in the woollen industry and often with a consequent decrease in population, may have adversely affected male literacy levels.

Other districts where male illiteracy had by 1871 become greater than female (though by less than 5 percentage points), where this had not been the case in 1856, included six of the twenty Devon districts, St. Columb (Cornwall), Shaftesbury and Sherborne (Dorset), Ledbury, Bromyard and Leominster (Herefords.), Thornbury (Glos.), Shifnal, Madeley and Newport (Shropshire), Clutton, Langport, Frome, Shepton Mallet and Axbridge (Som.), and Calne and Pewsey (Wilts.), most of which were purely agricultural or agricultural and old textile districts.

Detailed investigation of improvements in female literacy in Gloucestershire shows that it was concentrated in daughters of labourers; daughters of artisans were not proportionately more literate than sons of artisans. By 1865 some brides, such as daughters of the depressed weavers, were more likely to be illiterate than labourers' daughters. Indeed, from the 1840s there was a tendency for labourers in rural areas of Gloucestershire (as opposed to the towns) to keep their daughters at school longer than their sons.[228] Such tendencies may have been present in other parts of the West Country. A Somerset manufacturer in the early 1840s felt that in areas where there was little agricultural employment for girls they stayed at school much longer than boys and 'are generally well instructed in reading, writing and needlework'.[229]

At all events, for all the western counties the proportion of the population on the books of day schools rose between 1818 and 1833 and again between 1833 and 1851. By 1851 actual attendance on census day in Cornwall, Devon, Somerset and Shropshire was more or less at the national level, in Dorset and Wiltshire much above it, and in Gloucestershire, Monmouthshire and Herefordshire greatly below. And the last two counties had lower proportions of population on day-school books than any other English county (Appendix J).[230]

In the mining and industrial districts the incidence of full-time child labour affected schooling; in the widespread rural areas seasonal labour was a significant factor, for children often failed to return to the classroom quickly even when the work was finished.[231] Where small family farms predominated, moreover, farmers' children might leave school for full employment earlier than did those of labourers. But many labourers' offspring were affected by the common practice of men moving from farm to farm every year or two which militated against regular school attendance. In Dorset whole families were often hired with an obligation for boys to work for their father's employer. In rural Herefordshire, poor roads rendered schools inaccessible while low wages resulted in child labour and low levels of school attendance, particularly in the more sparsely populated districts. Herefordshire and Dorset, in particular, illustrated the difficulties of providing schools where villages were small and scattered, and the lack of decent schools was very common in the rural west generally.[232] In 1833 there were six places in Cornwall where the only school was a Sunday school and where it could not be presumed that children could attend any other school, fifteen in Devon, thirty-eight in Dorset, forty-eight in Gloucestershire, thirteen in Herefordshire, seventeen in Monmouthshire, thirty-eight in Somerset, six in Shropshire and thirty-six in Wiltshire.[233] In the 1840s there were reckoned to be fifty-seven Gloucestershire parishes with nothing but a Sunday school and thirty-four without a school of any kind. Some of these were growing Gloucester suburbs, others had access to schools near by, but many were small and remote rural parishes.[234] In north-west Devon at this time, where the labourers were particularly backward, such Church schools as existed were said to be in a deplorable state.[235] Rural Monmouthshire, too, and the mining districts of that county were particularly deprived.[236]

Despite the spread of schooling in some rural areas, the lack of schools persisted in the 1850s. Thus in 1853 seventy-four parishes in the Hereford diocese still had no school at all, fourteen of them with populations over 200.[237] Later in the decade the Newcastle Commission was told that Herefordshire and Worcestershire were short of public schools 'not because they had been superseded by private schools, but because in many large areas, particularly the Union of Bromyard, there are no schools at all'. In Dore district half the parishes had not even a Sunday school.[238] At that time it was reckoned that in Cornwall, Devon, Dorset and Somerset half the schools in parishes with populations of over 600 were public schools, but in smaller parishes there were far fewer. In Somerset there was only one inspected school in 282 rural parishes, in Dorset the proportion was one in seventeen, in Devon one in twenty-two, in Cornwall one in seventeen, in Herefordshire one in twenty-six. Although some children in these parishes had access to schools in other parishes, a large proportion had no decent school available.[239] In Wiltshire, however, the vast majority of parishes had day schools thought to be reasonable in 1858–9 and many had flourishing night schools.[240]

In the towns the situation was better. An investigation of 275 working-class families in Bristol about 1836 revealed that 57 per cent of children aged three to fourteen were at school, perhaps roughly the average in Gloucestershire as a whole fourteen years later.[241] About 1841 a general survey of Bristol showed 53 per cent of boys and 47 per cent of girls aged five to fifteen at day or evening school.[242] In 1852 the situation in Monmouthshire was far better in the market towns than the rural districts.[243] And less than a dozen of the forty-eight large and small West Country towns separately treated in the education census of 1851 had proportions of children on their rolls, or at their desks on census day, lower than those of the county in which they were set — only Plymouth and Torrington had worse proportions both on the books and in attendance (Appendixes J, K).[244]

If the pupils at school on census day, 1851, are expressed as percentages of children aged five to fourteen, nearly all the West Country towns included in a list of sixty-seven 'principal towns' had well above the average (52 per cent) for such towns: Dorchester 75 per cent, Poole 73, Truro 66, Salisbury 65, Exeter 64, Gloucester 61, Bath 60, Bristol 59, Hereford 58 and Shrewsbury 57 per cent. Only Bridgwater (50), Plymouth and Devonport (48), and Newport (Mon.) (41) of the western towns listed fell below average.[245]

By 1858 there had certainly been an extension of school attendance in the districts of the two largest towns, Bristol and Plymouth (Table 6·2). By then it was felt that few children in these two urban areas went entirely unschooled, though a deficiency of schools still existed in Plymouth and East Stonehouse.[246] Bristol was rather sanguinely thought to be well-off for schools, 'long famed for its charities and the zeal of its inhabitants for education, besides which it is surrounded by the wealth and charity of Clifton and its neighbourhood'.[247]

TABLE 6·2

Proportion of pupils in Bristol and Plymouth, 1851, 1858

Registration district	% pupils to population	
	1851	1858
Bristol	15	18
Bedminster	11	15
Plymouth	9	13
East Stonehouse	11	12
Stoke Damerel	14	17

By this time there were improvements in rural areas, too, as is illustrated by an analysis of several districts in Herefordshire and Dorset (Table 6·3). Even so it was reckoned that these proportions accounted for fewer than two-thirds of children aged four to twelve.[248]

A decade later the situation had improved in many parts of the western counties. In Herefordshire, only two parishes with over 500 population lacked a

TABLE 6·3
Proportion of pupils in twelve rural districts

Registration districts	% pupils to population	
	1851	1859
Sherborne	12	17
Dorchester	14	16
Cerne	13	15
Beaminster	11	14
Axminster	10	13
Yeovil	11	12
Hereford (with Dore)	10	12
Ross	7	12
Leominster	10	13
Bromyard	8	11
Ledbury	13	16
Upton on Severn	11	13

school,[249] but deficiences still existed. In the city of Hereford itself a thousand children were allegedly uncatered for.[250] In Shropshire there was an overall excess of school places over pupils but many schools were said to be unsatisfactory and a large tract of 450 square miles in the south-west of the county was still 'entirely without any good school'.[251] In similar districts of small farms, as in the Holsworthy area of north Devon and in the neighbourhood of St. Columb (Cornwall) there was still a dearth of schools,[252] while the only school in a ten-mile stretch of the Wye valley (Mon.) was allegedly held in a room provided by a farmer for fifteen children.[253] In Somerset, however, there was said to be ample provision in nearly every part of the county.[254] In 1868 Bristol ranked sixth of the sixteen largest English towns with respect to the percentage of children for whom school places were provided (though places did not match the topographical distribution of children) and seventh for average attendance rates.[255] But the very poor were insufficiently provided for, and an extensive survey by the Bristol School Board in 1871 revealed two parts of the city (St. Philip's and Bedminster) deficient in school places.[256] In Gloucestershire by the early 1870s most parishes possessed day schools of some sort,[257] and in Dorset there were enough schools for all, in but a few places, and very few school boards were required.[258] In the Forest of Dean, where there had been a general deficiency of schools in the 1840s, places in National schools were by the 1860s generally considered quite sufficient to meet the needs of the inhabitants; indeed, many school places remained vacant.[259] In Salisbury no board schools were felt to be needed in 1871,[260] and in Wiltshire as a whole only sixteen parishes had no school in 1872.[261]

There appears (Appendix I) to have been at county level a rough connection between the proportions of children aged five to fourteen not at school in 1851 and marriage mark levels in 1866. Application of the product moment correlation coefficient formula gives a correlation coefficient between school attendance levels in 1851 and proportions of marks in 1866 of -0.91 for Monmouthshire (by far the strongest relationship for any English county),[262] -0.63 for Gloucestershire, and -0.56 for Devon. This suggests that the schooling input into later literacy was perhaps about 80, 40, and 31 per cent respectively for these three counties. For the other western counties the relationship, measured in this way, appears weak, and in the case of Shropshire non-existent.[263] Taking all the registration districts of the region together, the correlation coefficient is -0.43, about the same as in the south midlands. Nevertheless the tendency for districts with higher school proportions in 1851 to have lower illiteracy rates fifteen years later is demonstrated in a rudimentary way in Table 6·4.

This tendency, however, is more evident in some counties than others (Appendix F). Every district in Monmouthshire and all the Cornish mining districts, except Launceston, Penzance and Falmouth,[264] had proportions at day school below the national level in 1851. Of these, only Chepstow (23 per cent), Bodmin (17) and Truro (26) had fewer than 29 per cent making marks in 1866. In Gloucestershire there is a discernible connection: all but two of the seven districts with below-average school attendance later had 30 per cent or more making marks.

In largely rural Dorset every district equalled or surpassed the national level

TABLE 6·4

Illiteracy rates and schooling

% of population in attendance at day school, 1851	Illiteracy rates, 1866: number of districts		
	8–22% marks (40 districts)	23–29% marks (44 districts)	30–55% marks (37 districts)
17	0	0	1
16	0	0	0
15	1	0	0
14	1	0	0
13	4 } 29	1 } 23	0 } 10
12	5	6	2
11	11	6	1
10	7	10	6
9	8	8	9
8	2	9	11
7	0	2	2
6	2 } 12	0 } 20	3 } 27
5	0	1	0
4	0	0	0
3	0	0	2

Note
Two districts which existed in 1866 but not in 1851 (Dulverton; Whitchurch (Shropshire)) do not appear here.
Source: Based on Appendix F.

for school attendance in 1851, and the same was so in Wiltshire except for Cricklade and Malmesbury. The school figures for 1858 for these two counties reflect the increased interest of landowners in the provision of schools.[265] Again a clear connection with later literacy levels is evident — in Dorset in only one district (Sturminster) did over 29 per cent make marks in 1866 (in most the percentages lay well below that), and in Wiltshire in only three districts (Cricklade, Marlborough and Pewsey).

The likelihood of levels of school attendance affecting later literacy levels, however, is less obvious in the other western counties. In Shropshire, of the eleven districts with below average attendance in 1851 only one had less than 29 per cent marks in 1866, but of the four with average or above average school attendances again only one had less than 29 per cent marks. In Herefordshire, all but one district had below average school attendance in 1851 but all but one (Bromyard)[266] had mark percentages of less than 28 per cent in 1866. Again in Devon though only two districts had less than 28 per cent with marks in 1866 (Torrington and Tavistock), only seven of the twenty districts had had average or above-average school attendance in 1851, among them Tavistock. And in only about half the Somerset districts does there seem to be any relationship between attendance and later literacy levels.

It seems very likely that school provision affected later literacy levels differently according to the occupational structure of the districts concerned. Detailed research into Gloucestershire suggests that while inadequate school provision had little effect on the children of artisans, ready availability of schooling did not necessarily have a beneficial effect on the later literacy levels of labourers, miners and watermen, who regarded education as less valuable than did artisans.[267] Even as late as 1859, 58 per cent of a sample of Gloucestershire labourers, 59 per cent of miners, and 40 per cent of watermen made marks on marriage. Again, while Bristol literacy levels were generally high, in the parish of St. Philip and St. Jacob, where there was a concentration of labourers, literacy levels were consistently lower (1820–70) than those in most other parishes of the city.[268] Indeed, differences in literacy levels reflected to a great extent the proportions of labourers in local communities.

As elsewhere, of course, migration and other factors render any exact correlation between schooling and later literacy levels unlikely. In Devon, for example, the higher literacy levels in districts containing towns were no doubt only partly due to schooling facilities, for there was in mid-century a considerable movement of population from the rural parishes into urban districts, especially into Plymouth, Exeter and the seaside towns.[269]

Official opinion favoured the view that public schools provided a better education than private ones, and certainly there was in all the nine counties, as elsewhere, a considerable increase between 1833 and 1851 in the proportion of day-school pupils attending public schools (Appendix J.) In Gloucestershire,

Herefordshire, Shropshire and Wiltshire public schools already by 1833 catered for a half or more of day-school pupils. By 1851 in those counties and in Dorset and Monmouthshire the high proportion of over 70 per cent was reached. Of the remaining three western counties all but Cornwall had over 60 per cent of day-school pupils at public schools by 1851. Indeed Devon and Cornwall consistently lagged behind in this respect[270] and by 1851 alone of the western counties had proportions at public day school lower than the national average.[271]

Attendance at private schools tended to be at a higher level in towns than in rural districts. Of the seven large towns (over 20,000) separately treated in the census of 1851 (Appendix K), Bath, Shrewsbury and Bristol had 74, 73 and 65 per cent respectively of day-school pupils on the books of public schools. Gloucester and the Devon towns of Plymouth, Devonport and Exeter, however, had 58, 56, 51 and 56 per cent, well below the average of their own county. Of the forty-one other towns (some quite small) for which discrete data is available, the proportions of public-school pupils varied greatly. Eighteen towns had between 67 and 88 per cent, thirteen below 56 per cent (seven of them in Cornwall and three in Devon). Only thirteen of the forty-one had proportions at public day school higher than those of their home county (Appendix J). County averages, too, disguise variations among registration districts. Some districts which embraced towns had particularly high levels at private schools. In the Yeovil district, for example, 49 per cent of elementary school children were still at private schools in 1858.[272] In Bedminster, Stoke Damerel and Stonehouse districts, essentially parts of Bristol and Plymouth, there was actually an increase in the proportions of school children at private schools between 1851 and 1859.[273]

Some private schools were middle-class but many, particularly for infants, catered for the working classes. The Newcastle Commission found that attendance rates in private schools were better than those in public schools in some rural districts of Dorset and Herefordshire and in the five districts comprising the cities of Plymouth and Bristol.[274] Private schools provided the only available day schooling in some Dorset and Hampshire country areas, and generally it was reported that dame schools were more successful in starting young children to read than public schools using the monitorial system,[275] though the same was not claimed for writing. Certainly many teachers in public schools were of a low calibre — as was reported of some in Gloucestershire and Monmouthshire in the 1840s.[276]

A distinction needs to be made between inspected and uninspected public schools, for by no means all the public schools were grant-aided. In Wiltshire in 1858–9, for instance, 14,306 children attended inspected schools and 11,850 uninspected ones, and of the latter group only some 1,900 were in dame schools.[277] An easy connection between the incidence of all public schooling and literacy levels is therefore unlikely, and examination of individual registration districts provides little evidence for any strong link (Appendix F), though beneficial effects from the growth of inspected schools may be suspected.

At all events the spread of public schools was attributable largely to the Established Church, which by 1851 (Appendix L) was schooling over 80 per cent of the public day pupils in all but two of the nine counties: Gloucestershire (71 per cent) and Monmouthshire (68). Dissent was strong in Monmouthshire, which undoubtedly suffered from the paucity of Anglican churches, some sited away from centres of population.[278] The Gloucestershire figures are probably affected by the inclusion of Bristol, for a much lower proportion of the city's population attended Church schools than was so for the county as a whole.[279]

By 1858 the nonconformists had improved their relative position slightly in Cornwall and Devon, and quite considerably in Monmouthshire, but otherwise the hold of the Church was maintained and, especially in Gloucestershire and Herefordshire, strengthened (Appendix L). Such a trend is confirmed by surveys, 1837–67, of proportions of the population at Church schools (Appendix M), which show a progressive expansion decade by decade in all nine counties. Only in nonconformist Cornwall and Monmouthshire did proportions fall considerably below the national average over that period. Other evidence shows that at Bristol in 1859 some 66 per cent of public schools were Anglican and at Bedminster 91 per cent.[280] By then a survey of twelve rural districts of Herefordshire and Dorset revealed that 92 per cent of public day-school pupils were at Church schools. By 1870 Dorset had almost ten times as many Church day schools as nonconformist ones, and of the 438 Gloucestershire parishes with public schools only seventy-nine were British, the vast majority of the rest being Anglican. Even in Monmouthshire three-quarters of public schools were Church ones.[281] In Devon it was often a choice of a Church school or none.[282]

To what extent did this situation reflect the natural outcome of local Anglican strength, the decidedly patchy interest of parish clergy noted above, or the general support of the Church and the National Society? Comparison of the religious and educational censuses of 1851 reveal some correlation between the proportion at Church day schools and the level of Anglican allegiance in Herefordshire, Dorset, Shropshire and Monmouthshire. But such a relationship is less obvious in the other western counties. None of the earliest diocesan boards of education included any covering the West Country.[283] Over the years 1838–9 two archidiaconal boards of education for Shropshire were established, and diocesan boards were founded for Bath and Wells (covering parts of Somerset), Exeter (Devon and Cornwall), Gloucester (Gloucestershire, parts of Wiltshire and Somerset), Lichfield (part of Shropshire), Llandaff (Monmouthshire) and Salisbury (Dorset, part of Wiltshire), and many district boards were also formed.[284] Not till 1849, however, was the Hereford Diocesan Board founded (Herefordshire and part of Shropshire). Although by 1860 diocesan teacher training colleges were to be found in the dioceses of St. Asaph, Exeter, Gloucester and Salisbury, as well as a non-diocesan Church college at Cheltenham,[285] the record does not suggest any sense of special urgency on the part of Church leaders as far as the West Country is concerned. The dangers of proliferating Dissent in centres of high population density, as in the northern industrial areas, were not apparently considered important in most of the west, even in Cornwall and Monmouthshire, despite the fact that, as noted above, the Newport risings of 1839 were attributed partly to a dearth of schools in the mining district of that area. Dorset, Gloucestershire and Wiltshire received government grants to public day schools (mostly Anglican) over the period 1833–59 above the national average, the last two named considerably above it, but the other western counties received less than the average, with Monmouthshire and Cornwall getting the least (Appendix O).

As for income other than government grants, of Anglican schools in 1858 (Appendix P), those of Cornwall and Monmouthshire again fell well below the national average, while those of the other western counties (except marginally Devon) enjoyed above average. Wiltshire's Church schools received almost twice the national average, against Cornwall's half that figure. The special difficulties of the Anglican clergy in Cornwall and the lack of generosity on the part of the National Society in the form of grants to Cornwall have been noted above.[286]

Organised dissenting education was financially weak. Income from other than government grants for British and nonconformist schools in the western counties in 1858 fell below the national average for such schools, except in Monmouthshire and Gloucestershire, and was particularly low in Shropshire and Herefordshire (Appendix P).

But statistics of school places and attendance do not provide the whole story. Empty school places, or full rolls, did not necessarily indicate generous provision. Children who were registered frequently attended irregularly and for short periods, many leaving at an age too young to have learnt a great deal. In 1844 the H.M.I. responsible for Anglican schools in the western district reported that shortness of school life and irregularity of attendance, because of the calls of agriculture, were the greatest hindrance to education in rural districts. Summer attendance was only half that of winter.[287] In the agricultural areas of Wiltshire, Dorset, Devon and Somerset in the early 1840s it had been felt that the majority of 'boys taken from school to be put out to farm labour can generally read, sometimes correctly, but they cannot often write with sufficient ease for useful purposes'. At Sunday school they could keep up their reading but rarely improve their writing, and on dairy or grazing farms might not be able to attend Sunday school, in which case they forgot much of what they had learnt.[288] Moreover in country districts distance and the weather made it difficult for small children to attend National schools, and when they were old enough they were soon removed for work.[289] Town schools, which were anyway often of higher quality, had better records of attendance than those in the mining, manufacturing and agricultural areas.[290]

The children of the depressed hand-loom weavers were particularly irregular attenders, reflecting the uncertainty of parental earnings. In the hand-loom weaving areas of Gloucestershire in 1840 the average length of school stay was three years.[291] At mid-century it was two years nine months in Wiltshire and little more than two years in Dorset.[292] Even in 1860 the average in Bristol was two years.[293] Such statistics, of course, reflect early leaving ages. In the Cornish mining areas in the 1840s boys left at aged eight or so. And in west Cornwall National schools in the 1850s the average age was seven and a half.[294] At two Monmouthshire schools in 1845, 51 per cent were under six years of age and only 15 per cent over ten.[295] In the inspected schools of Wiltshire and Berkshire in 1851 37 per cent of pupils were under age seven, and 63 per cent below nine; only 11 per cent were aged eleven upwards.[296] In Wiltshire in the late 1860s boys often left at nine at the oldest, and girls between ten and eleven.[297] At Bideford British School (Devon) in 1860 the average school stay was eighteen months for boys and nine months for girls, and half the children in the school had been there for less than a year.[298] In Dorset the average age of school children was low throughout the period, often below seven. In 1848, for example, 60 per cent of pupils in five inspected schools were under the age of nine; in 1850 75 per cent in such schools in Dorset were under ten, and the position was not very different in the 1860s, the usual leaving age varying from seven to eleven according to the relative poverty of the district, age eight being common.[299] About 1860 many Bristol children left by the age of ten, though some returned after a spell as errand boys.[300] In the late 1860s in Gloucestershire the leaving age was ten at the latest, preceded by irregular attendance, with children often being absent from spring to autumn.[301] In south-west Shropshire, a poor area of small farms, attendance at school even in the late 1860s became irregular from the age of eight,[302] and in 1870 in the 'Welsh' farming hill districts of Monmouthshire, farmers' children began work at eight years old, two years earlier than those of labourers who also attended more regularly. In the 'English' farming districts of the county children also attended irregularly and left at an early age.[303]

Statistics of attendance illustrate the extent of irregular attendance. In the mid-1840s in forty-five Devon schools the average attendance was 67 per cent of those on the books; in eighteen Dorset schools it was 71 per cent; in thirty-one Somerset schools 60 per cent; in fifty-one Gloucestershire schools 66 per cent; and in six Monmouthshire schools 68 per cent.[304] At Pontypool National school, with a roll of 385, the average attendance was 205; at Avering (Glos.) the

average was fifty-four for a roll of eighty.[305] School attendance in Monmouthshire improved in the 1850s and 1860s but in the 1870s attendance rates were
still low there and in the Forest of Dean. At Coleford and at Bream, for
example, they averaged 50 per cent. In Gloucester it was 'quite common to find
the number of absent children exceeding that of the present'.[306] Contemporary
reports of attendance rates, however, sometimes suggest a better state of affairs
than really existed. Thus in a survey of six Dorset and six Herefordshire
districts in 1859, 66 per cent and 79 per cent of those on the school books on
average attended school in the year, but the proportion that attended for 176
days or more was only between 20 and 49 per cent.[307]

A combination of irregular attendance and early leaving meant that at any
particular time many children between say five and thirteen were not at school,
though how many never attended school at all is difficult to determine. In
Monmouthshire and Brecon in 1840 it was reckoned that only 30 per cent of
working-class children attended day schools, the vast majority relying on
Sunday schools.[308] And although a high proportion of boys aged five to fifteen
in Penzance (Cornwall) was said to attend day school in 1839,[309] in seven
mining parishes in the county over half the children were not at school in
1840.[310] In Gloucestershire in 1846 about a third of children were reckoned to
attend only Sunday schools.[311] Indeed, many children of hand-loom weavers in
some areas rarely attended day schools except as infants.[312]

The 1851 census suggests a general extension of day-school attendance by
then, and official investigators were of the opinion that children were staying
longer at good schools.[313] But still many children aged five to fourteen were not
on school books at the time of the census (Appendix I). By the 1860s the
majority of children of artisans in Gloucestershire were attending school for a
reasonable period, but this could not be said of the children of many miners,
labourers and the extremely poor.[314] Very few Somerset children were by then
getting no education at all, but many still attended insufficiently long to enable
them to retain a great deal, and there were rural parishes, like Hentland
(Herefords.), where half the children still did not go to school.[315] Even in the
1870s nearly 10,000 children in Bristol were not, according to a school board
survey, attending school, to say nothing of irregular attenders.[316] Similarly in
Gloucestershire there were said to be in all the towns, particularly Gloucester
and its environs, and many of the larger villages 'multitudes of children who
attend no school whatever. Children who should have been at school were seen
to be playing in the streets — in their hundreds'.[317]

Some H.M.I.s and diocesan inspectors in the 1850s felt that extension of the
half-time system to rural districts would assist the West Country.[318] It is clear,
however, that both in agricultural, and in manufacturing, mining and town
districts the problem of general shortness and irregularity of attendance
rendered satisfactory educational provision by means of voluntary attendance

impossible. In 1870 the half-time system was laxly enforced in the manufacturing areas of Gloucestershire,[319] and as late as 1875 E. W. Colt Williams,
H.M.I., reporting on Herefordshire, Radnorshire and the Forest of Dean,
where there were still 5,000 empty places in aided schools, felt that 'education
in this district and in the rest of the country will never be general without the
aid of compulsion'.[320]

Other contemporaries had a sanguine view of the contribution of Sunday
schools to public education. The incumbent of Castle Combe (Wilts.) con-
tended in 1844 that many parish priests put Sunday before day schools and
that any survey of elementary education should take Sunday schooling into
account.[321] The actual educational impact of Sunday schools in the western
counties is, however, difficult to assess. According to the return of 1818 there
were then more children at day school than Sunday school in all the western
counties except Gloucestershire, Somerset and Wiltshire. How correct these
figures are is uncertain. Certainly the returns of 1833 show more at Sunday
school than day school in Cornwall, Dorset, Gloucestershire, Monmouthshire,
Somerset and Wiltshire, while only in Devon, Herefordshire and Shropshire
was the reverse so (Appendix J). In 1847 it was said of Monmouthshire that
education was generally 'little more than Sunday school instruction in the
Bible, in Welsh, owing to the obstacle of the language'.[322] Some places
throughout the region certainly relied entirely on Sabbath schools.

In only thirteen of all the registration districts in the nine counties were
there over 4 percentage points more of the population at Sunday schools than at
day schools in 1851 (Appendix F). These were districts where child labour was
extensively used: Melksham and Bradford (Wilts.), Chard and Yeovil (Som.),
Dursley, Stroud and Winchcomb (Glos.), Wellington and Oswestry (Shropshire), Redruth and Truro (Cornwall), and Abergavenny and Pontypool (Mon.).
In the last two districts nearly 15,000 attended Sunday school on census Sunday
as opposed to 5,000 day school on census day. Eight of these thirteen districts
ranked between eighty-seventh and 123rd of the 123 western districts for
literacy in 1866, suggesting that Sunday schooling there, if, as seems likely, a
substitute for day schools, was not a particularly effective one '(Appendixes
F, G).

In 1833 there were in Devon fifteen parishes with only Sunday schools, in
Dorset thirty-eight, in Gloucestershire forty-eight, in Herefordshire thirteen,
in Monmouthshire seventeen, in Shropshire six, in Somerset thirty-eight, in
Cornwall six and in Wiltshire thirty-six. The age range, too, was greater than in
the day schools, varying usually between four and fifteen, with sometimes older
youths and adults especially in Somerset and Monmouthshire.[323]

In 1851, at county level, Cornwall, Dorset, Wiltshire and Monmouthshire
had proportionately more Sunday-school pupils than was the case nationally
(Appendix J), but this appears to bear no discernible relationship to the later

literacy rates of those counties, except that the least literate county, Monmouthshire, had the highest proportion of its population at Sunday school.[324] Devon, Herefordshire and Shropshire had substantially lower proportions at Sunday school than the national level, and Gloucestershire and Somerset somewhat lower. These counties were, however, also below the national level for day-school attendance. Indeed, in fifty-seven of the 123 districts of the western counties Sunday-school attendance was below the national average (Appendix F), and that included every district in Herefordshire, most in Devon and about half in Gloucestershire. In the counties where it was most frequently at or above the average (Wiltshire and Dorset in particular) day-school attendance was also generally above the national level.[325] Only in Monmouthshire and some Somerset and Cornish districts does it seem likely that Sunday schools were being used as a substitute for day schooling on a large scale.[326]

In the towns day-school attendance was generally greater than Sunday-school, often considerably so. In none but Gloucester of the seven major towns (over 20,000 population) separately treated in the education census of 1851 did the numbers even approach those at day school (Appendix K). At Bristol, where in 1841 25 per cent of children aged five to fourteen and one-third of those attending any school went only to Sunday schools,[327] the proportion of the population at day school in 1851 was almost double that at Sunday school. In the forty-one smaller towns (under 20,000 population) separately treated in the census there was a higher proportion at Sunday than day school only in nine, and in most of those the excess was small. At Torrington, Tewkesbury and Chard, where considerably more attended Sunday than day school, the known incidence of child labour suggests that Sunday schools were substitutes for day schools. In many of the towns in this category, however, day-school exceeded Sunday-school attendance quite considerably, and the same is evident in some registration districts which embraced towns not separately treated in the census (Appendix F). These included Newton Abbot (11 per cent at day, 6 per cent at Sunday school), Stoke Damerel (12 and 6 per cent), East Stonehouse (9 and 4 per cent) and Cheltenham (11 and 7 per cent).

No doubt the strength of Dissent in the West Country contributed to the popularity of Sunday schools The nonconformists catered for many more Sunday than day pupils (Appendix L). Even so, in 1833 Anglican Sunday schools took a higher proportion of children than the chapel schools, except in Cornwall and Monmouthshire, where the reverse was decidedly so. Thus in Devon, Shropshire, Somerset, Gloucestershire and Wiltshire some 60 per cent of Sunday scholars were at Church Sunday schools, in Dorset 77 per cent and in Herefordshire 80 per cent. These, of course, are county averages. In Bristol in 1841 4,000 children attended Anglican Sunday schools as against 6,900 at nonconformist ones.[328] In Gloucestershire, with its historic

connection with Robert Raikes, nonconformist Sunday schools were strongest
in the towns and manufacturing districts. At Gloucester in 1833 400 children
attended nonconformist Sunday schools and 512 Anglican ones; at Cheltenham
1,137 and 1,035.[329]

By 1851 (Appendix L) nonconformist efforts had substantially changed the
situation in the counties. There had been considerable increases in the
proportions of pupils at dissenting Sunday schools in Cornwall and, particularly, in Devon, Dorset and Herefordshire, and some increase in Gloucestershire,
Shropshire and Somerset, and even in Monmouthshire, where by 1851 only 17
per cent of Sunday scholars attended Anglican establishments. Only in
Wiltshire was the state of affairs substantially what it had been in 1833. By
1858, except in Somerset, the Church Sunday schools had recovered some
ground, but in all the western counties except Gloucestershire and Wiltshire
the Church's share of Sunday-school pupils was lower than in 1833.

As for evening schools, there is little to suggest that they can have had any
great effect on educational standards. The numbers attending adult evening
schools in 1851 in the nine counties together was less than 3,700 (in fewer than
200 schools), of whom almost a third were in Monmouthshire.[330] Figures of
children (mainly boys) at evening schools in 1858 are larger, but there is
nothing to suggest any significant substitution for day schooling. Wiltshire and
Dorset, which had the highest day-school attendance rates of the nine counties
on census day 1851, also had the highest proportion of their population at
evening schools in 1858, and Devon, Cornwall, Shropshire and Herefordshire
had very few at such schools anyway (Appendixes J, Q). In 1865 there were only
nine night schools in Shropshire.[331]

The proportion of pupil teachers and of certificated teachers in the aided
schools increased in Devon, Cornwall, Dorset and Somerset very considerably in the period 1849–55 and capitation grant doubled in 1854–5.[332] The
inspectors' reports suggest gradually rising standards in the western counties
generally and this is borne out by the literacy figures. Nevertheless in the
1860s, as in the previous decade, the inspectorate was still dismayed at the
number of poorly staffed, ill equipped schools. In 1865 there were still thirteen
towns in Devon without an inspected Church school,[333] and two years later
only 36 per cent of schools in the census districts of Somerset were inspected
ones (varying from 60 per cent in the Bath district to 16 per cent in the rural
district of Williton).[334] In Wiltshire in 1858–9 uncertified and unregistered
teachers far outnumbered those who were certified and registered.[335] A report
on Monmouthshire in 1860 claimed that educational progress since 1853 was 'so
marked as to deserve especial notice'. The statistics provided, however, show
that the position achieved by 1860 was extremely modest. In that year there
were eighteen annual grant schools in the county and fourteen others under
simple inspection and the number of certified teachers in the county was

twenty-five and of pupil teachers fifty-three. Ten populous agricultural parishes had no inspected schools at all, and inspected schools in the towns of Monmouth and Usk were not in receipt of annual grant.[336]

Large parts of the western counties were rural, many parishes remote. Here school provision as well as school attendance was difficult, especially where large landowners were not present. In some parts of the West Country domestic industry as well as agriculture claimed child workers into the 1860s and beyond, while in other parts, especially in Monmouthshire and Shropshire, conditions similar to those in the Black Country prevailed. The H.M.I.s reported in the 1850s and 1860s that many children were still 'altogether without education', and that only further government assistance and perhaps the provision of central schools in sparsely populated districts could secure any further material advance.[337] It is difficult to dissent from that verdict.

CONCLUSION

Through a glass darkly

The reservoir of evidence available for the study of elementary schooling and literacy levels and their socio-economic background in the manifold communities of England, during the two generations before the 1870 Education Act, is enormous.[1] This study has relied largely on a restricted range of contemporary published data, much of it emanating from government and Church sources, and conclusions must, therefore, be regarded as preliminary and in some respects tentative.

The very considerable differences in educational provision and attainment between one part of the country and another, and between different types of urban and rural communities, have nevertheless been demonstrated quite clearly in the foregoing chapters. Moreover, not only did the extent of basic literacy vary greatly over different localities, but such variations have been found explicable in broad terms by reference to the typology of the community and other local phenomena, particularly of a demographic kind. The social and economic structures of individual communities affected the demand for schooling and the type of schools favoured, and school attendance was influenced by the demand for child labour and its nature and by parents' and employers' attitudes to education. The availability of public schooling, and whether or not it enjoyed government funding, depended, too, on the outlook and resources of local philanthropists, civic leaders, landowners and clergy, and indeed of the local middle class generally.

Religion was a significant ingredient of local educational standards mainly as it reflected the varying strength of the Established Church and the enthusiasm, energy and resources of its parish clergy towards school provision, and the extent to which funds collected in one part of the country were channelled elsewhere. There is little evidence that spatial differences in working-class enthusiasm for schooling stemmed from any particular religious or denominational conviction, as might have been the case in, for instance, Puritan areas in earlier times. Where nonconformity was strong and the Church weak, however, as in some northern and midland towns, the provision of public day schools might be adversely affected. And in parts of towns where poor Irish

Catholics were concentrated there was probably a tendency to avoid Anglican schools even when no other public schools were available.

Aside from the general improvement in literacy, school provision and attendance, over the period studied, the relative educational position of some towns and districts experienced ups and downs. Again, there are usually plausible explanations for such changes. In particular, population growth or decline was often important in variations in the educational standards of a district, though the actual effects differed according to circumstance. Thus, for instance, the rapid growth experienced by some northern towns and districts, associated as it often was with the influx of unskilled labourers, sometimes with concentrations of poor Irish attracted by employment opportunities for themselves and their offspring, had a depressing effect on literacy and schooling levels. On the other hand the growth of market and commercial centres, and London itself, as they syphoned off the better educated young from surrounding rural districts, might well have had the opposite effect on urban standards while weakening those of the milked countryside. In other areas, however, rural depopulation served to remove the least educated, keep labourers' wages up, and affect schooling and literacy levels beneficially.

As for gender differences, the proportions of literate brides relative to grooms varied geographically and the spatial pattern changed over the period for reasons that again are, at least partially, discernible. Particularly striking is the relative improvement in female literacy levels where opportunities for girl employment in agriculture and industry were affected by falling demand and legal restrictions and by the expansion of jobs in domestic service for those who were schooled (detailed in Chapter 2).

It has been suggested[2] that since the trend of illiteracy rates nationally was continuously downward, and decline was not accelerated by the introduction of board schools, then compulsory education, free schooling and the intrusion of the state in popular education, through legislation beginning in 1870, were unnecessary. The regional investigations undertaken in previous chapters, however, make it hard to support such a theory. The national literacy rate disguised, even on the eve of the 1870 Act, very considerable local differences, and in many grey and black areas the existing system of voluntary and private schools left much to be desired. Moreover, the attitudes and economic status of parents lowest in the social scale made it unlikely that their children would enjoy proper schooling unless it were free and compulsorily enforced. Even better-off working-class parents in some areas were insufficiently persuaded that regular school attendance over a period of four of five years, at ages when they were susceptible to instruction, was necessary or desirable. In some lingering domestic industries short-sighted parents put early introduction to their dying trades before the opportunities of schooling. Even sectors of urban communities in the period covered were 'not yet dominated by print or a mass need to confront it with a high level of ability[3] based on some schooling. Many parents and employers did not perceive its future functional necessity, and felt little cultural need of education. The half-time system, which some regarded as a possible national alternative to full-time compulsory schooling, was, outside the textile factory areas, often resented by those to whom it applied and disliked by employers, and its general extension became clearly impracticable as an educational programme.[4]

Moreover the decline in the proportions of illiterate spouses over the period should not lead to an over-sanguine assessment of the achievement of the voluntary and private schools. The value of marriage mark statistics as used in this study lies in their suitability as a comparative measure.[5] They indicate how one place compared with another in the likely proportion of young men and women who were completely or semi-illiterate. They measure over the years changes in the proportions of similar age cohorts in a locality who were unable to reach a certain, rather low, standard. They do not measure the actual level of literacy in the sense of the quality of achievement of those involved, or changes in that over time. Increased percentages of spouses able to sign their name in an area may have resulted merely from more young people attaining the same very low level of literacy, and do not demonstrate that the educational standards of those who were able to sign were improving. They do not, for example, indicate the extent if any to which those who could sign in 1865 were better educated than those who could sign in 1855.

Deductions based on statistical evidence of this kind must, therefore, be limited. Moreover, although many of those who could not sign their names could read, subjective evidence suggests that even in the 1860s the ability to 'read' and 'write' might have little practicability among those with a smattering of schooling. 'I found that what a child called "reading" was spelling out letter by letter words of one syllable, and arriving now and again at a correct pronunciation of the whole: they seemed quite satisfied, by this means, of their superiority over their illiterate companions,' reported H. W. Lord to the Children's Employment Commission in 1863.[6] And of bridal illiteracy statistics in 1864 the Registrar of Births, Deaths and Marriages suggested that they represented 'an understatement rather than an overstatement of the number of young women in England incapable of writing for any practical purpose'.[7] Sarah Limer, who had attended a Catholic day school and as a ten-year-old pottery worker in 1843 continued to attend Sunday school, professed to be able to write but her signature, reproduced here, indicates the value of that assertion.[8]

The Newcastle Commission's belief, based on a survey of children 'on school books', that by 1861 only a comparatively small proportion of English children were completely unschooled, is open to considerable doubt.[9] Even if true, however, it begs the question of the quality and value of such schooling.

The proportions in a locality of those basically literate, as measured by marriage signatures, has been shown in previous chapters to tend to relate to proportions previously at school there — but that such a relationship was far from perfectly matched.[10] Aside from the factor of migration between school and marriage, and the possibility of learning outside the school, the extent to which 'schooling' was of any practical value is significant. As W. L. Sargant wrote in 1867, 'the great question is, not how many children are at school, but how many children are educated, and retain their instruction'.[11] In 1838 the Manchester Statistical Society in a survey of Pendleton (Lancs.) found that of adults who could not read 'more have attended school than have not'.[12] And in 1851 the education census claimed that 'nearly all ... see the inside of a schoolroom', but, more realistically than the Newcastle Commission, added, 'although some do little more'.[13] Relevant here is the length of school life, the regularity of attendance, the age span during which schooling occurred, and the quality of instruction.

True, the introduction of board schools was not the only way school provision might have been improved in quantity and quality — grants to voluntary schools could have been increased and good private schools subsidised in return for inspection (as suggested by the Newcastle Commission)[14] — but much of the evidence discussed in previous chapters suggests that, even apart from the problem of the residue of children who never attended a day school, compulsion had by 1870 become a necessity if regular attendance over a reasonable number of years during an appropriate age span was to be ensured for all children. Moreover, while dame and other private schools may have assisted in the spread of the numbers able to achieve very basic levels of literacy, in many places an extension of better equipped, better staffed schools was essential if general standards were to rise.[15]

For parents at the lower end of the social scale 'school' was often conceived as a combination of 'creche' for infants and a place for older children to acquire a smattering of reading. It is not enough, however, to point to parental satisfaction with dame and other private schools which were little different in the 1860s than they had been in the 1830s, or to argue that they often taught reading tolerably well, perhaps better at times than in the lower classes of the voluntary schools during the monitorial period.[16] In many of these schools conditions must have been very poor. Over 700 teachers, for example, were said to have signed the 1851 education returns with marks.[17] Even in the 1860s, moreover, many unaided voluntary schools differed little from dame schools, were poorly equipped, often conducted by untrained teachers, and suffered from lack of funds[18] and from the restricted views of their promoters on what education for the poor should consist.

In 1870 it is likely that about a quarter of all working-class day pupils were attending private schools,[19] while unaided voluntary schools comprised about a third of all schools for the working classes.[20] Increasing numbers of children in the aided schools were enjoying an extended curriculum at the hands of trained teachers and reaching higher levels of education than earlier in the century. Even so, standards in many of the aided schools, too, left much to be desired.[21] Compulsion and extended public funding, at least, seem to have been essential for further progress.

In this exercise in comparative local history many questions have been left unanswered. The statistical data provided in the Appendixes could doubtless be made to yield further information. It has been said, however, though with some exaggeration, that 'almost all important questions are important precisely because they are *not* susceptible to quantitative answers',[22] and certainly what is now required is further investigation into the more subtle implications of literacy in the past. How significant was reading literacy as opposed to writing literacy? Why was literacy sought? What use was it actually put to — in work and in other aspects of life? How did it affect social, political, gender and family relationships? Was it related to family structures, to social or spatial mobility? As far as informal learning is concerned, how exactly was it transmitted? How was it affected by differing teaching styles, school organisation or curricular content? How important were different degrees of literacy? And in all these aspects to what extent and why were there geographical, chronological, class or occupational differences?

There is thus much scope for local investigations more detailed than has been possible here, for an examination of the minutiae of family life and for study of the intimacy of grass-root political, religious and socio-economic networks. And until such questions are tackled we are still looking through a glass darkly in viewing the significance of literacy and popular schooling in nineteenth-century provincial England — and indeed elsewhere.

NOTES

1 The inheritance of diversity (pp. 2–14)

1 D. Cressy, *Literacy and the Social Order*, Cambridge, 1980, pp. 53–61; R. Houston, 'The literacy myth? Illiteracy in Scotland, 1630–1760', *Past and Present*, XCVI, 1982, pp. 82–3; P. Collinson, 'The significance of signatures', *Times Literary Supplement*, 9 January 1981.

2 R. S. Schofield, 'The measurement of literacy in pre-industrial England', in J. Goody (ed.), *Literacy in Traditional Societies*, Cambridge, 1968, pp. 318–25; *27th A. R. Registrar General of Births, Deaths and Marriages*, PP 1866, XIX, pp. xiv, xxi; PP 1867–8, XIII, p. 62. See also L. Stone, 'Literacy and education in England, 1640–1900', *Past and Present*, XLII, 1969, pp. 118–9; E. G. West, *Education and the State*, London, 1965, p. 134; R. S. Schofield, 'Dimensions of illiteracy, 1750–1850', *Explorations in Economic History*, X, 1973, pp. 440–3; T. Laqueur, 'The cultural origins of popular literacy', *Oxford Review of Education*, II (3), 1976, p. 271 n. 1.

3 P. Gardner, *The Lost Elementary Schools of Victorian England: The People's Education*, Beckenham, 1984, p. 20; and see pp. 25–6, 158–9.

4 R. K. Webb, 'Working class readers in early Victorian England', *English Historical Rev.*, LXV, 1950.

5 The following is based on: Cressy, *Literacy*, chapters 4, 6, 7; Stone, 'Literacy'; R. A. Houston, 'The development of literacy: northern England, 1640–1750', *Ec. H. R*, 2nd ser. XXXV, 1982; R. A. Houston, 'Illiteracy in the diocese of Durham, 1663–89 and 1750–62: the evidence of marriage bonds', *NH*, XVIII, 1982; R. T. Vann, 'Literacy in seventeenth century England: some hearth-tax evidence', *Jnl. Interdisciplinary History*, V, 1974; Stephens (1977); W. B. Stephens, 'Male and female illiteracy in seventeenth century Cornwall', *JEAH*, XII, 1977; W. B. Stephens, 'Male illiteracy in Devon on the eve of the Civil War', *Devon Historian*, XI, 1975.

6 Cressy, *Literacy*, pp. 74–6; Stone, 'Literacy', pp. 100–1; Stephens (1977), p. 30; Houston, 'Development of literacy', pp. 209–11.

7 M. Spufford, *Contrasting Communities, English Villagers in the Sixteenth and Seventeenth Centuries*, Cambridge, 1974, pp. 173, 207, 218.

8 Houston, 'Development of literacy', pp. 214–5; Houston, 'Illiteracy in Durham', p. 250. See also Table 1.2, below, especially Yorkshire N. R. and E. R., 1754–62.

9 Schofield, 'Dimensions', pp. 445–6. Cf. App. D.

10 Issac Watts, *An Essay Towards the Encouragement of Charity Schools*, London, 1728, p. 15.

11 See Table 1.1, Dudley, and remarks on Stoke and Bushbury, below.

12 Stephens (1977), pp. 32–5.

13 W. B. Stephens, 'Illiteracy in Devon during the Industrial Revolution, 1754–1844', *JEAH*, VIII, p. 3.

14 F. O'Shaughnessy, *A Spa and its Children*, Warwick, 1979, pp. 1–4; and see note 12 to Table 1.1.

15 J. Grayson, 'Literacy, schooling and industrialization: Worcestershire, 1760–1850', in Stephens (1983), p. 57; R. A. Church, *Economic and Social Change in a Midland Town: Victorian Nottingham, 1815–1900*, London, 1966, Chapters 1–4; *VCH, Northants.*, III, p. 29; J. Foster, 'Nineteenth-century towns — A class dimension', in H. J. Dyos (ed.), *The Study of Urban History*, London, 1968, p. 291; and see below.

16 J. Bradshaw, 'Occupation and Literacy in the Erewash Valley coalfield', in Stephens (1983), p. 8.

17 T. W. Laqueur, 'Debate: literacy and social mobility in the Industrial Revolution in England', *Past and Present*, LXIV, 1974, p. 99. These include some of the towns in Table 1.1.

18 M. Sanderson, 'Literacy and social mobility in the Industrial Revolution in England', *Past and Present*, LVI, 1972, p. 85.

19 PP 1844, XVII, App. p. 86.

20 Schofield, 'Dimensions', p. 449.

21 M. Gratton, 'Aspects of literacy and 19th-century society: the environs of Liverpool', *JEAH*, XVII, 1985.

22 R. W. Unwin, 'Literacy patterns in rural communities in the Vale of York', in Stephens (1983), pp. 73, 75.

23 M. Yasumoto, 'Urbanization and population in an English town: Leeds during the Industrial Revolution', *Keio Economic Studies*, X, 1973, pp. 83–5.

24 G. Gomez, 'The endowed schools of Staffordshire in the eighteenth century', M. Phil. thesis, University of Leeds, 1977, p. 390.

25 D. Levine, 'Illiteracy and family life during the first Industrial Revolution', *Jnl. Social History*, XIV, 1980–1, pp. 28–9; D. Levine, 'Education and family life in early Industrial England', *Jnl.Family History*, IV, 1979, pp. 371–2.

26 Sanderson, 'Literacy and social mobility', pp. 82, 85.

27 Schofield, 'Dimensions', pp. 446–9.

28 G. Young, 'Educational development in a rural society: a study of the control and provision of schooling in Rutland in the nineteenth century', M. Ed. thesis, University of Leicester, 1980, p. 116.

29 Sanderson, 'Literacy and social mobility'; Laqueur, 'Debate' and M. Sanderson, 'A Rejoinder', *Past and Present*, LXIV, 1974; M. Sanderson, *Education, Economic Change and Society in England, 1780–1870*, London, 1983, pp. 9–16.

30 Laqueur, 'Debate'; Sanderson, 'Rejoinder'; M. Sanderson, 'Social change and elementary education in industrial Lancashire, 1780–1840', *NH*, III, 1968, pp. 136 ff; W. L. Sargant, 'On the progress of elementary education', *JSSL*, XXX, 1867, p. 91.

31 Stephens (1983), p. 4; Laqueur, 'Cultural origins', pp. 257, 259: D. W. Gallenson, 'Literacy and age in pre-industrial England: quantitative evidence and implications', *Economic Development and Social Change*, XXIX, 1980–1, p. 828.

32 T. W. Laqueur, *Religion and Respectability: Sunday Schools and Working Class Culture, 1780–1850*, London, 1976.

33 Based on data included in the sources for Table 1.1, q.v.

34 W. B. Stephens, 'Elementary education and literacy, 1770–1870', in D. Fraser (ed.), *A History of Modern Leeds*, Manchester, 1980, pp. 224–5.

35 Based on the sources cited for Table 1.2

36 Schofield, 'Dimensions', pp. 449–51; J. Campbell, 'Occupation and literacy in Bristol and Gloucestershire, 1755–1870', in Stephens (1983), pp. 26–31; Grayson, 'Literacy', p. 62; Unwin, 'Literacy patterns', p. 76; Sanderson, 'Literacy and social mobility', pp. 89–93; Stone, 'Literacy', pp. 108–12; Houston, 'Illiteracy in Durham', pp. 242–51; Houston, 'Development of literacy', p. 206; Levine, 'Illiteracy', p. 30; Gomez, 'Endowed schools of Staffordshire', p. 392; Levine, 'Education and family life', pp. 372–3; W. Couth, 'The development of the town of Gainsborough, 1754 to 1850', M. A. thesis, University of Wales, 1975, App. F. 2.

37 P. Laslett, *The World We Have Lost*, London, 1963, pp. 194–5.

38 Stephens (1977), p. 33.

39 Cf. Schofield, 'Dimensions', p. 453; Sanderson, 'Social change'; Bradshaw, 'Occupation and literacy', pp. 11–2; Grayson, 'Literacy', pp. 57–61; Houston, 'Illiteracy in Durham', pp. 245–6; S. A. Harrop, 'Literacy and educational attitudes as factors in the industrialization of north-east Cheshire, 1760–1830', in Stephens (1983), pp. 38–41.

40 A map based on the 1818 returns is in W. E. Marsden, 'Diffusion and regional variation in elementary education in England and Wales, 1800–1870', *History of Education*, XI, 1982, p. 175.

41 Houston, 'Development of literacy', pp. 214–5.

42 A statistical analysis of illiteracy rates in 1838–9 and schooling figures *c*.1820 (for England and Wales) produced a correlation coefficient of −0·44: G. R. Lucas, 'The diffusion of literacy in England and Wales in the nineteenth century', *Studies in Education*, III, 1958–63, pp. 247–8.

43 See maps in Marsden, 'Diffusion', p. 175 and Lucas, 'Diffusion', p. 242.

44 Cf. R. A. Houston, *Scottish Literacy and the Scottish Identity: Illiteracy and Society in Scotland and Northern England, 1600–1800*, Cambridge, 1985, pp. 193–5.

45 Levine, 'Education and family life', p. 4.

46 Cf. Stephens (1983), p. 6.

2   Schooling and literacy: Regional characteristics and influences (pp. 15–53)

1 E. Johansson, *The History of Literacy in Sweden in Comparison with some Other Countries*, Umeå, 2nd edn. 1977, pp. 71–2. Marriage mark percentages for 1855, 1865, 1870 were, for England and Wales: 36, 27, 24; for Wales alone: 54, 43, 35; for Scotland: 17, 17, 15; for Ireland: ? , 46, 42; for France: 40, 34, 34; for Italy the rates in 1867 and 1870 were 69 and 68 per cent. See App. D; *16th A. R. Registrar General of Births, Deaths and Marriages in Scotland*, PP 1874, XIV, p. xx; *2nd* and *7th A. R.s Registrar General of Births, Deaths and Marriages in Ireland*, PP 1870, XVI, p. vii; 1873, XX, p. 7; C. M. Cipolla, *Literacy and Development in the West*, Harmondsworth, 1969, pp. 121–4.

2 *8th A. R. Registrar General of Births, Deaths and Marriages*, PP 1847–8, XXV, p. xxx.

3 Stephens (1973), p. 9.

4 Cf. L. Stone, 'Literacy and education in England, 1640–1900', *Past and Present*, XLII, 1969, p. 124.

5 See also App. F, statistics of children at school by registration districts.

6 *Education Census, 1851*, p. cxxxii.

7 There were three exceptions: female illiteracy in the West Riding was untypically lower than male in 1865, and the same was so in Westmorland and Warwickshire in 1875. These counties are not included in the numbers cited.

8 PP 1887, XXX, p. 738; and see below.

9 See, e.g., K. D. M. Snell, *Annals of the Labouring Poor: Social Change and Agrarian England, 1660–1900*, Cambridge, 1985, pp. 128–30, which seeks to demonstrate a considerable fall in farm wages, 1835–50, in the southern, midland and eastern counties.

10 See pp. 54–5, 70–1, 102–3, 164–5, 207, 210–11.

11 W. L. Sargant, 'On the progress of elementary education', *JSSL*, XXX, 1867; F. Hill, *National Education: Its Present State and Future Prospects*, I, London, 1836, pp. 247ff.; *29th A. R. Registrar General of Births, Deaths and Marriages*, PP 1867–8, XIX, p. vi; *ibid*, 32nd A. R., PP 1871, XV, p. xiii; PP 1887, XXX, pp. 737–9.

12 J. Fletcher, 'Moral and educational statistics of England and Wales', *JSSL*, X, 1847, pp. 193–233. Fletcher's figures are reproduced in *CCE, 1846(2)*.

13 Kent, Middlesex and Surrey are omitted from these calculations.

14 E.g., *29th A. R. Registrar General of Births, Deaths and Marriages*, PP 1867–8, XIX, pp. v–vi.

15 *45th A. R. Registrar General of Births, Deaths and Marriages*, PP 1882, XIX, p. xiv.

16 Fletcher, 'Moral and educational statistics', p. 210. Kent and Middlesex are omitted from these calculations.

17 *Education Census, 1851*, pp. xxxix–xl.

18 M. Sanderson, 'Social change and elementary education in industrial Lancashire, 1780–

1840', *NH*, III, 1968, p. 153; *CCE, 1840–1*, pp. 160, 425–6; J. Campbell, 'Occupation and literacy in Bristol and Gloucestershire, 1755–1870', in Stephens (1983), p. 28. And see pp. 78–9.

19 M. Johnson, *Derbyshire Schools in the Nineteenth Century*, Newton Abbot, 1970, pp. 59–60; J. Bradshaw, 'Occupation and literacy in the Erewash Valley coalfield', in Stephens (1983), p. 19. And see pp. 125, 128.

20 'Report on the state of education in Birmingham', *JSSL*, III, 1840, p. 26.

21 See pp. 122–3, 125–7.

22 D. F. Mitch, 'The spread of literacy in nineteenth-century England', Ph.D. dissertation, University of Chicago, 1982, pp. 418–22, in a statistical analysis, concludes that living standards made only a very modest contribution to literacy levels.

23 The nature of domestic service at this time is, however, complex, and the following discussion must necessarily here be at a general and perhaps superficial level; but cf. E. Higgs, 'Domestic servants and households in Victorian England', *Social History*, VIII, 1983.

24 Omitting Kent, Middlesex, Surrey.

25 Mitch, 'Spread of literacy', pp. 92, 109, 111–4, 140–1; PP 1867, XVI, p. 109; PP 1868–9, XIII, (b), p. 433; PP 1887, XXX, p. 738.

26 See pp. 73, 88, 114, 172, 218.

27 P. E. H. Hair, 'Children in society, 1850–1980', in T. Barker and M. Drake (eds.), *Population and Society in Britain, 1850–1980*, London, 1982, pp. 47–8; P. M. Tillott, 'Sources of inaccuracy in the 1851 and 1861 censuses', in E. A. Wrigley (ed.), *Nineteenth-Century Society*, Cambridge, 1972, pp. 122–5 (but based on a very localised sample); Mitch, 'Spread of literacy', pp. 272, 282.

28 See p. 169.

29 Mitch, 'Spread of literacy', p. 509.

30 *Censuses, 1851, 1871*; PP 1867–8, XVII, (a), p. xvii.; *Newcastle*, II, p. 147.

31 Cf. Hair, 'Children in society', pp. 49–50.

32 Cf. *Hansard*, 3rd ser., vol. cxciv, col. 1194; and see pp. 61, 92, 147, 259.

33 See pp. 172–3, 176. Cf. J. S. Hurt, 'Professor West on early nineteenth-century education', *Ec.H.R.*, 2nd ser., XXIV, 1971, p. 626.

34 See App. F.

35 Fletcher, 'Moral and educational statistics', p. 109.

36 Mitch, 'Spread of literacy', pp. 234–50, found that contemporary biographies and surveys of working-class life testify to the increasing tendency for literacy skills to be learnt at school rather than elsewhere by mid-century.

37 See p. 13.

38 Mitch, 'Spread of literacy', p. 243, found a correlation coefficient between day schooling at county level in 1833 and literacy in 1851 of +0·75 (this excluded the Yorkshire ridings, Kent, Middlesex and Surrey: ex inf. Dr. Mitch).

39 Application of the Pearsonian formula to the relationship between county illiteracy rates in 1866 and percentages of children not at school in 1851 (App. I) yields correlation coefficients of +0·75 (males) and +0·77 (females), indicating a fairly close connection. Cf. also G. R. Lucas, 'The diffusion of literacy in England and Wales in the nineteenth century', *Studies in Education*, III, 1958–63, pp. 247–8; Mitch 'Spread of literacy', p. 243.

40 R. Pallister, 'The determinants of elementary school attendance about 1850', *Durham Research Rev.*, V, 1969, pp. 385–8.

41 F. J. Williams, 'The development of elementary education in Widnes, 1840–80', M. A. thesis, University of Sheffield, 1983, pp. 193–4.

42 P. Gardner, *The Lost Elementary Schools of Victorian England: The People's Education*, Beckenham, 1984, chapter 5; D. Leinster-Mackay, 'A question of ephemerality: the longevity of 19th-century private schools', *JEAH*, X, 1978; D. Leinster-Mackay, 'Dame schools: a need for review', *BJES*, XXIV, 1976.

43 See pp. 152, 255.

44 See, e.g., pp. 76, 149, 204, 262.

45 *Education Census, 1851*, pp. cxxxii, cxxxix.

46 E.g., PRO, H.O. 129/495; and see p. 60.

47 See, e.g., National Society, *Summaries of the Returns to the General Inquiry...into... Schools of the Established Church...*, 1856–7, 1868.

48 See pp. 99, 149, 198, 255–6.

49 J. Hurt, *Education in Evolution*, London, 1971, p. 221.

50 D. W. Sylvester, *Robert Lowe and Education*, Cambridge, 1974, pp. 84–93. Recent literature on the Revised Code is too extensive for citation here. See, A. J. Marcham, 'Recent interpretations of the Revised Code of Education, 1862', *History of Education*, VIII, 1979; A. J. Marcham, 'The Revised Code of Education, 1862: reinterpretations and misinterpretations', *ibid.*, X, 1981.

51 Stephens (1973), p. 11.

52 Stone, 'Literacy', p. 76; Sanderson, 'Social change'; T. W. Laqueur, *Religion and Respectability: Sunday Schools and Working-Class Culture, 1780–1850*, London, 1976, pp. 61, 259; Stephens (1973), pp. 11–12; W. B. Stephens, 'Elementary education and literacy, 1770–1870', in D. Fraser (ed.), *A History of Modern Leeds*, Manchester, 1980, pp. 224–6; and see pp. 86–8.

53 Laqueur, *Religion and Respectability*, pp. 54–60.

54 *Ibid.*, pp. 258–60.

55 Mitch, 'Spread of literacy', pp. 256–60. Mitch also suggests that to say that there was no relationship between day and Sunday school rates is too strong. Across counties a positive correlation existed in 1818, suggesting that Sunday schooling then was largely complementary to day schooling, while in 1833 (and to a less extent in 1851) the reverse was so, showing Sunday schools being used to some extent as substitutes for day schools. Mitch found, too, a negative correlation in 1851 across ninety-two registration districts in Lancashire, the West Riding, Durham, Glamorganshire, Caernarvonshire and Staffordshire. But across boroughs there was a positive correlation, suggesting that there substitution was not strong.

56 App. J. Overlap only in Warwickshire, Worcestershire, Middlesex, Devon, Herefordshire.

57 Mitch, 'Spread of literacy', pp. 242–4, 255.

58 *Abstract of Returns of the Different Parishes in York made by a Committee of the Society of Friends, 27th January 1826.*

59 Laqueur, *Religion and Respectability*, p. 100.

60 *Education Census, 1851*, pp. cxlii–cliv. Cf. A. H. Robson, *The Education of Children Engaged in Industry, 1833–1876*, London, 1931, *passim*.

61 A. A. Fry, 'Report of the inspectors of factories on the effects of the educational provisions of the Factories' Act', *JSSL*, II, 1839, p. 174.

62 *Education Census, 1851*, p. ccviii. This does not include mechanics' and literary institutes.

63 National Society, *Statistics of Church of England Schools for the Poor in England and Wales for the Years 1866 and 1867*, 3rd edn., London, n.d., p. 19.

64 *Newcastle*, I, pp. 82, 388. Industrial ragged schools for children committed by the courts not included here.

65 Stephens (1973), p. 5; W. B. Stephens, 'An anatomy of illiteracy in mid-Victorian Devon', in J. Porter (ed.), *Education and Labour in the South West*, Exeter, 1975, *passim*.

66 E.g., Campbell, 'Occupation and literacy', pp. 22 ff.; Bradshaw, 'Occupation and literacy', p. 13; J. Grayson, 'Literacy, schooling and industrialization: Worcestershire, 1760–1850', in Stephens (1983), pp. 61–3; M. Sanderson, 'Literacy and social mobility in the Industrial Revolution in England', *Past and Present*, LVI, 1972, pp. 79 ff.; Williams, 'Education in Widnes', pp. 181–5; J. M. Gratton, 'Literacy, educational provision and social structure in the first half of the nineteenth century: the case of Liverpool's suburban periphery', M. Ed. thesis, University of Liverpool, 1982,

Chapter 5; R. S. Schofield, 'Dimensions of illiteracy, 1750–1850', *Explorations in Economic History*, X, 1973, pp. 450–1.

67 W. Clare (ed.), *A Young Irishman's Diary (1836–1847)*, 1928, p. 65.

68 Sanderson, 'Literacy and social mobility', pp. 79 ff.; D. Levine, 'Education and family life in early industrial England', *Jnl. Family History*, IV, 1979, p. 375; Mitch, 'Spread of literacy', pp. 369–85; Campbell, 'Occupation and literacy', pp. 30–6; Bradshaw, 'Occupation and literacy', pp. 15–9.

69 A. Everitt, 'The Banburys of England', *Urban History Year Book*, 1974.

70 Cf. B. I. Coleman, 'The incidence of education in mid-century', in Wrigley (ed.), *Nineteenth Century Society*, pp. 404–5.

71 Revd. Canon Trevor, 'Elementary schools in small town populations', *TNAPSS*, 1864, pp. 412–20.

72 PP 1887, XXX, p. 738.

73 *VCH, Yorks., City of York*, pp. 269 ff. The effect of the railway on York is, however, debatable: A. Armstrong, *Stability and Change in an English County Town*, Cambridge, 1974, pp. 37 ff.

74 R. Newton, *Victorian Exeter, 1837–1914*, Leicester, 1968, pp. 74 ff. Newton's interpretations of the figures for children at school in Exeter (pp. 103–4), however, are incorrect. He has taken 1 in 6.77 to mean that 6.77 per cent of Exeter's population were on the books of schools, and consequently Exeter had a smaller proportion at school than York, Birmingham, Leicester, Newcastle and Sunderland, when in fact the opposite was the case.

75 J. Murphy, *The Religious Problem in English Education: The Crucial Experiment*, Liverpool, 1959.

76 *CCE, 1844 (2)*, p. 272.

77 *Newcastle*, IV, p. 379. For want of schooling in Liverpool, however, see pp. 89, 99.

78 The census provides statistics of ages only in quinquennial groups.

79 For a full list of towns and statistics, see Stephens (1977), p. 39.

80 Stephens (1973), p. 9.

81 T. W. Laqueur, 'Debate: literacy and social mobility in the Industrial Revolution in England', *Past and Present*, LXIV, 1974, p. 102; and see pp. 62–3.

82 Quoted in Sanderson, 'Social change', pp. 141–2; A. Redford, *Labour Migration in England, 1800–1850*, Manchester, 1964 edn. (ed. and revised W. H. Chaloner), pp. 150 ff., map G; J. A. Banks, 'The contagion of numbers', in H. J. Dyos and M. Wolff (eds.) *The Victorian City: Images and Realities*, London, 1973, I, p. 118; and see pp. 86, 89, 90, 92.

83 Redford, *Labour Migration*, pp. vii–viii, 62, ff., 182–4.

84 Cf. E. H. Hunt, 'Labour productivity in English agriculture, 1850–1914', *Ec. H. R.*, 2nd ser. XX, 1967, p. 284.

85 PP 1868–9, XIII, (a), p. 37.

86 Cf. C. A. Anderson, 'Patterns and variability in distribution and diffusion of schooling', in C. A. Anderson and M. J. Bowman (eds.), *Education and Economic Development*, London, 1966, pp. 330–2.

87 For the backwardness of rural Norfolk, see D. Jones, 'Thomas Campbell Foster and the rural labourers; incendiarism in East Anglia in the 1840s', *Social History*, I, 1976.

88 Stephens, 'Anatomy', pp. 12–4.

89 W. B. Stephens, 'Literacy in maritime districts of England and Wales in the mid-nineteenth century', unpublished paper read at the Exeter Seminar on Maritime History, Dartington, 1984. Districts (including Welsh ones) are those identified by Welton (1860).

90 E.g., W. Couth, 'Development of the town of Gainsborough, 1750 to 1850', M. A. Thesis, University of Wales, 1975; S. Ville, 'Literacy in the merchant marine, 1788–1815', *Mariners' Mirror*, LXVIII, 1982, pp. 125–6; *CCE, 1853–4*, pp. 922–5.

91 Stephens (1977), pp. 46–7.

92 W. B. Stephens, 'Early Victorian Coventry: education in an industrial community, 1830–51', in A. E. Everitt (ed.) *Perspectives in English Urban History*, London, 1973, p. 170. Many young children were still employed in the Coventry ribbon trade in the 1860s.

93 E.g. J. A. Davies, *Education in a Welsh Rural County, 1870–1973*, Cardiff, 1973, p. 10; R. W. Unwin and W. B. Stephens (eds.), *Yorkshire Schools and Schooldays*, Leeds, 1976, p. 41; Sanderson, 'Social change', pp. 151–2; *CCE, 1847–8*, p. 30; Stephens (1973), p. 11.

94 Laqueur, *Religion and Respectability*, pp. 90, 100.

95 J. Bingham, *The Period of the Sheffield School Board, 1870–1903*, Sheffield, 1949, introd. p. 2; E. R. Wickham, *Church and People in an Industrial City*, London, 1957, p. 83; *Education Census, 1851*, pp. clxxxvi, clxxxix, cxci; *VCH, Warwicks.*, VII, p. 486.

96 Sargant, 'Elementary education', pp. 108–9; H. Fawcett, rep. in *Economist*, 13 October 1866, pp. 1192–3. Cf. Hill, *National Education*, I, p. 247.

97 W. B. Stephens, 'Schooling and literacy in rural England, 1800–1914', *History of Education Quarterly*, Spring 1982, pp. 73–82. Cf. R. K. Webb, 'Working class readers in early Victorian England', *EHR*, LXV, 1950, pp. 237–9.

98 *BFSS*, 1831, quoted Hill, *National Education*, I, p. 265.

99 PP 1837–8, VII, pp. 94–5; W. F. Hook, *On the Means of Rendering More Efficient the Educaton of the People — A Letter to the Lord Bishop of St. David's*, London, 1846.

100 Sanderson, 'Social change', pp. 147–51.

101 R. J. Smith, 'Education, society and literacy: Nottinghamshire in the mid-nineteenth century', *University of Birmingham Historical Jnl.*, XII, 1969, pp. 44, 49–53.

102 PP 1867–8, XVII, (a), p. 85.

103 *CCE, 1847–8(2)*, p. 182. Quotation cited E. S. Bellamy, 'Elementary education in the Staffordshire Potteries, 1780–1870', B. Phil. dissertation, University of Hull, 1974, p. 79 (without adequate reference). Cf. *VCH, Staffs.*, VIII, p. 257. See also p. 116.

104 See Chapter 5.

105 Stephens, 'Anatomy'; J.S. Hurt, *Elementary Schooling and the Working Classes, 1860–1918*, London, 1979, p. 39.

106 F. M. L. Thompson, *English Landed Society in the Nineteenth Century*, London, 1963, pp. 32, 114–7.

107 Quot. Hill, *National Education*, I. p. 269.

108 PP 1887, XXX, p. 738.

109 D. C. Coleman, 'Growth and Decay...in East Anglia', *Scandinavian Economic History Rev.*, X, 1962, pp. 117–27; A. Charlesworth (ed.), *An Atlas of Rural Protest in Britain, 1548–1900*, London, 1983, pp. 146–55, 158–63.

110 Cf. P. Horn, *The Victorian Country Child*, Kineton, 1974, pp. 71–93.

111 Stephens, 'Anatomy'; K. Shahidullah, 'Literacy in mid-nineteenth century Devon and Suffolk', M. A. thesis, University of British Columbia, 1979, pp. 40–1.

112 *CCE, 1839–40*, pp. 176–7.

113 A. R. Education Board for the Archdeaconry of Llandaff and Monmouth, 1852, pp. 5–6.

114 Thompson, *English Landed Society*, pp. 33, 114, 118.

115 See p. 57.

116 *Newcastle*, II, p. 147.

117 *Ibid.*, pp. 26–7.

118 PP 1868–9, XIII, (a), pp. 29, 71–2.

119 *Ibid.*, p. 150.

120 PP 1867–8, XVII, (b), p. 286.

121 PP 1868–9, XIII, (a), p. 23; Hurt, *Elementary Schooling*, p. 58.

122 *Newcastle*, II, pp. 151, 165; PP 1868–9, XIII, (a), p. 148.

123 PP 1868–9, XIII, (a), p. 527.

124 *Education Census, 1851,* p. xxxix.

125 Several works on the history of the Church in this period devote some attention to the Church and education. For the National Society, C.K.F. Brown, *The Church's Part in Education, 1833–1941,* London, 1942, and H. S. Burgess and P. A. Welsby, *A Short History of the National Society, 1811–1961,* London, 1961, are useful though brief.

126 Cf. R. A. Soloway, *Prelates and People: Ecclesiastical Social Thought in England, 1783–1852,* London, 1969, pp. 374–5; G. F. A. Best, 'The religious difficulties of national education in England, 1800–70', *Cambridge Historical Jnl.,* XII (2), p. 163.

127 Reports for these are among the National Society's collections.

128 Soloway, *Prelates and People,* pp. 387–8, 406.

129 W. Otter, *Reasons for Continuing the Education of the Poor at the Present Crisis,* Shrewsbury, 1820, pp. 5–8.

130 Cf. G. F. A. Best, *Temporal Pillars,* Cambridge, 1964, pp. 153ff.; O. J. Brose, *Church and Parliament: The Reshaping of the Church of England, 1828–1860,* London, 1959, pp. 181–93; Soloway, *Prelates and People,* pp. 388–9, 392–400, 407–8.

131 *Newcastle,* I, pp. 575–6; *29th A. R. Nat. Soc.,* 1840, pp. 37–40, 45; *39th A. R. Nat. Soc.,* 1850, p. 271; *Diocesan and Local Boards of Education formed during the Years 1838–9 in connection with the National Society,* 1839; *CCE, 1850–1,* pp. 216–7; *5th Report National Schools Society for Archdeaconry of Coventry,* 1818; *2nd Report Windsor and Eton Church Union Society,* 1839, App., p. 5. Cf. N. Ball, *Educating the People,* London, 1983, pp. 57–8.

132 Cf. Brose, *Church and Parliament,* pp. 193–4.

133 Burgess and Welsby, *National Society,* p. 18; *Newcastle,* I, p. 576; *29th A. R. Nat. Soc.,* 1840, App. II, pp. 27–37; *CCE, 1850–1,* pp. 216–7.

134 Soloway, *Prelates and People,* p. 419.

135 Brose, *Church and Parliament,* p. 198; Soloway, *Prelates and People,* pp. 408, 413–4. Cf. W. L. Mathieson, *English Church Reform, 1815–1840,* London, 1923, pp. 17–8.

136 Cf. G. K. Clark, *Churchmen and the Condition of England, 1832–1885,* London, 1973, pp. 125–6.

137 *Education Census, 1851,* p. cxxiii.

138 *Newcastle,* I, pp. 55, 80, 592.

139 Deduced from PP 1867–8, LIII.

140 The rather high proportion for Staffordshire includes infant school children in much larger numbers than in other counties.

141 Cf. also 1857 percentages at Church day and evening schools (App. M) with 1858 percentages at all public schools (App. J), for an indication of those counties where non-Anglican public schools were most important.

142 *Summaries of the Return to the General Inquiry made by the National Society . . .,* 1858, pp. iii–iv; W. E. Marsden, 'Diffusion and regional variation in elementary education in England and Wales, 1800–1870', *History of Education,* XI, 1982, pp. 183–7; M. Sanderson, 'The National and British societies in Lancashire, 1803–1839: the roots of Anglican supremacy in English education', in T. G. Cook (ed.), *Local Studies and the History of Education,* London, 1972.

143 Marsden, 'Diffusion', pp. 184–7.

144 See, e.g., *39th A. R. Nat. Soc.;* *Newcastle,* VI, p. 578.

145 Stephens (1973), pp. 14–5, 29, 33.

146 Marsden, 'Diffusion', p. 181; Sanderson, 'National and British Societies', *passim;* Stephens (1973), pp. 16–7. Cf. A. Everitt, 'Nonconformity in the English countryside', in Cook, *Local Studies;* D. Bowen, *The Idea of the Victorian Church,* Montreal, 1968, pp. 202–3.

147 Stephens (1973), p. 16.

148 Marsden, 'Diffusion', pp. 177–81.

149 Stephens (1973), pp. 13–20; Stephens, 'Elementary education', pp. 230–1.

150 Cf. Best, *Temporal Pillars*, pp. 409–10; Brown, *The Church's Part in Education*, pp. 37, 133; *Newcastle*, V, pp. 410–23.

151 M. Cruickshank, *Church and State in English Education: 1870 to the Present Day*, London, 1963, p. 17.

152 National Society, *Schools for the Poor in England and Wales for the Years 1866 and 1867*, n.d., pp. 34–5.

153 PP 1870, LIV. Cf. Hurt, *Elementary Schooling*, pp. 52–7.

154 There is a large literature: see F. M. L. Thompson, 'Social control in Victorian Britain', *Ec.H.R.*, 2nd ser., XXXIV, 1981, and works cited there.

155 Cf. T. W. Laqueur, 'Working-class demand and the growth of English elementary education, 1750–1850', in L. Stone (ed.), *Schooling and Society*, London, 1976.

156 Laqueur, *Religion and Respectability*, pp. 148–60.

157 The same sort of pattern existed in 1858: App. J.

158 Hurt, *Elementary Schooling*, pp. 46–51.

159 This is discussed by Mitch, 'Spread of literacy', Chapter 2.

160 Cf. T. W. Laqueur, 'The cultural origins of popular literacy', *Oxford Review of Education*, II (3), 1976.

161 See pp. 136–7, 180, 233.

162 PP 1863, XVIII, p. 146; *Newcastle*, II, p. 398. Cf. Mitch, 'Spread of literacy', pp. 32 ff., 59–60, 154–5.

163 *Education Census, 1851*, pp. xl–xli.

164 Cf. Stephens (1973), pp. 8–9.

165 For poverty as a cause of lack of schooling, see above p. 20.

166 See pp. 122–4, 138, 175–6, 222, 225–6.

167 *Education Census, 1851*, pp. xl–xli.

168 Cf. PP 1840, XXIV (Hickson), p. 45; *Newcastle*, II, pp. 203–4; Hurt, *Elementary Schooling*, p. 33; Mitch, 'Spread of literacy', pp. 33–5; and see pp. 32–3, 38, 59, 78, 142, 193, 244–5.

169 Sanderson, 'Social change'; Stephens (1973), pp. 7–8; R. M. Hartwell, *The Industrial Revolution and Economic Growth*, London, 1971, Chapter 11; Stephens (1977), pp. 31–4; Schofield, 'Dimensions'; Mitch, 'Spread of literacy', pp. 133–4; E. G. West, 'Literacy and the Industrial Revolution', *Ec.H.R.* 2nd ser. XXXI, 1978.

170 Sanderson, 'Literacy and social mobility', pp. 102–3; T. W. Laqueur, 'Debate', and M. Sanderson, 'Rejoinder', *Past and Present*, LXIV, 1974.

171 See, e.g., R. K. Webb, *The British Working Class Reader, 1780–1848*, London, 1955; R. D. Altick, *The English Common Reader: A Social History of the Mass Reading Public, 1800–1900*, Chicago, 1957.

172 Laqueur, 'Debate', p. 104.

173 West, *Education and the Industrial Revolution*, pp. 107–8, 110; G. Sutherland, *Elementary Education in the Nineteenth Century*, London, 1971, p. 19; *Newcastle*, I, pp. 84, 654. Cf. Pallister, 'Determinants of elementary education', p. 386.

174 See pp. 58, 89, 153–4, 200, 258.

175 See pp. 79, 92, 125, 176–8, 226–9; Hurt, *Elementary Schooling*, Chapters II, III. The need for compulsion does not necessarily support the view that board schools were needed: E. G. West, *Education and the State*, London, 1965, pp. 12–3.

176 Information from the official censuses and the reports of the Registrar General of Births, Deaths and Marriages, are for 'registration' counties; other evidence is often for 'administrative' counties. The differences are not so great as to require adjustments in the conclusions arrived at.

177 Some changes in district boundaries occurred over the period, especially in Lancashire and Yorkshire, but they are not so extensive as to create any great difficulties for this investigation.

178 I have to some extent been influenced by the regions adopted by E. H. Hunt in his *Regional Wage Variations in Britain, 1850–1914*, Oxford, 1973.

3 A survey of northern and eastern England (pp. 54–100)

1 The registration county of Rutland embraced some Lincolnshire parishes, but no attempt has been made to adjust findings to take that into account.

2 L. Stone, 'Literacy and education in England, 1640–1900', *Past and Present*, XLII, 1969, pp. 123–4; W. E. Marsden, 'Diffusion and regional variation in elementary education in England and Wales, 1800–1870', *History of Education*, XI, 1982, pp. 188–90; A. E. Dobbs, *Education and Social Movements, 1700–1850*, London, 1919, pp. 52–3; PP 1887, XXX, pp. 737–8; R. A. Houston, *Scottish Literacy and the Scottish Identity: Illiteracy and Society in Scotland and Northern England, 1600–1800*, Cambridge, 1985, pp. 146–7.

3 D. J. Rowe, 'The economy of the north east in the nineteenth century: a survey', *NH*, VI, 1971; A. E. Smailes, 'Population changes in the colliery districts of Northumberland and Durham', *Geographical Jnl.*, XCI, 1938. See also App. A.

4 Cf. App. L. This is supported by the rather low proportion at public schools in 1833: App. J.

5 See, e.g., PP 1842, XVI, pp. 144, 151, 302, 529; *Newcastle*, II, pp. 321 ff.; *Reps. Mining Districts, passim; CCE, passim*; R. K. Webb, 'Working class readers in early Victorian England', *EHR*, LXV, 1950, p. 340.

6 PP 1842, XVI, pp. 151, 529–30, 535, 729; *Reps. Mining Districts, passim; Newcastle*, II, pp. 347–50.

7 PP 1846, XXIV, p. 26; PP 1850, XXIII, pp. 55–6; *CCE, 1853–4*, p. 912.

8 R. Pallister, 'Educational investment by industrialists in the early part of the nineteenth century in County Durham', *Durham University Jnl.*, NS XXX, 1968, pp. 36–7; PP 1851, XXIII, pp. 25–7; PP 1842, XVI, p. 686; PP 1842, XVII, pp. 749–50; *CCE, 1840–1*, p. 149.

9 *Newcastle*, II, pp. 344 ff.; PP 1847, XVI, pp. 7–8; PP 1843, XV, pp. 710–11; R. Colls, '"Oh Happy English Children": coal, class and education in the north-east', *Past and Present*, LXXIII, 1976, pp. 92–5; R. Moore, *Pit-Men, Preachers and Politics*, Cambridge, 1974, pp. 79–80.

10 E.g., PP 1842, XVI, p. 531; PP 1846, XXIV, pp. 13–20; PP 1850, XXIII, pp. 43–6, 49–51; *Newcastle*, II, p. 344.

11 *Reps. Mining Districts, passim; CCE, passim*.

12 J. Benson, 'The motives of 19th-century colliery owners in promoting day schools', *JEAH*, III, 1970, p. 16.

13 Pallister, 'Educational investment', p. 33; PP 1842, XVI, p. 711.

14 Benson, '19th-century colliery owners', pp. 15–7; S. Pollard, 'The factory village in the industrial revolution', *EHR*, LXXIX, 1964, pp. 527–8.

15 Cf. *Newcastle*, II, pp. 344–5.

16 PP 1852–3, XL. p. 9.

17 E.g., PP 1846, XXIV, pp. 13, 27; PP 1847, XVI, pp. 7–8; PP 1849, XXII, p. 4; PP 1850, XXIII, pp. 50–1; PP 1842, XVI, p. 710.

18 *CCE, 1840–1*, pp. 125–52; *CCE, 1853–4*, pp. 926–8; *CCE, 1867–8*, p. 178; PP 1842, XVI, pp. 144, 534, 726; PP 1850, XXIII, pp. 49–50; PP 1851, XXIII, p. 29; 'Education in the mining districts of Durham and Northumberland', *TNAPSS*, 1870, pp. 345–6.

19 Cf. Stone, 'Literacy', p. 123; and above p. 54.

20 PP 1868–9, XIII, (a), pp. 148–50. Cf. PP. 1867–8, XVII, (a), p. 60.

21 Quot. F. Hill, *National Education: Its Present State and Future Prospects*, I, London, 1836, p. 246. Cf. J. D. Marshall, 'Some aspects of the social history of 19th century Cumbria: migration and literacy', *Trans. Cumberland and Westmorland Antiquarian and Archaeological Society*, NS LXVI, 1969.

22 CCE, 1868–9, p. 343. Cf. Marsden, 'Diffusion', pp. 187–90.

23 PP 1867–8, XVII, (a), pp. 62–3. Cf. PP 1868–9, XIII, (a), p. lxv.

24 Quot. Marsden, 'Diffusion', p. 189.

25 PP 1868–9, XIII, (a), pp. xiv. 148; Newcastle, II, p. 354. Cf. CCE, 1866–7, p. 145.

26 Newcastle, II, pp. 323–4; Marsden, 'Diffusion', pp. 192–3.

27 B. A. King, 'Literacy and schooling in Cumberland and Westmorland, c.1841–c.1885', M. Ed. research exercise, University of Leeds, 1980, (LME), pp. 83 ff.

28 See, e.g., PP 1867–8, XXVIII, pt. vii., pp. 265 ff.; pt. viii, pp. 901–9.

29 PP 1868–9, XIII, (a), p. 148.

30 Ibid., pp. 148–50.

31 CCE, 1851–2, p. 788; CCE, 1856–7, pp. 477, 480.

32 CCE, 1863–4, pp. 98, 100, 110. Cf. CCE, 1851–2, p. 792; County of Rutland Society for Promoting the Education of the Poor, 1838 (Report), n.d., p. 4.

33 See p. 47.

34 PP 1867–8, XVII, (a), pp. 61–2; PP 1868–9, XIII, (a), p. lxv.

35 'Report of a committee of the Manchester Statistical Society on the state of education in the county of Rutland in the year 1838', JSSL, II, 1839, pp. 303–6; G. Young, 'Educational development in a rural society: a study of the control and provision of schooling in Rutland in the nineteenth century', M. Ed. thesis, University of Leicester, 1980, pp. 39–40.

36 Rep. Rutland Deanery Board of Education for 1851, n.d., p. 8.

37 Cf. CCE, 1862–3, pp. 31–4.

38 Newcastle, II, p. 147.

39 E.g., CCE, 1866–7, pp. 59–61.

40 J. Obelkevich, Religion and Rural Society: South Lindsey, 1825–1875, Oxford, 1976, pp. 79–80; W. Wright, 'On the improvements in the farming of Yorkshire', JRAS, XXII, 1861, p. 127.

41 PP 1867–8, XVII, (a), p. 84.

42 CCE, 1850–1, pp. 459–60.

43 Cf. PP 1867–8, XVII, (a), pp. 84–5; CCE, 1864–5, p. 139.

44 Obelkevich, Religion and Rural Society, pp. 53–4; CCE, 1862–3, pp. 31–4; CCE, 1865–6, p. 190; CCE, 1867–8, pp. 230, 273; PP 1867–8, XVII, (a), pp. 84–6; Newcastle, V. pp. 9, 13; D. Macrae, 'The improvements of waste lands', JRAS, NS V, 1969, p. 91.

45 T. H. Bamford, The Evolution of Rural Education: Three Studies of the East Riding of Yorkshire, Hull, 1965, pp. 7–13, 80; CCE, 1864–5, pp. 127–9; P. M. Crossley, 'Educational provision and literacy in the East Riding of Yorkshire, 1818–1870', M. Ed. research exercise, University of Leeds, 1983, (LME), p. 33. Cf. W. P. Baker, Parish Registers and Illiteracy in East Yorkshire, York, 1961, pp. 15–22.

46 See also Tables 2·2, 2·3 pp. 31, 33.

47 App. K, 'on census day'.

48 Grimsby had no inspected schools in 1850: CCE, 1850–1, p. 459.

49 E.g., CCE, 1864–5, pp. 130–2; CCE, 1866–7, p. 66; Young, 'Educational development', pp. 3, 24, 95, 117.

50 VCH, Yorks. City of York, p. 288; F. Hill, Victorian Lincoln, Cambridge, 1974, pp. 142–6, 273.

51 Newcastle, III, pp. 229–30.

52 W. Cargill, 'Educational, criminal, and social statistics of Newcastle-upon-Tyne', JSSL, I, 1838, pp. 355–9.

53 CCE, 1853–4, pp. 909, 919–22; F. W. D. Manders, A History of Gateshead, Gateshead, 1973, p. 197; 41st A. R. of the Society for the Encouragement of Parochial Schools in the Diocese of Durham, 1852, 1853, p. 7; 43rd A. R., ibid., 1854, 1855, pp. 6–7. Cf. App. K.

54 R. P. Hastings, More Essays in North Riding History, [Northallerton], 1984, p. 91, Cf.

A. Briggs, *Victorian Cities*, Harmondsworth, 1968 edn., p. 245–8.

55 *CCE*, *1864–5*, p. 127; *CCE*, *1866–7*, p. 63; *26th A. R. Wesleyan Education Committee*, 1865, pp. 58–9.

56 E.g., *43rd A. R. of the Society for the Encouragement of Parochial Schools ... Durham, 1854*, 1856, p. 6.

57 Cf. M. G. Mason, 'The history of elementary education on Tyneside before 1870', *Durham Research Rev.*, I, 1950–4, pp. 22–6; *CCE*, *1866–7*, pp. 63–4.

58 PP 1863, XVIII, p. 81.

59 Cargill, 'Educational statistics', p. 358; *Newcastle*, III, pp. 235–6; PP 1863, XVIII, p. 82; *CCE*, *1866–7*, p. 63.

60 About 10 percentage points more children were 'on the books' than attended on census day.

61 Cargill, 'Educational statistics', p. 360; *CCE*, *1866–7*, p. 61.

62 *CCE*, *1853–4*, p. 920.

63 E. H. Hunt, *Regional Wage Variations in Britain, 1850–1914*, Oxford, 1973, pp. 62–3. See also *CCE*, *1865–6*, p. 184; A. Rogers, *History of Lincolnshire*, Henley-on-Thames, 1970, p. 68; J. A. Clarke, 'Farming in Lincolnshire', *JRAS*, XII, 1851, p. 160.

64 PP 1867–8, XVII, (a), pp. 73, 80–2; *Newcastle*, V, p. 10; T. W. Beastall, *The Agricultural Revolution in Lincolnshire*, Lincoln, 1978; B. Metcalfe, 'Aspects of illiteracy in England in the period 1840–1880, with special reference to Lincolnshire', M. Ed. thesis, University of Leeds, 1983, pp. 109, 114–20, 124–8.

65 PP 1867–8, XVII, (a), p, 73.

66 *Newcastle*, II, p. 328; PP 1868–9, XIII, (a), pp. xii–xiii, 136.

67 PP 1867–8, XVII, (a), p. 74; PP 1868–9, XIII, (a), p. xi.

68 E.g., *Newcastle*, III, p. 235.

69 PP 1842, XVI, pp. 123, 299–300, 523, 724–5; PP 1846, XXIV, p. 457; PP 1847, XVI, p. 4; *TNAPSS*, 1870, p. 377.

70 E.g., PP 1842, XVI pp. 686–7; PP 1843, XIII, *passim*; PP 1843, XV, pp. 15, 66, 77, 139–41, 146; PP 1863, XVIII, p. 81; PP 1865, XX, pp.207–8, 214–17, 238–42, 244–9, 261–4.

71 *CCE*, *1840–1*, p. 126; *CCE*, *1850–1*, p. 259; *CCE*, *1853–4*, p. 921;*CCE*, *1857–8*, pp. 473–6, 483; PP 1868–9, XIII, (a), p. ix.

72 *Newcastle*, II, p. 328.

73 *CCE*, *1850–1*, p. 259; *CCE*, *1857–8*, pp. 473–6, 483.

74 *CCE*, *1864–5*, p. 126. Cf. *VCH*, *Yorks. East Riding*, I, p. 352; *CCE*, *1850–1*, p. 266.

75 E.g., *CCE*, *1864–5*, pp. 130–3; *Newcastle*, III, pp. 223–4, 229–30; *65th BFSS*, 1870, pp. 71–2.

76 PP 1851, XXIII, p. 29.

77 E.g., PP 1842, XVI, p. 532; PP 1851, XXIII, pp. 29–30; *CCE*, *1864–5*, pp. 132–3; *CCE*, *1866–7*, p. 59; PP 1867–8, XVII, (a), pp. 63–4, (b), p. 382. See also C. B. Freeman, *Mary Simpson of Boynton Vicarage*, York, 1972; Crossley, 'Educational provision', pp. 26–31.

78 E.g., PP 1842, XVI, pp. 532–3, 687, 709; Cargill, 'Educational statistics', p. 356; *Newcastle*, II, p. 338, III, pp. 223–4; *29th A. R. National Society*, 1840, p. 146; *CCE*, *1840–1*, pp. 144–8; Mason, 'Education on Tyneside', p. 26.

79 London figures excluded.

80 Metcalfe, 'Aspects of illiteracy', pp. 243–51, 285–6.

81 Some of these had unusually large numbers of Presbyterians: King, 'Literacy in Cumberland and Westmorland', pp. 114–15.

82 Welton (1860), pp. 50–1.

83 King, 'Literacy in Cumberland and Westmorland', p. 20.

84 *CCE*, *1840–1*, p. 150; *Newcastle*, II, pp. 323, 333. Cf. PP 1842, XVII, pp. 722–3.

85 R. Wood, *West Hartlepool: The Rise and Fall of a Victorian New Town*, West Hartlepool,

1967, pp. 113–15; *VCH, Durham*, II, pp. 307–8.

86 *Censuses, 1861, 1871*.

87 *CCE, 1864–5*, p. 127; *CCE, 1866–7*, p. 65.

88 J. D. Marshall and C. A. Dyehouse, 'Social transition in Kendal and Westmorland, *c.* 1760–1860', *NH*, XII, 1976, pp. 128, 136, 153–4.

89 D. J. Rowe, 'Occupations in Northumberland and Durham, 1851–1911', *NH*, VIII, 1973, p. 127. Cf. B. Harrison and P. Hollis (eds.), *Robert Lowery, Radical and Chartist*, London, 1979, p. 82; *VCH, Yorks. East Riding*, I, pp. 412 ff.

90 E. Riding, −0·13; Lincolnshire, −0·15; Cumberland, +0·17; Westmorland, +0·04 (3 readings only). Rutland had only two districts.

91 E.g., *CCE, 1854–5*, p. 25; *CCE, 1867–8*, pp. 179–80; PP 1846, XXIV, p. 27; PP 1854, XIX, p. 42; *TNAPSS*, 1870, p. 346.

92 App. A.

93 Cf. App. H, paupers relieved.

94 A. Digby 'The labour market and the continuity of social policy after 1834: the case of the eastern counties', *Ec. H. R.*, 2nd series XXVIII, 1975, pp. 78–80; W. Ashworth, *An Economic History of England, 1870–1939*, London, 1960, p. 63; J. Thirsk and J. Imray (eds.), *Suffolk Farming in the Nineteenth Century*, Suffolk Records Society Publications, I, 1958, pp. 31–4.

95 *VCH, Essex*, II, pp. 313, 325–9, 403, 484–5; *VCH, Suffolk*, III, pp. 253, 276–7; D. C. Coleman, 'Growth and decay during the Industrial Revolution: the case of East Anglia', *Scandinavian Economic History Rev.*, X, 1962; PP 1840, XXIII, pp. 285–301, 329–34; N. Evans, *The East Anglian Linen Industry: Rural Industry and Local Economy, 1500–1850*, Aldershot, 1985, pp. 152–68.

96 G. E. Fussell, '"High Farming" in the east midlands and East Anglia, 1840–1880', *Economic Geography*, XXVII, 1951, pp. 85–8.

97 PP 1840, XXIII, pp. 301–50; J. K. Edwards, 'The decline of Norwich textiles industry', *Yorkshire Bulletin of Economic and Social Research*, XVI, 1964; *CCE, 1840–1*, pp. 426–8, 438; *White's History, Gazetteer and Directory of Suffolk*, 1844, pp. 49–50, 497, 499–500, 505; *White's History, Gazetteer and Directory of Norfolk*, 1846, pp. 232–5; *VCH, Suffolk*, III, p. 252; H. Rainbird, 'On the farming of Suffolk', *JARS*, VIII, 1847, p. 266.

98 *VCH, Essex*, V, pp. 10–16; R. Baker, 'On the farming of Essex', *JARS*, V, 1845, pp. 1, 39.

99 *VCH, Middlesex*, I, p. 97.

100 F. W. Jessup, *A History of Kent*, London, 1958, p. 172.

101 J. Caird, *English Agriculture in 1850–1*, London, 1852, pp. 94, 128, 130.

102 *VCH, Kent*, III, pp. 420–4; D. Harvey, 'Fruit growing in Kent in the nineteenth century', *Archaeologia Cantiana*, LXXIX, 1964, pp. 96–7; G. Buckland, 'On the farming of Kent', *JRAS*, VI, 1845, pp. 267, 273; H. Evershed, 'On the farming of Surrey', *JRAS*, XIV, 1853, pp. 400, 403, 405; J. C. Clutterbuck, 'The farming of Middlesex', *JRAS*, 2nd series V, 1869, pp. 9–10, 14, 18.

103 J. R. McCulloch, *A Descriptive and Statistical Account of the British Empire*, London, 1847 edn., I, pp. 196–200.

104 J. Wilkinson, 'The farming of Hampshire', *JRAS*, XXII, 1861, pp. 268–70, 272; Hunt, *Regional Wage Variations*, pp. 10, 52–3; Ashworth, *Economic History*, p. 63.

105 *VCH, Hampshire*, V, pp. 423–4. Cf. App. H, paupers relieved.

106 Wilkinson, 'Farming of Hampshire', p. 258; Evershed, 'Farming of Surrey', pp. 410, 412; Caird, *English Agriculture*, pp. 88–9, 95, 124, 126.

107 Even if children not 'on school books' rather than not 'in attendance' on census day is taken, the same wide differences remain.

108 Cf. *Report of the Western Division of the Sussex Society for the Education of the Infant Poor*, 1822, p. 4.

109 Use of data for Middlesex, Surrey and Kent is complicated by the fact that some sources do

282 NOTES

not distinguish the extra-metropolitan parts from the metropolitan.

110 Some fifty British schools functioned in Hampshire 1810–70: B. V. Spence, 'The development of elementary education in Hampshire, 1800–1870', M. Ed. thesis, University of Durham, 1973, pp. 27–8.

111 But day pupils at public schools as a proportion of all day scholars were below the national average in Kent, Norfolk, Suffolk, Sussex.

112 For Kent the 1851 extra-metropolitan population was much larger than that of its London districts.

113 *CCE, 1861–2*, pp. 17–8; *CCE, 1867–8*, pp. 245, 249–50.

114 *CCE, 1856–7*, p. 383; *CCE, 1858–9*, p. 88; *CCE, 1862–3*, p. 7; *CCE, 1870–1*, pp. 82–3.

115 *CCE, 1848–9*, pp. 4–5, 7–8. Cf. *Report on the State of Education in the Rural Deanery of Godstone*, 1840, p. 8.

116 'Results of an enquiry into the conditions of the working classes in five parishes in the county of Norfolk', *Central Society of Education, Third Publication*, London, 1839; *CCE, 1840–1*, pp. 449–59; *4th A. R. of the Lynn and and Marshland National Schools Society*, 1842, p. 1.

117 *CCE, 1844 (2)*, p. 154; *1st Report of the Essex Branch of the London Diocesan Board of Education*, 1841, p. 7.

118 *CCE, 1857–8*, p. 342. Cf. *CCE, 1851–2*, p. 398.

119 *CCE, 1867–8*, p. 188.

120 *Census, 1851*.

121 *CCE, 1854–5*, p. 466.

122 *CCE, 1863–4*, pp. 92–5.

123 *CCE, 1850–1*, pp. 392–3; *CCE, 1855–6*, p. 393; Thirsk and Imray (eds.), *Suffolk Farming*, p 32.

124 *CCE, 1846 (1)*, p. 280

125 E.g. *21st A. R. of the County of Essex Society for the Education of the Infant Poor*, 1833, p. 5; *6th A. R. of the Diocesan Society of the Archdeaconry of Suffolk for Promoting Education, 1845*, 1846, pp. 1–2, 9–10; *10th A. R. ibid., 1849–50*, 1851, pp. 9–10; *35th A. R. of the Norwich Diocesan Society for the Education of the Poor*, 1847, p. 10.

126 *CCE, 1844 (2)*, p. 156; *CCE, 1863–4*, pp. 94–5; *CCE, 1866–7*, p. 87; *CCE, 1867–8*, p. 19; *CCE, 1872–3*, p. 178.

127 Cf. PP 1867–8, XVII, (a), p. 19.

128 *CCE, 1844 (2)*, p. 156; *CCE, 1850–1*, p. 393.

129 *CCE, 1840–1*, p. 460; *CCE, 1850–1*, pp. 390–3, 402–3; *CCE, 1855–6*, 393; *CCE, 1857–8*, pp. 343–2; *CCE, 1864–5*, pp. 111–12; *CCE, 1865–6*, pp. 142–3; *CCE, 1867–8*, pp. 30, 190.

130 *CCE, 1870–1*, p. 90.

131 *CCE, 1868–9*, p. 82.

132 *CCE, 1844 (2)*, p. 161; *CCE, 1845 (1)*, pp. 157–8. Cf. PP 1867–8, XVII, (a), pp. 24–5.

133 *CCE, 1856–7*, p. 340–1; *CCE, 1872–3*, p. 178.

134 *CCE, 1850–1*, pp. 392, 395; *CCE, 1863–4*, p. 95; *CCE, 1865–6*, p. 146; *CCE, 1867–8*, p. 190; PP 1867–8, XVII, (a), pp. 11–2.

135 *CCE, 1844 (2)*, pp. 154–5; *CCE, 1866–7*, p. 84; *CCE, 1867–8*, p. 19; *VCH, Suffolk*, II, pp. 253–4; *VCH, Essex*, II, pp. 375–9; PP 1867–8, XVII, (a), p. 34; and see p. 176.

136 E.g., E. Melling, *Kentish Sources IV: The Poor*, Maidstone, 1964, pp. 148, 186–7.

137 E.g., *7th A. R. of the Canterbury Diocesan Board of Education*, 1846; *27th Report of the Hampshire Society for the Education of the Poor*, 1837, p. 9.

138 'State of the peasantry in the county of Kent', *Central Society of Education, Third Publication*, London, 1839, pp. 109, 118–19, 122–3. Cf. *3rd A. R. of the Canterbury Diocesan Board of Education*, 1842, p. 9; and see p. 41.

139 *Canterbury Diocesan Board of Education, General Report on Parochial Schools*, 1858.

140 PP 1868–9, XIII, (a), pp. 7, 15; *CCE, 1857–8*, p. 466; *CCE, 1863–4*, p. 112; P. Horn, *Education in Rural England, 1800–1914*, Dublin, 1978, p. 138; Spence, 'Education in Hampshire', p. 133.

141 *CCE, 1847–8 (2)*, p. 272.

142 *CCE, 1855–6*, p. 510; *CCE, 1870–1*, p. 65; PP 1861, XLVIII, p. 13.

143 *CCE, 1848–9*, p. 20; *CCE, 1855–6*, p. 459; *CCE, 1857–8*, p. 463; *CCE, 1858–9*, p. 58; *CCE, 1862–3*, p. 75; *2nd Report of the Winchester Diocesan Board of Education*, 1842, p. 17.

144 *CCE, 1855–6*, pp. 384–5; *CCE, 1856–7*, p. 383.

145 *CCE, 1863–4*, p. 160.

146 *CCE, 1863–4*, p. 113; *CCE, 1864–5*, p. 106; PP 1868–9, XIII, (a), p. 7.

147 *CCE, 1867–8*, p. 263.

148 *CCE, 1872–3*, pp, 200–1.

149 *CCE, 1863–4*, p. 115.

150 *CCE*. *1842 (2)*, pp. 86–7.

151 *Report of the Western Division of the Sussex Society for the Education of the Infant Poor*, 1831, pp. 5–6; *CCE, 1864–5*, p. 106; *CCE, 1870–1*, p. 101.

152 *CCE, 1850–1*, p. 521; *CCE, 1855–6*, p. 459; *DNB*, Sumner; Horn, *Education in Rural England*, pp. 232, 328. The example of the extraordinary King's Somborne school was said to be influential in Hampshire; the inspectors' reports were enthusiastic. See also, W. A. C. Stewart and W. P. McCann, *The Educational Innovators, 1750–1850*, London, 1967; D. Layton, *Science for the People*, London, 1973; R. Dawes, *Hints on an Improved and Self-supporting System of National Education*, London, 1847.

153 E.g., *23rd Report of the Hampshire Society for the Education of the Infant Poor*, 1833, 1834, p. 8; *28th Report, ibid.*, 1838, pp 7–8.

154 *33rd Report of the Hampshire Society*, 1843, p. 1; *3rd Report of the Winchester Diocesan Board of Education*, 1843, 1844, p. 5; *5th Report, ibid.*, 1845, 1846, p. 6; *6th Report, ibid.*, 1846, 1847, p. 5; *7th Report, ibid.*, 1847, 1848, pp. 1, 16; *12th Report, ibid.*, 1853, 1854, p. 7; Spence, 'Education in Hampshire', pp. 15–7, 56–7.

155 *CCE, 1870–1*, pp. 61, 65.

156 See Table 2·2, p. 31 (includes only towns for which data is provided in the *Census*).

157 Cf. Table 2·3, p. 33.

158 Cf. Table 2·2, p. 31.

159 Spence, 'Education in Hampshire', pp. 152–3. Cf. *1st Report of the Winchester Diocesan Board of Education*, 1840.

160 As far as represented in App. K.

161 Cf. A. T. Patterson, *A History of Southampton, 1700–1914*, II, Southampton, 1971, pp. 108–9, 131–2, 152ff.; *CCE, 1855–6*, p. 459; G. Meason, *Official Illustrated Guide to the South-Eastern Railway*, 1858, pp. 75–8.

162 *CCE, 1863–4*, pp. 158–9.

163 E. W. Gilbert, *Brighton: Old Ocean's Bauble*, London, 1954, pp. 197–8.

164 *55th BFSS*, 1860, p. 57.

165 *CCE, 1863–4*, p. 112; J. Stanford and A. T. Patterson, 'The condition of the children of the poor in mid-Victorian Portsmouth', *Portsmouth Papers*, XXI, 1974, pp. 12–13.

166 E.g., J. M. Russell, *The History of Maidstone*, Rochester, 1881, p. 322.

167 *4th A. R. of the Lynn and Marshland National Schools Society*, 1842, p. 1.

168 PP 1840, XXIII, pp. 321–4, 327; *CCE, 1840–1*, pp. 425–9, 438–42.

169 PP 1863, XVIII, pp. 77–80.

170 *CCE, 1845 (1)*, p. 167.

171 *CCE, 1844 (2)*, pp. 153–4; *CCE, 1851–2*, pp. 396, 398, 600–1.

172 J. Glyde, *The Moral, Social and Religious Condition of Ipswich in the Middle of the*

Nineteenth Century, Ipswich, 1850, pp. 159–65.

173 *CCE, 1850–1*, p. 396; *CCE, 1852–3*, pp. 621–2; *CCE, 1855–6*, pp. 391–2; *CCE, 1863–4*, p. 93; *CCE, 1864–5*, pp. 116–17; *CCE, 1865–6*, p. 141; *CCE, 1866–7*, pp. 84–5; *Newcastle*, III, pp. 215–21, 231–47; H. J. Hillen, *History of the Borough of King's Lynn*, II, Norwich, 1907, p. 642; *General Report of the Diocesan Society of the Archdeaconry of Suffolk for Promoting Education, 1849–50*, 1851, p.9.

174 *CCE, 1867–8*, pp. 189–90.

175 References here to Kent, Middlesex and Surrey are to the extra-metropolitan parts of those counties.

176 Cf. Table 2·4, p. 35 (Bury St. Edmunds, King's Lynn, Ipswich, Yarmouth).

177 Risbridge, Sudbury, Cosford, Bosmere, Halstead, Dunmow, Lexden, Saffron Walden.

178 Cf. Table 2·4, p. 35.

179 East Grinstead, Uckfield, Ticehurst, Godstone; Hambledon, Midhurst, Petworth, Thakeham.

180 For comment on this exercise, see above, p. 68.

181 *VCH, Essex*, II, pp. 375–9.

182 *Religious Census, 1851*, p. 12.

183 Richmond, Kingston, Croydon, Epsom.

184 Hendon, Edmonton, Brentford, with Barnet (in Middlesex registration county).

185 Fell in rank by 1871, probably consequent on the advent of military establishments.

186 Experienced rise in mark percentages, 1866–71, perhaps with influx of railway navvies in this period.

187 Cf. Table 2·4, p. 35 (Southampton, Portsmouth). Ipswich and King's Lynn districts were also in the least illiterate group in 1856 but not in 1866, nor 1871.

188 See above.

189 Cf. *CCE, 1863–4*, pp. 159–60.

190 Cf. App. I.

191 Cf. *CCE, 1863–4*, pp. 116–8; PP 1867–8, XVII, (a), p. 10; PP 1868–9, XIII, (a), p. 7.

192 PP 1867–8, XVII, (a), p. 33; Spence, 'Education in Hampshire', pp. 52–3.

193 Laqueur, *Religion and Respectability*, pp. 49–52.

194 Cf. *Newcastle*, III, p. 224.

195 W. Palin, 'The farming of Cheshire', *JRAS*, V, 1845, pp. 58, 87; W. J. Garnett, 'The farming of Lancashire', *JRAS*, X, 1849, pp. 1, 5–6, 16–20, 23, 35–6, 49; J. Charnock, 'On the farming of the West Riding of Yorkshire', *JRAS*, IX, 1848, pp. 289, 293–4, 301, 311; PP 1868–9, XIII, pp. 226–7; C. S. Davies, *The Agricultural History of Cheshire, 1750–1850*, Chetham Society, 3rd ser. X, 1960, pp. ix, 13 ff., 91.

196 D. Sylvester, *A History of Cheshire*, Henley-on-Thames, 1971, p. 49; Davies, *Agricultural History of Cheshire*, p. 77.

197 Hunt, *Regional Wage Variations*, pp. 37–8, 115–16, 164–6.

198 R. A. Soloway, *Prelates and People: Ecclesiastical Social Thought in England, 1783–1852*, London, 1969, pp. 412, 415.

199 PP 1863, XVIII, pp. 160 ff.; PP 1852–3, XL, pp. 10–13; *CCE, 1844 (2)*, pp. 279–80; W. B. Stephens, *Adult Education and Society in an Industrial Town: Warrington, 1800–1900*, Exeter, 1980, pp. 9–10.

200 Children aged 8–11 had hours restricted in silk mills, 1844.

201 Charnock, 'Farming of the West Riding', p. 311; PP 1843, XII, pp. 309, 345; PP 1843, XV, pp. 57–8; PP 1868–9, XIII, (b), pp. 559–60; *CCE, 1844 (2)*, p. 280; *CCE, 1848–50*, p. 206; *CCE, 1850–1*, pp. 297, 322; *CCE, 1853–4*, p. 512; H. C. Cottam, 'Literacy in the Doncaster poor law union, 1801 to 1860', M. Ed. research exercise, University of Leeds, 1984, (LME), pp. 19–51; M. Sanderson, 'Social change and elementary education in industrial Lancashire, 1780–1840', *NH*,

III, 1968, pp. 131–5.

202 See pp. 111, 169.

203 The 29,000 children in textile factories in 1838 had grown to 80,000 in 1868: A. H. Robson, *The Education of Children Engaged in Industry in England, 1833–1876*, London, 1931, p. 82.

204 PP 1870, LIV, p. 164.

205 Census schedules: S. Wilson, 'The regional study of elementary education and literacy in the 19th century, with two case studies', M. Ed. research exercise, University of Leeds, 1979, (LME), p. 29.

206 *CCE, 1840–1*, p. 177; *CCE, 1847–8*, p. 31; *Newcastle*, II, pp. 180, 188, V, p. 183; *35th BFSS*, 1840, p. 59; PP 1852 XI, pp. 468–71.

207 E.g. *CCE, 1871–2*, pp. 78–9.

208 Sanderson, 'Social change'; Stephens (1973); W. B. Stephens, 'Elementary education and literacy, 1770–1870', in D. Fraser (ed.), *A History of Modern Leeds*, Manchester, 1980.

209 Cf. M. Sanderson, 'The National and British school societies in Lancashire 1803–1830: the roots of Anglican supremacy in English education', in T. G. Cook (ed.), *Local Studies and the History of Education*, London, 1972, pp. 12–13, 18.

210 *CCE, 1851–2*, p. 462.

211 *CCE, 1854–5*, p. 429; *CCE, 1865–6*, p. 128. Cf. *CCE, 1845 (2)*, p. 177.

212 *21st A. R. Wesleyan Education Committee*, 1860, p. 54.

213 PP 1870, LIV, pp. 78–9, 149–50, 167–8, 174; J. S. Hurt, *Elementary Schooling and the Working Classes, 1860–1918*, London, 1979, pp. 54–6.

214 *CCE, 1840–1*, pp. 160–2; *CCE, 1844 (2)*, pp. 271–2; *CCE, 1845 (2)*, p. 173; *CCE, 1846 (1)*, p. 457; *CCE 1846 (2)*, pp. 27, 30; *CCE, 1848–50*, p. 135; *CCE, 1850–1*, p. 274; *CCE, 1853–4*, pp. 518–19; *CCE, 1854–5*, p. 428; *CCE, 1855–6*, p. 358; *CCE, 1856–7*, p. 290; *CCE, 1858–9*, pp. 52–3, 90; *CCE, 1859–60*, pp. 41–2; *CCE, 1860–1*, pp. 54–5; *CCE, 1861–2*, p. 65; *CCE, 1871–2*, p. 79; PP 1852, XI, pp. 40, 376–7; *Newcastle*, II, p. 235; W. F. Hook, *On the Means of Rendering More Efficient the Education of the People–A Letter to the Lord Bishop of St. David's*, London, 1846; *21st A. R. Wesleyan Education Committee*, 1860, p. 54; J. Hole, *'Light More Light!' On the Present State of Education Amongst the Working Classes of Leeds*, London, 1969 edn., pp. 9–10; F. Watkins, *A Letter to His Grace the Archbishop of York on the State of Education in the Church Schools of Yorkshire*, Leeds, 1860, pp. 8, 10, 13, 18, 31.

215 CCE, 1855–6, p. 348. Cf. *50th BFSS*, 1855, p. 52.

216 *CCE, 1844 (2)*, p. 277; Sanderson, 'Social change', p. 151.

217 *CCE, 1844 (2)*, pp. 276–7, 442; *CCE, 1845 (2)*, p. 178; *CCE, 1847–8*, pp. 22, 25; *CCE, 1850–1*, p. 265; *CCE, 1851–2*, pp. 466–7; *CCE, 1853–4*, p. 765; *CCE, 1854–5*, pp. 438–9; *CCE, 1855–6*, p. 348; *CCE, 1858–9*, p. 104; *CCE, 1868–9*, p. 217; *CCE, 1870–1*, p. 136; PP 1852, XI, p. 416; Watkins, *Letter to the Archbishop of York*, pp. 14–15; *Newcastle*, II, pp. 189–92.

218 *CCE, 1851–2*, pp. 462, 464; *CCE, 1854–5*, pp. 438–9; *CCE, 1856–7*, p. 291.

219 *CCE, 1844 (2)*, pp. 443–5; *CCE, 1854–5*, p. 517; *CCE, 1863–4*, pp. 136–7; *CCE, 1865–6*, p. 206; *12th A. R. Wesleyan Education Committee*, 1850, pp. 47–54; *Newcastle*, II, p. 188; J. H. Robson, 'Educational attainment of the working-class female in the West Riding of Yorkshire, 1850 to 1870', M. A. research exercise, University of Leeds, 1976, (LME), pp. 40–5.

220 *CCE, 1871–2*, p. 79.

221 *CCE, 1844 (2)*, pp. 273, 522; *CCE, 1847–8 (1)*, p. 188; *CCE, 1851–2*, p. 463; *CCE, 1860–1*, p. 13; *CCE, 1868–9*, p. 159; *CCE, 1871–2*, p. 79; Stephens, 'Elementary education', pp. 244–5; *Report of the Chester Diocesan Board*, 1842; *Newcastle*, II, p. 187; Hole, *'Light More Light!'*, p. 8.

222 Cf. R. B. Walker, 'Religious changes in Cheshire, 1750–1850', *Jnl. Ecclesiastical History*, XVII, 1866, pp. 85–94; Sanderson, 'Social change', p. 33; A. Redford, *Labour Migration in England*,

1800–1850, Manchester, 2nd edn. ed. W. H. Chaloner, 1964, pp. 150 ff., Map G 1; R. Glen, *Urban Workers in the Early Industrial Revolution*, London, 1984, pp. 22–3.

223 [R. S. Bayley], *The Substance of a Lecture on National Education*, Sheffield, 1837 (in Sheffield Central Library).

224 *CCE, 1840–1*, pp. 176–7; Stephens, 'Elementary education', p. 239.

225 E.g., *CCE, 1866–7*, pp. 162–3.

226 See pp. 46–7. Cf. Apps. O, P; Watkins, *Letter to the Archbishop of York*, p. 10.

227 *CCE, 1840–1*, p. 177; *CCE, 1845 (2)*, pp. 110, 177; *CCE, 1846 (1)*, pp. 408–15; *CCE, 1847–8*, p. 6; *CCE, 1851–2*, p. 700; *CCE, 1853–4*, pp. 751–3; *CCE, 1854–5*, pp. 517–19; *CCE, 1855–6*, p. 458; PP 1852, XI, pp. 202–5.

228 E.g., *CCE, 1844 (2)*, p. 270; *CCE, 1845 (2)*, p. 78; *CCE, 1850–1*, p. 297; *CCE, 1851–2*, p. 463; *CCE, 1855–6*, p. 352; Cottam, 'Literacy in Doncaster union', pp. 40–1; W. A. Peers, 'Church, labour and education in an industrial city: an account of educational provision in Sheffield, 1836 to 1870', M. A. research exercise, University of Leeds, 1981, (LME), p. 20

229 S. A. Harrop, 'Literacy and educational attitudes as factors in the industrialization of north-east Cheshire, 1760–1830', in Stephens (1983), p. 48; Peers, 'Church, labour and education', p. 44.

230 *CCE, 1853–4*, pp. 758–9.

231 *Bradford Observer*, 7 September 1854.

232 *CCE, 1844 (2)*, pp. 447–8, 450–2; *CCE, 1846 (2)*, pp. 27, 30; *CCE, 1869–70*, pp. 319–21; *Education Census, 1851*, p. clxii; PP 1870, LIV, p. 88; PP 1852, XI, pp. 456, 462, 553; Stephens, 'Elementary education', pp. 231–2; Stephens (1973), pp. 18–19; D. Fraser, 'Voluntarism and West Riding politics in the mid-nineteenth century', *NH*, XIII, 1977; M. Sanderson, 'National and British school societies'; D. Smith, *Conflict and Compromise: Class Formation in English Society, 1830–1914*, London, 1982, pp. 127–30; N. L. Pole, 'The development of elementary education in the borough of Macclesfield, 1833–1918', M. A. thesis, University of Sheffield, 1975, p. 72; G. W. Fenn, 'The development of education in an industrial town', *Researches and Studies*, V, 1952, p. 34.

233 Marsden, 'Diffusion', pp. 179–80.

234 E.g., J. A. Bremner, 'Education of the manual labour class', *TNAPSS*, 1866, pp. 309, 311; *CCE, 1849–50 (1)*, p. 155; *CCE, 1851–2*, pp. 699–700; S. Pollard and C. Holmes (eds.), *Essays in the Economic and Social History of South Yorkshire*, Sheffield, 1976, p. 265.

235 *2nd. A. R. Catholic Poor School Committee*, 1849, pp. 143–4. Cf. PP 1870, LIV, pp. 88–91; T. C. Barker and J. R. Harris, *A Merseyside Town in the Industrial Revolution, St. Helen's, 1750–1900*, London, 1959, p. 392; J. Murphy, 'The rise of public elementary education in Liverpool; Pt. Two, 1819–35', *Trans. Historic Society of Lancashire and Cheshire*, CXVIII, 1966, pp. 113–14.

236 J. Fletcher, 'Moral and educational statistics of England and Wales', *JSSL*, X, 1847, pp. 198–9; A. Gatty, *Sheffield Past and Present*, London, 1873, p. 300; *CCE, 1840–1*, p. 319; *CCE, 1846 (2)*, pp. 27–8; *CCE, 1848–50 (2)*, p. 188; *CCE, 1860–1*, p. 89; *CCE, 1861–2*, p. 66; Peers, 'Church, labour and education', p. 2; C. Knight, *Passages of a Working Life*, II, London, 1864, p. 83.

237 This is a vast subject which can only be touched on here. See, especially, M. Sanderson, 'Education and the factory in industrial Lancashire, 1780–1840', *Ec. H. R.*, 2nd ser. XX, 1967; Robson, *Education of Children in Industry*; W. G. Rimmer, *Marshalls of Leeds, Flaxspinners, 1788–1886*, Cambridge, 1960; R. S. Fitton and A. P. Wadsworth, *The Strutts and Arkwrights, 1758–1830*, Manchester, 1958; M. Cruickshank, *Children and Industry*, Manchester, 1981; G. Ward, 'The education of factory child workers, 1833–50', *Economic Jnl. Supplement*, February 1935; W. C. R. Hicks, 'The education of the half-timer', *Economic History*, IV, 1939; J. C. Hammond, 'The factory school of John Ward and William Walker', *Foster Society Bulletin*, 1971; *VCH, Cheshire*, III, p. 208; PP 1842, XVII, p. 859; PP 1852 XL, pp. 11–13.

238 E.g., PP 1839, XLII (Reps.), p. 26.

239 E.g., PP 1857, XL, pp. 54–8; *CCE, 1855–6*, p. 355; *CCE, 1857–8*, p. 305; *CCE, 1866–7*, p. 176; *CCE, 1868–9*, p. 195. Cf. J. James, *The History and Topography of Bradford*, Bradford, 1841, p. 19.

240 E.g., PP 1845, XXVII, pp. 24–9, 32; PP 1852–3, XL, p. 20; PP 1857 (2), XVI, pp. 7–10.

241 *VCH, Cheshire*, III, p. 208; W. H. Chaloner, *The Social and Economic Development of Crewe, 1780–1923*, Manchester, 1950, pp. 61–4.

242 PP 1842, XVI, p. 20; PP 1842, XVII, p. 75.

243 *CCE, 1853–4*, p. 764.

244 Peers, 'Church, labour and education', pp. 3–4; Smith, *Conflict and Compromise*, pp. 128–9; *Newcastle*, V, pp. 184–5.

245 D. Bythell, *The Hand-loom Weavers*, Cambridge, 1969, p. 147.

246 PP 1868–9, XIII, (a), p. 11.

247 Cottam, 'Literacy in Doncaster union', pp. 33, 40–1

248 *CCE, 1855–6*, p. 355.

249 Garnett, 'Farming in Lancashire', p. 16; W. Clare (ed.), *A Young Irishman's Diary (1836–1847)*, 1928, p. 65.

250 Davies, *Agriculture in Cheshire*, p. 91.

251 Watkins, *Letter to the Archbishop of York*, p. 28.

252 PP 1868–9, XIII, (a), pp. 154–5.

253 E.g., *CCE, 1844 (2)*, pp. 270, 273; *CCE, 1857–8*, p. 305; *CCE, 1860–1*, p. 89; *CCE, 1865–6*, p. 128.

254 PP 1842, XVII, p. 823.

255 PP 1854–5, XV, p. 6.

256 Cf. *Newcastle*, II, pp. 195–6, 202–4; *CCE, 1868–9*, p. 229. But see C. Nardinelli, 'Corporal punishment and children's wages in nineteenth century Britain', *Explorations in Economic History*, XIX, 1982, pp. 233–4.

257 'On the state of education in the township of Pendleton, 1838', *JSSL*, II, 1839, pp. 69–70; PP 1842, XVII, p. 833.

258 Smith, *Conflict and Compromise*, pp. 116–7.

259 PP 1845, XXVII, pp. 30–1; Bremner, 'Education of the manual labour class', p. 312.

260 PP 1842, XVII, p. 856.

261 PP 1842, XVI, pp. 197–200.

262 PP 1863, XVIII, pp. lxxvii, 162, 165, 168, 173–81.

263 *CCE, 1845 (2)*, p. 79; *CCE, 1851–2*, pp. 465–6.

264 *CCE, 1857–8*, p. 305.

265 PP 1857, XI, p. 31.

266 *Ibid.*, pp. 32, 51, 54–7.

267 W. E. Axon, 'Education in Salford: retrospective and prospective', *Transactions Manchester Statistical Society*, 1852–3, pp. 192–3; Sanderson, 'Social change', pp. 136–41. Cf., e.g., PP 1840, XXIII, pp. 493, 543–4, 568–70; PP 1840, XXIV, pt. IV, p. 339, pt. V. p. 609.

268 PP 1852, XI, pp. 70–1, 376. Cf. J. Kay-Shuttleworth, *Four Periods of Public Education*, London, 1862, pp. 152–3.

269 Bremner, 'Education of the manual labour class', pp. 307–8, 311–2; PP 1870, LIV, pp. 167–8, 174.

270 *2nd A. R. Catholic Poor School Committee*, 1849, pp. 142–5; Glen, *Urban Workers*, pp. 22–4, 280.

271 *Newcastle*, II, pp. 200–1.

272 C. J. Morgan, 'Demographic change', in Fraser (ed.), *Modern Leeds*, pp. 61–2; Stephens, 'Elementary education', pp. 232–6, 244–5; A. B. Reach, *The Yorkshire Textile Districts in 1849*,

Helmshore, ed. C. Aspin, 1974, *passim*; A. B. Reach, *Manchester and the Lancashire Textile Districts in 1849*, Helmshore, ed. C. Aspin, 1974, *passim*.

273 Stephens, *Warrington*, pp. 19–20.

274 Cf. Watkins, *Letter to the Archbishop of York*, p. 27; T. Laqueur, 'Working-class demand and the growth of English elementary education, 1750–1850', in L. Stone (ed.), *Schooling and Society, 1750–1850*, London, 1976, pp. 197–8.

275 PP 1852, XI, p. 376.

276 *60th BFSS*, 1865, pp 69–71; *CCE, 1863–4*, pp. 81–2; *CCE, 1865–6*, p. 120.

277 P. J. Dixon, 'School attendance in Preston: some socio-economic influences', in R. Lowe (ed.), *New Approaches to the Study of Popular Education, 1851–1902*, Leicester, 1979, p. 55; D. J. Oddy, 'Urban famine in nineteenth-century Britain: the effects of the Lancashire cotton famine on working-class diets and health', *Ec. H. R.*, 2nd ser. XXXVI, 1983, p. 75; N. Longmate, *The Hungry Mills*, London, 1978, chapter 14; *CCE, 1862–3*, p. 44; *CCE, 1865–6*, p. 120.

278 Sanderson, 'Education and the factory'; H. Silver, 'Ideology and the factory child: attitudes to half-time education', in P. McCann (ed.), *Popular Education and Socialization in the Nineteenth Century*, London, 1977; *CCE, 1864–5*, pp. 178–9.

279 E.g., PP 1837–8, VII, pp. 63–5; PP 1840, XXIII, p. 544; PP 1843, XXVII, pp. 22–3.

280 *CCE, 1844 (2)*, p. 445; *CCE, 1866–7*, pp. 175–6; *CCE, 1868–9*, p. 159; *Newcastle*, II, pp. 228–39; J. A. Bremner, 'The half-time system', *TNAPSS*, 1875, pp. 394–6; PP 1870, LIV, pp. 18–19, 140, 145–6; PP 1876, XXX, pp. 485, 498.

281 *Newcastle*, II, p. 230.

282 See. e.g., J. F. C. Harrison, *Learning and Living, 1790–1960*, London, 1961; B. Simon, *The Two Nations and the Educational Structure, 1780–1870*, London, 1974; T. Kelly, *George Birkbeck, Pioneer of Adult Education*, Liverpool, 1957; R. K. Webb, *The British Working Class Reader, 1790–1848*, London, 1955; R. D. Altick, *The English Common Reader: A Social History of the Mass Reading Public, 1800–1900*, Chicago, 1957; M. Tylecote, *The Mechanics' Institutes of Lancashire and Yorkshire before 1851*, Manchester, 1957; Stephens, *Warrington*; Glen, *Urban Workers*, pp. 219, 225–9, 266, 269–70, 277; N. Kirk, *The Growth of Working Class Reformism in Mid-Victorian England*, London, 1985, pp. 208–12.

283 Cf. E. Baines Jr., *The Social, Educational and Religious State of the Manufacturing Districts*, London, 2nd edn. 1843, pp. 20–5; Laqueur, *Religion and Respectability*, pp. 61, 259; PP 1852, XI, pp. 287–301, 458–61.

284 Cf. Table 2·5, p. 39: 10 of the 21 towns listed are in Lancashire, the West Riding and Cheshire; A. P. Wadsworth, 'The first Manchester Sunday schools', in M. W. Flinn and T. C. Smout (eds.), *Essays in Social History*, Oxford, 1974, pp. 116, 119–20; N. B. Roper, 'The contribution of the non-conformists to the development of education in Bradford in the nineteenth century', M. Ed. thesis, University of Leeds, 1967, chapter 1.

285 Baines, *State of the Manufacturing Districts*, pp. 39–52; 'Report on Pendleton', pp. 72, 75; 'Statistics of Sunday schools in Manchester and Salford', *JSSL*, XXVII, 1864, pp. 421–6; G. C. Holland, *Vital Statistics of Sheffield*, Sheffield, 1843, p. 221; PP 1837–8, VII, p. ix; *Children's Employment Commission Reports*, *passim*; PP 1840, XXIII, pp. 544–5; *Newcastle*, II, pp. 192–3, 236, IV, p. 388; *CCE, 1844 (2)*, pp. 252–4; *CCE, 1847–8 (2)*, p. 30; *CCE 1850–1*, p. 585; I. Chen, 'Variations in educational attainment in Lancashire during the mid-nineteenth century', M. A. research exercise, University of Leeds, 1978, (LME), pp. 12–17; Laqueur, *Religion and Respectability*, pp. 98–101; Sanderson, 'Social change', pp. 146–51.

286 PP 1842, XVII, p. 859.

287 Murphy, 'Education in Liverpool', pp. 126–8.

288 E.g., *CCE, 1847–8 (2)*, p. 30.

289 Laqueur, *Religion and Respectability*, pp. 102–3, 123; H. F. Mathews, *Methodism and the Education of the People, 1791–1851*, London, 1949, p. 53; PP 1845, XXVII, pp. 43–9.

290 Wadsworth, 'Manchester Sunday schools', p. 119.

291 Cf. PP 1842, XVII, pp. 833–5; Laqueur, *Religion and Respectability*, Chapter 5.

292 Stephens, 'Elementary education', p. 228; P. Joyce, *Work, Society and Politics: The Culture of the Factory in later Victorian England*, Brighton, 1980, p. 178; Laqueur, *Religion and Respectability*, pp. 92–3; PP 1843, XIII, p. 154; Hole, *'Light More Light!'*, pp. 36–8; M. Dick, 'The myth of the working-class Sunday school', *History of Education*, IX, 1980, p. 32.

293 PP 1845, XXVII, pp. 43–9; Laqueur, *Religion and Respectability*, pp. 119–23; *Children's Employment Commission Reports, passim*.

294 PP 1842, XVII, p. 104. Cf. PP 1845, XXVII, pp. 34–5, 41.

295 Figures available only for Yorkshire as a whole.

296 *CCE, 1845 (2)*, pp. 176–7; *CCE, 1851–2*, p. 476; *CCE, 1859–60*, p. 43; *CCE, 1860–1*, pp. 49, 94; *CCE, 1861–2*, p. 190. Cf. Robson, 'Working-class female', p. 59.

297 E.g., PP 1842, XVII, pp. 183, 835–6, 859–60; PP 1845, XXVII, pp. 33, 35.

298 PP 1842, XVII, pp. 77–81, 186.

299 PP 1845, XXVII, pp. 43–9.

300 Harrop, 'Literacy in north-east Cheshire', pp. 49–50.

301 Chen, 'Educational attainment in Lancashire', p. 8, figs. 5A, 5B.

302 Cf. I. T. Cunliffe, 'The development of literacy in the county of Cheshire, 1840–1884', M. A. research exercise, University of Leeds, 1983, (LME), p. 9.

303 Cf. App. F; Robson, 'Working-class female', pp. 10–1, 21.

304 For a comment on this exercise, see above p. 68.

305 Ulverston, Lancaster, Garstang, Sedbergh, Pateley Bridge, Great Ouseburn, Ripon, Otley, Knaresborough, Wetherby.

306 Pateley Bridge, Sedbergh, Knaresborough, Lancaster, Garstang: *Census, 1851*.

307 Saddleworth, Wortley, Hemsworth, Doncaster, Goole, Thorne, Selby.

308 Fylde, Clitheroe, Halifax, Huddersfield, Skipton, Settle, Tadcaster, Pontefract, Nantwich (containing Crewe), Runcorn, Congleton, Macclesfield (containing residential Alderley).

309 Wilson, 'Elementary education and literacy', pp. 43, 81, 100.

310 Stockport registration district included some land in Lancashire.

311 Note the improvement in the position of Fylde which contained Blackpool: App. G.

312 Chen, 'Educational attainment in Lancashire', pp. 6–7.

313 See S. A. Harrop, 'Adult education and literacy', *History of Education*, XIII, 1984.

314 Cheshire: -0.20. Cunliffe, 'Literacy in Cheshire', p. 27, using the Spearman rank correlation coefficient formula found for Cheshire districts no correlation between literacy levels in 1866 and either day or Sunday schooling levels in 1851.

315 Cf. *CCE, 1844 (2)*, p. 522; *CCE, 1868–9*, p. 219.

316 Numbers of districts changed 1851–61.

317 Cf. App. I, girls not at school.

318 E.g., *CCE, 1840–1*, p. 174; *CCE, 1847–8*, pp. 2–3; *CCE, 1850–1*, pp. 38, 296; *CCE, 1861–2*, p. 175; *CCE, 1863–4*, p. 150; *CCE, 1865–6*, p. 206; Robson, 'Working-class female', *passim*; *Education Census, 1851*, p. xxxii; *Newcastle*, II, pp. 180, 188.

319 See p. 147.

320 Robson, 'Working-class female', pp. 24–6.

321 *CCE, passim*; PP 1852, XI, pp. 518–9; PP 1870, LIV, pp. 130–5, 150–2.

322 E.g., *CCE, 1872–3*, p. 98; Stephens, 'Elementary education', p. 229; PP 1870, LIV, pp. 3, 105–6.

323 Cf. p. 49. D. F. Mitch, 'The spread of literacy in nineteenth-century England', Ph. D. dissertation, University of Chicago, 1982 (pp. 193 ff., 393–4, 397), found in Rochdale and Bradford that an upturn in literacy was linked to an increase in aided public schools.

324 Robson, *Education of Children in Industry*, p. 82.

325 E. A. G. Clark, 'Education in Congleton', in W. B. Stephens (ed.), *History of Congleton*, Manchester, 1970, p. 281. Cf. PP 1840, XXIV, pt. IV, p. 339.

326 *CCE, 1866–7*, p. 176; PP 1870, LIV, p. 144.

327 PP 1845, XXVII, pp. 32, 40; PP 1863, XVIII, pp. 172–8; PP 1870, LIV, p. 164; and see above.

328 PP 1870, LIV, p. 144.

329 'Report on Pendleton'; P. McDowall, 'Statistics of Ramsbottom', *Report of the 8th Meeting of the British Association*, 1838; PP 1842, XVII, pp. 77–82; R. K. Webb, 'Working class readers in early Victorian England', *EHR*, LXV, 1950, pp. 339, 342–3; S. A. Harrop, 'The place of education in the genesis of the Industrial Revolution, with special reference to Stalybridge, Dukinfield and Hyde', M. Ed. thesis University of Manchester, 1976, p. 86; *Report of a Committee of the Manchester Statistical Society on the Condition of the Working Classes in an Extensive Manufacturing District in 1834, 1835, and 1836*, 1838, Table 4, p. xii.

330 PP 1870, LIV.

331 E.g., Bremner, 'Education of the manual labour class', pp. 312–13; Manchester Education Society cited S. E. Maltby, *Manchester and the Movement for National Elementary Education, 1800–1870*, Manchester, 1918, p. 97; *CCE, 1861–2*, p. 71.

332 W. R. W. Stephens, *The Life and Letters of Walter Farquar Hook*, II, London, 1880 edn., pp. 205–12.

333 Maltby, *Manchester ... Education*, pp. 100–2; E. Baines, *National Education*, London, 1867; A. Miall, *Life of Edward Miall*, London, 1884, pp. 231–5; J. Murphy, *Church, State and Schools in Britain, 1800–1970*, London, 1971, p. 45; D. Fraser, 'Edward Baines', in P. Hollis (ed.), *Pressure from Without in Early Victorian England*, London, 1974, pp. 201–2.

4 The midland counties (pp. 102–61)

1 For population figures, see App. A. The following paragraphs draw on: *Censuses*; Welton (1860); G. C. Allen, *The Industrial Development of Birmingham and the Black Country, 1860–1927*, London, 1929; D. M. Palliser, *The Staffordshire Landscape*, London, 1976; T. G. Raybould, *The Economic Emergence of the Black Country*, Newton Abbot, 1973; *VCH, Staffordshire*, II, VIII; *VCH, Derbyshire*, II.

2 C. C. Owen, *The Development of Industry in Burton upon Trent*, Chichester, 1978, pp. 10–11.

3 Welton (1860), p. 77.

4 Calculated from data in C. H. Lee, *British Regional Statistics, 1841–1971*, Cambridge, 1979, Series A tables.

5 The following draws on: *Censuses*; Welton (1860); W. Felkin, *History of the Machine-Wrought Hosiery and Lace Manufactures*, London, 1867; D. M. Smith, 'The British hosiery industry at the middle of the nineteenth century', *Trans. Institute of British Geographers*, XXXII, 1963; *VCH, Leicestershire*, II, III; *VCH, Derbyshire*, II; PP 1845, XV; PP 1840, XXIV, pt. IV; R. A. Church, *Economic and Social Change in a Midland Town: Victorian Nottingham, 1815–1900*, London, 1960; J. D. Chambers, *Nottinghamshire in the Eighteenth Century*, London, 1966 edn.; F. A. Wells, *The British Hosiery and Knitwear Industry*, Newton Abbot, 1972; C. J. Erickson, *British Industrialists: Steel and Hoisery, 1850–1950*, Cambridge, 1959; A. T. Patterson, *Radical Leicester*, Leicester, 1954; J. Simmons, *Leicester Past and Present*, I, London, 1974; E. G. Nelson, 'The English framework knitting industry', *Jnl. Economic and Business History*, II, 1930; P. Head, 'Putting out in the Leicestershire hosiery industry in the middle of the nineteenth century', *Trans. Leicestershire Archaeological and Historical Society*, XXXVII, 1961–2.

6 Church, *Economic and Social Change*, p. 207.

7 The following draws on: W. B. Stephens, 'Social history from 1700', *VCH, Warwickshire*, VIII; W. B. Stephens, 'Early Victorian Coventy: education in an industrial community, 1830–1851', in A. E. Everitt (ed.), *Perspectives in Urban History*, London, 1973; D. M. Smith, 'The silk industry in the east midlands', *East Midland Geographer*, III, 1962.

8 PP 1843, XIV, pp. C17–18; PP 1840, XXIV, pt. IV, pp. 350 ff. Cf. *VCH, Staffordshire*, II, pp. 209 ff.

9 The following draws on: J. N. Bartlett, *Carpeting the Millions*, Edinburgh, [1977]; *VCH, Worcestershire*, II, p. 298; [B. Gibbons], *Notes and Suggestions for a History of Kidderminster*, Kidderminster, 1859; I. L. Wedley, *Kidderminster and its Borderland*, Kidderminster, 1936, p. 52; J. N. Bartlett, 'The mechanization of the Kidderminster carpet industry', *Business History*, IX, 1967; *Jnl. Design and Manufactures*, 1850, pp. 171–7; PP 1833, XX, pp. B1, 11 ff; PP 1843, XIV, pp. C21 ff.

10 Owen, *Industry in Burton upon Trent*, pp. 78, 82–3, 178, 237.

11 Raybould, *Black Country*, pp. 182 ff; J. E. Williams, *The Derbyshire Miners*, London, 1962, pp. 18 ff, 35 ff; A. R. Griffin, *Mining in the East Midlands, 1550–1947*, London, 1971, pp. 28–33; *VCH, Derbyshire*, II, pp. 334, 355; PP 1842, XV, pp. 39 ff; PP 1842, XVI, pp. 1, 89; PP 1843, XIII, (Mines), pp. lxxxiv–lxxxvi.

12 PP 1850, XXIII, p. 15.

13 Raybould, *Black Country*, pp. 146 ff.

14 A. Birch, *The Economic History of the British Iron and Steel Industry, 1784–1879*, London, 1967, pp. 114, 151, 153, 197, 254, 276, 284; K. Warren, *The British Iron and Steel Sheet Industry since 1840*, London, 1970, pp. 16–17.

15 The following draws on: A. Briggs, *Victorian Cities*, Harmondsworth, 1968 edn., Chapter 5; Allen, *Birmingham and the Black Country*, 152 ff; *VCH, Warwickshire*, VII, pp. 109 ff, 126, 133, 135; PP 1843, XIV, p. F18.

16 PP 1843, XIV, pp. F17, f179.

17 *Ibid.*, F23–4, f121 ff; PP 1889, XIII, pp. 219–23; and see p. 118.

18 The following draws on: W.H.B. Court, *Rise of the Midland Industries, 1600–1838*, London, 1938, pp. 196–216; S. Timmins (ed.), *Birmingham and the Midland Hardware District*, Birmingham, 1866, p. 114; Allen, *Birmingham and the Black Country*, pp. 75, 153, 272–3; G. W. Hilton, *The Truck System*, Cambridge, 1960, pp. 10 ff.

19 *VCH, Derbyshire*, II, p. 362.

20 PP 1843, XV, p. Q 88.

21 L. Weatherill, *The Pottery Trade and North Staffordshire, 1660–1760*, Manchester, 1971, chapter 4; J. Thomas, 'The pottery industry and the Industrial Revolution', *Economic History*, III, 1937, pp. 403, 407–10; PP 1843, XIV, pp. C2–3; W. H. Warburton, *History of Trade Union Organisation in the North Staffordshire Potteries*, London, 1931, chapters 8, 9.

22 PP 1847, XVI, p. 26; PP 1850, XXIII, p. 12.

23 See, e.g., W. G. Hoskins, *Making of the English Landscape*, London, 1957, pp. 218 ff; J. Prest, *The Industrial Revolution in Coventry*, London, 1960, p. 26; *VCH, Warwickshire*, VIII, pp. 149–50; PP 1843, XIV, p. F16; PP 1844, XVII, pp. 130–8, 151; PP 1845, XVIII, pp. 1–50.

24 'Education in the mining and manufacturing district of south Staffordshire', *JSSL*, X, 1847, pp. 235–7.

25 PP 1843, XIII, pp. iv-v; E. Burritt, *Walks in the Black Country and its Green Borderland*, Kineton, 1976 edn., p. 181; D. Levine, *Family Formation in an Age of Nascent Capitalism*, New York, 1977, *passim*; C. Shaw, *When I was a Child*, Wakefield, 1903, repr. 1969, pp. 27 ff; Palliser, *Staffordshire Landscape*, pp. 218 ff; G. J. Barnsby, *Social Conditions in the Black Country, 1800–1900*, Wolverhampton, 1980, *passim*.

26 The following draws on: PP 1833, V, pp. 83 ff, 394 ff, 565 ff, 587 ff; PP 1836, VIII, p. 227; J. Caird, *English Agriculture in 1850–1*, London, 1852; the 'Prize Essays' in *JRAS*: VI, 1845

(Notts.), XIV, 1853 (Derbys.), XVII, 1856 (Warwicks.), 2nd ser. II, 1864 (Leics.), III, 1867, (Worcs.), V, 1869 (Staffs.); *VCH, Derbyshire*, II, pp. 184, 237, 308, 312 ff; *VCH, Nottinghamshire*, II, pp. 376–7; *VCH, Leicestershire*, II, p. 245; *VCH, Warwickshire*, II, p. 276; *VCH, Worcestershire*, II, pp. 310, 313, IV, p. 463; PP 1867–8, XVII, (a), pp. 75, 83; PP 1868–9, XIII, (a), p. 107.

27 F. M. L. Thompson, *English Landed Society in the Nineteenth Century*, London, 1963, pp. 32, 114–17.

28 E. H. Hunt, *Regional Wage Variations in Britain, 1850–1914*, Oxford, 1973, pp. 27 ff, 62–3, 198: J. D. Marshall, 'Nottinghamshire labourers in the early nineteenth century', *Trans. Thoroton Society*, LXIV, 1960, p. 62; A. L. Bowley, 'Rural population in England and Wales', *JRSS*, LXXVII, 1914, App. III; G. J. Barnsby, 'The standard of living in the Black Country during the nineteenth century', *Ec. H. R.*, 2nd ser. XXIV, 1971, and debate in *ibid.*, XXVI, 1973; E. Hopkins, 'Small town aristocrats and their standard of living, 1840–1914', *Ec. H. R.*, 2nd ser. XXVIII, 1975, p. 231; W. Forrest, 'Chainmakers of Cradley Heath', *TNAPSS*, 1859; *VCH, Warwickshire*, VIII, p. 183; PP 1867–8, XVII (a), (b); PP 1868–9, XIII, (a), (b), *passim*; *JRAS*, VI, 1845, 39; PP 1850, XXVII, pp. 127, 129 ff., 136, 141–2; PP 1850, XXIII, p. 9; PP 1861, L, p. 9.

29 See pp. 21–3.

30 PP 1864, XXII, 3rd report, pp. 157 ff; W. L. Sargant, 'On the progress of elementary education', *JSSL*, XXX, 1867, p. 122.

31 PP 1843, XIV, p. F95.

32 PP 1843, XIII, p. 50.

33 J. P. Norris, 'Notes on popular education in Staffordshire', *TNAPSS*, 1858, p. 295, Cf. p. 41.

34 Cf. PP 1863, XVIII, p. 45 ff.

35 *Ibid.*, p. 29.

36 PP 1843, XIII, pp. 8–9, 17, 54.

37 PP 1843, XIV, pp. C4–6; PP 1843, XV, pp. 1–2.

38 PP 1863, XVIII, pp. viii ff., xxxvi–xxxvii, 332.

39 *Ibid.*, p. 2.

40 G. Lambert, *Traité Pratique de la Fabrication des Faiences Fines et Autres Poteries*, Paris, 1865, p. 294. Cf. Shaw, *When I was a Child*, chapters 1, 2.

41 PP 1871, LXII, p. 38.

42 PP 1864, XXII, 3rd report, p. 39; PP 1866, XXIV, pp. vi, 152 ff.

43 Burritt, *Walks in the Black Country*, pp. 115–8.

44 PP 1842, XV, p. 35–6; Williams, *Derbyshire Miners*, p. 64.

45 PP 1833, XXI, pp. C3, 7; PP 1842, XV, pp. 9–11, 24–5, 106–7; PP 1842, XVI, pp. 8, ff., 89 ff; PP 1842, XVII, pp. 271, 283, 286, 293; PP 1843, XV, p. Q64 (Bilston); *VCH, Derbyshire*, II, p. 355.

46 PP 1854–5, XV, p. 6; PP 1859 (2), XII, p. 24; J. Bradshaw, 'Occupation and literacy in the Erewash Valley coalfield', in Stephens (1983), pp. 15–16.

47 J. P. Norris, *The Education of the People*, London, [1869], p. 43.

48 PP 1843, XIII, p. 19.

49 PP 1843, XV, p. Q47; PP, 1864, XXII, 3rd report, pp. iv, 36, 40; I. Pinchbeck, *Women Workers and the Industrial Revolution, 1750–1850*, London, 1977, p. 274.

50 Cf. *Newcastle*, II, 246, ff, 286, ff.

51 Allen, *Birmingham and the Black Country*, p. 168; PP 1833, XX, BI, pp. 7–8; PP 1843, XIII, p. 7; PP 1843, XIV, pp. F18–9, 23–4, 41, f119, 134 ff.; PP 1864, XXII, 3rd report, p.x; *VCH, Warwickshire*, VII, p. 135.

52 PP 1843, XIII, p. 7; PP 1843, XIV, pp. C20–1; *Newcastle*, II, pp. 247–8; Allen, *Birmingham and the Black Country*, p. 169; Burritt, *Walks in the Black Country*, pp. 247–8.

53 PP 1843, XV, pp. Q6–7.

54 PP 1837, V, p. 156.

55 PP 1843, XIII, p. 21; Patterson, *Radical Leicester:* M. I. Thomis, Politics and Society in Nottingham, Oxford, 1969, pp. 18–26.

56 PP 1843, XIII, pp. 10–2, 21; PP 1843, XIV, pp. F5–10, 13, f64 ff; PP 1845, XV, p. 113 and *passim.*

57 PP 1845, XV, p. 199.

58 PP 1843, XIV, pp. F9, f62.

59 D. Wardle, *Education and Society in Nineteenth-Century Nottingham,* Cambridge, 1971, pp. 25, 27; Church, *Economic and Social Change,* p. 87.

60 PP 1843, XIV, pp. F6–9, F13–4; PP 1845, XV, p. 113.

61 Quot. Wardle, *Education and Society,* p. 27.

62 PP 1843, XIV, p. F16. Cf. PP 1843, XIII, p. 25.

63 PP 1854–5, XIV, pp. 164, 179; PP 1863, XVIII, pp. lxxx, 13, 236, 265; PP 1864, XXII, 2nd report, pp. xi ff., xxvi ff; 'The Children's Employment Commission', *Quarterly Rev.,* CXIX, 1866.

64 PP 1850, XXVII, p. 127.

65 PP 1863, XVIII, p. 275.

66 PP 1839, XLII, pp. 75, 137, 221, 257, 263.

67 Stephens, 'Victorian Coventry', p. 164; *VCH, Warwickshire,* VIII, p. 228. Cf. PP 1833, XX, p. 131–which stated that no children under ten were employed.

68 PP 1866, XXIV, pp. xiii, 114 ff.

69 PP 1843, XIV, pp. C17–8; PP 1840, XXIV, pt. IV, p. 346; *VCH, Staffordshire,* II, pp. 210–1, 214.

70 PP 1833, XX, pp. BI, 11 ff; PP 1839, XLII, pp. 134–5; PP 1843, XIV, pp. C22–3, c108.

71 Simmons, *Leicester Past and Present,* II, p. 23.

72 PP 1843, XIV, p.f 191–2; PP 1863, XVIII, pp. 242–3; *CCE, 1868–9,* p. 210.

73 Owen, *Burton upon Trent,* p. 230.

74 PP 1843, XIV, pp. A13–4, a57–8.

75 PP 1837, V, p. 96; PP 1861, L, pp. 8, 22, 29; PP 1867–8. XVII, (a), pp. 75, 87; PP 1868–9, XIII, (a), pp. xiii, 87, 186–7, 318–9.

76 *CCE, 1856–7,* pp. 255–6; PP 1861, L. p. 9; PP 1868–9, XIII, (a), pp. 53, 60, 111.

77 PP 1867–8, XVII, (a), pp. xvii–xix, 75, 86–7; 'Agricultural gangs', *Quarterly Rev.,* CXXIII, 1867.

78 PP 1868–9, XIII, (a), pp. 113, 118; (b), 85–6, 89, 223, 294, 415–7, 428; *VCH, Leicestershire,* II, p. 238; D. R. Mills, 'The geographical effects of the laws of settlement in Nottinghamshire', *East Midland Geographer,* V, 1970.

79 D. Levine, 'Illiteracy and family life during the first Industrial Revolution', *Jnl. Family History,* XIV, 1980–1.

80 Levine, *Family Formation,* p. 29.

81 See pp. 126, 131–2.

82 *Newcastle,* II, p. 253, Cf. J. Grayson, 'Literacy, schooling and industrialization: Worcestershire, 1760–1850', in Stephens (1983), pp. 63–4.

83 *Newcastle,* II, pp. 246–7, 249–50.

84 *CCE, 1850–1,* p. 207, Cf. *CCE, 1851–2,* pp. 730–1.

85 *Newcastle,* II, p. 249.

86 *VCH, Warwickshire,* VII, p. 135.

87 PP 1850, XXIII, pp. 12, 25–6, 33–4; PP 1851, XXIII, p. 9. Cf. PP 1843, XIII (Mines), pp. xliii, cxxxix. Cf. Grayson, 'Literacy: Worcestershire', p. 63.

88 *Newcastle,* II, p. 249.

89 *Ibid.,* p. 305.

90 *Ibid.,* p. 249. Cf. Grayson, 'Literacy: Worcestershire', p. 354.

91 *Newcastle*, II, pp. 249–50, 267–8.

92 PP 1868–9, XIII, (a), pp. 61, 117; (b), 88, 417, 423.

93 *Newcastle*, II, pp. 268, 275–6.

94 Grayson, 'Literacy: Worcestershire', p. 60–3.

95 *Newcastle*, II, p. 251.

96 *Abstract, 1833*, p. 997.

97 PP 1837–8, VII, p. 124; PP 1843, XIV, p. c15, 19, 106, ff., and *passim*; PP 1863, XVIII, p. 29.

98 *Newcastle*, II, pp. 304–7. Cf. PP 1842, XVII, p. 143; PP 1843, XV, p. Q13.

99 PP 1842, XVI, p. 101.

100 PP 1843, XIV, p. f 84; PP 1845, XV, p. 54 Cf. M. Caplan, 'The poor law in Nottinghamshire, 1836–71', *Trans. Thoroton Society*, LXXIX, 1970, pp. 91–2.

101 E.g., PP 1843, XIV, pp. c59, f87; PP 1845, XV, pp. 790, 853.

102 PP 1840, XXIV, pt. IV, p. 340; PP 1866, XXIV, p. 87.

103 *CCE, 1853–4*, pp. 401–2.

104 PP 1867–8, XVII, (a), p. 88.

105 PP 1843, XIV, p. C27; PP 1843, XV, pp. Q93, q50–1, q81.

106 PP 1843, XIII, p. 194; PP 1843, XIV, pp. f161, 166.

107 PP 1850, XXIII, p. 24; PP 1851, XXIII, pp. 1–2, 41; PP 1852–3, XL, p. 33.

108 Hunt, *Regional Wage Variations*, p. 121.

109 PP 1854, XIX, p. 32.

110 *Stratford Herald*, 14 September 1860.

111 *CCE, 1846 (1)*, pp. 177–8, 199–200.

112 PP 1842, XVI, p. 26; PP 1850, XXIII, p. 24.

113 PP 1843, XIII, p. 193.

114 PP 1864, XXII, 3rd report, p. 36. Cf. 'Children's Employment Commission'.

115 PP 1843, XIV, pp. c64, C10, F10, f42.

116 Stephens, 'Early Victorian Coventry', p. 180.

117 PP 1843, XIII, p. 193, Cf. PP 1843, XV, p. Q74.

118 PP 1868–9, XIII, (a), pp. 13, 61–2; (b), 294.

119 PP 1847, XVI, p. 26.

120 PP 1843, XV, p. q55.

121 *CCE, 1856–7*, p. 255.

122 PP 1864, XXII, 3rd report, p. 40.

123 PP 1834, XIX, p. 258.

124 PP 1843, XV, p. Q26.

125 PP 1864, XXII, 3rd report, p. 37.

126 *Newcastle*, II, p. 285.

127 E. Hopkins, 'Working-class attitudes in the Black Country in the mid-nineteenth century', *Bulletin History of Education Society*, XIV, 1974, p. 45.

128 E.g., PP 1845, XV, pp. 35, 128, 180, *inter alia*.

129 *CCE, 1851–2*, p. 726. Cf. Norris, *Education of the People*, p. 58.

130 Relevant pp. in: PP 1849, XXII; PP 1850, XXIII; PP 1851, XXIII; PP 1852, XXI: PP 1852–3, XL; PP 1854, XIX; PP 1854–5, XV; PP 1857 (2), XVI; PP 1859 (2), XII; PP 1861, XLVIII (letter); PP 1864, XXII, 3rd report, pp. 37, 60; *CCE, 1854–5*, 738 ff; *CCE*, 1855–6, p. 472 ff.; *CCE, 1856–7*, pp. 114 ff. See also E. Hopkins, 'Tremenheere's prize schemes in the mining districts', *Bulletin History of Education Society*, XV, 1975.

131 PP 1864, XXII, 3rd report, p. 162.

132 PP 1845, XV, p. 313.

133 PP 1854–5, XIV, p. 269, Cf. Bradshaw, 'Occupation and literacy', p. 14.

134 Bradshaw, 'Occupation and literacy', p. 19.

135 *CCE, 1853–4*, pp. 400–1; *Newcastle*, II, p. 285 ff. Cf. *CCE, 1845 (1)*, p. 257.

136 Burritt, *Walks in the Black Country*, p. 120.

137 D. Smith, *Conflict and Compromise: Class Formation in English Society, 1830–1914*, London, 1982, p. 118.

138 *CCE, 1869–70*, p. 347.

139 PP 1845, XV, p. 112. Cf. *Leicestershire Mercury*, 7 June, 1845.

140 PP 1851, XXIII, pp. 3–5; PP 1852–3, XL, pp. 32–3.

141 *Newcastle*, II, p. 305.

142 G. Barnsby, *A History of Education in Wolverhampton, 1800 to 1972*, (typescript), 1972 , p.6; G. J. Barnsby, *The Working Class Movement in the Black Country, 1750 to 1867*, Wolverhampton, 1977, pp. 101–2.

143 *Flint Glass Makers Magazine*, I, 1851, quot. Hopkins, 'Working-class attitudes', p. 41.

144 J. Rowley, 'Education and the working class in the Black Country in the mid-nineteenth century: a further dimension', *Bulletin History of Education Society*, XXI, 1978, pp. 21–3.

145 Cf. PP 1843, XV, p. Q25.

146 D. Bythell, *The Handloom Weavers*, Cambridge, 1969, p. 216.

147 T. Cooper, *Life of Thomas Cooper by Himself*, London, 1886 edn., pp. 172–3.

148 J. Simmons, *Life in Victorian Leicester*, 1971, pp. 68–9.

149 *Dudley Weekly Times*, 26 September 1857.

150 Rowley, 'Education and the working class', pp. 18–9.

151 PP 1843, XV, p. Q11.

152 *Newcastle*, II, pp. 248, 287.

153 E.g., PP 1843, XIII, p. 181.

154 E.g., PP 1833, XXI, p. C3; PP 1842, XVII, p. 129; PP 1847, XVI, p. 27; PP 1850, XXIII, pp. 8–9.

155 PP 1843, XV, pp. Q21–2.

156 *Ibid.*, pp. Q13, 24; PP 1847, XVI, p. 19; PP 1850, XXIII, p. 9; PP 1854–5, XV, p. 6.

157 PP 1843, XIV, p. c4.

158 PP 1847, XVI, pp. 26–7.

159 PP 1850, XXIII, pp. 9–10.

160 'Infant labour', *Quarterly Rev.*, LXVII, 1840; 'Children's Employment Commission', *ibid.*, CXIX, 1866; 'Children in mines and collieries', *Westminster Rev.*, XXXVIII, 1842.

161 E.g., PP 1850, XXIII, pp. 8, 12.

162 E.g., PP 1854–5, XIV, p. iv.

163 This sort of unrest is the subject of controversy and cannot be pursued here. See Thomis, *Politics and Society in Nottingham*; E. P. Thompson, *The Making of the English Working Class*, Harmondsworth, 1968 edn., pp. 580–603; R. A. Church and S. D. Chapman, 'Gravener Henson and the making of the English working class', in C. E. Mingay and E. L. Jones (eds.), *Essays in Honour of J. D. Chambers*, London, 1967; Patterson, *Radical Leicester*; Barnsby, *Working Class Movement*; Shaw, *When I was a Child*; M. Hovell, *The Chartist Movement*, Manchester, 1918, p. 260; *VCH, Warwickshire*, VII, pp. 277 ff., 298 ff.; D. Philips, 'Riots and public order in the Black Country, 1838–1860', in R. Quinault and J. Stevenson (eds.), *Popular Protest and Public Order*, London, 1974; F. C. Mather, 'The general strike of 1842 'in *ibid.*

164 Cf. 1843, XIIII (Mines), pp. cxxvii-cxxxiii, cxlii.

165 *CCE, 1844 (2)*, p. 522.

166 PP 1850, XXIII, p. 15.

167 PP 1852, XXI, p. 47. Cf. Norris, 'Popular education in Staffordshire', pp. 291–2, 300.

168 PP 1850, XXIII, pp. 26–31; PP 1851, XXIII, pp. 5–6.

169 Norris, *Education of the People*, p. 61. Cf. *CCE, 1866–7*, pp. 200–1.

170 *CCE, 1850–1*, p. 210; *CCE, 1856–7*, p. 269.

171 Cf. *Newcastle*, II, p. 258.

172 PP 1843, XIV, p. c69.

173 *CCE, 1847–8 (2)*, pp. 182–3.

174 *Report of the Leicester Domestic Mission Society, 1846–7*, p. 76.

175 J. Ward, *History of the Borough of Stoke on Trent*, London, 1847 repr. 1869, p. 31.

176 Smith, *Conflict and Compromise*, pp. 130–1.

177 *Warwick Advertiser*, 18 January 1845.

178 *11th Report of the County of Leicester Society for the Education of the Infant Poor*, 1823, p. 6.

179 PP 1842, XVI, pp. 25–6.

180 PP 1837–8, VII, pp. 44–5; Sargant, 'On the progress of elementary education', p. 233.

181 PP 1850, XXIII, pp. 9–12; PP 1854–5, XV, pp. 6–7.

182 PP 1837–8, VII, p. 95.

183 PP 1854, XIX, pp. 15–16.

184 *Newcastle*, II, p. 311.

185 PP 1842, XVII, p. 283.

186 *Newcastle*, II, pp. 256–8.

187 PP 1852, XXI, pp. 32 ff.

188 *Newcastle*, II, p. 285, Cf. PP 1863, XVIII, pp. 8–9 and *passim*.

189 PP 1864, XXII, 3rd report, pp. 40, 62.

190 PP 1842, XVII, p. 101.

191 *Berrows Worcester Jnl.*, 10 December 1846.

192 PP 1843, XV, p. Q92; PP 1854, XIX, pp. 10–15; *Worcestershire Chronicle*, 2 July 1856.

193 Burritt, *Walks in the Black Country*, pp. 152–3; PP 1851, XXIII, pp. 23–4; *Newcastle*, I, pp. 270–1, II, p. 257; *CCE, 1856–7*, pp. 425–6.

194 *Newcastle*, II, pp. 249, 257, 285–6; PP 1843, XV, p. Q92; PP 1864, XXII, 3rd report, p. xxii. See also, Barnsby, *Social conditions in the Black Country*, pp. 163–4.

195 *Reps. Mining Districts*, *passim*.

196 PP 1842, XVII, p. 128; PP 1850, XXIII, p. 38 ff.; PP 1854, XIX, pp. 15–6, 38; *Newcastle*, I, pp. 267–9; *CCE, 1856–7*, pp. 422–3.

197 PP 1843, XIV, pp. F37–8.

198 *Ibid.*, p. f13; PP 1854–5, XIV, pp. 77, 79.

199 Quot. Smith, *Conflict and Compromise*, p. 133.

200 PP 1843, XIV, pp. f129 ff., 148, 152.

201 PP 1844, XVI, p. 62.

202 *Ibid.*, pp. 62–3; PP 1851, XXIII, p. 24.

203 PP 1849, XXII, p. 22. Cf. R. H. Mottram and C. R. Coote, *Through Five Generations: the History of the Butterley Company*, London, 1950.

204 J. Benson, 'The motives of 19th-century colliery owners in promoting day schools', *JEAH*, III, 1970, p. 17.

205 PP 1843, XIII, pp. 185–6.

206 PP 1850, XXIII, pp. 33–4.

207 PP 1852–3, XL, p. 39.

208 PP 1850, XXIII, pp. 34, 40–1, Cf. PP 1854, XIX, p. 37.

209 PP 1867–8, XVII, (b), pp. 320–1.

210 PP 1868–9, XIII, (b), pp. 225, 294.

211 PP 1868–9, XIII, (a), p. 118.

212 *Newcastle*, II, p. 257.

213 B. J. Biggs, 'Early Victorian schools in north Nottinghamshire', *Trans. Thoroton Society*, LXXXI, 1977, p. 67.

214 PP 1868–9, XIII, (a), p. 116; (b), p. 416; *CCE, 1841–2*, p. 161.

215 *CCE, 1867–8*, pp. 94, 96–7.

216 PP 1868–9, XIII, (b), pp. 225, 294.

217 *Stratford Herald*, 11 March 1870.

218 PP 1868–9, XIII, (b), pp. 84–6.

219 See Chapter 5, and Map 13.

220 See Chapter 3, and Maps 6, 7.

221 For comment on this exercise, see p. 68.

222 Cf. Grayson, 'Literacy; Worcestershire'.

223 Bradshaw, 'Occupation and literacy', pp. 8, 11, 13, 17. Cf. Levine, *Family Formation*, p. 28.

224 Grayson, 'Literacy: Worcestershire'.

225 S. M. Stewart, 'Literacy in Warwickshire, 1840–1870', M. Ed. research exercise, University of Leeds, 1979, (LME), pp. 35–6: based on H.M.I. reports.

226 See p. 114.

227 See pp. 41–2.

228 See above.

229 Much the same impression is given if pupils 'on the books' (rather than in attendance on census day) are considered.

230 Stephens, (1977), p. 39; and see pp. 34–5.

231 *CCE, 1866–7*, pp. 47–8.

232 PP. 1864, XXII, 3rd report, p. 157.

233 *CCE, 1867–8*, p. 130; *CCE 1868–9*, pp. 207 ff.

234 *CCE, 1866–7*, pp. 47–8.

235 Barnsby, *Education in Wolverhampton*, p. 3.

236 See pp. 40–1.

237 *CCE, 1868–9*, pp. 203–4; PP 1864, XXII, 2nd report, p. vi.

238 *CCE, 1866–7*, p. 194.

239 Cf. R. J. Smith, 'Education, society and literacy: Nottinghamshire in the mid-nineteenth century', *University of Birmingham Historical Jnl.*, XII, 1969, p. 51; PP 1867, XVI, p. 84; PP 1867–8 XVII, (a), p. 85; PP 1852, XXI, p. 47.

240 Cf. the comparison of Worcester and Dudley in Grayson, 'Literacy: Worcestershire'.

241 Cf. *CCE, 1868–9*, pp. 50–1.

242 E.g., over half the private schools in two Birmingham parishes declined to make returns: *Abstract, 1833*, p. 991.

243 *CCE, 1850–1*, p. 472; *CCE, 1851–2*, pp. 726–8.

244 PP 1870, LIV, pp. 36–7.

245 See App. J., public day school pupils as percentage of total population, 1858.

246 *VCH, Warwickshire*, VIII, pp. 539–40, 299–300.

247 See pp. 47–8.

248 K. S. Inglis, 'Patterns of Religious Worship in 1851', *Jnl. Ecclesiastical History*, XI, 1960, p. 83; *VCH, Warwickshire*, VII, p. 427; *Education Census, 1851*, p. clvii; PP 1870, LIV, p. 296.

249 *VCH, Warwickshire*, VII pp. 489 ff.; M. Cruickshank, *Church and State in English Education*, London, 1964, pp. 16 ff.; Smith, *Conflict and Compromise*, p. 135.

250 *Education Census, 1851*, p. clxiii; Wardle, *Education and Society*, pp. 49–55.

251 Cf. *CCE, 1847–8 (2)*, p. 182.

252 Stephens, (1973), p. 33.

253 W. E. Marsden, 'Diffusion and regional variation in elementary education in England and Wales, 1800–1870', *History of Education*, XI, 1982, pp. 184–7; and see pp. 46–7.

254 E. S. Bellamy, 'Elementary education in the Staffordshire Potteries, 1780–1870', B. Phil. thesis, University of Hull, 1974, pp. 64–7.

255 Grayson, 'Literacy: Worcestershire', p. 59.

256 PP 1843, XIII, p. 141; PP 1863, XVIII, p. 27; PP 1868–9, XIII, (a), pp. 13, 17; (b), p. 87; *CCE, 1842–3*, pp. 56–9; *CCE, 1848–50*, p. 4; M. Johnson, *Derbyshire Village Schools*, Newton Abbot, 1970, pp. 59–60.

257 E.g., *Newcastle*, II, pp. 292–3; *CCE, 1867–8*, pp. 121–2.

258 E. g., F. D. How, *A Memoir of Bishop Sir Lovelace Stamer, Baronet, D. D.*, London, 1910, pp. 95–6.

259 *CCE, 1845 (1)*, pp. 256–7.

260 *CCE, 1844 (2)*, p. 575; *CCE, 1847–8 (2)*, p. 185; PP 1854, XIX, pp. 35–6.

261 *Newcastle*, II, p. 293.

262 Johnson, *Derbyshire Schools*, p. 60.

263 Simmons, *Leicester, Past and Present*, I, p. 174; *VCH, Leicestershire*, IV, p. 330; *Leicestershire Mercury*, 5 October 1839, 31 July 1841.

264 PP 1868–9, XIII, (a), pp. 13, 17, 60; (b), 87; Johnson, *Derbyshire Schools*, pp. 63 ff.

265 *CCE, 1846 (1)*, p. 150.

266 *CCE, 1844 (2)*, p. 523; *CCE, 1846 (2)*, p. 189.

267 *CCE, 1846 (1)*, pp. 206, 209.

268 *CCE, 1847–8 (2)*, pp. 192–3; *CCE, 1853–4*, pp. 674–5; *CCE, 1855–6*, p. 425.

269 *CCE, 1848–50 (2)*, pp. 5, 9–11; *CCE, 1850–1*, p. 463; *CCE, 1853–4*, p. 849; *CCE, 1855–6*, p. 420.

270 PP 1867–8, XVII, (a), p. 87.

271 PP 1863, XVIII, p. 272.

272 PP 1864, XXII, 3rd report, pp. 90–1, 132.

273 *CCE, 1845 (1)*, pp. 257, 276 ff. Cf. *CCE, 1846 (1)*, pp. 150–2.

274 'Education in the mining and manufacturing district of south Staffordshire', *JSSL*, X, 1847, pp. 238–9; PP 1847, XVI, p. 26. 8 per cent were of unrecorded age. Cf. Hill, *National Education*, I, pp. 248, 259.

275 PP 1843, XIV, p. C27.

276 PP 1852, XXI, p. 47. Cf. *CCE, 1850–1*, pp. 622–3.

277 PP 1864, XXII, 3rd report, pp. 32–3.

278 'Report on the state of education in Birmingham', *JSSL*, III, 1870, p. 41. Cf. *CCE, 1846 (1)*, p. 151.

279 PP 1864, XXII, 3rd report, p. 157.

280 PP 1843, XIV, p. c65. Cf. *ibid.*, p. c60.

281 *CCE, 1852–3*, p. 813.

282 PP 1854, XIX, p. 34, q.v. for other examples.

283 PP 1863, XVIII, p. 25.

284 PP 1864, XXII, 3rd report, pp. vi–vii.

285 PP 1866, XXIV, p. 86.

286 PP 1843, XIV, p. F37.

287 *CCE, 1857–8*, pp. 364–5.

288 PP 1863, XVIII, p. 271.

289 PP 1845, XV, p. 452; PP 1854–5, XIV, p. 269.

290 *CCE, 1846 (1)*, p. 150.

291 *CCE, 1850–1*, p. 625; *CCE, 1856–7*, pp. 254–5; PP 1863, XVIII, pp. 24–5.

292 *CCE, 1866–7*, pp. 199–200.

293 PP 1868–9, XIII, (a), pp. 59, 116; (b), 423, 428.

294 PP 1863, XVIII, pp. 24–5. Cf. *CCE, 1851–2*, p. 735; *CCE, 1852–3*, p. 813.

295 PP 1867–8, XVII, (a), p. 85.

296 PP 1867–8, XVII, (a), pp. 86–7, (b), pp. 332–3.

297 'Education in the mining district of south Staffordshire', p. 242; PP 1852, XXI, pp. 46–7; PP 1852–3, XL, p. 33. Cf. *CCE, 1841–2*, p. 149.

298 PP 1846, XXII, 3rd report, p. 33.

299 *Leicestershire Chronicle*, 18 September 1845; W. Biggs, *Report on Lecture on National Education*, 1849; PP 1863, XVIII, pp. 292-3.

300 PP. 1843, XIII, p. 168.

301 *CCE, 1854–5*, p. 422–3.

302 Cf. *CCE, 1850–1*, p. 462.

303 PP 1868–9, XIII, (a), p. 136.

304 E.g., PP 1868–9, XIII, (a), p. 332; (b), pp. 3,301.

305 *CCE, 1845 (1)*, p. 228.

306 *Abstract, 1833*.

307 PP 1834, XIX, pp. 102–4; 'State of education in Birmingham', pp. 25 ff.; Stephens, 'Early Victorian Coventry', p. 165; PP 1843, XIV, pp. C18, 26, f108, 110; Patterson, *Radical Leicester*, pp. 245, 372. Cf. S. D. Chapman, 'The evangelical revival and education in Nottingham', *Trans. Thoroton Society*, LXVI, 1962, pp. 40–4.

308 *1st Report of the Birmingham Education Society*, 1869.

309 Cf. Table 2·5, p. 39.

310 PP. 1834, XIX, p. 102.

311 'State of education in Birmingham', pp. 25 ff.; Laqueur, *Religion and Respectability*, p. 99.

312 PP 1843, XIII, pp. 142, 153, 167.

313 Calculated from, 'Report on the state of education among the working classes in the parish of West Bromwich', *JSSL*, II, 1839, p. 377.

314 PP 1843, XV, pp. C9–10. Cf. J. Ward, *Stoke upon Trent*, pp. 92–6, 245, 403, 497, 546, 554, 571; PP 1834, XIX, pp. 102–3.

315 Laqueur, *Religion and Respectability*, pp. 46–7; PP 1840, XXIV, pt. IV, p. 347.

316 Smith, 'Education, society and literacy', p. 50.

317 PP 1845, XV, p. 277. Cf. *ibid.*, pp. 8, 79, 89, 194; PP 1840, XXIV, pt. IV, p. 349; PP 1843, XIII, p. 142; PP 1854–5, XIV, p. 220.

318 PP 1845, XV, p. 218.

319 PP 1864, XXII, 3rd report, p. 159.

320 PP 1834, XIX, pp. 102–3; PP 1843, XIV, p. C19; 'Education in West Bromwich', p. 277.

321 'Education in the mining district of south Staffordshire', pp. 240–2.

322 Laqueur, *Religion and Respectability*, p. 99.

323 *Ibid.*, p. 103; PP 1845, XV, p. 114; *Leicestershire Mercury*, 7 June 1845.

324 Biggs, 'Early Victorian schools', p. 69. But cf. *ibid.*, p. 70.

325 *VCH, Staffordshire*, VIII, p. 298.

326 *Ibid.*, p. 278; *Newcastle*, II, pp. 279–80.

327 PP 1842, XVI, p. 24; PP 1842, XVII, pp. 144–5, 258, 286; PP 1843, XIV, pp. C10–11

328 PP 1843, XIV, pp. C26, f109.

329 PP 1845, XV, p. 194.

330 E.g., PP 1833, XX, pp. B1, 3 ff., 12, Cf. PP 1833, XXI, pp. C3, 7.

331 PP 1843, XIV, pp. f 98–9.

332 *Ibid.*, pp. f 200–3.

333 E.g. *Ibid.*, pp. f 34–25.

334 *Ibid.*, p. f127.

335 PP 1843, XIII, p. 169; PP 1843, XIV, pp. c10–11, 13, 69, F35, f109, Q51–2, q68. Cf. PP 1837–8, VII, p. 126; PP 1843, XIV, pp. 265, 277.

336 PP 1843, XIII, p. 152; PP 1863, XVIII, 187 ff., 225, 277, 328; PP 1864, XXII, 3rd report, pp. 61, 77, 132.

337 PP 1843, XIII, p. 153.

338 PP 1863, XVIII, pp. xl, 25–6.

339 PP 1850, XXIII, pp. 35–6; PP 1851, XXIII, p. 23; PP 1864, XXII, 3rd report, pp. 32–3, 159, 162.

340 *Education Census, 1851*, p. ccviii. Members of mechanics' and literary institutes not included.

341 *Newcastle*, II, pp. 291, 298–9.

342 PP 1843, XIII, pp. 146–7.

343 PP 1864, XXII, 3rd report, pp. 33–4.

344 Smith, *Conflict and Compromise*, pp. 135–6.

345 See pp. 166–7, 178.

346 *CCE, 1867–8*, pp. 366–8; *CCE, 1868–9*, p. 209; *CCE, 1869–70*, p. 355.

347 PP 1866, XXIV, p. 115.

348 Cf. *CCE, 1867–8*, p. 241.

349 *CCE, 1868–9*, pp. 51, 210–11. And see pp. 114, 147.

350 PP 1841, X, pp. 120–5.

5 The south midlands (pp. 162–205)

1 Welton (1860); *Censuses*. See also App. F.

2 Calculated from data in C. H. Lee, *British Regional Statistics, 1841–1971*, Cambridge, 1979, Series A tables.

3 The following draws on J. B. Spearing, 'On the agriculture of Berkshire', *JRAS*, XXI, 1860; W, Bennett, 'The farming of Bedfordshire', *JRAS*, XVIII, 1857; W. Bearn, 'On the farming of Northamptonshire', *JRAS*, XIII, 1852; S. Jonas, 'The farming of Cambridgeshire', *JRAS*, VII, 1846; J. Caird, *English Agriculture in 1850–1*, London, 1852; G. E. Fussell, ' "High Farming" in the east midlands and East Anglia', *Economic Geography*, XXVII, 1951; W. Hasbach, *A History of the English Agricultural Labourer*, trans. R. Kenyon, London, 1908.

4 N. Hammond, *Rural Life in the Vale of the White Horse, 1780–1914*, Reading 1974, p. 89.

5 *VCH Hertfordshire*, IV, pp. 226–7.

6 Hammond, *Rural Life*, p. 47.

7 F. M. L. Thompson, *English Landed Society in the Nineteenth Century*, London, 1963, pp. 32, 114–7.

8 E. H. Hunt, *Regional Wage Variations in Britain, 1850–1914*, Oxford, 1973, pp. 62–3; Caird, *English Agriculture*, p. 480; A. L. Bowley, 'Rural population in England and Wales', *JRSS*, LXXVII, 1914, App. III.

9 A. Digby, 'The labour market and the continuity of social policy after 1834: the case of the eastern counties', *Ec. H. R.*, 2nd ser. XXVIII, 1975, p. 82; W. Meyer, 'Driving the Irish', *Records of Huntingdonshire*, 1981; D. H. Morgan, *Harvesters and Harvesting, 1840–1900*, London, 1982, pp. 76–83.

10 Cf. Digby, 'Labour market', pp. 70, 74; D. R. Mills, 'The quality of life in Melbourne, Cambridgeshire, in the period 1800–50', *International Rev. of Social History*, XXIII, 1978.

11 *VCH, Cambridgeshire*, II, pp. 116–7, 119; Spearing, 'Agriculture of Berkshire'.

12 N. E. Agar, *The Bedfordshire Farm Worker in the Nineteenth Century*, Bedfordshire Historical Record Society, LX, 1981; J. Godber, 'Some documents relating to riots', *ibid.*, XLIX, 1970; A. F. Cirket, 'The 1830 riots in Bedfordshire, background and events', *ibid.*, LVII, 1978.

13 Welton (1860), pp. 13–14.

14 J. Vaizey, *The Brewing Industry, 1886–1951*, London, 1960, pp. 3–9; J. H. Clapham, *Economic History of Modern Britain*, I, Cambridge, 1926, p. 170; II, 1932, pp. 122–3, 259.

15 D. C. Coleman, *The British Paper Industry, 1495–1860*, Oxford, 1958, pp. 220–4, 292–5; *VCH, Hertfordshire*, IV, pp. 256–7; PP 1843, XIII, pp. 18, 22; PP 1865, XX, p. xxxvii.

16 Welton (1860), pp. 13–4; *VCH, Oxfordshire*, II, pp. 165–6, 202–5, 227–8, 250–1, 268–70; A. Everitt, 'The Banburys of England', *Urban History Year-book*, 1974; A. Plummer and R. E. Early, *The Blanket Makers, 1669–1969*, London, 1969, pp. 73–5; *VCH, Hertfordshire*, IV, pp. 248–51.

17 Cf. W. H. Derbyshire, *The History of Dunstable*, Dunstable, 2nd edn. [*c.* 1882], p. 100.

18 Cf. P. Horn, 'The employment of children in Victorian Oxfordshire', *Midland History*, IV, 1977, pp. 68–9; and p. 214.

19 Welton (1860), p. 66.

20 See below.

21 D. Bythell, *The Sweated Trades*, London, 1978, pp. 102–4.

22 PP 1863, XVIII, p. 257.

23 P. Horn, *Labouring Life in the Victorian Countryside*, Dublin, 1976, pp. 110–1.

24 Bythell, *Sweated Trades*, pp. 104–5; PP 1843, XIII, pp. 97, 111.

25 The following draws on: F. Davis, *The History of Luton, with its Hamlets*, Luton, 1855, pp. 155, 159–60; *VCH, Bedfordshire*, II, pp. 121–2; *VCH, Hertfordshire*, IV, pp. 253–6; Bythell, *Sweated Trades*, pp. 119–22; PP 1843, XIII, p. 132; PP 1843, XIV, pp. 248–9, 253, 256.

26 Welton (1860), pp. 97–8.

27 *VCH, Hertfordshire*, IV, p. 254; P. Horn, 'Child workers in the pillow lace and straw plait trades of Victorian Buckinghamshire and Bedfordshire', *Historical Jnl.*, XVII, 1974, p. 789; P. L. R. Horn, 'The Buckinghamshire straw plait trades in Victorian England', *Records of Buckinghamshire*, XIX, 1971, pp. 44 ff.

28 Welton (1860), p. 10, Cf. P. R. Mountfield, 'The footwear industry of the east midlands, III, Northamptonshire, 1700 to 1911', *East Midlands Geographer*, III, 1962–5, pp. 434–7.

29 PP 1864, XXII, 2nd Report, pp. 168–70; PP 1865, XX, pp. 124–6; J. Stafford, *Life in Old Northampton*, Northampton, 1975, pp. 40–3; Bythell, *Sweated Trades*, pp. 11–17; Mountfield, 'Footwear industry', pp. 442–8; K Brooker, 'The Northampton shoemakers' reaction to industrialisation', *Northamptonshire Past and Present*, VI (3), 1980, p. 151; V. A. Hatley, 'Some aspects of Northampton's history', *ibid.*, III (6), 1965–6, pp. 243, 246; R. A. Church, 'Labour supply and innovation, 1800–1860: the boot and shoe industry', *Business History*, XII.

30 Hunt, *Regional Wage Variations*, p. 143.

31 Cf. Horn, 'Children in Victorian Oxfordshire', p. 69.

32 Bucks. County Record Office, Clergy Visitation Returns, Buckingham Archdeaconry, MS Oxf. Dioc. Pp. d. 179, 1857.

33 The following draws on: *VCH, Buckinghamshire*, II, p. 108; PP 1843, XIII, pp. 97–111; PP 1863, XVIII, pp. lxxxi, 185, 256–63; Horn, 'Child workers'; Horn, 'Buckinghamshire straw plait trades'; P. L. R. Horn, 'Pillow lace-making in Victorian England: the experience of Oxfordshire', *Textile History*, III, 1972; Bythell, *Sweated Trades*.

34 PP 1863, XVIII, p. 258.

35 *VCH, Buckinghamshire*, II, pp. 119, 121; PP 1843, XIII, p. 132.

36 Quot. Horn, 'Buckinghamshire straw plait trades', p. 789.

37 Quot. *ibid.*, p. 790.

38 PP 1843, XIV, p. a56.

39 Horn, *Labouring Life*, p. 115.

40 PP 1868–9, XIII, (a), pp. 80–1.

41 *CCE, 1857–8*, pp. 451–2.

42 Hatley, *Northampton's History*, p. 246.

43 Stafford, *Old Northampton*, p. 40.

44 PP 1864, XXII, 2nd Report, pp. 168–70; PP 1865, XX, pp. 124–6, 135–6.

45 PP 1843, XIII, pp. 13–4, 49, 63, 93, 99; PP 1865, XX, pp. xxxvii–xxxviii, 149–50, 161–4; Coleman, *Paper Industry*, pp. 292, 294–5.

46 PP 1867–8, XVII, (a) pp. 111, 126; Hasbach, *English Agricultural Labourer*, pp. 227–8, 257–8, 265–70, 406–8; Horn, 'Child Workers', pp. 66–7.

47 PP 1867, XVI, pp. viii–xxiv, 11; PP 1867–8, XVII, pp. ix, 155–6. See also Morgan, *Harvesters*, pp. 58–9.

48 *CCE, 1847–8*, pp. 51–2; PP 1843, XIII, p. 181.

49 E.g., *CCE, 1848–50 (2)*, pp. 25–6; *CCE 1865–6*, p. 181.

50 PP 1840, XXIV, pt. V, pp. 551–2.

51 See above. Cf. Horn, 'Buckinghamshire straw plait trades', pp. 791–2; Horn, 'Child workers', pp. 50–2.

52 *CCE, 1850–1*, p. 207.

53 Cf. Horn, 'Buckinghamshire straw plait trades', pp. 45–7.

54 PP 1863, XVIII, pp. 256–9.

55 E.g., *ibid.*, p. 185.

56 Cf. PP 1876, XXX, p. 158.

57 *CCE, 1848–50 (2)*, p. 26.

58 *CCE, 1844 (2)*, pp. 171–3.

59 J. S. Hurt, *Bringing Literacy to Rural England: the Hertfordshire Example*, Chichester, 1972, p. 10.

60 Horn, 'Buckinghamshire straw plait trades', p. 48; *Report of the Board of Education for the Archdeaconry and County of Bedford*, 1846, p. 15; *CCE, 1848–50 (2)*, p. 26; PP 1863 XVIII, p. 185.

61 PP 1864 XXII, 2nd Report, pp. 168–9.

62 *CCE 1865–6*, pp. 181–2.

63 PP 1865, XX, p. 150.

64 *CCE, 1847–8*, p. 52.

65 *CCE, 1867–8*, pp. 96–7.

66 *CCE, 1857–8*, pp. 451–2.

67 *CCE, 1865–6*, p. 183.

68 *CCE, 1867–8*, p. 97.

69 Horn, 'Child workers', pp. 788–9.

70 *CCE, 1844 (2)*, p. 172; PP 1843, XIII, p. 132.

71 *CCE, 1850–1*, p. 206, Cf. Hurt, *Bringing Literacy*, p. 11.

72 Quot. Horn, 'Buckinghamshire straw plait trades', p. 45.

73 *CCE, 1865–6*, p. 177; *CCE, 1867–8*, p. 92.

74 *CCE, 1857–8*, p. 450.

75 *CCE, 1864–5*, p. 141.

76 See p. 199.

77 Cf. *CCE, 1867–8*, p. 92.

78 *CCE, 1862–3*, pp. 32–3; PP 1863, XVIII, pp. 257–9.

79 PP 1868–9, XIII, (a), p. 88.

80 PP 1868–9, XIII, (b), p. 401.

81 PP 1863, XVIII, p. 259.

82 Cf. *Newcastle*, V, pp. 311–2.

83 PP 1867–8, XVII, (a), p. 134.

84 PP 1876, XXIX, p. 86; XXX, p. 158; PP 1863, XVIII, pp. 257–9; Hurt, *Bringing Literacy*, pp. 13–4.

85 PP 1876, XXIX, pp. 158–9, 188. Cf. Bythell, *Sweated Trades*, p. 121.

86 Quot. Horn, *Labouring Life*, p. 112.

87 Cf. Horn, 'Children in Victorian Oxfordshire', pp. 61, 64–5.

88 Agar, *Bedfordshire Farm Worker*, pp. 164, 166.

89 Cf. P. Horn (ed.), *Village Education in Nineteenth Century Oxfordshire*, Oxfordshire Record Society, LI, 1979, p. xxiii; Horn, 'Children in Victorian Oxfordshire', pp. 62–3, 66.

90 *VCH, Cambridgeshire*, V, p. 45.

91 PP 1843, XIII, p. 132.

92 PP 1867–8, XVII, (a), pp. 113–4. Cf. *VCH, Cambridgeshire*, VIII, p. 29.

93 Horn, 'Children in Victorian Oxfordshire', p. 63.

94 PP 1876, XXX, p. 160.

95 Cf. Hurt, *Bringing Literacy*, p. 22.

96 *CCE, 1845 (1)*, p. 151; Agar, *Bedfordshire Farm Worker*, pp. 161–2; Morgan, *Harvesters*, p. 63.

97 PP 1867–8, XVII, (b), p. 439.

98 *Newcastle*, V, pp. 311–2; *CCE, 1845 (1)*, p. 151; *CCE, 1867–8*, pp. 94, 96–7.

99 *CCE, 1865–6*, p. 177.

100 See p. 176.

101 PP 1867–8, XVII, (a), p. 130; *CCE, 1870–1*, p. 23.

102 Hurt, *Bringing Literacy*, p. 24.

103 *CCE, 1844 (2)*, p. 171; *CCE, 1845 (1)*, p. 150; *CCE, 1850–1*, pp. 150–1; *CCE, 1866–7*, p. 19; *CCE, 1867–8*, p. 94; *CCE, 1872–3*, p. 95; PP 1868–9, XIII, (a), pp. 88–9.

104 See below.

105 *Report of the Northamptonshire Society for Promoting and Extending Education*, 1856, p. 11. Cf. *17th A.R. Oxford Diocesan Board of Education, 1846*, p. 20.

106 *CCE, 1867–8*, p. 94.

107 *CCE, 1866–7*, pp. 19–20.

108 *CCE, 1844 (2)*, pp. 6, 171.

109 Quot. Horn, *Village Education*, p. xv, q.v. for other examples.

110 *CCE, 1866–7*, p. 23. Cf. D. McClatchy, *Oxfordshire Clergy, 1777–1869*, Oxford, 1960, pp. 141–4.

111 PP 1868–9, XIII, (a), p. 91.

112 Horn, *Village Education*, p. xv.

113 *A.R. of the Diocesan Association of Schoolmasters in the Diocese of Oxford*, 1857, p. 38. For Wilberforce, see G. K. Clark, *Churchmen and the Condition of England, 1832–1885*, London, 1973, pp. 144–5.

114 *CCE, 1844 (2)*, pp. 8–9.

115 Hurt, *Bringing Literacy*, p. 21.

116 *CCE, 1843–4*, pp. 36–7. Cf. *CCE, 1845 (1)*, p. 158.

117 PP 1867–8, XIII, (a), p. 98.

118 *CCE, 1866–7*, p. 23; *CCE, 1870–1*, p. 23.

119 See below, pp. 197–8, and App. L.

120 E. Legg, 'Education in Fenny Stratford', *Records of Buckinghamshire*, XXII, 1980, p. 41.

121 Hurt, *Bringing Literacy*, pp. 20–1.

122 *CCE, 1850–1*, p. 218.

123 Cf. *CCE, 1845 (1)*, p. 151.

124 *CCE, 1844 (2)*, p. 6; *CCE, 1864–5*, p. 141. Cf. A. D. Gilbert, *Religion and Society in Industrial England: Church, Chapel and Social Change, 1740–1914*, London, 1976, p. 98.

125 *CCE, 1844 (2)*, pp. 6–7.

126 *CCE, 1851–2*, p. 598.

127 *CCE, 1863–4*, p. 128; *CCE, 1864–5*, pp. 141–2.

128 F. Hill, *National Education: Its Present State and Future Prospects*, I, London, 1836,

p. 270; *CCE, 1858–9*, p. 113.

129 PP 1868–9, XIII, (a), p. 88.

130 PP 1887, XXX, p. 735. Cf. App. H, persons of independent means.

131 J. S. Hurt, 'Landowners, farmers and clergy in the financing of rural education before 1870', *JEAH*, I, 1968–9; Hurt, *Bringing Literacy*, pp. 14 ff. Cf. *CCE, 1847–8*, p. 51.

132 *CCE, 1844 (2)*, pp. 7–8.

133 Hurt, *Bringing Literacy*, pp. 25–6.

134 PP 1868–9, XIII, (a), p. 118.

135 *Ibid.*, pp. viii–ix, 87–90; PP 1867–8, XVII, (a), pp. 126, 129–31.

136 PP 1868–9, XIII, pp. xi, 91.

137 PP 1867–8, XVII, (a), pp. 113–6.

138 E.g., PP 1876, XXX, p. 160.

139 *CCE, 1863–4*, p. 128.

140 Cf. R. S. Schofield, 'Dimensions of illiteracy in England, 1750–1850', *Explorations in Economic History*, X, 1973, pp. 447–9.

141 For comment on this exercise, see p. 68.

142 See p. 8.

143 C. F. Tebutt, *St. Neot's*, London, 1978, p. 18.

144 V. A. Hatley, 'Literacy at Northampton', *Northamptonshire Past and Present*, IV, 1966–71, p. 379.

145 See p. 202.

146 Hill, *National Education*, p. 271.

147 *VCH, Cambridgeshire*, II, p. 354.

148 *Abstract, 1833*.

149 Cf. Stephens (1977), p. 35.

150 *Ibid.*, p. 39.

151 D. W. Bushby, 'Elementary education in Bedford, 1868–1903', *Bedfordshire Historical Records Society*, LIV, 1975, p. 12. And see *ibid.*, chapter 1; *CCE, 1844 (2)*, p. 35; *VCH, Bedfordshire*, II, p. 149. At Reading 8 per cent of the population was at school in 1838 (PP 1837–8, VII, p. viii), compared with 11 per cent in Berkshire in 1833 (App. L).

152 *CCE, 1844 (2)*, pp. 174–6; Stephens (1977), p. 39.

153 *CCE, 1844 (2)*, pp. 3, 171–2. Cf. *Dunstable Chronicle*, 10 October 1861.

154 Hill, *National Education*, p. 271.

155 Hurt, *Bringing Literacy*, pp. 19–21.

156 *CCE, 1872–3*, pp. 71–4.

157 *CCE, 1862–3*, p. 63.

158 *CCE, 1844 (2)* pp. 2–3.

159 See Map 10.

160 *CCE, 1844 (2)*, pp. 3–5, 171–4.

161 *CCE, 1848–50*, p. 5; *CCE, 1854–5*, p. 489; *CCE, 1857–8*, pp. 446–7; *CCE, 1860–1*. p. 66.

162 Horn, *Village Education*, p. xxiii.

163 *CCE, 1857–8*, pp. 446–7; *CCE, 1868–9*, p. 33; PP 1864, XXII, 2nd Report, p. 191.

164 PP 1868–9, XIII, (a), pp. 85–7; *CCE, 1872–3*, p. 71. Cf. *CCE, 1858–9*, p. 113; Hammond, *Rural Life*, p. 131; Spearing, 'Agriculture of Berkshire', p. 44.

165 *CCE, 1855–6*, p. 416; *CCE, 1862–3*, p. 31.

166 *CCE, 1862–3*, pp. 66–70; *CCE, 1865–6*, pp. 176–7.

167 PP 1867–8, XVII, (a), p. 113; *The Times*, 10 April 1868.

168 *CCE, 1855–6*, p. 417.

169 *CCE, 1864–5*, pp. 144–6; *CCE, 1868–9*, pp. 230–1, 234.

170 PP 1867–8, XVII, (a), pp. 128–9; PP 1867–8, LIII, pp. 195–6; PP 1874, XIII, p. 10.

171 *CCE, 1872–3*, p. 91.

172 *VCH, Cambridgeshire*, VIII, pp. 48, 53, 123.

173 *CCE, 1872–3*, p. 94.

174 *VCH, Cambridgeshire*, VIII, p. 29.

175 see pp. 169–70.

176 See p. 190.

177 Bucks. −0·47; Cambs. −0·24; Berks. −0·06; Hunts. +0·03 (3 readings only).

178 *CCE, 1850–1*, p. 217.

179 See. App. N. Cf. B. I. Coleman, 'Southern England in the Census of Religious Workship, 1851', *Southern History*, V, 1983, p. 165.

180 See above.

181 See p. 147.

182 See Apps. G. H. The districts were: Hertford (% marks 18, % of population at all day schools 16); Woodstock (25, 13); Bedford (25, 10); Wokingham (27, 10); Hardingstone (27, 8); Aylesbury (28, 8); Faringdon (32, 11); Caxton (36, 11); Newport Pagnell (40, 7); Woburn (40, 9).

183 *Report of the Northamptonshire Society for Promoting and Extending Education*, 1856, p. 10.

184 B. S. Trinder, *Victorian Banbury*, Chichester, 1982, p. 104.

185 E.g., *CCE, 1844 (2)*, pp. 36–7; *CCE, 1848–50 (2)*, p. 28; *Newcastle*, II, p. 167. Cf. *CCE, 1845 (1)*, p. 158; *CCE, 1861–2*, p. 101.

186 Bucks. County Record Office, Clergy Visitation Returns, Buckingham Archdeaconry, MS Oxf. Dioc. Pp. d.179, 1857, and see pp. 172, 176.

187 PP 1863, XVIII, pp. 13, 258, 262–3, and *passim*.

188 *CCE, 1855–6*, p. 301; *CCE, 1853–4*, p. 329.

189 PP 1867–8, XIII, (a), pp. 127–9; *CCE, 1867–8*, p. 92.

190 *CCE, 1852–3*, p. 349.

191 *CCE, 1868–9*, p. 20.

192 PP 1867–8, XVII, (a), pp. 127–9; PP 1868–9, XIII, (a), pp. 85–7.

193 *CCE, 1855–6*, p. 301. Cf. *CCE, 1853–4*, p. 329.

194 Cf. *CCE, 1850–1*, p. 207.

195 *CCE, 1850–1*, p. 147.

196 *CCE, 1868–9*, p. 328.

197 *CCE, 1845 (1)*, p. 158; *CCE, 1846 (1)*, p. 277.

198 *CCE, 1868–9*, p. 230.

199 *CCE, 1871–2*, pp. 31–2, Horn, 'Children in Victorian Oxfordshire', pp. 64–5.

200 PP 1863, XVIII, p. 261.

201 *Abstract, 1833*, and App. J.

202 Abingdon, Northampton, Maidenhead, Wycombe, St. Albans, Chipping Norton.

203 PP 1840, XXIV, pt. V, p. 522.

204 *Education Census, 1851*, p. ccviii.

205 PP 1867–8, XVII, (a), p. 129; PP 1868–9, XIII, (a), pp. 87–8. Spearing, 'Agriculture of Berkshire', p. 44; *CCE, 1845 (1)*, pp. 159–60. Cf. PP 1863, XVIII, pp. 256–63; McClatchy, *Oxfordshire Clergy*, pp. 159–62.

206 PP 1867–8, XVII, (a), pp. 115–16.

207 Cf. *CCE, 1844 (2)*, p. 6; Hurt, *Bringing Literacy, passim*.

208 Cf. *VCH, Cambridgeshire*, II, p. 319.

209 Hurt, *Bringing Literacy*, p. 15.

210 E.g., *CCE, 1848–50*, p. 7; *CCE, 1866–7*, p. 21.

211 *CCE, 1845 (1)*, pp. 168–9. Cf. *CCE, 1847–8*, pp. 52–3; *CCE, 1851–2*, p. 598.

212 *CCE, 1851–2*, p. 602, Cf. *CCE, 1867–8*, p. 94.

213 *CCE, 1868–9*, p. 230.

214 *CCE, 1850–1*, pp. 150–5; *CCE, 1857–8*, pp. 443–7; *CCE, 1858–9*, p. 113; *CCE, 1866–7*, pp. 18–19.

215 *CCE, 1855–6*, p. 416; *CCE, 1866–7*, pp. 20–1.

216 *CCE, 1850–1*, p. 147.

217 *CCE, 1845 (1)*, pp. 162–3, Cf. *CCE, 1850–1*, p. 149; *CCE, 1855–6*, p. 417.

218 *CCE, 1846 (1)*, p. 275.

219 *CCE, 1872–3*, pp. 71–2.

220 CCE, 1850–1, pp. 158–62.

221 PP 1868–9, XIII, (a), p. 88.

222 *CCE, 1870–1*, p. 23; *CCE, 1871–2*, pp. 31–2. Cf. *CCE, 1872–3*, pp. 71–3.

223 *CCE, 1865–6*, pp. 177–83.

6 The western counties (pp. 206–63)

1 For county populations, see App. F.

2 Kingsbridge, Plympton St. Mary, Totnes, Honiton, Axminster. Cf. J. Saville, *Rural Depopulation in England and Wales, 1851–1951*, London, 1957, chapter 5.

3 South Molton, Crediton, Okehampton, Torrington, Holsworthy, Bideford.

4 Dursley, Thornbury, Chipping Sodbury, Chippenham, Cricklade, Calne, Bradford, Frome, Shepton Mallet.

5 A. L. Bowley, 'Rural population in England and Wales', *JRAS*, LXXVII, (1914), p. 605.

6 Cf. T. A. Welton, 'Forty years of industrial change in England and Wales', *Trans. Manchester Statistical Society*, 1897–8, p. 210.

7 Calculated from data in C. H. Lee, *British Regional Statistics, 1841–1971*, Cambridge, 1979, Series A tables.

8 The following paragraphs draw on: relevant VCH volumes; J. Caird, *English Agriculture in 1850–1*, London, 1852; Prize essays in *JRAS*, V, 1844; VI, 1845; IX, 1848; XI, 1850; XIV, 1853; XIX, 1858; VI NS, 1870; W. G. Hoskins, *Devon*, London, 1954; W. J. Rowe, *Cornwall in the Age of the Industrial Revolution*, Liverpool, 1953, chapter 6; *Census, 1851*; E. H. Hunt, *Regional Wage Variations in Britain, 1850–1914*, Oxford, 1960; articles by G. E. Fussell in *Economic Geography*, XXIV, 1948; XXV, 1949; XXVII, 1951; E. Girdleston, 'Landowners, land and those who till it', *Fraser's Magazine*, LXXVIII, 1868.

9 F. M. L. Thompson, *English Landed Society in the Nineteenth Century*, London, 1963, pp. 32, 114–7.

10 F. E. Halliday, *A History of Cornwall*, London, 1975 edn., pp. 300–1.

11 W. B. Stephens, 'An Anatomy of Illiteracy in Mid-Victorian Devon', in J. Porter (ed.), *Education and Labour in the South West*, Exeter, 1975, p. 8.

12 Thompson, *English Landed Society*, pp. 32, 114–7.

13 The other two were Nottinghamshire and Worcestershire.

14 Bowley, 'Rural Population', App. III; Hunt, *Wage Variations*, pp. 14–5, 62–3; *VCH, Wiltshire*, IV, p. 80; *VCH, Dorset*, I, p. 262; J. H. Bettey, *Dorset*, Newton Abbot, 1974, p. 57; A. E. W. Salt, 'Agricultural labourers in Herefordshire', *Trans. Woolhope Club*, 1947, p. 95.

15 M. Baker, 'Aspects of the life of the Wiltshire agricultural labourer, *c.* 1850' *Wiltshire Archaeological Magazine*, LXXIV–LXXV, 1981; S. G. Osborne, *A View of the Low Moral and Physical Condition of the Agricultural Labourer*, London, 1844.

16 Royal Naval personnel not included.

17 Welton (1860).

18 The following draws on: *VCH, Cornwall*, I, pp. 554 ff; A. K. Jenkin, *The Cornish Miner*,

London, 1927, pp. 158 ff, 204 ff; Rowe, *Cornwall in the Industrial Revolution*, Chapter 4; D. B. Barton, *A History of Tin Mining and Smelting in Cornwall*, Truro, 1967, Chapters 1, 2; L. L. Price, '"West Barbary" or notes on the system of work and wages in the Cornish Mines', 1851, reprinted in R. Burt (ed.), *Cornish Mining*, Newton Abbot, 1969, pp. 125, 133–53, 160–3; various vols. of the Children's Employment Commissioners' reports.

19 Halliday, *Cornwall*, pp. 299–300; R. M. Barton, *A History of the Cornish China-Clay Industry*, Truro, 1960, Chapters 2, 3.

20 PP 1842, XVI, p. 78; PP 1847–8, XXVI, pp. 2, 555–6; B. Trinder, *The Industrial Revolution in Shropshire*, London, 1973, Chapter 3.

21 PP 1840, XXIII, pp. 407–17, 437, 448 ff.

22 PP 1840, XXIV, pt. V, pp. 409, 425–30.

23 PP 1840, XXIII, pp. 412–3, 445; PP 1840, XXIV, pt. V, p. 436.

24 *VCH, Wiltshire*, IV, pp. 170 ff.

25 A. Redford, *Labour Migration in England*, ed. W. H. Chaloner, Manchester, 1976, p. 46; *VCH, Wiltshire*, IV, pp. 170 ff; PP 1840, XXIII, p. 442.

26 PP 1833, XX, pp. B1, 80. Cf. PP 1843, XIII, p. 25.

27 D. Bythell, *The Sweated Trades*, London, 1978, pp. 102–4; PP 1863, XVIII, pp. 246–7; PP 1843, XIII, pp. 246–86; *VCH, Somerset*, II, pp. 426–7; and see pp. 215–23.

28 Bythell, *Sweated Trades*, pp. 117–9; *VCH, Wiltshire*, IV, pp. 236–7.

29 Bythell, *Sweated Trades*, p. 72.

30 PP 1840, XXIII, p. 447; *Census, 1851.*

31 PP 1843, XIV, p. d43; PP 1866, XXIV, pp. 102–4, 106; *VCH, Dorset*, I, pp. 350 ff.

32 See pp. 20–1.

33 Welton (1860), pp. 42–3.

34 Dorset, 12·7 per cent; Cornwall, 10·6; Herefordshire, 14·2; Monmouthshire, 11·8; Wiltshire, 13·2: calculated from Welton (1860). Cf. App. H, (but note that in Cornwall and Monmouthshire the figures included some indoor farm workers). See also p. 20.

35 Welton (1860), pp. 15–6.

36 Cf. E. H. Hunt, *British Labour History, 1815–1914*, London, 1981, pp. 14–5. And see pp. 20–1.

37 Exceptions: Devon and Cornwall, 1871 (5–10)

38 Jenkin, *Cornish Miner*, p. 223; PP 1842, XV, pp. 205–8, 211, 214–6; PP 1843, XIII, p. 160.

39 Jenkin, *Cornish Miner*, pp. 22, 241.

40 PP 1842, XV, pp. 229–36; PP 1842, XVI, pp. 764, 807; Jenkin, *Cornish Miner*, pp. 232–7.

41 PP 1864, XXIV, pp. 121–2.

42 PP 1842, XV, pp. 36–7; PP 1847–8, XXVI, p. 3.

43 *VCH, Somerset*, II, p. 386; PP 1842, XV, pp. 22 ff., 36, 98; PP 1842, XVI, pp. 77 ff; PP 1842, XVII, pp. 49 ff, 428; N. K. Buxton, *The Economic Development of the British Coal Industry*, London, 1978, p. 129; Trinder, *Industrial Revolution in Shropshire*, pp. 352–4.

44 PP 1842, XVII, pp. 534–5, 537; PP 1846, XXIV, pp. 30–1.

45 PP 1842, XV, pp. 98, 103–4, 112.

46 PP 1843, XIV, pp. d45–6; 01–2.

47 PP 1842, XVI, pp. 79–80.

48 PP 1850, XXIII, pp. 61 ff.

49 PP 1833, XX, pp. BI, 29–30, 62–8, 90 ff; PP 1834, XIX, pp. 24, 35; PP 1834, XX, section B1, *passim.*

50 PP 1843, XIV, p. d43.

51 PP 1866, XXIV, pp. 102–4. Cf. *Newcastle*, II, p. 26.

52 PP 1866, XXIV, pp. 106–7.

53 PP 1843, XIV, p. D5.

54 PP 1833, XX, p. B1, 80–3; PP 1834, XIX, p. 31; PP 1834, XX, pp. B1, 1; PP 1843, XIII, p. 11.

55 PP 1864, XXII, 2nd Report, p.v.

56 PP 1843, XIII, p. 11; PP 1863, XVIII, pp. 247 ff.

57 Quot. Bythell, *Sweated Trades*, 103.

58 PP 1864, XXII, 2nd Report, pp. xxix–xxxii; Bythell, *Sweated Trades*, 102, 104–5.

59 I. Pinchbeck, *Women Workers in the Industrial Revolution, 1750–1850*, London, 1977 impression, pp. 224–6.

60 PP 1843, XIII, pp. 128–30; PP 1843, XIV, pp. D2–6, d34–9.

61 *Newcastle*, II, p. 26; PP 1864, XXII, 2nd Report, pp. 175–8, 194.

62 PP 1865, XX, pp. xxxvi–xxxvii, 129–30.

63 PP 1843, XIII, pp. 9, 18, 20; PP 1843, XIV, pp. d46–7.

64 PP 1843, XV, p. 01.

65 PP 1843, XV, pp. 03, 08; PP 1866, XXIV, p. 53.

66 PP 1843, XII, pp. 28, 43 ff. Cf. E. W. Martin, *The Shearers and the Shorn*, London, 1965, pp. 53–4.

67 PP 1868–9, XII, (a), p. 35.

68 Jenkin, *Cornish Miner*, p. 241.

69 *Census, 1851*; PP 1868–9, XIII, (a), pp. 12–3.

70 PP 1870, XIII, pp. 58–65, Cf. *CCE, 1850–1*, p. 203.

71 PP 1843, XII, p. 29; PP 1868–9, XIII, (a), pp. xiii–xv, 3–4; (b), pp. 5 ff; Cf. *Report on the State of Parochial Education in the Diocese of Salisbury*, 1840, p. 26.

72 PP 1867–8, XVII, (a), pp. 9–10; (b), pp. 3–4. Cf. *CCE, 1850–1*, p. 206.

73 PP 1868–9, XIII, (a), pp. 121–2.

74 *Ibid.*, pp. 51–2; *CCE, 1850–1*, pp. 201–3.

75 *Newcastle*, II, pp. 56–61, 66.

76 *Newcastle*, III, pp. 30–1.

77 *Ibid.*, p. 66.

78 See chapter 4.

79 *Churchman's Family Magazine*, Aug. 1865.

80 PP 1847, XXVII, pp. 393–4. Cf. *CCE, 1845(2)*, p. 199.

81 PP 1846, XXIV, p. 31. Cf. PP 1847, XXVII, pp. 370–1.

82 PP 1850, XXIII, p. 64.

83 PP 1846, XXIV, p. 38. Cf. *CCE, 1839–40*, p. 184.

84 PP 1850, XXIII, pp. 59–64; R. Pallister, 'The determinants of elementary school attendance about 1850', *Durham Research Rev.* V, 1969, p. 389.

85 D. R. A. Williams, 'Elementary education in the Forest of Dean, 1698–1870', M. A. thesis, University of Bristol, 1962, p. 251.

86 PP 1847–8, XXVI, pp. 3–4.

87 I. Wilks, *South Wales and the Rising of 1839: Class Struggle as Armed Struggle*, London, 1984.

88 Jenkin, *Cornish Miner*, pp. 198–9; Rowe, *Cornwall in the Industrial Revolution*, p. 311. Cf. *Quarterly Rev.*, CII, 1857, pp. 288, 329; Burt, *Cornish Mining*, p. 125.

89 *CCE, 1844(2)*, pp. 189–90; *40th BFSS*, 1845, pp. 93, 118.

90 PP 1842, XVI, p. 758.

91 *Newcastle*, III, pp. 101, 105, 113, 119.

92 *12th Report Wesleyan Education Committee*, 1850, p. 63.

93 E.g., PP 1847–8, XXVI, p. 3.

94 *CCE, 1840–1*, pp. 195 ff.

95 *CCE, 1839–40*, pp. 182–3; *CCE, 1840–1*, pp. 202–3.

96 PP 1847, XXVII, p. 377.

97 *CCE, 1839–40*, pp. 177, 182.

98 *CCE, 1840–1*, pp. 209–10.

99 Jenkin, *Cornish Miner*, pp. 222, 230; Halliday, *Cornwall*, pp. 255–6.

100 *CCE, 1839–40*, p. 182.

101 PP 1843, XIII, p. 194.

102 E.g., PP 1868–9, XIII, pp. 37, 126–7.

103 *Newcastle*, III, pp. 5, 35, 100.

104 E.g., PP 1840, XXIII, p. 412; PP 1840, XXIV, pt. V, pp. 491, 493–4; *Newcastle*, III, p. 34.

105 PP 1840, XXIV, pt. V, pp. 499 ff.

106 *Ibid.*, p. 498.

107 *Ibid.*, pp. 428, 503–4.

108 PP 1840, XXIV, pt. IV, pp. 461–3.

109 J. Campbell, 'Occupation and literacy in Bristol and Gloucestershire, 1755–1870', in Stephens (1983), pp. 28, 31.

110 PP 1840, XXIV, pt. V, pp. 487–8, 503.

111 PP 1840, XXIII, p. 413.

112 *Ibid.*, p. 448.

113 *Ibid.*, pp. 424–6.

114 *Ibid.*, p. 443.

115 PP 1840, XXIV, pt. V, p. 504.

116 Pinchbeck, *Women Workers*, p. 235.

117 PP 1843, XIII, pp. 128–30; 1843, XIV, p. d36.

118 PP 1868–9, XIII, (a), 132.

119 Pinchbeck, *Women Workers*, p. 232.

120 PP 1843, XII, p. 16, Cf. PP 1843, XIV, p. D8.

121 *Newcastle*, III, pp. 31–2, 59–60, Cf. *35th BFSS*, 1840, p. 72.

122 *Newcastle*, III, pp. 35, 37, 94–5, 147, 155, 157, 160, 193.

123 *55th BFSS*, 1860, pp. 48–9.

124 Campbell, 'Occupation and literacy', pp. 23–4, 31.

125 PP 1843, XII, pp. 36–43.

126 *CCE, 1844(2)*, p. 213.

127 PP 1845, XII, pp. 67, 71, 109.

128 PP 1868–9, XIII, (a), p. 61.

129 PP 1843, XII, p. 99.

130 PP 1868–9, XIII, (a), 29–32.

131 PP 1843, XII, pp. 44–5, 97.

132 *CCE, 1844(2)*, pp. 220–1. Cf. *Newcastle*, II, pp. 57–61.

133 *18th Report of the Bath and Wells Diocesan Church Building Society and the 16th Report of the Diocesan Board of Education*, 1854, p. 15.

134 PP 1868–9, I, p. 2; *Report of the State of Parochial Education in the Diocese of Salisbury*, 1840, p. 26. Cf. *Newcastle*, V, pp. 346–7.

135 *CCE, 1870–1*, p. 64.

136 National Society, *Church Schools Inquiry, 1846–7*, 1849.

137 *CCE, 1853–4*, pp. 563–4.

138 PP 1868–9, XIII, (a), p. 37. Cf. *ibid.*, pp. 61–2.

139 *Newcastle*, II, pp. 57–61.

140 PP 1868–9, XIII, (a), p. 126.

141 *Ibid.*, (a), pp. 12–3.

142 PP 1868–9, (b), pp. 145–6, 209.

143 PP 1868–9, (a), pp. 38–40, 61–2.

144 *CCE, 1855–6*, pp. 373–4.

145 *CCE, 1847–8(1)*, pp. 112–7.

146 *CCE, 1840–1*, pp. 29–33; *CCE, 1844 (2)*, pp. 224–6; *CCE, 1847–8(1)*, p. 114; PP 1846, XXIV, pp. 31–7; PP 1850–1, XXIII, pp. 64–5; PP 1856, XVIII, pp. 24 ff.

147 PP 1846, XXIV, p. 38.

148 PP 1847–8, XXVI, p. 10.

149 J. McFall, 'Education in the Madeley Union of Shropshire in the 19th century', M. A. thesis, University of Keele, 1973, pp. 32–3, 253–4; A. Raistrick, *Dynasty of Ironfounders*, London, 1953, p. 265.

150 Rowe, *Cornwall in the Industrial Revolution*, pp. 156–7.

151 *Quarterly Rev.*, CII, pp. 102, 289–339.

152 Jenkin, *The Cornish Miner*, pp. 108–9; Rowe, *Cornwall in the Industrial Revolution*, 311.

153 *CCE, 1840–1*, p. 194; *CCE, 1855–6*, p. 374. Cf. W. B. Stephens, 'Elementary education in the Cornish mining areas in the mid-nineteenth century', *Devon and Cornwall Notes and Queries*, XXXI (5), 1969.

154 *CCE, 1840–1*, pp. 29–31; *CCE, 1845(2)*, pp. 199–201.

155 *VCH, Wiltshire*, IX, p. 159.

156 PP 1840, XXIV, pt. V, p. 492.

157 PP 1843, XIV, p. 246.

158 *CCE, 1845(1)*, p. 86.

159 *CCE, 1845 (2)*, p. 192; PP 1870, XIII, p. 63.

160 A. Charlesworth (ed.), *An Atlas of Rural Protest in Britain, 1548–1900*, London, 1983, p. 154.

161 W. F. E. Gibbs, 'The development of elementary education in Dorset from the early nineteenth century to 1870', M. A. thesis, University of Southampton, 1960, pp. 29–34, 40 and App. III.

162 *VCH, Wiltshire*, V, p. 352; *CCE, 1858–9*, p. 116.

163 Cf. *CCE, 1844(2)*, p. 86.

164 *CCE, 1847–8(2)*, p. 111.

165 A. Platts and G. H. Hainton, *Education in Gloucestershire: a Short History*, Gloucester, 1954, pp. 54–5.

166 G. H. Hainton, 'The development of elementary education in Gloucestershire, 1698–1846', M. A. thesis, University of Bristol, 1952, p. 100.

167 PP 1868–9, XIII, (a), p. 62. Cf. *CCE, 1853–4*, pp. 563–4; *CCE, 1855–6*. p. 373.

168 *Newcastle*, II, pp. 69–71. Cf. *ibid.*, pp. 132–7; PP 1868–9, XIII, pp. 50–73.

169 *Eddowes Jnl.*, 12 October 1870.

170 F. Hill, *National Education: its Present State and Future Prospect*, I, London, 1836, p. 271.

171 PP 1843, XII, pp. 40–1, 64; *CCE, 1844(2)*, pp. 213–4; *CCE, 1847–8*, p. 60; *CCE, 1855–6*, p. 374; PP 1868–9, XIII, (b), pp. 75–6; *Newcastle*, V, pp. 412–5.

172 PP 1868–9, XIII, (a), p. 12.

173 *Shrewsbury Jnl.*, 10 January 1872.

174 PP 1868–9, XIII, (a), pp. 41, 127. Cf. *CCE, 1844(2)*, p. 214.

175 PP 1868–9, XIII, (a), pp. 6, 58, 62, 126. Cf. Bettey, *Dorset*, p. 139.

176 PP 1843, XII, pp. 88, 105, 108, 112.

177 *Newcastle*, II, p. 105.

178 PP 1867–8, XVII, (a), p. 102.

179 PP 1868–9, (a), pp. 37–9.

180 *CCE, 1870–1*, p. 31.

181 *CCE, 1844(2)*, pp. 229–31; *CCE, 1870–1*, p. 29.

182 H. V. Bailey, *A Charge Delivered to the Clergy of the Archdeaconry of Stow*, 1826, p. 12.

183 *2nd Report of the Gloucester Diocesan Board of Education*, 1841, p. 4. Cf. *ibid.*, *3rd Report*, 1842, p. 4.

184 *7th A. R. Exeter Diocesan Board of Education*, 1846, p. 25.

185 *Newcastle*, V, pp. 412–5. Cf. PP 1840, XXIV, pt. V, p. 487.

186 *CCE, 1844(2)*, pp. 221–3; *CCE, 1845 (1)*, pp. 86, 182–3.

187 *Newcastle*, II, p. 70.

188 PP 1868–9, XIII, (a), p. 126.

189 Gibbs, 'Education in Dorset', App. III.

190 *CCE, 1868–9*, pp. 242, 247; *CCE, 1870–1*, p. 31.

191 *CCE, 1863–4*, p. 76.

192 *Newcastle*, II, p. 83. Cf. *ibid.*, p. 142; *CCE, 1863–4*, p. 77; *CCE, 1865–6*, p. 32.

193 PP 1868–9, XIII, (a), p. 39.

194 *35th BFSS*, 1840, pp. 54–5; *40th BFSS*, 1845, p. 118.

195 *CCE, 1870–1*, p. 28.

196 PP 1847–8, xxvi, pp. 4–6. Cf. Williams, 'Education in the Forest of Dean', pp. 133 ff., 231–5.

197 *Report on State of Parochial Education in the Diocese of Salisbury*, 1840, p. 27.

198 *Cheltenham Jnl.*, 28 August 1842; 18 December 1843.

199 *A Series of Reports...to the Bishop of Bath and Wells on the State of National, Parochial and Middle Schools*, 1841, p. 60.

200 *A. R. Education Board for the Archdeaconry of Llandaff and Monmouth*, 1852, pp. 5–6.

201 E. T. Davis, *Monmouthshire Schools and Education to 1870*, Newport, Mon., 1957, pp. 83–8.

202 W. E. Marsden, 'Diffusion and regional variation in elementary education in England and Wales, 1800–1870', *History of Education*, XI, 1982, pp. 184–7.

203 *A. R. Education Board for the Archdeaconry of Llandaff and Monmouth*, 1857, p. 5.

204 See, e.g., J. Stevenson, *Popular Disturbances in England, 1700–1870*, London, 1979, pp. 238–9.

205 App. E. Except that the number of illiterate brides in Herefordshire was slightly larger in 1871 than 1866.

206 The high and unrepresentative 61 per cent for Okehampton is perhaps erroneous. The percentages of marks for Okehampton for 1857 are: 46 grooms, 42 brides; and the average, 44 per cent, is shown in brackets in Map 11.

207 Stephens, 'Anatomy', p. 8.

208 This group connected with a similar group in Berkshire: Faringdon, Hungerford, Abingdon, Wantage, Wallingford. See Map 10, pp. 186–7 and p. 208.

209 The adjoining Malmesbury district shows an unrepresentatively high 84 per cent illiteracy, and is undoubtedly incorrect. The percentages of marks for the district in 1857 are: 29 grooms, 33 brides, 31 overall. The overall percentage for 1855 was also 31.

210 For comment on this exercise, see p. 68.

211 N.b. The Malmsbury figures for 1856 have been disregarded, and those for 1857 used instead: see App. F, note 15, and note 209 above.

212 Cf. PP 1843, XIII, p. 160. Cf. Hill, *National Education*, I. p. 261: of Redruth, 'not more than three-fourths of the population above 12 years of age can read; and not one half of the inhabitants above that age can write'.

213 Cf. *Newcastle*, III, pp. 23 ff.; Stephens, 'Anatomy', p. 8.

214 Cf. W. L. Sargant, 'On the progress of elementary education', *JSSL*, XXX, 1867, pp. 134–5, Calculations based on Sargant's figures show that Cheltenham and Bath in 1846 and 1847 had substantially better rates than the average for the counties in which they were set (Gloucestershire and Somerset). Cf. Stephens (1977), pp. 42–3.

215 Hoskins, *Devon*, p. 500.

216 *Ibid.*, p. 350.

217 K. Shahidulla, 'Literacy in mid-nineteenth century Devon and Suffolk', M.A. thesis, University of British Columbia, 1979, pp. 30, 32, 34, found that Devon districts with greater proportions of town dwellers were generally more literate than more rural districts in the county. Cf. W. B. Stephens, 'Illiteracy in Devon during the Industrial Revolution, 1754–1844', JEAH, VIII, 1976, pp. 1–4.

218 Stephens, Anatomy', p. 7; Shahidulla, 'Literacy in Devon and Suffolk', pp. 39–41.

219 M. J. Campbell, 'The development of literacy in Bristol and Gloucestershire: 1755–1870', Ph.D. thesis, University of Bath, 1980, pp. 142–5. Cf. *CCE, 1870–1*, pp. 30–1.

220 Five districts were equally thirty-eighth.

221 R. A. Kunicki, 'Educational provision and literacy levels in Herefordshire, 1830–1870', M. Ed. exercise, University of Leeds, 1981, (LME), pp. 57–8.

222 Cf. *Census, 1861*, I, p. 418.

223 *CCE, 1870–1*, p. 29.

224 In Wilton itself a fall in population 1831–41 was due to 'relinquishment of a factory'. Cf. J. de la Mann, *The Cloth Industry in the West of England from 1640 to 1880*, Oxford, 1971, pp. 160, 191n, 196.

225 This is confirmed by detailed investigation of Gloucestershire parish registers and bishop's transcripts: Campbell, 'Literacy in Bristol and Gloucestershire', pp. 135–6, 148, 331–2; Campbell, 'Occupation and literacy', p. 23, Table 3.2.

226 Some showed equal proportions for brides and grooms.

227 *Censuses*.

228 Campbell, 'Literacy in Bristol and Gloucestershire', pp. 331–2; Campbell, 'Occupation and literacy', pp. 33–4; Sargant, 'Elementary education', p. 111.

229 PP 1843, XII, 124.

230 Cf. Stephens (1973), App. I.

231 PP 1843, XII, pp. 38–9; *CCE, 1853–4*, pp. 280–1; *CCE, 1870–1*, pp. 225–6; PP 1870, XIII, pp. 63–5.

232 *Newcastle*, II, pp. 27–8; *ibid.*, V, pp. 344–9; *VCH, Dorset*, II, p. 262; Kunicki, 'Educational provision in Herefordshire', pp. 6, 35–6, 62. Cf. R. R. Sellman, *Devon Village Schools in the Nineteenth Century*, Newton Abbott, 1967, p. 21.

233 *Abstract, 1833*.

234 Hainton, 'Education in Gloucestershire', pp. 99–100.

235 *CCE, 1845(2)*, p. 192.

236 *CCE, 1839–40*, pp. 176–8; *CCE, 1840–1*, pp. 28–33; Davies, *Monmouthshire Schools*, pp. 79–82.

237 *4th A. R. Hereford Diocesan Board of Education, 1853; Church Schools Inquiry, 1846–7*, p. 7.

238 *Newcastle*, II, pp. 36–7, 120, 126–8.

239 *Newcastle*, V, pp. 412–5. Cf. *CCE, 1859–60*, p. 54.

240 *CCE, 1858–9*, pp. 117–8, 120–6. Cf. PP 1859(1), XXI, (2), p. 66.

241 C. B. Fripp, 'Report of an enquiry into the condition of the working classes of the city of Bristol', JSSL, II, 1839, p. 373. Cf. PP 1837–8 VII, p. viii.

242 'Statistics of education in Bristol', *JSSL*, IV, 1841, p. 253.

243 *A. R. Education Board for the Archdeaconry of Llandaff and Monmouth*, 1852, pp. 5–6.

244 The others were: Tewkesbury, Bridgnorth, Wenlock (lower proportion on the books); Truro, Bridport, Devizes, Chard, Glastonbury, Oswestry (lower proportions in attendance).

245 See Stephens (1977), p. 39.

246 *Newcastle*, III, pp. 56, 59, 82.

247 *Newcastle*, II, p. 21.

248 *Ibid.*, pp. 31, 57.

249 PP 1868–9, XIII, (a), p. 60.

250 *CCE, 1867–8*, p. 611. Cf. *Newcastle*, II, pp. 36–7.

251 *CCE, 1865–6*, p. 80.

252 PP 1868–9, XIII, (a), pp. 39, 41.

253 PP 1870, XIII, p. 63.

254 PP 1868–9, XIII, (a), p. 127. Cf. *CCE, 1865–6*, p. 32, *CCE, 1867–8*, pp. 54–5.

255 *CCE, 1870–1*, pp. 27–9.

256 Campbell, 'Literacy in Bristol and Gloucestershire', p. 131.

257 *CCE, 1872–3*, p. 39; Williams, 'Education in the Forest of Dean', p. 282.

258 National Society, *Schools for the Poor in England and Wales for the Years 1866 and 1867*, n.d., pp. 7, 10.

259 Hainton, 'Education in Gloucestershire', pp. 99–100; Williams, 'Education in the Forest of Dean', pp. 249, 284–6.

260 PRO, Ed. 16/322.

261 *VCH, Wiltshire*, V, p. 352.

262 But based on only 5 readings.

263 Coefficients: Wiltshire, -0.21; Dorset, -0.48; Cornwall, -0.39; Somerset, -0.14; Herefordshire, -0.48; Shropshire, -0.09. Overall for the region: -0.43.

264 R. Edmonds, 'A statistical account of the parish of Madron, Cornwall', *JSSL*, II, 1839, p. 224.

265 *VCH, Wiltshire*, V, p. 352; *CCE, 1855*, p. 372; *CCE, 1858–9*, pp. 114–6; Gibbs, 'Education in Dorset', pp. 29–34, 40, App. III.

266 An area of small farms with a high proportion of parishes lacking schools: Kunicki, 'Educational provision in Herefordshire', p. 62.

267 But see the case of weavers, below, p. 259.

268 Campbell, 'Literacy in Bristol and Gloucestershire', pp. 112, 117, 185, 199, 332. Cf. Campbell, 'Occupation and literacy', pp. 20–3.

269 Stephens, 'Anatomy', pp. 7–8.

270 Cf. *Newcastle*, V, pp. 5, 57, 82, 412–5.

271 See also the 1858 proportion of the population at public schools: App. J.

272 *Newcastle*, II, p. 29.

273 *Newcastle*, III, p. 82.

274 *Newcastle*, II, p. 33; *ibid.*, III, p. 73.

275 *Newcastle*, II, pp. 35–8.

276 Platts and Hainton, *Education in Gloucestershire*, pp. 69–70; Davies, *Monmouthshire Schools*, pp. 108–9.

277 PP 1959(1), XXI (2), p. 66.

278 PP 1846, XXIV, p. 33.

279 *Newcastle*, III, p. 23.

280 *Newcastle*, II, p. 39.

281 Gibbs, 'Education in Dorset', pp. 198, 205; Williams, 'Education in the Forest of Dean', p. 282.

282 Sellman, *Devon Village Schools*, p. 26.

283 See p. 43.

284 Cf. *29th A. R. Nat. Soc.*, 1840, pp. 51, 69; *A. R. Exeter Diocesan Board of Education*, 1839.

285 *Newcastle*, I, p. 576; *Report of the Hereford Board of Education, 1850*.

286 See p. 46.

287 *CCE, 1844(2)*, p. 220.

288 PP 1843, XII, p. 37.

289 *7th A. R. Exeter Diocesan Board of Education*, 1846, p. 25.

290 *CCE, 1844(2)*, p. 231.

291 PP 1840, XXIV, pt. V, pp. 503–4. Cf. *12th A. R. Wesleyan Education Committee*, 1850, pp. 63–6.

292 *CCE, 1850–1*, p. 146; Gibbs, 'Education in Dorset', .pp. 157–8.

293 Campbell, 'Literacy in Bristol and Gloucestershire', p. 109, Cf. *CCE, 1870–1*, p. 28.

294 *CCE, 1844(2)*, p.223; *National Society Monthly Paper*, LXVII, June, 1852, p. 171.

295 *CCE, 1845(2)*, p. 199.

296 *CCE, 1851–2*, p. 353.

297 PP 1868–9, XIII, (a), p. 59.

298 *55th BFSS*, 1860, pp. 45–6. Cf. *60th BFSS*, 1865, pp. 52–4.

299 *CCE, 1845–50*, pp. 298–9, 304–5, 308–9; *CCE, 1850–1*, p. 343; *CCE, 1868–9*, pp. 248–9; PP 1868–9, XIII, (a), p. 6; Gibbs, 'Education in Dorset', pp. 157–8, citing visitation returns.

300 Campbell, 'Literacy in Bristol and Gloucestershire', p. 109.

301 PP 1867–8, XVII, (a), p. 13.

302 PP 1868–9, XIII, (a), p. xii.

303 1870, XIII, pp. 63–4. Cf. *CCE, 1839–40*, p. 179.

304 *CCE, 1845(2)*, pp. 193–8.

305 *CCE, 1844(2)*, pp. 225, 229.

306 Marsden, 'Diffusion', p. 192; *CCE, 1872–3*, pp. 39, 188.

307 *Newcastle*, II, pp. 32–4. Cf. *CCE, 1867–8*, p. 54.

308 PP 1846, XXIV, p. 33.

309 Edmonds, 'Madron', p. 224.

310 *CCE, 1840–1*, pp. 192–3. Cf. Stephens, 'Cornish mining areas', p. 137.

311 Platts and Hainton, *Education in Gloucestershire*, p. 45.

312 See pp. 220, 227–8.

313 E.g., *CCE, 1851–2*, pp. 352–3.

314 Campbell, 'Occupation and literacy', p. 110.

315 PP 1868–9, XIII, (a), pp. 59, 128. Cf. *4th A. R. Hereford Board of Education*, 1853.

316 *TNAPSS*, 1877, p. 440.

317 *CCE, 1872–3*, p. 39.

318 E.g., *CCE, 1855–6*, pp. 374–6; *18th Report of the Bath and Wells Diocesan Building Society and the 16th Report of the Diocesan Board of Education*, 1854, pp. 15–6.

319 *CCE, 1870–1*, p. 31.

320 *CCE, 1875–6*, pp. 438–9.

321 *CCE, 1844(2)*, p. 37.

322 J. Fletcher, 'Moral and educational statistics of England and Wales', *JSSL*, X, 1847, p. 197.

323 *Abstract, 1833*.

324 Cf. App. N.

325 Wiltshire and Dorset had the highest proportion of population at evening school in 1858 of all the western counties: App. Q.

326 Stephens, 'Anatomy', p. 12.

327 'Statistics of education in Bristol', *JSSL*, IV, 1841, pp. 255–6.

328 *Ibid.*, p. 255.

329 Platts and Hainton, 'Education in Gloucestershire', pp. 51–2.

330 *Education Census, 1851*, p. ccviii (not including mechanics' and literary institutes).

331 *CCE, 1865–6*, p. 81.

332 *Ibid.*, p. 16.

333 *CCE, 1855–6*, pp. 376–7.

334 *CCE, 1867–8*, p. 55 (excluding Wellington, Taunton, Langport, Chard, Yeovil).

335 PP 1859(1), XXI (2), p. 66.

336 *CCE, 1860–1*, p. 33.

337 *CCE, 1853–4*, pp. 561–2; *CCE, 1855–6*, pp. 372–3; *CCE, 1857–8*, p. 317; *CCE, 1859–60*, p. 54; *CCE, 1862–3*, pp. 15–6; *CCE, 1865–6*, p. 81; *CCE, 1870–1*, pp. 27, 30. Cf. *Newcastle*, V. pp. 411 ff.

Conclusion: Through a glass darkly (pp. 264–8)

1 Cf. W. B. Stephens, 'Statistical evidence for schooling and literacy in nineteenth-century England and Wales', unpublished paper read at the Seminar on the Application of Statistical Methods to the Study of History, at Bellagio, Italy, Easter 1984.

2 See E. G. West, *Education and the State*, London, 1965, pp. 132–5, 153–4; E. G. West, 'Literacy and the Industrial Revolution', *Ec. H. R.*, 2nd ser. XXI, 1978, pp. 380–2.

3 H. J. Graff, 'Literacy and Social Development in North America: On Ideology and History', in Stephens (1983), p. 93.

4 See pp. 99, 115, 160, 178–9, 205, 259–60. Cf. H. Silver, 'Ideology and the factory child; attitudes to half-time education', in P. McCann (ed.), *Popular Education and Socialization in the Nineteenth Century*, London, 1977.

5 R. S. Schofield, 'The measurement of literacy in pre-industrial England', in J. Goody (ed.), *Literacy in Traditional Societies*, Cambridge, 1968, p. 318; L. Soltow and E. Stevens, 'Economic aspects of school participation in mid-nineteenth-century United States', *Jnl. of Interdisciplinary History*, VIII, 1977, p. 225.

6 PP 1863, XVIII, p. 174; and see pp. 152–3, 159, 199.

7 *27th A. R. Registrar General of Births, Deaths and Marriages*, PP 1866, XIX, p. xxi.

8 PP 1843, XIV, p. c38.

9 *Newcastle*, I, p. 293, Sunday and evening schooling ignored. See J. S. Hurt, *Elementary Schooling and the Working Classes, 1860–1918*, London, 1979, pp. 52–9; P. E. H. Hair, 'Children in society, 1850–1980', in T. Barker and M. Drake (eds.), *Population and Society in Britain, 1850–1980*, London, 1982, pp. 51–2.

10 See pp. 69–70, 84–5, 98–9, 147–9, 196–7, 252–4.

11 W. L. Sargant, 'On the progress of elementary education', *JSSL*, XXX, 1867, p. 85.

12 'Report on the state of education in the township of Pendleton, 1838', *JSSL*, II, 1839, p. 73.

13 *Education Census, 1851*, p. xxx.

14 *Newcastle*, I, p. 96.

15 Cf. Hair, 'Children in society'; N. Ball, 'Elementary school attendance and voluntary effort before 1870', *History of Education*, II, 1973.

16 See P. Gardner, *The Lost Elementary Schools of Victorian England: The People's Education*, London, 1984, chapter 5.

17 *Hansard*, 3rd ser. CXXXVIII, col. 1811.

18 See pp. 26, 74–7, 89–90, 149, 181–2, 194–5, 203–4, 234–6, 262–7.

19 Gardner, *Lost Elementary Schools*, p. 188.

20 P. McCann, 'Elementary education in England and Wales on the eve of the 1870 Education Act', *JEAH*, II, 1969, p. 22.

21 See, e.g. McCann, 'Elementary education', pp. 27–8; *CCE, 1870–1*, p. xii.

22 A. Schlesinger, 'The humanist looks at empirical social research', *American Sociological Rev.*, XXVII, 1962, p. 770.

APPENDICES

Appendix A   Males aged twenty and over engaged in agriculture, mining and manufacturing, 1851 (%)

Registration county	Agriculture	Mining	Manufacturing
Cumberland	35·4	8·6	11·2
Durham	13·7	21·8	10·1
Lincolnshire	50·8	0·1	1·6
Northumberland	23·1	11·4	7·6
Rutland	50·1	0·2	0·7
Westmorland	45·9	2·0	10·1
Yorkshire, E.R.	31·8	0·1	5·0
Yorkshire, N.R.	48·2	3·2	3·5
Cheshire	25·4	3·1	18·4
Lancashire	10·7	4·2	30·5
Yorkshire, W.R.	15·8	5·2	36·6
Derbyshire	24·2	10·4	10·2
Leicestershire	30·0	2·3	24·7
Nottinghamshire	27·6	3·6	24·8
Staffordshire	17·3	14·0	24·1
Warwickshire	19·2	0·9	24·8
Worcestershire	26·4	3·1	20·8
Essex	48·6	0·0	2·5
Hampshire	31·9	0·1	2·0
Kent	36·0	0·3	2·2
Middlesex	28·5	0·0	2·6
Norfolk	44·6	0·1	4·1
Suffolk	51·1	0·1	2·5
Surrey	39·2	0·2	2·3
Sussex	41·7	0·1	1·4
Bedfordshire	51·2	0·0	1·1
Berkshire	44·2	0·0	1·8
Buckinghamshire	48·3	0·0	2·1
Cambridgeshire	49·9	0·0	1·3
Hertfordshire	47·4	0·0	2·0
Huntingdonshire	53·9	0·0	1·1
Northamptonshire	42·1	0·1	2·5
Oxfordshire	45·4	0·1	3·3
Cornwall	32·7	24·8	2·2
Devon	37·5	1·9	3·0
Dorset	42·9	1·3	1·9
Gloucestershire	27·0	1·9	7·2
Herefordshire	54·2	0·9	1·4
Monmouthshire	20·7	21·4	12·9
Shropshire	42·5	7·3	4·9
Somerset	37·1	3·6	4·8
Wiltshire	47·8	0·4	6·3
London	2·3	0·0	10·6
N. Wales	43·1	12·6	4·7
S. Wales	31·3	13·9	8·0
England and Wales	26·5	4·4	13·2

Source: Welton (1860), pp. 1–2, 42–3.

Appendix B   Children returned as occupied in the censuses of 1851 and 1871

Registration county	Children aged 5–9							
	1851				1871			
	Boys		Girls		Boys		Girls	
	No. occupied	% of age group	No. occupied	% of age group	No. occupied	% of age group	No. occupied	% of age group
Cumberland	48	0.4	29	0.3	17	0.1	7	0.05
Durham	233	0.9	33	0.1	108	0.2	26	0.05
Lincolnshire	190	0.8	24	0.1	171	0.6	18	0.07
Northumberland	124	0.7	28	0.2	20	0.08	12	0.05
Rutland	8	0.5	2	0.1	12	0.9	0	0
Westmorland	23	0.7	7	0.2	4	0.1	2	0.05
Yorkshire, E.R.	35	0.2	11	0.1	20	0.1	16	0.09
Yorkshire, N.R.	39	0.3	27	0.2	11	0.08	13	0.09
Cheshire	350	1.4	331	1.3	218	0.7	237	0.7
Lancashire	3266	2.8	1842	1.6	2544	1.5	2199	1.3
Yorkshire, W.R.	4026	5.1	2939	3.7	2845	2.6	3016	2.7
Derbyshire	299	1.9	309	2.0	144	0.7	108	0.5
Leicestershire	572	4.1	674	4.9	160	1.0	146	0.9
Nottinghamshire	601	3.5	766	4.4	145	0.7	229	1.0
Staffordshire	1254	3.3	402	1.0	228	0.4	204	0.4
Warwickshire	919	3.4	383	1.4	167	0.4	134	0.4
Worcestershire	473	3.1	173	1.1	78	0.4	111	0.5
Essex	600	2.7	335	1.6	225	0.8	76	0.3
Hampshire	255	1.1	29	0.1	47	0.2	6	0.02
Kent	203	0.7	47	0.2	202	0.5	10	0.03
Middlesex	28	0.3	7	0.1	17	0.1	15	0.1
Norfolk	533	2.1	55	0.2	272	1.1	59	0.2
Suffolk	519	2.5	228	1.1	234	1.1	101	0.5
Surrey	118	1.0	6	0.05	46	0.2	7	0.03
Sussex	238	1.1	26	0.1	169	0.7	9	0.04
Bedfordshire	974	11.9	1732	21.4	460	4.9	981	10.5
Berkshire	220	1.8	38	0.3	46	0.3	5	0.03
Buckinghamshire	484	5.5	970	11.1	204	2.1	323	3.3
Cambridgeshire	331	2.7	82	0.7	403	3.5	57	0.5
Hertfordshire	631	5.7	796	7.4	299	2.5	518	4.3
Huntingdonshire	111	2.9	77	2.0	93	2.5	25	0.7
Northamptonshire	550	4.3	888	6.9	335	2.2	209	1.4
Oxfordshire	220	2.1	85	0.8	121	1.1	39	0.3
Cornwall	612	2.6	124	0.5	180	0.8	223	1.0
Devon	315	0.9	380	1.1	116	0.3	147	0.4
Dorset	350	3.3	139	1.3	134	1.2	48	0.4
Gloucestershire	413	1.7	116	0.5	233	0.8	51	0.2
Herefordshire	86	1.5	14	0.2	16	0.2	10	0.1
Monmouthshire	126	1.2	24	0.2	28	0.2	16	0.1
Shropshire	188	1.3	49	0.3	30	0.2	32	0.2

Children aged 10–14

England & Wales	21,483	2·0	14,939	1·4	1·7	11,511	0·9	9949	0·7	0·8
Cumberland	2666	24·3	1396	13·4	19·0	2592	21·9	1575	13·5	17·7
Durham	8349	36·6	1678	7·6	22·3	12,696	30·7	3320	8·3	19·7
Lincolnshire	5846	26·2	2288	10·5	18·5	7128	30·3	3437	14·8	22·6
Northumberland	4615	28·9	1254	7·9	18·4	5402	25·6	1808	8·9	17·4
Rutland	386	27·3	118	9·2	18·7	409	26·8	162	12·3	20·1
Westmorland	686	21·4	439	13·7	17·5	692	19·3	544	15·1	17·2
Yorkshire, E.R.	3903	30·4	1793	13·9	22·2	3787	23·6	2519	16·1	19·9
Yorkshire, N.R.	2889	27·1	1288	12·7	20·1	2936	22·5	1827	14·5	18·5
Cheshire	8706	37·3	7098	30·5	33·9	9486	32·9	8229	28·5	30·7
Lancashire	48,391	43·7	37,149	33·7	38·7	62,307	41·5	54,235	28·2	38·7
Yorkshire, W.R.	39,373	51·6	26,896	35·9	43·8	42,839	43·3	34,794	28·7	39·3
Derbyshire	6083	41·7	4957	33·8	37·7	6890	38·2	5048	28·7	33·5
Leicestershire	5593	43·5	4218	33·1	38·3	5775	38·3	4153	28·2	33·3
Nottinghamshire	6785	42·2	5682	35·1	38·6	7070	36·3	5633	28·7	32·5
Staffordshire	16,860	46·5	7981	22·6	34·7	17,286	34·5	10,160	20·7	27·7
Warwickshire	11,610	44·8	6461	24·8	34·8	12,383	35·8	7864	23·2	29·6
Worcestershire	5852	41·0	3060	21·9	31·6	5756	30·9	3895	21·0	25·9
Essex	6888	35·8	2578	13·6	24·8	7971	30·9	3304	13·5	22·4
Hampshire	7189	34·4	1849	9·0	21·9	6784	24·5	2840	10·5	17·6
Kent	7307	27·2	1998	7·7	17·6	7782	23·1	2932	8·9	16·1
Middlesex	1557	18·0	599	7·6	13·0	2057	13·0	1391	9·9	11·6
Norfolk	8285	35·5	2312	10·1	23·0	8437	35·6	3373	14·6	25·2
Suffolk	6104	32·4	2209	12·1	22·4	6957	34·2	3117	16·2	25·5
Surrey	3271	28·2	903	8·3	18·5	3754	19·9	1938	10·4	15·2
Sussex	6545	33·8	1801	9·6	22·0	6734	28·9	2867	12·8	21·0
Bedfordshire	3587	49·6	3710	50·6	50·1	3908	44·4	3957	46·4	45·4
Berkshire	4291	38·5	1192	11·2	25·2	4385	34·2	1552	12·8	23·8
Buckinghamshire	3594	44·0	2627	34·0	39·1	3452	39·3	2430	27·8	33·6
Cambridgeshire	3573	34·2	1061	10·2	22·2	4494	42·6	1591	15·4	29·2
Hertfordshire	4165	42·2	2439	25·7	34·1	4136	37·0	2552	24·3	30·9
Huntingdonshire	1454	42·2	547	15·9	29·0	1660	48·5	606	18·4	33·7
Northamptonshire	5560	47·6	3707	32·1	39·9	6327	45·2	3757	27·5	36·4
Oxfordshire	3522	37·7	1249	13·7	25·9	4008	37·7	1536	15·3	26·8
Cornwall	9814	46·7	3298	16·3	31·7	8299	39·6	3296	16·2	28·0
Devon	10,838	36·0	5789	19·5	27·9	9442	29·0	5814	18·1	23·6
Dorset	4146	42·5	1510	16·0	29·5	3838	36·0	1556	15·1	25·7
Gloucestershire	6868	31·6	3224	15·1	23·4	7553	29·1	4125	15·6	22·3
Herefordshire	1663	32·2	651	12·7	22·5	1716	25·3	919	14·0	19·8
Monmouthshire	3990	43·1	1021	11·1	27·2	4313	36·1	1480	12·6	24·5
Shropshire	4827	35·2	2045	15·3	25·4	4296	28·7	2558	17·5	23·2
Somerset	9132	36·4	5068	20·5	28·5	9553	34·9	5318	20·1	27·6
Wiltshire	5810	42·4	2056	15·7	29·4	6125	42·9	2379	17·5	30·5
London	24,620	23·0	12,951	11·9	17·4	30,533	19·9	20,454	13·1	16·5
England & Wales	352,599	36·6	188,977	19·9	28·3	392,241	32·1	246,824	20·5	26·4

Source: Censuses 1851, 1871.

Appendix C   Occupied persons under 20 years of age in certain 'principal' towns, 1851 (%)

	Males	Females	Males and Females
Durham	25	16	20
Sunderland	27	11	19
Newcastle upon Tyne	27	15	21
Whitehaven	25	13	19
Hull	27	16	21
Lincoln	23	16	20
Stockport	37	36	37
Bolton	33	29	31
Blackburn	36	32	34
Liverpool	24	15	19
Manchester and Salford	31	26	28
Oldham	37	31	34
Preston	34	32	33
Bradford	40	38	39
Leeds	33	25	29
Sheffield	31	16	23
Wolverhampton	31	16	23
Birmingham	33	21	27
Coventry	34	32	33
Leicester	32	29	30
Nottingham	35	38	37
Derby	34	32	33
Brighton	23	20	21
Portsmouth	23	14	19
Southampton	22	15	18
Norwich	28	23	26
Cambridge	23	19	21
Bedford	23	20	21
Plymouth and Devonport	23	15	19
Bath	25	25	25
Bristol	24	19	22

Source: Census, 1851.

Appendix D Proportions of illiterate brides and grooms, 1839–85 (%)

Registration county	1841			1845			AVERAGE 1839–45			1850			1855			1856			1858			1859		
	M	F	T	M	F	T	M	F	T	M	F	T	M	F	T	M	F	T	M	F	T	M	F	T
Cumberland	16	36	26	16	36	26	16	36	26	16	32	24	16	29	23	17	30	24	18	34	26	21	34	28
Durham	26	49	38	25	48	37	25	48	37	27	47	37	28	47	38	27	44	36	28	43	36	27	43	35
Lincolnshire	32	47	40	32	47	40	32	46	39	27	40	34	30	36	33	29	34	32	28	33	31	24	28	26
Northumberland	18	38	28	19	38	29	19	37	28	20	39	30	21	38	29	20	36	28	18	32	25	18	31	25
Rutland	40	36	38	25	30	28	31	34	33	24	29	27	14	24	19	18	22	20	22	24	23	26	23	25
Westmorland	20	34	27	19	34	27	20	35	28	19	35	27	21	24	28	17	21	19	17	17	17	13	23	18
Yorkshire, E.R.	21	38	30	19	37	28	20	39	30	20	37	29	21	34	28	20	35	28	18	32	25	18	30	24
Yorkshire, N.R.	22	38	30	22	38	30	23	40	32	19	34	27	21	31	26	20	29	25	18	27	23	18	29	24
Cheshire	38	62	50	36	60	48	36	61	49	33	56	45	32	50	41	32	52	42	29	47	38	29	47	38
Lancashire	38	67	53	40	68	54	39	67	53	37	64	51	33	59	46	33	58	45	29	47	42	30	55	43
Yorkshire, W.R.	37	63	50	37	64	51	38	64	51	34	64	49	29	51	40	29	51	40	26	44	37	26	48	37
Derbyshire	30	48	39	31	49	40	30	49	40	28	47	38	28	40	34	25	39	32	24	37	31	24	35	30
Leicestershire	32	44	38	33	48	41	33	50	42	33	46	40	28	39	34	29	37	33	26	35	31	27	36	32
Nottinghamshire	33	49	41	34	53	44	34	53	44	32	49	41	30	44	37	29	42	36	26	35	33	29	42	36
Staffordshire	42	59	51	47	63	55	43	60	52	47	61	54	44	57	52	44	57	52	42	55	49	42	53	48
Warwickshire	32	47	40	31	47	40	32	48	40	32	45	39	29	38	34	29	40	35	28	37	33	28	37	33
Worcestershire	46	60	53	48	62	54	45	60	53	37	47	42	33	40	37	35	40	38	33	39	36	30	39	35
Essex	47	53	50	46	52	50	47	53	50	43	46	45	44	39	42	40	37	39	39	32	36	37	32	35
Hampshire	32	41	37	31	38	35	31	39	35	28	33	31	26	29	28	25	28	27	24	24	24	23	26	23
Kent*	30	40	35	30	39	35	29	39	34	28	33	31	32	37	32	27	28	28	25	25	25	25	26	26
Middlesex*	31	35	33	32	33	33	32	35	34	31	31	31	25	27	26	26	21	24	25	20	23	22	21	22
Norfolk	42	48	45	46	50	48	44	50	47	41	44	43	41	39	40	40	38	39	38	35	37	36	35	36
Suffolk	47	52	50	48	52	50	46	52	49	47	50	48	42	41	42	43	39	41	41	36	39	41	36	39
Surrey*	33	35	34	40	34	37	36	37	37	35	28	32	28	23	26	28	23	25	25	20	23	26	19	23
Sussex	28	39	34	33	38	36	35	39	35	30	30	30	27	23	25	26	23	25	24	20	22	24	20	22
Bedfordshire	49	62	56	49	63	56	51	64	58	47	59	53	44	53	49	43	50	47	41	48	45	40	50	45
Berkshire	41	44	43	41	43	42	41	44	43	40	41	41	36	30	33	37	32	35	35	31	33	33	29	31
Buckinghamshire	41	50	46	45	55	50	43	55	49	41	50	46	39	45	42	37	41	39	36	39	38	37	39	38
Cambridgeshire	47	56	52	46	55	51	46	55	51	41	47	44	40	43	42	40	44	42	40	41	41	37	37	37
Hertfordshire	50	56	53	53	58	56	51	56	54	48	50	49	49	46	48	50	44	46	43	40	42	44	38	41
Huntingdonshire	43	52	48	46	57	52	45	54	50	40	48	44	44	44	44	43	43	43	40	40	40	33	37	35
Northamptonshire	38	51	45	38	51	45	38	51	45	32	42	37	33	40	37	30	38	34	29	37	33	29	36	33
Oxfordshire	35	46	41	34	38	41	35	44	40	36	41	39	33	31	32	33	34	33	31	29	30	31	27	29
Cornwall	35	55	45	37	54	46	36	55	46	35	52	44	36	49	43	36	47	42	36	46	41	34	44	39
Devon	28	40	34	28	41	35	28	41	35	26	37	32	27	33	30	26	29	33	24	29	27	24	30	27
Dorset	30	38	34	38	46	42	34	43	39	35	36	36	31	36	34	33	33	32	31	33	32	31	29	30
Gloucestershire	28	41	35	28	40	34	29	42	36	26	37	32	26	31	29	26	31	29	21	30	26	26	29	28
Herefordshire	38	45	42	38	44	41	38	44	41	41	41	41	42	31	38	40	58	48	36	36	36	40	31	36
Monmouthshire	51	64	58	53	67	60	51	65	58	50	62	56	48	60	54	48	58	54	43	53	48	44	55	50
Shropshire	41	52	47	42	53	48	42	53	48	42	52	47	39	47	43	40	46	43	38	41	40	39	43	41
Somerset	37	49	44	35	46	41	37	48	43	34	43	39	33	36	34	33	36	34	32	33	34	31	33	33
Wiltshire	43	55	49	43	52	48	44	54	49	41	43	42	36	38	37	35	36	36	34	33	34	34	31	33

Registration county	1860 M	1860 F	1860 T	1865 M	1865 F	1865 T	1866 M	1866 F	1866 T	1870 M	1870 F	1870 T	1871 M	1871 F	1871 T	1875 M	1875 F	1875 T	1880 M	1880 F	1880 T	1885 M	1885 F	1885 T
Cumberland	20	36	28	19	30	25	18	30	24	15	26	21	17	28	23	15	23	19	13	19	16	9	13	11
Durham	26	42	34	23	38	31	25	38	32	24	37	31	23	36	30	21	31	26	18	30	24	14	19	17
Lincolnshire	21	28	25	22	23	22	22	21	22	18	18	18	18	18	18	14	14	15	12	12	12	10	9	10
Northumberland	16	31	24	17	28	23	15	26	21	13	23	18	14	23	18	12	21	17	11	18	15	8	12	10
Rutland	18	21	20	21	17	19	20	15	18	15	11	13	18	9	14	11	10	11	14	5	10	6	2	4
Westmorland	15	22	18	9	16	13	15	17	16	11	15	13	11	12	12	8	8	8	6	10	8	3	5	4
Yorkshire, E.R.	16	29	23	18	26	23	15	26	21	14	22	18	14	23	19	13	21	17	10	16	13	8	11	10
Yorkshire, N.R.	18	26	22	17	22	20	17	24	21	16	23	20	16	21	19	17	20	19	15	19	17	11	12	12
Cheshire	27	45	36	24	38	31	24	38	31	19	30	25	19	32	26	17	27	22	14	20	17	10	14	12
Lancashire	29	54	42	24	46	35	24	37	31	21	39	30	21	38	30	18	34	26	14	27	21	10	18	14
Yorkshire, W.R.	25	47	36	46	41	44	22	40	31	20	36	28	19	35	27	18	31	25	14	25	20	11	17	14
Derbyshire	22	36	29	22	29	26	23	28	26	20	26	23	18	25	22	16	21	19	13	18	16	11	12	12
Leicestershire	25	34	30	22	30	26	22	29	26	21	27	24	20	26	23	18	23	21	13	19	16	9	12	11
Nottinghamshire	28	39	34	25	35	30	24	32	28	22	31	27	21	31	26	20	26	23	15	21	18	10	13	12
Staffordshire	40	52	46	30	48	39	35	45	40	36	44	40	35	44	40	30	37	44	25	31	28	17	22	20
Warwickshire	26	36	31	23	31	27	23	31	27	22	29	26	23	30	27	30	26	28	17	22	20	12	16	14
Worcestershire	30	36	33	27	33	30	25	30	28	23	28	26	23	27	26	20	25	24	18	19	19	13	14	14
Essex	37	31	34	31	26	29	29	24	27	25	18	22	22	17	19	20	15	18	16	11	14	12	7	10
Hampshire	23	24	24	17	16	17	16	16	16	16	15	16	15	14	15	12	11	12	9	8	9	9	5	7
Kent*	24	24	24	21	20	21	19	18	19	17	16	17	15	14	15	15	12	14	12	10	11	7	6	8
Middlesex*	21	20	21	18	16	17	17	14	16	16	12	14	13	11	11	12	9	11	11	9	10	7	5	6
Norfolk	35	30	33	32	27	30	32	27	30	30	24	27	28	22	25	26	20	23	21	14	18	17	11	14
Suffolk	38	30	34	34	28	31	33	26	30	31	22	27	28	22	25	26	19	23	22	16	19	19	11	15
Surrey*	24	18	21	18	15	17	19	14	17	14	10	12	12	11	12	12	9	11	8	6	7	6	4	5
Sussex	23	18	21	20	16	18	19	14	17	17	13	15	16	11	13	15	10	13	12	7	10	8	4	6
Bedfordshire	41	45	43	35	41	38	33	40	37	33	36	35	30	33	32	26	30	28	24	28	26	19	16	18
Berkshire	29	24	27	24	19	21	25	19	22	15	15	15	19	14	17	17	12	15	13	11	12	10	6	8
Buckinghamshire	32	35	34	28	29	29	31	34	33	21	24	25	25	27	26	25	21	23	19	17	18	15	12	14
Cambridgeshire	36	34	35	31	27	29	27	29	28	28	25	27	26	21	24	25	17	21	19	16	18	18	11	15
Hertfordshire	39	33	36	33	30	32	33	27	30	30	24	27	29	25	27	27	20	24	23	18	21	18	11	15
Huntingdonshire	37	32	35	30	28	30	32	30	31	28	23	26	25	21	23	24	22	22	20	13	17	19	11	15
Northamptonshire	27	31	29	25	26	26	23	25	24	20	23	21	21	22	22	16	18	17	14	15	15	10	8	9
Oxfordshire	30	28	29	24	22	23	22	19	21	20	15	18	19	16	18	19	14	17	14	11	13	10	7	9
Cornwall	35	43	39	30	38	34	26	35	31	24	29	27	24	29	27	22	25	24	20	20	20	17	17	17
Devon	22	27	25	18	23	21	18	22	20	17	19	17	15	18	17	13	17	15	10	11	11	8	9	9
Dorset	29	29	29	25	25	25	21	21	22	19	19	20	21	20	20	15	15	17	12	12	12	13	7	10
Gloucestershire	23	27	25	20	22	21	20	22	21	18	19	19	17	18	18	16	17	17	14	14	14	11	11	11
Herefordshire	31	29	30	31	25	28	29	21	28	26	23	25	21	21	24	18	15	17	14	12	14	13	9	11
Monmouthshire	44	51	48	41	48	45	37	46	42	37	44	41	35	40	38	27	31	29	18	32	31	21	22	22
Shropshire	36	40	38	30	34	32	31	33	32	26	27	26	27	29	28	25	31	29	23	13	20	15	13	14
Somerset	30	31	31	27	26	27	26	26	26	22	21	21	23	21	22	20	18	18	16	15	16	14	11	13
Wiltshire	31	30	31	26	24	25	25	22	24	21	19	20	22	18	18	19	15	17	15	10	13	13	7	10
England and Wales	26	36	31	22	31	27	22	30	26	20	27	24	19	27	23	17	23	20	14	19	17	11	13	12

M: Males; F: Females; T: Total.
*: extra-metropolitan.
Source: Annual Reports of the Registrar of Births, Deaths and Marriages.

Appendix E   Numbers of illiterate brides and grooms, 1856, 1866, 1871

Registration county	1856			1866			1871		
	M	F	T	M	F	T	M	F	T
Cumberland	174	311	485	284	480	764	295	485	780
Durham	1166	1918	3084	1390	2087	3477	1532	2369	3901
Lincolnshire	864	1030	1894	666	639	1305	572	566	1138
Northumberland	534	981	1515	545	935	1480	487	834	1321
Rutland	28	33	61	30	23	53	26	13	39
Westmorland	60	76	136	59	70	129	51	55	106
Yorkshire, E.R.	501	866	1367	434	734	1168	388	661	1049
Yorkshire, N.R.	313	460	773	297	392	689	301	382	683
Cheshire	1096	1759	2855	966	1539	2505	803	1368	2171
Lancashire	6897	12,514	19,411	6394	12,305	18,699	5774	10,653	16,427
Yorkshire, W.R.	3484	6288	9772	3633	6435	10,068	3284	5936	9220
Derbyshire	514	847	1361	602	729	1331	494	691	1185
Leicestershire	518	672	1190	495	644	1139	449	592	1041
Nottinghamshire	766	1114	1880	663	900	1563	723	1055	1778
Staffordshire	2839	3672	6511	2643	3322	5965	2766	3473	6239
Warwickshire	1301	1795	3096	1185	1564	2749	1271	1674	2945
Worcestershire	810	937	1747	627	770	1397	682	761	1443
Essex	928	862	1790	739	614	1353	591	457	1048
Hampshire	977	1059	2036	635	654	1289	618	578	1196
Kent*	1062	1129	2191	932	876	1808	664	626	1290
Middlesex*	228	183	411	227	190	417	186	158	344
Norfolk	1292	1239	2531	1025	855	1880	866	694	1560
Suffolk	1134	1027	2161	769	621	1390	708	548	1256
Surrey*	394	314	708	417	323	740	277	253	530
Sussex	635	551	1186	591	427	1018	472	341	813
Bedfordshire	447	522	969	380	461	841	326	368	694
Berkshire	532	450	982	379	300	679	293	214	507
Buckinghamshire	371	412	783	318	349	667	255	279	534
Cambridgeshire	540	590	1130	333	352	685	351	286	637
Hertfordshire	481	407	888	395	323	718	360	316	676
Huntingdonshire	193	192	385	128	120	248	101	85	186
Northamptonshire	558	710	1268	397	439	836	384	411	795
Oxfordshire	443	458	901	288	245	533	216	189	405
Cornwall	1059	1335	2394	651	865	1516	590	706	1296
Devon	1246	1540	2786	872	1064	1936	698	872	1570
Dorset	424	426	850	285	276	561	270	228	498
Gloucestershire	949	1132	2081	799	924	1723	727	788	1515
Herefordshire	286	258	544	206	151	357	193	154	347
Monmouthshire	857	1024	1881	680	847	1527	666	776	1442
Shropshire	718	831	1549	559	635	1194	455	489	944
Somerest	1035	1145	2180	878	859	1737	753	680	1433
Wiltshire	563	588	1151	412	368	780	371	297	668

M: Males; F: Females; T: Total.
*: extra-metropolitan.
Source: Annual Reports of the Registrar of Births, Deaths and Marriages.

Appendix F   Proportions of illiterate spouses, 1856, 1866, 1871 and statistics of school attendance, 1851

Illiteracy: M: Males; F: Females; T: Total

Registration District	Population			% Marks 1856			% Marks 1866			% Marks 1871			% Population at School, March 1851				% of Day Schools at Public Schools, 1851
													Day			Sunday	
	1851	1861	1871	M	F	T	M	F	T	M	F	T	M	F	T	T	
Cumberland: (Population (000's): 1841–178; 1851–195; 1861–205; 1871–220)																	
Alston	6816	6404	5680	20	44	32	16	36	26	16	31	24	6	6	12	17	87
Penrith	22,307	22,322	23,737	8	19	14	12	18	15	10	16	13	6	5	11	8	72
Brampton	11,323	10,866	10,608	3	11	7	4	25	15	12	13	13	5	2	7	8	56
Longtown	9696	10,469	8365	9	10	7	12	18	14	4	15	10	6	5	11	6	50
Carlisle	41,557	44,820	46,627	7	28	19	10	31	22	10	25	18	6	5	11	7	63
Wigton	23,661	23,273	22,691	7	16	12	11	19	15	8	18	13	7	5	12	5	68
Cockermouth	38,510	41,292	46,545	19	29	24	21	32	27	21	34	28	7	5	12	8	56
Whitehaven	35,614	39,950	47,572	29	44	37	30	38	34	28	39	34	6	5	11	9	60
Bootle	6008	5880	8525	12	20	16	8	10	9	14	14	14	6	6	12	6	79
Durham: (Population (000's): 1841–326; 1851–412; 1861–542; 1871–742)																	
Darlington	21,618	26,122	40,812	33	26	30	16	19	18	16	19	18	8	6	14	12	61
Stockton	52,934	57,099	99,705	24	39	32	22	31	26	24	33	28	6	6	12	9	51
Auckland	30,083	50,491	69,159	47	55	51	31	48	40	31	44	38	6	5	11	8	68
Teesdale	19,813	20,880	20,398	18	25	22	14	25	21	14	19	17	7	6	13	10	68
Weardale	14,567	16,418	19,155	16	39	23	20	26	23	20	25	23	6	4	10	12	63
Durham	55,951	70,274	91,798	35	53	44	31	34	33	31	42	37	6	5	11	8	63
Easington	21,795	27,293	33,694	35	62	49	24	54	45	26	45	36	5	5	10	11	68
Houghton	19,564	21,773	26,171	37	59	48	27	44	35	28	44	36	5	3	8	12	50
Chester-le-Street	20,907	27,660	33,300	71	44	58	27	45	36	31	45	39	6	4	10	8	63
Sunderland	70,576	90,704	112,643	26	44	35	20	41	33	21	37	29	6	5	11	8	46
South Shields	35,790	44,849	74,949	24	41	33	18	37	30	20	32	26	6	6	12	11	58
Gateshead	48,081	59,409	80,271	27	47	37	23	37	32	24	34	29	7	5	12	10	56
Hartlepool[1]		29,153	39,970				17	37	25	19	32	26					
Lincolnshire: (Population (000's): 1841–356; 1851–400; 1861–404; 1871–428)																	
Stamford	19,755	18,213	17,821	24	29	28	17	24	21	14	16	16	8	7	15	9	52
Bourne	22,362	20,113	19,981	15	39	37	15	17	16	17	21	21	5	5	10	11	55
Spalding	21,290	22,129	23,184	23	35	34	18	21	20	21	20	20	6	6	12	12	67
Holbeach	19,134	18,402	19,351	32	38	36	26	32	31	26	26	26	5	5	10	13	48
Boston	38,444	37,969	38,836	24	34	30	22	24	24	26	20	20	6	4	10	9	65
Sleaford	24,551	24,919	25,834	24	40	37	22	24	24	20	20	20	5	5	10	12	53
Grantham	29,850	28,886	30,606	21	24	24	11	18	15	12	13	12	6	4	10	8	72
Lincoln	42,062	47,063	52,290	10	12	11	14	17	16	11	15	15	7	5	12	12	60
Horncastle	25,089	24,718	28,764	21	37	34	22	21	19	16	22	19	5	5	10	12	56
Spilsby	28,937	28,799	29,246	19	29	29	15	19	17	14	19	15	6	5	11	12	70
Louth	33,427	34,711	34,808	27	35	32	23	19	21	20	20	19	5	5	10	8	62
Caistor	34,291	37,517	48,885	19	40	34	17	25	22	21	19	19	6	4	10	10	51
Glanford Brigg	33,786	34,731	36,239	30	41	36	16	20	19	19	21	19	6	6	12	12	55
Gainsborough	27,258	25,973	27,230	25	34	30	17	22	20	18	19	19	6	6	12	11	56

Appendix F Proportions of illiterate spouses, 1856, 1866, 1871 and statistics of school attendance, 1851

Illiteracy: M: Males; F: Females; T: Total

Registration District	Population			% Marks 1856		% Marks 1866			% Marks 1871			% Population at School, March, 1851				% of Day Schools at Public Schools, 1851
												Day			Sunday	
	1851	1861	1871	M	F	M	F	T	M	F	T	M	F	T	T	
Northumberland: (Population (000's), 1841–266; 1851–304; 1861–343; 1871–387)																
Newcastle	89,156	110,968	130,198	23	41	16	29	23	16	28	22	5	4	8	5	55
Tynemouth	64,248	77,955	94,583	21	37	20	32	26	15	24	20	5	5	10	9	48
Castle Ward	13,897	14,943	16,911	9	20	10	13	12	2	11	7	6	5	11	8	74
Hexham	30,346	31,850	32,543	13	27	11	19	15	12	17	15	7	5	12	9	72
Haltwhistle	7286	6693	6987	6	19	20	13	17	8	8	8	6	4	10	7	68
Bellingham	6553	7080	7080	4	11	11	10	11	3	6	5	6	5	11	7	78
Morpeth	18,127	24,003	31,027	12	30	10	27	19	11	19	15	6	6	12	7	71
Alnwick	21,122	21,053	19,799	7	20	4	16	10	4	12	8	7	5	12	9	79
Belford	6871	6260	5,847	0	0	2	17	10	11	5	8	7	5	12	9	60
Berwick	24,093	21,862	21,397	10	26	6	10	8	6	8	7	7	7	14	9	64
Glendale	14,348	13,211	12,188	0	6	7	9	8	4	7	6	7	5	12	8	82
Rothbury	7431	7147	7081	6	0	2	14	8	9	9	9	7	5	12	4	82
Rutland: (Population (000's), 1841–23; 1851–24; 1861–23; 1871–23)																
Oakham	11,513	11,112	11,142	15	21	19	17	19	15	12	16	7	6	12	11	59
Uppingham	12,759	12,367	12,243	22	22	17	14	17	22	6	12	6	5	11	12	63
Westmorland: (Population (000's), 1841–57; 1851–58; 1861–61; 1871–65)																
East Ward	13,660	15,411	16,937	10	16	2	17	10	12	14	13	7	5	12	12	63
West Ward	8155	8072	8248	16	14	11	11	11	8	5	8	7	6	13	8	82
Kendal	36,572	37,463	39,345	19	25	18	18	18	11	11	11	7	6	13	10	72
Yorkshire, East Riding: (Population (000's), 1841–221; 1851–254; 1861–274; 1871–307)																
York	54,324	59,909	64,908	18	29	11	21	16	11	16	13	8	6	14	7	75
Pocklington	16,095	16,710	15,964	20	34	14	26	20	13	22	18	6	6	12	9	48
Howden	14,436	15,001	14,227	33	52	24	40	32	21	34	27	6	5	11	7	54
Beverley	20,040	21,029	21,450	15	23	15	21	18	11	18	14	7	5	12	9	63
Sculcoates	44,719	51,956	68,142	20	38	16	27	22	15	29	22	5	5	10	9	40
Hull	50,670	56,888	68,316	17	36	14	28	21	14	27	20	5	5	10	6	52
Patrington	9407	9681	9115	32	28	6	27	17	16	27	21	5	5	10	6	52
Skirlaugh	9279	9654	9778	22	20	19	10	15	18	13	15	6	5	12	7	74
Driffield	18,265	19,226	19,265	25	38	23	30	27	14	23	18	7	5	12	11	59
Bridlington	14,322	14,371	15,415	18	29	16	31	26	11	22	17	7	6	13	9	56
Yorkshire, North Riding: (Population (000's), 1841–186; 1851–195; 1861–211; 1871–235)																
Scarborough	29,615	30,425	36,560	19	30	11	17	14	15	22	19	7	5	12	8	60
Malton	23,128	23,463	22,882	24	34	21	21	21	16	24	20	7	6	13	10	73
Easingwold	10,211	10,148	10,026	21	37	13	22	18	18	24	21	7	5	12	9	49
Thirsk	12,760	12,299	12,161	22	24	18	21	20	17	18	18	7	5	12	11	54
Helmsley	12,455	11,832	11,716	21	36	21	26	23	12	18	15	6	5	11	10	66
Pickering	9978	10,549	12,737	21	22	12	27	20	19	16	17	5	4	9	11	52
Whitby	21,592	23,633	25,804	17	27	21	28	25	16	24	20	6	5	11	9	52

(Yorkshire, continued)

Place	Pop I	Pop II	Pop III														%?
Leyburn	10,057	10,105	8705	12	20	16	12	14	13	11	9	10	5	5	10	11	60
Askrigg[2]	5635	5649	5473	3	11	7	9	26	18	12	12	12	7	4	11	14	58
Reeth	6820	6196	5370	24	36	30	12	29	21	11	32	22	5	4	9	17	73
Richmond	13,846	13,457	13,555	17	17	17	20	14	17	11	13	12	7	7	14	10	71

Cheshire: (Population (000's), 1841–368; 1851–424; 1861–475; 1871–539)

Place	Pop I	Pop II	Pop III														%?
Stockport	90,208	94,360	97,709	38	68	53	34	51	43	19	32	45	5	3	8	17	33
Macclesfield	63,827	61,543	59,339	27	52	45	17	26	28	16	25	34	5	4	10	7	68
Altrincham	34,043	40,517	49,913	27	35	31	21	26	24	13	16	18	6	5	11	13	61
Runcorn	25,797	26,792	30,534	42	52	47	28	35	32	26	29	32	6	6	12	13	68
Northwich	31,202	33,338	37,310	45	55	50	35	42	39	33	36	39	6	7	12	10	72
Congleton	30,512	34,328	36,281	37	55	46	33	34	34	20	25	30	6	6	10	15	69
Nantwich	35,941	40,955	53,767	34	51	43	30	39	35	20	25	30	5	6	11	9	69
Great Boughton[3]	52,950	58,501	72,049	25	40	33	22	33	28	17	22	26	5	7	12	9	68
Wirral[4]	57,157	18,420	23,149	16	24	20	16	23	20	18	17	15	5	6	10	6	64
Birkenhead[4]		61,420	79,464	16				23	20	14	19	17	5	6	10		

Lancashire: (Population (000's), 1841–1699; 1851–2067; 1861–2465; 1871–2849)

Place	Pop I	Pop II	Pop III														%?
Liverpool	258,236	269,742	238,411	27	47	37	25	40	33	24	31	38	4	5	9	4	75
West Derby	153,279	225,845	342,295	16	27	22	10	19	15	9	13	16	5	6	12	5	74
Prescot	56,074	73,127	92,551	46	63	55	39	54	47	37	42	47	5	6	11	7	70
Ormskirk	38,307	46,252	59,310	44	59	52	28	35	32	22	25	27	5	6	11	10	71
Wigan	77,539	94,561	111,874	50	71	61	49	68	59	39	48	57	4	4	8	12	68
Warrington	36,164	43,875	54,394	51	70	61	32	50	41	28	33	38	4	6	11	9	74
Leigh	32,734	37,700	41,924	43	75	59	39	65	52	34	42	50	5	4	7	15	70
Bolton	114,712	130,269	158,408	39	67	54	29	53	41	22	33	44	3	5	8	18	65
Bury	88,815	101,135	109,155	34	65	45	20	45	33	17	28	38	4	5	9	17	64
Bartun-upon Irwell	31,585	39,038	51,571	17	63	48	23	43	33	22	29	36	4	6	11	16	66
Chorlton	123,841	169,579	211,384	28	40	29	10	26	18	11	17	22	5	5	8	10	46
Salford	87,523	105,335	128,890	34	57	43	24	52	38	22	35	48	3	4	7	11	59
Manchester	228,433	243,988	251,956	24	54	39	17	44	31	15	27	38	3	4	7	15	68
Ashton	119,199	134,753	130,626	44	72	53	22	51	37	17	22	33	3	5	8	16	49
Oldham	86,788	111,276	126,982	40	81	63	24	57	41	22	28	38	3	4	7	16	46
Rochdale	72,515	91,574	109,558	36	73	57	25	52	39	16	27	32	4	5	9	20	61
Haslingden	50,424	69,781	79,956	41	67	52	27	53	38	20	32	43	4	6	9	19	68
Burnley	63,968	75,595	87,809	22	70	56	24	58	43	25	37	49	5	5	8	19	79
Clitheroe	22,368	20,476	21,081	42	50	36	22	34	29	12	19	25	5	6	10	18	76
Blackburn	90,738	119,942	143,510	39	75	59	32	63	48	34	39	44	6	5	8	17	83
Chorley	37,701	41,678	43,004	26	70	55	24	48	36	21	33	33	5	5	9	12	83
Preston	96,545	110,523	115,846	33	73	56	32	60	46	27	40	52	5	5	9	10	68
Fylde	22,002	25,682	30,626	23	44	35	22	26	24	24	25	25	8	8	14	13	73
Garstang	12,695	12,425	12,196	23	39	31	23	29	29	15	18	21	7	7	12	12	70
Lancaster	34,660	35,927	32,661	15	37	30	15	23	19	16	18	19	7	7	13	9	67
Ulverston[5]	30,556	35,738	55,053	26	39	34	26	31	29	24	26	28	6	6	12		48
Lunesdale[5]			6975							9	7	5	5				

Appendix F   Proportions of illiterate spouses, 1856, 1866, 1871 and statistics of school attendance, 1851

Illiteracy: M: Males; F: Females; T: Total

Registration District	Population			Illiteracy									% Population at School, March, 1851						% of Day Schools at Public Schools, 1851
				% Marks 1856			% Marks 1866			% Marks 1871			Day			Sunday			
	1851	1861	1871	M	F	T	M	F	T	M	F	T	M	F	T	M	F	T	
Yorkshire, West Riding: (Population (000's), 1841–1177; 1851–1340; 1861–1530; 1871–1854)																			
Sedbergh	4574	4391	4990	14	43	29	18	5	11				9	4	13			16	79
Settle	13,762	12,528	15,134	35	35	35	12	19	14				7	6	13			15	71
Skipton	28,766	31,343	32,398	29	37	37	17	25	20				5	4	10			17	69
Pateley Bridge	9334	9534	8686	26	56	41	5	18	18				5	4	9			14	71
Ripon	16,041	15,742	15,967	25	35	30	6	16	17				5	5	11			9	68
Great Ouseburn	12,167	14,534	11,697	23	27	25	13	20	16										
Knaresborough	15,473	18,117	19,088	25	33	29	7	17	12				6	6	14			11	65
Wetherby	5129	6486	14,874	21	29	25	12	12	10										
Otley[6]	28,541	18,669		25	38	32	13	30	21				7	5	12			14	65
Keighley	45,903	43,122	52,141	33	62	48	17	37	27				6	5	11			14	71
Todmorden	29,727	31,113	32,323	34	75	55	10	40	33				6	5	10			18	53
Saddleworth	17,799	18,631	19,923	15	47	31	13	28	19				5	4	9			18	49
Huddersfield	123,860	134,336	140,151	25	58	42	14	44	31				6	4	10			16	61
Halifax	120,958	128,673	153,266	29	62	46	19	39	29				6	5	11			14	62
Bradford	181,964	196,475	257,713	35	63	49	28	50	38				5	4	9			15	57
Hunslet[7]	88,679	25,763	46,274	23	47	35	20	47	37				6	5	11			14	52
Leeds	101,343	117,566	162,421	24	48	37	26	38	29				6	5	10			15	57
Dewsbury	71,768	92,883	124,286	34	65	50	23	52	39				6	5	11			10	44
Wakefield	48,956	54,899	68,786	32	50	41	29	33	28				6	5	11			15	69
Pontefract[8]	29,973	14,635	34,498	35	44	40	15	31	30				6	5	10			12	62
Hemsworth	8158	7793	8114	24	34	28	31	14	19				8	7	15			11	78
Barnsley	34,980	45,797	57,212	41	58	50	18	47	41				5	4	10			9	67
Wortley	32,012	38,511	44,985	25	42	34	20	26	24				5	5	10			14	71
Ecclesall Bierlow	37,514	63,618	87,432	19	81	50	25	30	26				5	5	9			12	45
Sheffield	103,626	128,951	162,271	30	47	39	23	40	34				5	5	10			7	60
Rotherham	33,082	44,350	57,396	32	45	39	13	36	31				6	6	12			8	61
Doncaster	34,675	39,388	45,205	22	28	25	24	20	17				6	5	11			13	63
Thorne	15,886	16,011	17,011	27	40	34	14	37	32				5	4	9			10	33
Goole	13,686	15,153	17,276	26	37	32	25	37	34				5	5	10			12	59
Selby	15,672	16,001	16,380	27	38	33	17	22	24				7	6	13			11	68
Tadcaster[9]	19,710	19,954	21,080	17	65	41		23	20				8	6	14			11	51
Bramham[9]		5996																	
Wharfedale		12,936					16	16	16										
Kirkstall		15,453	39,142				14	23	23			19							
Holbeck		49,440					16	30	27										
Bramley		15,824	21,617				18	35	34		36	27							
Castleford[8]		11,391	44,441				22	45	21		23	24							
Derbyshire: (Population (000's), 1841–240; 1851–261; 1861–294; 1871–325)																			
Shardlow	32,322	31,113	33,925	26	29	28	18	23	22	18	20	19	6	6	12			17	63
Derby	43,684	51,049	62,333	17	37	27	13	18	18	13	24	19	5	5	10			13	69
Belper	46,872	51,711	52,864	30	42	36	22	30	30	22	26	24	6	5	11			17	72

Hayfield	29,712	32,176	32,425	30	60	45	20	36	28	13	29	21	5	4	8	20	54
Leicestershire: (Population (000's), 1841–220; 1851–235; 1861–244; 1871–275)																	
Lutterworth	16,194	15,515	14,257	36	33	35	18	13	16	11	11	11	4	4	8	9	59
Market Harborough	15,839	16,059	16,081	31	29	30	19	11	15	16	8	12	5	4	10	10	63
Billesdon	7009	7272	7509	25	18	22	11	13	12	10	7	9	5	4	9	11	65
Blaby	14,190	14,305	14,814	46	49	48	19	31	25	28	21	25	6	5	11	18	49
Hinckley	16,558	16,374	16,148	39	57	48	39	52	46	35	50	43	5	4	9	16	60
Market Bosworth	13,631	13,428	13,746	33	41	37	33	28	31	15	13	14	7	6	12	13	82
Ashby de la Zouche	25,895	28,543	31,532	39	41	40	26	31	30	27	27	27	7	6	13	13	76
Loughborough	25,368	24,147	24,141	25	36	31	25	26	26	22	25	24	6	5	11	14	73
Barrow-on-Soar	20,059	19,778	21,562	36	43	40	27	28	28	22	27	25	6	5	11	16	62
Leicester	60,642	65,256	95,220	20	34	27	20	31	26	17	29	23	5	4	8	10	62
Melton Mowbray	20,533	20,171	17,926	27	33	30	14	11	13	12	10	11	7	6	13	13	70
Nottinghamshire: (Population (000's), 1841–271; 1851–294; 1861–324; 1871–355)																	
East Retford	22,758	22,677	23,035	22	40	31	23	23	23	18	16	17	5	5	10	10	59
Worksop	19,153	20,704	25,347	23	21	22	21	28	25	24	17	21	6	7	13	9	62
Mansfield	30,146	30,547	35,833	32	50	41	41	44	41	30	39	35	5	4	9	13	52
Basford	64,923	74,357	84,561	39	56	48	28	37	33	31	41	36	5	4	9	16	48
Radford	26,776	30,479	33,789	23	40	32	24	40	32	21	41	31	4	3	6	8	40
Nottingham	58,419	74,693	82,621	26	42	34	19	33	26	16	31	25	5	4	9	12	51
Southwell	25,616	24,425	21,937	32	30	31	15	18	22	13	17	15	5	5	10	13	66
Newark	30,348	30,186	29,616	20	30	25	17	16	17	13	14	14	6	5	11	12	54
Bingham	16,241	15,670	14,665	35	33	34	19	27	23	17	14	16	6	5	11	17	65
Staffordshire: (Population (000's), 1841–529; 1851–631; 1861–769, 1871–877)																	
Stafford	22,787	24,474	26,768	33	40	37	15	26	21	21	27	24	5	5	10	9	67
Stone	19,344	21,926	24,686	38	53	46	23	26	25	20	24	22	6	6	12	10	63
Newcastle under Lyme	20,814	24,567	30,225	38	46	42	25	37	31	26	34	30	5	5	9	13	65
Wolstanton	41,916	54,356	68,932	46	64	55	40	53	47	38	51	45	4	4	8	15	53
Stoke-on-Trent	57,942	71,308	89,262	39	56	48	33	43	38	32	43	38	5	4	9	11	55
Leek	23,031	24,080	28,093	30	48	39	25	41	33	25	37	31	4	3	8	13	69
Cheadle	18,142	20,988	21,199	38	43	41	29	29	29	11	22	21	6	6	12	12	82
Uttoxeter	15,140	14,787	14,325	29	29	29	13	14	14	19	18	15	5	6	11	8	61
Burton-on-Trent	31,843	41,065	52,628	26	34	30	17	18	18	20	20	20	6	5	11	11	73
Tamworth	13,996	15,504	16,809	35	29	27	23	26	25	12	12	17	7	6	13	11	74
Lichfield	25,279	27,541	32,165	29	25	25	25	22	24	20	16	18	7	6	13	9	69
Penkridge	16,850	18,662	23,705	39	41	40	28	30	29	38	40	39	4	4	8	9	62
Wolverhampton	104,158	126,902	136,053	47	60	54	31	44	38	35	44	40	4	3	7	9	70
Walsall	43,044	59,908	71,834	47	62	55	37	45	41	41	48	42	4	4	8	10	54
West Bromwich	60,729	92,480	106,626	37	53	45	30	36	33	30	36	33	4	3	7	11	66
Dudley	106,530	130,267	134,125	57	70	64	54	62	58	53	64	59	4	3	7	13	57

Appendix F Proportions of illiterate spouses, 1856, 1866, 1871 and statistics of school attendance, 1851

Illiteracy: M: Males; F: Females; T: Total

Registration District	Population 1851	Population 1861	Population 1871	% Marks 1856 M	F	T	% Marks 1866 M	F	T	% Marks 1871 M	F	T	% at School Day M	F	T	Sunday T	% of Day Schools at Public Schools, 1851
Warwickshire: (Population (000's), 1841–409; 1851–480; 1861–561; 1871–630)																	
Birmingham	173,951	212,621	231,105	28	44	36	25	38	32	26	36	31	5	4	8	7	56
Aston	66,852	100,522	146,818	24	34	29	21	30	26	25	32	29	5	3	7	5	51
Meriden	11,267	11,290	10,994	32	32	32	18	12	15	16	2	9	5	4	9	4	83
Atherstone	11,448	12,118	11,875	30	40	35	19	22	21	26	18	22	6	6	12	15	60
Nuneaton	13,532	13,054	12,432	32	57	45	32	46	39	20	41	32	5	5	9	14	80
Foleshill	18,527	19,997	17,250	46	70	58	31	44	38	27	46	37	3	2	6	8	80
Coventry	36,811	41,647	40,113	29	49	39	19	36	28	18	32	25	4	3	7	8	45
Rugby	23,477	24,436	25,048	26	23	25	18	8	13	12	16	14	8	6	13	11	78
Solihull	11,931	13,231	15,341	19	24	22	19	15	17	13	11	11	6	4	9	8	69
Warwick	41,934	44,047	48,840	18	19	19	15	8	12	9	11	10	6	5	11	6	73
Stratford-on-Avon	20,789	21,249	22,373	38	27	33	30	16	23	16	12	14	6	5	11	13	69
Alcester	17,482	16,878	18,172	44	46	45	36	27	32	24	28	26	4	3	6	10	72
Shipston-on-Stour	20,651	19,852	19,677	38	30	34	23	18	22	23	14	19	6	5	11	10	86
Southam	10,509	10,392	10,524	37	33	35	22	13	18	16	11	14	6	6	12	13	67
Worcestershire: (Population (000's), 1841–230; 1851–259; 1861–295; 1871–336)																	
Stourbridge	57,350	68,726	73,386	51	62	57	38	39	39	38	47	43	5	5	10	12	56
Kidderminster	32,917	30,307	34,948	40	50	45	31	36	34	24	29	27	7	4	11	9	74
Tenbury	7047	7366	7828	51	43	47	25	28	27	36	25	31	4	3	8	6	68
Martley	18,811	15,098	16,308	46	40	43	30	21	26	28	14	21	4	4	8	7	85
Worcester	27,677	30,969	32,416	26	35	31	20	27	24	19	21	20	6	4	10	8	63
Upton-on-Severn	18,070	21,010	23,376	34	32	33	20	16	18	15	9	12	5	4	9	4	78
Evesham	14,463	14,767	15,623	46	51	49	37	31	34	27	20	24	5	4	9	11	76
Pershore	13,553	13,865	14,142	43	40	42	30	30	30	28	14	21	4	3	8	9	60
Droitwich	18,152	19,237	22,443	29	36	33	24	25	25	25	24	25	4	5	10	7	65
Bromsgrove	24,822	26,259	29,003	49	57	53	27	39	33	40	37	39	5	4	8	11	59
Kings Norton	30,871	47,349	66,803	15	17	16	11	17	14	12	18	15	5	4	8	7	55
Essex: (Population (000's), 1841–321; 1851–344; 1861–380; 1871–441)																	
West Ham	3395	59,319	99,142	14	17	16	15	14	15	7	9	8	7	5	12	5	73
Epping	15,631	16,549	20,240	46	28	37	35	18	27	30	11	21	7	6	10	6	66
Ongar	11,855	11,317	11,523	49	41	45	31	17	24	14	8	11	5	5	10	7	81
Romford	24,607	26,965	30,389	37	32	35	22	19	21	24	19	22	5	5	10	7	66
Orsett	10,642	11,595	13,172	44	38	41	44	25	35	19	17	18	6	5	10	9	71
Billericay	13,787	15,031	17,862	39	27	33	29	26	28	29	13	21	3	4	8	5	67
Chelmsford	32,272	32,765	33,712	48	34	41	14	16	15	22	12	17	5	6	11	8	74
Rochford	15,838	18,282	20,580	49	43	46	31	23	27	29	9	19	5	5	10	8	68
Maldon	22,137	22,556	23,732	34	32	33	31	31	31	26	22	24	5	5	11	8	61
Tendring	27,710	27,105	28,718	43	46	45	38	29	34	36	22	29	3	3	7	8	48
Colchester	19,443	23,815	26,345	18	30	24	16	17	17	10	23	17	4	4	10	8	55
Lexden	21,666	22,950	24,110	49	43	46	37	37	37	31	21	26	5	5	10	10	60
Witham	16,099	16,324	15,864	41	43	42	34	21	28	24	20	22	7	5	12	9	61
Halstead	19,273	18,482	18,453	56	65	61	48	48	48	27	30	29	5	5	10	12	66
Braintree	17,561	17,170	17,142														

Union													
Havant													
Portsea Island[10]	72,126	94,828	113,595	21	32	27	13	21	17	11	18	15	45
Alverstoke	16,908	22,653	22,644	27	42	35	14	24	19	12	16	14	53
Fareham	13,924	14,864	16,801	28	29	29	17	13	15	21	11	16	63
Isle of Wight	50,324	55,362	66,219	18	21	20	23	10	12	9	10	10	67
Lymington	12,153	12,094	12,396	42	23	33	13	11	18	27	22	22	70
Christchurch	8482	10,438	16,338	18	15	17	13	17	13	17	16	16	66
Ringwood	5675	5357	5397	30	27	29	14	25	16	21	14	18	63
Fordingbridge	6834	6377	6441	26	10	18	30	12	28	29	21	22	58
New Forest	13,540	13,509	13,496	27	19	23	17	15	16	10	4	7	78
Southampton	34,098	43,414	48,055	15	19	17	15	12	12	13	13	13	52
South Stoneham	15,974	25,542	32,201	22	21	22	16	10	13	14	13	13	71
Romsey	10,810	10,771	10,892	25	25	25	20	22	21	22	12	19	72
Stockbridge	7480	7286	7317	39	28	34	28	9	20	18	15	13	88
Winchester	25,661	26,607	29,269	24	17	21	9	7	8	31	7	22	68
Droxford	10,697	10,665	11,750	53	38	46	39	21	30	30	12	18	77
Catherington[11]	2493	2497	2769	57	7	32	18	14	16	21	5	22	68
Petersfield	7814	7853	9672	38	21	30	24	19	19	21	17	18	79
Alresford	7418	7182	7270	37	35	36	23	13	18	24	14	19	78
Alton	11,910	12,063	14,999	55	40	48	27	21	24	22	14	20	83
Hartley Wintney	11,223	11,480	20,601	38	24	31	16	21	19	24	28	20	79
Basingstoke	17,466	17,429	18,105	44	29	37	33	16	24	26	16	21	83
Whitchurch	5619	5522	5606	42	44	43	26	33	22	36	15	28	78
Andover	17,266	17,132	17,590	41	33	37	22	26	17	24	19	22	77
Kingsclere	8909	8517	8576	59	55	57	36	31	34	42	25	34	92

Kent (extra metropolitan): (Population (000's), 1841–447; 1851–485; 1861–549; 1871–629)

Union													
Bromley	17,637	20,368	32,184	25	31	28	16	17	17	11	11	5	79
Dartford	27,330	32,316	42,344	36	36	36	24	22	20	20	10	9	75
Gravesend	16,633	18,782	21,265	21	21	21	14	11	13	13	12	5	56
North Aylesford	16,569	19,121	21,561	26	32	29	24	23	24	21	20	9	55
Hoo	2845	2861	3143	60	60	60	46	31	39	35	35	12	46
Medway	42,796	51,805	59,150	22	35	29	16	19	19	14	14	8	50
Malling	19,579	21,447	23,383	34	33	34	26	21	25	17	17	8	65
Sevenoaks	22,095	22,039	24,262	28	25	27	25	23	21	19	19	8	74
Tunbridge	28,545	34,271	44,668	29	27	28	18	16	18	15	10	7	65
Maidstone	36,097	36,670	42,017	24	31	28	14	17	17	14	17	6	64
Hollingbourn	13,751	13,584	14,047	37	26	32	34	19	27	20	14	9	66
Cranbrook	13,069	13,412	14,005	32	33	33	19	20	20	19	19	9	57
Tenterden	11,279	10,947	10,871	26	22	24	16	8	12	16	9	8	68
West Ashford	13,314	15,137	16,730	22	29	26	12	12	12	12	9	6	78
East Ashford	11,960	12,286	13,016	37	24	31	24	15	20	21	16	5	74
Bridge	11,164	11,316	11,139	40	30	35	30	24	29	29	23	7	76
Canterbury	14,100	16,642	16,510	20	31	26	16	18	22	22	14	9	55
Blean	14,661	16,161	18,269	30	26	28	28	17	24	15	13	10	50
Faversham	16,684	18,867	22,346	40	34	37	30	24	26	20	8	11	52
Milton	12,026	14,775	19,217	35	22	29	27	26	26	26	23	8	65
Sheppey	13,385	18,494	18,565	32	34	33	21	15	27	15	21	9	34
Thanet	31,798	31,842	42,129	14	19	17	15	23	14	9	10	5	63
Eastry	25,162	25,900	27,229	28	26	27	23	19	21	17	14	8	52
Dover	28,325	31,575	35,249	19	17	18	12	11	11	7	8	9	60
Elham	18,780	26,925	29,747	25	19	22	22	18	18	12	14	9	63
Romney Marsh	5437	5708	6080	24	24	24	15	13	13	10	3		44

Appendix F Proportions of illiterate spouses, 1856, 1866, 1871 and statistics of school attendance, 1851

Illiteracy: M: Males; F: Females; T: Total

Registration District	Population 1851	Population 1861	Population 1871	% Marks 1856 M	F	T	% Marks 1866 M	F	T	% Marks 1871 M	F	T	% Pop. at School, March 1851 — Day M	F	T	Sunday T	% of Day Schools at Public Schools, 1851
Middlesex (extra metropolitan): (Population (000's), 1841–141; 1851–151; 1861–187; 1871–264)																	
Staines	13,973	15,976	20,199	30	29	30	20	12	16	18	12	15	6	5	11	7	70
Uxbridge	19,475	23,155	25,538	38	29	34	26	23	25	20	15	18	8	6	12	9	63
Brentford	41,325	50,534	71,933	22	23	23	17	17	17	12	13	13	8	6	14	6	62
Hendon	15,916	19,220	37,160	19	15	17	16	11	14	11	10	10	9	6	15	7	75
Barnet	14,619	19,128	25,169	26	20	23	12	9	11	17	10	14	9	7	16	7	74
Edmonton	45,298	59,312	84,855	21	15	18	14	11	13	9	8	9	7	6	13	5	63
Norfolk: (Population (000's), 1841–405; 1851–434; 1861–427; 1871–431)																	
Yarmouth	26,880	30,338	35,166	32	36	34	25	25	25	22	19	21	6	5	11	6	47
Flegg	8497	8631	9382	53	38	46	35	38	37	46	28	37	6	5	11	7	68
Tunstead	15,614	14,516	14,407	56	44	50	37	29	33	39	19	29	4	5	9	9	75
Erpingham	21,772	20,874	19,841	52	42	47	33	24	29	28	24	26	6	5	11	9	65
Aylsham	20,007	19,052	18,115	45	44	45	36	26	31	33	21	27	5	5	10	9	56
St. Faiths	11,890	11,298	10,901	36	39	38	36	25	31	34	30	32	4	5	9	9	64
Norwich	68,195	74,891	80,386	26	35	31	22	25	24	16	21	19	5	4	9	7	65
Forehoe	13,565	12,818	12,308	51	43	47	32	26	29	40	34	37	6	5	11	9	61
Henstead	11,545	11,290	10,726	47	32	40	40	16	28	28	17	23	5	5	10	5	71
Blofield	11,574	11,521	11,325	44	52	48	39	31	38	39	19	29	5	5	9	7	58
Loddon	13,095	14,242	13,670	40	33	37	36	31	33	29	24	26	4	5	9	7	67
Depwade	26,395	25,248	24,272	51	37	44	36	26	31	26	25	25	4	5	9	8	65
Guiltcross	12,744	11,541	11,257	54	39	47	40	34	37	27	23	25	4	5	9	10	70
Wayland	12,141	11,562	11,094	47	38	43	39	33	37	36	29	33	5	5	10	12	68
Mitford	29,389	28,020	27,567	41	39	40	33	28	31	33	28	30	6	5	11	8	63
Walsingham	21,883	21,118	20,051	43	38	40	35	29	33	35	23	28	6	6	13	10	60
Docking	18,148	17,596	17,302	48	42	45	34	28	31	28	16	22	6	6	12	9	60
Freebridge Lynn	13,557	13,486	18,439	47	40	44	28	22	24	25	23	25	5	4	10	11	64
King's Lynn	20,530	16,701	17,132	18	28	23	18	12	15	15	12	15	5	4	9	6	40
Downham	20,985	20,264	20,585	41	43	42	26	23	24	31	24	31	4	6	9	10	58
Swaffham	14,320	13,747	13,608	53	41	47	38	24	30	31	30	31	5	6	12	10	70
Thetford	19,040	18,694	18,104	44	40	42	27	20	36	24	20	24	6	5	11	12	64
Suffolk: (Population (000's), 1841–315; 1851–336; 1861–336; 1871–347)																	
Risbridge	18,125	17,432	18,417	61	61	61	51	53	52	50	46	48	4	3	7	10	53
Sudbury	30,815	31,415	31,793	52	49	51	37	36	37	36	30	33	5	5	10	9	67
Cosford	18,107	17,376	17,094	56	48	52	43	30	37	41	31	36	6	6	11	10	66
Thingoe	19,014	18,224	17,614	47	35	41	37	22	30	31	19	25	5	6	11	8	71
Bury St. Edmunds	13,900	13,318	14,928	31	28	30	14	17	16	14	13	14	5	4	9	6	64
Mildenhall	10,354	9595	9223	44	37	41	34	32	33	28	19	24	5	4	9	14	67
Stow	21,110	20,908	20,997	40	43	42	38	24	31	26	19	23	5	5	11	10	52
Hartismere	19,028	17,665	16,742	54	42	48	43	38	41	41	30	35	4	4	8	7	67
Hoxne	15,900	14,694	14,404	54	54	54	35	41	38	41	28	35	4	4	7	8	62

Place	P1	P2	P3	1	2	3	4	5	6	7	8	9	10	11	12	13	14
Plomesgate	21,477	20,720	20,718	45	44	45	27	22	25	27	21	24	6	5	10	9	56
Blything	27,883	26,848	26,424	41	32	37	37	23	30	30	18	24	6	6	11	10	57
Wangford	14,014	13,619	14,037	50	45	48	26	22	24	43	21	32	6	5	11	7	63
Mutford	20,163	24,050	31,364	33	29	31	18	18	19	22	16	19	6	5	11	7	60

Surrey (extra metropolitan): (Population (000's), 1841—188; 1851—203; 1861—261; 1871—365)

Place	P1	P2	P3	1	2	3	4	5	6	7	8	9	10	11	12	13	14
Epsom	19,040	22,409	30,291	29	14	22	18	12	15	10	7	9	8	6	13	4	61
Chertsey	16,148	18,642	23,038	37	25	29	27	19	23	14	11	13	6	6	12	8	76
Guildford	25,012	29,330	35,667	31	25	28	26	9	18	19	11	15	5	5	9	6	66
Farnham	11,743	30,707	39,867	36	27	32	17	22	20	12	20	16	5	5	10	4	82
Farnborough	7839	14,318		30	38	34	37	24	19	27	17	22	5	5	10	8	76
Hambledon	13,552	13,907	15,276	48	27	38	23	11	31	19	8	14	5	5	11	8	67
Dorking	11,353	12,445	14,869	23	25	24	17	7	17	11	10	11	5	5	10	4	72
Reigate	14,329	20,109	27,303	31	23	27	17	7	12	23	21	22	5	5	12	3	81
Godstone	8868	9642	13,541	58	38	48	33	19	26	10	9	10	7	4	15	10	70
Croydon	31,888	46,474	83,853	22	19	21	17	17	17	10	9	10	8	5	12	5	75
Kingston	26,783	36,479	55,929	17	12	15	11	8	10	10	9	10	6	6	13	6	64
Richmond	15,906	18,802	26,145	17	11	14	7	8	8	5	8	7	7	6	13	4	58

Sussex: (Population (000's), 1841—302; 1851—340; 1861—367; 1871—421)

Place	P1	P2	P3	1	2	3	4	5	6	7	8	9	10	11	12	13	14
Rye	12,349	11,927	11,998	24	33	29	28	12	20	14	17	16	6	5	11	11	61
Hastings	21,215	26,631	35,642	14	13	14	9	7	8	9	4	7	7	6	12	8	79
Battle	14,232	12,680	13,763	31	32	32	19	13	16	14	13	14	4	4	8	6	74
Eastbourne	8347	10,721	15,726	20	13	17	9	12	11	7	6	7	8	7	15	9	53
Hailsham	13,289	12,680	13,021	22	22	22	26	19	23	15	17	17	6	6	13	10	55
Ticehurst	15,507	14,626	16,717	35	41	32	28	22	25	17	14	20	6	6	11	9	75
Uckfield	17,631	17,260	19,314	39	40	40	34	27	31	32	23	28	6	5	11	5	48
East Grinstead	13,216	14,097	16,304	43	36	40	27	20	24	24	21	23	6	5	10	9	76
Cuckfield	15,607	17,163	20,180	42	27	35	23	8	16	19	6	13	6	6	12	6	61
Lewes	25,719	26,995	29,942	24	21	14	16	13	15	11	9	11	6	6	12	7	55
Brighton	65,569	77,693	90,011	13	14	18	11	12	12	13	13	12	7	6	11	4	47
Steyning	16,867	24,053	31,473	18	18	30	16	15	16	23	7	10	7	5	13	8	60
Horsham	14,018	15,313	19,331	31	29	30	35	15	25	23	10	17	5	7	11	7	68
Petworth	9629	9397	10,138	54	44	44	34	24	29	31	15	22	6	5	10	7	49
Thakeham	7434	7567	8422	44	31	38	47	23	35	31	21	26	5	6	13	8	64
Worthing	18,746	18,921	21,591	32	15	24	16	8	12	11	6	9	6	6	11	7	66
Westhampnett	15,248	14,811	18,860	38	21	21	28	15	22	13	9	15	6	5	12	8	70
Chichester	14,438	14,775	8205	16	12	14	21	9	15	18	10	14	8	6	15	6	60
Midhurst	13,599	12,581	13,051	51	30	41	40	22	31	30	14	22	5	5	9	4	70
Westbourne	6944	6957	7221	35	18	27	34	23	29	10	8	9	5	6	11	6	75

Bedfordshire: (Population (000's), 1841—112; (1851—130; 1861—140; 1871—152)

Place	P1	P2	P3	1	2	3	4	5	6	7	8	9	10	11	12	13	14
Bedford	35,528	38,072	41,662	36	40	38	23	27	25	20	22	21	6	4	10	15	89
Biggleswade	23,436	25,393	27,887	49	49	49	48	47	48	37	33	35	4	4	8	12	76
Ampthill	16,542	16,970	17,526	56	61	59	33	47	40	39	39	35	4	5	8	18	70
Woburn	12,075	11,684	11,529	46	60	53	36	43	40	36	40	38	6	3	9	19	82
Leighton Buzzard	17,142	17,648	18,667	49	61	55	32	37	35	39	45	42	6	5	11	16	45
Luton	25,087	30,712	34,268	36	51	44	31	42	37	27	36	32	5	3	8	18	54

Appendix F   Proportions of illiterate spouses, 1856, 1866, 1871 and statistics of school attendance, 1851

Illiteracy: M: Males; F: Females; T: Total

Registration District	Population			% Marks 1856			% Marks 1866			% Marks 1871			% Population at School, March, 1851				% of Day Schools at Public Schools, 1851
													Day			Sunday	
	1851	1861	1871	M	F	T	M	F	T	M	F	T	M	F	T	T	
Berkshire: (Population (000's), 1841–190; 1851–199; 1861–206; 1871–226)																	
Newbury	20,815	19,999	20,641	38	31	35	26	19	23	27	14	21	6	6	12	10	68
Hungerford	20,404	19,852	19,349	60	51	56	29	25	27	21	21	25	5	6	11	13	69
Faringdon	15,732	15,688	15,091	38	36	37	35	29	32	18	20	19	5	6	11	9	83
Abingdon	20,946	20,801	21,561	46	37	42	25	28	27	20	18	19	6	4	10	10	67
Wantage	17,488	17,308	17,360	51	48	50	44	21	33	32	21	27	7	6	13	10	75
Wallingford	14,163	14,017	14,648	43	33	38	26	21	24	28	13	21	6	6	11	9	70
Bradfield	16,380	15,771	15,853	50	32	41	35	27	31	23	19	21	4	4	9	4	64
Reading	22,175	25,876	33,340	27	24	26	16	16	15	11	11	11	6	7	12	8	61
Wokingham	13,668	14,465	16,195	36	24	30	27	20	27	12	9	11	5	4	10	7	83
Cookham	11,767	13,081	14,873	31	25	28	19	12	16	18	9	14	6	7	13	16	74
Easthampstead	6352	7436	10,632	26	15	21	9	11	10	15	13	14	4	4	8	3	50
Windsor	19,889	21,801	26,725	18	13	16	21	10	16	8	3	6	8	6	14	7	72
Buckinghamshire: (Population (000's), 1841–138; 1851–144; 1861–147; 1871–155)																	
Amersham	18,637	18,240	18,511	43	44	44	32	40	36	33	25	29	6	6	12	13	61
Eton	21,490	22,353	24,928	32	28	30	24	18	21	14	7	11	8	6	14	5	67
Wycombe	33,562	35,138	38,366	41	51	46	36	37	37	27	36	32	5	5	10	13	69
Aylesbury	23,071	23,600	24,617	38	43	41	24	31	28	24	25	25	5	3	8	14	83
Winslow	9376	9265	9082	47	45	46	44	33	39	33	39	36	5	3	9	15	49
Newport Pagnell	28,109	24,855	25,867	31	36	34	35	44	40	25	29	27	4	3	7	16	81
Buckingham	14,410	13,756	13,636	29	40	35	23	32	28	18	26	22	5	3	8	13	70
Cambridgeshire: (Population (000's), 1841–170; 1851–192; 1861–182; 1871–192)																	
Caxton	11,065	10,966	11,661	50	54	52	41	30	36	32	27	30	5	5	11	12	85
Chesterton	25,170	25,083	27,948	41	43	42	26	23	25	31	18	25	6	7	13	11	67
Cambridge	27,815	26,361	30,078	18	20	19	10	16	13	8	10	9	6	5	11	10	65
Linton	14,148	13,510	13,768	46	51	49	33	34	34	30	24	27	6	6	12	12	59
Newmarket	30,655	28,675	29,498	46	48	47	34	39	37	33	23	28	5	4	9	9	78
Ely	22,896	21,928	22,284	52	58	55	35	32	34	31	27	30	6	5	10	9	59
North Witchford	16,243	14,791	15,585	41	39	40	35	38	37	21	26	24	6	5	11	7	44
Whittlesey	7687	6966	7002	37	35	36	25	20	23	30	24	27	6	6	11	7	37
Wisbech	36,215	33,323	34,209	37	46	42	24	29	27	27	23	25	5	4	8	9	58
Hertfordshire: (Population (000's), 1841–162; 1851–174; 1861–177; 1871–195)																	
Ware	16,482	16,515	17,460	53	30	42	31	21	26	21	10	16	7	7	14	5	71
Bishop's Stortford	20,356	20,212	21,620	55	34	45	40	18	29	30	15	23	6	6	12	8	78
Royston	26,355	25,014	26,180	48	35	35	38	26	32	30	19	25	5	5	11	14	78
Hitchin	24,729	2560	27,656	53	63	58	38	43	40	38	40	39	6	5	11	10	68
Hertford	15,090	15,301	16,009	46	26	36	25	11	18	24	14	19	9	7	16	8	83

Town	Pop.	Pop.	Pop.	23	50	56	53	26	29	31	30	5	4	9	15	72
Berkhampstead	12,527	13,204	14,099	23	50	56	53	26	29	31	30	5	4	9	15	72

Huntingdonshire: (Population (000's), 1841–56; 1851–56; 1861–59; 1871–58)

Town	Pop.	Pop.	Pop.	23	50	56	53	26	29	31	30	5	4	9	15	72
Huntingdon	20,900	20,518	20,711	34	39	40	33	34	18	23	21	6	6	12	12	68
St. Ives	20,594	19,654	18,824	28	45	39	32	30	35	20	28	7	7	14	14	70
St. Neots	18,825	18,965	18,511	27	45	49	31	29	21	21	21	5	4	9	14	66

Northamptonshire: (Population (000's), 1841–199; 1851–214; 1861–231; 1871–248)

Town	Pop.	Pop.	Pop.	23	50	56	53	26	29	31	30	5	4	9	15	72
Brackley	13,747	13,471	13,512	21	36	35	32	27	24	19	22	6	5	11	13	75
Towcester	12,806	13,004	12,987	36	23	35	27	32	26	27	27	5	4	9	16	75
Potterspury	10,663	11,632	11,717	22	31	50	22	22	17	17	17	5	2	7	10	65
Hardingstone	9157	9928	10,650	25	41	49	29	27	25	31	28	5	4	8	16	83
Northampton	33,857	41,152	50,743	23	20	36	19	21	18	26	22	6	5	11	13	61
Daventry	21,926	20,600	19,452	22	22	29	17	20	20	20	20	6	6	12	13	67
Brixworth	14,771	15,367	13,866	23	31	36	23	23	11	11	11	6	5	11	13	75
Wellingborough	21,367	24,224	28,998	35	44	55	33	34	30	30	30	4	3	8	16	71
Kettering	18,097	18,995	20,113	28	35	45	18	23	17	17	17	6	5	11	15	70
Thrapston	12,841	14,065	14,319	26	43	39	29	28	24	27	26	5	5	10	16	72
Oundle	15,655	15,463	14,619	18	39	31	23	21	33	14	24	6	6	12	10	68
Peterborough	28,957	33,178	37,219	21	28	31	17	19	17	18	18	6	5	11	7	62

Oxfordshire: (Population (000's), 1841–163; 1851–170; 1861–171; 1871–178)

Town	Pop.	Pop.	Pop.	23	50	56	53	26	29	31	30	5	4	9	15	72
Henley	17,895	18,200	18,915	15	47	35	20	18	26	18	22	6	7	13	9	59
Thame	15,640	15,305	15,003	24	39	45	25	25	33	23	28	6	5	12	10	77
Headington	15,771	17,185	21,686	14	21	26	17	16	8	8	8	7	6	13	6	55
Oxford	20,172	20,037	21,016	13	19	29	13	10	10	13	12	7	5	12	4	66
Bicester	15,562	15,555	15,587	29	38	36	30	30	27	24	26	4	5	9	12	65
Woodstock	14,453	14,286	14,070	18	30	37	32	25	28	21	25	7	6	13	11	83
Witney	23,558	23,238	22,905	31	54	48	36	34	25	17	21	6	5	11	11	61
Chipping Norton	17,427	17,806	17,268	11	37	34	22	17	19	16	18	6	6	12	13	79
Banbury	29,769	30,171	31,208	20	22	23	18	19	15	18	17	5	5	11	10	68

Cornwall: (Population (000's), 1841–343; 1851–357; 1861–365; 1871–358)

Town	Pop.	Pop.	Pop.	23	50	56	53	26	29	31	30	5	4	9	15	72
Stratton	8580	8028	7844	26	40	23	12	19	35	35	35	5	4	9	11	72
Camelford	8448	7784	8417	31	30	40	26	29	26	20	23	4	3	7	10	38
Launceston	18,305	17,005	17,142	20	34	34	22	21	22	22	22	5	5	10	12	63
St. Germans	16,545	17,631	17,999	17	25	36	13	15	16	16	16	5	5	10	8	58
Liskeard	33,831	33,562	34,192	37	38	47	27	32	26	32	29	5	5	9	9	41
Bodmin	20,493	19,691	19,776	23	30	36	10	17	16	18	17	5	4	9	8	55
St. Columb	17,402	16,754	16,799	27	36	47	30	29	25	23	24	5	4	9	8	39
St. Austell	32,069	43,797	31,194	39	40	51	21	35	28	30	29	5	4	8	11	33
Truro	42,270	43,070	41,722	31	34	40	31	31	11	23	23	6	5	11	12	55
Falmouth	22,056	23,332	25,098	30	26	32	20	25	23	18	15	4	4	8	9	48
Helston	28,402	30,036	28,420	40	37	50	32	36	33	33	28	4	4	8	11	61
Redruth	53,629	57,173	58,503	46	53	65	36	41	0	43	38	6	6	11	16	40
Penzance	53,517	54,554	54,160	34	33	48	13	28	26	32	29	9	5	17	11	36
Scilly Isles	2627	2431	2090	50	11	5	8	32		22	11		9		17	10

Appendix F Proportions of illiterate spouses, 1856, 1866, 1871 and statistics of school attendance, 1851

Illiteracy: M: Males; F: Females; T: Total

Registration District	Population			% Marks 1856			% Marks 1866			% Marks 1871			% Population at School, March, 1851				% of Day Schools at Public Schools, 1851
													Day			Sunday	
	1851	1861	1871	M	F	T	M	F	T	M	F	T	M	F	T	T	
Devon: (Population (000's), 1841–537; 1851–572; 1861–589; 1871–606)																	
Axminster	20,303	19,758	20,059	37	31	34	23	26	25	33	19	26	5	4	9	10	57
Honiton	23,824	22,729	22,291	33	31	32	29	25	27	17	14	16	5	3	8	8	73
St. Thomas	48,806	48,805	49,308	21	24	23	16	13	15	13	11	12	5	4	9	5	56
Exeter	32,823	33,742	34,652	16	18	17	9	18	14	11	12	12	7	6	13	4	53
Newton Abbot	52,306	59,063	68,203	16	18	17	14	15	15	8	9	9	6	5	11	6	58
Totnes	34,022	32,942	35,557	27	24	26	18	19	19	20	19	20	6	4	11	10	45
Kingsbridge	21,377	19,394	19,706	25	32	29	35	19	27	17	16	18	4	6	9	9	38
Plympton St. Mary	19,723	20,502	22,190	30	32	31	24	22	23	17	16	17	5	3	8	6	63
Plymouth	52,231	62,599	68,883	22	36	29	21	24	21	10	21	16	5	3	8	6	53
East Stonehouse	11,979	14,343	14,585	37	46	42	24	30	26	20	25	23	5	4	9	4	65
Stoke Damerel	38,180	50,440	49,449	24	37	32	11	20	16	9	19	14	6	5	12	6	47
Tavistock	27,850	35,265	31,240	35	43	39	20	35	29	20	19	20	5	4	10	9	64
Okehampton[12]	20,401	18,580	19,249	33	89	61	21	20	21	26	28	26	4	4	8	7	42
Crediton	21,728	20,274	19,406	38	39	39	26	16	24	23	25	23	4	4	9	6	66
Tiverton	32,540	30,875	29,720	33	33	31	21	16	19	16	22	16	5	4	9	9	69
South Molton	20,566	19,532	18,975	28	35	32	16	28	26	18	15	16	5	5	10	7	66
Barnstaple	38,178	36,293	37,406	25	25	25	20	19	20	13	24	15	5	5	9	6	57
Torrington	17,491	16,876	16,334	30	37	34	31	40	31	27	17	30	5	4	9	10	64
Bideford	19,607	17,790	19,506	29	36	33	19	19	17	20	33	20	6	6	11	13	60
Holsworthy	9350	9876	9427	37	33	35	20	31	27	20	40	30	6	2	5	8	48
Dorset: (Population (000's), 1841–188; 1851–177; 1861–182; 1871–189)																	
Shaftesbury	13,025	12,986	13,137	28	30	29	23	21	22	22	17	20	6	6	11	9	85
Sturminster	10,382	10,340	10,861	34	40	37	43	30	37	38	25	32	5	5	10	10	59
Blandford	14,837	14,821	14,634	34	31	33	18	14	16	18	15	17	6	7	15	12	67
Wimborne	17,284	17,253	17,323	38	24	31	27	15	21	19	9	17	5	5	10	12	86
Poole	12,890	13,742	14,734	29	27	28	16	21	19	19	14	17	7	7	13	13	35
Wareham	17,417	17,072	17,226	33	23	28	24	17	19	20	16	15	6	6	11	13	74
Weymouth	22,037	27,291	31,216	17	22	20	13	14	14	12	17	22	6	5	11	13	51
Dorchester	25,002	24,810	26,044	36	21	29	14	29	25	24	19	21	6	6	12	9	70
Sherborne	13,081	13,463	13,982	31	37	34	21	20	24	22	19	21	5	5	10	12	68
Beaminster	14,276	13,587	13,111	36	39	38	28	21	23	26	28	27	5	5	12	12	68
Bridport	16,866	16,828	16,732	41	48	45	28	30	28	24	24	24	6	5	13	13	64
Gloucestershire: (Population (000's), 1841–396; 1851–420; 1861–444; 1871–489)																	
Bristol	65,716	66,027	62,662	21	31	26	19	26	23	17	21	21	7	5	12	9	66
Clifton	77,450	94,687	128,084	22	31	28	20	24	22	15	21	18	5	5	9	7	68
Chipping Sodbury	18,526	18,763	18,656	55	48	52	40	23	32	23	18	23	4	4	9	9	72
Thornbury	16,454	16,499	17,320	40	40	40	22	8	15	21	20	21	5	5	9	9	65
Dursley	14,803	13,331	13,077	23	32	28	23	22	23	23	16	20	7	5	12	16	70

Stroud	37,386	36,448	39,357	38	32	26	16	20	18	11	14	11	13	6	5	13	11	72
Tetbury	6254	6110	6132	14	20	26	37	43	40	28	19	10	24	5	5	24	12	79
Cirencester	21,327	20,934	21,364	38	33	32	34	14	18	21	15	21	18	6	5	18	10	76
Northleach	10,984	10,895	10,584	38	39	39	27	16	25	23	13	23	18	5	6	18	13	81
Stow-on-the-Wold	9930	9687	9621	23	28	32	41	12	20	16	12	36	14	5	5	14	10	81
Winchcomb	10,136	10,082	10,330	49	51	49	11	26	34	31	17	37	24	3	3	24	11	71
Cheltenham	44,184	49,792	53,166	16	17	16	11	9	10	10	9	26	10	5	6	10	7	68
Tewkesbury	15,131	14,908	14,288	38	39	38	44	31	38	23	20	28	21	4	4	22	9	68

Herefordshire: (Population (000's), 1841–97; 1851–99; 1861–119; 1871–121)

Ledbury	13,139	14,880	13,102	40	45	49	22	20	20	25	23	25	24	5	5	24	5	86
Ross	15,502	16,306	16,604	33	35	36	28	29	19	19	20	19	29	3	3	29	6	54
Hereford	35,154	39,287	42,574	32	35	38	28	25	23	23	17	23	20	4	4	20	5	69
Weobly	8718	9018	9031	42	39	35	30	27	25	36	14	36	25	4	3	25	8	86
Bromyard	11,697	11,811	11,934	53	52	50	46	38	27	37	36	38	37	3	5	37	4	76
Leominster	14,910	15,494	15,411	35	37	39	26	25	23	26	24	26	25	5	3	25	4	72
Kington[13]			12,067							28	21	28	25				9	

Monmouthshire: (Population (000's), 1841–151; 1851–177; 1861–197; 1871–220)

Chepstow	19,057	17,941	18,341	41	42	42	25	23	21	21	18	23	20	4	4	20	7	72
Monmouth	27,319	30,244	31,598	36	41	45	31	29	31	31	26	29	29	5	5	29	8	73
Abergavenny	59,229	67,092	74,625	74	70	65	47	55	45	45	54	55	50	3	3	50	17	66
Pontypool	27,993	30,288	33,892	66	60	54	44	55	45	45	54	44	50	3	3	50	16	75
Newport	43,472	51,412	61,252	46	42	38	26	30	20	20	26	34	23	3	4	23	11	59

Shropshire: (Population (000's), 1841–242; 1851–245; 1861–260; 1871–267)

Ludlow	17,051	17,721	18,078	40	40	39	37	32	24	24	24	32	24	4	5	24	5	76
Clun	10,119	10,615	10,801	41	42	43	31	31	35	35	22	31	29	3	3	29	3	76
Church Stretton	6167	6289	6343	39	42	52	19	21	17	17	17	21	17	3	3	17	1	76
Cleobury Mortimer	8663	8304	8317	42	50	58	22	39	32	32	27	34	30	3	4	30	6	74
Bridgnorth	15,608	15,920	15,448	51	47	43	26	29	25	25	31	32	28	3	4	28	6	74
Shiffnal	11,483	11,994	12,787	49	46	49	32	43	34	34	32	44	33	3	5	33	7	66
Madeley	27,627	30,403	30,364	52	46	39	44	43	41	41	40	40	41	4	5	41	11	77
Atcham	19,174	19,455	18,313	48	50	52	34	25	34	34	30	32	—	5	4	17	5	81
Shrewsbury	23,104	25,784	27,252	33	27	20	32	18	25	25	19	16	17	5	5	17	4	72
Oswestry	27,795	23,817	26,849	41	38	35	16	20	22	22	25	20	24	4	4	24	12	78
Ellesmere	15,239	14,611	14,465	42	37	31	20	31	17	17	22	31	20	5	6	20	8	64
Wem	10,625	10,644	10,879	54	52	50	30	36	25	25	13	36	19	6	7	19	7	78
Whitchurch[14]		11,272	11,424	52	44	40	31	28	27	27	43	31	35			35		
Market Drayton	14,160	14,260	14,656	44	42	40	33	31	18	18	22	33	20	4	7	20	10	70
Wellington	20,725	23,873	25,184	60	58	56	49	53	39	39	48	57	44	4	4	44	12	52
Newport	15,620	15,447	15,844	52	50	48	28	31	32	32	31	33	32	4	5	32	5	77

Somerset: (Population (000's), 1841–449; 1851–456; 1861–463; 1871–483)

Williton	19,985	19,918	19,807	27	34	41	30	33	33	33	29	35	31	5	5	31	10	65
Dulverton	6023	6158	5794	19	20	20	24	25	21	21	17	24	19			19		
Wellington	22,121	20,480	20,777	42	44	45	24	30	27	27	20	30	24	5	4	24	10	56
Taunton	35,114	35,601	35,522	37	34	31	22	24	24	24	17	22	21	5	5	21	10	59
Bridgwater	33,188	34,420	34,871	43	42	40	25	25	27	27	22	25	21	5	5	21	9	62
Langport	18,587	18,077	17,650	47	47	46	39	40	30	30	28	41	29	4	4	29	11	66
Chard	26,085	25,591	26,437	45	44	43	33	35	37	37	28	37	34	5	5	34	13	69
Yeovil	28,463	28,489	28,852	47	40	47	32	32	25	25	31	35	31	5	5	31	13	48
Wincanton	21,311	21,500	21,059	50	47	43	29	28	33	33	26	34	26	6	6	26	11	61
Frome	25,325	23,704	24,271	38	34	29	24	24	17	17	16	29	16	5	5	17	14	66
Shepton Mallet	16,957	16,619	16,003	43	42	41	44	41	30	30	26	43	28	4	5	28	10	60

Appendix F Proportions of illiterate spouses, 1856, 1866, 1871 and statistics of school attendance, 1851

Illiteracy: M: Males; F: Females; T: Total

Registration District	Population 1851	Population 1861	Population 1871	% Marks 1856 M	F	T	% Marks 1866 M	F	T	% Marks 1871 M	F	T	Day M	F	T	Sunday T	% of Day Schools at Public Schools, 1851
Wells	21,342	21,889	22,368	30	38	34	22	23	26	22	23	23	5	4	9	5	66
Axbridge	33,059	36,106	89,221	40	40	45	21	21	27	21	19	20	4	4	8	8	65
Clutton	25,227	23,721	23,725	51	39	21	27	23	30	27	23	25	6	5	11	13	66
Bath	69,847	68,336	69,591	19	22	43	11	11	17	11	11	11	6	6	12	7	69
Keynsham	21,115	21,802	22,892	38	48	26	29	40	35	29	38	34	6	6	12	13	68
Bedminster	38,143	41,257	53,872	22	30		15	19	19	15	16	16	5	4	9	5	70
Wiltshire: (Population (000's), 1841–243; 1851–241; 1861–236; 1871–245)																	
Highworth	17,020	19,237	25,679	38	40	39	26	32	29	17	17	17	5	5	10	11	77
Cricklade	11,402	11,470	12,128	35	32	34	34	33	34	27	15	21	4	4	8	9	80
Malmesbury[15]	14,809	14,556	14,711	85	83	84	24	22	23	20	16	18	4	4	8	10	53
Chippenham	21,407	22,029	21,834	36	31	34	27	18	23	24	14	19	6	6	12	10	67
Calne	9173	8885	8923	34	34	34	26	17	22	14	13	14	7	7	14	11	82
Marlborough	10,267	9774	9986	43	38	41	31	28	30	36	11	24	6	6	12	12	84
Devizes	22,236	21,680	21,250	47	47	47	22	22	22	27	17	22	6	5	11	8	78
Melksham	18,815	17,233	18,417	20	35	28	15	19	17	15	22	19	6	5	11	15	67
Bradford	11,607	10,646	10,646	59	46	53	31	23	28	31	25	28	7	6	13	16	76
Westbury	12,330	11,751	11,526	24	30	27	20	19	20	18	22	20	6	5	11	16	75
Warminster	17,067	15,942	15,260	32	35	34	27	31	29	18	22	20	6	5	11	9	72
Pewsey	12,508	12,466	11,917	42	44	43	44	25	35	36	34	35	5	5	10	11	78
Amesbury	8250	8127	7953	34	32	33	32	15	24	18	12	16	5	5	10	12	88
Alderbury	14,908	1477	16,322	22	31	27	14	18	16	10	10	10	6	5	11	12	81
Salisbury	8930	9034	9912	10	18	14	8	8	8	10	10	10	7	6	13	10	67
Wilton	10,742	10,647	10,500	33	24	29	31	23	29	31	18	25	6	7	13	14	80
Tisbury	10,181	9862	9898	35	34	35	26	17	21	26	15	21	6	6	12	11	85
Mere	8433	8057	8105	37	56	47	36	21	27	36	26	31	6	5	11	13	80

Sources: *Censuses, 1851, 1861, 1871; Education Census, 1851; Annual Reports of the Registrar of Births, Deaths and Marriages.*
1. 1851–6 included in Stockton.
2. Called Aysgarth in 1871.
3. Boundary altered 1871, increase in acreage c. 12 per cent.
4. Birkenhead formed out of Wirral, 1861.
5. Four parishes taken from Lancaster district.
6. 1861 Wharfedale removed from this district which ceased to exist in 1871.
7. Reduced in size 1861, when Kirkstall, Holbeck, Bramley districts formed.
8. Pontefract in 1861 lost over half acreage as Castleford district formed: this was returned to Pontefract in 1871.
9. Tadcaster lost acreage to Bramham 1861. Bramham a distinct district in 1866, but in Wetherby, 1871.
10. Largely Portsmouth borough.
11. Only 14 marriages 1856.
12. Okehampton figures for 1856 are untypical, perhaps erroneous. Percentages for 1857, male 46, female 42, total 44.
13. Formerly in Radnor, Wales.
14. Formed out of Wem district and part of Malpas (Cheshire).
15. Malmesbury figures for 1856 are very untypical. Percentages for 1855, male 29, female 32, total 31; for 1857, male 29, female 33, total 31.

Appendix G   Illiteracy by registration districts, 1856, 1866, 1871

1856		Registration District	1866		1871		% Population change	
Rank	% Marks		Rank	% Marks	Rank	% Marks	1851–61	1861–71

Counties of the Far North and North-East

Rank	% Marks		Rank	% Marks	Rank	% Marks	1851–61	1861–71
19	18	Bedale	1	6	33	17	−4	−3
19	18	Berwick			3	7	−9	−2
2	3	Glendale	2	8	2	6	−8	0
2	3	Rothbury			9	9	−4	−1
16	16	Bootle	5	9	22	14	−2	+45
12	14	Alnwick			5	8	0	−6
1	0	Belford	6	10	5	8	−9	−7
10	13	East Ward			17	13	+13	+10
7	8	Bellingham	9	11	1	5	+8	0
14	15	West Ward			5	8	−1	+2
14	15	Castle Ward	11	12	3	7	+8	+13
16	16	Leyburn	12	13	10	10	+1	−13
4	7	Longtown	13	14	10	10	+8	−21
39	25	Scarborough			43	19	+24	+20
4	7	Brampton			17	13	−4	−2
24	20	Hexham	15	15	24	15	+5	+2
12	14	Penrith			17	13	+1	+6
25	21	Skirlaugh			24	15	+4	+1
9	12	Wigton			17	13	−2	−3
67	37	Bourne	20	16	56	21	−10	−1
34	24	York			17	13	+10	+8
10	13	Haltwhistle			5	8	−8	+4
8	11	Lincoln	22	17	24	15	+12	+11
50	30	Patrington			56	21	+3	−6
18	17	Richmond			13	12	−3	+1
27	22	Uppingham			13	12	−3	−1
4	7	Askrigg			13	12	0	−3
22	19	Beverley	27	18	22	14	+5	+2
50	30	Darlington			37	18	+21	+56
44	29	Easingwold			56	21	−1	−1
34	24	Grantham			13	12	−3	+6
27	22	Kendal			12	11	+2	+7
44	29	Spilsby			24	15	−1	+2
62	34	Horncastle	33	19	43	19	−2	+16
25	21	Morpeth			24	15	+33	+29
19	18	Oakham			31	16	−4	0
50	30	Gainsborough			43	19	−5	+5
27	22	Pickering	37	20	33	17	+6	+21
40	27	Pocklington			37	18	+4	−4
32	23	Thirsk			37	18	−4	−1
66	36	Glanford Brigg			43	19	+3	+4
40	27	Hull	41	21	49	20	+12	+20
44	29	Malton			49	20	+2	−3
34	24	Northallerton			37	18	−2	−5
50	30	Reeth			59	22	−9	−13
42	28	Stamford			31	16	−8	−2
42	28	Stokesley			24	15	+20	+4
27	22	Teesdale			33	17	+5	+2
62	34	Caistor	49	22	43	19	+9	+30
22	19	Carlisle			37	18	+8	+4
44	29	Sculcoates			59	22	+16	+31
62	34	Spalding			49	20	+4	+5
56	32	Louth			43	19	+4	0

1856 Rank	% Marks	Registration District	1866 Rank	% Marks	1871 Rank	% Marks	% Population change 1851–61	1861–71
56	32	Newcastle	53	23	59	22	+24	+18
32	23	Weardale			62	23	+13	+17
50	30	Boston	56	24	49	20	−1	+2
67	37	Sleaford			49	20	+2	+4
—	—	Hartlepool	58	25	65	26	0	+37
27	22	Whitby			49	20	+10	+9
56	32	Alston			63	24	−6	−11
34	24	Bridlington			33	17	0	+7
55	31	Guisborough	60	26	63	24	+81	+76
56	32	Stockton			69	28	+10	+75
44	29	Tynemouth			49	20	+21	+21
34	24	Cockermouth	65	27	69	28	+7	+13
56	32	Driffield			37	18	+5	0
44	29	Helmsley	67	29	24	15	−5	−1
61	33	South Shields	68	30	65	26	+25	+67
67	37	Gateshead			71	29	+24	+35
71	38	Holbeach	69	32	65	26	−4	+5
72	43	Howden			68	27	+4	−5
73	44	Durham	72	33	76	37	+26	+31
65	35	Sunderland			71	29	+29	+24
67	37	Whitehaven	74	34	73	34	+12	+19
74	48	Houghton	75	35	74	36	+11	+20
77	58	Chester-le-Street	76	36	78	39	+32	+20
76	51	Auckland	77	40	77	38	+68	+37
75	49	Easington	78	45	74	36	+25	+23

Counties of the North-West

1856 Rank	% Marks	Registration District	1866 Rank	% Marks	1871 Rank	% Marks	% Population change 1851–61	1861–71
3	25	Wetherby	1	10	8	14	+27	+129
7	29	Sedbergh	2	11	17	18	−4	+14
7	29	Knaresborough	3	12	3	10	+17	+5
22	35	Settle	4	14	11	16	−9	+21
2	21	West Derby	5	15	7	13	+47	+52
3	25	Great Ouseburn	6	16	4	11	+19	−20
—	—	Bramham[1]			—	—	—	—
10	30	Ripon	8	17	2	9	−2	+1
3	25	Doncaster			8	14	+14	+15
7	29	Chorlton	10	18	13	17	+37	+25
33	41	Pateley Bridge			4	11	+2	−9
6	28	Hemsworth			6	12	−5	+4
10	30	Lancaster	12	19	17	18	+4	−9
12	31	Saddleworth			24	22	+5	+7
26	37	Skipton			10	15	+9	+3
33	41	Tadcaster	15	20	23	21	−70	+252[1,4]
1	20	Wirral			13	17	—	+26[2]
—	—	Birkenhead			13	17	—	+29[2]
15	32	Otley	19	21	—	—	−35	—[3]
—	—[4]	Bramley			29	24	—	+290
—	—[3]	Wharfedale	21	23	20	19	—	+153[3]
12	31	Altrincham			11	16	+19	+23
17	33	Selby			29	24	+2	+2
19	34	Wortley	22	24	28	23	+20	+17
22	35	Fylde			31	25	+17	+19
47	50	Ecclesall Bierlow	26	26	37	26	+68	+37
—	—[4]	Kirkstall	27	27	—	—	—	—
43	48	Keighley			22	20	−6	+21

	1856	Registration District	1866		1871		% Population change	
Rank	% Marks		Rank	% Marks	Rank	% Marks	1851–61	1861–71
12	31	Garstang			17	18	−2	−2
17	33	Great Boughton			24	22	+11	+23[5]
19	34	Ulverston	29	28	37	26	+17	+54
33	41	Wakefield			52	32	+12	+25
39	45	Macclesfield			31	25	−4	−4
25	36	Clitheroe			20	19	−8	+3
26	37	Leeds	34	29	37	26	+16	+38
40	46	Halifax			24	22	+6	+19
32	40	Pontefract[6]	37	30	52	32	−51[5]	+136[5]
29	39	Rotherham			40	27	+34	+29
29	39	Manchester	38	31	40	27	+7	+3
36	42	Huddersfield			40	27	+9	+4
19	34	Thorne			45	28	+1	+6
58	56	Ormskirk	41	32	31	25	+21	+28
42	47	Runcorn			48	29	+4	+14
26	37	Liverpool			51	31	+5	−12
43	48	Barton upon Irwell	44	33	48	29	+24	+32
45	49	Bury			45	28	+14	+8
55	55	Todmorden			31	25	+5	+4
15	32	Goole			13	17	+11	+14
29	39	Sheffield	48	34	52	32	+24	+26
40	46	Congleton			31	25	+12	+6
—	—[4]	Holbeck			40	27	—	+37
37	43	Nantwich	52	35	31	25	+14	+31
55	55	Chorley	53	36	57	33	+11	+3
22	35	Hunslet	54	37	62	37	−71[4,5]	+80
52	53	Ashton			24	22	+13	−3
37	43	Salford			60	35	+20	+22
45	49	Bradford	56	38	48	29	+8	+31
51	52	Haslingden			52	32	+38	+15
61	57	Rochdale			40	27	+26	+20
47	50	Dewsbury			64	38	+29	+34
47	50	Northwich	60	39	61	36	+7	+12
—	—	Castleford[6]			—	—	—	—
63	66	Oldham	63	40	45	28	+28	+14
47	50	Barnsley			64	38	+31	+25
54	54	Bolton	64	41	57	33	+14	+22
66	60	Warrington			57	33	+21	+24
58	56	Burnley	67	42	62	37	+18	+16
52	53	Stockport	68	43	52	32	+5	+4
58	56	Preston	69	46	67	40	+15	+5
55	55	Prescot	70	47	68	42	+30	+27
63	59	Blackburn	71	48	66	39	+32	+20
62	58	Leigh	72	52	68	42	+15	+11
63	59	Wigan	73	59	70	48	+22	+18
—	—	Lunesdale	—	—	1	7	—	—

Midland Counties

2	19	Warwick	1	12	3	10	+5	+11
3	22	Billesdon			1	9	+4	+3
16	30	Melton Mowbray	3	13	4	11	−2	−1
7	25	Rugby			9	14	+4	+3
1	16	Kings Norton	5	14	14	15	+53	+41
14	29	Uttoxeter			14	15	−2	−3
16	30	Market Harborough	7	15	7	12	+1	0
24	32	Meriden			1	9	0	−3
33	35	Lutterworth	9	16	4	11	−4	−8

1856		Registration District	1866		1871		% Population change	
Rank	% Marks		Rank	% Marks	Rank	% Marks	1851–61	1861–71
6	23	Chapel-en-le-Frith			22	18	+22	+13
7	25	Newark	10	17	9	14	−1	−2
3	22	Solihull			4	11	+11	+16
16	30	Burton-on-Trent			27	20	+29	+28
9	27	Derby			24	19	+17	+22
33	35	Southam	13	18	9	14	−1	+1
27	33	Upton-on-Severn			7	12	+16	+11
16	30	Ashborne			14	15	−1	0
33	35	Atherstone	18	21	34	22	+6	−2
38	37	Stafford			37	24	+7	+9
12	28	Shardlow			24	19	−4	+9
30	34	Shipston on Stour	20	22	24	19	−4	−1
20	31	Southwell			14	15	−5	−11
12	28	Bakewell			18	16	+5	−6
30	34	Bingham	23	23	18	16	−4	−6
20	31	East Retford			20	17	0	+2
27	33	Stratford-on-Avon			9	14	+2	+5
9	27	Lichfield	27	24	22	18	+9	+17
20	31	Worcester			27	20	+12	+5
58	48	Blaby			41	25	+1	+4
27	33	Droitwich			41	25	+6	+17
56	46	Stone	29	25	34	22	+13	+13
24	32	Tamworth			20	17	+11	+4
3	22	Worksop			29	21	+8	+22
14	29	Aston			49	29	+50	+46
9	27	Leicester			36	23	+12	+40
20	31	Loughborough	34	26	37	24	−5	+1
50	43	Martley			29	21	−20	+8
30	34	Nottingham			41	25	+28	+16
57	47	Tenbury	39	27	52	31	+5	+6
42	40	Barrow-on-Soar			41	25	−1	+9
40	39	Coventry	40	28	41	25	+13	−4
51	45	Hayfield			29	21	+8	+1
48	42	Pershore			29	21	+2	+2
46	41	Cheadle	44	29	29	21	+16	+1
42	40	Penkridge			62	39	+11	+27
42	40	Ashby de la Zouche	46	30	47	27	+10	+10
36	36	Belper			37	24	+10	+2
38	37	Market Bosworth			9	14	−2	+2
48	42	Newcastle under Lyme	48	31	50	30	+18	+23
51	45	Alcester			46	26	−3	+8
36	36	Birmingham	50	32	58	36	+22	+9
24	32	Radford			52	31	+14	+11
58	48	Basford			58	36	+15	+14
63	53	Bromsgrove			62	39	+6	+10
40	39	Leek	53	33	52	31	+5	+17
51	45	West Bromwich			56	33	+33	+15
62	49	Evesham	57	34	37	24	+2	+6
51	45	Kidderminster			47	27	−8	+15
42	40	Chesterfield	59	37	50	30	+35	+25
68	58	Foleshill			60	37	+8	−14
58	48	Stoke-on-Trent	60	38	61	38	+23	+25
64	54	Wolverhampton			64	40	+22	+7
51	45	Nuneaton			55	32	−4	−5
67	57	Stourbridge	63	39	66	43	+20	+7
46	41	Mansfield			57	35	+1	+17
65	55	Walsall	65	41	65	42	+39	+20

	1856	Registration District	1866		1871		% Population change	
Rank	% Marks		Rank	% Marks	Rank	% Marks	1851–61	1861–71
58	48	Hinckley	67	46	66	43	−1	−1
65	55	Wolstanton	68	47	68	45	+30	+27
69	64	Dudley	69	58	69	59	+22	+3

East Anglia and the South-Eastern Counties

	1856	Registration District	1866		1871		% Population change	
Rank	% Marks		Rank	% Marks	Rank	% Marks	1851–61	1861–71
1	14	Hastings			1	7	+26	+34
1	14	Richmond	1	8	1	7	+18	+39
17	21	Winchester			23	13	+4	+10
5	15	Kingston	4	10	11	10	+36	+53
24	23	Barnet			34	14	+31	+32
12	18	Dover	5	11	5	8	+12	+12
7	17	Eastbourne			1	7	+28	+47
1	14	Brighton			22	12	+19	+16
7	17	Christchurch			53	16	+23	+57
16	20	Isle of Wight			11	10	+10	+20
39	27	Reigate	8	12	18	11	+40	+36
7	17	Southampton			23	13	+27	+11
30	24	Tenterden			23	13	−3	−1
37	26	West Ashford			45	15	+14	+10
30	24	Worthing			7	9	+1	+14
12	18	Edmonton			7	9	+31	+43
17	21	Gravesend			23	13	+13	+13
30	24	Romney Marsh	16	13	11	10	+5	+7
20	22	South Stoneham			23	13	+60	+26
7	17	Hendon	20	14	11	10	+21	+93
7	17	Thanet			11	10	0	+32
102	41	Chelmsford			58	17	+2	+3
1	14	Chichester			34	14	+2	−44[7]
20	22	Epsom			7	9	+18	+36
49	29	Fareham	22	15	53	16	+7	0
24	23	Ipswich			53	16	+16	+13
24	23	Lewes			18	11	+5	+11
6	16	West Ham			5	8	+70	+67
65	32	Battle			34	14	−11	+8
56	30	Bury St. Edmunds			34	14	−4	+12
65	32	Catherington			64	18	0	+11
79	35	Cuckfield	29	16	23	13	+10	+18
24	23	New Forest			1	7	0	0
49	29	Ringwood			64	18	−11	+1
56	30	Staines			45	15	+14	+27
12	18	Steyning			11	10	+43	+31
24	23	Brentford			23	13	+22	+42
44	28	Bromley			18	11	+16	+58
37	26	Canterbury			34	14	+18	−1
30	24	Colchester	37	17	58	17	+23	+11
17	21	Croydon			11	10	+5	+81
30	24	Dorking			34	14	+10	+23
44	28	Maidstone			45	15	+2	+15
39	27	Portsea Island			45	15	+31	+20
83	36	Alresford			70	19	−3	+1
20	22	Elham			23	13	+43	+11
44	28	Guildford	45	18	45	15	+17	+22
30	24	Havant			34	14	0	+13
69	33	Lymington			88	22	−1	+3
44	28	Tunbridge			34	14	+20	+30
79	35	Alverstoke			34	14	+34	0
74	34	Farnborough			—	—	+83	—

1856		Registration District	1866		1871		% Population change	
Rank	% Marks		Rank	% Marks	Rank	% Marks	1851–61	1861–71
61	31	Hartley Wintney	51	9	79	20	+2	+79
49	29	Medway			58	17	+21	+14
61	31	Mutford			70	19	+19	+30
56	30	Petersfield			70	19	+1	+23
85	37	Andover			88	22	−1	+3
65	32	Farnham			53	16	+293[8]	
69	33	Cranbrook	57	20	70	19	+3	+4
61	31	East Ashford			99	23	+3	+6
49	29	Rye			53	16	−3	+1
74	34	Stockbridge			70	19	−3	0
39	27	Eastry			34	14	+3	+5
79	35	Romford	63	21	88	22	+10	+13
36	25	Romsey			23	13	0	+1
39	27	Sevenoaks			45	15	0	+10
83	36	Dartford	67	22	82	21	+18	+31
56	30	Westhamphett			45	15	−3	+27
49	29	Chertsey	69	23	23	13	+16	+24
20	22	Hailsham			58	17	−5	+3
131	48	Alton			79	20	+1	+24
44	28	Blean			23	13	+10	+13
98	40	East Grinstead			99	23	+7	+9
24	23	King's Lynn	71	24	45	15	−19	+3
49	29	North Aylesford			82	21	+15	+13
61	31	Norwich			70	19	+10	+7
102	41	Ongar			18	11	−5	+2
131	48	Wangford			131	32	−3	+3
112	43	Whitchurch			123	28	−2	+2
56	30	Horsham			58	17	+9	+26
74	34	Malling			64	18	+10	+9
117	45	Plomesgate			104	24	−4	
97	39	Samford	80	25	70	19	+3	
92	38	Ticehurst			79	20	−6	
74	34	Uxbridge			64	18	+19	
74	34	Yarmouth			82	21	+13	
85	37	Faversham	87	26	70	19	+13	
131	48	Godstone			88	22	+9	
85	37	Epping			82	21	+6	
121	46	Rochford	89	27	70	19	+15	
69	33	Sheppey			64	18	+38	0
85	37	Woodbridge			99	23	−4	−1
69	33	Billericay			82	21	+9	+19
79	35	Bridge			34	14	+1	−2
139	52	Dunmow			104	24	−4	0
12	18	Fordingbridge	93	28	88	22	−7	+1
114	44	Freebridge Lynn			129	31	−1	+37
98	40	Henstead			99	23	−2	−5
108	42	Witham			88	22	+1	−3
85	37	Basingstoke			82	21	0	+4
114	44	Braintree			140	36	−2	0
126	47	Erpingham			115	26	−4	−5
126	47	Forehoe	100	29	142	37	−6	−4
49	29	Milton			111	25	+23	+30
136	49	Petworth			88	22	−2	+8
39	27	Westbourne			7	9	0	+4
85	37	Blything			104	24	−4	−2
121	46	Droxford	107	30	88	22	0	+10
126	47	Swaffham			129	31	−4	−1
102	41	Thingoe			111	25	−4	−3

	1856	Registration District		1866		1871		% Population change	
Rank	% Marks		Rank	% Marks		Rank	% Marks	1851–61	1861–71
117	45	Aylsham				121	27	−5	−5
114	44	Depwade				115	26	−4	−4
92	38	Hambledon				88	22	+3	+10
65	32	Hollingbourn				58	17	−1	+3
69	33	Maldon	111	31		104	24	+2	+5
102	41	Midhurst				88	22	−8	+4
92	38	St. Faiths				131	32	−5	−4
108	42	Stow				99	23	−1	0
98	40	Uckfield				123	28	−2	+12
92	38	Walsingham				121	27	−4	−5
121	46	Saffron Walden	121	32		115	26	−5	−1
85	37	Loddon				104	24	+9	−4
102	41	Mildenhall	122	33		104	24	−7	−4
98	40	Mitford				131	32	−5	−2
137	50	Tunstead				125	29	−7	−1
142	57	Kingsclere	126	34		134	34	−4	+1
117	45	Tendring				125	29	−2	+6
102	41	Orsett	128	35		64	18	+9	+14
92	38	Thakeham				115	26	+2	+12
108	42	Thetford	130	36		104	24	−2	−3
139	52	Cosford				140	36	−4	−2
108	42	Downham				111	25	−3	+2
121	46	Flegg				142	37	+2	+9
126	47	Guiltcross	131	37		111	25	−9	−3
121	46	Lexden				115	26	+6	+5
138	51	Sudbury				134	33	+2	+1
112	43	Wayland				134	33	−5	−4
131	48	Blofield	138	38		125	29	−1	−2
141	54	Hoxne				137	35	−8	−2
117	45	Docking	140	39		88	22	−3	−2
143	60	Hoo				137	35	+1	+10
131	48	Hartismere	142	41		137	35	−7	−5
126	47	Bosmere	143	47		115	26	−6	−3
144	61	Halstead	144	49		125	29	−2	0
144	61	Risbridge	145	52		144	48	−4	+6

South Midland Counties

3	21	Easthampstead	1	10		9	14	+17	+43
5	24	Oxford	2	13		8	12	−1	+5
2	19	Cambridge				3	9	−5	+14
7	26	Reading	4	15		4	11	+17	+29
1	16	Windsor				1	6	+7	+25
9	28	Cookham	6	16		9	14	+11	+14
5	24	Headington				2	8	+9	+26
22	36	Chipping Norton	8	17		15	18	−1	0
22	36	Hertford	9	18		17	19	+1	+5
34	41	Henley				28	22	+2	+4
4	23	Banbury	11	19		12	17	+1	+3
12	30	Peterborough				15	18	+15	+12
7	26	Daventry	13	20		20	20	−6	−6
12	30	Eton				4	11	+4	+12
9	28	Northampton	14	21		28	22	+22	+23
19	35	Oundle				35	24	−1	−6
34	41	Potterspury	17	22		12	7	+9	+1
28	38	Watford				32	23	+8	+34
22	36	Whittlesey				45	27	+10	+1
15	34	Brixworth	18	23		4	11	+4	−10

1856 Rank	% Marks	Registration District	1866 Rank	% Marks	1871 Rank	% Marks	% Pop. change 1851–61	1861–71
31	40	Kettering			12	17	+5	+6
19	35	Newbury			21	21	−4	+3
15	34	Hatfield	23	24	32	23	−1	+3
28	38	Wallingford			21	21	−1	+5
28	38	Bedford			21	21	+7	+9
39	42	Chesterton	25	25	37	25	0	+12
39	42	Thame			50	28	−2	−2
15	34	Woodstock			37	25	−2	−1
62	53	Berkhampstead	29	26	56	30	+4	+7
39	42	Ware			11	16	0	+6
39	42	Abingdon			17	19	0	+3
22	36	Brackley			28	22	−2	0
48	45	Hardingstone	31	27	50	28	+8	+1
66	56	Hungerford			37	25	−3	−3
39	42	Wisbech			37	25	−8	+3
12	30	Wokingham			4	11	+6	+12
34	41	Aylesbury			37	25	+2	+4
19	35	Buckingham	37	28	28	22	−5	−1
34	41	Thrapston			43	26	+10	+2
48	45	Bishop's Stortford	40	29	32	23	−1	+7
53	47	St Neots			21	21	+1	−2
26	37	Bicester	42	30	43	26	0	0
39	42	St. Ives			50	28	−5	−4
34	41	Bradfield	44	31	21	21	−4	+1
26	37	Faringdon			17	19	0	−4
39	42	Royston	45	32	37	25	−5	+5
11	29	Towcester			45	27	+2	0
57	50	Wantage	48	33	45	27	−1	0
64	55	Ely			56	30	−4	+2
31	40	Huntingdon			21	21	−2	+1
55	49	Linton			45	27	−5	+2
50	46	St. Albans	49	34	50	28	+5	+11
57	50	Wellingborough			56	30	+13	+17
59	51	Witney			21	21	−1	−1
64	55	Leighton Buzzard	55	35	68	42	+3	+6
46	44	Amersham			55	29	−2	+2
60	52	Caxton	56	36	56	30	−1	+6
60	52	Hemel Hempstead			62	35	+6	+6
46	44	Luton			60	32	+22	+12
31	40	North Witchford	59	37	35	24	−9	+5
53	47	Newmarket			50	28	−6	+3
50	46	Wycombe			60	32	+5	+9
50	46	Winslow	63	39	65	36	−1	−2
68	59	Ampthill			62	35	+3	+3
67	58	Hitchin			67	39	+4	+8
15	34	Newport Pagnell	64	40	45	27	−12	+4
62	53	Woburn			66	38	−3	−1
55	49	Biggleswade	68	48	62	35	+8	+9

Western Counties

1856 Rank	% Marks	Registration District	1866 Rank	% Marks	1871 Rank	% Marks	1851–61	1861–71
1	14	Salisbury	1	8	2	10	+1	+10
2	17	Cheltenham	2	10	2	10	+13	+7
2	17	Exeter	3	14	6	12	+3	+3
5	20	Weymouth			12	15	+24	+14
2	17	Newton Abbott			1	9	+13	+16
34	32	St. Germans	5	15	16	16	+7	+2
9	23	St. Thomas			6	12	0	+1
75	40	Thornbury			56	21	0	+5

1856		Registration District	1866		1871		% Population change	
Rank	% Marks		Rank	% Marks	Rank	% Marks	1851–61	1861–71
16	27	Alderbury	9	16	2	10	−1	+11
40	33	Blandford			23	17	0	−1
34	32	Stoke Damerel			10	14	+32	−2
8	21	Bath	12	17	5	11	−2	+2
40	33	Bideford			44	20	−9	+10
40	33	Bodmin			23	17	−4	0
20	28	Melksham			38	19	−8	+7
40	33	Cirencester			32	18	−2	+2
16	27	Shrewsbury	16	18	23	17	+12	+6
34	32	Stroud			9	13	−3	+8
40	33	Wheatenhurst			6	12	−2	0
13	26	Bedminster	20	19	16	16	+8	+31
11	25	Gloucester			12	15	+9	+19
20	28	Poole			23	17	+7	+7
34	32	Stratton			114	35	−6	−2
58	35	Tisbury			56	21	−3	0
30	31	Tiveston			16	16	−18	−4
13	26	Totnes			44	20	−3	+8
11	25	Barnstaple	27	20	12	15	−5	+3
99	45	Ledbury			74	24	+13	−12
9	23	Stow-on-the-Wold			10	14	−3	−1
16	27	Westbury			44	20	−5	−2
102	46	Church Stretton	31	21	23	17	+2	+1
46	34	Launceston			63	22	−7	+1
95	44[9]	Okehampton			89	26	−9	+4
24	29	Plymouth			16	16	+21	+10
58	35	Ross			44	20	+5	+2
20	28	Wareham			32	18	−2	+1
30	31	Wimborne			16	16	0	0
46	34	Calne			38	19	−3	0
16	27	Clifton	38	22	32	18	+22	+35
106	47	Devizes			63	22	−3	−2
24	29	Shaftesbury			44	20	0	+1
67	38	Beaminster			91	27	−5	−4
119	53	Bradford			92	28	−10	+2
15	26	Bristol			38	19	+1	−5
83	42	Chepstow	42	23	44	20	−6	+2
46	34	Chippenham			38	19	+3	−1
20	28	Dursley			44	20	−10	−2
30	31[9]	Malmesbury			32	18	−2	+1
30	31	Plympton St. Mary			23	17	+4	+8
40	33	Amesbury			16	16	−2	−2
69	39	Crediton			68	28	−7	−4
46	34	Frome	50	24	23	17	−6	+2
46	34	Sherborne			56	21	+3	+4
46	34	Taunton			56	21	+1	0
112	50	Atcham			23	17	+2	−6
46	34	Axminster			89	26	−3	+2
24	29	Dorchester			63	22	−1	+5
5	20	Dulverton	55	25	38	19	+2	−6
24	29	Falmouth			12	15	+6	+8
58	35	Hereford			44	20	+12	+9
63	37	Leominster			34	25	+4	−1
69	39	Northleach			32	18	−1	−3
83	42	East Stonehouse			68	23	+20	+2
34	32	South Molton	63	26	56	21	−5	−3
63	37	Truro			68	23	+2	−3
46	34	Wells			68	23	+2	+2

1856 Rank	% Marks	Registration District	1866 Rank	% Marks	1871 Rank	% Marks	% Pop. change 1851–61	% Pop. change 1861–71
75	40	Axbridge			44	20	+9	+9
83	42	Bridgwater			84	25	+4	+1
34	32	Honiton			16	16	−5	−2
58	35	Holsworthy	67	27	104	30	+6	−5
24	29	Kingsbridge			32	18	−9	+2
106	47	Mere			108	31	−5	+1
69	39	Weobly			84	25	+3	0
99	45	Bridport			74	24	0	−1
79	41	Penzance	74	28	97	29	+2	−1
79	41	Whitchurch			115	35	−1	+1
106	47	Bridgnorth			92	28	+2	−3
58	35	Camelford			65	23	−8	+8
69	39	Highworth			23	17	+13	+33
79	41	Monmouth			97	29	+11	+5
83	42	St. Columb	77	29	74	24	−4	0
69	39	Tavistock			74	24	+27	−11
46	34	Warminster			44	20	−7	−4
116	52	Wem			38	19	0	+2
24	29	Wilton			84	25	−1	+3
106	47	Wincanton			104	30	+1	−2
99	45	Clutton			84	25	−6	0
79	41	Marlborough			74	24	−5	+2
51	42	Newport (Mon.)	87	30	68	23	+22	+19
67	38	Oswestry			74	24	+5	+13
95	44	Wellington (Som.)			74	24	−7	+2
91	48	Westbury-on-Severn			97	29	+11	+12
83	42	Clun			97	29	+5	+2
83	42	Market Drayton	93	31	44	20	+1	+1
112	50	Newport (Shrops.)			110	32	−1	+3
46	34	Torrington			104	30	−2	−3
116	52	Chipping Sodbury			56	21	+1	−1
91	43	Liskeard	97	32	97	29	−1	+2
75	40	Ludlow			74	24	+4	+2
63	37	Ellesmere	100	33	44	20	−4	−1
46	34	Williton			108	31	0	−1
46	34	Cricklade			56	21	+1	+6
115	51	Winchcomb	102	34	74	24	−1	−3
75	40	Yeovil			92	28	0	+1
95	44	Chard			113	34	−2	+3
91	43	Keynsham	105	35	113	34	+1	+5
91	43	Pewsey			115	35	0	−4
102	46	St. Austell			97	29	+5	−8
95	44	Helston	109	36	92	28	+6	−5
102	46	Madeley	110	37	120	41	+10	0
63	37	Sturminster			110	32	0	+5
116	52	Bromyard			118	37	+1	+1
106	47	Newent	112	38	63	22	−1	−3
69	39	Tewkesbury			63	22	−2	−4
112	50	Cleobury Mortimer	115	39	104	30	−4	0
106	47	Langport	116	40	97	29	−3	−2
5	20	Tetbury			74	24	−2	0
121	59	Redruth	118	41	119	38	+7	+3
102	46	Shiffnal	119	43	112	33	+5	+7
83	42	Shepton Mallet			92	28	−2	−4
122	60	Pontypool	121	50	122	50	+8	+12
.20	58	Wellington (Shrops.)	122	53	124	44	+15	+6
123	70	Abergavenny[10]	123	55	122	50	+13	+11

Sources: Annual Reports of the Registrar of Births, Deaths and Marriages; Censuses, 1851, 1861, 1871.

1. Tadcaster lost acreage to Bramham, 1861. Bramham in Wetherby, 1871.
2. New district of Birkenhead formed (out of Wirrall) 1861.
3. Otley lost acreage to new Wharfedale district, 1861; disappeared 1871.
4. Kirkstall, Holbeck, Bramley were new districts, 1861, and Hunslet was reduced in size.
5. Boundary changes.
6. Pontefract lost acreage to new district of Castleford, 1861. Castleford reabsorbed into Pontefract, 1871.
7. Between 1861 and 1871, the district lost over 90 per cent of its acreage, thus the loss of nearly half the population, 1861–71.
8. For various reasons, the 1851–1861 and the 1861–71 population changes are difficult to establish: the overall increase 1851–71 is given.
9. 1856 figures for Malmesbury and Okehampton are suspect: 1857 figures are used.
10. Includes Bedwellty district when that formed.

Appendix H   Statistics of various social phenomena in the 1840s

Percentage above (+) and below (−) National Average

Registration County	No. of Persons per 100 acres, 1841	Persons of Independent means, 1841	Marriages under 21, 1844	Illegitimate births, 1842	Paupers relieved, 1844[1]	Deposits in Savings Banks, 1844[2]	No. of Domestic Servants per 1000 of Population, 1841	% Spouses making marks 1839–45
Cumberland	18	+32	−26	+70	−31	−23	66	26
Durham	46	−9	−26	−16	−12	−60	47	37
Lincolnshire	22	−11	+4	−7	−19	−8	73	39
Northumberland	21	−2	−8	+1	−1	+19	56	28
Rutland	22	−30	−67	+1	+4	—	67	33
Westmorland	12	+44	−38	+38	+19	−71	76	28
Yorkshire, E.R.	31	+17	−32	+2	−8	+84	70	30
Yorkshire, N.R.	16	+12	−43	+26	−11	+11	67	32
Cheshire	59	−24	+40	+40	−30	−4	61	49
Lancashire	147	−29	+8	+29	−15	−20	44	53
Yorkshire, W.R.	70	−33	+68	+5	−20	−35	37	51
Derbyshire	41	−32	+10	+21	−44	−18	56	40
Leicestershire	42	−28	+111	+7	+18	−43	61	42
Nottinghamshire	47	−31	+58	−47	−26	+13	53	44
Staffordshire	67	−43	+34	+10	−26	−37	46	52
Warwickshire	70	−20	—	−24	−24	−22	59	40
Worcestershire	50	−20	+17	−7	−12	+13	47	53
Essex	35	−23	+40	−21	+50	−14	59	50
Hampshire	34	+18	−60	−5	+22	+1	64	35
Kent	55	+21	−41	−13	+1	+15	66	34[3]
Middlesex	874	+73	−63	−49	−12	+82	99	34[3]
Norfolk	32	−10	+29	+47	+30	−15	56	47
Suffolk	33	−15	+17	+20	+36	−24	56	49
Surrey	120	+50	−62	−48	−13	−15	76	37[3]
Sussex	32	+6	+4	+1	+43	−8	75	35
Bedfordshire	36	−43	+148	+15	+27	−23	44	58
Berkshire	34	+6	−3	+9	+19	+50	72	43
Buckinghamshire	33	−30	+69	+9	+50	−43	56	49
Cambridgeshire	28	−17	+104	+7	+28	−45	58	41
Hertfordshire	39	−16	+113	+5	+18	−46	65	54
Huntingdonshire	25	−30	+115	−24	+9	−33	60	50
Northamptonshire	31	−32	+58	−5	+20	−15	53	45
Oxfordshire	33	−15	+8	+11	+47	+21	59	40
Cornwall	40	−5	−13	−37	−30	−4	59	46
Devon	32	+36	−54	−24	+1	+86	79	35
Dorset	27	+14	+26		+43	+57	54	39
Gloucestershire	54	+32	−5	−10	−3	+25	72	36
Herefordshire	21	+3	−46	+58	+2	+23	98	41
Monmouthshire	42	−30	−39	−31[4]	−32	−57	56	58
Shropshire	28	−21	−47	+38	−3	+60	73	48
Somerset	41	+22	+7	−7	+26	+6	66	43

Sources: J Fletcher, 'Moral and educational statistics of England and Wales', *JSSL*, X, 1847, pp. 215–17; *Annual Reports of the Registrar General of Births, Deaths and Marriages* (for last column).

1. Poor-law counties differ slightly from administrative counties.
2. Bank districts do not coincide exactly with county boundaries.
3. Extra-metropolitan.
4. Fletcher, 'Moral and educational statistics' pp. 202–3, suggests that this is an underestimate.

Registration county	Boys not at School, 1851		Grooms making marks, 1866		Girls not at school, 1851		Brides making marks, 1866	
	%	Rank Order	%	Rank Order	%	Rank Order	%	Rank Order
Cumberland	45	37	18	35	55	26	30	15
Durham	49	30	25	16	57	21	38	7
Lincolnshire	51	24	21	29	56	24	21	33
Northumberland	48	32	15	41	57	23	26	21
Rutland	47	34	20	31	53	33	15	39
Westmorland	38	41	14	42	48	40	17	37
Yorkshire, E.R.	42	40	15	40	50	39	26	23
Yorkshire, N.R.	43	39	17	37	54	29	22	27
Cheshire	51	21	24	19	59	15	38	6
Lancashire	54	13	24	21	65	4	45	2
Yorkshire, W.R.	51	22	22	25	59	14	40	4
Derbyshire	51	19	23	23	58	20	28	18
Leicestershire	51	20	22	27	58	17	29	17
Nottinghamshire	56	9	24	20	61	11	32	11
Staffordshire	61	3	35	2	66	3	44	3
Warwickshire	57	6	23	22	64	7	31	12
Worcestershire	56	7	25	15	62	10	31	12
Essex	55	12	29	11	57	22	24	26
Hampshire	44	38	16	39	47	41	16	38
Kent	46	36	20	32	53	30	18	36
Middlesex	36	42	17	38	46	42	14	41
Norfolk	54	16	32	7	55	27	27	20
Suffolk	55	11	32	5	58	18	26	22
Surrey	47	35	19	34	51	36	14	40
Sussex	50	29	19	33	53	34	14	42
Bedfordshire	56	8	33	4	68	2	39	5
Berkshire	50	27	25	18	52	35	19	34
Buckinghamshire	54	15	31	8	64	8	34	9
Cambridgeshire	54	14	27	12	58	19	29	16
Hertfordshire	50	26	33	3	54	28	27	19
Huntingdonshire	51	25	32	6	53	32	30	14
Northamptonshire	52	18	23	24	59	16	25	25
Oxfordshire	48	33	22	26	50	38	19	34
Cornwall	60	4	26	14	65	5	35	8
Devon	53	17	18	36	60	12	22	30
Dorset	49	31	22	28	51	36	21	32
Gloucestershire	50	28	21	30	56	25	22	29
Herefordshire	62	2	29	10	65	6	21	31
Monmouthshire	66	1	37	1	70	1	46	1
Shropshire	59	5	31	9	62	9	33	10
Somerset	55	10	26	13	60	13	26	24
Wiltshire	51	23	25	17	53	31	22	28

Sources: *Annual Report of the Registrar General of Births, Deaths and Marriages* for 1866; Census, 1851; Education Census, 1851.

% Not at school' = proportion of age group 5–14 not in attendance on census day. Percentages given here to nearest whole number: hence differences in ranking for some apparantly equal percentages.

Appendix J   County statistics of schooling, Sunday and day, 1818, 1833, 1851, 1858 (%)

County	Day-school Pupils as % of Total Population				Sunday-school Pupils as % of Total Population				Public Day-School Pupils as % of Total Population	Sunday School Pupils as % of Total Population	Public Day-School Pupils as % of all Day-School Pupils	
	1818	1833	1851 on books	1851 census day	1818	1833	1851 on books	1851 census day	1858	1858	1833[1]	1851 on books
Cumberland	10·1	12·7	13·0	11·2	4·1	8·7	10·4	7·9	8·9	9·0	30	66
Durham	10·2	12·1	12·6	10·8	4·5	9·6	12·2	9·2	7·1	11·6	32	60
Lincolnshire	8·6	12·0	12·8	10·9	2·5	10·0	14·0	10·5	9·5	14·6	33	62
Northumberland	9·3	11·0	12·3	10·4	2·3	7·6	9·8	7·4	6·7	8·0	31	64
Rutland	10·6	13·9	14·8	11·5	6·5	14·1	14·6	11·6	11·6	13·5	44	65
Westmorland	13·2	13·2	15·4	12·8	2·6	8·5	12·9	10·4	12·7	11·1	36	73
Yorkshire, E.R.[2]	9·1	12·1	13·1	11·6	4·1	9·0	10·5	7·9	[8·1][3]	[13·7][3]	44	61
Yorkshire, N.R.	10·4	12·0	13·7	11·7	1·6	9·1	12·5	9·8			39	64
Cheshire	5·7	9·6	12·1	10·2	6·7	14·9	14·9	11·1	7·9	13·3	34	65
Lancashire	4·7	7·3	10·6	8·9	6·2	17·0	15·9	11·9	7·5	13·0	37	70
Yorkshire, W.R.	6·2	7·6	12·2	10·4	7·7	14·4	16·9	13·0	[8·1][3]	[13·7][3]	30	62
Derbyshire	8·1	10·3	12·6	10·5	6·1	16·5	19·2	14·6	9·4	17·2	38	67
Leicestershire	6·5	9·8	12·3	10·3	8·1	15·8	15·4	12·4	8·4	15·0	41	68
Nottinghamshire	8·0	9·5	11·5	9·4	6·2	14·3	16·3	12·5	7·4	14·6	34	58
Staffordshire	6·4	8·7	10·9	8·6	6·6	12·9	15·3	11·2	8·4	15·3	48	67
Warwickshire	6·5	7·7	10·8	8·8	5·4	10·2	10·6	7·7	6·7	9·3	54	67
Worcestershire	6·1	8·4	11·0	9·3	5·9	9·8	12·4	8·9	7·4	11·5	49	70
Essex	7·1	10·4	12·6	10·4	5·1	9·3	10·7	8·1	11·5	11·6	49	71
Hampshire	8·1	12·3	14·3	11·9	3·8	10·3	11·2	8·6	9·2[4]	10·1	47	69
Kent[5]	7·8	11·2	13·9	11·5	2·6	7·8	9·4	7·6	10·2	10·4	40	65
Middlesex[5]	4·1	7·5	15·8	13·6	1·8	3·8	5·9	6·4	7·7	5·7	66	69
Norfolk	7·0	9·0	12·3	10·2	3·4	7·8	11·1	8·5	8·8	10·9	41	65
Suffolk	7·1	9·7	12·3	10·1	6·2	10·2	6·5	8·3	9·5	11·6	39	65
Surrey[5]	6·0	9·4	13·7	11·8	2·9	4·6	8·8	5·5	8·3	7·0	54	70
Sussex	9·5	12·1	13·7	11·5	3·4	7·9	8·8	6·6	9·1	9·1	47	64
Bedfordshire	6·2	6·9	10·4	9·1	7·2	16·6	19·8	16·1	8·6	18·0	51	74
Berkshire	8·7	11·4	13·3	11·4	4·3	9·7	11·2	8·9	10·8	12·3	54	73
Buckinghamshire	6·4	7·4	11·6	9·6	7·6	14·1	16·0	12·7	9·9	15·9	49	73
Cambridgeshire	9·6	10·9	13·1	10·3	3·9	9·8	12·5	9·5	7·5	12·0	37	67
Hertfordshire	7·4	11·0	14·0	11·4	4·6	9·8	13·2	10·2	10·9	13·1	50	77
Huntingdonshire	8·4	10·9	14·0	11·7	3·4	11·9	16·6	13·2	10·1	14·1	44	72
Northamptonshire	7·9	10·2	12·5	10·3	8·3	15·8	15·8	12·7	10·3	16·5	53	72
Oxfordshire	6·9	10·5	13·8	11·6	4·8	11·0	11·8	9·4	12·0	13·5	51	70
Cornwall	6·6	10·5	10·9	9·1	5·0	11·4	16·6	11·4	6·2	15·6	26	49
Devon	8·0	11·1	11·3	9·6	2·6	8·8	10·1	7·4	8·0	9·2	35	61
Dorset	8·0	11·4	13·6	11·4	7·6	12·5	15·0	11·5	11·0	14·3	41	69
Gloucestershire	5·2	8·3	12·2	7·2	9·3	10·6	12·6	9·3	10·4	12·3	57	73
Herefordshire	6·1	7·9	9·9	8·0	2·9	6·8	7·9	5·4	8·9	8·7	57	76
Monmouthshire	5·8	6·8	9·0	7·1	1·0	12·8	16·9	13·0	8·8	13·9	45	71
Shropshire	7·1	8·9	14·0	9·0	3·6	8·4	9·9	7·6	8·7	12·4	50	75
Somerset	5·4	8·9	12·1	9·7	6·0	10·6	13·0	9·9	8·7	12·7	37	68
Wiltshire	5·5	8·5	13·7	11·1	7·7	13·0	14·8	11·4	12·8	16·1	50	78

Sources: 1818: *Tables Showing the State of Education in England, Scotland and Wales*, PP 1820 XII, pp. 342–3, 346–7;
1833: *Abstract, 1833*; 1851: *Education Census, 1851*; pp. xxxviii, 4–7; 1858: *Newcastle*, I, pp. 596 ff., 614 ff. (based on estimated populations,

1. The 1833 returns do not provide data for exact figures because of difficulties of classification. Schools classed as providing education by fees 'at the ex[...] of the parents' are taken here to be 'private' schools; schools categorized as 'supported by subscription', 'financed from fees and subscriptions', 'endo[...] are taken to be 'public'.
2. City of York not included, 1833 (day 12·2, Sunday 11·4).
3. Yorkshire as a whole.
4. Includes Channel Isles.
5. Includes parts of London, 1818, 1833, 1858. For 1851, extra-metropolitan only.

Appendix K   Schooling statistics, municipal cities and boroughs, 1851

	Population	% on Books		% attending on 31 March, 1851		% Day scholars on books of public schools
		Day Schools	Sunday Schools	Day Schools	Sunday Schools	
COUNTIES OF THE FAR NORTH AND NORTH-EAST Cumberland (C), Durham (D), Lincolnshire (L), Northumberland (N), Westmorland (W), Yorkshire E.R. (E.R.), Yorkshire N.R. (N.R.)						
Towns over 20,000						
Carlisle (C)	26,598	12	10	10	7	69
Gateshead (D)	25,568	12	10	10	7	49
Hull (E.R.)	85,549	12	9	10	7	50
Newcastle upon Tyne (N)	87,784	10	7	9	5	59
South Shields (D)	28,974	15	15	13	12	60
Sunderland (D)	64,673	12	10	11	7	46
Tynemouth (N)	29,170	10	8	8	7	53
York	36,303	16	11	14	7	76
Towns under 20,000						
Berwick (N)	15,094	12	7	11	6	62
Beverley (E.R.)	8915	17	15	14	12	69
Boston (L)	15,132	16	10	14	8	73
Durham (D)	18,334	10	6	8	4	61
Grantham (L)	5375	14	8	12	5	75
Grimsby (L)	8860	11	13	10	10	28
Hartlepool (D)	9503	13	12	11	9	53
Kendal (W)	11,829	18	16	15	13	66
Lincoln (L)	17,536	17	13	15	9	57
Louth (L)	10,467	15	4	11	2	70
Morpeth (N)	4120	18	20	16	14	78
Richmond (N.R.)	4106	19	14	16	11	74
Scarborough (N.R.)	12,915	15	10	12	7	51
Stamford (L)	9066	18	15	15	12	44
Stockton (D)	10,172	17	11	15	8	70

Appendix K   Schooling statistics, municipal cities and boroughs, 1851

	Population	% on Books		% attending on 31 March, 1851		% Day scholars on books of public schools
		Day Schools	Sunday Schools	Day Schools	Sunday Schools	
COUNTIES OF THE NORTH-WEST Cheshire (C), Lancashire (L), Yorkshire W.R. (W.R.)						
Towns over 20,000						
Ashton under Lyne (L)	35,218	8	22	7	16	50
Blackburn (L)	46,536	9	19	8	15	83
Bolton (L)	61,171	10	18	8	15	65
Bradford (W.R.)	103,778	9	15	8	12	62
Chester (C)	27,964	13	9	11	8	64
Halifax (W.R.)	47,826	13	16	11	11	68
Leeds (W.R.)	174,809	12	14	10	12	60
Liverpool (L)	388,319	12	6	10	4	78
Macclesfield (C)	41,189	10	18	9	12	66
Manchester (L)	303,382	9	14	7	10	62
Oldham (L)	52,820	8	17	7	13	49
Preston (L)	69,542	11	16	9	11	69
Salford (L)	63,850	8	16	7	11	64
Sheffield (W.R.)	135,310	12	11	9	8	60
Stockport (C)	56,073	7	19	6	14	25
Wakefield (W.R.)	30,314	14	13	11	10	77
Warrington (L)	23,363	12	11	9	8	74
Wigan (L)	31,941	12	22	9	16	72
Towns under 20,000						
Clitheroe (W.R.)	7244	14	26	11	19	69
Congleton (C)	10,520	13	24	11	19	76
Doncaster (W.R.)	12,052	11	8	9	6	53
Lancaster (L)	14,604	13	18	11	14	61
Pontefract (W.R.)	5106	16	—	13	—	87
Ripon (W.R.)	6160	17	11	13	8	66
MIDLAND COUNTRIES Derbyshire (D), Leicestershire (L), Nottinghamshire (N), Staffordshire (S), Warwickshire (Wa), Worcestershire (Wo)						
Towns over 20,000						
Birmingham (Wa)	244,501	9	10	7	6	59
Coventry (Wa)	36,208	8	11	7	8	59
Derby (D)	40,609	13	19	10	13	72
Leicester (L)	61,078	9	13	8	9	67
Nottingham (N)	57,407	10	16	9	12	56
Walsall (S)	26,822	12	12	9	8	65
Wolverhampton (S)	49,985	8	11	6	8	82
Worcester (Wo)	29,104	12	11	10	8	69
Towns under 20,000						
Bewdley (Wo)	3435	14	16	11	11	83
Chesterfield (D)	7101	10	13	16	10	67

Newcastle under Lyme (S)	10,569	14	20	12	14	69
Retford, East (N)	2943	25	21	20	14	54
Stafford (S)	13,042	12	14	10	10	62
Stratford-on-Avon (Wa)	3372	15	6	12	5	62
Tamworth (S)	8655	13	11	10	8	66
Warwick (Wa)	10,973	15	9	10	7	59

EAST ANGLIA AND THE SOUTH-EASTERN COUNTIES Essex (E), Hampshire (H), Kent (K), Norfolk (N), Suffolk (S), Surrey (Su), Sussex (Sx), Isle of Wight (I of W)

Towns over 20,000

Dover (K)	22,772	10	6	8	4	71
Ipswich (S)	35,014	12	5	11	4	66
Maidstone (K)	20,740	14	9	12	6	67
Norwich (N)	68,195	11	10	10	7	67
Portsmouth (H)	72,096	13	6	12	5	48
Southampton (H)	35,305	16	10	12	7	58
Yarmouth (N)	30,879	11	8	10	6	49

Towns under 20,000

Andover (H)	5187	20	14	18	8	73
Arundel (Sx)	2748	20	16	16	13	66
Basingstoke (H)	4263	15	10	13	8	64
Beccles (S)	4398	15	8	13	5	71
Bury St Edmunds (S)	13,900	11	8	7	6	66
Canterbury (K)	18,662	14	7	12	5	61
Chichester (Sx)	8968	18	10	15	7	66
Colchester (E)	19,443	12	11	10	9	59
Deal (K)	7067	14	11	13	9	23
Eye (S)	2587	12	6	12	5	57
Faversham (K)	4595	21	10	18	8	59
Folkestone (K)	6726	17	11	14	7	52
Gravesend (K)	16,633	13	8	12	5	58
Guildford (Su)	8082	19	11	16	8	65
Harwich (E)	4451	11	13	9	10	52
Hastings (K)	17,625	15	11	13	8	80
Hythe (K)	2857	18	17	16	13	66
Kings Lynn (N)	19,355	11	8	9	6	46
Kingston upon Thames (Su)	12,144	13	7	11	6	69
Lymington (H)	4182	21	15	16	12	66
Maldon (E)	4558	22	12	18	9	66
Newport (I of W)	17,242	16	15	14	11	71
Rochester (K)	16,580	12	9	10	7	57
Romsey (H)	2080	19	43[1]	15	30	91
Rye (Sx)	4592	15	13	13	9	65
Saffron Walden (E)	5911	17	13	15	10	75
Sandwich (K)	2966	14	9	12	7	29
Southwold (S)	2109	19	16	16	13	60
Sudbury (S)	6043	20	11	15	9	88
Tenterden (K)	3958	18	9	15	6	69
Thetford (N)	4075	17	18	15	13	52
Winchester (H)	14,005	14	11	11	8	62

Appendix **K**   Schooling statistics, municipal cities and boroughs, 1851

	Population	% on Books		% attending on 31 March, 1851		% Day scholars on books of public schools
		Day Schools	Sunday Schools	Day Schools	Sunday Schools	
SOUTH MIDLAND COUNTIES Bedfordshire (B), Berkshire (Be), Buckinghamshire (Bu), Cambridgeshire (C), Hertfordshire (H), Huntingdonshire (Hu), Northamptonshire (N), Oxfordshire (O)						
Towns over 20,000						
Cambridge (C)	27,815	14	13	11	10	71
Kidderminster (N)	20,852	13	12	11	8	77
Northampton (N)	26,657	13	16	11	12	61
Oxford (O)	28,061	12	5	11	4	67
Reading (Be)	21,456	16	11	13	8	64
Towns under 20,000						
Abingdon (Be)	6848	13	17	11	12	71
Banbury (O)	4026	17	15	14	11	70
Bedford (B)	11,693	16	12	15	10	88
Buckingham (Bu)	4020	15	17	12	12	69
Chipping Norton (O)	2932	17	23	14	18	72
Daventry (N)	4430	15	16	14	14	79
Godmanchester (Hu)	2337	15	14	13	11	67
Hertford (H)	7982	20	10	18	7	78
Huntingdon (Hu)	3882	20	18	18	14	61
Maidenhead (Be)	7866	15	20	12	16	77
Newbury (Be)	6574	15	16	14	13	56
St. Albans (H)	9380	11	14	9	10	79
Wallingford (Be)	2819	13	12	11	9	63
Windsor (Be)	11,217	17	6	14	4	72
Wisbech (C)	10,594	16	7	13	5	63
Wycombe (Bu)	3588	21	27	16	19	82
WESTERN COUNTIES Cornwall (C), Devon (D), Dorset (Do), Gloucestershire (G), Herefordshire (H), Monmouthshire (M), Shropshire (S), Somerset (So), Wiltshire (W)						
Towns over 20,000						
Bath (So)	52,240	13	9	11	6	74
Bristol	139,883	13	10	12	7	65
Devonport (D)	38,180	13	9	12	6	51
Exeter (D)	32,818	15	6	13	4	56
Gloucester (G)	21,104	12	11	10	8	58
Plymouth (D)	52,221	9	9	8	6	56
Shrewsbury (S)	23,104	12	6	10	4	73
Towns under 20,000						
Barnstaple (D)	12,484	13	11	11	8	54
Bideford (D)	5775	20	16	17	13	71
Blandford (Do)	3948	22	8	18	6	50
Bodmin (C)	4705	13	11	12	8	46
Bridgnorth (S)	6328	12	13	10	9	74

Town	Population				
Chippenham (W)	4559				
Dartmouth (D)	4508	12	14	11	11	51
Devizes (W)	8172	12	9	10	7	77
Dorchester (Do)	6660	17	8	14	6	74
Falmouth (C)	8151	17	16	14	10	48
Glastonbury (So)	3125	12	12	9	9	69
Helston (C)	3355	19	17	16	11	52
Hereford (H)	12,823	13	8	12	6	60
Honiton (D)	3427	13	16	11	12	48
Launceston (C)	3397	18	15	16	11	78
Leominster (H)	5214	11	8	9	4	57
Liskeard (C)	6128	16	17	14	10	48
Ludlow (S)	4691	16	4	13	3	62
Marlborough (W)	3908	29	11	26	11	86
Monmouth (M)	5967	16	9	14	7	61
Newport (M)	19,892	11	11	8	8	58
Oswestry (S)	8796	10	10	8	7	74
Penryn (C)	3959	18	8	16	5	53
Penzance (C)	9214	15	14	13	9	35
Poole (Do)	9255	18	18	16	14	33
St Ives (C)	6525	20	16	17	11	32
Salisbury (W)	11,947	14	13	12	9	68
Shaftesbury (Do)	2641	26	24	15	18	88
South Molton (D)	4482	15	18	12	15	69
Tewkesbury (G)	5878	10	20	8	15	59
Tiverton (D)	11,144	12	14	11	11	85
Torrington (D)	3308	9	23	8	19	76
Totnes (D)	4866	19	12	17	9	60
Truro (C)	16,277	12	15	9	10	80
Wells (So)	7401	12	4	11	3	63
Wenlock (S)	18,728	12	13	10	10	80
Weymouth (Do)	9458	18	16	16	13	59

Source: Education Census, 1851, Table T. Towns are confined to those listed in this source. Populations cited are those of the areas for which the schooling figures pertain, and sometimes differ from the actual bourough/city populations.

1. This figure seems excessive, but is correct according to the source.

Appendix L   Religious affiliation of day and Sunday schools, 1833, 1851, 1858

	Day Schools								
	Approx. Nos. of Schools			% Public Day Scholars					
	1833[a]			1851[b]			1858[c]		
County	Church of England	Dissent	Roman Catholic	Church of England	Dissent	Roman Catholic	Church of England	Dissent	R Ca
Cumberland	8	3	1	78	17	4	87	9	
Durham	45	4	5	82	13	4	79	13	
Lincolnshire	47	12	1	79	20	1	84	16	
Northumberland	16	4	2	68	23	9	66	19	
Rutland	13	1	0	100	0	0	99	1	
Westmorland	7	25		82	17	1	87	12	
Yorkshire, E.R.[1]	27	3	4	80	16	4	[73]	[22]	
Yorkshire, N.R.[1]	39	11	3	79	18	2	[73]	[22]	
Cheshire	22	4	1	79	17	4	79	18	
Lancashire	88	65	32	64	24	12	61	22	
Yorkshire, W.R.[1]	63	33	4	72	26	2	[73]	[22]	
Derbyshire	25	12	0	78	20	2	86	14	
Leicestershire	30	4	1	78	18	4	79	20	
Nottinghamshire	43	21	2	88	9	3	89	7	
Staffordshire	63	14	15	74	20	6	76	16	
Warwickshire	58	18	7	76	17	7	78	12	
Worcestershire	28	13	5	83	13	3	88	10	
Essex	58	24	3	74	25	0	81	18	
Hampshire	118	32	1	83	16	1	86	12	
Kent	111	13	1	85	14	1	83	13	
Middlesex[2]	69	79	23	68	28	6	68	20	
Norfolk	71	13	1	83	16	1	93	6	
Suffolk	65	13	0	85	15	0	89	10	
Surrey	72	27	2	75	22	3	71	22	
Sussex	89	25	2	85	14	1	89	9	
Bedfordshire	15	13	0	77	23	0	81	19	
Berkshire	38	6	0	88	11	1	83	15	
Buckinghamshire	23	10	0	79	21	0	85	15	
Cambridgeshire	28	12	0	77	23	0	82	18	
Hertfordshire	33	10	1	83	16	1	84	15	
Huntingdonshire	13	3	0	76	24	0	81	19	
Northamptonshire	38	16	1	84	16	0	87	13	
Oxfordshire	34	13	0	85	14	1	86	13	
Cornwall[3]	47	13	0	82	18	0	79	20	
Devon	67	23	1	84	15	1	83	16	
Dorset	28	11	1	85	14	1	85	14	
Gloucestershire	43	30	1	71	27	2	76	21	
Herefordshire	27	4	0	88	11	1	93	6	
Monmouthshire	13	6	0	68	26	6	56	40	
Shropshire	37	13	2	88	10	2	90	9	
Somerset	59	21	4	85	14	0	87	12	
Wiltshire	41	22	0	84	15	1	85	14	

	Sunday Schools						
	% of all Scholars						
1833(d)		1851(e)			1858(f)		
...rch ...nd Roman Catholic	Dissent & Roman Catholic	Church of England	Dissent	Roman Catholic	Church of England	Dissent	Roman Catholic
	35	48	51	0	53	43	4
	42	28	72	0	25	70	4
	38	44	55	0	45	55	0
	42	31	68	1	35	60	5
	23	66	33	1	69	30	0
	33	60	39	1	66	33	1
	40	41	58	0	[37]	[62]	[1]
	30	51	48	1			
	50	36	61	3	41	56	3
	55	37	57	5	41	53	5
	56	31	68	1	[37]	[62]	[1]
	47	40	58	2	42	58	0
	48	47	52	1	49	50	1
	55	40	59	1	44	56	0
	45	39	58	3	40	57	3
	46	50	48	3	51	46	3
	43	51	48	1	52	41	7
	26	61	39	0	64	36	0
	40	53	47	0	66	34	0
	41	42	57	0	58	42	0
	53	38	60	1	56	43	1
	36	55	45	0	62	38	0
	31	63	38	0	67	33	0
	41	48	52	0	58	41	0
	33	59	41	0	71	29	1
	41	48	52	0	51	49	0
	24	55	45	1	65	35	0
	42	55	45	0	57	43	0
	32	50	50	0	54	45	0
	37	55	45	0	60	40	0
	34	56	44	0	58	41	0
	30	58	42	0	60	40	0
	35	68	32	0	71	28	0
	55	20	80	0	22	78	0
	40	44	56	0	56	43	0
	23	65	35	0	68	32	0
	43	47	52	1	58	41	1
	20	69	31	0	76	24	0
	75	17	82	1	23	77	0
	42	48	51	0	53	47	0
	37	58	42	0	56	44	0
	44	57	43	0	64	36	0

Sources: (a) Abstract, 1833. Very approximate estimates from this source, the data in which is often too vague for easy categorization. Schools are here counted as Church of England if the cleric played a significant part in management or financial support or paid for one-third or more of the pupils. Where the clergyman paid for only a minority of pupils or was one of a number of subscribers, then such schools are omitted here. Schools wholly or partly supported by the parishioners, by endowments or by local dignitaries are also omitted, as are boarding schools. Dissenting and Roman Catholic schools are those so designated in the source. Anglican schools are probably underestimated.

(b) Education Census, 1851, Table O, pupils on the books of Class III schools. British schools are included under Dissent unless indicated as Anglican. Figures for Middlesex, Surrey, and Kent include metropolitan districts.

(c) Calculated from Newcastle, I, pp. 596 ff. British schools are included under Dissent.

(d) As (a).

(e) Education Census, 1851, Table R.

(f) Newcastle, I, pp. 617 ff.

1. 1858 figures are for Yorkshire as a whole. City of York, 1833, numbers of schools, 3, 23, 0; 1851, numbers of schools, 44, 28, 28, Sunday schools, 40, 52, 7.
2. Jewish schools excluded.
3. Includes Scilly Isles, 1833.

Appendix M   Percentage of population on the books of Church of England day and evening schools, 1837–67

County	1837	1847	1857	1867
Cumberland	1·7	6·6	7·0	8·1
Durham	5·0	5·5	7·0	7·2
Lincolnshire	1·6	6·9	8·2	10·0
Northumberland	3·0	4·2	4·8	4·4
Rutland	4·5	10·1	11·4	15·1
Westmorland	0·9	8·5	8·8	11·7
Yorkshire, E.R. }[1] Yorkshire, N.R. }	[1·6] }	[5·6] }	[6·0] }	[7·8] }
Cheshire	2·7	5·7	6·3	8·5
Lancashire	1·2	4·4	4·9	7·8
Yorkshire, W.R.[1]	[1·6]	[5·6]	[6·0]	[7·8]
Derbyshire	1·4	6·5	7·9	8·7
Leicestershire	2·8	5·9	6·6	9·6
Nottinghamshire	1·5	6·0	6·8	9·6
Staffordshire	3·2	6·2	7·1	7·4
Warwickshire	2·4	5·1	6·4	7·8
Worcestershire	2·4	6·5	6·8	9·0
Essex	5·3	7·4	9·0	10·4
Hampshire	4·2	7·1	8·1	8·3
Kent	3·1	6·4	7·8	8·4
Middlesex	1·0	4·1	4·9	6·2
Norfolk	2·2	6·8	8·1	10·1
Suffolk	2·5	6·8	8·5	10·5
Surrey	4·2	4·9	5·8	7·4
Sussex	3·8	8·5	8·5	9·1
Bedforshire	0·8	4·9	7·4	9·1
Berkshire	2·6	8·0	8·9	12·0
Buckinghamshire	1·7	5·5	8·1	11·2
Cambridgeshire	2·2	6·3	6·3	9·3
Hertfordshire	3·0	7·6	8·9	10·9
Huntingdonshire	1·4	8·2	8·3	12·0
Northamptonshire	2·6	8·1	9·0	11·1
Oxfordshire	3·2	8·0	10·1	12·1
Cornwall	2·3	4·2	4·9	5·5
Devon	2·3	6·1	6·7	7·5
Dorset	3·5	8·0	9·9	12·5
Gloucestershire	2·5	6·0	7·7	9·3
Herefordshire	2·3	7·2	8·1	9·4
Monmouthshire	1·5	4·6	4·9	5·8
Shropshire	2·2	6·2	7·0	10·1
Somerset	2·6	6·1	8·1	10·7
Wiltshire	2·1	7·4	10·6	13·3
England and Wales	3·1	5·7	6·4	7·7

Sources: National Society, 27th Annual Report, 1838; National Society, Church School Inquiry, 1846–7, London, 1849; National Society, Summaries to the Returns to the General Inquiry ... into ... Schools ... of the Established Church ... 1856–7, London, 1858; National Society, Schools for the Poor in England and Wales for the Years 1866 and 1867, London, n.d. All percentages are based on populations in the previous decennial census. Figures for 1837 are for day schools only.

1. Yorkshire figures do not distinguish the three Ridings.

Appendix N   Religious allegiance and the importance of Sunday Schools, 1851

County	Rank in order of % of dissenting sittings	Rank in order of % of Sunday-School pupils to population
Monmouthshire	1	3
Cornwall	2	5
Northumberland	3	37
Durham	3	24
Yorkshire, W.R.	5	3
Yorkshire, E.R.	6	32
Nottinghamshire	7	6
Derbyshire	8	2
Bedfordshire	8	1
Yorkshire, N.R.	10	24
Lincolnshire	11	16
Cambridgeshire	11	18
Huntingdonshire	13	15
Leicestershire	14	10
Cheshire	14	11
Lancashire	16	8
Wiltshire	17	14
Northamptonshire	18	9
Gloucestershire	19	19
Cumberland	19	33
Buckinghamshire	19	7
Staffordshire	22	12
Devonshire	22	35
Hertfordshire	24	23
Norfolk	25	28
Worcestershire	26	21
Warwickshire	26	33
Somerset	26	21
Essex	26	31
Berkshire	26	29
Middlesex	31	42
Suffolk	32	30
Shropshire	33	36
Hampshire	33	26
Kent	35	38
Dorset	35	13
Westmorland	37	19
Surrey	37	41
Sussex	39	39
Oxfordshire	40	26
Rutland	41	17
Herefordshire	42	40

Sources: *Education Census, 1851*, p. lxxvi; *Religious Census, 1851*, p. ccxcvii; A. Everitt, 'Nonconformity in country parishes', *Agricultural History Rev.*, XVIII, supplement, 1970, p. 181, adapted to include Monmouthshire.

Appendix O   Government grants to day-schools per head of population, 1833–59
(based on 1851 populations)

County	
Cheshire	4s. 6d.
Gloucestershire	4s. 4d.
Yorkshire	4s. 3d.
Wiltshire	4s. 1d.
Hampshire	4s. 0d.
Lancashire	3s. 10d.
Staffordshire	3s. 10d.
Dorset	3s. 9d.
Hertfordshire	3s. 9d.
Surrey	3s. 6d.
Kent	3s. 5d.
Derbyshire	3s. 3d.
Durham	3s. 3d.
Somerset	3s. 3d.
Middlesex	3s. 2d.
Berkshire	3s. 1d.
Cambridgeshire	3s. 1d.
Worcestershire	3s. 0d.
Warwickshire	3s. 0d.
Sussex	3s. 0d.
Herefordshire	3s. 0d.
Bedfordshire	2s. 11d.
Cumberland	2s. 11d.
Shropshire	2s. 11d.
Leicestershire	2s. 10d.
Oxfordshire	2s. 9d.
Huntingdonshire	2s. 8d.
Devon	2s. 7d.
Suffolk	2s. 7d.
Nottinghamshire	2s. 6d.
Cornwall	2s. 6d.
Northumberland	2s. 6d.
Rutland	2s. 6d.
Buckinghamshire	2s. 5d.
Essex	2s. 5d.
Lincolnshire	2s. 5d.
Monmouthshire	2s. 3d.
Northamptonshire	2s. 2d.
Westmorland	2s. 0d.
Norfolk	1s. 10d.
England	3s. 4d.

Source: Deduced from *Newcastle*, I, p. 585.

(*Income* = 1858; *Population* = 1851)

County	*Total*	*C.E.*	*British*	*R.C.*	*Wesleyan*	*Congst.*	*Baptist*	*Unitarian*	*Jewish*
Westmorland	2*s*. 2¾*d*.	2*s*. 1¼*d*.	1½*d*.	—	—	—	—	—	—
Rutland	1*s*. 9½*d*.	1*s*. 8¾*d*.	—	—	—	—	¾*d*.	—	—
Huntingdonshire	1*s*. 9¼*d*.	1*s*. 6¼*d*.	2*d*.	—	1*d*.	—	—	—	—
Wiltshire	1*s*. 8½*d*.	1*s*. 6¾*d*.	1¼*d*.	—	¼*d*.	¼*d*.	—	—	—
Oxfordshire	1*s*. 7¾*d*.	1*s*. 6¼*d*.	1¼*d*.	—	¼*d*.	—	—	—	—
Northamptonshire	1*s*. 6¾*d*.	1*s*. 5¼*d*.	1¼*d*.	—	¼*d*.	—	—	—	—
Essex	1*s*. 6¾*d*.	1*s*. 4¼*d*.	2¼*d*.	—	—	¼*d*.	—	—	—
Hertfordshire	1*s*. 6*d*.	1*s*. 4¼*d*.	1½*d*.	—	—	¼*d*.	—	—	—
Berkshire	1*s*. 5½*d*.	1*s*. 3¾*d*.	1¼*d*.	—	½*d*.	—	—	—	—
Lincolnshire	1*s*. 5*d*.	1*s*. 3¼*d*.	½*d*.	—	1¼*d*.	—	—	—	—
Sussex	1*s*. 4¾*d*.	1*s*. 3¾*d*.	¾*d*.	—	¼*d*.	—	—	—	—
Bedfordshire	1*s*. 4¼*d*.	1*s*. 2*d*.	1½*d*.	—	¾*d*.	—	—	—	—
Kent	1*s*. 4¼*d*.	1*s*. 2½*d*.	1¼*d*.	—	¼*d*.	¼*d*.	—	—	—
Hampshire & Channel Isles	1*s*. 3¾*d*.	1*s*. 2¾*d*.	¾*d*.	—	—	¼*d*.	—	—	—
Shropshire	1*s*. 3¼*d*.	1*s*. 2¼*d*.	¾*d*.	—	¼*d*.	—	—	—	—
Worcestershire	1*s*. 3¼*d*.	1*s*. 1¾*d*.	½*d*.	—	½*d*.	—	—	½*d*.	—
Buckinghamshire	1*s*. 3¼*d*.	1*s*. 1¼*d*.	2*d*.	—	—	—	—	—	—
Gloucestershire	1*s*. 3*d*.	1*s*. 0¼*d*.	2¼*d*.	¼*d*.	¼*d*.	—	—	—	—
Herefordshire	1*s*. 3*d*.	1*s*. 2¼*d*.	½*d*.	—	—	—	¼*d*.	—	—
Somerset	1*s*. 2¾*d*.	1*s*. 1¼*d*.	1*d*.	—	¼*d*.	¼*d*.	—	—	—
Dorset	1*s*. 2¾*d*.	1*s*. 1¼*d*.	1½*d*.	—	—	¼*d*.	—	—	—
Cumberland	1*s*. 2½*d*.	1*s*. 1*d*.	¾*d*.	¼*d*.	¼*d*.	—	—	—	—
Surrey	1*s*. 2½*d*.	1*s*. 0¼*d*.	1¾*d*.	—	¼*d*.	¼*d*.	—	—	—
Leicestershire	1*s*. 2¼*d*.	1*s*. 0*d*.	1¼*d*.	¼*d*.	¼*d*.	¼*d*.	—	¼*d*.	—
Suffolk	1*s*. 2¼*d*.	1*s*. 1¼*d*.	¾*d*.	—	—	¼*d*.	—	—	—
Norfolk	1*s*. 1¾*d*.	1*s*. 0½*d*.	¾*d*.	—	—	¼*d*.	—	¼*d*.	—
Staffordshire	1*s*. 1¾*d*.	11¾*d*.	¼*d*.	½*d*.	1*d*.	¼*d*.	—	—	—
Yorkshire	1*s*. 1½*d*.	11½*d*.	¾*d*.	—	1*d*.	¼*d*.	—	—	—
Cheshire	1*s*. 1½*d*.	11¼*d*.	¾*d*.	¼*d*.	1*d*.	¼*d*.	—	—	—
Derbyshire	1*s*. 1½*d*.	1*s*. 0*d*.	1*d*.	—	½*d*.	—	—	—	—
Middlesex	1*s*. 1½*d*.	10½*d*.	1*d*.	—	¼*d*.	½*d*.	—	—	1*d*.
Devon	1*s*. 0*d*.	10¾*d*.	1*d*.	—	¼*d*.	—	—	—	—
Cambridgeshire	11¾*d*.	10½*d*.	1¼*d*.	—	—	—	—	—	—
Warwickshire	11½*d*.	10*d*.	½*d*.	½*d*.	—	¼*d*.	—	—	¼*d*.
Nottinghamshire	11*d*.	10¼*d*.	¼*d*.	¼*d*.	¼*d*.	—	—	—	—
Northumberland	9¾*d*.	7¾*d*.	1¼*d*.	½*d*.	¼*d*.	—	—	—	—
Lancashire	9¾*d*.	7½*d*.	1*d*.	½*d*.	½*d*.	¼*d*.	—	—	—
Durham	9¾*d*.	8½*d*.	½*d*.	¼*d*.	½*d*.	—	—	—	—
Monmouthshire	9¼*d*.	7¼*d*.	1*d*.	—	—	¾*d*.	¼*d*.	—	—
Cornwall	7¼*d*.	6*d*.	½*d*.	—	¾*d*.	—	—	—	—
England	1*s*. 1¾*d*.	11¾*d*.	1*d*.	¼*d*.	½*d*.	¼*d*.	—	—	—

Source: Deduced from *Newcastle*, I, p. 584.
C.E. = Church of England; R.C. = Roman Catholic; Congst. = Congregationalist.

Appendix Q   Pupils at evening schools, 1858

County	Males	Females	M: F Ratio	Totals	As % of 1851 Population
Bedfordshire	1040	321	3·2:1	1361	1·09
Northamptonshire	1370	619	2·2:1	1989	0·94
Hertfordshire	1173	201	5·8:1	1374	0·82
Wiltshire	1744	287	6·1:1	2031	0·80
Lancashire	7902	7361	1·1:1	15,263	0·75
Oxfordshire	1091	175	6·2:1	1266	0·74
Cheshire	1929	1389	1·4:1	3318	0·73
Buckinghamshire	878	283	3·1:1	1161	0·71
Dorset	1072	237	4·5:1	1309	0·71
Rutland	143	20	7·1:1	163	0·71
Warwickshire	1903	1455	1·3:1	3358	0·71
Suffolk	1727	309	5·6:1	2036	0·60
Nottinghamshire	939	679	1·4:1	1618	0·60
Somerset	1789	709	2·5:1	2498	0·56
Cambridgeshire	864	140	6·2:1	1004	0·54
Huntingdonshire	194	139	1·4:1	333	0·52
Derbyshire	1006	541	1·9:1	1547	0·52
Berkshire	774	90	8·6:1	864	0·51
Leicestershire	642	535	1·2:1	1177	0·51
Essex	1399	438	3·2:1	1837	0·50
Norfolk	2028	193	10·5:1	2221	0·50
Worcestershire	808	313	2·6:1	1121	0·40
Gloucestershire	1239	537	2·3:1	1776	0·39
Sussex	1107	138	8·0:1	1245	0·37
Middlesex	3994	2600	1·5:1	6594	0·35
Yorkshire	3379	2507	1·3:1	5886	0·33
Hampshire	1543	116	13·3:1	1659	0·33
Monmouthshire	253	253	1:1	506	0·32
Cumberland	329	282	1·2:1	611	0·31
Northumberland	599	341	1·8:1	940	0·31
Surrey	1367	627	2·2:1	1994	0·29
Durham	851	192	4·4:1	1043	0·27
Kent	1369	309	4·4:1	1678	0·27
Lincolnshire	963	151	6·4:1	1114	0·27
Cornwall	808	69	11·7:1	877	0·25
Staffordshire	868	553	1·6:1	1421	0·23
Devon	793	370	2·1:1	1163	0·21
Westmorland	45	68	1:1·5	113	0·19
Shropshire	257	53	4·8:1	310	0·14
Herefordshire	59	—		59	0·05
England	52,238	25,600	2:1	77,838	0.46

Source: Newcastle, I, pp. 628–35.

INDEX

Counties indicated are those pertaining in the nineteenth century. Place names with the suffix RD are census registration districts, which are distinct from the towns from which they took their names. County names attached to RD entries are those of relevant registration counties, usually, but not invariably, covering the same areas as administrative counties. In entries for individual counties no distinction has been made between registration and administrative countries.

The following abbreviations have been used for county names:

Beds., Bedfordshire; Berks., Berkshire; Bucks., Buckinghamshire; Cambs., Cambridgeshire; Ches., Cheshire; Cumb., Cumberland; Derbys., Derbyshire; Glos., Gloucestershire; Hants, Hampshire; Herefs., Herefordshire; Herts., Hertfordshire; Hunts., Huntingdonshire; Lancs., Lancashire; Leics., Leicestershire; Lincs., Lincolnshire; Mddx., Middlesex; Mon., Monmouthshire; Northants, Northamptonshire; Northumb., Northumberland; Notts., Nottinghamshire; Oxon., Oxfordshire; Shrops., Shropshire; Som., Somerset; Staffs., Staffordshire; Warws., Warwickshire; Westm., Westmorland; Wilts., Wiltshire; Worcs., Worcestershire; Yorks. ER, Yorkshire, East Riding; Yorks. NR. Yorkshire, North Riding; Yorks. WR, Yorkshire West Riding.

Abel-Smith, *family*, 183

Abergavenny (Mon.), (RD), 211, 242, 248, 260, 337, 348

Abingdon (Berks.), 166, 193, 356

Abingdon (RD) (Berks.), 188, 192, 311*n*., 334, 346

agriculture, *see* economic and social structure; child labour

Agricultural Children's Act (1873), 179

Agricultural Gangs Act (1867), 75, 179

Alcester (Warws.), 139, 142, 330, 342

Alderbury (RD) (Wilts.), 242, 244, 338, 347

Alderley (Ches.), 289*n*.

Aldershot (Hants), 84

Allen, John, 182

Alnwick (RD) (Northumb.), 326, 339

Alresford (RD) (Hants), 331, 343

Alston (RD) (Cumb.), 62, 68, 325, 340

Alton (RD) (Hants), 80, 331, 344

Altrincham (RD) (Ches.), 86, 95, 327, 340

Alverstoke (RD) (Hants), 84, 331, 343

Amersham (Bucks.), 166

Amersham (RD) (Bucks.), 188, 334, 346

Amesbury (RD) (Wilts.), 244, 338, 347

Ampthill (Beds.), 195

Ampthill (RD) (Beds.), 188, 189, 192, 202, 333, 346

Andover (Hants), 31, 32, 77, 355

Andover (RD) (Hants), 84, 331, 344

America, 188, 190

archidiaconal boards of education, *see* boards of education

Arnold (Notts.), 152

Arundel (Sussex), 31, 77, 355

Ashborne (Derbys.), 142

Ashborne (RD) (Derbys.), 142, 328, 342

Ashby de la Zouche (Leics.), 125,

135

Ashby de la Zouche (RD) (Leics.), 140, 143, 329, 342

Ashton (RD) (Lancs.), 29, 327, 341

Ashton-under-Lyne (Lancs.), 7, 8, 33, 49, 90, 354

Ashton-under-Lyne (RD) (Lancs.), 94, 95, 97, 98

Askrigg (RD) (Yorks. NR), 68, 326, 339

Aston (Warws.), 35, 103

Aston (RD) (Warws.), 144, 330, 342

Atcham (RD) (Shrops.), 242, 245, 337, 347

Atherstone (RD) (Warws.), 330, 342

Auckland (RD) (Durham), 63, 68, 325, 340

Audley (Staffs.), 151

Australia, 188, 190

Austria, 16

Avering (Glos.), 258–9

Avon valley (Warws.) 110

Axbridge (Som.), 223